Lars Borin and Anju Saxena (Eds.)
Approaches to Measuring Linguistic Differences

Trends in Linguistics
Studies and Monographs 265

Editor
Volker Gast

Editorial Board
Walter Bisang
Jan Terje Faarlund
Hans Henrich Hock
Natalia Levshina
Heiko Narrog
Matthias Schlesewsky
Amir Zeldes
Niina Ning Zhang

Editor responsible for this volume
Volker Gast

De Gruyter Mouton

Approaches to Measuring Linguistic Differences

edited by
Lars Borin
Anju Saxena

De Gruyter Mouton

ISBN 978-3-11-048808-1
e-ISBN 978-3-11-030525-8
ISSN 1861-4302

Library of Congress Cataloging-in-Publication Data
A CIP catalog record for this book has been applied for at the Library of Congress.

Bibliographic information published by the Deutsche Nationalbibliothek
The Deutsche Nationalbibliothek lists this publication in the Deutsche Nationalbibliografie; detailed bibliographic data are available in the Internet at http://dnb.dnb.de.

© 2013 Walter de Gruyter GmbH, Berlin/Boston
Typesetting: Frank Benno Junghanns
Printing: Hubert & Co. GmbH & Co. KG, Göttingen
♾ Printed on acid-free paper
Printed in Germany
www.degruyter.com

Preface

This volume contains a selection of contributions to the *Workshop on comparing approaches to measuring linguistic differences* held in Gothenburg on 24–25 October, 2011. All contributions have been thoroughly reworked for inclusion in the volume. The workshop was a joint arrangement by the University of Gothenburg, Uppsala University and the Max Planck Institute for Evolutionary Anthropology in Leipzig.

The work on preparing the volume has been funded in part by the Swedish Research Council (*Vetenskapsrådet*).

The volume editors would like to express their gratitude to Bernard Comrie and Östen Dahl for taking on the substantial task of thoroughly reviewing all the contributions, to the TiLSM series editor Volker Gast for his final vetting of the volume, to Kjell Edgren for his help in preparing the final manuscript version, and last but absolutely not least, to the always helpful and unerringly professional people at Mouton de Gruyter under whose watchful eyes the volume went from idea to finished product: Uri Tadmor, Birgit Sievert and Julie Miess.

Lars Borin
Anju Saxena

Contents

Preface... v

Introduction

The why and how of measuring linguistic differences 3
Lars Borin

Case studies

Contrasting linguistics and archaeology in the matrix model:
GIS and cluster analysis of the Arawakan languages................. 29
Gerd Carling, Love Eriksen, Arthur Holmer and Joost van de Weijer

Predicting language-learning difficulty 57
Michael Cysouw

How aberrant are divergent Indo-European subgroups? 83
Folke Josephson

Measuring socially motivated pronunciation differences 107
*John Nerbonne, Sandrien van Ommen, Charlotte Gooskens
and Martijn Wieling*

Distance-based phylogenetic inference algorithms in the
subgrouping of Dravidian languages............................... 141
Taraka Rama and Sudheer Kolachina

Carving Tibeto-Kanauri by its joints: Using basic vocabulary lists
for genetic grouping of languages................................. 175
Anju Saxena and Lars Borin

The effect of linguistic distance across Indo-European mother
tongues on learning Dutch as a second language 199
Job Schepens, Frans van der Slik and Roeland van Hout

Using semantically restricted word-lists to investigate relationships
among Athapaskan languages....................................... 231
Conor Snoek

Languages with longer words have more lexical change 249
Søren Wichmann and Eric W. Holman

Methods and tools

The Intercontinental Dictionary Series – a rich and principled
database for language comparison 285
Lars Borin, Bernard Comrie and Anju Saxena

Towards automated language classification: A clustering approach 303
Armin Buch, David Erschler, Gerhard Jäger and Andrei Lupas

Dependency-sensitive typological distance 329
Harald Hammarström and Loretta O'Connor

Degrees of semantic control in measuring aggregated lexical distances   353
Kris Heylen and Tom Ruette

Word similarity, cognation, and translational equivalence 375
Grzegorz Kondrak

Comparing linguistic systems of categorisation 387
William B. McGregor

Black box approaches to genealogical classification and their
shortcomings 429
Jelena Prokić and Steven Moran

Semantic typologies by means of network analysis of bilingual
dictionaries 447
Ineta Sejane and Steffen Eger

Measuring morphosemantic language distance in parallel texts 475
Bernhard Wälchli and Ruprecht von Waldenfels

Information-theoretic modeling of etymological sound change 507
Hannes Wettig, Javad Nouri, Kirill Reshetnikov and Roman Yangarber

Index 533

Introduction

The why and how of measuring linguistic differences

Lars Borin

> *The Gileadites captured the fords of the Jordan leading to Ephraim, and whenever a survivor of Ephraim said, "Let me cross over," the men of Gilead asked him, "Are you an Ephraimite?" If he replied, "No," they said, "All right, say 'Shibboleth.'" If he said, "Sibboleth," because he could not pronounce the word correctly, they seized him and killed him at the fords of the Jordan. Forty-two thousand Ephraimites were killed at that time.*
>
> The Bible (New International Version), Judges 12: 5–6

1. Introduction

The present volume collects contributions addressing different aspects of the measurement of linguistic differences, a topic which probably is as old as language itself – see the Bible quotation introducing this chapter – but which has acquired renewed interest over the last decade or so, reflecting a rapid development of data-intensive computing in all fields of research, including linguistics.

In this volume, the measuring of linguistic differences refers to differences *between language systems* (languages, language varieties, "lects", down to and including idiolects). In contrast, especially in computational linguistics there has been a substantial body of work on measuring differences within language systems, e.g., for the automatic identification in texts of the different senses of homonymous or polysemous words (so-called *word sense disambiguation and word sense induction*; Navigli 2009). Such work on measuring intra-language differences falls outside the scope of the present volume, although insofar as some of the methods and tools are common to the two problem areas, occasional mention will be made of this.

This introductory chapter gives a brief overview of the problem area and sets the individual contributions against this background. Motives and means for measuring linguistic differences are outlined in section 2, brief synopses of the individual contributions are presented in section 3, and the introduction is wrapped up with an outlook in section 4. References to the papers in this volume are given with authors' names in boldface.

2. Measuring linguistic differences

2.1. Why measure linguistic differences?

In the days of the ascent of generative linguistics with its insistence on the native speaker's linguistic intuition as the empirical basis par excellence for the study of language, it was not uncommon to see statements in linguistic papers to the effect that the presented data and analysis concerned "my idiolect", in an uneasy acknowledgement of the fact that individuals obviously differ in their linguistic behavior and their intuitions about language, and that there may in fact be more to the analysis of a language than can even in principle be worked out from introspection alone.

In order to work with anything other than "idiolects", we need to be able to group individual linguistic behaviors and linguistic products – including entire language systems – into larger aggregates, or categories, by characterizing them as being "the same" or, conversely, "different". But in a world where every individual has her own unique linguistic system, this is equivalent to being able to gauge the relative closeness or distance between such systems, so that we can say, e.g., "this woman sounds like she is from the west coast of Sweden, although not from Gothenburg".

In such cases, we presumably resort to some estimation of the similarity between two language systems. We will assume that such an estimation can in principle be placed along a numerical scale, and refer to it as a *linguistic distance measure*.[1] Such a measure gives us not only the means for determining when two individual language systems or linguistic products should be considered to represent the same language – using some kind of (motivated) threshold – but also for grouping languages in more encompassing categories and placing them relation to each other in some kind of abstract space. Since there are many bases for grouping languages, there are also many potential linguistic distance measures, which could be used alone or in combination to achieve a categorization.

A linguistic distance measure need not be formalized. In the example given above, the listener would probably simply have used her experience of being exposed to various Swedish varieties in order to place the speaker geographically, in a process perhaps no more or less accessible to conscious introspective analysis than, e.g., recognizing the face of somebody that we have met before. In the same way, experienced linguists will be able to make similarity judgments about linguistic phenomena without necessarily being able also to account explicitly for all the reasoning involved. However, because of the ubiquity of the computer in all kinds of research and the increasing availability of text and speech data in digital form, recent interest has focused on measures than can be computerized and automatically applied to large linguistic datasets. As a concrete manifestation of this interest there has been a number of recent workshops on the theme of measuring linguistic distances, including the 2011 workshop at the University of Gothenburg which resulted in the present volume: in general (Nerbonne and Hinrichs 2006b), as well as for the purpose of genetic linguistics (Nerbonne, Ellison, and Kondrak 2007), language typology (Cysouw and Wälchli 2007), or language variation studies (Hinrichs and Jäger 2012).

Linguistic distance measures – whether formalized or not – have been and are used for distinguishing idiolects, e.g., for author identification in literary studies (e.g., Kjetsaa et al. 1984) and forensic linguistics (Tiersma and Solan 2002). They are also finding increasing use in typological and areal linguistics, and in the present volume **Nerbonne, van Ommen, Gooskens, and Wieling** present a sociolinguistic case study.

However, the by far most popular application area – also among the contributions to this volume – is genetic linguistics, including dialectology. Turning to the literature, we find that interest in computational procedures for determining linguistic distances among language varieties – and through these genetic grouping of these varieties – has a long history in genetic linguistics, whereas the application of these methods to dialect grouping – often under the heading of "dialectometry" – is somewhat more recent. By and large, we would expect the same kind of methods to be useful in both cases, if only for the reason that the boundary between "languages" and "dialects" is anything but sharp. It is well-known that there is no purely linguistic criterion by which we can determine that two related language varietes are to be considered dialects of one language or two separate languages. Instead, languagehood (of closely related varieties) is mainly a political matter.

Thus we find an overlap in methodology between (computational) dialectometry and genetic linguistics. It seems that the main differences are that dialect studies take the language as axiomatic and as their sampling frame, and consequently that both the data collection and the design of distance measures for dialectological investigations tend to be informed by what is already known about the language, as in the case of the Tibeto-Burman varieties investigated in **Saxena and Borin**'s contribution.

What we find in the literature is a continuum with purely dialectological investigations at one end (see Chambers and Trudgill 1998 for the classical references) and large-scale genetic-areal investigations at the other end (e.g., Bakker et al. 2009), lexicostatistical and glottochronological studies falling somewhere in-between (e.g., Swadesh 1948, 1950, 1952, 1955; Lees 1953;

Kruskal, Dyen, and Black 1973; Dyen, Kruskal, and Black 1992), together with the traditional comparative method in historical linguistics and also, at least in part, with areal and typological linguistics.

Of course, dialectology, lexicostatistics and comparative-historical linguistics differ from areal and typological linguistics in the hypothesized origin of similarities between the language varieties under scrutiny, i.e., genetic relatedness, as opposed to language contact in areal linguistics and intrinsic features of human languages in typological linguistics. In all these fields, the other sources of similarities among language varieties must be recognized, however, in order to be eliminated as irrelevant to the investigation at hand.

2.2. How are linguistic differences measured?

Even if the purpose is known for comparing two or more language systems, there is still a question of means: How should the distance measure be designed? This has (at least) two aspects, namely (1) which linguistic features to use as input; and (2) how to turn the features into a distance measure. In genetic linguistics, there is generally an additional third aspect: (3) how to use the computed distances for constructing a tree or network representation reflecting the genetic connections among the languages. Here, the focus is on (1) and (2), although we note that distance measures are more often than not evaluated by constructing a tree or network (see section 4 below). The papers in the present volume form no exception in this regard.

2.2.1. *Linguistic features*

In order to be objective, the judgment and measurement of similarity must ultimately boil down to the comparison of concrete linguistic (surface) features in an explicit and repeatable way. This is consequently an important methodological dimension in language comparison, i.e., which linguistic features to investigate and how to rank them. In the literature we find various proposals for linguistic features to use as input to inter-language distance measures (for the general case, and not only for genetic linguistics). These include: character n-grams (Cavnar and Trenkle 1994; Singh and Surana 2007; Rama 2012); phonetic feature n-grams (Rama and Singh 2009); syllable sequences (List 2012); part-of-speech tag sequences (Borin and Prütz 2004; Nerbonne and Wiersma 2006), dependency syntax trees (Homola and Kuboň 2006); translation equivalents automatically extracted from parallel corpora (Rama and Borin 2011; **Buch, Erschler, Jäger, and Lupas**; **Kondrak**; **Wälchli and von Waldenfels**) or from bilingual dictionaries (**Sejane and Eger**); word distributions in corpora (**Heylen and Ruette**); etymological or dialectological lexical data (**Nerbonne, van Ommen, Gooskens, and Wieling**; **Rama and Kolachina**; **Snoek**; **Wettig, Reshetnikov, and Yangarber**); selected grammatical features (Ringe, Warnow, and Taylor 2002; Wichmann and Holman 2009; **Cysouw**; **Hammarström and O'Connor**; **Josephson**; **McGregor**; **Rama and Kolachina**); and the sound structure of (a subset of) the vocabulary (Ellison and Kirby 2006). However, the by far most used kind of linguistic input data is some form of (short) basic vocabulary list, or Swadesh list (**Buch, Erschler, Jäger, and Lupas**; **Carling, Eriksen, Holmer, and van de Weijer**; **Prokić and Moran**; **Rama and Kolachina**; **Saxena and Borin**; **Schepens, van der Slik, and van Hout**; **Wichmann and Holman**).

Traditionally, dialectological investigations have focused mainly on vocabulary and pronunciation, whereas comparative-historical linguists put much stock in grammatical features, but we get conflicting messages from the literature about which features are the most important. Chambers and Trudgill (1998: 99) suggest that the order of importance of linguistic features for distinguishing dialects should be grammatical – phonological – lexical, where the grammatical features carry most weight. Their ranking of lexical features – words – as the least reliable finds support from, e.g., Nerbonne (2003: 7), who notes that "[...] pronunciation is the better measure, and we suspect that this is due to the fact that lexis is simply more volatile than pronunciation. While pronunciations tend to be stable, we acquire new words easily and in great numbers."

How do we reconcile this with the fact that the data set of choice in automated genetic linguistic investigations – and often the only data set used – is a Swadesh-style word list, i.e. a lexical data set of similar size to that referred to by Nerbonne (and certainly not an order of magnitude larger). We even find claims in the literature (e.g., by Holman et al. 2008) to the effect that the optimal size Swadesh list for lexicostatistically based construction of genealogical trees for languages is on the order of 40 items (word senses), whereas in later work the same group of researchers (Bakker et al. 2009) show that on the order of 85 grammatical features from *The world atlas of language structures* (WALS; Haspelmath et al. 2005) give the optimal genetic classification of the WALS languages. Combining the lexical and grammatical features gives an improved classification (Bakker et al. 2009), but the lexical component still accounts for the by far larger part of the distance measure (Holman et al. 2008).

The findings of Nerbonne and his colleagues seem to contradict the results achieved in large-scale lexicostatistics, but in fact it is possible that they do not. The 40 word senses used by Holman et al. (2008) are the most stable items in the Swadesh list, stability being defined as a high degree of cognacy in recognized language families. E.g., the word sense 'TWO' – being among the 40 – would be expected to be expressed by cognate items among the Indo-European languages, which is what we actually find for this word sense and this language family.

Holman et al. (2008) work with a much more coarse-grained language classification than dialectologists do – the smallest recognized grouping lying two or more levels above the "dialect" level – and in fact the way stability is defined in their work logically implies that their chosen 40 senses would be expressed by the same (i.e., closely cognate) words in dialects of one language, and consequently be fairly uninteresting in the context of dialect grouping. The lexical items useful in dialectometry, on the other hand, would be rejected as indicators in large-scale lexicostatistics because of their ephemeralness. Thus, "lexical features" actually refer to two different – non-overlapping – sets of lexical items in the two contexts.

Finally, there may be all kinds of pragmatically based reasons for using particular kinds of linguistic data, not least the substantial effort required to collect large quantities of detailed linguistic data (**Borin, Comrie, and Saxena**). In large-scale comparative linguistic investigations such as those typical of language typology research or indeed modern-day lexicostatistics, data sources will often not offer comparable phonetic information even at the fairly coarse level of detail which is commonly used in traditional dialectological studies, which tend to be feasible only for the very few languages where there are already centuries of linguistic research to build upon. When we work with secondary sources or when the primary data is collected over a short period of time with limited human and economic resources – as in many language description and documentation projects – the least common denominator and basis for comparison must be sought among such linguistic data as is normally available in word lists and reference grammars, i.e., ranging from phonology, over basic vocabulary, to some central grammatical (morphological and syntactic) features. The finer points of pronunciation, most of the intricacies of individual grammars, and almost all of semantics and pragmatics will inevitably be left out of such comparisons.

2.2.2. Calculating distances

There are three kinds of representations which are commonly compared when calculating inter-language distances:

Sets of features (grammatical, lexical, or phonological). A feature – often called a "character" in the context of computational historical linguistics – can be binary, so that the distance measure can be based on the cardinality of the intersection of the two sets. Alternatively, features can take one of a (small) number of nominal values. In this case a commonly used distance measure is one borrowed from computational biology: the tree distance in a perfect phylogeny computed from the feature sets on the assumption that feature values express developmental states of characters (McMahon and McMahon 2005; Nichols and Warnow 2008).

Probability distributions of linguistic features. Distance measures can be standard measures for comparing probability distributions (see, e.g., Ellison and Kirby 2006; Satterthwaite-Phillips 2011).

Symbol sequences, e.g., words in a standard orthography or in some phonetic transcription. In this case, distance measures are often string similarity measures, such as those used in information retrieval or spell checkers.

In practice, the most commonly encountered method for measuring linguistic distances is the last of the three, based on a small diagnostic word list where the words expressing the same concept in the two languages are compared using some variant of Levenshtein distance (also referred to as edit distance; Levenshtein [1965] 1966).

The use of diagnostic word lists comes out of at least two traditions in linguistics – dialectology as practiced since the mid-19th century (Chambers and Trudgill 1998) and Swadesh lists (Swadesh 1948, 1950, 1952, 1955) – and is consequently well-motivated and firmly entrenched in an internal linguistic methodological tradition. In dialectology, the items for the lists are chosen on the basis of the researchers' pre-knowledge of linguistic phenomena likely to exhibit geographical variation in the language in question. Swadesh's original lists were compiled to contain items highly resistant to lexical replacement using "a combination of intuition and experience following certain guidelines" (Oswalt 1971: 422), e.g., avoiding items judged to express culture-specific concepts or to be not fully arbitrary (e.g., onomato-poetic or sound-symbolic), etc. (Swadesh 1955).

Why Levenshtein distance is so much in favor is more of an enigma, especially to somebody coming from a background in computational linguistics with its close connections to computer science. The almost exclusive popularity that Levenshtein distance enjoys in linguistics is in all likelihood traceable back to the influential volume on sequence comparison edited by Sankoff and Kruskal (1983; new edition 2001). However, in various computer science fields and also in bioinformatics, many other sequence comparison measures have been proposed over the years for different tasks, including comparison of words and other linguistic units, e.g. in the context of information retrieval or database access, and the properties of the various measures have been systematically investigated in these contexts (e.g., Cohen, Ravikumar, and Fienberg 2003). This development seems to have gone largely unnoticed in linguistics, except for some small studies (e.g., Inkpen, Franza, and Kondrak 2005; Heeringa et al. 2006; Kondrak and Sherif 2006), but there is nothing comparable to, e.g., Pecina's (2010) exhaustive comparative evaluation of methods for collocation extraction from text corpora. Rama and Borin (in prep.) have now initiated a comparative evaluation of some 20 different string distance measures found in the computational literature on the task of automatic language classification using the ASJP database (Holman et al. 2008), a selection of languages comprising more than 70% of the world's languages.

Levenshtein distance is often modified in various ways. In its basic version the algorithm assigns a unit cost to all edit operations (insertion, deletion, replacement, and sometimes swap). Modified versions may penalize some operations in relation to others, and/or base the cost of a replacement operation on the particular segments involved, e.g., on the basis of phonetic similarity (Kondrak 2002; Heeringa 2004; Kessler 2005) or by an a priori grouping of segments into equivalence classes (**Buch, Erschler, Jäger, and Lupas; Saxena and Borin**). If the compared sequences are words, this raises the issue of a common phonetic space (Ellison and Kirby 2006), or rather of comparability of the written representations used in this work.[2] This issue is dealt with in various ways in the literature. With small, well-controlled data sets, the data can be normalized manually, as the ASJP data set, where the lexical items in a modified short Swadesh list are rendered in a coarse phonetic transcription where some phonological distinctions are ignored (Holman et al. 2008; **Wichmann and Holman**). For larger data sets – both those written in traditional orthography and those rendered in some phonetic transcription (of which there are many in addition to the IPA) – and the general case, we are still waiting for an interoperability solution along the lines of the proposals by Hughes, Gibbon, and Trippel (2006) and Moran (2009).

Another issue which normally arises in connection with the use of Levenshtein distance is that of (length) normalization. This seems to be an underresearched problem, at least with respect to linguistic data. A common way of normalizing for length is through division by the length of the longer of the two compared sequences (or by the average of their lengths), which serves to scale all individual conparisons into the interval [0,1]. On the one hand it is easy to see why one would like to normalize for length, since otherwise longer sequences would by necessity tend to display larger distances. On the other hand, e.g., Heeringa et al. (2006) found that when working with dialect data, the best results came from not normalizing for length at all. Cf. the contributions by **Kondrak** and **Wichmann and Holman** to this volume

There is an unstated assumption in most linguistic work using normalized Levenshtein distance that the best normalization is linear in the length of the compared sequences, rather than some other function of the length (e.g., logarithmic, polynomial, or exponential), and that the length of (one of) the sequences should be the basis for the normalization, rather than, e.g., the length of the segment alignment produced as a by-product of the distance computation (but see Heeringa 2004: 130ff). This is equal to a kind of independence assumption: Each segment makes an independent, equally large contribution to the result (before the division), so that the normalization changes the scale of the result and nothing else. But in principle it could be the case that each added segment would make a non-equal contribution – smaller or larger – than the one before it, and perhaps even a context-dependent contribution. Cf., e.g., soundex and similar algorithms, which do not make this assumption. In soundex it is assumed, on the contrary, that vowels and any segment beyond the first four consonants make no contribution at all to the similarity measure (National Archives 2007). Normalization by sequence length (as well as post-normalization by alignment length as used by Heeringa 2004) is characterized as "suboptimal" by Marzal and Vidal (1993), who propose a more complex normalization technique based on editing paths. Note that **Buch, Erschler, Jäger, and Lupas** and **Wichmann and Holman** apply different versions of Levenshtein distance – both with regard to the way segments are compared and with regard to length normalization.

3. This volume

The papers in this volume have been arranged into two sections: *Case studies* and *Methods and tools*, in this order. This order reflects the bottom-up nature of the problem area under discussion. However, placement of a paper in one of the sections does not indicate that it is irrelevant to the other topic. In fact, most of the contributions contain elements of both methodological development and concrete case studies, since especially computational methods by their very nature cry out for proof-of-the-pudding type demonstrations of their applicability in concrete problem-solving settings. Thus, which heading a paper has been placed under reflects its main emphasis, as perceived by the editors of this volume.

3.1. Case studies

Carling, Eriksen, Holmer, and van de Weijer represent a cross-disciplinary collaboration involving linguistics, human ecology, and archeology. In their contribution *Contrasting linguistics and archaeology in the matrix model: GIS and cluster analysis of the Arawakan languages* they investigate the spread and contact of languages and socio-cultural features using a combination of computational methods, such as Geographical Information Systems (GIS) and clustering techniques using linguistic distance measures between 100-item lexical lists annotated with manual cognacy judgments.

Both the contribution by **Cysouw** (*Predicting language-learning difficulty*) and that by **Schepens, van der Slik, and van Hout** (*The effect of linguistic distance across Indo-European mother tongues on learning Dutch as a second language*) describe the use of linguistic distance measures between a language learner's native language (L1) and a second/foreign language (L2) as a predictor of the learning difficulty, i.e., the time and effort needed to attain a particular level of proficiency in the L2 with a given L1 background. The two studies are complementary, in two respects: (1) In **Cysouw**'s study the L1 is fixed to be English, while a number of L2s are investigated, and in the study by **Schepens, van der Slik, and van Hout**, the L2 is Dutch in all cases, while the L1s are a number of Indo-European languages. (2) **Cysouw** bases his measure on genealogical and geographical distance, writing system and typological features taken from the WALS database (Haspelmath et al. 2005), while **Schepens, van der Slik, and van Hout** work with two lexicostatistical measures, one using the expert cognacy judgments in the Indo-European (IE) Swadesh list database of Dyen, Kruskal, and Black (1992), and the other the normalized Levenshtein distance developed in the ASJP project (Holman et al. 2008). There is a number of IE L2s in **Cysouw**'s study, making it possible to compare the findings of the two studies. Both studies agree that linguistic distance between L1 and L2 correlates well with L2-learning difficulty, even though their way of measuring linguistic distance is very different. **Cysouw**'s measure is optimized for the particular purpose to which it is put here, and it does not seem likely that the three or four broad typological binary features that he ends up with could be useful predictors of much else, and specifically not the genealogical relationships that the lexical data used in the other study were originally designed to uncover.

Josephson (*How aberrant are divergent Indo-European subgroups?*) discusses the placement of the Anatolian languages in the Indo-European family tree, on the basis of various grammatical characters representing innovations and retentions in Anatolian and other branches of IE. This is a piece of traditional comparative linguistics, but **Josephson** notes that his results are not in contradiction to the character-based computational genetic classification presented by Ringe, Warnow, and Taylor (2002).

Nerbonne, van Ommen, Gooskens and Wieling address the problem of *Measuring socially motivated pronunciation differences* using data and methods for dialectometry developed by the Groningen group over a number of years (Nerbonne and Heeringa 2010). Specifically, they muster this methodological toolbox to investigate the notion of regional language (or *regiolect*) in the Dutch-speaking area. They take the speech of local radio announcers as representing such a variety, and use their speech to test the hypothesis – found in the literature – that a regiolect will measure in somewhere between the standard language and the regional dialect, but closer to the regional language. Interestingly, this hypothesis is falsified in most cases, and the authors conclude that regiolects – or at least the speech of these popular local radio announcers – are perhaps to be regarded as "the (situated) varietal performance of a regional identity rather than as a natural koiné", i.e., as sociolectal rather than dialectal in nature.

Rama and Kolachina's contribution *Distance-based phylogenetic inference algorithms in the subgrouping of Dravidian languages* continues a long line of works where lexicostatistical methods are applied to the problem of establishing the internal genealogical structure of the Dravidian language family. The authors make a thorough comparison of the combinations of four different datasets plus distance measures with two different tree inference methods. As a by-product of the experiments, they make some valuable observations about the quality of the etymological data available for Dravidian. Unfortunately, none of the trees inferred in the eight experiments agrees with the current expert consensus view on the subgrouping of the Dravidian language family, and the authors consequently conclude that further work is needed.

Rather than relying on a general sequence-comparison method such as Levenshtein distance, **Saxena and Borin** explore a linguistically motivated rule-based technique in their paper *Carving Tibeto-Kanauri by its joints: Using basic vocabulary lists for genetic grouping of languages*. They compare seventeen Tibeto-Burman (TB) language varieties spoken (with one exception) in the Indian Himalayan region, using an extended Swadesh list. The items are compared using correspondence rules formulated by a linguist, an expert on these languages, and the resulting judgments are binary (i.e., not Levenshtein-style item–item distances), so that the whole procedure is equivalent to that of using manual cognacy judgments, with the difference that the equivalence statements are based on the automatic application of the rules. The main advantages of this procedure – which is more in line with older work, e.g., by Hewson (1974, 1977), Borin (1988), or Lowe and Mazaudon (1994), than with recent work in lexicostatistics – are its complete consistency and replicability. The aim of the comparison was to get a better understanding of the low-level genealogical relationships among these TB language varieties, and one noteworthy result is that the Upper Kinnaur varieties should be classified as Tibetic rather than West Himalayish.

In his paper *Using semantically restricted word-lists to investigate relationships among Athapaskan languages*, **Snoek** focuses on a particular semantic domain denoting time-stable and culture-independent referents, parts and fluids of the human body. The domain is in turn divided into three subdomains; body parts, "ephemera" (e.g., 'fingernails', 'warts'), and "effluvia" (e.g., 'blood', 'urine'). A noteworthy finding of **Snoek**'s study is that effluvia terms turn out to be diachronically more stable in the Athabaskan language family than the other two semantic domains. This is interesting among other things because Swadesh's original lists do not contain many effluvia terms. Among the 222 items discussed by Swadesh (1955), only two (or three, if 'spit' is taken as a noun) of **Snoek**'s 12 effluvia terms are present ('blood' and 'vomit').

The title of **Wichmann and Holman**'s contribution summarizes a serendipitous finding which emerged from their work in the ASJP project (Holman et al. 2008): *Languages with longer words have more lexical change*. While investigating the correlation between language distance – as measured both by the ASJP version of Levenshtein distance and by a traditional cognacy-judgment based distance measure – and various typological features of language systems, they found that while most investigated features did not show a strong correlation with distance, surprisingly, word length did. It correlates significantly with both the traditional and the ASJP measure. The reasons for this still await further research (but cf. **Kondrak**'s contribution to this volume).

3.2. Methods and tools

Borin, Comrie, and Saxena describe *The Intercontinental Dictionary Series – a rich and principled database for language comparison*. The IDS is a long-term project aiming at providing a broader basis for comparative linguistic studies than the short Swadesh-type word lists used at present in much computational and other work, including many of the contributions to this volume. The authors point out that the size of the IDS list is about one order of magnitude larger than, e.g., the ASJP list, which probably is significant for linguistic data, which tend to display a Zipfian – or power-law – distribution. This means that, e.g., doubling the size of a Swadesh list would not be expected to lead to significantly better performance on the uses to which such a list is normally put. The IDS team strongly advocates the view – still rarely met with in linguistics, unfortunately, but slowly gaining ground even in this community – that basic research data in digital form should be openly and freely available along the same lines as open source computer software.

In *Towards automated language classification: A clustering approach*, **Buch, Erschler, Jäger, and Lupas** explore an alternative visualization of sets of distances among languages. They point out that the standard phylogenetic algorithms borrowed into linguistics from computational biology have some disadvantages which can potentially be avoided by the use of carefully designed statistics-based clustering algorithms instead. The paper presents a number of proof-of-concept experiments aiming to show this.

In their contribution *Dependency-sensitive typological distance*, **Hammarström and O'Connor** investigate to what extent the independence assumption often tacitly made when comparing languages using linguistic features influences the resulting grouping of languages. Given that there are well-known dependencies among many of the linguistic features collected in typological databases, it could in principle be essential to weed out such dependencies before calculating language distances using these datasets. Using a dataset of 81 features for 35 languages spoken on and around the land bridge between the two American continents, **Hammarström and O'Connor** calculate both the redundancy of the features – about 35 features or 43% are predictable from the rest – and to what extent the dataset gives evidence of shared but unusual feature combinations ("quirks"). Their results with regard to the investigated dataset are that while there are many dependencies among the features, they are nevertheless evenly distributed in it and that consequently the effect of disregarding them is marginal. The same goes for unusual feature combinations.

16 *Lars Borin*

Heylen and Ruette (*Degrees of semantic control in measuring aggregated lexical distances*) describe an experiment aimed at investigating lexical variation using a large corpus material (1.8 billion words of Dutch from Belgium and the Netherlands), reflecting a mixture of formal and informal genres, and automatically lemmatized and annotated for part of speech. A well-established technique from computational linguistics – semantic vector space models – was used to cluster text lemmas into near-synonym sets. They then go on to show how controlling for word use in two different ways – roughly: Which lemmas are used in which kinds of texts? and: Which members of a near-synonym set are chosen in which kinds of texts? – yields complementary views on lexical variation in the corpus material.

Kondrak explores the relationship among the three phenomena making up the title of his contribution – *Word similarity, cognation, and translational equivalence* – in a concrete case study aiming at testing the hypothesis that "words that are phonetically similar across different languages are more likely to be mutual translations". In the case study **Kondrak** examines translation equivalents between English and French on the basis of an aligned parallel corpus and an automatically generated phrase translation dictionary. He finds that the empirical study supports the hypothesis, and observes that this points to potential synergies between computational historical linguistics and machine translation research. However, it turns out that not only actually related words (cognates and loanwords), but also unrelated translation equivalents systematically exhibit greater similarity across languages than random bilingual pairs. After confirming this observation on a larger set of language pairs, the author traces the similarity to an artefact of the similarity measure. The way length normalization is done when calculating this measure tends to raise the similarity of pairs close in length, which we can expect translation equivalents to be on independent grounds, having to do with the distributional properties of words. (Cf. also the contribution by **Wichmann and Holman.**)

McGregor discusses the comparison of linguistic systems on the level of grammatical constructions in his contribution *Comparing linguistic systems of categorisation*. His point of departure is a verbal construction type common among the languages of northern Australia. The *compound verb construction* (CVC) involves a combination of an uninflected and an inflected verb, and least in some of its functions is reminiscent of English support verb constructions. After reviewing and comparing a number of formal properties and semantic features of CVCs, **McGregor** presents a detailed study of three lexical features of CVCs in several languages of the area, in order to set the stage for a more principled cross-linguistic numerical comparison of

CVCs. This comparison gives promising results which by and large are in accord with the known genealogical facts, but also makes some erroneous predictions, which call for an explanation and further research.

Prokić and Moran (*Black-box approaches to genealogical classification and their shortcomings*) compare four "black-box" approaches to calculating family trees for languages. In their terminology, *black-box* approaches are those which "take into account very limited or no linguistic knowledge" in performing the calculation. Three of the approaches investigated use sequence similarity measures for comparing items in Swadesh-style word lists (Levenshtein distance and shared unigrams and bigrams) and the fourth compares file compression ratios for pairs of languages (see also **Wettig, Nouri, Reshetnikov, and Yangarber**). The resulting language-distance matrix was then used as input to a standard genealogical network algorithm (neighbor-net as implemented in SplitsTree). Their conclusions are somewhat negative: No sequence similarity measure stood out from the others, meaning that the greater complexity of calculating the Levenshtein distance is essentially wasted in this case. The compression-based measure came out consistently behind the sequence similarity measures. In all cases the authors point out some obvious shortcomings, which could be overcome with access to expert linguistic knowledge.

Sejane and Eger (*Semantic typologies by means of network analysis of bilingual dictionaries*) explore bilingual dictionaries as means for computing distances between languages. Their methodology works by building networks of glosses in a pivot language (English in their case) for all languages to be compared, under the hypothesis that these networks will reflect the lexical-semantic system of the languages, but crucially expressed in a comparable way, since each node in each network is an English word or phrase. The task of measuring the distance between two languages then turns into that of determining the similarity between the corresponding graphs, a task which has been thoroughly explored in the computational literature. The authors then go on to cluster 22 languages according to this measure. Their results are interesting, but as the authors themselves state, it is not completely clear what kind of classification is actually expected to come out as a result – genealogical, areal or typological. In the experiment as reported by **Sejane and Eger** there are also some issues with data quality and evaluation of the results, which need to be further explored in future research along these lines.

In their paper *Measuring morphosemantic language distance in parallel texts* **Wälchli and von Waldenfels** illustrate one possible direction in which the database for comparative linguistic investigations can be broadened. The measure that they propose is based on translation equivalent distributions in aligned parallel corpora. Even with the fairly small – by today's standards in corpus linguistics – corpora used (the New Testament in 60 languages, and Bulgakov's novel *The master and Margarita* in 28 languages) it is obvious that the number of items used in the comparison will be many times that in Swadesh-type word lists. The authors also point out that working with unannotated corpora in this way means that the distance measures reflect both lexicon and grammar, since the compared items are (bilingual) text word correspondences, i.e., carrying inflectional, derivational and possibly clitic elements in some languages. They find that the measure reflects the factors generally considered as biases in typological research, and suggest that one useful application could be sampling for typological investigations, "since measuring morphosemantic distance is actually measuring typological bias".

Wettig, Nouri, Reshetnikov, and Yangarber (*Information-theoretic modeling of etymological sound change*) address the problem of discovering recurring regular sound correspondences among known cognates in a particular language family, the Uralic languages in their case. The correspondences are automatically inferred using an information-theoretic technique known as minimum description length (MDL; Rissanen 1978), basically the same as a file compression method such as that used by the zip program (Ziv and Lempel 1978; see also the contribution by **Prokić and Moran**). The authors describe some ways in which the quality of the discovered correspondences can be verified, both manually and automatically. A particularly intriguing and promising form of semi-automatic control is imputation: The correspondences can be used to transduce a word in one language into its (putative) cognate in another of the Uralic languages. This can be seen as the next logical step taking a procedure developed in one of the pioneering efforts in computational language reconstruction – that of Hewson (1974, 1977) – to a higher level.

4. Outlook

Most of the contributions in this volume are concerned with using linguistic distance measures for automatic genetic classification of languages. As already meantioned, this normally involves performing two computational steps: (1) calculation of inter-language distances; (2) inference of a phylogenetic tree from the distance measures. For the second step, a small number of methods are used, mostly standard software solutions from the field of computational biology. Because of the intractability of the problem itself, these methods are in general not guaranteed to find the globally optimal tree or network, but only the locally best solution within a bounded number of computational steps. It behooves us to remember that these methods were actually designed to solve a different problem from that of classifying languages, and that it may be a mistake for linguists to use them as black boxes (this is an additional black box to those discussed by **Prokić and Moran**) which take as input distance measures and produce genealogical trees.

In computational linguistics, in the wake of the so-called statistical revolution in natural language processing, classification currently rules the roost, variously referred to as machine learning, language modeling, or data-driven language processing. Consequently, computational linguistics has a wide and growing array of tools to offer for attacking the problem of language classification. Linguists have been slower to adapt these tools than the ones from computational biology – possibly because of a steeper learning curve – but hopefully we will see more interaction between linguistics and computational linguistics in this exciting field over the coming years.

A lasting and beneficial change that the statistical revolution has brought about in computational linguistics is the insistence on formal evaluation of systems and methods, a requirement which is now also put in equal measure on rule-based systems. It is true that it not always clear that a particular proposed evaluation method actually will be the best possible way of evaluating a particular task, or even that it in fact does evaluate what it purports to evaluate. There is still much methodological groundwork to do in this area, but crucially, there is a consensus in the computational linguistics community about the need for well-documented, formal, replicable procedures for evaluating different language processing tasks, based on ground-truth consensus datasets, or *gold standards*. This consensus is still lacking in data-intensive linguistics. Although some authors do provide numerical scores quantifying the differences between trees output by tree-inferring software and established linguistic genealogies (e.g., Pompei, Loreto, and Tria 2011), in the overwhelming number of cases the results are still largely eyeballed and "evaluated" in prose descriptions.

This volume (and, e.g., Nerbonne and Hinrichs 2006b) is about linguistic distances, but evaluation is normally done on something that is one (black-box) step removed from the computed distances themselves, the genealogical trees or networks resulting from feeding the distance or character data to a tree-inferring algorithm designed for recovering biological phylogenies, but where the output is not always guaranteed to be the "right" tree. It would be good to have a gold standard for linguistic distances directly. There are some proposals in this direction, where computed linguistic distance data is correlated with data from human judgments (Heeringa et al. 2006), from geographical distance (Nerbonne and Kleiweg 2007), from second-language learning effort (Schepens 2012; **Cysouw; Schepens, van der Slik, and van Hout**), from pairwise comparisons of distances in established genealogies (Greenhill 2011), and from imputation of unseen data (**Wettig, Nouri, Reshetnikov, and Yangarber**). These efforts are fragmented, however, and it is clear that the field would benefit from a concerted effort aiming at establishing rigorous evaluation procedures for language comparison methods.

Looking at the considerable and wide-ranging literature on measuring linguistic differences, and trying to assess how the papers in this volume can advance the state of the art, is like watching the beginning stages of the assembly of a large jigsaw puzzle. There are tantalizing glimpses of the larger picture, and one senses something about what would be needed to connect some of the as yet unconnected portions. For instance: We still have much to learn about the relationship between the linguistic features that we choose as input to a distance measure and the purpose of the comparison carried out with this measure. In other words, we need to uncover the "hidden variables" in the similarity relations (Nerbonne and Hinrichs 2006a: 1), and understand how to collect and curate the necessary linguistic data for investigating them fully. It seems that the kind of work exemplified by **Wettig, Nouri, Reshetnikov, and Yangarber** if systematically pursued could provide a handle on our current lack of statistical data on sound changes in the world's languages (Kessler 1995: 63), which could provide better word comparison methods at least for genetic classification of languages. Finally, the standards of evaluation need to be brought up at least to the level of those normally assumed in computational linguistics. Perhaps the time is ripe for initiating a broad research program on computational comparative linguistics which would allow us to assemble larger fragments of the unfinished jigsaw puzzle that we see when attempting to measure linguistic differences.

Notes

1. It is desirable (but not always the case, and arguably not always motivated [Kondrak 2002: 48f]) that the measure be a metric in the mathematical sense, i.e., that distances are non-negative and symmetric: $d(x,y) = d(y,x) \geq 0$; that (only) the distance between an object and itself is 0: $d(x,x) = 0$; and that distances obey the triangle inequality: $d(x,z) \leq d(x,y) + d(y,z)$.
2. To my knowledge, so far there has been no work dealing directly with digitized speech as input data for the kind of investigations discussed here. It is probably just a matter of time before we will see the first such attempts, however.

References

Bakker, Dik, André Müller, Viveka Velupillai, Søren Wichmann, Cecil H. Brown, Pamela Brown, Dmitry Egorov, Robert Mailhammer, Anthony Grant, and Eric W. Holman
    2009   Adding typology to lexicostatistics: A combined approach to language classification. *Linguistic Typology* 13: 167–179.

Borin, Lars
    1988   A computer model of sound change: An example from Old Church Slavic. *Literary and Linguistic Computing* 3 (2): 105–108.

Borin, Lars and Klas Prütz
    2004   New wine in old skins? A corpus investigation of L1 syntactic transfer in learner language. In *Corpora and Language Learners*, Guy Aston, Silvia Bernardini, and Dominic Stewart (eds.), 69–89. Amsterdam: John Benjamins.

Cavnar, William B. and John M. Trenkle
    1994   N-gram-based text categorization, *Proceedings of SDAIR-94, 3rd Annual Symposium on Document Analysis and Information Retrieval*, 161–175.

Chambers, Jack K. and Peter Trudgill
    1998   *Dialectology*. Second edition. Cambridge: Cambridge University Press.

Cohen, William W., Pradeep Ravikumar, and Stephen Fienberg
    2003   A comparison of string metrics for matching names and records. *KDD Workshop on Data Cleaning and Object Consolidation*.

Cysouw, Michael and Bernhard Wälchli (eds.)
    2007   Parallel texts. Using translational equivalents in linguistic typology. Thematic issue of *Sprachtypologie & Universalienforschung STUF 60 (2)*.

Dyen, Isodore, Joseph Kruskal, and Paul Black
    1992   An Indoeuropean classification: A lexicostatistical experiment. *Transactions of the American Philosophical Society* 82 (5).

Ellison, T. Mark and Simon Kirby
    2006   Measuring language divergence by intra-lexical comparison. *Proceedings of COLING-ACL 2006*, 273–280. Sydney: ACL.

Greenhill Simon J.
    2011   Levenshtein distances fail to identify language relationships accurately. *Computational Linguistics* 37 (4): 689–698.

Haspelmath, Martin, Matthew S. Dryer, David Gil, and Bernard Comrie (eds.)
    2005   *The World Atlas of Language Structures*. Oxford: Oxford University Press.

Heeringa, Wilbert
    2004   Measuring dialect pronunciation differences using Levenshtein distance. Ph.D. thesis, University of Groningen.

Heeringa, Wilbert, Peter Kleiweg, Charlotte Gooskens, and John Nerbonne
   2006   Evaluation of string distance algorithms for dialectology. In Nerbonne and Hinrichs 2006b, 51–62.

Hewson, John
   1974   Comparative reconstruction on the computer. In *Historical Linguistics I*, John M. Anderson and Charles Jones (eds.), 191–197. Amsterdam: North-Holland.

Hewson, John
   1977   Reconstructing prehistoric languages on the computer: The triumph of the electronic neogrammarian. *Proceedings of COLING 1973*, 264–273. Florence: Leo S. Olschki Editore.

Hinrichs, Erhard and Gerhard Jäger (eds.)
   2012   ESSLLI workshop on computational approaches to the study of dialectal and typological variation. Online proceedings <http://www.sfs.uni-tuebingen.de/~gjaeger/conferences/essli_2012/>, accessed on 15th July, 2012.

Holman, Eric W., Søren Wichmann, Cecil H. Brown, Viveka Velupillai, André Müller, and Dik Bakker
   2008   Explorations in automated language classification. *Folia Linguistica* 42: 331–354.

Homola, Petr and Vladislav Kuboň
   2006   A structural similarity measure. In Nerbonne and Hinrichs 2006b, 91–99.

Hughes, Baden, Dafydd Gibbon, and Thorsten Trippel
   2006   Feature-based encoding and querying language resources with character semantics. *Proceedings of LREC 2006*, 939–944. Genoa: ELRA.

Inkpen, Diana, Oana Franza, and Grzegorz Kondrak
   2005   Automatic identification of cognates and false friends in French and English. *Proceedings of RANLP-2005*, 251–257. Borovets, Bulgaria.

Kessler, Brett
   1995   Computational dialectology in Irish Gaelic. *Proceedings of EACL 1995*, 60–66. Dublin: ACL.

Kessler, Brett
   2005   Phonetic comparison algorithms. *Transactions of the Philological Society* 103 (2): 243–260.

Kjetsaa, Geir, Sven Gustavsson, Bengt Beckman, and Steinar Gil
   1984   *The Authorship of* The Quiet Don. Oslo: Solum.

Kondrak, Grzegorz
   2002   *Algorithms for language reconstruction*. Ph.D Thesis, University of Toronto.

Kondrak, Grzegorz and Tarek Sherif
   2006   Evaluation of several phonetic similarity algorithms on the task of cognate identification. In Nerbonne and Hinrichs 2006b, 43–50.

Kruskal, Joseph B., Isidore Dyen, and Paul Black
  1973 Some results from the vocabulary method of reconstructing language trees. In *Lexicostatistics in genetic linguistics*, Isidore Dyen (ed.), 30–55. The Hague: Mouton.

Lees, Robert B.
  1953 The basis of glottochronology. *Language* 29 (2): 113–127.

Levenshtein, Vladimir I.
  1966 Binary codes capable of correcting deletions, insertions, and reversals. *Soviet Physics Doklady* 10: 707–710. (Original publication: Левенштейн, В.И. 1965. Двоичные коды с исправлением выпадений, вставок и замещений символов. Доклады Академий Наук СССР 163 (4): 845–848.)

List, Johann-Mattis
  2012 Improving phonetic alignment by handling secondary sequence structures. In Hinrichs and Jäger (2012).

Lowe, John and Martine Mazaudon
  1994 The Reconstruction Engine: A computer implementation of the comparative method. *Computational Linguistics* 20 (3): 381–417.

Marzal, Andrés and Enrique Vidal
  1993 Computation of normalized edit distance and operations. *IEEE Transactions on Pattern Analysis and Machine Intelligence* 15 (9): 926–932.

McMahon, April and Robert McMahon
  2005 *Language Classification by Numbers.* Oxford: Oxford University Press.

Moran, Steven
  2009 An ontology for accessing transcription systems (OATS). *Proceedings of the EACL 2009 Workshop on Language Technologies for African Languages – AfLaT* 2009, 112–120. Athens: ACL.

National Archives
  2007 The soundex indexing system. Available at <http://www.archives.gov/research/census/soundex.html>, accessed 23rd July, 2012.

Navigli, Roberto
  2009 Word sense disambiguation: A survey. *ACM Computing Surveys* 41 (2/10): 1–69.

Nerbonne, John
  2003 Linguistic variation and computation. *Proceedings of the 10th Conference of the EACL*, 3–10. Budapest: ACL.

Nerbonne, John, T. Mark Ellison, and Grzegorz Kondrak (eds.)
  2007 *Computing and Historical Phonology. Proceedings of the Ninth Meeting of the ACL Special Interest Group in Computational Morphology and Phonology.* Prague: ACL.

Nerbonne, John and Wilbert Heeringa
    2010   Measuring dialect differences. In *Language and Space: An International Handbook of Linguistic Variation. Volume 1: Theories and Methods*, Jürgen Erich Schmidt and Peter Auer (eds.), 550–567. Berlin: De Gruyter Mouton.
Nerbonne, John and Erhard Hinrichs
    2006a   Linguistic distances. In Nerbonne and Hinrichs 2006b, 1–6.
Nerbonne, John and Erhard Hinrichs (eds.)
    2006b   *Linguistic Distances. Proceedings of the Workshop*. Sydney: ACL.
Nerbonne, John and Peter Kleiweg
    2007   Toward a dialectological yardstick. *Journal of Quantitative Linguistics* 14 (2): 148–166.
Nerbonne, John and Wybo Wiersma
    2006   A measure of aggregate syntactic distance. In Nerbonne and Hinrichs 2006b, 82–90.
Nichols, Johanna and Tandy Warnow
    2008   Tutorial on computational linguistic phylogeny. *Language and Linguistics Compass* 2 (): 760–820.
Oswalt, Robert L.
    1971   Towards the construction of a standard lexicostatistic list. *Anthropological Linguistics* 13 (9): 421–434.
Pecina, Pavel
    2010   Lexical association measures and collocation extraction. *Language Resources and Evaluation* 44: 137–158.
Pompei, Simone, Vittorio Loreto, and Francesca Tria
    2011   On the accuracy of language trees. *PLoS ONE* 6 (6): e20109.
Rama, Taraka
    2012   N-gram approaches to the historical dynamics of basic vocabulary. In Hinrichs and Jäger (2012).
Rama, Taraka and Lars Borin
    2011   Estimating language relationships from a parallel corpus. A study of the Europarl corpus. *NODALIDA 2011 Conference Proceedings*, 161–167. Riga: NEALT.
Rama, Taraka and Lars Borin
    in prep.   Comparative evaluation of string comparison measures for automatic language classification.
Rama, Taraka and Anil Kumar Singh
    2009   From bag of languages to family trees from noisy corpus. *Proceedings of RANLP-2009*, 355–359. Borovets, Bulgaria: ACL.
Ringe, Don, Tandy Warnow, and Ann Taylor
    2002   Indo-European and computational cladistics. *Transactions of the Philological Society* 100 (1): 59–129.
Rissanen, Jorma
    1978   Modeling by shortest data description. *Automatica* 14 (5): 465–471.

Sankoff, David and Joseph B. Kruskal (eds.)
   1983   *Time Warps, String Edits, and Macromolecules: The Theory and Practice of Sequence Comparison*. New York: Addison-Wesley.

Satterthwaite-Phillips, Damian
   2011   Phylogenetic inference of the Tibeto-Burman languages or on the usefulness of lexicostatistics (and "megalo"-comparison) for the subgrouping of Tibeto-Burman. Stanford University Anthropological Sciences PhD dissertation. Available online at <http://purl.stanford.edu/wv919xj7158>, accessed on 21st July, 2012.

Singh, Anil Kumar and Harshit Surana
   2007   Can corpus based measures be used for comparative study of languages? In Nerbonne, Ellison, and Kondrak 2007, 40–47.

Swadesh, Morris
   1948   The time value of linguistic diversity. Paper presented at the *Viking Fund Supper Conference for Anthropologists*, 12th March, 1948. (Abstract in part: Swadesh 1952: 454.)

Swadesh, Morris
   1950   Salish internal relationships. *International Journal of American Linguistics 16* (4): 157–167.

Swadesh, Morris
   1952   Lexico-statistic dating of prehistoric ethnic contacts: with special reference to North American Indians and Eskimos. *Proceedings of the American Philosophical Society* 96 (4): 452–463.

Swadesh, Morris
   1955   Towards greater accuracy in lexicostatistic dating. *International Journal of American Linguistics* 21 (2): 121–137.

Tiersma, Peter and Lawrence Solan
   2002   The linguist on the witness stand: Forensic linguistics in American courts. *Language* 78 (2): 221–239.

Wichmann, Søren and Eric W. Holman
   2009   *Temporal Stability of Linguistic Typological Features*. LINCOM Studies in Theoretical Linguistics, Bd. 42. Munich: LINCOM Europa.

Ziv, Jacob and Abraham Lempel
   1978   Compression of individual sequences via variable-rate coding. *IEEE Transactions on Information Theory* 24 (5): 530–536.

Case studies

Contrasting linguistics and archaeology in the matrix model: GIS and cluster analysis of the Arawakan languages

Gerd Carling, Love Eriksen, Arthur Holmer and Joost van de Weijer

1. Language contact, linguistic distance and the emergence of socio-cultural identity: The matrix model[1]

Scientific research on the pre-Columbian cultures of lowland South America has taken a great leap forward during the first decade of the new millennium. In terms of material culture, the excavations of large-scale settlements with Amazonian Dark Earths (ADE), more commonly known as terra preta soils, indicating the remains of large-scale systems of indigenous intensive agriculture (Lehmann et al. 2003; Glaser and Woods 2004; Woods et al. 2009), and the recent discovery of the huge earthwork complex in the Brazilian state of Acre where so far more than 250 geometric figures, many of them measuring 200–300 meters across (Schaan et al. 2007; Mann 2008; Saunaluoma 2010), are just two examples of archaeological discoveries of great significance for our view of pre-Columbian Amazonian societies. At the same time, linguistic research, aided by new developments in software technology and computer capacity, has moved toward large-scale comparison projects where new ways of measuring linguistic distance are supplying new evidence of genetic relationships as well as contact scenarios (Muysken 2011; Danielsen et al. 2011; Walker and Ribeiro 2011; O'Connor and Muysken 2012). Seen as a whole (a perspective strongly advocated by the current investigators), these discoveries calls for methodological advance in order to integrate the results from different academic disciplines into a more comprehensive picture of pre-Columbian Amazonian societies and their mutual interaction.

The great development in the sciences devoted to the study of the material cultures and languages of indigenous Amazonians has also demanded new theoretical models for the socio-cultural expansion of the large-scale, contact-seeking, pre-Columbian societies of the region. Several attempts at synthesizing this knowledge have also appeared (Hornborg 2005; Eriksen 2011; Hornborg and Hill 2011), all advocating the need for an integrated perspective, joining together expertise from archaeology, anthropology, and linguistics in order to understand the development of material culture, socio-cultural organization, and language as a whole. It may sound like an understatement to say that the need for an integrated perspective on these research questions stems from the fact that language is always used in a cultural context and that the study of a particular language therefore always should include the study of the cultural context in which the language is used, but since this is not always the case, we wish to emphasize that this is exactly what the present study is devoted to doing. We therefore constantly seek to contrast the results of our linguistic investigations with those of archaeology and anthropology in order to acquire a more comprehensive picture of the cultural and linguistic development in pre-Columbian Amazonia.

As for Arawak, the language family to which this study is mainly devoted, one attempt to synthesize the current knowledge across scientific disciplines appeared in the publication Comparative Arawakan histories: Rethinking language family and culture area in Amazonia (Hill and Santos-Granero 2002), in which a cultural matrix model in which socio-cultural and linguistic features of Arawak-speaking societies in space and time were joined together into a cultural matrix composed of the following elements:

- suppression of endo-warfare,
- a tendency to establish socio-political alliances with linguistically related groups,
- a focus on descent and consanguinity as the basis of social life,
- the use of ancestry and inherited rank as the foundation for political leadership, and
- an elaborate set of ritual ceremonies that characterizes personal, social, as well as political life (Santos-Granero 2002: 42ff).

Furthermore, Eriksen (2011: 9) defined a complementary set of features related to the material culture typical of Arawak-speaking societies:

- the use of various types of high-intensity landscape management strategies as the basis of subsistence (Hill 2011),
- a tendency to situate their communities in the local and regional landscapes through the use of such techniques as "topographic writing", extensive systems of place-naming, and rock art (Santos-Granero 1998),
- an elaborate set of rituals including a repertoire of sacred musical instruments and extensive sequences of chanting, often performed as part of place-naming rituals (Hill 2007),

- a proclivity to establish settlements along major rivers and to establish trade and other social relations through river transportation (Hornborg 2005).

In a cultural matrix model, the matrix feeds information to its users by acting as a cultural backbone and the features of the matrix are displayed by the users in order to communicate the ethnic identity and distinctiveness of the group *vis-à-vis* other ethnic groups when in contact with them. Viewed as a whole, the Arawak cultural complex formed an integrated unit in which material as well as non-material culture and language helped construct and spread a cultural package across Amazonia with the present-day distribution of Arawak-speaking societies as the persisting result.

Since a majority of the features of the Arawak matrix can be related precisely to situations of social (and linguistic) contact (e.g. trade, ceremonies, political leadership), it is impossible to overlook the importance of the connection between language, material culture and ethnic identity when analyzing the spread of linguistic features among Arawak languages. We therefore view language as an integrated part of the ethnic identity of Arawak-speakers and carefully take the importance of ethnic identity into consideration when evaluating the mechanisms of language contact involving Arawak languages. Finally, we also believe that the powerful cultural matrix of the Arawaks and the strong ethnic identity derived from it was an important element in the vast expansion of Arawak languages across South America and the Antilles during the pre-Columbian period.

2. Implementing the model – general problems

The basic aim of the current project is to develop tools for the implementation and interpretation of the culture matrix model into an existing set of data. The data from the region in question – both in terms of cultural and linguistic data – is indeed huge, which requires sophisticated tools for handling and organizing it.

Since the matrix model relates both to material and non-material culture as well as language as important markers of ethnic identity, the data collected and contrasted consists of material and non-material culture, as well as language. At present, a selected number of relevant items of both types will be contrasted (cf. sections 4–5).

First of all, the implementation of a general, theoretical framework on a set of data like this is typically connected to problems of defining *boundaries*.

This is in particular relevant when it comes to defining or narrowing down data into standardized data formats, which is a necessary prerequisite for applications of the type that is being done in the current project. The problems appear at all levels: on the one hand when a complex setup is simplified and narrowed down to a simple Y/N alternative or when complex patterns have to be simplified or generalized in order to be squeezed into a simple formula, and on the other hand when the outcome of the computer generated applications is open to a number of alternative interpretations.

In the current project, the main focus has been on the tools and methods of implementing the questions arising from the culture matrix model described in the previous section. When data is being collected, analyzed and projected onto applications two basic parameters are taken into fundamental consideration: expected *stability* and expected *contact sensitiveness*. With *stability* we mean the probability of the system remaining stable without changing, with *contact sensitivity* we mean the probability of being substitutions arising in a contact situation (see further 2.1–2.2.). Prerequisites for the applications are that data are a first analyzed and grouped according to these parameters and thereupon projected against each other, using a *layering technique*, which will be described further in section 3.

A necessary basic tool for investigating and understanding contact-related features as well as the spread of features over large areas is constituted by GIS-technology, which will be described further under 3.1. Cladograms, NeighborNets, and cluster analysis can give information about a number of correspondences, depending on the nature of the input data and the methods of applying them. Cladograms in the form of trees basically give information on linguistic distance and sub-grouping of dialects as well as dialectal nodes (cf. 3.2.). Unrooted trees (NeighborNets), which are favored in a number of current studies of the Arawakan family (e.g., Walker and Ribeiro 2011; Danielsen et al 2011), both group languages into subgroups and show linguistic distance, as do (rooted) trees, but they are also able to give information on shared similarities, depending on either retention or contact.

2.1. Calculating stability in language – how could it be done?

For any linguistic property shared across two or more languages, be it a lexical item, a morphological form, a construction or a general principle of structure, there are logically speaking four possible reasons for the similarity: (a) shared inheritance; (b) loans under contact; (c) shared language-internal typological pressure (as expressed in universals or universal tendencies); and

(d) coincidence. Depending on the factors underlying the shared property and the type of property involved, we speak variously of areal features (loans of structural properties), calques (loans of constructions), lexical loans, universals (e.g. grammatical properties resulting from communication requirements), core vocabulary etc.[2]

Under the assumption that all similarities derive from one of these four factors, it remains an empirical issue to determine which types of property are more likely to derive from which factor. Which properties are more likely to be diffused by areal contact, which tend to survive unchanged across time (i.e. to be inherited diachronically from earlier stages of a language), and which are susceptible to typological pressure? We will discount the fourth alternative, coincidence, here, partly because it is theoretically uninteresting, and partly because we assume that it will behave like random noise across the various categories, and will therefore not be expected to be a major confounding factor either.

The concept of diachronic stability is therefore the propensity to be inherited, i.e. to resist both contact-induced change and typologically induced change, while the concept of contact sensitivity is the propensity to be loaned across language boundaries. That these two concepts can be addressed separately and are not in a directly inverse relation is due to the fact that a feature which is neither contact sensitive nor diachronically stable might be particularly sensitive to typological pressure. Examples of typological pressure include the cross-linguistic correlation between SOV and overt case morphology (Greenberg 1963: 96).

As for vocabulary the situation is somewhat different. Here typological pressure is not directly applicable, so stability and borrowability are more or less in an inverse relationship: The core vocabulary is a feature with typically high stability *and* low borrowability, while cultural vocabulary is typically more unstable and contact sensitive (cf. Tadmor and Haspelmath 2009). The whole concept of glottochronology of lexicostatistics is based on this assumption, namely, that certain parts of the lexicon are more stable for classification (Swadesh 1952; Greenhill et al. 2010).

2.2. Calculating stability in material culture

The four different categories used for explaining linguistic similarity that were outlined in section 2.1 can also be used for describing the occurrence of similar forms of material culture occurring at two or more geographical locations. In terms of "translating" the scenarios of linguistic contact into those of material culture, categories a, b, and d (shared inheritage, loans under contact, and coincidence) are relatively self-explanatory also in the context of material culture, while category c, shared language-internal typological pressure, is translated into an artifact's use-value or cultural affordance; i.e. its ability to retain its position in a given society despite constant technological development occurring through time (e.g. an artifact such as the scythe has greatly decreased in terms of numbers and importance in Europe due to the mechanization of agriculture during the 19th and 20th century; its ability to fit into the new conditions is low, and its use will therefore decrease through time).

Although material culture may behave differently from language in terms of its tendency to be transformed in contact scenarios, different types of material culture can nevertheless be measured according to its tendency to show stability vs. contact sensitivity in different social contexts. An important point to mention here is that although the material aspects of artifacts may be preserved for almost indefinite time (archaeologists may recover stone tools dating back millions of years back in time), their cultural context regulating e.g. meaning, techniques, functions, etc. can easily be lost if the artifact is separated from its cultural context or if the cultural context ceases to exist (as in the example with the scythe above). The use of a particular artifact and the raw material from which it is made may also change significantly over time, e.g. in the case of the large amounts of gold that was stolen by the Spanish from the Incas, taken to Europe and transformed into coins and objects with new social functions that today are being used to manufacture computers, items of high significance in Western society, but nevertheless very different from the role of the Inca goldwork in pre-Columbian South America.

Apart from the extremely abrupt changes caused by the European colonization of the New World, Amazonian material culture displays many interesting examples of stability as well as contact sensitivity among its material cultures, some of which will be discussed in greater detail in this section. Overall, the ceramic material of pre-Columbian Amazonia (ceramic items generally being the most well-preserved artifacts of Amazonian archaeological contexts) show long temporal continuities, stretching millennia back in time. The oldest pottery of the New World is found along the lower Amazon River (Roosevelt et al 1991) and it spread rather extensively in northern South America already during 5000–6000 BC (Eriksen 2011: 228f). It is likely that once the knowledge of manufacturing solid ceramic vessels of good quality had appeared and been diffused across the continent, the technique was not reinvented again, but passed on to new potters from generation to generation. This would indicate a high degree of stability in the ceramic technology itself, and traces of contact sensitivity should therefore be sought for in such features as the design and composition of the ceramic material.

Interestingly, while several Amazonian ceramic traditions, e.g. Zoned-Hachured, Barrancoid, Saladoid, and Amazonian Polychrome, spread across vast areas during timespans of up to 2 000 years, some ceramic traditions, e.g. Camani, Paredão, and Cedeñoid, continued to be locally produced during almost equally extensive time spans (Eriksen 2011). The expansion of the major ceramic traditions in Amazonia was most likely conducted through indigenous exchange systems (as opposed to migratory spread) (Hornborg 2005; Eriksen 2011), resulting in the adoption of particular ceramic traditions by new ethno-linguistic groups through contact (e.g. trade, ritual exchange, etc.). This indicates a high degree of inherent stability in the material culture, but also, to a certain degree, contact sensitivity, because the major ceramic traditions were split up into many subtraditions (so called ceramic phases) that were locally or regionally manufactured, but with a certain set of features still in common with the overarching ceramic tradition to which they were associated.

In contrast to the widely distributed ceramic traditions, characteristic locally produced ceramic styles were maintained by some groups for millennia without adapting the style of their pottery despite long periods of contact and outer pressure from major ceramic tradition. One such example is the Camani phase of the Araracuara area of Southeastern Colombia, which despite close geographical contact with groups manufacturing Barrancoid and Amazonian Polychrome pottery for at least 600 years maintained their distinctive ceramics, until around 1000 AD when they finally shifted their ceramics (Eriksen 2011: 175). Another example is the Paredão phase (AD 700–1200 (Eriksen 2011: 99)) of the middle Amazon in which locally produced ceramic style was maintained for more than 1500 years despite close geographical proximity to the Barrancoid and Amazonian Polychrome traditions. A third case of this type of scenario is the conservatism of the makers of the Cedeñoid ceramics of the middle Orinoco Valley, who started to produce a distinctive kind of ceramics dated by C^{14}-sampling to 1050 BC (Zucchi et al. 1984) and kept on doing so up until the time of European colonization (for further discussion, see Eriksen 2011: 232).

These three cases may serve as examples of stability in the archaeological material, while the spread of the major ceramic traditions indicate a high degree of contact sensitivity among the material cultures of the ethno-linguistic groups that shifted their traditional wares to the new ceramics of the major traditions. However, it should be pointed out that the spread of major ceramic traditions took place through processes of transformation, whereby new ethno-linguistic groups were incorporated into the major cultural complexes through the adaption of their material culture (and in many instances also their non-material culture and language) to those of the major traditions. Such shifts also affected the style and composition of the major ceramic traditions through a recursive process feeding back traits from the newly incorporated ceramic styles into the previously established tradition, a phenomena indicating a certain degree of contact sensitivity among the major ceramic traditions of Amazonia. This ability to transform and to be transformed also indicates that a certain degree of contact sensitivity was advantageous in terms of successfully navigating in the socio-cultural landscape of pre-Columbian Amazonia.

3. Methods and materials – a description

In this section, methods and materials used in the present project will be described. First of all we use GIS-technology, then cluster analysis and finally a combination of the techniques, which is described under 3.3. The organization of the database and problems connected with the organization is described in 3.4. Applications and evaluations are given in section 4.

3.1. Geographical Information Systems

Although GIS, Geographical Information Systems, trace their background to physical geography and the natural sciences, its applicability in the humanistic and social sciences is great, and its potential in linguistic research has perhaps been overlooked so far. However, new internet-based applications such as The World Atlas of Language Structures (WALS) Online (http://wals.info/), allowing anyone from interested laymen to academic scholars to search and display the distribution of linguistic features around the world, are currently breaking new ground in the spatial dimensions of linguistic research. While WALS Online effectively shows the great potential of what the results of a spatial analysis of linguistic features have to offer to linguists, another motive for using GIS in linguistic research would be in order to open the field up for transdisciplinary comparisons with spatially distributed data derived from other scientific disciplines. Since spoken languages are always situated in a socio-cultural and ecological context, spatially distributed data from archaeology, ethnography, economy, and ecology, may tell us much about the context in which the language is spoken, and hence about the external factors influencing language use and language contact.

GIS offers a tool for transdisciplinary investigations of the interplay between language, culture, and materiality. In the present investigation, GIS is used for researching the socio-cultural context in which Arawak languages have expanded across Amazonia, and to investigate how linguistic distance has been affected by contact and isolation between groups of speakers in different parts of lowland South America during the past 2 000 years. More concretely, we are using spatially distributed data from linguistics, archaeology, ethnography, ethnohistory, and physical geography in order to investigate the relationship between languages of the Arawak family and to map out the features of the Arawak cultural matrix (see section 1). Since a given language is used in a particular socio-cultural context and at defined spatial locations, GIS either allows us to investigate other types of data related to the socio-cultural context of the language (e.g. a specific tribe and its material culture) *or* the distribution of other types of data at the specific location in which the language is currently spoken (changes in the historical/archaeological data or alterations in the physical geography of a language setting). Such analyses have been made possible through large-scale data collection in the project "Nature and Culture in Prehistoric Amazonia" (Eriksen 2011), in which large amounts of transdisciplinary data with a particular focus on features relating to the Arawak language family and the Arawak matrix have been collected and analyzed, allowing for broad-scale comparison with linguistic features in space and time.

Technically speaking, the interplay between the linguistic and the socio-cultural/ecological data stored in a GIS takes place through the linking of our SQL-database (3.4.) containing linguistic features, to the GIS database containing socio-cultural features for the same groups, *and* geographical coordinates for them. Due to the nature of the construction of these databases, using a common denominator, e.g., an identity code (in this case the names of the ethno-linguistic groups), the two data sets can easily be linked together through a so called "join operation", resulting in the so called combined applications (see 3.3.). This operation immediately allows the two data sets to share all features – linguistic as well as non-linguistic – with each other in a new, spatially distributed data set. The operation results in a new data set in which the spatial distribution of linguistic features can be examined and compared to the spatial distribution of the socio-cultural features of the Arawak matrix, thereby allowing for true transdisciplinary work to take place.

3.2. Cluster analysis of cladograms

In the present study, we have performed a cluster analysis of 100 basic lexical concepts (including pronouns, adjectives, nouns, verbs). The data has been provided by Walker and Ribeiro (2011). For these concepts, the number of different lexical variants range from 1 to 16, yielding a total of 694 variants. Cognates are identified in 60 languages. These are entered into a data set that indicates whether a variant occurs in a language or not. We have created a distance matrix for binary data and performed the cluster analysis (hierarchical cluster analysis, divisive approach) on this matrix. The results are represented by the tree diagram in figure 1. On the whole, the results of the analysis are rather similar to those reported by Walker and Ribeiro (2011), that is, that languages which shared many variants in our study were also similar in theirs.

We have looked for a reasonable division of the clusters which was not too general on the one hand, and not too detailed (e.g., yielding clusters with only one language) on the other hand. Trying out different numbers of groups, we finally decided on dividing the clusters into 10 groups as indicated by the grey rectangles in figure 1. The reason for selecting 10 groups is described in more detail in section 5: most important would be that the difference between clusters A and B becomes apparent first from 8 clusters (i.e., not yet at 7 clusters). For the application, see figure 2.

3.3. Combined applications and layering technique

In the current project, the main focus is laid on *combined* and *layered applications* (cf. 3.1.). The organization of the data into the Amazonian database (see 3.4.) is adjusted towards maximum applicability of these applications. The following *combined applications* are made possible:

- Cultural/archaeological data are projected onto:
  - Maps, showing geographic distribution of features in time and space
  - Maps with linguistically derived information
- Linguistic data (typological/lexical) are projected onto:
  - Maps, showing geographic distribution
  - Cladograms, showing linguistic distance and subgrouping
  - Combinations of maps and cladograms by means of cluster analysis, showing linguistic distance/subgrouping in relation to geographical distance.

Contrasting linguistics and archaeology in the matrix model

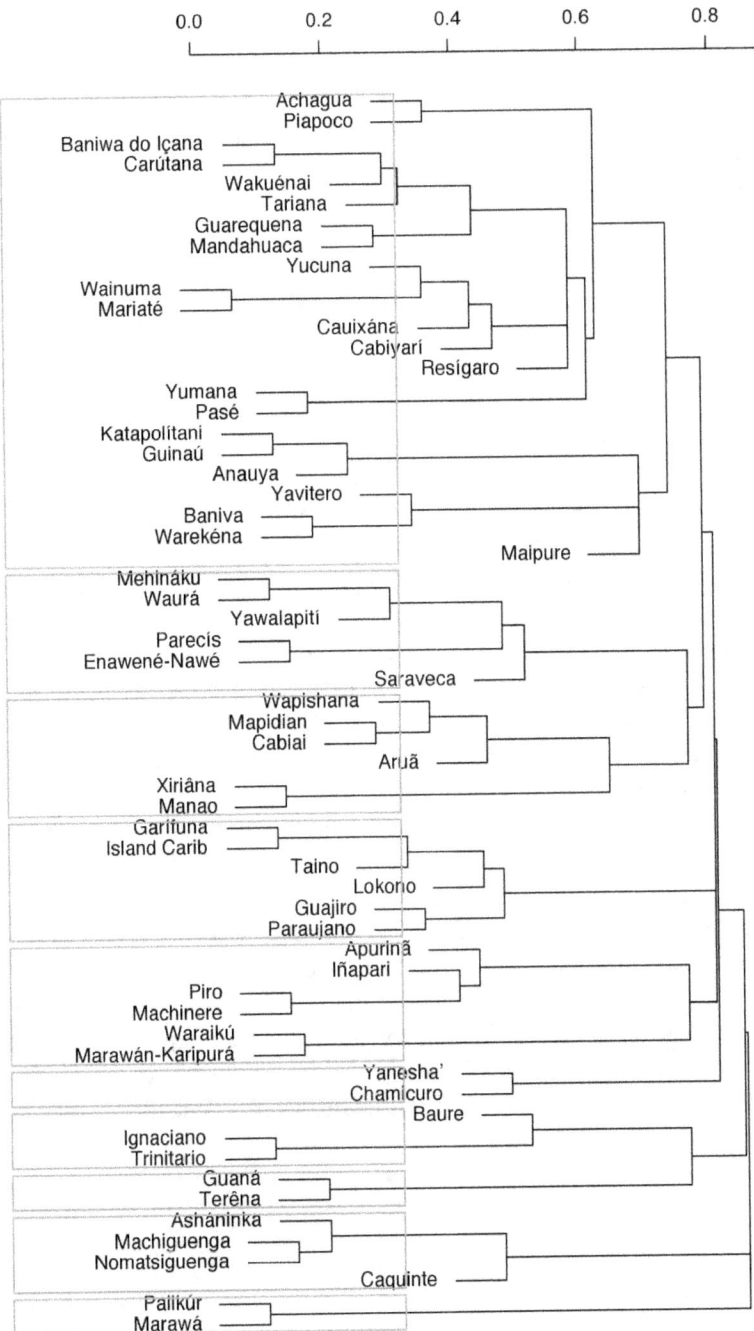

Figure 1. The language tree with the ten clusters (A–J).

The *layered applications* (see section 5) make possible a further step of combining features: here, combinations derived from language data could be projected onto maps with cultural/archaeological data, either general or more specific. Individual features of interest oculd be projected onto groups or clusters of features. The possible combinations and projections of general and individual data in the database are in principle endless.

3.4. The Amazonian database – a short description

The "database" used in the current description consists in fact of two physically separated databases, based on the same identification system: one database with *archaeological/cultural data* (basis for Eriksen 2011) and one with *linguistic data*. The underlying identification system is based on labels of "ethno-linguistic" groups, given a certain *identification number*, which is complemented by a series of GIS-coordinates (see 3.1.). These ethno-linguistic groups are based primarily on linguistic descriptions (see Eriksen 2011). Since the Amazonian situation is particularly complex with alternative names of groups, mismatches between descriptions (anthropological/linguistic) and identical or similar names of different groups can occur, the database distinguishes several columns with alternative names beside the standardized name, used in applications. Reference columns are also inserted. The database contains a huge number of groups from 20 different families and a number of isolates. After the id-number and name columns follows a column with linguistic family affiliation, e.g., Arawak, Tupi, Carib, based either on resources like Ethnologue or individual descriptions (Payne 1991; Aikhenvald 1999). Thereupon follow the columns with the various data, lexical or typological. Each feature (lexical/typological) normally requires three or four columns, e.g., for typological data: (1) actual data (including internal variations), (2) standardization for the purpose of applications and (3) references, or, for lexical data: (1) actual forms (including variation), (2) cognate identification or reconstruction of forms, (3) references.

4. The applicability of language data: lexical and typological features compared

4.1. Lexical data

The lexical data in the project are selected and applied in accordance with two basic parameters: (1) expected stability versus contact sensitivity, (2) correlation with the features distinguished in the matrix (see section 1). Both these parameters might be problematic, in particular if seen as oppositional. At a general level, studies of typology of borrowability like Haspelmath and Tadmor (2009) are indeed useful, but at a regional level, a number of separate factors have to be taken into consideration before stability or contact sensitivity is calculated. If the definition of a matrix is regarded as a set of features typical for the Common or Proto-Arawakan linguistic and cultural area, then several matrix-related items could count as belonging to a "stable" part of language. An item reconstructed as belonging to the basic vocabulary of one language family could be an outsider in another language family, depending on the ecological habitats of speakers. Further, the probability of borrowing, even if the item belongs to the reconstructable proto-vocabulary, is there in any case, in particular in the Amazonian region, where intra-linguistic cultural borrowing seems to be very frequent (Payne 1991; Danielsen et al. 2011) and the huge impact of colonizing languages (Spanish, Portuguese) blurs the patterns (cf. Brown 1999). A further problem (which counts for Arawak as well as other Amazonian languages with no old written sources) is constituted by the great difficulties in defining relative chronologies, a prerequisite for distinguishing true cognates from early loans in cultural vocabulary.

However, the layering technique, enabled by the GIS-technology, opens a number of possibilities. Here, individual items of interest, be it crops, kinships terms, flutes or names for various animals, could be either lumped with other items of the basic vocabulary and used in clusters, or projected (against maps) either individually or in groups of relevance.

In this study, two different methods of reconstruction are used. For the purpose of creating cladograms and clusters, we identify cognates in order to enable Y/N or numerical marking. For the purpose of GIS applications of individual items, we produce *ad hoc reconstructions*, in which not only cognates are identified, but the actual reconstructed forms are also presented (cf. the method by Payne 1991).[3] This kind of reconstruction can be done within a well established language family by looking at the actual forms of ascertained semantic notions (e.g., maize, manioc) and excluding speculative etymologies. Expected paths of sound change, both general (cf. Campbell 2004: 40ff.) and language-specific (cf. Payne 1991) are then taken into consideration by comparing forms of languages and setting up a tentative tree of forms. This type of reconstruction can, to a certain extent, distinguish more preserved forms from more changed, as well as – to a certain extent – identify sub-nodes, but it can hardly distinguish true cognates from early loans. For this a greater amount of data for comparison would be required. In figure 2, an ad hoc-reconstruction of words for "maize" in a number of languages of various families (data basically from Birket-Schmidt 1943, see also Brown 2006) has been worked out (fig. 2). The various forms in these languages can be boiled down to 19 reconstructed forms plus a number of isolated forms (not included). Of these forms, several can be reconstructed into sub-nodes (*mahikʲi, e.g., Palikur *mahikí*, versus *makanasi, e.g., Mandahuahca *makanaži* and *awatʲi, e.g. Manao *auâty*, and *aNatʲi, e.g., Chamicuro *n'atši*).

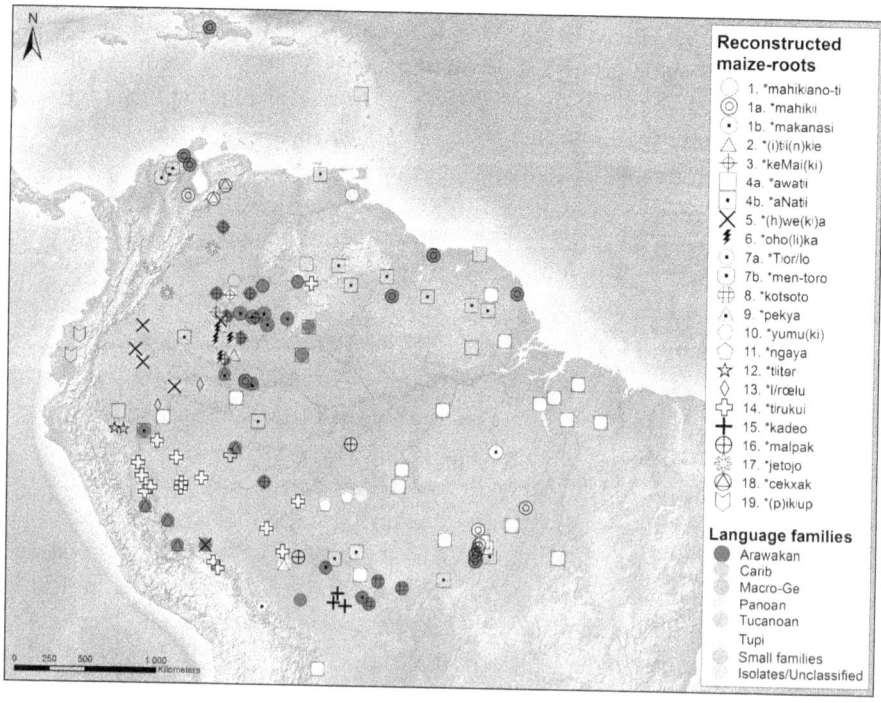

Figure 2. The spatial distribution of reconstructed maize roots in Amazonia.

4.2. Typological data

What has been described in the previous section for the lexicon holds equally for typological data: the basic dichotomy concerns the distinction between stability and contact sensitivity. However, there is an important difference between lexicon and typology: while the lexicon of a language is to a large extent arbitrary, and can display almost limitless cross-linguistic variation, the structural properties of language are (a) much more restricted and (b) often functionally motivated. This has important consequences for our investigation. For one thing, given that the number of possible options for any typological feature is highly limited, chance similarities become a potential problem: if two languages share SVO word order this is very possibly coincidental. Even highly marked combinations such as VSO word order and postpositions could surface independently as a matter of chance (as indeed appears to have happened: the combination is found in both Guajajara, cf. Harrison 1986, and Yagua,[4] which are spoken at more or less opposing ends of the Amazonian region, and there is no evidence of genetic relationship between them: Yagua is a Peba-Yaguan language and Guajajara is a Tupí-Guaraní language).

Further, structural properties are more likely to be affected by internal typological pressure: if a languge displays one property along one dimension, it is also more likely than otherwise to display another, seemingly unrelated property. Going back all the way to Greenberg (1963), one such correlation is that between VSO word order and the existence of prepositions, another is the tendency for SVO languages not to have a case system (and even stronger, the near-universal tendency for SVO languages not to have an ergative case alignment).[5] We are hestitant to use the term "universals" coined by Greenberg, since few, if any, of the generalizations are actually universal.[6] However, the idea of typological pressure expresses the same intuitions. In situations dealing strictly with word order, it corresponds to Hawkins' (1983) concept of cross-categorial harmony, and otherwise more closely to Nichols' (1992: 100ff) discussion of typological correlations. We assume that consistent correlation patterns which are statistically significant and attested cross-linguistically reflect a tendency towards maximal efficiency and economy in the language system.[7] We also assume that the tendency itself is universally valid but may be overshadowed locally or regionally by other factors.

The typological issue is particularly a concern if a set of languages shares a number of unusual features, in which case it might be tempting to posit areal contact based on only typological evidence. However, the set of features might equally well be the result of one feature being shared by coincidence, and a whole cluster of concomitant features arising due to typological pressure exerted by this one chance feature.[8]

Given typological properties shared across languages, and again assuming that coincidence will at most represent troublesome noise in the data, we are faced with the issue of whether these properties are the result of inheritance, areal contact or typological pressure, and which properties are most likely to be the result of which factor.

Previous studies have focused primarily on the borrowability of typological features (cf. Aikhenvald 2002: 12 and works cited therein) and diachronic stability (cf. in particular Nichols 1992: 167ff.). Both concepts are highly relevant to our study, but the contribution of the present approach will be to focus on teasing apart typologically motivated characteristics and areal features by systematic comparisons of linguistic data with attested contacts (both contemporary and historical), as evidenced by the spread of cultural artefacts and culture words, supplemented by archaeological data.

Among typological features, some appear to be genetically more stable than others (Nichols 1992: 167ff). In particular, morphological complexity and case alignment are properties which are shared across members of the same genetic phylum (and thus presumably diachronically relatively stable), head- and dependent marking are less so, whereas, at the other extreme, word order is more likely to be an areal feature.[9] There are differences in this respect between different parts of the world, but unfortunately, for sampling reasons, Nichols (1992) does not include Amazonian data in the relevant section. However, Aikhenvald (2002: 102) observes that in Tariana, an Arawakan language areally influenced by Tucanoan languages, case alignment to a certain extent follows the inherited Arawakan split-ergative / active pattern, whereas Tariana shares with Tucano a mixture of head and dependent marking (other Arawakan languages are more consistently head marking).[10] Further, Tariana is more typically Tucano-like in being strictly postpositional and displaying a tendency towards verb-final structure (ibid. 167).

Note that the relative genetic stability of case alignment does not imply total stability: from various language families, we have evidence of languages switching case alignment: e.g. from the Kartvelian split-ergative alignment found in Georgian, Laz has developed into a fully ergative language, while Megrelian has developed into a fully (marked) accusative language (Harris 1985: 26ff); in Indo-European, it is a matter of debate whether the proto-language was active or accusative (cf. Drinka 1999), but the family as such contains (partially) ergative, active and accusative languages.

Thus, word order and case alignment appear to be the features which are maximally distinct when it comes to genetic stability versus contact sensitivity. It is therefore important to point out that these two features are also typologically very closely connected. Here we should expect to find cases where word order may have changed due to areal influence, while case alignment is genetically preserved, leading to a mismatch between word order and case-alignment. How this tension is resolved in various languages is an interesting issue.[11]

In the present database we include word order at various levels in the clause (adpositions, noun-modifier and clause-level) and case-alignment of different types,[12] various kinds of subordination construction, polar and content interrogativity as well as various properties of the verbal paradigm. One aim is to chart in greater detail the various degrees of genetic stability and contact-sensitivity displayed by different typological features, as well as to examine how well the general tendencies shown by Nichols carry over to a specifically Amazonian setting, with its very special characteristics.

As a principle, we expect typological pressure to be universally valid.[13] Insofar as certain geographical areas seem on the surface to be partially exempt from this, i.e. to be rife with exceptions to generally valid cross-linguistic generalizations (impressionistically, Amazonia seems to be a case in point, although this remains to be confirmed), we must conclude that some other factor may be overriding typological pressure.

One factor which might be involved is general instability in the language systems caused by widespread language attrition in various populations, partly today, but quite probably also in connection with the sudden demographic changes caused by European contact: between disease and genocide, European contact led to the untimely death of more than half of the population of the American continent, even according to cautious and conservative estimates (Cook 1998 and sources cited therein), and the aftermath led to a diaspora of various peoples scattered across the whole of Amazonia.

Further, given the principle of linguistic exogamy found in various Amazonian populations (Hornborg 1988; Aikhenvald 2002: 22), multilingualism is widespread, and structural loans across typologically diverse languages could possibly lead to unusual combinations of features surfacing within a single language.

Whatever constellations of features have appeared as a result of this, it is possible that the time elapsed since then has not been sufficient for typological pressure to act on the languages. To evaluate this account would require some kind of knowledge of the rate of change of the typological features involved.

A final, more speculative, hypothesis might derive inspiration from Barth's (1969) seminal study on the construction of ethnic identity and ethnic boundaries, and propose that linguistic properties can be actively exaggerated by speakers to emphasize ethnic distinctions in a multilingual setting. If this is the case, it should be possible to show independently that certain linguistic properties are consciously accessible to speakers.

5. Results of combined applications

The interpretations proposed by the current investigation take as their point of departure the discussion of expected stability versus expected contact sensitivity among the linguistic and cultural features. To start with, Arawak languages display a certain degree of overall stability in the sense that they still share some overarching genetic similarities despite a very large degree of separation in space and time. Furthermore, Arawak cultures also share similarities through the Arawak matrix, indicating that certain cultural features (both material and non-material) also show considerable stability over time. This section seeks to outline which features are subject to a high degree of stability, and which features are to a greater degree contact sensitive.

In terms of the language tree (fig. 1.) and its clusters, it is in itself indicative of a certain kind of macro-stability given that the basic vocabulary of the languages are still similar to a certain degree despite considerable spatial and temporal division between many of the languages of the tree. The fact that the languages do cluster may indicate that at the micro level, e.g. in a given spatial area, a certain kind of contact sensitivity contributed to making the languages more similar through areal contacts among the languages within the respective clusters. However, the purpose of using the most stable part of language, i.e., basic vocabulary, for clustering, is precisely to being able to contrast contact-sensitivity to stability at a micro level.

The parallels between linguistic and geographical clustering are confirmed by figure 3, showing that the clusters in the language tree display themselves in particular geographical settings according to their position in the language tree (this is not in any way implied in the cladistics analysis, which only indicates the degree of separateness in terms of basic vocabulary and thus contains no spatial component whatsoever).

Figure 3 shows, (a) that lexical similarities reflect spatial closeness within the clusters, but (b), that spatial separation is not a direct reflection of lexical distance (cluster B is located far from cluster A and C, the clusters with which it shares basic vocabulary most closely). This finding is indicative of the fact that other factors besides geographical distance are influential in the distribution of basic vocabulary among members of the Arawak family.

Contrasting linguistics and archaeology in the matrix model 47

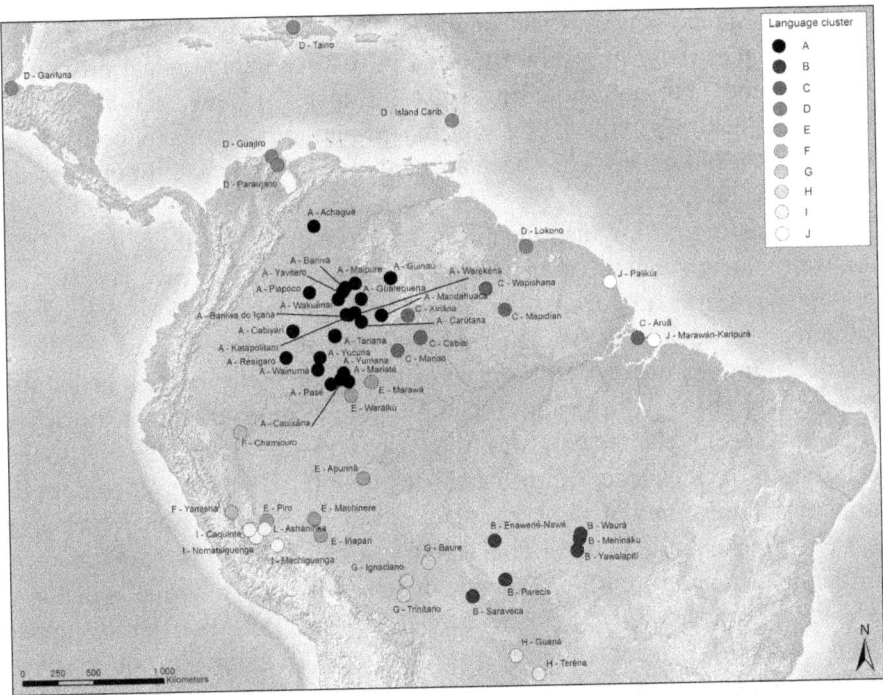

Figure 3. The spatial distribution of the language clusters.

The fact that cluster B is geographically located far from cluster A and C is noteworthy, particularly in the light of the proposed north-south split in the Arawak languages suggested by Aikhenvald (1999). This finding is confirmed by the interpretation of Walker and Ribeiro (2011: 3), who provided the original data set on which this conclusion is based.

Furthermore, the spatial analysis of the language tree identifies cluster I and J at two opposite ends of the continent. It is interesting to see that these two clusters share close lexical similarities despite no indications of socio-cultural contacts between speakers of these languages for at least a millennium (Eriksen 2011). Regarding the spatial distribution of clusters A, C, and D, their positions are located at reasonably expected distances from each other given some kind of geographical diffusion process from a common proto-language. This is also the case for clusters E and F, and in the case of Apurinã, Machinere, Iñapari, and Piro of cluster E, it indicates that these languages rather share a common history with Marawá and Waraikú, the two other languages of cluster E, and ultimately with the Arawak languages of the northwest Amazon, than with the languages of cluster I; Asháninka,

Caquinte, Machiguenga, Nomatsiguenga. This finding is of course noteworthy given that these groups are located in relative geographical proximity to each other, but not surprising since the historical amnesia among the Arawak-speaking groups of cluster E regarding their common ancestry with the languages of cluster I has been attested by ethnographers for quite some time (Gow 2002: 153).

In terms of non-linguistic features, many of the cultural features of the Arawak matrix show remarkable temporal stability, a fact that has allowed previous research to reconstruct an Arawak-mediated regional exchange system as far back as 900 BC in the northern part of the continent (Eriksen 2011). An interesting observation that can be made in this context is that the present-day pottery of the upper Xingú region (a multi-ethnic area heavily acculturalized by its Arawak-speaking groups) shows direct analogies to the ceramics of the Orinoco Valley dated back to 900 BC (the Barrancoid tradition) at the locations of the early nodes of the Arawak regional exchange system (Heckenberger 2005). This is a strong indication of *stability* in terms of the material culture of the Arawak matrix. Also worth noting is that due to the historical ethno-linguistic production specialization of the upper Xingú region (Eriksen 2011: 88), Arawak-speaking female potters have been responsible for the region-wide pottery production, meaning that other ethno-linguistic groups have been subjected to both Arawak material culture and language when in trade contacts with the Arawaks, a process that has been ongoing for a considerable time depth.[14] This may be interpreted as indicative of a greater degree of contact sensitivity among the languages of the non-Arawak-speaking groups of the upper Xingú region, but it is also indicative of the strong cultural influence conducted by the Arawak-speaking groups.

The fact that the reconstructed words for maize (fig. 2) are borrowed throughout the area is in itself an indication of the close socio-linguistic contact of the region. As seen in figure 5, the distribution of root 1a, *$mahik^ji$, is clearly an Arawak-dominated root spread through the exchange system and to some non-Arawak-speaking groups through socio-cultural contact. Thus, the distribution of root 1a is clearly a stable feature that is borrowed only in certain types of social contexts like the close interaction sphere of the upper Xingú area. Overall, we see a clear effect of social interaction through socio-cultural exchange on the distribution of lexical features (fig. 3), but an even more detailed picture can be painted by examining the distribution of individual lexical features and their relationship to the exchange system. As for the distribution of the proto-forms for maize, a close examination indicates that socio-cultural contact through the Arawak exchange system

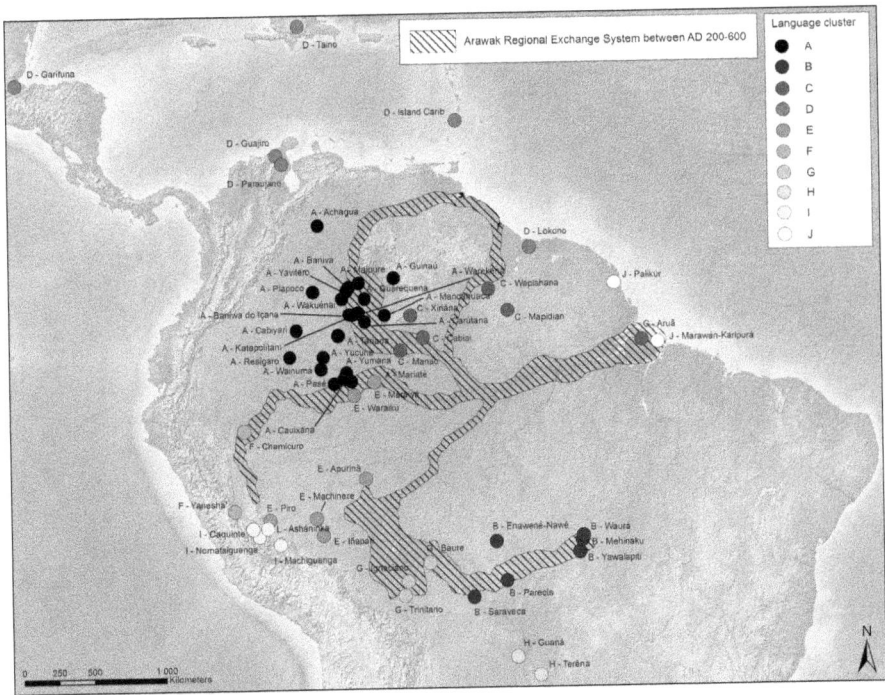

Figure 4. The spatial distribution of the language clusters and the extent of the Arawak regional exchange system at AD 200–600.

was a much more influential force in the distribution of the proto-words than the genetic relationship between the languages, indicating that certain types of language contact situations occurred after the initial geographic dispersal of the languages of the Arawak family.

Nichols (1992: 166ff) notes that word order is a feature which readily spreads areally between unrelated languages. The distribution of verb-initial ordering (VSO/VOS) in the Arawakan languages is a case in point. While verb-initial order is found in several Arawakan languages, it is largely concentrated to the western areas of Amazonia (cf. fig 6), in areas where there are several other non-Arawakan languages which display verb-initial ordering. In other regions of Amazonia, Arawakan languages tend to display other word order patterns (particularly SVO in northen areas, and SOV further south). In contrast, the active verb agreement pattern (with prefixes cross-referencing agentive arguments and suffixes cross-referencing patientive arguments) is found throughout Amazonia.

In summary, the Arawak matrix developed and spread through a regional exchange system initiated around 900 BC in the Orinoco area. In terms of

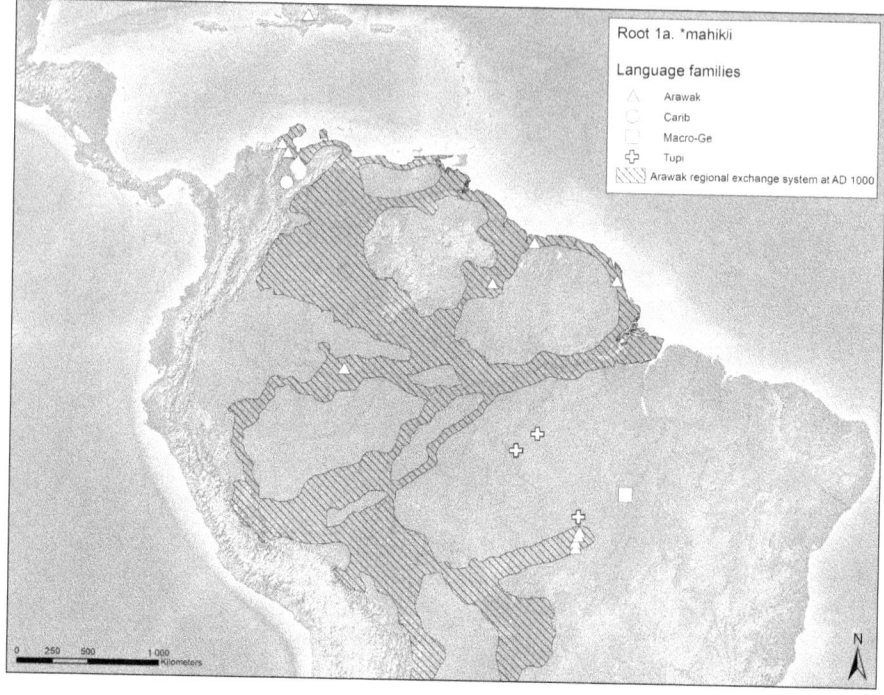

Figure 5. The spatial distribution of maize root 1a, and the extent of the Arawak regional exchange system at AD 1000.

the present study, the most important time period in the system is between AD 200 and 600, a time period when the system displays its greatest internal similarities in terms of material culture. At this point in time, the materiality of the Arawak matrix displays similarities so great that the same type of ceramic adornos (a decorative feature of the Arawak pottery) was used in an area stretching from the Antilles to Central Amazonia. Comparing the extension of the regional exchange system at this point in time to the distribution of clusters A, B, C, and D in the language tree may explain the high degree of lexical similarities between cluster A and B despite great geographical separation of the speakers; the distribution of the lexical features is the result of language contact up to AD 600. After this period, the internal homogenization of the system was less powerful, perhaps as a consequence of the constant geographical expansion of the trade networks that kept on linking more and more distant areas of Amazonia together. By AD 1000 (fig. 3) the system experienced its greatest territorial extent, but, as mentioned above, the internal similarities in terms of material culture and language had constantly decreased after AD 600. After AD 1000, a slow internal

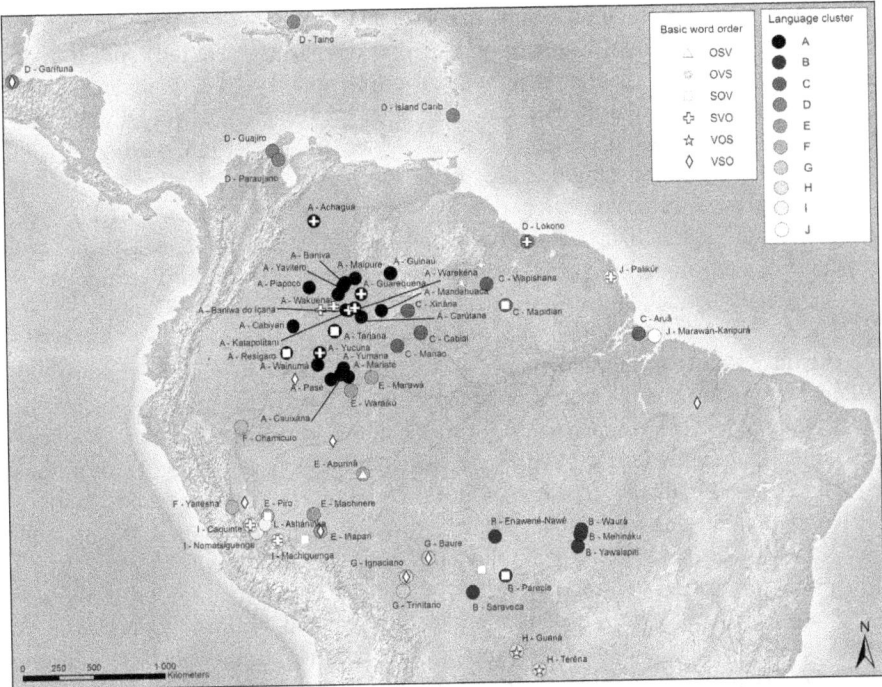

Figure 6. The distribution of basic word order among the Arawak languages in the sample, and the spatial distribution of the language clusters.

fragmentation process continued up until AD 1200, when the expansion of the Tupian languages (Lathrap 1970: 150f; Meggers 1971: 122–130; Neves et al 2004: 133; Rebellato et al 2009: 22, 27) finally broke the Arawak regional exchange system apart once and for all. What remained of the system after AD 1200 were the current Arawak-speaking groups, and small sections of the formerly great regional exchange system still upheld by these local Arawak-speaking communities.[15]

Notes

1. We thank Alf Hornborg and Chris Sinha for valuable comments. We also thank Judith Josephson for correcting our English. The research has been funded by Centre for Cognitive Semiotics/Bank of Sweden Tercentenary Foundation and the Human Ecology Division, Lund University.
2. The assumption made here is that the same factors hold for lexical items, grammatical constructions and basic language structure alike, albeit in different degrees

(which is part of the topic of this paper). Thus, as pointed out by an anonymous reviewer, e.g. calques are simply a special (construction-based) subset of the more general phenomenon of areal features (or, conversely, areal features can be described as clusters of calques). The label of "typological pressure" can be taken to mean non-coincidental features which are neither inherited nor loaned, but are in some way functionally or cognitively motivated. Under this reading, a lexical parallel to typological pressure can possibly be found, namely iconicity (e.g. sound-symbolism, onomatopoeia). However, we will not deal further with the issue of iconicity, since its effect in creating surface similarities across languages is much lower than that of inheritance or loans.

3. Here, an IPA-based system of writing reconstructed forms is used, which also includes a more traditional historical-linguistic method (e.g., Szémerenyi 1990): in case of the occurrence of palatalization and/or fricativization in a number of languages, the reconstructed form is marked by a non-palatalized plosive + palatalization marker /ʲ/. In case of reflexes in languages that yield several possibilities, e.g., bilabial plosives /p/ or /b/ as being the possible reconstructions, capitals (referring to the most likely form) are being used, e.g., */B/ = bilabial plosives (/b/ /p/), */T/ = dental/alveolar/postalveolar plosives (/t/ /d/), */N/ = nasals (/n/ /m/, more probably /n/), */M/ = nasals (/m/ /n/, more probably /m/). For problematic vocalic reconstructions, the classical "schwa" */ə/ is used.

4. The Yagua data is open to various interpretations, but one possible interpretation is that Yagua adpositions are postpositions, either suffixed directly to nouns, or suffixed to agreement clitics which precede the noun, which gives the appearance of agreeing prepositions (Payne and Payne 1990: 363ff).

5. Here WALS cites a single exception, not surprisingly, perhaps, a language in Amazonia: the Arauan language Paumarí, spoken in western Brazil, on the Purus river.

6. Indeed, Evans and Levinson (2009) refer to the "myth of language universals", capitalizing on the fact that they are tendencies rather than exceptionless universals, although they do admit that certain strong tendencies are due to functional economy (op. cit. 445). We are aware of the non-universality of Greenbergian "universals", of which there is perhaps more evidence in Amazonia than elsewhere. However, our basic assumption (to be empirically tested) is that several tendencies are so strong that they cannot be the product of mere chance.

7. Efficiency and economy can be measured in terms of the degree to which structures can be re-used for different types of constructions in the language (e.g. head-final structures appearing both in OV verb phrases and in postpositional phrases), and the degree to which unnecessary redundancy is done away with.

8. As is argued in Holmer (2006) to be the explanation of the striking similarities at the syntactic and morphological levels between Basque, Georgian, Burushaski and Chukchi (including polypersonal agreement and prefixed morphology), namely that they all derive from typological pressure exerted by the one coincidentally shared property of ergativity.

9. An anonymous reviewer points out that gender is another feature which correlates highly with language family, i.e. is, in our parlance, genetically stable.
10. One reason is that Tariana has borrowed overt case marking from Tucano (although the alignment itself is not fully accusative as it is in Tucano).
11. Or if it is resolved at all: strictly speaking, it is an ergative alignment of the case marking system which is more or less excluded in SVO languages, whereas the split-ergative / active alignment found in Amazonia concerns verb agreement paradigms. WALS does, indeed, list 6 languages which combine SVO word order with an active verb agreement alignment, 4 of them in Amazonia, and three of these (Apurinã, Arawak [Lokono] and Warekena) actually belonging to the Arawakan family.
12. e.g. whether the alignment pattern is instantiated by case-marking, verb agreement or syntactic relations.
13. *pace* Dunn et al. 2011, who argue that many instances of typological correlations are lineage-specific, i.e. represent shared inheritance.
14. Heckenberger (2005: 31) estimates that the Arawak population of the upper Xingú dates back to AD 500.
15. The scattered remains of the Arawak exchange system were often transformed into multi-ethnic interaction spheres around the centuries of European colonization (Eriksen 2011: 197). This process was intensified as a response to the pressures of the colonial powers on indigenous communities across Amazonia, and it is likely that there were also substantial effects on language use accompanying this process.

References

Aikhenvald, Alexandra
    1999   Arawak languages. In *Amazonian Languages*. Robert Dixon and Alexandra Aikhenvald (eds.), 487–517. Cambridge: Cambridge University Press.

Aikhenvald, Alexandra
    2002   *Language contact in Amazonia*. Oxford: Oxford University Press.

Barth, Fredrik
    1969   Introduction. In *Ethnic Groups and Boundarie*, Fredrik Barth (ed.), 9–38. Oslo: Scandinavian University Press.

Birket-Schmidt, Kaj
    1943   *The Origin of Maize Cultivation*. Copenhagen: Ejnar Munksgaard.

Brown, Cecil H.
    1999   *Lexical Acculturation in the Native American Languages*. Oxford: Oxford University Press.

Brown, Cecil H.
  2006   Glottochronology and the chronology of maize in the Americas. In *Histories of Maize. Multidisciplinary Approaches to the Prehistory, Linguistics, Biogeography, Domestication, and Evolution of Maize*, John E. Staller, Robert H. Tykot, and Bruce F. Benz (eds.), 647–663. London: Academic Press.

Campbell, Lyle
  2004   *Historical Linguistics. An Introduction.* Edinburgh: Edinburgh University Press.

Cook, Noble David
  1998   *Born to Die: Disease and New World conquest, 1492–1650.* Cambridge: Cambridge University Press

Danielsen, Swintha, Michael Dunn, and Peter Muysken
  2011   The spread of the Arawakan languages: A view from structural phylogenetics. In: Hornborg and Hill 2011.

Dunn, Michael, Simon Greenhill, Stephen Levinson, and Russell Gray
  2011   Evolved structure of language shows lineage-specific trends in word-order universals. *Nature.* Published online April 2011.

Eriksen, Love
  2011   *Nature and Culture in Prehistoric Amazonia: Using G.I.S. to reconstruct ancient ethnogenetic processes from archaeology, linguistics, geography, and ethnohistory.* Ph.D. diss., Human Ecology Division, Lund University.

Evans, Nicholas and Stephen Levinson
  2009   The myth of language universals: Language diversity and its importance for cognitive science. *Behavioral and Brain Sciences* 32: 429–492.

Glaser, Bruno and William I. Woods (eds.)
  2004   *Amazonian dark earths: Explorations in space and time.* Berlin: Springer.

Gow, Peter
  2002   Piro, Apurinã, and Campa: Social dissimilation and assimilation as historical processes in southwestern Amazonia. In *Comparative Arawakan Histories: Rethinking language family and culture area in Amazonia*, Jonathan D. Hill and Fernando Santos-Granero (eds.), 147–170. Urbana: University of Illinois Press.

Greenberg, Joseph
  1963   Some universals of grammar with particular reference to the order of meaningful elements. In *Universals of Language*, Joseph Greenberg (ed.), 73–113. London: MIT Press.

Harris, Alice
  1985   *Diachronic Syntax: The Kartvelian Case.* (Syntax & Semantics, Vol 18). Orlando: Academic Press

Harrison, Carl
   1986   Verb prominence, verb initialness, ergativity and typological disharmony in Guajajara. In *Handbook of Amazonian languages, Vol 1*, Desmond Derbyshire and Geoffrey Pullum (eds.), 407– 439. Berlin/New York: Mouton de Gruyter.

Haspelmath, Martin and Uri Tadmor
   2009   *Loanwords in the World's Languages. A Comparative Handbook.* Berlin/New York: Mouton de Gruyter.

Hawkins, John
   1983   *Word Order Universals.* New York: Academic Press

Heckenberger, Michael J.
   2005   *The Ecology of Power: Culture, Place, and Personhood in the Southern Amazon, AD 1000–2000.* New York: Routledge.

Hill, Jonathan D.
   2007   Sacred landscapes as environmental histories in Lowland South America. Paper prepared for session on "Long-Term Patterns of Ethnogenesis in Indigenous Amazonia," Jonathan Hill and Alf Hornborg, organizers. Annual Meetings of the American Anthropological Association, Washington D.C., November 30, 2007.

Hill, Jonathan D.
   2011   Sacred landscapes as environmental histories in Lowland South America. In *Ethnicity in Ancient Amazonia: Reconstructing Past Identities from Archaeology, Linguistics, and Rthnohistory*, Alf Hornborg, and Jonathan D. Hill (eds.), 259–278. Boulder: University Press of Colorado.

Hill, Jonathan D. and Fernando Santos-Granero (eds.)
   2002   *Comparative Arawakan Histories: Rethinking Language Family and Culture Area in Amazonia.* Urbana: University of Illinois Press.

Holmer, Arthur
   2006   Polypersonal agreement, convergent evolution and the Basque-Caucasian hypothesis. In *Andolin Gogoan. Essays in honour of Professor Eguzkitza.* Fernández, Beatriz, and Laka, Itziar (eds.), 477–495. Bilbao: University of the Basque Country.

Hornborg, Alf
   1988   *Dualism and Hierarchy in Lowland South America. Trajectories of Indigenous Social Organization.* Uppsala: Uppsala Studies in Cultural Antropology 9.

Hornborg, Alf
   2005   Ethnogenesis, regional integration, and ecology in prehistoric Amazonia. *Current Anthropology* 46 (4): 589–620.

Hornborg, Alf and Jonathan D. Hill (eds.)
   2011   *Ethnicity in Ancient Amazonia: Reconstructing Past Identities from Archaeology, Linguistics, and Ethnohistory.* Boulder: University Press of Colorado.

Lehmann, Johannes, Dirse C. Kern, Bruno Glaser, and William I. Woods (eds.)
   2003   *Amazonian Dark Earths: Origin, Properties, management*. Dordrecht: Kluwer.
Mann, Charles C.
   2008   Ancient earthmovers of the Amazon. *Science* 321 (5893): 1148–1152.
Muysken, Pieter C.
   2011   Contacts between indigenous languages in South America. In *Historical Linguistics of South America*, Lyle Campbell and Veronica Grondona (eds.), 235–258. Berlin/Boston: Mouton de Gruyter.
Nichols, Johanna
   1992   *Linguistic Diversity in Space and Time*. Chicago: University of Chicago Press.
O'Connor, Loretta and Pieter C. Muysken (eds.)
   2012   *The Native Languages of South America: Origins, Development, Typology*. [Forthcoming]
Payne, Doris and Thomas Payne
   1990   Yagua. In *Handbook of Amazonian languages, Vol 2*, Desmond Derbyshire and Geoffrey Pullum (eds.), 249–474. Berlin/New York: Mouton de Gruyter.
Payne, David
   1991   A classification of Maipuran (Arawakan) languages based on shared lexical retentions. In *Handbook of Amazonian languages, Vol 3*, Desmond Derbyshire and Geoffrey Pullum (eds.), 355–499. Berlin/New York: Mouton de Gruyter.
Santos-Granero, Fernando
   1998   Writing history into the landscape: Space, myth, and ritual in contemporary Amazonia. *American Ethnologist* 25: 128–148.
Saunaluoma, Sanna
   2010   Pre-Columbian earthworks of the Riberalta region of the Bolivian Amazon. *Amazônica* 2 (1): 85–115.
Schaan, Denise, Alceu Ranzi, and Martti Pärssinen.
   2007   *Arqueologia da Amazônia Occidental: Os Geoglifos do Acre*. Belém: EDUFPA.
Walker, Robert S. and Lincoln A. Ribeiro
   2011   Bayesian phylogeography of the Arawak expansion in lowland South America. *Proceedings of the Royal Society 2011*, published online 19 January 2011.
WALS Online   *World Atlas of Language Structures*.
   Online version available at: http://wals.info/. Accessed 2011-10-12)
Woods, William I., Wenceslau G. Teixeira, Johannes Lehmann, Christoph Steiner, Antoinette WinklerPrins, and Lilian Rebellato (eds.)
   2009   *Amazonian Dark Earths: Wim Sombroek's Vision*. New York: Springer.

Predicting language-learning difficulty

Michael Cysouw

1. Introduction[1]

The difficulty people have in learning a foreign language strongly depends on how different this language is from their native tongue (Kellerman 1979). Although this statement seems uncontroversial in the general form as it is formulated here, the devil lies in the detail, namely in the problem how to define differences between languages. In this paper, I investigate various factors that quantify differences between languages, and explore to which extend these factors predict language learning difficulty. This investigation results in concrete predictive formulas that derive the learning difficulty for native English speakers depending on a small selection of linguistic factors of the language to be learned.

Section 2 presents the data for language learning difficulty that will be used in this paper. This data originates at the Foreign Services Institute (FSI) of the US Department of State and it includes only approximate average learning times of foreign languages for English speakers. The data is rather rough, but it is highly interesting because it gives comparable estimates for language learning difficulty for a large number of strongly different languages from all over the world. Section 3 investigates the relation of these estimates for language learning difficulty to very general predictors like geographical distance and genealogical affiliation. In both cases, the further away a language is from English, both geographically and genealogically, the more difficult a language is expected to be. All empirical effects point in the expected direction, though the factor Germanic vs. non-Germanic turns out to be the strongest predictor for language-learning difficulty.

Section 4 takes up the differences in writing systems as used for the various languages in the current sample. Using the Universal Declaration of Human Rights, the orthographic similarity between English and other languages is established. For languages with a Latin script, there is a strong correlation between language learning difficulty and the similarity in frequency distribution of orthographic symbols. Section 5 investigates structural grammatical properties of languages using data from the World Atlas of Language Structures. I establish which structural differences from

English most strongly correlate with language learning difficulty for English speakers.

Section 6 combines all these factors and searches for suitable models to predict language-learning difficulty. Two different kinds of models are proposed: one based on agglomerative similarity values between English and other languages and one based on more practical binary predictors describing actual characteristics of the languages to be learned. In the agglomerative models, language learning difficulty can be predicted by a strong factor related to structural typological similarity and a weaker subsidiary factor related to the writing system. In the binary models, the main factors were related to having a Latin script or not, being an Indo-European language or not, and various structural characteristics, namely prepositions vs. postpositions, accusative vs. ergative alignment and the presence vs. absence of obligatory plural marking of nouns.

2. Measurements of language learning difficulty

For this paper, I will use two different measurements of the difficulty English speakers appear to have when learning specific foreign languages. Both these rather rough measurements originate at the Foreign Services Institute (FSI) of the US Department of State. They arose in the context of planning the amount of resources necessary for language teaching when preparing US citizens for foreign detachment.

The first measurement of language learning difficulty is an assessment of the number of class hours it takes to achieve general proficiency in speaking and reading in a foreign language (where "general proficiency" is defined by the language skill level descriptions from the Interagency Language Roundtable). It is basically a three-level scale (I for "easy", II for "middle", III for "hard"), which Jackson and Kaplan (2001: 77) explain as follows:

> "The categories indicate gross differences in how hard it is for native speakers of American English to learn different languages. [...] These categories [...] are based solely on FSI's experience of the time it takes our learners to learn these languages. [...] The more commonalities a language shares with English – whether due to a genetic relationship or otherwise – the easier and faster it is for a native English speaker to learn that language. [...] The more dissimilar a new language is – in structure, sounds, orthography, implicit world view, and so on – the longer learning takes." (Jackson and Kaplan 2001: 77)

Actual assessments for different languages are not currently available through any documentation from the FSI. However, there used to be a website from the FSI with information about the languages of the world, which can still be accessed through the Internet Archive. On this website a classification of various languages is given according to the three-level scale, as reproduced here in table 1.2 In addition, it is noted that various languages are "somewhat more difficult for native English speakers to learn than other languages in the same category". These languages are marked with a star in the table. Further, German is specifically indicated to fall in between category I and I*, so I have added a separate category for German. I will use the resulting seven-level scale as a measurement of difficulty and refer to this measurement "FSI-level" in the remainder of this paper. If not specifically indicated, I will interpret the seven levels as a linear numerical scale from one to seven, as shown in table 1.

The second measurement of language learning difficulty used in this paper is reported in Hart-Gonzales and Lindemann (1993), as cited in Chiswick and Miller (2005: 5–6). As above, I have not been able to get hold of the original source by Hart-Gonzales and Lindemann, so I am simply using the numbers as presented in Chiswick and Miller. They explain this measurement as follows:

"The paper by Hart-Gonzalez and Lindemann (1993) reports language scores for 43 languages for English-speaking Americans of average ability after [24 weeks] of foreign language training. [...] The range is from a low score (harder to learn) of 1.00 for Japanese to a high score (easier to learn) of 3.00 for Afrikaans, Norwegian and Swedish. The score for French is 2.50 and for Mandarin 1.50. These scores suggest a ranking of linguistic distance from English among these languages: Japanese being the most distant, followed by Mandarin, then French and then Afrikaans, and Norwegian and Swedish as the least distant." (Chiswick and Miller 2005: 5)

I will refer to this measurement as the "24-week ability" score in the remainder of this paper. The individual scores from Hart-Gonzales and Lindemann are reproduced here in table 2.

These two measurements of language learning difficulty are strongly correlated (Pearson $r = -0.85$, $p = 1.8e-12$). The correlation is negative because more difficult languages have a high FSI-level score, but learners will have a low ability after 24 weeks of language training. Although the two measurements are highly correlated, there are still notable differences (e.g. concerning the position of Danish and Spanish). Also, there are more

Table 1. FSI levels of difficulty for various languages (higher levels represent greater difficulty).

FSI Level	Languages
1 (I)	Afrikaans, Danish, Dutch, French, Italian, Norwegian, Portuguese, Romanian, Spanish, Swedish
2 (I)	German
3 (I*)	Indonesian, Malay, Swahili
4 (II)	Albanian, Amharic, Armenian, Azerbaijani, Bengali, Bosnian, Bulgarian, Burmese, Czech, Greek, Hebrew, Hindi, Icelandic, Khmer, Lao, Latvian, Lithuanian, Macedonian, Nepali, Pashto, Persian, Polish, Russian, Serbo-Croatian, Sinhalese, Slovak, Slovenian, Swahili, Tagalog, Turkish, Ukrainian, Urdu, Uzbek, Xhosa, Zulu
5 (II*)	Estonian, Finnish, Georgian, Hungarian, Mongolian, Thai, Vietnamese
6 (III)	Arabic, Cantonese, Korean, Mandarin
7 (III*)	Japanese

Table 2. Average ability scores for various languages after 24 weeks of foreign language training (low values represent less communicational ability).

24-week ability	Languages
1.00	Japanese, Korean
1.25	Cantonese
1.50	Arabic, Lao, Mandarin, Vietnamese
1.75	Bengali, Burmese, Greek, Hindi, Nepali, Sinhalese
2.00	Amharic, Bulgarian, Czech, Finnish, Hebrew, Hungarian, Indonesian, Khmer, Mongolian, Persian, Polish, Serbo-Croatian, Sinhalese, Tagalog, Thai, Turkish
2.25	Danish, German, Spanish, Russian
2.50	French, Italian, Portuguese
2.75	Dutch, Malay, Swahili
3.00	Afrikaans, Norwegian, Romanian, Swedish

languages with an FSI-level than with a 24-week ability score, which makes the somewhat more coarse-grained FSI-level scale more telling for quantitative comparisons. For these reasons, I will use both measurements in the rest of this paper.

It should be noted that these measurements of language learning difficulty are extremely rough. Not only do they just distinguish a few levels of "difficulty", they also do not include any information about the background of the learners and the process of the learning itself, both factors known to have significant influence on the language learning difficulty (cf. Schepens, van der Slik and van Hout, this volume). However, given the origin of the current data, it can be assumed that the kind of people entering the learning and the kind of lessons presented to them are rather homogeneous, so that ignoring these factors – while unfortunate – is probably not influencing the current results significantly.

3. Geography and genealogy

The difficulty in learning a language is supposedly related to the degree of difference between the language(s) a learner already knows and the language the learner wants to learn. There are two factors that are known to be strongly correlated to the degree of difference between languages. First, the closer two languages are geographically, the smaller the differences are expected to be. And, second, the closer the genealogical relationship between two languages, the smaller the differences will be.

To assess the geographical distance between English and the other languages considered in this paper, I will locate English in the City of London. This is of course a completely illusory point of origin considering the current world-wide distribution of English speaking communities. At best, it represents the most prestigious location of English speakers up until a century ago. Likewise, I will use point locators for all the other languages listed in Section 2, which in many cases are also spoken over widely dispersed territories. The measurements of geographical proximity are thus to be taken as very rough approximations (verging on the nonsensical) of the actual social distance between real speakers. In practice, I will use the coordinates as listed in the *World Atlas of Language Structures* (WALS, Haspelmath et al. 2005) as the point locations for the computation of geographical distance between languages.

As the distance between two point locators representing languages, I will use the distance "as the bird flies", i.e. the great-circle distance, further assuming the world to be a perfect sphere and ignoring elevation difference. Such a simplistic assumption will of course further lessen any real-world impact of the current conceptualization of geographical distance between languages. However, the correlation between this notion of geographical distance and language learning difficulty is still clearly significant, though not very strong (FSI-levels: $r = 0.38$, $p = 0.003$; 24-week ability scores: $r = -0.43$, $p = 0.004$). So, indeed, languages that are further away geographically from English are in general more difficult to learn for English speakers. As expected, Afrikaans, Swahili, Malay and Indonesian are the most extreme outliers to the one side, being much easier to learn than expected from their large geographical distance from English. In contrast, Arabic is more difficult to learn compared to the relative geographical proximity to English (see figure 1).

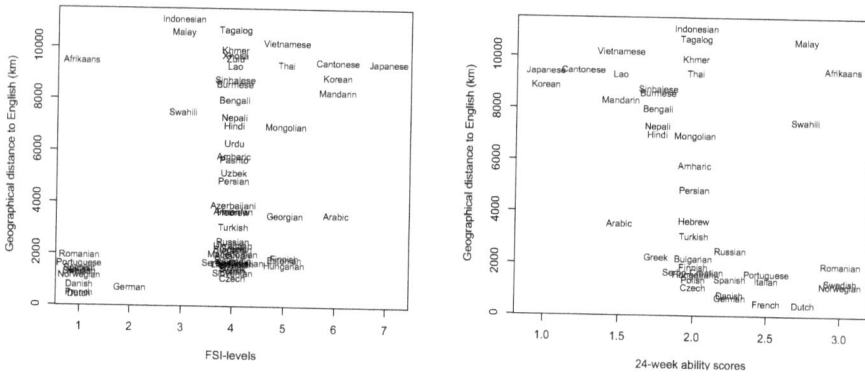

Figure 1. Correlations between geographical proximity to English and language learning difficulty, FSI-levels to the left and 24-week ability scores to the right.

Genealogically closely related languages – i.e. languages from the same language family – are also expected to be relatively similar, and thus be easier to learn. Closely related languages are often structurally similar and also share part of the lexicon, which might ease learning. A substantial amount of shared lexicon of course also increases the chance of the occurrence of false friends, inhibiting ease of learning. However, this effect is probably not relevant for the relatively low proficiency levels with which we are dealing in this paper. Further complicating matters is that it is not immediately obvious how to quantify genealogical proximity of languages. Although it is clear that English is genealogically closer to German than to Greek, Hindi, or Cantonese (in decreasing order), giving numbers to such qualifications strongly depends on the details of the historical reconstruction. As a practical solution, I will use the two-level genealogical classification from Dryer (2005b). Dryer distinguishes a level of closely related languages ("genus") and a level of more distantly related languages ("family").

As expected, languages from within the same genus as English, viz. Germanic, are easier to learn for English speakers than languages from different genera (FSI-levels: Germanic mean 1.57 vs. non-Germanic mean 4.00, $t = -5.27$, $p = 7.5\text{e-}4$; 24-week ability scores: Germanic mean 2.71 vs. non-Germanic mean 1.95, $t = 4.52$, $p = 0.002$). Similarly, languages from the same family as English, viz. Indo-European (IE), are easier to learn for English speakers than languages from different families (FSI-levels: IE mean 3.06 vs. non-IE mean 4.58, $t = -4.86$, $p = 9.2\text{e-}6$; 24-week ability scores: IE mean 2.27 vs. non-IE mean 1.83, $t = 3.16$, $p = 0.003$).

So, languages that are geographically far away, and such that are non-Germanic or better still non-Indo-European, are difficult to learn for English speakers. But, these three factors are to some extend measuring the same facts and are clearly all related to each other (cf. Cysouw 2012). Non-Indo-European languages are by definition also non-Germanic languages, and both these groups of languages will generally be geographically far away. To assess the relative impact of these factors for language learning difficulty, I combined the three factors in a linear regression model, as shown in table 3.

These numbers can be interpreted as follows. For the FSI-levels, the default level to learn a foreign language is at 1.52 (viz. the intercept estimate), while the presence of any of the other factors increases the difficulty of the language: geographical distance leads to an increase of 0.25 per 10.000 km, being non-Germanic increases learning difficulty with 1.85, and being non-Indo-European increases learning difficulty with 1.03. For example, for Hindi (located at about 7.000 km from English) this model predicts an FSI-level of 3.55 (=1.52+0.25·0.70+1·1.85+0·1.03), while the actual FSI-level is at 4. However, the geographical factor is not significant, and removing this factor indeed results in a simpler model with equal residual deviance. So, while both genealogical levels are significant factors, the influence of geographical distance is already accounted for to a large extend by the genealogical factors.

For the 24-week ability the results in table 3 are similar, though in this case the factor non-Indo-European is also not significant. Further note that the intercept estimate (2.77) here represents the maximum ability after 24 weeks, while all factors reduce the predicted ability. Again taking Hindi as an example, the model predicts an ability of 2.00 (=2.77−0.28·0.70−1·0.57−0·0.19), while the actual ability as listed in the data used in this paper is 1.75.

In this table, only the Germanic vs. non-Germanic parameter is significant, and this parameter was also the strongest in the calculations for the FSI-levels. This suggests that the strongest effect for language learning difficulty stem from the rather local effect of whether a language is Germanic or not.

Table 3. Regression model of geographical and genealogical factors.

	Estimate	Std. Error	t-value	Pr(> |t|)
FSI-levels				
Intercept	1.52	0.44	3.45	0.001 **
Geography	0.25	5.18	0.49	0.62
Non-Germanic	1.85	0.48	3.88	0.0002 ***
Non-Indo-European	1.03	0.37	2.79	0.007 **
24-week ability				
Intercept	2.77	0.18	15.72	< 2e-16 ***
Geography	− 0.28	2.17	− 1.29	0.21
Non-Germanic	− 0.57	0.20	− 2.85	0.007 **
Non-Indo-European	− 0.19	0.17	− 1.02	0.31

4. Writing system

Another obvious factor influencing the effort needed to learn a foreign language is the writing system that is used. Languages with a similar writing system to English are expected to be easier to learn than languages with a completely different writing system. To quantitatively assess the similarities of writing systems between languages I used the translations of the Universal Declaration of Human Rights as prepared in Unicode encoding by Eric Muller.[3] For several languages there is more than one translation available. For German and Romanian, I chose the version with the most recent orthography. For Chinese I chose the simplified orthography and for Greek the version with the monotonic script. For Malay, Bosnian and Azerbaijani I selected the translation using the Latin script, while for Serbian I chose the Cyrillic script, because these scripts seem to have the most widespread usage for these languages. Finally, for Sinhalese and Cantonese no translations were available.

It is well known that the orthographic structure of texts is a good approximation for language similarity (Damashek 1995). The most widespread application of this finding is the usage of so-called "n-gram" statistics for the identification of languages or even individual authors. The same statistics can also be used to approximate genealogical relationships (Huffman 2003; Coppin 2008). The basic idea of n-gram statistics is that the number of occurrences of each sequence of *n* character is counted in the text. I will here basically use 1-gram statistics, i.e. the simple frequency of each character. However, the situation is a bit more complicated, because sequences of Unicode characters that include combining characters are treated as one character. For Latin scripts, the most widespread combining characters are various diacritics, like tildes and accents. All possible combinations of letters with diacritics are treated as separate characters of the orthographic structure in this paper. This makes the Devanagari scripts of Indian languages especially complicated, because the syllabic combinations of consonants and vowels are treated as one character.[4] Further, not taken into account here is the widespread occurrence of multigraphs in orthographies all over the world, i.e. combinations of multiple letters to signify one element of the orthography, like <sh> or <ng>. Languages with frequent multigraphs will be estimated here to have a simpler orthography than they in reality have.

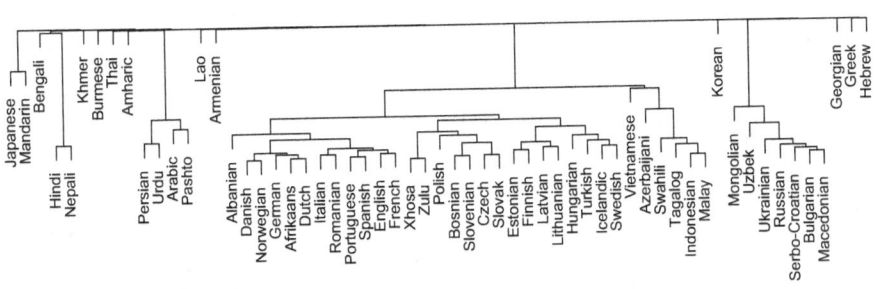

Figure 2. Dendrogram of 1-gram similarities of writing systems.

The similarity between two orthographies is computed by taking the Pearson correlation coefficient between the frequencies of occurrence of each character per language. The correlation matrix of all pairs of languages can be used to make a hierarchical clustering of orthographies (see figure 2). In this hierarchical clustering, the following groups are clearly discernible:

– A large cluster with all Latin scripts, including Vietnamese as an outlier;
– A cluster with the Cyrillic scripts of Mongolian, Uzbek, Ukrainian, Russian, Serbian, Bulgarian and Macedonian;

- A cluster with the Arabic scripts of Persian, Pashto, Urdu, and Arabic;
- The Devanagari script of Hindi and Nepali cluster together with a minor link to Bengali (which has its own Unicode range of characters, though uses the same separation sign as Devanagari, viz. the "danda", Unicode U+0964).
- Japanese and Mandarin cluster together based on the frequent usage of Chinese Kanji in Japanese;
- The scripts of Khmer, Burmese, Thai, Amharic, Lao, Armenian, Korean, Georgian, Greek and Hebrew do not cluster with any other script in the current set of languages.

The similarity between the English orthography and the orthographies of other languages (as measured by the Pearson correlation coefficient) is strongly negatively correlated with the difficulty of learning the language (FSI-levels: $r = -0.56$, $p = 4.6\text{e-}6$; 24-week ability scores: $r = 0.66$, $p = 2.9\text{e-}6$). So, the more different a script is from English, the more difficult it is to learn the language for an English speaker. This correlation only makes a statement about languages that have a Latin script. For all other languages the similarity to the English script is basically zero, so they are all treated as "just different". Yet, intuitively there seems to be a great difference between learning the Cyrillic characters of Russian and the Kanji of Japanese. Simply because there are much more Kanji, the Japanese script should be more difficult. For all languages that do not have a Latin script, I investigated the difficulty of learning the languages in relation to the number of different characters used in the script. Although there is a trend discernible, this trend is not significant (FSI-levels: $r = 0.32$, $p = 0.11$; 24-week ability scores: $r = -0.39$, $p = 0.097$). The crucial outliers in this correlation are Korean and Arabic, which are both far more difficult to learn than the (limited) size of their orthographic inventory would predict. Removing these outliers from the correlation makes the correlation between size of the orthographic inventory and the difficulty in learning the language highly significant (FSI-levels: $r = 0.51$, $p = 0.01$; 24-week ability scores: $r = -0.73$, $p = 0.0009$).

5. Language structure

A further factor influencing the difficulty of language learning is the structural similarity between languages. The more similar the grammatical structure of two languages is, the easier it is – supposedly – for speakers of the one language to learn the other language. The notion of "grammatical structure" is interpreted here rather all-encompassing, including phonological, morphological, syntactical, lexical, semantic and discourse structures. To quantitatively assess the similarity of grammatical structure, I will use the data from the *World Atlas of Language Structures* (WALS, Haspelmath et al. 2005). This atlas provides data on the worldwide distribution of 142 structural typological parameters, including parameters concerning all above-mentioned domains of grammar. The data on sign languages and on writing systems in WALS will not be used in this paper, so there are 139 remaining structural parameters to be included in the comparison here.

There are numerous different ways to derive an overall measure of structural similarity between languages from the WALS data (cf. Albu 2006; Cysouw 2012). For this paper I will use the most basic measure of similarity, namely a relative Hamming distance. This similarity is defined as the number of similar parameters between two languages divided by the number of comparisons made. For example, English and Hindi differ in 55 structural parameters from WALS, but are similar in 69 parameters. For the remaining 15 parameters (=139–55–69) there is no data available for both languages, so no comparison can be established. This results in a structural similarity of $69/(55+69) = 0.56$ between English and Hindi. On this scale, a value of one would indicate complete structural identity, while a value of zero would signify that the two languages do not share any characteristic in WALS. Because of limited data availability in WALS, Afrikaans, Malay, Slovak and Bosnian are excluded from the computations in this section.

The overall structural similarity between English and all other languages is strongly negatively correlated with the difficulty of learning those languages (FSI-levels: $r = -0.65$, $p = 4.8e-8$; 24-week ability scores: $r = 0.69$, $p = 7.4e-7$). So, the more different a language is structurally from English, the more difficult it is to learn this language. Even more interesting is the question, which of the 139 structural parameters correlate strongly with language learning difficulty, because such parameters are indicative of structural characteristics that are difficult to learn for English speakers.

For all parameters individually, I computed the absolute value of the Goodman-Kruskal gamma for the distribution of same vs. different compared to English across the seven FSI-levels. Likewise, I computed the probability values of t-tests testing the difference of the 24-week ability scores between the set of languages with similar vs. different structure compared to English. The resulting rankings of parameter-difficulty are strongly correlated (Spearman's $\rho = -0.73$, $p = 2.2e-16$), arguing that both difficulty measures roughly agree on which parameters from WALS are difficult for English language learners. The combination of the two assessments of difficulty is plotted in figure 3, higher values indicating more difficult features. For reasons of better visibility, the negative logarithm of the probability values of the t-test is shown in this figure.

There are various interesting structural parameters that end up high in both rankings. I will specifically discuss here those parameters that have a t-test probability of less than 0.01 (for the 24-week ability scores) and, at the same time, an absolute value of gamma that is higher than 0.60 (for the FSI-levels). These boundaries do not have any special meaning. They are only used here as a practical limitation to restrict the discussion of individual features. The following WALS parameters are strongly correlated with language learning difficulty.

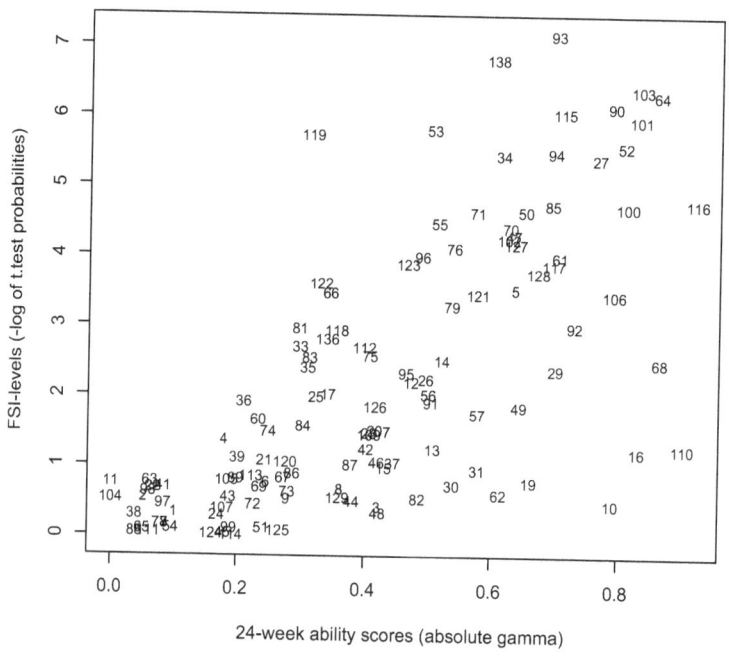

Figure 3. Difficulty assessment of individual WALS features (numbers refer to the chapters in WALS).

The parameters 93: "Position of interrogative phrases in content questions" (Dryer 2005g) and 116: "Polar questions" (Dryer 2005f) both relate to the structure of questions. Apparently, it is difficult for English speakers to learn a language in which the structure of questions is different from English. With regard to parameter 93, English consistently places the content interrogate (*who*, *what*, etc.) in the first position of the sentence, like most European languages. The most widespread other option used among the world's languages is the so-called "in-situ" interrogative, which appears in the same position in the sentence as the corresponding answer. Concerning parameter 116, English – like all Germanic languages – uses a special word order for polar questions (the so-called "inversion" construction, triggering *do*-support in English). This is a highly unusual construction from a world-wide perspective. Most languages use a special interrogative particle to formulate polar questions.

The parameters 100: "Alignment of verbal person marking" (Siewierska 2005a), 101: "Expression of pronominal subjects" (Dryer 2005a) and 103: "Third-person zero of verbal person marking" (Siewierska 2005b) all relate to the person cross-referencing as marked on the verb (so-called "person inflection", also often called "agreement"). Apparently it is difficult for English speakers to learn a language that uses a different kind of person inflection compared to English. Regarding parameter 100, English uses accusative alignment, i.e. the intransitive subject and the transitive subject trigger the same inflection. This is the most widespread strategy from a world-wide perspective. Other approaches, like ergative or active alignment, make a language more difficult to learn for English speakers. Concerning parameter 101, English needs obligatory pronouns in subject position. Most languages do not force such marking ("pro-drop"), again apparently making learning difficult for English speakers. Finally, with regard to parameter 103, English overtly marks a third person singular subject by verb inflection (with the suffix *-s*, though not in all tenses), whereas all other persons are unmarked. This is a highly idiosyncratic structure from a world-wide perspective. Languages with another distribution of zero person inflection are relatively more difficult for English learners. However, this difficulty actually conflates two phenomena. First, languages without any person inflection (i.e. all person marking is zero) are generally more difficult for English learners, but, likewise, are languages with person inflection for all persons, though zero-marked in the third person.

The parameters 52: "Comitatives and instrumentals" (Stolz, Stroh and Urdze 2005) and 64: "Nominal and verbal conjunction" (Haspelmath 2005b) both relate to the semantic distribution of linguistic structures. In both parameters, English – like all European languages – does not differentiate formally between the coding of two different semantic structures. Languages that do differentiate are apparently more difficult for English Learners. Concerning parameter 52, English uses the same construction for comitatives (*John went to the cinema* **with** *Mary*) and instrumentals (*John fixed the lamp* *with a screwdriver*), which is actually a minority pattern from a worldwide perspective. Similarly, English uses the same conjunction between noun phrases (***The lion and the monkey** eat bananas*) and verb phrases (*The lion **eats and sleeps***). Such an identity of conjunction structure is widespread, though roughly half of the world's languages would use different marking in these two situations.

The parameters 85: "Order of adposition and noun phrase" (Dryer 2005c), 90: "Order of relative clause and noun" (Dryer 2005e) and 94: "Order of adverbial subordinator and clause" (Dryer 2005d) all relate to the ordering of elements in the sentence. Ever since Greenberg's (1963) seminal paper on word order universals, there has been a strong interest in the interrelation between such parameters (cf. Dryer 1992 as a major reference). It is not completely clear why exactly these three parameters (and not any of the other word-order parameters) end up high on the scale of difficult to learn grammatical characteristics. It appears to depend on the rather limited set of languages in the current sample. Yet, it is clear that languages with different word-order characteristics from English are difficult to learn for English speakers.

There are various other parameters that appear to make languages difficult to learn for English speakers, for example the use of reduplication as a structural mechanism in the grammar of a language (parameter 27, Rubino 2005) and the fact that nouns with a plural meaning are not always obligatorily marked as such (parameter 34, Haspelmath 2005c). The remaining parameters high on the difficulty scale are less obvious to explain. Parameter 115: "Negative indefinite pronouns and predicate negation" (Haspelmath 2005a) described the difference whether negative indefinites like *nowhere, nobody* or *nothing* can co-occur with a further negation in the sentence. However, English is described as having "mixed behavior", so almost all the world's languages are different from English in this respect. Finally, parameter 138: "The word for *tea*" (Dahl 2005) classifies languages as to whether they use a word for *tea* derived from Sinitic *cha,* or from Min Nan Chinese *te*. Although it is slightly amusing that such a parameter appears to be correlated with learning difficulty, it simply seems to be an accidental side effect that will be ignored subsequently in this paper.

6. Predicting language learning difficulty

Given the numerous factors that strongly correlate with language learning difficulty for English speakers, it seems likely that we can reverse the approach and predict the difficulty of a language from these factors. Such a prediction might be useful to get an indication of expected difficulty for languages that are not included in the FSI data used here. Furthermore, statistical predictive models offer a more detailed indication of the relative importance of the various factors discussed in this paper. However, remember that the following predictive models are based on the very restricted difficulty-assessments as prepared by the FSI. For example, that data does not include any control for the individual background of the learners, but treats all English speakers as equal. Differently formulated, the current factors only deal with the target of the learning, while better models should also include factors relating to the background and personality of the learners. Also, the levels of difficulty distinguished are rather rough, and the number of languages available for the establishment of the models is rather limited. The models that will be proposed in this section should thus be interpreted with these limitations in mind.

The basic approach to find suitable predictive models is to include various factors into a linear regression model and try to find a model by reducing the number of factors, while optimizing the relative goodness of fit as measured by the Akaike information criterion (AIC).[4] By including many factors it will almost always be possible to produce well-fitting predictive models. However, the more factors included, the less clear the interpretation of such models becomes. It is thus more interesting to search for models with a limited number of factors that still predict the observed measurements to a reasonable degree.

Before turning to the concrete models, there is one further problem with the current data. The problem is that the values to be predicted (i.e. the values of language learning difficulty) are strongly biased towards mid values. In the FSI-levels, the largest group of languages is of level 4 (viz. 34 of 60 languages, i.e. more than half of the sample, cf. table 1), while for the 24-week ability scores, the largest group of languages has a score of 2.00 (viz. 15 of 42 languages, cf. table 2). To counterbalance this skewed distribution, I weighted all observations in the regression model by the inverse of the number of languages in the level. For example, the languages with FSI-level 4 were weighted as counting only 1/34.

Table 4. Predictive model of language-learning difficulty with continuous factors.

	Estimate	Std. Error	t-value	Pr(> |t|)
FSI-levels				
Intercept	8.98	0.68	13.21	< 2e-6 ***
Typology	−7.25	1.50	−4.82	1.34e-5 ***
Writing System	−2.19	0.46	−4.71	1.93e-5 ***
24-week ability				
Intercept	0.72	0.29	2.53	0.016 *
Typology	1.77	0.59	3.00	0.0049 **
Writing System	0.66	0.19	3.51	0.0013 **

The first kind of model to predict language-learning difficulty consists mainly of continuous factors. I included the following factors in the search for optimal models (the actual values used can be found in the Appendix A):

- Typological similarity, defined as a value between 1 (completely similar to English) and 0 (completely dissimilar from English), cf. Section 5;
- Geographical distance from London, defined as the great circle distance in kilometers;
- Orthographic similarity, defined as a value between 1 (completely similar to English) and 0 (completely dissimilar from English), cf. Section 4;
- Size of the orthographic system, defined as the number of Unicode graphemes used in the writing system;
- Genealogical similarity to English, defined as two binary parameters: first, whether the language belongs to the Germanic genus or not, and, second, whether the language belongs to the Indo-European family or not.

The optimal models only include the typological similarity and the orthographic similarity, as shown in table 4. For the FSI-levels, this model starts from an intercept of almost 9, which can be interpreted as saying that language learning is very difficult. Then, depending on the typological and orthographic similarity to English, the FSI-level is reduced. The typological similarity counts for a relative reduction of 7.25, while the orthographic similarity only results in a relative reduction of 2.19. Consider for example Norwegian, with an FSI-level of 1 (i.e. easy to learn for English speakers). Based on the typological similarity of Norwegian to English of 0.78 and a writing system similarity to English of 0.93, the linear regression in table 4 predicts an FSI-level of 1.29 (=8.98−7.25·0.78−2.19·0.93). For the 24-week ability scores, the model starts from an intercept of 0.72, which likewise represents maximum language learning difficulty. Typological similarity adds a fraction of 1.77, while orthographic similarity adds a fraction of 0.66 to this score. Again taking Norwegian as an example (24-week ability score of 3.00) the model predicts a score of 2.71 (=0.72+1.77·0.78+0.66·0.93). Only by including these two factors, a reasonable good prediction can be made of the learning difficulty of a language for English speakers.

Although the models in table 4 have a good predictive power, they are not very practical in actual usage. To predict language-learning difficulty with these models it is necessary to assess the complete typological similarity to English based on the WALS data. Furthermore, an extensive analysis of the writing system is necessary. To obtain simpler predictive models, I searched for optimal models using only binary factors, i.e. simple yes/no questions about the languages in question. A well-fitting model with only a few such simple questions could be of enormous practical value for predicting the difficulty English speakers might have when learning a foreign language. I included the following factors in the search for optimal models:

– Whether the language has a Latin script, or not;
– Whether the language is of the same genus as English (i.e. Germanic), or not;
– Whether the language is of the same family as English (i.e. Indo-European), or not;
– Whether the language has the same grammatical structure as English for any of the WALS parameters as discussed above with reference to figure 2, i.e. parameters 93, 116, 100, 101, 52, 64, 85, 90, 94, 27, and 34.[6]

To be able to search through all combinations of WALS parameters, a complete data table for the 11 parameters is necessary. Unfortunately, the data in WALS is highly incomplete, so I had to reduce the number of languages even more for this search. In the end, I decided on a set of 28 languages for which the parameters are almost completely available, and added the missing data points by choosing the parameter values most commonly attested in closely related languages and/or in the linguistic area in which the language is spoken (see Appendix B and C). The resulting predictive models (after optimizing for AIC, as above) are shown in table 5. With only four binary factors (as with the FSI-levels model) it is maximally possible to predict $2^4 = 16$ different levels of learning difficulty. With only three factors (as with the 24-week ability scores model) the number of possibly difficulty levels is even less, namely only $2^3 = 8$ levels. These models can thus not be very precise in their predictions. Statistically, it seems to be possible to reduce the number of factors even further, but I have decided to add more typological parameters as statistically necessary for an optimal model to get somewhat more different levels of prediction (which leads to non-significance of some of the parameters).

I will take Greek as an example for how these models predict language-learning difficulty. First, Greek has an FSI-level of 4, while the model in table 5 predicts a level of 3.41 (=6.46−0·1.72−1·1.68−1·0.84−1·0.53), based on the facts that Greek does not have a Latin script, but is Indo-European, has (predominantly) prepositions, and has accusative alignment. Second, Greek has a 24-week ability score of 1.75, while the model in table 5 predicts a score of 1.99 (=1.21+0·0.47+1·0.28 +1·0.50). The predications are equally accurate for all other languages investigated.

Table 5. Predictive model of language-learning difficulty with only binary factors.

	Estimate	Std. Error	t-value	Pr(> |t|)
FSI-levels				
Intercept	6.46	0.30	21.68	< 2e-6 ***
Latin script	− 1.72	0.43	− 4.00	5.70e-4 ***
Indo-European	− 1.68	0.40	− 4.21	3.32e-4 ***
Prepositions (85)	− 0.84	0.41	− 2.04	0.052
Accusative (100)	− 0.53	0.47	− 1.13	0.27
24-week ability				
Intercept	1.21	0.12	9.83	2.63e-9 ***
Latin script	0.47	0.15	3.18	0.0045 **
Prepositions (85)	0.28	0.16	1.71	0.10
Nominal plural (34)	0.50	0.15	3.27	0.0037 **

7. Conclusion

Language learning becomes more difficult the more different the language to be learned is from the learner's native tongue. There are many different ways in which differences between languages can be quantified, and this paper has investigated a few possibilities. It turns out that, indeed, larger differences between languages are correlated with larger difficulty, though not all differences are equally important. For English native speakers it appears to be particularly difficult to learn a language that does not have a Latin script, is non-Indo-European, has postpositions, is ergatively aligned and does not have obligatory nominal plural. The fact that such differences make a language difficult to learn is not very surprising. The more interesting result of this paper is, first, exactly which factors are the strongest predictors amongst the many possible factors quantifying similarity between languages, and, second, the detailed quantitative predictions of language learning difficulty based on such few characteristics of the language to be learned.

Appendix A: Complete data for continuous factors

WALS code	Language name	FSI-level	24-week score	Germanic	Indo-Europ.	Geograph. distance	Typology similarity	Script similarity	Script invent.
afr	Afrikaans	I	3.00	+	+	9469	NA	0.912	53
dsh	Danish	I	2.25	+	+	789	0.848	0.929	60
dut	Dutch	I	2.75	+	+	412	0.750	0.915	59
fre	French	I	2.50	−	+	467	0.662	0.954	60
ita	Italian	I	2.50	−	+	1343	0.696	0.947	60
nor	Norwegian	I	3.00	+	+	1112	0.782	0.935	58
por	Portuguese	I	2.50	−	+	1571	0.638	0.929	62
rom	Romanian	I	3.00	−	+	1929	0.657	0.920	61
spa	Spanish	I	2.25	−	+	1368	0.615	0.947	60
swe	Swedish	I	3.00	+	+	1283	0.862	0.934	63
ger	German	I*	2.25	+	+	684	0.698	0.916	70
ind	Indonesian	I**	2.00	−	−	11086	0.481	0.766	52
mly	Malay	I**	2.75	−	−	10553	NA	0.750	58
swa	Swahili	I**	2.75	−	−	7476	0.463	0.687	62
alb	Albanian	II	NA	−	+	1947	0.590	0.858	62
amh	Amharic	II	2.00	−	−	5787	0.446	0.000	164
arm	Armenian	II	NA	−	+	3651	0.494	0.000	83
aze	Azerbaijani	II	NA	−	−	3858	0.415	0.668	70
ben	Bengali	II	1.75	−	+	7924	0.439	0.000	383
bos	Bosnian	II	NA	−	+	1674	NA	0.850	62
bul	Bulgarian	II	2.00	−	+	2145	0.620	0.000	68
brm	Burmese	II	1.75	−	−	8573	0.373	0.000	357
cze	Czech	II	2.00	−	+	1070	0.630	0.849	78
grk	Greek	II	1.75	−	+	2225	0.581	0.000	67
heb	Hebrew	II	2.00	−	−	3620	0.562	0.000	31
hin	Hindi	II	1.75	−	+	6968	0.556	0.000	390
ice	Icelandic	II	NA	+	+	1737	0.689	0.855	61

WALS code	Language name	FSI-level	24-week score	Germanic	Indo-Europ.	Geograph. distance	Typology similarity	Script similarity	Script invent.
khm	Khmer	II	2.00	–	–	9905	0.402	0.000	336
lao	Lao	II	1.50	–	–	9288	0.432	0.000	268
lat	Latvian	II	NA	–	+	1635	0.580	0.816	69
lit	Lithuanian	II	NA	–	+	1612	0.565	0.821	72
mcd	Macedonian	II	NA	–	+	2000	0.692	0.000	68
nep	Nepali	II	1.75	–	+	7260	0.426	0.000	352
psh	Pashto	II	NA	–	+	5654	0.429	0.000	34
prs	Persian	II	2.00	–	+	4842	0.430	0.000	48
pol	Polish	II	2.00	–	+	1364	0.605	0.841	70
rus	Russian	II	2.25	–	+	2488	0.652	0.000	66
scr	SerboCroatian	II	2.00	–	+	1662	0.608	0.000	64
snh	Sinhalese	II	1.75	–	+	8739	0.523	NA	NA
svk	Slovak	II	NA	–	+	1447	NA	0.870	81
slo	Slovenian	II	NA	–	+	1277	0.677	0.885	51
tag	Tagalog	II	2.00	–	–	10653	0.387	0.607	56
tur	Turkish	II	2.00	–	–	3044	0.437	0.861	56
ukr	Ukrainian	II	NA	–	+	2336	0.659	0.000	73
urd	Urdu	II	NA	–	+	6285	0.500	0.000	30
uzb	Uzbek	II	NA	–	–	5148	0.442	0.000	75
xho	Xhosa	II	NA	–	–	9697	0.360	0.808	61
zul	Zulu	II	NA	–	–	9569	0.397	0.812	60
tha	Thai	II*	2.00	–	–	9336	0.455	0.000	249
hun	Hungarian	II*	2.00	–	–	1540	0.511	0.851	56
est	Estonian	II*	NA	–	–	1796	0.583	0.862	52
fin	Finnish	II*	2.00	–	–	1858	0.593	0.863	56
geo	Georgian	II*	NA	–	–	3454	0.400	0.000	46
vie	Vietnamese	II*	1.50	–	–	10181	0.423	0.649	117
kha	Mongolian	II*	2.00	–	–	6903	0.432	0.000	54
aeg	Arabic	III	1.50	–	–	3520	0.504	0.000	60
cnt	Cantonese	III	1.25	–	–	9450	0.447	NA	NA
kor	Korean	III	1.00	–	–	8855	0.453	0.000	64
mnd	Mandarin	III	1.50	–	–	8286	0.462	0.001	532
jpn	Japanese	III*	1.00	–	–	9379	0.385	0.000	505

Appendix B: Data added to WALS

Language	WALS	Feature	Value	Notes
Burmese	brm	34	1	common in South-East Asia
Burmese	brm	52	2	common in South-East Asia
Burmese	brm	64	1	common in South-East Asia
Dutch	dut	27	3	same as all of Europe
Dutch	dut	52	1	same as all of Europe
Dutch	dut	64	1	same as all of Europe
Dutch	dut	93	1	same as all of Europe
Georgian	geo	116	6	
Georgian	geo	90	1	
Hindi	hin	101	2	same as most Indic
Italian	ita	93	1	same as all of Europe
Khalka	kha	115	1	typical Eurasian
Khalka	kha	64	2	same as Mangghuer
Khmer	khm	101	5	common in South-East Asia
Khmer	khm	64	1	common in South-East Asia
Korean	kor	34	4	
Latvian	lat	27	3	same as most of Europe
Mandarin	mnd	94	5	same as Cantonese
Persian	prs	34	6	same as all Iranian and European
Spanish	spa	52	1	same as all of Europe
Swahili	swa	64	2	same as most Bantu
Tagalog	tag	101	1	
Tagalog	tag	85	2	same as all Austronesian
Thai	tha	34	1	common in South-East Asia
Vietnamese	vie	52	2	common in South-East Asia
Zulu	zul	52	2	typical Bantu

Appendix C: Complete data for WALS parameters

WALS	100	101	103	93	116	52	64	115	34	27	90	94	85
dut	2	1	2	1	4	1	1	2	6	3	1	1	2
fre	2	1	2	1	1	1	1	3	6	3	1	1	2
ita	2	2	2	1	6	1	1	3	6	3	1	1	2
spa	2	2	2	1	4	1	1	3	6	3	1	1	2
ger	2	1	2	1	4	1	1	2	6	3	1	1	2
ind	2	1	2	3	1	3	1	1	4	2	1	1	2
swa	2	2	2	2	1	2	2	1	6	1	1	1	2

WALS	100	101	103	93	116	52	64	115	34	27	90	94	85
brm	1	5	1	2	2	2	1	1	1	2	2	4	1
grk	2	2	2	1	1	1	1	1	6	3	1	1	2
heb	2	6	4	1	1	1	1	1	6	1	1	1	2
hin	2	2	2	2	1	2	1	1	6	1	4	1	1
khm	1	5	1	2	1	2	1	1	4	1	1	1	2
lat	2	1	4	1	1	1	1	1	6	3	1	1	2
prs	2	2	4	2	1	1	1	1	6	1	1	1	2
rus	2	1	2	1	1	3	1	1	6	3	1	1	2
tag	1	1	1	1	1	2	1	1	4	1	1	1	2
tur	2	2	4	2	1	1	1	1	6	1	2	5	1
zul	2	2	2	2	1	2	2	1	6	2	1	1	2
tha	1	5	1	2	1	2	1	1	1	1	1	1	2
hun	2	2	2	2	1	3	1	1	6	1	7	1	1
fin	2	6	4	1	1	2	1	1	6	3	1	1	1
geo	2	4	2	2	6	3	1	3	6	1	1	1	1
vie	1	5	1	2	1	2	1	1	4	1	1	1	2
kha	1	5	1	2	1	2	2	1	4	1	2	2	1
aeg	2	2	4	2	1	2	1	1	6	1	1	1	2
kor	1	5	1	2	2	2	2	1	4	1	2	2	1
mnd	1	5	1	2	1	2	2	1	2	1	2	5	2
jpn	1	5	1	2	1	2	2	1	2	2	2	2	1

Notes

1. I thank the editors and the anonymous reviewers for their assistance with the preparation of the current paper. This research was supported by ERC Starting Grant 240816 "Quanthistling".
2. The following FSI website contains the assessments of language difficulty: http://www.nvtc.gov/lotw/months/november/learningExpectations.html. This website is available through the internet archive at http://www.archive.org/. A website at WikiBooks claims to have information about the FSI-levels for an even larger number of languages, but I have not been able to trace the origin of these additional assessments, so I have not used them for this paper: http://en.wikibooks.org/wiki/Language_Learning_Difficulty_for_English_Speakers (all pages accessed on 22 March 2011).
3. Available online at http://unicode.org/udhr/.
4. For some reason, the Unicode standard treats the Hangul script of Korean differently, as the syllabic combinations are not treated as combining. This results

in Korean being treated here rather differently from Devanagari, while the difference in the script structure is not that profound.
5. In practice, I used the implementation step as available in the statistical environment R (R Development Core Team 2010) for this optimization.
6. The parameters 103 and 115 are not included, because their similarity/difference to English is difficult to interpret. Also parameter 138 is not included because of lack of relevance (cf. the discussion in Section 5).

References

Albu, Mihai
    2006   Quantitative analyses of typological data. Ph.D. Thesis, University of Leipzig.

Chiswick, B. R. and P. W. Miller
    2005   Linguistic distance: A quantitative measure of the distance between English and other languages. *Journal of Multilingual and Multicultural Development* 26(1). 1–11.

Coppin, Ben
    2008   Automatic language similarity comparison using n-gram analysis. Master Thesis, Queens' College: Cambridge.

Cysouw, Michael
    2012   Disentangling geography from genealogy. In: Benedikt Szmrecsanyi (ed.), *Space in language and linguistics: geographical, interactional, and cognitive perspectives*. Berlin/Boston: De Gruyter Mouton.

Dahl, Östen
    2005   Tea. In: Martin Haspelmath et al. (eds.), 554–557.

Damashek, M.
    1995   Gauging similarity with n-grams: Language-independent categorization of text. *Science* 267 (5199). 843.

Dryer, Matthew S.
    1992   The Greenbergian word order correlations. *Language* 68(1). 80–138.

Dryer, Matthew S.
    2005a   Expression of pronominal subjects. In: Martin Haspelmath et al. (eds.), 410–413.

Dryer, Matthew S.
    2005b   Genealogical language list. In: Martin Haspelmath et al. (eds.), 582–642.

Dryer, Matthew S.
    2005c   Order of adposition and noun phrase. In: Martin Haspelmath et al. (eds.), 346–349.

Dryer, Matthew S.
    2005d   Order of adverbial subordinator and clause. In: Martin Haspelmath et al. (eds.), 382–385.

Dryer, Matthew S.
2005e Order of relative clause and noun. In: Martin Haspelmath et al. (eds.), 366–369.
Dryer, Matthew S.
2005f Polar questions. In: Martin Haspelmath et al. (eds.), 470–473.
Dryer, Matthew S.
2005g Position of interrogative phrases in content questions. In: Martin Haspelmath et al. (eds.), 378–381.
Hart-Gonzalez, Lucinda and Stephanie Lindemann
1993 Expected achievement in speaking proficiency. School of Language Studies, Foreign Services Institute, Department of State: Washington DC.
Greenberg, Joseph H.
1963 Some universals of grammar with particular reference to the order of meaningful elements. In: Joseph H. Greenberg (ed.), *Universals of Language*, 73–113. Cambridge, MA: MIT Press.
Haspelmath, Martin
2005a Negative indefinite pronouns and predicate negation. In: Martin Haspelmath et al. (eds.), 466–469.
Haspelmath, Martin
2005b Nominal and verbal conjunction. In: Martin Haspelmath et al. (eds.), 262–265.
Haspelmath, Martin
2005c Occurrence of nominal plurality. In: Martin Haspelmath et al. (eds.), 142–145.
Haspelmath, Martin, Matthew S. Dryer, Bernard Comrie, and David Gil (eds.)
2005 *The World Atlas of Language Structures*, Oxford University Press: Oxford.
Huffman, Stephen M.
2003 The genetic classification of languages by n-gram analysis. PhD Thesis, Georgetown University: Washington, D.C.
Jackson, F. H. and M. A. Kaplan
2001 Lessons learned from fifty years of theory and practice in government language teaching. In: James A. Alatis and Ai-Hui Tan (eds.), *Language in Our Time*, 71–87. Georgetown UP: Washington, D.C.
Kellerman, Eric
1979 Transfer and Non-Transfer: Where We Are Now. *Studies in Second Language Acquisition* 2 (1). 37–57.
R Development Core Team
2010 R: A Language and Environment for Statistical Computing. R Foundation for Statistical Computing: Vienna, Austria.
Rubino, Carl
2005 Reduplication. In: Martin Haspelmath et al. (eds.), 114–117.

Schepens, Job, Frans van der Slik, and Roeland van Hout
　this vol.　The effect of linguistic distance across Indo-European mother tongues on learning Dutch as a second language.
Siewierska, Anna
　2005a　Alignment of verbal person marking. In: Martin Haspelmath et al. (eds.), 406–409.
Siewierska, Anna
　2005b　Third-person zero of verbal person marking. In: Martin Haspelmath et al. (eds.), 418–421.
Stolz, Thomas, Cornelia Stroh, and Aina Urdze
　2005　Comitatives and Intrumentals. In: Martin Haspelmath et al. (eds.), 214–217.

How aberrant are divergent Indo-European subgroups?

Folke Josephson

1. Introduction

This paper contains a comparison between results obtained by mathematical cladistics as applied to relations between Indo-European subgroups and subgrouping in the field of Indo-European comparative linguistics.
　　Ringe et al. (2002) apply computational cladistics to Indo-European. Some of their observations are relevant for a comparison with the ongoing discussion of divergence and subgrouping within Indo-European linguistics. The authors accept the fundamental notion that subgroups should share significant innovations. They mention that phonetic changes have played an important role in traditional reconstruction but emphasize that phonetic changes can be repeated in different lines of descent (p. 66) and provide less information than might be supposed. They also state that in inflectional morphology parallel developments are less prevalent but if we work from the terminal nodes of the tree we often do not know which inflectional markers are ancestral and which are innovations (p. 68) and lexical evidence is even more problematic (p. 69). Character-based cladistics gives serious problems for mathematical reasons (p. 72). However, when the methods are tested on Indo-European lexical items they give the best tree (p. 87).
　　There has been strong emphasis on vocabulary in modern cladistics but comparatively less so in Indo-European linguistics. At the beginning of Indo-European studies reconstruction was mainly based on morphology but phonological reconstruction became the stable basis of the comparative method. Meillet considered reconstruction of shared morphology to be of prime importance for establishing family relationships, followed by phonological correspondences and lexical reconstruction. In more recent times there has been increased emphasis on word formation and syntax.
　　Reconstruction of inflectional and derivational morphemes, the functions of morphological categories, patterns of accentuation, and ablaut as means of derivation are areas in focus in Indo-European linguistics. Reconstruction of syntax and evaluation of common syntactic traits are intensively cultivated fields and questions of diachronic and areal typology are seen as highly

relevant. Attention to the historical development of morphological, grammatical, and semantic categories in different branches of Indo-European plays an important role in contemporary research.

2. Reconstruction of Proto-Anatolian

Hittite, Palaic and Luvian are cuneiform Anatolian languages of the Bronze Age. The Palaic corpus is small and belongs to an early period. The Hittite corpus is the largest one and there were important changes in the language during the course of the centuries of its attested history. The main corpus of Luvian hieroglyphic inscriptions belongs to the early Iron Age after the fall of the Hittite empire. The later Lydian, Carian, Lycian, and some additional minor western Anatolian languages are attested in alphabetic script. Reconstruction of Proto-Anatolian and efforts to establish an Anatolian language tree show that Lycian is a close relative of Luvian and that these languages formed a "Luvic" subgroup, to which Carian probably also belongs. Attempts are being made to place Lydian in its proper position. The position of the scantily preserved Palaic is difficult to determine.

Reconstruction of Proto-Anatolian and Proto-Tocharian is fundamental for present-day Indo-European research.

Anatolian has been securely established as belonging to the *centum* type after some earlier hesitation about Luvian palatalisation of dorsal stops (cf. Melchert to appear c). The vocabulary of Anatolian is of Indo-European origin to a much higher degree than those of Classical Greek and Old Indic and shows important affinities to Italic, Germanic and Slavic. Tocharian also has significant vocabulary in common with western Indo-European. Anatolian should be seen in the light of differences of structures and developmental tendencies between western and eastern Indo-European subgroups.

Anatolian shows many differences from traditionally reconstructed Indo-European patterns and lacks several Indo-European grammatical categories.

Early separation of Proto-Anatolian from the main body of Indo-European is a widely held opinion and some scholars believe that Proto-Tocharian left the main body earlier than Anatolian. It has been claimed that Proto-Anatolian occupied a central position in a dialectal continuum.

We shall assess to what degree Proto-Anatolian is different from other branches of Indo-European and give attention to what contemporary research reveals about archaism and renewal of morphology and the expression of grammatical categories in different branches of Indo-European in comparison with Anatolian.

3. Innovation and retention

The question of archaism or innovation in the Anatolian branch is of fundamental importance for Indo-European reconstruction. The "Indo-Hittite" hypothesis of Sturtevant and others, which implies early separation of Proto-Anatolian from the rest of Indo-European, can only be verified if a sufficient number of innovations common to the non-Anatolian branches can be demonstrated.

The grammatical categories of traditionally reconstructed Proto-Indo-European that are not present in Anatolian include such important categories of tense and aspect as the sigmatic aorist of Greek, Indo-Iranian and Slavic and the synthetic perfect. Anatolian has no fully grammaticalised aorist category but some preterits look like root aorists of other IE languages. There is no future tense. The subjunctive and optative moods are missing and Anatolian shows no relic forms of the optative, which is surprising because the suffix *-ieh_1/ih_1- of the IE athematic optative has an archaic structure. Optative may have been grammaticalised late in PIE and optative and subjunctive may have been formed on the basis of the verbal root rather than on a particular tense-aspect stem as in Tocharian (Clackson 2007: 136–137). Rix (1986) argued for a secondary character of the IE moods (cf. Clackson 2007: 156). Anatolian has no feminine gender and no dual. It has been claimed that many or all of the missing IE categories had been lost in accordance with the so called "Schwund-hypothese". The "Indo-Hittite" hypothesis of Sturtevant was accepted by Cowgill, Jasanoff, and others, but variants of the "Schwund-hypothese" have been favoured by some scholars. Critical and balanced views on these problems based on significant advances in the analysis of Anatolian language structure have recently been presented by Rieken (2009) and Melchert (to appear a).

4. Aorist

Latin has strongly developed tense categories but possesses no aorist category though inherited sigmatic aorist forms are found in its perfect paradigm. Archaic Latin shows some examples of the earlier opposition between aorist and perfect (cf. Haverling 2008: 12). Reduplicated and thematic aorists cannot be reconstructed for Proto-Italic. Celtic has no aorist category and also preserved aorist forms as part of the perfect paradigm. Archaic Latin has a sigmatic future and the sigmatic desiderative and sigmatic future forms are found in Sabellian. The Celtic future is similar to the Old Indian sigmatic desiderative (McCone 1991: 141–182) and, as remarked by Clackson (2007: 119), reconstruction of a desiderative *s*-present may make it unnecessary to reconstruct a PIE future. As mentioned above, Anatolian has no future category.

Germanic has no aorist category and shows no trace of the sigmatic aorist. It does not have the Indo-European subjunctive but optative is preserved in Gothic. The tense/aspect system of Germanic is typologically similar to that of Anatolian. Tense takes precedence over aspect, and both groups developed periphrastic perfects and pluperfects. Indo-European languages which had a clear predominance of tense over aspect were not innovative in creating aspectual forms. Celtic and Italic also belonged to this type but a new and original aspectual system evolved in Insular Celtic (cf. Ó Corráin to appear).

Actionality of verbal stems was of paramount importance in PIE and performed aspectual functions based on a fundamental role of actional parameters.

The time of the onset of the productivity of the sigmatic aorist cannot be pinpointed and Strunk (1997) believed that it was late. The Greek aorist was telic (cf. Napoli 2006). Napoli shows that the distribution of root aorists and sigmatic aorists in Homeric Greek reflects a situation in which the *s*-suffix came to be used as a mark of perfectivity when applied to durative (non-punctual) verbs. According to Jasanoff (2003: 214) the classical sigmatic aorist was an innovation of "Inner PIE" after Hittite and Tocharian separated from the rest of Indo-European, which he calls "Nuclear IE". Completives formed by -*s* had developed to anteriors, witness the -*s* endings of Hittite. Preterits of telic roots were understood as perfective by implicature.

Jasanoff (2003: 221) believes that the creation of a fully sigmatic active indicative was a common innovation of the non-Anatolian and non-Tocharian branches, which emerge as a proper subgroup of Indo-European. In a "shallow" stage of pre-PIE a presigmatic aorist and a stative-intransitive aorist (Jasanoff 2003: 220–221) were specialisations of the *-h_2e-conjugation which underlies the Hittite *ḫi*-conjugation of the present tense. In pre-PIE, the *-h_2e-conjugation and the normal IE middle were represented by a single category, which Jasanoff calls "proto-middle".

5. Clitics and prefixes

Preverbs with actional and aspectual meaning are an important trait of Slavic languages and serve as a perfectivising device. Germanic *ga-* may be perfectivising though this is doubted by some. *ga-* is related etymologically to the Latin verbal prefix *co(m)-*, Old Irish *com-,* and Hittite *-kan. -kan* is one of several local clitics that found a place in the final slot of the extensive Wackernagel chain of clitics when they transformed into parts of a phrasal affixation system, in which the affixes were sensitive to the lexical features of the verb (Garrett 1996: 126). *-kan* has a strongly completive meaning but it had not been completely grammaticalised as a mark of perfective aspect in the manner of Slavic verbal prefixes (Josephson 2008: 143 – 144). *-kan* and *-san*, which is related to Skt. *sam* (IE **sem/som*) and Greek *sun(-)* that also occurs in the final Wackernagel position, have actional meanings similar to those of Latin *co(m)-* and Greek *sun-*. *-san* has a fundamentally adessive, adlative, and comitative meaning and commonly indicates direction to a goal. The mutually exclusive clitics *-kan* and *-san* can also modify the meaning of local adverbs and play such static or dynamic roles that are inherent parts of the meaning of Germanic, Slavic, Latin, Sabellian, and Greek local adverbs/preverbs. The facts that *-kan* can refer to the initial point of an action and that *-san* indicates DIRECTED and EXTENDED PATH explain why these elements can modify the meaning of local adverbs. The directional meaning of *-san* is similar to that belonging to the Latin preverb/ preposition *ad(-)* and English *to*, which explains the common occurrence of *-san* with the allative case and with the dative/locative when it has dative function (Josephson to appear). *-kan* occurs with locatives that do not have dative function and because it can indicate the initial point of a motion it frequently occurs together with the ablative case (Josephson to appear).

Latin possesses no preverb that is related to Skt. *sam-* and Greek *sun(-)*, but Latin *co(m)-* which refers to the term of an action can also have the directive function of Greek *sun-*, which is semantically close to that of Latin *ad-* (Haug 2007: 86, Josephson to appear) and was used in Late Latin in order to translate Greek *sun-*. *ad-* indicates gradual change as in *adsuesco* "get used to gradually", whereas *consuesco* "get used to" is terminative (Haverling 2008: 76). Latin completive *co(m)-* focuses on achievement (Haverling 2000: 256). Latin *ob-* has a function that "emphasizes a change, especially a sudden one, a leap into a new situation" (Haverling 2000: 324). Old Hittite *-apa* is a Wackernagel clitic like *-kan* and *-san*. *-san* expresses DIRECTED and EXTENDED PATH and serves as a goal modifier expressing gradual change, whereas an action qualified by *-apa* is exhaustive and reaches full measure. When preceded by *-apa* the verb *arai-* "(a)rise" refers to getting into a standing position in order to be able to act and immediate completion and equals the related Latin *oborior* (Josephson 2010: 187) whereas Latin *adorior* refers to direction and passage towards a goal. Latin *ob-* has the spatial function of face-to-face (García Hernández 1980: 184, Josephson 2010: 186) and the actional function of change from one state to another (Haverling 2000: 115 –123). Hittite -*apa* ... *ed-* 'eat up' and -*apa* ... *karāp-* 'consume', 'devour' have the exhaustive transformative meaning described by Johanson (2000: 69) and -*apa* ... *suwa-* means 'fill (something) up'.

This shows that three of the originally five Hittite local particles are materially identical with verbal prefixes of other IE languages and possess similar functions. It is therefore not strange that they became parts of a phrasal affixation system in which elements were sensitive to actional and lexical features of the verb.

The Hittite clitics have semantic contents that belong to the meaning of etymologically related preverbs/prepositions of other IE languages but they have a wider set of functions.

Slavic verbal prefixes have "directional and measurement usages" (Filip 2003). They are mostly of prepositional or adverbial origin and serve as SOURCE/GOAL modifiers. The telicity status of prefixed verbs is shown by the spatial orientation indicated by directional prefixes.

Because of their interplay with local adverbs, most obviously with those directional and static local adverbs that in Middle Hittite lost their original lexical distinction between static and directional functions, they allow an insight into the Proto-Indo-European system of local and directional adverbs/prepositions/preverbs (Josephson to appear).

This illustrates how a combination of lexical, syntactic, and semantic comparison based on synchronic and diachronic analysis of data obtained by the study of related languages reveals the structure of a prehistoric spatial and actional system. They illustrate how form and function can be reconstructed conjointly.

6. Inheritance and loan

The Anatolian chains of Wackernagel clitics, which comprise sentence connectives and a modal particle in the first slot, a citation particle, a modal particle, enclitic pronouns, and a reflexive particle in a fixed order, with one of the originally five local/directional particles in the final slot, were listed by Watkins (2001: 55) as one of several traits of Anatolian that may have been caused by Hurrian and Hattic influence in a more extensive linguistic area. These chains clitic elements are however very different from the Hurrian and Hattic structures. The establishment of the clitics in Wackernagel position seems to have been caused by internal factors rather than by outside influence (Josephson 2012). There is little evidence of Hurrian and Hattic influence outside of the domains of phonology and some vocabulary though some syntactical traits have recently been claimed to be due to substrate or adstrate Hurrian influence. The lexical loans from Hurrian and Hattic mainly belong to the religious and technical domains.

There was an extensive Anatolian area of closely interrelated Indo-European languages. Hittite and Luvian, which are the best attested and most widespread of the Anatolian languages, probably entered Anatolia at different periods and probably from the West. Luvian advanced eastwards from South-West Anatolia, and close contact with Hittite was established before the beginning of attested history. There was widespread Hittite-Luvian bilingualism in the Middle and Late Hittite periods (cf. Yakubovich 2010: 302–413). These interrelations, which mainly imply a strong Luvian influence on Hittite, led to several parallel developments in the two languages (Yakubovich 2010: 305–308) and to strengthening of already existing common developmental tendencies. Hittite functional categories were adapted to the Luvian system, which resulted in such changes as reduction of the number of cases by which ablative and instrumental became one category in Hittite and loss of distinction between nominative and accusative plural. This presupposes a stable contact situation (Rieken 2009: 48). The period of prehistoric contacts between Hittite and Luvian was compared by Yakubovich (2010: 198) to the period of koineization described by Dawson (2003) that explains the wide impact of Norse on the structure of English that was caused by genetic and typological similarity between the two languages that enabled speakers of one language to understand the other without learning to speak it. The establishment of local clitics in final Wackernagel position was a common Anatolian development and their number was gradually reduced in Luvian and Hittite in a parallel historical development. Both languages reduced their number to two and Luvian *-tar* and Hittite *-san* acquired similar functions as illustrated by Yakubovich (2010: 141–145).

Directionality, extension, and perlative meaning belonged to Luvian *-tar* (Josephson to appear b) and to Hittite *-san* but the Luvian clitic did not have the original adessive meaning of *-san*. Both indicated DIRECTED PATH including GOAL and the *to*-meaning of *-tar* was stronger than what was demonstrated by Yakubovich (Josephson to appear b). Luvian *-tta* was opposed to *-tar* in the same way that Hittite *-kan* to *-san*. Hittite *-san* and Luvian *-tar* disappeared in a final stage of a protracted *Abbau*-tendency of the "sentence particles" that was common to both languages.

Another example of Luvian influence on Hittite is the Luvian reflexive particle *-ti*, which developed from an IE dative pronoun **toi* "to you" as demonstrated by Rieken (2004: 183) and was borrowed as Hittite *-z(a)* (Yakubovich 2010: 192–193). *-z(a)* also developed into an accessory of middle forms as in -*za...esari* "he sits down" but differently from the development in Germanic the Anatolian reflexive did not become a true middle.

7. Macro-areal typology

In an article on Proto-Bantu and Proto-Niger-Congo, Güldemann (2010) discussed the relation between macro-areal typology and linguistic reconstruction, a question that is highly relevant for the Anatolian situation. As opposed to the Macro-Sudan belt, which was the result of linguistic convergence processes, the Bantu area involves languages with a great number of shared linguistic features that show inheritance from a common ancestor language. It is "not only typologically but also genealogically homogeneous" and had probably "been subject to a relatively recent expansion of languages" (Güldemann 2010). Güldemann believes that there were "multiple contact events within a compact zone of closely related languages and other types of areal pressure".

The Anatolian area can be characterized as a "spread zone" of an already established subgroup of languages, whose members had originated in some unknown close-knit area before a long period of separation followed by the renewed meeting of Luvian and Hittite in Central Anatolia where close contact was reestablished between them. There was some areal pressure from languages of different structure in the larger macro-area as a result of intensive symbiosis. Some early Hattic influence is found in Hittite; Hurrian affected Luvian language and culture and spread to Hittite because of the strong Luvian influence on Hittite culture and ritual and Hittite-Luvian bilingualism.

The Italic subgroup of IE may have had a similar prehistory and differences between Latin and Sabellian make it probable that they entered the area at different times. When Sabellian languages spread across Italy they came into close contact with Latin and there were mutual influences between the two groups. The degrees and effects of outside pressure on Anatolian and Italic are of course not identical and the factors that determined the degree of tenacity of resistance to external pressure were not equal.

8. Indo-European language groups

Proto-Italic was recognised as a node from the very beginning of IE linguistics. Devoto (1929) argued that Italic and Sabellic were two separate branches and that there was a separate process of convergence. Weiss (2009: 467–472) makes a survey of the question and lists shared phonological innovations, which he considers to be most probative, possible Pre-Italic innovations, problematic cases where relative chronology appears to show independence of changes, and such where the phenomenon is dubious or verging on trivial. There were many important common morphological innovations which seem "too numerous and integrated to be the result of secondary approximation" (Weiss 2009: 471) but there are many differences as in the formation of the perfect.

Among lexical items that Italic shared with Celtic there are several that belong to the legal and religious areas and are also found in Indo-Iranian and they may therefore be due to a geographically marginal position (Vendryes 1918). Weiss lists common features worthy of consideration, the most convincing of which are the phonological development *CRHC to CrāC (Latin *granum* 'grain' = Old Irish *grán*), the *a*-subjunctive, the common superlative formant, and the primary 3rd person middle endings *-*tro*/ *-*ntro*. Weiss believes that the numerous shared lexical items should be placed at a much lower level of importance for reconstruction than phonological and morphological innovations. He leaves the Italo-Celtic question open but stresses that Italic shares more innovative features with Celtic than with any other branch. Many words are shared by Italic, Celtic and Germanic (the so called Northwest vocabulary) and there is also some shared Italic and Germanic vocabulary.

A marginal and isolated position of Proto-Anatolian in relation to the rest of the languages and an early separation of Anatolian from the main body of PIE can explain such archaic traits as the retention of two of the three phonemes (later called laryngeals) that were reconstructed by Saussure for theoretical reasons before the discovery of Hittite. Anatolian retains the second and third laryngeals in most, but not all, phonetic environments, and beside the *mi*-conjugation of the present and past tenses it possesses a *ḫi*-conjugation, characterized by the first person ending *-h_2e of the Indo-European perfect.

Jasanoff (2003) believes that Anatolian, Tocharian, and Italo-Celtic departed early from the rest of Indo-European (Jasanoff 2003: 46, n. 42, with a reference to Schindler). The prehistory of the *ḫi*-conjugation plays an important role in his argumentation for an original status of this conjugation as a "proto-middle", which had the endings that are characteristic of the PIE perfect active. It had middle-like semantics but more archaic endings than the PIE middle. Another theory sees the h_2-forms as a stative opposed to an active paradigm.

9. The Middle in prehistory and history

Jasanoff's analysis of archaic derivational processes in PIE (Jasanoff 2003) is based on the insight that the Anatolian *ḫi*-conjugation with its affinity to the IE perfect was a Pre-PIE category and his reconstruction of a proto-middle (Jasanoff 2003: 221) leads him to discuss the value of an attempt to define the functions of a pre-Proto-IE proto-middle and the conditions under which some of its forms were renewed as middles (Jasanoff 2003: 222) but he acknowledges that this endeavour can be seen to press the comparative method to its limits.

The Middle category (commonly called medio-passive) is best preserved in Indo-Iranian, Anatolian, and Greek, on the basis of which a fundamental function of personal involvement in the action has been reconstructed. It also has reflexive and reciprocal meanings and a passive meaning, which is the main characteristic of the Latin and Gothic medio-passive.

Hittite, Tocharian, and Italo-Celtic middle endings show the addition of a final *-r* but in Anatolian and Tocharian this element is not found in the past tense. In Hittite, the present tense shows *-r(i)* in the singular but the oldest texts show an absence of *-r(i)* in most forms except the 3rd singular of the thematic *-a*-verbs.

Pinault (2010: 293) reconstructs a third person plural middle perfect ending *-*ntro* on the basis of Tocharian and Italo-Celtic, which adds to already existing evidence for close affinity between Common Tocharian and Western Indo-European.

The further development of the medio-passive in certain IE branches has been studied by scholars who stress the importance of valency and intransitivity.

In an article on valency-changing function of derivational categories in Indo-Aryan and Indo-European Kulikov (2009) observes that for a long time there has been an imbalance of synchronic and diachronic typological studies and proceeds to demonstrate the feasibility of retrospective diachronic typological studies as he tries to reconstruct possible sources of valence-changing categories in the Indo-European proto-language. He states that there was a decline of Middle in Indo-Aryan, where non-characterized middle forms are extremely rare in passive usages, an emergence of new valence-changing categories, and a decline of labile patterning. He presents evidence to show that the middle category degrammaticalized in Indo-Aryan and that this process was supported by grammaticalization of several new categories (Kulikov 2009: 84). Passive is expressed by characterized formations. The Old Indic *-āna*-participles are transitive as well as intransitive and middle perfects are stative. The middle has a reflexive intransitivising function which is normally anticausative, but not only middles are anticausative (Kulikov 2009: 81). They are opposed to causatives with nasal affixes like Old Indic *pavate* 'becomes clean' to active *punāti* 'makes clean' and class IV *riyate* 'flows' to *rināti* 'makes flow'. There was decay of middle of intransitive verbs, verbs of perception and consumption, and intransitive/transitive verbs. Passives formed by *-ya-* increase productivity. Labile valency, which may originate in the predominant intransitivity of the IE perfect, is mostly secondary but labile syntax is found, especially in thematized V, IX, and VII nasal classes. The decline of the middle was due to new valency-changing categories formed by *-ya-, -aya-,* etc. Western IE languages have a new formally reflexive middle voice and lability increases in Greek, Romance, and Baltic.

Evidence from Germanic is presented in Ottosson (to appear). The Indo-European middle was used in part to express anticausative content. It survived into Germanic, but is only attested in Gothic, where it has become restricted to passive use and the active form expresses medioactive. There was therefore an opening for new expressions of the anticausative. Germanic shows transition from aspect to valency and systematizes transitive versus unaccusative (anticausative). *ja*-causatives were inherited from Proto-Germanic. Germanic languages have thriving anticausative *-na-*, which puts more focus on the effect. The Germanic new reflexive middle does not seem to have developed at the Common Germanic or Proto-Germanic stage. The Old Nordic middle and the OHG reflexive are mainly anticausative. The synthetic passive of Proto-Germanic is found in Gothic in the present tense but is extinct in the other Old Germanic languages.

Hoffner and Melchert (2008: 302–305) present evidence from Hittite: Active verbs are transitive or intransitive. Some medio-passives show active function and may be transitive or intransitive. Other medio-passives function as passives to corresponding active verbs. Some agentless passives are equivalent to intransitives but can also be stative. Passives are formed periphrastically with *-ant*-participle and *es-* "be" and this construction is often stative (Hoffner and Melchert 2008: 304, 312). Because of association of medio-passive with intransitive, there is a tendency in New Hittite for medio-passives of transitive meaning to be converted to active *ḫi*-verbs.

Hittite denominal verbs with *-ē-* suffix are stative but mostly indicate change-of-state (Watkins 1973: 67, Hoffner and Melchert 2008: 177). When referring to change-of-state the *-ē-*suffix was substituted by *-ēss-*. The suffix *-nu-* forms causative verbs and factitives of adjectives.

10. Ergativity, agentivity, and animacy

Meillet suggested in 1931 that PIE had only two genders motivated by ANIMACY and based on a syntactic feature AGENS, which was later replaced by SUBJECT. There were restrictions on nouns as being subjects of certain categories of verbs. In most Indo-European languages NATURAL SEX and form determine the assignment to concord classes and ANIMACY plays no role. Weitenberg (1987) discussed Proto-Indo-European nominal classification in the light of Old Hittite. Hittite possesses two CONCORD classes, common and neuter. One can reconstruct a perfectly motivated (ANIMACY) two member classification based on a syntactic feature AGENS. CONCORD class neuter nouns are restricted as to SUBJECT. It cannot be excluded that the original motivation for Proto-Indo-European nominal classification was related to the feature SUBJECT.

In Hittite, neuter nouns do not function as grammatical subjects of transitive verbs. *wātar* 'water' cannot be a subject but is found in this function as *wetenanza*, which is commonly considered as an ergative form, the plural nominative of which is *wetenantes*, which is provided with the nominative ending -*es*. *kas tuppiyanza* 'this tablet' is the subject of *wemizzi* 'finds' in a passage of a Hittite letter which shows one example of the nominative form of demonstrative pronouns together with the -*anza* form of the neuter noun *tuppi*. The use of these forms is conditioned by neuter gender and subjecthood of transitive verbs (Hoffner and Melchert 2008: 67). Though -*anz(a)* could be an ablative form reanalyzed as derivational as claimed by Garrett (1990: 265) the plural nominative -*antes* and the nominative of the demonstratives followed by a noun with a singular -*anza* may make an alternative analysis more probable. Garrett (1990) claimed that Hittite shows a split ergative system and has been followed by Melchert (2011) and others. A split ergative structure of a specific kind that has typological parallels (Melchert 2011) is a trait of Anatolian and -*ant* is found in Luvian as well as Hittite. It applies to Anatolian but as has always been maintained by Comrie (cf. 2001: 27) it does not imply that an ergative structure will have to be accepted for Proto-Indo-European.

According to Josephson (2004) Hittite -*ant* is a multifunctional derivational morpheme that is singulative, decollectivizing, and agentive and plays a syntactic role, most importantly in its facilitating function as Instigator in effective construction and entrance into a role of Subject. The agentive role is one that the inanimate neuter cannot play with the transitive verb and it needs the addition of the individualizing and agentive suffix -*ant*- in order to play that role. The suffix is syntactic as well as semantic and therefore belongs to the third of the three suffix classes defined by Fruyt (1984: 255–264), who advocates multifunctionality of suffixes (cf. Josephson 2004: 115–116.)

There are reasons to believe that a whole continuum of functions of *-ant-* belonged to the suffix -*-*ent*- in Indo-European prehistory. A derivational agentive function may be a better explanation for the origin of Hittite -*anz(a)* than an original ergative based on an ablative, in which case it would represent the agentive suffix -*ant* followed by the -*s* of the nominative (Josephson 2004: 115–116). This view is shared by Kloekhorst (2008: 184–185) who does not consider -*anz(a)* to be a real case ending although he calls it "ergative".

11. Participles

The Latin -*nt*- participle is active. This formation is also found in Anatolian and it is the only Hittite participle. It usually refers to an attained state. In Luvian it occurs only as lexicalized. In non-Anatolian Indo-European the *-*ent*- participle is active and processual (cf. Kuryłowicz (1964: 167). Melchert (to appear a) states that these are different specializations of a verbal adjunct that was not yet a participle in PIE and that it is possible that the development of the derived adjective in *-*ent* into a participle occurred separately in Anatolian and non-Anatolian.

The only Luvian participial formation has -*Vm(m)a/i)*- which mostly refers to an attained state like Hittite -*ant*-, but it is sometimes transitive. It should probably be connected with the IE suffix *-*men*- which serves for nominal derivation and does not have agentive meaning (cf. Melchert to appear a). The development of a one-participle system is a trait of Common Anatolian. The Indo-European *-*to*- and -*no*-participles are not found in Anatolian (Hittite *akkant*- 'dead' translates Lat. *mortuus*) though it is found as a nominal suffix. Participial -*wes*- of the IE perfect is not found in Anatolian, which has not inherited the perfect, and this would be due to its non-existence in Pre-Proto-IE if we accept the Indo-Hittite hypothesis.

12. Common innovations and archaism

Melchert (to appear a) presents some common innovations of non-Anatolian Indo-European as evidence supporting the Indo-Hittite hypothesis as compared with contradicting evidence:

Common innovations of non-Anatolian:
- Feminine gender.
- True participles with fixed diathesis built on tense-aspectual stems.
- *-i*-verbs renewed as *-ye/yo*-verbs.
- Possibly the perfect.
- Development of the fully sigmatic aorist as an innovation of non-Anatolian.
- Dative plural formations *-m-os* and *-bhy-os* replacing *-os* are post-Anatolian innovations.
- Post-Anatolian expansion of simple thematic verbs. (There are simple thematic verbs in Anatolian but they are very rare.)
- **-to* of the deverbative type is possibly a post-Anatolian innovation.

Innovation in Anatolian and non-Anatolian:
- Anatolian preserved and extended the h_2e-conjugation, whereas non-Anatolian renewed it by various thematic types.
- Anatolian *-ant* is only occasionally active but **-ent* is active and processual in other IE languages. These may be different specializations of an adjective.

Anatolian loss:
- Dual was lost in Anatolian.
- Anatolian may have lost the distinction perfective/imperfective stem, which would in that case not be an innovation of non-Anatolian.

Inherited structure:
- Anatolian present stem formation was as rich as in classical IE.
- Gen.**-e/o-so* is inherited.
- PIE had a set of root presents with an **ó/é*-ablaut *ḫi*-verb attested by Hittite *karāp-/karēp-* 'consume, devour' and other verbs. (The reconstruction of this ablaut was doubted by Kloekhorst (2008: 142–143).

Melchert (to appear a) suggests a revision but not a radical one. A marginal position of Proto-Anatolian can explain archaic traits and retentions as well as losses. The common innovations of non-Anatolian are explained as due to a marginal position of Anatolian, which would explain retentions as well as losses.

A new observation can be added to Melchert's non-trivial innovations of non-Anatolian. According to Kim (2011: 200) the PIE non-suffixed thematic present was characterized by the same stress and ablaut alternations as athematic presents. The agreement among the classical IE languages in having full-grade root suggests that this was a common innovation of "Nuclear IE" following the departure of Anatolian and Tocharian, rather than a parallel independent development.

Luraghi (2011) and Melchert (to appear b) are two important contributions towards solving the question of the origin of the feminine gender. Development of the feminine grammatical gender is an innovation of Core Indo-European. The *-eh_2 suffix of abstracts had animate gender. An endocentric *-eh_2 derived grammatically animate substantives and like other endocentric suffixes it took on adjectival function which helped the development of the agreement pattern that was crucial for establishing the feminine as a true grammatical gender. Luraghi (2009: 4–5 and 2011) cites problems with the derivation of the feminine gender from the collective function of *-h_2 and there is no basis for supposing that there was any association between animate collective nomina tantum nominative-accusative in *-eh_2 and animate abstracts with *-eh_2. She shows that the creation of the feminine gender resulted from a split within the animate gender as argued by Meillet (1931) and that when the new distinction was extended to the demonstrative by adding the nominal ending *-eh_2 to the animate *so (Hittite sentence introductory sa-) and according to Melchert this may have been a crucial step in the development of a grammatical gender. Luraghi proposes a scale of noun classification devices on which referent tracking gender systems "from below" and classificatory systems "from above" rank differently. The two-gender system of PIE was changed into a three-gender system based on sex starting from the new feminine demonstrative *seh_2 and spreading to adjectives in accordance with the agreement hierarchy of Corbett (1991).

Rieken (2009: 49) suggests that *-eh_2 could not be used for the feminine because it also formed the collective and that loss of that category and other categories such as optative *-yeh_1/-ih_1 and the comparative morpheme *-ero- can be the result of language contact in a multilingual surrounding.

Jasanoff (2003: 174–179) offers a solution for the morpheme -s-, and shows that the "classical" s-aorist cannot have arisen from an earlier partly sigmatic paradigm found in Tocharian and in the preterit of the Hittite ḫi-conjugation. The standard theory of the s-aorist cannot be correct and the mixed paradigm of Hittite and Tocharian was a feature of the parent language itself. The PIE ancestor of the s-aorist was the "presigmatic" aorist, whose non-3rd sg. forms of the active were non-sigmatic and took the perfect endings. Jasanoff reconstructs it as a subset of h_2e-conjugation aorists with active semantics, which was not associated with the stative-intransitive system that became the ancestor of the Hittite and Tocharian categories. An original mixed inflection of the inaccurately named s-aorist would therefore be a simpler solution than to assume two separate suppletions, one in Hittite and one in Tocharian. This illustrates the importance of distinguishing between the synchronic grammar of Late PIE and the explanation of this synchronic grammar, which can only be achieved by internal reconstruction (Jasanoff 2003: 179).

Rieken (2009) believes that the morpheme -s- was possibly not functional because it was found in aorists as well as present forms. According to Rieken, 3rd sg. preterite active -s of the ḫi-conjugation *nais* "turned" which corresponds to Old Indian *anaiḥ* shows that the aspectual opposition existed in Anatolian.

Tremblay (2004: 125–127) states that it is possible that Hittite did not possess the perfect, aorist and present categories but that its paradigms are nevertheless not very simple. In comparative grammar, typological comparison of morphological categories does not yield results but only comparison of forms. Categories may have been lost but the three Indo-Greek temporal forms of present, aorist and perfect are attested by Hittite forms.

13. Subgrouping

Anatolian and Tocharian have a structured set of lexical isoglosses in common with western Indo-European (Puhvel 1994, Melchert 1998: 28) and Hittite has important vocabulary in common with Italic. *kwo/i as a relative pronoun can be understood as a shared innovation if Proto-Anatolian separated from a western Indo-European neighbourhood (Melchert 1998: 28) as well as the -r of the middle, which is common to the central area and the west.

Germanic shares interesting traits with Anatolian such as transitivisation as against detransitivising tendencies in the eastern part of the IE area (Luraghi 2012) as well as the suffixation by which transitivisation is achieved. These groups also share the completive meaning of Germanic *ga-* and Hittite *-kan*.

Jasanoff continues to produce arguments for early separation of Anatolian and Tocharian, to which he adds Italo-Celtic (a marginal group according to Meillet (1931: 2–5), and he claims that the thematic optative was created in a large core dialect that remained after the departure of those three groups, when a "southern" dialect group (Greek-Armenian, Indo-Iranian) and a "northern" group (Germanic, Balto-Slavic) remained. All these dialects have the thematic optative except Celtic, which lost the optative completely (Jasanoff 2009: 17).

14. Conclusion

Ringe et al. (2002) state that there seems to be a node of Tocharian and Italo-Celtic, a Greek-Germanic node and a node joining Slavic and Indo-Iranian, all based on shared states. Germanic behaves in an anomalous way. If Germanic is omitted the best tree shows separation of Italo-Celtic, followed by Greek-Armenian, then Indo-Iranian, and lastly Slavic (p. 90). Anatolian is one last-order subgroup and the other languages together is the other. Other alternatives for a last-order subgroup are Anatolian and Tocharian, Anatolian-Tocharian and Italo-Celtic, Tocharian and Italo-Celtic. The first alternative is the best one (p. 97). One should accept as evidence only what is mathematically ineluctable (pp.105–106). There is a solution for Germanic: Germanic is a subgroup with Anatolian, Tocharian and Italo-Celtic that lost contact in the east and came in close contact with the languages in the west followed by lexical borrowing before any distinctive sound-changes (p.110). It occupied a central position in the family and belonged to the residue after the departure of Anatolian, Tocharian, and Italo-Celtic (pp. 110–111).

If we compare the results of Indo-European subgrouping presented by Ringe et al. and the present state of Indo-European research concerning common innovations and archaism, possible nodes, and prehistoric dialect geography we will find many similarities.

Grammatical and derivational categories play an important role in Indo-European research but only a marginal one in Ringe et al. which however contains a discussion about thematic aorists and optatives.

There is near agreement on possible nodes between these results based on mathematical cladistics and the present discussion in the field of Indo-European linguistics. The relative positions of the core dialects that remained after the departure of Anatolian and Tocharian based on the opinion of Meid (1988) are similar to the conclusions of Ringe et al. (2002 : 110–111), which are more detailed.

Some revision of "classical" Indo-European is required to account for the genuine archaisms of Anatolian as stated by Melchert (to appear a). A prehistoric position of Anatolian as separated from Core Indo-European explains why it did not share in several common innovations and this also applies to Tocharian.

Melchert (to appear a) summarises his results stating that the number of common non-Anatolian innovations is modest: the feminine gender and the true particle with fixed diathesis and perhaps the perfect. There were few innovations with creation and loss of categories but the $*-h_2e$-conjugation was lost and there was a marked expansion of the simple thematic stem.

References

Clackson, James
   2007   *Indo-European Linguistics. An Introduction.* Cambridge: Cambridge University Press.
Comrie, Bernard
   2001   Typology and the History of Language. In *Aspects of Typology and Universals,* Walter Bisang (ed.), 21–25. Berlin: Akademie Verlag.
Corbett, Greville
   1991   *Gender.* Cambridge: Cambridge University Press.
Dawson, Hope
   2003   Defining the outcome of language contact: Old English and Old Norse. *The Ohio State University. Working Papers in Linguistics* 57: 40–57.
Devoto, Giacomo
   1929   Italo-greco e italo-celtico. In *Silloge linguistica dedicata alla memoria di Graziadio Isaia Ascoli nel primo centenario della nascita,* 200–240. Torino: Giovanni Chiantore.
Filip, Hana
   2003   Prefixes and the delimitation of events. *Journal of Slavic Linguistics* 11: 55–101.
Fruyt, Michèle
   1984   Approche méthodologique de la suffixation en Latin et en Français. *Zeitschrift für Vergleichende Sprachforschung* 97.2: 246–264.
García Hernández, Benjamín
   1980   Sistema y desarollo semasiológico de los preverbios en la lengua Latina. In *Semántica estructural y lexemática del verbo,* Benjamín García Hernández (ed.), 123–241. Barcelona: Avesta.
Garrett, Andrew
   1990   The origin of NP split ergativity. *Language* 66 (2): 261–296.
Garrett, Andrew
   1996   Wackernagel's law and unaccusativity in Hittite. In *Approaching Second,* Aaron L. Halpern and Arnold M. Zwicky (eds.), 85–133. Stanford CA: GSLI.
Güldemann, Tom
   2010   Proto-Bantu and Proto-Niger-Congo: macro-areal typology and linguistic reconstruction, In *International Symposon of the Center of Corpus-based Linguistics and Language Education (CbLLE),* Christa König and Osamu Hieda (eds.), 109–142. Amsterdam/Philadelphia: John Benjamins.
Haug, Dag
   2007   The prefix *co(m)-* with motion verbs in Plautus; philological study and etymological implications, In *Greek and Latin from an Indo-Eu-*

ropean Perspective. George Coulter, Matthew McCullagh, Benedicte Nielsen, Antonia Ruppel, and Olga Tribulato (eds.), 80–88. Cambridge: Cambridge University Press.

Haverling, Gerd
2000   *On Sco-verbs. Prefixes and Semantic Functions. A Study in the Development of Prefixed and Unprefixed Verbs from Early to Late Latin.* Göteborg: Studia Graeca et Latina Gothoburgiensia.

Haverling, Gerd
2008   On the development of actionality, tense, and viewpoint from Early to Late Latin. In *Interdependence of Diachronic and Synchronic Analyses,* Folke Josephson and Ingmar Söhrman (eds.), 73–104. Amsterdam/Philadelphia: John Benjamins.

Hoffner, Harry A. Jr. and H. Craig Melchert
2008   *A Grammar of the Hittite Language, Part 1 Reference Grammar.* Winona Lake, Indiana: Eisenbrauns.

Jasanoff, Jay H.
2003   *Hittite and the Indo-European Verb.* Oxford: Oxford University Press.

Jasanoff, Jay H.
2009   Notes on the internal history of the PIE optative. In *East and West: Papers in Indo-European Studies,* Kazuhiko Yoshida and Brent Vine (eds.), 47–68. Bremen: Hempen.

Johanson, Lars
2000   Viewpoint operators in European languages. In *Tense and Aspect in the Languages of Europe,* Östen Dahl (ed.), 27–187. Berlin/New York: Mouton de Gruyter.

Josephson, Folke
2004   Semantics and typology of Hittite *-ant.* In *Indo-European Word Formation,* James Clackson and Birgit Anette Olsen (eds.), 91–118. Copenhagen: Museum Tusculanum Press.

Josephson, Folke
2008   Actionality and aspect in Hittite. In *Interdependence of Diachronic and Synchronic Analyses,* Folke Josephson and Ingmar Söhrman (eds.), 131–147. Amsterdam/Philadelphia: John Benjamins.

Josephson, Folke
2010   Hittite *-apa, -san,* and *-kan* as Actional Modifiers. In *Ex Anatolia Lux. Anatolian and Indo-European studies in honor of H. Craig Melchert on the occasion of his sixty-fifth birthday,* Ronald Kim, Norbert Oettinger, Elisabeth Rieken, and Michael Weiss (eds.), 184–190. Ann Arbor/New York: Beech Stave Press.

Josephson, Folke
2011   Allative in Indo-European. In *Grammatical Case in the Languages of the Middle East and Europe, Acts of the International Colloquium:*

Variations, Concurrence et Evolution des Cas dans Divers Domaines Linguistiques Paris, 2–4 avril 2007, Michèle Fruyt, Michel Mazoyer, and Denis Pardee (eds.), 143–150. Chicago: Oriental Institute of the University of Chicago.

Josephson, Folke
2012   Transfer of morphemes and grammatical structure in Ancient Anatolia. In *Copies vs. cognates in bound morphology*, Lars Johanson and Martine Robbeets (eds.), 337–353. Leiden: Brill.

Josephson, Folke
to appear   Directionality, case and actionality in Hittite. In *Diachronic and Typological Perspectives on Verbs*, Folke Josephson and Ingmar Söhrman (eds.), Amsterdam/Philadelphia: John Benjamins.

Kim, Ronald I.
2011   Possible Tocharian evidence for root Ablaut in PIE thematic presents? In *Ex Anatolia Lux. Anatolian and Indo-European studies in honor of H. Craig Melchert on the occasion of his sixty-fifth birthday*, Ronald Kim, Norbert Oettinger, Elisabeth Rieken, and Michael Weiss (eds.), 191–203, Ann Arbor/New York: Beech Stave Press.

Kulikov, Leonid
2009   Valency-changing categories in Indo-Aryan and Indo-European: A diachronic typological portrait of Vedic Sanskrit. In *Multilingualism. Proceedings of the 23rd Scandinavian Conference of Linguistics*, Anju Saxena and Åke Viberg (eds.), 75–92. Uppsala: Acta Universitatis Upsaliensis.

Kuryłowicz, Jerzy
1964   *The Inflectional Categories of Indo-European*. Heidelberg: Winter.

Luraghi, Silvia
2009   The origin of the feminine gender in PIE. In *Grammatical Change in Indo-European Languages. Papers Presented at the Workshop on Indo-European Linguistics at the XVIIIth International Conference on Historical Linguistics, Montreal 2007*, Vit Bubenik, John Hewson, and Sarah Rose (eds.), 3–13. Current Issues in Linguistic Theory Volume 305. Amsterdam and Philadelphia: John Benjamins.

Luraghi, Silvia
2011   The origin of the Proto-Indo-European gender system: Typological considerations. *Folia Linguistica* 45 (2): 435–464.

Luraghi, Silvia
2012   Basic valency orientation and the middle voice in Hittite. *Studies in Language* 36 (1): 1–32.

McCone, Kim
1991   *The Indo-European Origins of the Old Irish Nasal Presents, Subjunctives and Futures*. Innsbruck: Innsbrucker Beiträge zur Sprachwissenschaft.

Meid, Wolfgang
　1988　　*Indogermanisch und Keltisch.* Innsbruck: IBS.
Meillet, Antoine
　1931　　Essai de chronologie des langues indo-européennes. *Bulletin de la Société de Linguistique de Paris* 32: 1–28.
Melchert, H. Craig
　1998　　The dialectal position of Anatolian within Indo-European. In *Proceedings of The Twenty-Fourth Annual Meeting of the Berkeley Linguistics Society February 14–16, 1998. Special Session on Indo-European Subgrouping and Internal Relations February 14, 1998.* Benjamin K. Bergen, Madelaine C. Plauché, and Ashlee C. Bailey (eds.), 24–31. Berkeley: Berkeley Linguistics Society.
Melchert, H. Craig
　2011　　The problem of the ergative case in Hittite. In *Grammatical Case in the Languages of the Middle East and Europe, Acts of the International Colloquium: Variations, Concurrence et Evolution des Cas dans Divers Domaines Linguistiques Paris, 2–4 avril 2007,* Michèle Fruyt, Michel Mazoyer, and Denis Pardee (eds.), 161–168. Chicago: Oriental Institute of the University of Chicago.
Melchert, H. Craig
　to app. a　The position of Anatolian. In *Handbook of Indo-European Studies,* Andrew Garrett and Michael Weiss (eds.), Oxford: Oxford University Press.
Melchert, H. Craig
　to app. b　PIE *-eh_2 as an "individualizing" Suffix and the Feminine Gender. In *Kollektivum und Femininum: Flexion oder Wortbildung? Zum Andenken an Johannes Schmidt,* Robert Schuhmann & Sergio Neri (eds.), Leiden: Brill.
Melchert, H. Craig
　to app. c　Luvo-Lycian Dorsal Stops Revisited. In *The Sound of Indo-European 2,* Roman Sukač and Václav Blažek (eds.).
Napoli, Maria
　2006　　*Aspect and actionality in Homeric Greek. A contrastive analysis.* Milano: FrancoAngeli.
Ó Corráin, Ailbhe
　to appear　On the evolution of verbal aspect in Insular Celtic. In *Diachronic and Typological Perspectives on Verbs,* Folke Josephson and Ingmar Söhrman (eds.). Amsterdam/Philadelphia: John Benjamins.
Ottosson, Kjartan
　2008　　The Old Nordic middle voice in the pre-literary period: Questions of grammaticalisation and cliticization. In *Interdependence of Diachronic and Synchronic Analyses,* Folke Josephson and Ingmar Söhrman (eds.), 185–219. Amsterdam/Philadelphia: John Benjamins.

Ottosson, Kjartan
to appear   The anticausative and related categories in the Old Germanic Languages. In *Diachronic and Typological Perspectives on Verbs*, Folke Josephson and Ingmar Söhrman (eds.), Amsterdam/Philadelphia: John Benjamins.
Pinault, Georges-Jean
2010   On the r-endings of the Tocharian Middle. In *Ex Anatolia Lux. Anatolian and Indo-European studies in honor of H. Craig Melchert on the occasion of his sixty-fifth birthday*, Ronald Kim, Norbert Oettinger, Elisabeth Rieken, and Michael Weiss (eds.), 285–295. Ann Arbor/ New York: Beech Stave Press.
Puhvel, Jaan
1994   Western Indo-European affinities of Anatolian. In *Früh-, Mittel-, Spätindogermanisch (Akten der IX. Fachtagung der Indogermanischen Gesellschaft vom 5. bis 9. Oktober 1992 in Zurich)*, George E. Dunkel (ed.), 315–324. Wiesbaden: Reichert.
Rieken, Elisabeth
2004   Das Präteritum des Medio-Passivs im Hieroglyphen-Luwischen. *Historische Sprachforschung* 117: 179–188.
Rieken, Elisabeth
2009   Der Archaismus des Hethitischen: Eine Bestandsaufnahme. *Incontri Linguistici* 32: 37–52.
Ringe, Don, Tandy Warnow, and Ann Taylor
2002   Indo-European and computational cladistics. *Transactions of the Philological Society* 100 (1): 59–129.
Rix, Helmut
1986   *Zur Entstehung der urindogermanischen Modussystems*. Innsbruck: Institut für Sprachwissenschaft der Universität Innsbruck.
Strunk, Klaus
1967   *Nasalpräsentien und Aoriste. Ein Beitrag zur Morphologie des Verbums im Indoiranischen und Griechischen*. Heidelberg: Winter.
Tremblay, Xavier
2004   Review of Onofrio Carruba and Wolfgang Meid (eds.), *Anatolisch und Indogermanisch*. Bulletin de la Société de Linguistique XCIX, 2: 124–141.
Watkins, Calvert
1973   Hittite and Indo-European studies. The denominative statives in -e-. *Transactions of the Philological Society* 104: 51–93.
Watkins, Calvert
2001   An Indo-European Linguistic Area: Ancient Anatolia. Areal Diffusion as a Challenge to the Comparative Method? In *Areal Diffusion and Genetic Inheritance*, Alexandra Y. Aikhenwald and Robert M. W. Dixon (eds.), 44–63. Oxford: Oxford University Press.

Weiss, Michael
    2009   *Outline of the Historical and Comparative Grammar of Latin.* Ann Arbor/New York: Beech Stave Press.

Weitenberg, Jos J. S.
    1987   Proto-Indo-European Nominal Classification and Old Hittite. *Münchner Studien zur Sprachwissenschaft* 48: 213–250.

Yakubovich, Ilya
    2010   *Sociolinguistics of the Luvian Language.* Leiden/Boston: Brill.

Measuring socially motivated pronunciation differences

John Nerbonne, Sandrien van Ommen, Charlotte Gooskens and Martijn Wieling

1. Introduction[1]

This paper applies a measure of linguistic distance to differences in pronunciation which have been observed as a consequence of modern speakers orienting themselves to standard languages and larger regions rather than local towns and villages, resulting in what we shall call REGIONAL SPEECH. We examine regional speech, other local "varieties" in the Dutch of the Netherlands and Flanders, and also standard Netherlandic Dutch and Belgian Dutch.[2] Because regional speech is difficult to study, as it may not constitute a linguistic variety in the usual sense of the word, we focus on the speech of professional announcers employed by regional radio stations. We examine their speech in light of Auer and Hinskens' (1996) cone-shaped model of the speech continuum, which includes REGIOLECTS, which they define as a sort of comprise between standard languages and local dialects (more below). In this examination we use a measure of pronunciation difference which has been successful in dialectology (see Nerbonne & Heeringa 2009 for an overview) and which has been demonstrated to be valid both for measuring dialect differences and also for measuring speech differences due to limited auditory acuity (cochlear implants). We thereby introduce a technique into sociolinguistics to *measure* the difference between regional speech and standard Dutch as well as the difference between regional speech and the local speech of towns and villages, providing a perspective on the issue of whether regional speech functions as "standard" within more restricted areas or whether it serves rather to mark regional identity.

1.1. Sociolinguistic background

In the Netherlands and Flanders, Dutch is said to have reached an advanced stage of linguistic standardization (Smakman 2006). As Haugen (1966) states, the last stages of standardization are an elaboration of the function of a language and the acceptance of this language by the community.[3] This elaboration of function means that the standard language is used in contexts in which once a prestigious foreign language was used (an exoglossic standard (Auer 2005), i.e. Latin in medieval Europe or French in the era of enlightenment in most of Europe). Importantly, virtually all speakers have at least a passive mastery of the standard language, which is used in the mandatory educational system, in a large number of national and bi-national radio and television broadcasts, and in many civic and governmental functions. The local dialects of individual towns and villages (hence: BASE DIALECTS or BASILECTS) are used in fewer and fewer situations, and their distinctive properties are therefore being lost or LEVELED extensively. Base dialects, in this stage, may be reminiscent of old forms of dress (see Smakman 2006, for an overview and references), which are protected as a kind of cultural heritage. There is ample evidence that dialects are "leveling" to become more like standard languages (Hinskens 1998, to appear; Kerswill 2003; Streck 2012).

New regional forms are nonetheless springing up (Hinskens, Auer & Kerswill 2005), namely REGIOLECTS, regionally flavored speech, which may also serve new sociolinguistic functions (the concept is due to Hoppenbrouwers 1983, Hoppenbrouwers1990). In general a regiolect is not identical to any single basilect, but is easily understood within its region and is identifiable as originating from that region. Regiolects are considered to involve forms intermediate between basilects and standard language, an assumption we will examine in the current paper. We cannot be sure that the speech of the announcers in the regional radio broadcasts qualifies as regiolectal in Auer and Hinskens' sense (see below), but we shall nonetheless examine it from the perspective of their model.

The last formulation prompts a remark about terminology. We shall examine some instances of distinctly REGIONAL SPEECH in this paper and also show that it does not conform to the predictions made in Auer and Hinskens' model. We shall not refer to the samples we collect as 'regiolects' simply because we are not confident that they qualify as such. We shall elaborate on this below.

In this paper regional speech is examined phonetically. We wish to locate regional speech in the speech continuum, in particular with respect to the base dialects and the standard. We investigate how regional speech relates to base dialects and the standard, and how well it represents its region. In our examination we proceed from Auer and Hinskens' (1996) conical model, shown in figure 1 (which they attribute to Chambers and Trudgill 1980: 10–11). This figure shows the language situation which is assumed to exist in the Netherlands and Flanders. There is a layer of base dialects at the base

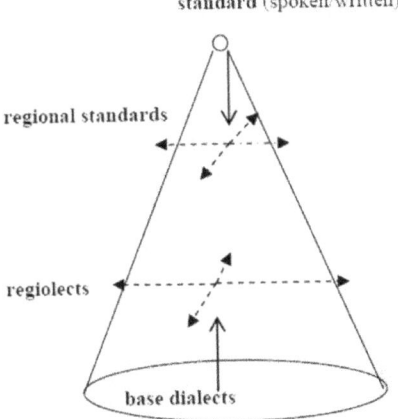

Figure 1. Model from Auer (2005), cone-shaped speech continuum reflecting diaglossic situations. The convergence of base dialects to each other and toward the standard leads to intermediate, regional, varieties.

of the cone (where the horizontal plane represents regional heterogeneity); there is a standard at the top of the cone (the vertical axis represents types of speech differentiation with respect to social status and context); and there are intermediate varieties within a three-dimensional socio-geographic continuum, where we explicitly do not attempt to identify a specific height or even potentially inclined plane that must contain regiolects. The variability of these intermediate forms is meant to be suggested by the arrows.

Our primary descriptive goal in this paper is to examine the speech of some professional representatives of regional speech, namely the announcers at regional radio stations. Since they are paid professional speakers of regionally colored speech, it is interesting to ask where their speech falls in Auer and Hinskens' conical model.

A second goal is to suggest how sociolinguistic discussions of the sort Auer and Hinskens (1996) and Auer (2005) exemplify might benefit from quantitative assessments of sociolinguistic conjectures and postulates. This should be a natural step given the geometric nature of the model, and also given discussions about it, which abound in references to one form of speech being "closer" to another, in references to the "space" between varieties, and in discussions of how a given speech form must be understood as the "convergence" of one form toward another. A great deal of this discussion appeals to an intuitive notion of linguistic distance which is advantageous to operationalize. We return to this in section 5 below.

2. Regiolects and speakers

In this section we first review the literature on regiolects to compile expectations on the linguistic qualities regional speech should have and then second, consider how one is to study regiolects – i.e. how to obtain samples of regiolectal speech. While we do not wish to insist that broadcasters' speech be regarded as regiolectal in Auer and Hinskens' sense, it is accepted within a sizable region as representative. It may be different in being more consciously controlled, however.

2.1. The sociolinguistics of regiolectal formation

As can be seen in figure 1, we use the notion of 'dialect' for a language variety bounded above by a related (ENDOGLOSSIC, see Auer 2005) standard. Between the dialectal level and the standard at the top of the cone, a continuum is imagined, representing other regional varieties.

> A diaglossic repertoire is characterized by intermediate variants between standard and (base) dialect. The term regiolect (or regional dialect) is often used to refer to these intermediate forms, although the implication that we are dealing with a separate variety is not necessarily justified. (Auer 2005: 22)

We shall return below to Auer's important qualification that regiolects may not be true varieties,[4] and our examination will show that the regional speech we have sampled is not intermediate between the standard and base dialects. For this reason we shall refer to our samples as regional speech and not as regiolects. We return to this in the discussion (below).

But we first wish to collect some thoughts on regiolects. What Auer calls intermediate forms (regiolects) are presumed to be more standard than dialects, but more regionally colored than the standard. Regiolects may arise due to various social forces, especially through a process of dialect leveling (koineization) and standardization. Sobrero (1996), analyzing the modern Italian situation, distinguishes three types of koineization (see also Hinskens, Auer, and Kerswill 2005):

1. Active koineization: The spread of a koiné of a strong urban center into the neighboring territory (e.g. Milanese and Neapolitan).
2. Passive koineization: Dialectal diversity is leveled under the influence of the standard.

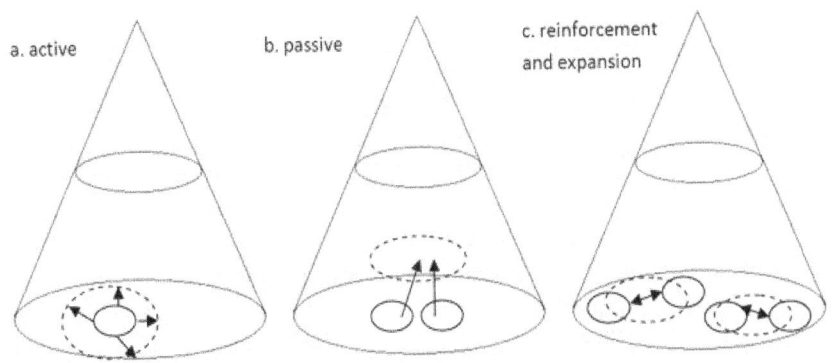

Figure 2. Three types of koineization, after Sobrero (1996). The dashed-line circles represent the result of the koineization.

3. Reinforcement and expansion: Horizontal leveling decreases distinctiveness on a local level in favor of distinctiveness on a regional level, which means the leveled regional varieties are more distinctive from each other than the original transition zone dialects.

In figure 2 these three types of koineization are visualized. Hinskens, Auer, and Kerswill (2005) describe the formation of koiné as "structural convergence between closely related linguistic systems, eventually leading to the stabilization of some compromise variety." According to Trudgill (1986), this koineization does not remove all variation and the remaining variation is assigned new functions. Thus, koineization results in a *re-allocation* of linguistic and extra-linguistic functions to different variants.

In figure 2a the active spread of an urban center increases the homogeneity of regional speech, because a single variety is used in a larger geographical region. In figure 2b, the standard influences the dialectal varieties. Because all the base dialects are influenced by the same standard, dialectal variation becomes smaller. The situation in figure 2c is comparable to the situation in figure 2b, in the sense that dialects converge, but in this situation the leveling results from their converging to each other and is not imposed by the standard or by a dominant (metropolitan) center. The result is that the homogeneity *within* a region increases, which at the same time results in more distinctiveness *between* (some) varieties on an inter-regional level. The figure suggests that dialect convergence and divergence take place simultaneously. Howell (2006) gives a concise overview of the literature on the influence of some migration processes on urban Dutch koineization and advocates a bottom-up view. He shows that a wide variety of Dutch dialects, through immigration, influenced the urban Dutch vernaculars, which contrasts with the view that prestigious dialects expanded. In sum, dialect convergence is the result of complicated interactions, normally leading to an increase in homogeneity on the regional level.

Following Auer (2005), we may assume regiolects are not merely a product of koineization, but also of standardization (although these influences may be intertwined, see figure 2b, where koineization is influenced by the standard). In the stage of standardization that Netherlandic and Belgian Dutch have reached, the influence of the standard is of great importance.

Van Coetsem (1988) describes four sorts of unidirectional interactions (ADVERGENCE, as posited by Mattheier 1996) which result in dialects becoming more like the standard. Van Coetsem focuses on the situation of language users, in particular whether a situation primarily involves speakers of base dialects who adopt standard forms while maintaining their own dialect. In this sort of situation the dialect speaker *actively* borrows from the standard. On the other hand, Van Coetsem also observed speakers of the standard language (or other dialects) who shift to a local dialect, e.g., as a consequence of moving to the dialect area. In this situation the immigrant speaker typically imposes other features onto (his rendering of) the dialect, which, however, is unlikely to change unless there is a substantial number of immigrants. Van Coetsem recognized that the processes were only separate in the ideal case, and that concrete contact situations often involve several factors. Van Coetsem (1988) conjectured that regional varieties typically evolve in situations in which the dialect is the active recipient, taking up (lexical) items from the standard.

If we summarize the descriptions of the regiolect we have noted thus far, we can state that regiolects are varieties on a continuum between dialects and standard, resulting from a process of koineization and standardization, including an imposition of the standard on dialects. Regiolects are thus (*inter alia*) phonetically distinct from the standard, but, through leveling, representative of a larger region than a base dialect. What, then, is the sociolinguistic role of this regiolect in the region?

Since a regiolect is a more standard-like variety of a dialect, and the standard is universally intelligible, a regiolect should be intelligible in a larger region than a base dialect would be. The regiolect, seen from this perspective, fulfills a communicative function. But dialects within one region are closely related and mostly mutually intelligible, which obviates the (communicative) need for a regiolect in intra-regional communication. On the other hand, a regiolect, as a regionally colored variety of the standard allows speakers to display their regional loyalty and regional identity without risking ineffective communication. This may be comparable to a situation Van Coetsem (1988) describes, where the standard absorbs phonetic features of the regional variety. One envisages a dynamic in which a regiolect is intelligible in a larger area than a base dialect, and where regional color in pronunciation allows the speaker to express affiliation with the region. Auer (2005) describes regiolects as a sociolinguistic tool in a similar way:

> The intermediate forms often fulfill a sociolinguistic function by enabling their users to act out, in the appropriate contexts, an identity which could not be symbolized through the base dialects (which may have rural, backwardish or non-educated connotations) nor through the national standard (which may smack of formality and unnaturalness and/or be unable to express regional affiliation). (Auer 2005: 23)

The two views differ in the function they attribute to regiolects. A regiolect produced by koineization, i.e. the convergence of dialects toward each other and toward the standard may facilitate communication, while on the other hand a regiolect as a means of expressing solidarity with a region, even regional identity, functions primarily as means of regional identification (social marking). Note that these two functions correspond to different directions from which regiolects arise in the cone of linguistic variation. The first, communicatively motivated force is attracted by the standard and represents an upward dynamic within the cone of variation, while the second, socially motivated force, reacts to the standard and ought to be seen as proceeding downwardly in the cone, from the standard to the regional varieties. A regiolect may well have both functions, and which function is most important may depend on the level of standardization of a language. If the standard language is accepted for all usage contexts (Smakman 2006; Haugen 1966), then the regiolect has no communicative function at all and may be used only to express regional affiliation. In a situation where regional (dialectal) speech is still the language of first language acquisition, there is no reason to see the use of regiolects as a reaction to standardization, but rather as a means of communication that is less formal than the standard.

2.2. Regional speech

If we wish to study regiolects, we need to obtain samples of them, concrete, representative examples. The task is not as straightforward in the study of regiolects as it is in other branches of variationist linguistics, which famously have their own challenges with respect to data collection, as witnessed by

Labov's (1972) discussion of the paradox of the observer. The reason for our added caution is hinted at in a qualifying clause in Auer's definition, which we repeat for convenience:

> A diaglossic repertoire is characterized by intermediate variants between standard and (base) dialect [...] *although the implication that we are dealing with a separate variety is not necessarily justified.* (Auer 2005: 22, emphasis added by the authors)

If regiolects are indeed not varieties, that is, relatively stable collections of speech habits that serve as a means of communication in a well-defined community, then regiolects are more ephemeral manners of speaking that are intermediate between base dialect and standard. Auer's admonishing clause suggests that regiolectal speech manners might be a sort of compromise between base dialects and standard that is within the competence of most diaglossic (standard-dialect) speakers. If this is correct, then we shall never encounter monolingual speakers of regiolect, nor, indeed, native speakers. The challenge is to find authentic and commensurable samples of regiolectal speech.

In light of these potential problems the existence of regional radio stations and regional programs is a most fortunate circumstance. These stations aim to serve areas much larger than single towns or villages, and they regularly transmit entire programs in regionally colored speech with the aim of reaching audiences throughout entire regions. They have existed for several decades now, and therefore appear to satisfy a need, which, moreover, is recognized commercially. While it may be true, as Auer tangentially suggests, that it would be incorrect to view regiolects as varieties, there are nonetheless professional speakers of locally colored language who aim to reach wide ranges of dialect speakers in a given region. Our strategy in probing the regiolectal landscape will therefore be to seek out such speakers and to investigate their speech as regiolectally representative.

It would of course be preferable to record more such professional regiolectal speakers for each region, but there are not many, and they are professionals who expect compensation for their speech. We are fortunate in having one per region, but we concede that more would be beneficial.

We shall examine the speech of regional radio announcers from the perspective of Auer and Hinskens's model of regiolects, and we shall examine the questions of where their regional speech fits within Auer's cone of variation, whether it faithfully represents the speech of its region, and whether it appears to be motivated more by a need to facilitate communication or by a wish to express regional identity. Even if it turns out that the speech of the broadcasters should not be regarded as regiolectal *sensu stricto*, the analysis below will be interesting if it shows the range that is possible for "professional" regional speakers, since their speech is accepted by many as representative of the region.

2.3. The Netherlands and Flanders

In both the Netherlands and in Flanders, Dutch is the standard language, but Standard Netherlandic Dutch is not the exact same language as Standard Belgian Dutch (see endnote 1). Even though the formal (written) standard does not differ much between Belgian and Netherlandic Dutch, the spoken standards have phonetically diverged (van de Velde 1996), resulting in two separate (but closely related) standard varieties. These varieties may be very similar, but they have evolved separately. The Eighty Years' War (1558–1648) politically isolated Flanders from the Netherlands, stalling the standardization of Dutch in Flanders, where French assumed many supra-regional communicative functions (Grondelaers et al. 2001). In the 19th and 20th centuries Dutch was again installed as the official standard in Flanders, leading to a new impulse to standardization. There was no Belgian Dutch standard, so the Netherlandic Dutch standard was accepted as the norm (Geeraerts 2001). Grondelaers et al. (2001) refer to one consequence of this interrupted standardization as SYNCHRONIC STRATIFICATION, i.e. a larger distance between regional and supra-regional speech.

We shall not examine in detail whether the Belgian differentiation is larger than the Dutch but we shall pay attention to the issue below, and we shall check for differences between the two Dutch speech continua.

We focus on the role of the regional speech – whether it functions primarily as koiné or as an expression of regional identity. We develop these hypotheses in section 3 (below).

3. The role of regiolects: Hypotheses

In the current paper, the phonetic proximity of regional speech to standard and dialect is used to investigate the function of regional speech. We expect pronunciation dissimilarities to be an important difference between regional and standard speech. This is irrespective of whether one proceeds from the assumption that the regional speech arises from a local variety which absorbs lexical items from the standard, whose pronunciation then "pulls" the local variety toward the standard, or from the assumption that regional speech is a variety of the standard which has absorbed local phonetic coloration. The latter likewise contributes to pronunciation differences. We compute pronunciation dissimilarities by the use of the Levenshtein distance (see below). Pronunciation differences between words are expressed in a distance, and distances between the many words in a sample together constitute the so-called dialect distance between two varieties.

For the current study these distances may be analyzed to reveal more about the role of regional speech in the Netherlands and Flanders. We distill our interests in the function of regional speech to the three questions below. We begin by noting that the conical model predicts an intermediate position for regional speech, which we shall, of necessity, test in two parts. Thinking geometrically, we view the position of the regional speech first from the perspective of the base dialects, and then from that of the standard.

1. Are the base dialects in the region really closer to the regional speech than they are to the standard, so that the regional speech might be easier to use (than the standard) and thus offer benefits in communication in the region? And how different are the standard and regional manners of speech as candidate koinés (again seen from the point of view of the base dialects)?
2. Is the regional speech also closer to the standard than the base dialects are, as the conical model predicts? This question is not the same as above (1), where we looked at two pairs of distances, namely base-standard and base-regional. We examine here the standard-regional and the standard-base distances to verify a second consequence of the conical model, namely that the regional manner of speaking is a compromise in the direction of the standard. Regional speech might be closer to the based dialects by emphasizing non-standardness even more than the base dialects, perhaps due to its function in displaying regional identity.
3. Is regional speech a loyal representative of its region? In other words, is the regiolect closer to base dialects in its own region than to other base dialects?

Our first questions (1 and 2) are aimed at verifying whether the conical model in fact obtains and at identifying possible instances where it does not. We do this in order to check on the most important functions of the regional speech, i.e. to see whether it might facilitate communication in limited regions or whether it instead functions primarily to express regional solidarity and regional identity.

We think the third question will most likely be answered positively, since there can be no motivation for disloyal regional speech, but we add this question partly in view of our samples, the speech of radio announcers. If they are performing poorly, e.g., simply adding regionalisms a bit randomly to their speech, then they may turn out to represent "general regional speech" better than they represent the regional speech of their own region. In any case it is a non-trivial task – perhaps not possible at all for many speakers – to place one's speech between the standard and a large number of base dialects.

We also tried to ask whether a given speech sample is a *fair* representative in its region, and not e.g., a slightly more standard variant of a base dialect from a dominant city or town in the region or from the place where the speaker comes from. However, we shall not test fairness strictly, as we have not found a way to do this quantitatively. We first hypothesized that for a given region, we might measure *all* the pair-wise distances not only among all the base dialects but also between the regiolect and all the base dialects, noting in particular the mean distance to the base dialects (for each base dialect and for the regiolect). If we then compared, for each base dialect and for the regional speaker's speech, its mean distance to the other base dialects, we might see where the regional speech lies in the distribution of mean differences. But we abandoned this idea due to the problem that various regiolects might *fairly* represent a region at different average distances from the base dialects (as the imaginary regiolect gets closer to the standard).

As noted in section 2.3 (above), the role of regiolects in Flanders and the Netherlands may differ, so we shall likewise pay attention to differences in the countries which might be due to the late standardization of Belgian Dutch, or to the very dominant position of the standard language in the Netherlands. We expect base dialects in the Netherlands to be more similar linguistically to the standard and to their regiolects (less vertical variation than in Flanders), which might in turn mean that regiolects in the Netherlands will also differ less from the standard (than those in Flanders). This is not a focus of our study, but we shall not neglect it.

4. Material

4.1. Geographic regions

In this study regions are mainly defined by provinces, which are governmental entities (Impe et al. 2008). We focus on the regions of the provinces Antwerp (FL), Brabant (FL), Belgian Limburg (FL), West Flanders (FL),

North Brabant (NL), Netherlandic Limburg (NL) and Groningen (NL) and the agglomeration *Randstad* (NL) shown in figure 3. The reader might wish to note that the province name 'Brabant' is used both for a province in the Netherlands and for one in Belgium. We shall refer to these respectively as 'North Brabant' or 'Brabant (NL)' and 'Brabant (FL)'.

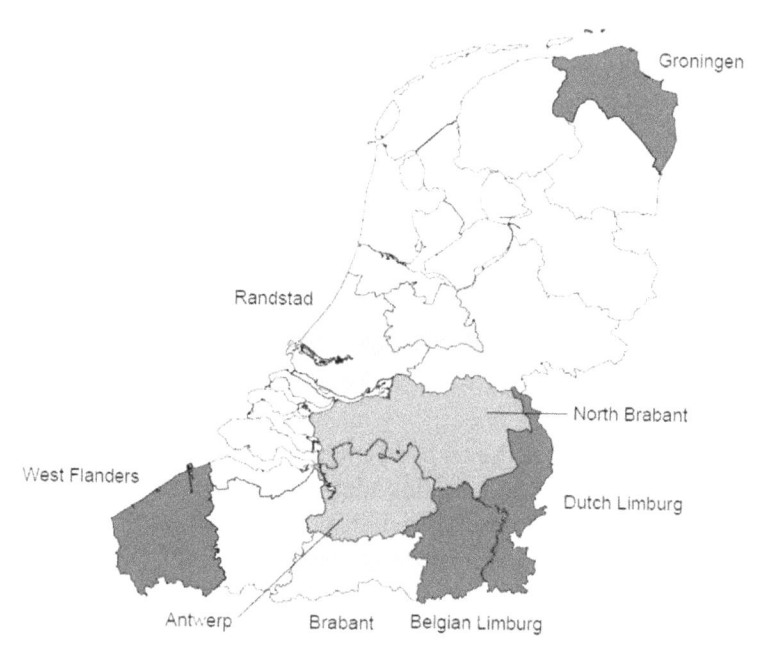

Figure 3. Map of the Netherlands and Flanders, indicating the regions.

The areas chosen differ with respect to their political and economic importance in their respective countries. The regions Brabant and *Randstad* are the most central areas (both containing the capital city[5]) in Flanders and the Netherlands, respectively. Besides the regions' economic and cultural importance both regions have dominant positions in the media in their respective countries. The regions West Flanders, Belgian Limburg, Groningen and Dutch Limburg, on the other hand, are peripheral areas, where dialectal language use is better preserved than in the other areas. The regions Antwerp and North Brabant are considered intermediate areas: they are closer to the central region than the peripheral areas.

The *Randstad* in reality is a region consisting of two provinces (Utrecht and South Holland) and a part of the province of North Holland. Since the *Randstad* is an agglomeration of cities in the Netherlands, crossing provincial borders, these provinces cannot, for the purpose of this study, be taken apart as separate regions. Because the regions mentioned above are defined by province borders (not dialectal areas), the borders of the *Randstad* are defined by state conventions as well, following VROM (Ministry of Housing, Spatial Planning and the Environment, *Randstadmonitor* 2006).

4.2. Pronunciation data

We wish to compute the phonetic distance between dialectal, regional and standard speech, which makes it necessary to use pronunciations from several sources. Regional pronunciations were selected from a project on mutual intelligibility in the Netherlands and Flanders where eight male regional radio commentators (four from each country) pronounced 300 words as they would as professional regional speakers (Impe et al. 2008). Every announcer was between the age of 27 and 34 at the time of testing, and born, raised and still living in the region he represents. The speakers reported using both regionally colored and standard speech regularly for personal and professional ends. The announcers were asked to pronounce the words in isolation, without making lexical changes to the words. This allows us to compare the pronunciations with the pronunciations of the base dialect respondents, who had the same task (see below). The instruction given to the speakers was to use "informal regionally accented speech, comprehensible in the speaker's entire region". All pronunciations were transcribed by the same person (the second author, whose native language is Netherlandic Dutch). The transcriptions were discussed with a second transcriber at an early stage, to ensure consistency and correctness. For the purpose of the current study the Belgian Dutch transcriptions were checked by a transcriber whose first language is Belgian Dutch.

Dialectal pronunciations in 318 places located in the eight regions were taken from a 562-word subset of the Goeman-Taeldeman-Van Reenen-Project (GTRP; Goeman & Taeldeman 1996). The words were selected by Wieling et al. (2007) for a computational analysis of Dutch dialect pronunciation, where words that were spoken in isolation were favored in order to facilitate the identification and extraction of the necessary material. We used the overlapping words in the two data sets for the comparison in this study (37 words: 2 nouns, 17 adjectives and 18 verbs). We transcribed the standard pronunciation of these 37 words ourselves according to Gussenhoven (2007; Dutch) and Verhoeven (2005; Belgian Dutch). The list of words used in the analysis can be found in the appendix.

The regional, standard and Belgian dialect transcriptions were all based on the same subset of IPA sound segments consisting of 55 sounds. As reported by Wieling et al. (2007), the dialect transcriptions in the Netherlands in the GTRP were transcribed using a much larger set of about 80 sounds. To make these transcriptions more comparable we automatically merged the sounds occurring only in the Netherlandic transcriptions with the most similar sounds occurring in the smaller set. This approach was proposed and discussed in detail by Wieling and Nerbonne (2011). The procedure of automatically determining sound distances (needed to determine the most similar sounds) is also discussed in the next section.

5. Method

As we noted in the introduction, we suggest as well that this paper may contribute a quantitative perspective to this sociolinguistic discussion. We noted further in the discussion of the literature on regiolects that the sociolinguistic discussion concerning regiolects repeatedly refers to the "distances" between varieties without actually attempting to define that notion precisely. We suggest in this paper that a dialectometric technique for assessing the differences between varieties quantitatively may serve to define one aspect of linguistic distance, i.e. pronunciation distance. Other work has shown that pronunciation distance correlates strongly with lexical and syntactic distances (Spruit, Heeringa, and Nerbonne 2009). Since it is also readily implemented, the Levenshtein distance effectively measures 'pronunciation distances' for sociolinguistic purposes. Our contention is thus that we are now in a position to operationalize the notion 'linguistic distance' effectively. We first explain how this is done and note work that has been done to validate the measure.

To determine the phonetic distance between dialects, regiolects and standard, we used a modified version of the Levenshtein distance (Levenshtein 1965). The regular Levenshtein distance counts the minimum number of insertions, deletions and substitutions to transform one string into the other. For example, the Levenshtein distance of two Dutch dialectal pronunciations of the word 'to bind', [bɪndən] and [bɛində], is 3:

bɪndən	insert ɛ	1
bɛɪndən	substitute i/ɪ	1
bɛindən	delete n	1
bɛində		
		3

The corresponding alignment is:

b	ɪ	n	d	ə	n
b	ɛ	i	n	d	ə	
	1	1				1

The regular Levenshtein distance does not distinguish vowels and consonants and may well align a vowel with a consonant. To enforce linguistically sensible alignments (and distances), we added a syllabicity constraint to the Levenshtein distance so that it does not align vowels with (non-sonorant) consonants. In addition, in the standard Levenshtein procedures, if one sound is replaced by another in the alignment, the Levenshtein distance is always increased by one. Intuitively this does not always make sense. A substitution of [i] for [y] should have a smaller effect on the pronunciation distance than a substitution of [i] for [A] as the former sounds are much more similar than the latter. To reflect this, we modified the Levenshtein distance to use more sensitive sound distances. We automatically determined the sound distances based on the relative frequency with which they align using Levenshtein distance. Pairs of sounds co-occurring relatively frequently are assigned relatively low costs and sounds occurring relatively infrequently are assigned high costs. This method was introduced and found to be superior over the Levenshtein distance with syllabicity constraint by Wieling et al. (2009). Furthermore Wieling et al. (2012) show that the automatically derived sound distances are linguistically sensible (showing a substantial correlation with acoustic distances ($0.6 < r < 0.8$).

It is important that measures not only be well defined, but also that they be shown *valid* for the task to which they are employed, i.e. that they measure what one intends to measure (Howitt and Cramer, 2008: 265–271). Levenshtein distance has indeed been shown valid for measuring pronunciation dissimilarity by Gooskens and Heeringa (2004), who showed that aggregate Levenshtein distance correlated well with Norwegian dialect speakers' perceptions of dialect dissimilarity. Similarly, Sanders and Chin (2009) have verified that Levenshtein distance is a valid measure of pronunciation difference when used to measure the degree to which the speech of cochlear implant patients differs from that of healthy controls, which we regard as further confirmation of validity (of Levenshtein distance as a measure of pronunciation difference). We postulate that no independent validation is needed for the application to the social differences we are concerned with, i.e. the differences between the speech of the radio broadcasters and that of the local dialects. The perceptual situation is similar, as is the measurement task. Naturally, this postulate could be in error, and we are interested in criticism of other researchers and in empirical testing.

We are also aware of Greenhill's (2011) criticism of the use of Levenshtein distance in order to detect genealogical relations among languages, but we suspect that the difficulty lies not in the capability of the Levenshtein algorithm to measure string dissimilarity but rather in using a good measure of string dissimilarity to ascertain genealogical (un)relatedness. In fact, historical linguists have always emphasized that it is not superficial similarity which is interpreted as evidence of genealogical relatedness, but rather shared innovations, normally realized as regular sound correspondences (Campbell 2004: 197).

After determining the distance between each pair of pronunciations (transcriptions) of each word, the distance between every pair of varieties (e.g., standard and regional, or standard and a dialect) is calculated by averaging all 37 word distances. This means we have a mean phonetic distance between every pair of varieties, based on the difference between these varieties in each pair of pronunciations.

Finally we should not conclude this section without noting that it is unusual in sociolinguistic research to pay attention to aggregate differences of any sort (phonetic, morphological, etc.). Sociolinguists have largely focused on the analysis of single variables such as the allophonic variation of a single phoneme, e.g., /æ/, and the social meaning attached to different allophones (Chambers, 2003). This has led to progress in understanding the motivation for individual sound changes. We do not presume to suggest replacing the usual focus on single features with aggregate analyses, but we do suggest including aggregate analyses in the set of methods available to sociolinguistics. The single-feature perspective risks becoming myopic when used to study the broad range of changes typically introduced by koneization, standardization, or the formation of regional varieties. We present an analysis of the aggregate differences below, and we claim that it provides a more insightful perspective of the sweeping changes brought about as standards influence dialects.

6. Results

6.1. Tests of hypotheses

We asked several questions pertaining to the structure and function of regional speech, trying to test whether the conical model was right in always placing the regional speech between the standard and the base dialects, and whether the regional speech is a loyal representative of the region. The conical model postulates that regional speech should be intermediate between base dialects and the standard, but we can only test relative distances. For this reason we separately test two consequences of the hypothesis that regional speech is intermediate.

1. From the point of view of the base dialects, which is closer, the regional or the standard speech?

It is a consequence of the conical model that all varieties are roofed by the standard. If regional speech takes a position between the base dialects and the standard (see figure 1), then the base dialects have to be closer to regional than to standard speech.

2. From the point of view of the standard, is the regional speech phonetically closer than the base dialects are?

This is also clearly a consequence of the conical model, which, however, we need to test separately because we are using distances to test the hypothesis that regional speech is intermediate. Note that we might have a positive answer to the question in (1) even where the regional speech is *less* standard than the base dialects. We therefore additionally check whether the regional speech is indeed more standard-like than the base dialects, ruling out cases where base dialects are closer to regional speech (than to the standard) only because the regional speech is actually *less* like the standard (than the base dialects are). The latter would be the case if the regional speech emphasized non-standardness even more than the base dialects, perhaps due to its function in displaying regional identity. If the regional speech is to function as a koiné, facilitating communication outside its region, then it must also be closer to the standard than (most) basilects.

3. Is the regional speech more similar to base dialects in its own region than to other base dialects?

We answer these questions by computing the pronunciation differences, using Levenshtein distance, as explained above. Figure 4 displays the distances of base dialects within each region to (left) the standard and (right) the regional speech of the same region. The box-and-whisker plots in figure 4 show the median (dark central horizontal line) and central 50% of distribution (within the boxes) of the distances. The lowest and highest quartiles of the distribution are shown in the "whiskers" of the graphs. We have added a dashed line to each graph showing the difference between the regional speech and the standard. The regions are ordered by country, with the Netherlands above and Belgian Flanders below. Each row is then ordered by centrality, where the region on the left is the most central and the region on the right the most peripheral.

We first examine the data graphic in figure 4 (below) in light of the first question, adopting the perspective of the base dialects and asking whether they are indeed closer to the regional speech than to the standard, as Auer and Hinskens' (1996) model predicts. In terms of box-and-whisker plots, we expect to see the plot of distances with respect to the standard (the left box-and-whiskers plot in each of the eight charts) to be above the plot of distances with respect to the regional speech (the box-and-whiskers plot on the right). As figure 4 shows, several samples of regional speech indeed conform to the predictions of the conical model: the base dialects in Dutch Limburg, Groningen and West Flanders are significantly closer to their regional speech of their regions than to the standard ($p<0.001$ in all cases). On the other hand, the pattern is not general. In Antwerp, there is no significant difference between the standard and the regional speech in their proximity to the base dialects, and in the four other regions, i.e., the *Randstad*, North Brabant, Belgian Brabant and Belgian Limburg, where the base dialects are actually closer to the standard than they are to the regional speech![6] This result is surprising given the theoretical discussion about regiolects above, which has emphasized their potentially facilitating role in multi-varietal situations. It turns out that the standard language is usually better suited for this role than the regional speech we examine, which, in turn suggests that this regional speech is not primarily used to facilitate communication within their regions, a task to which the standard language is better suited. Their attractiveness must lie elsewhere.

We next ask examine regional speech from the perspective of the standard, asking whether it is indeed closer to the standard than the base dialects are. It is also a consequence of the conical model that the regional speech of the radio announcers should be closer to the standard than the base dialects are. That is, regional speech should be properly intermediate between the standard and the base dialects. So we shall compare the distance of the base dialects to the standard against the distance between the regional speech and the standard. Linguistically, we are cautiously checking whether the regional speech might be emphasizing non-standardness even more than the base dialects, perhaps due to its function in displaying regional identity.

So we check further whether the regional speech is genuinely intermediate between the basilects and the standard by checking whether the horizontal dashed line – showing the distance between the regional speech and the standard – is below most of the basilects in the box-and-whisker plot on the left. Only in this case have we encountered a situation compatible with the predictions of the conical model. In case the dashed line is below most of the base dialects' distances to the regional speech, then the base dialect speakers might reasonably adopt the regional speech as means of accommodating speakers from outside the region (and even speakers within it). In this case the regional speech may be facilitating communication.

We turn then to an examination of the charts in figure 4. The distance between the standard and the regional speech is shown by the dashed horizontal lines in the eight charts, which we now compare to the box plots on the *left* side of each chart showing the distribution of distances from the different base dialects to the standard. Wherever we find the dashed line below most of the basilectal distances to the standard (considerably below the box in the box plots on the left side in each pair, say above the 95th percentile in proximity), we find it plausible that the regional speech may be facilitating communication between dialectal speakers in the region and speakers from outside, including standard speakers (assuming a positive answer to question one above). The regional speech in North Brabant (NL) and in Belgian Brabant are indeed substantially closer to the standard than the base dialects in their regions are (top 95th percentile or closer), and the regional speech in West Flanders is closer to the standard than 90% of the base dialects are. This circumstance is favorable to the putative function of these regional speech forms as facilitating communication – both between dialect speakers in the region and speakers from other regions or speakers of standard Dutch, in accordance with the views implicit in the conical model. The regional speech in the (Dutch) *Randstad*, Dutch Limburg and Belgian Limburg is closer to the standard when compared to the base dialects (64th to 80th percentiles), but only at a level we might attribute to chance.

But two samples of regional speech are particularly extreme, those in Groningen and Antwerp, which are *further* from the standard than most of the base dialects in their respective regions are. For these regional forms, it is implausible to attribute a facilitating, primarily communicative function as they would need to be closer to the standard to serve that function.

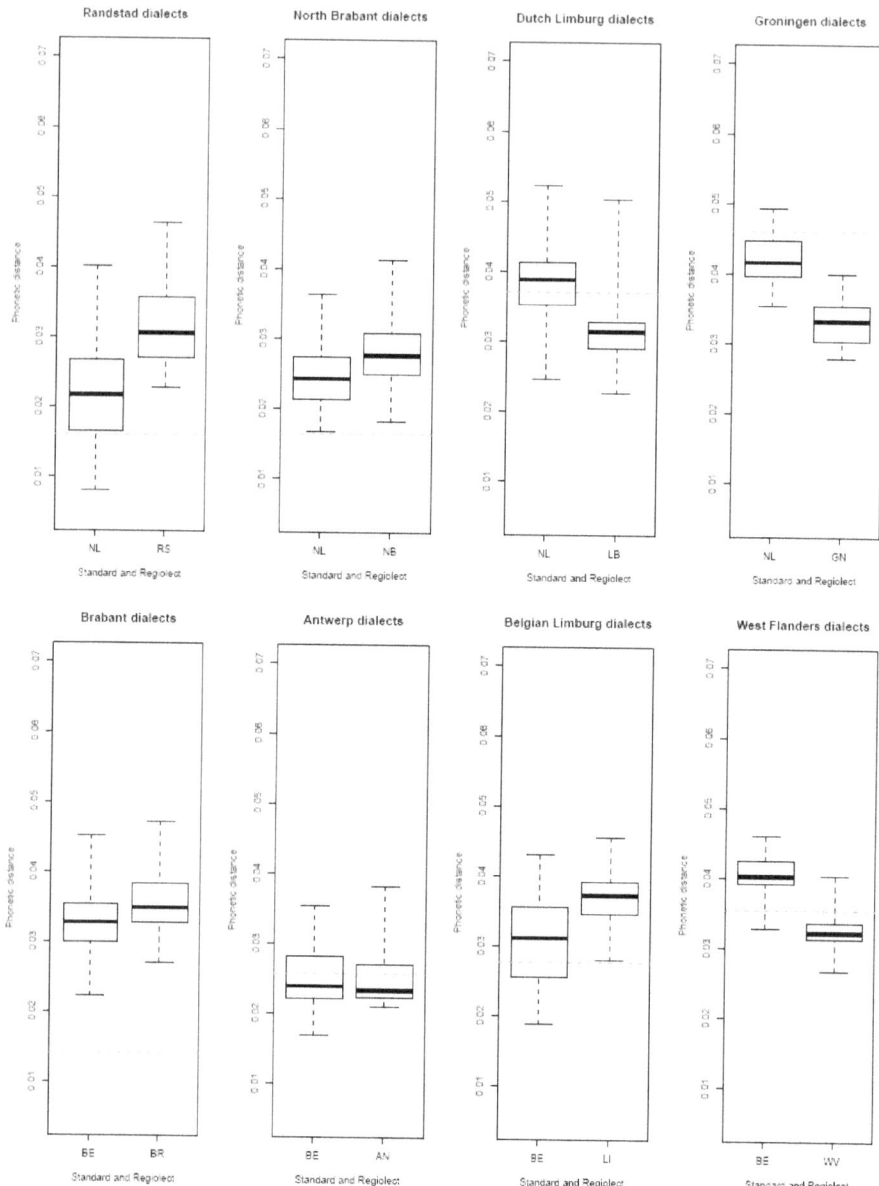

Figure 4. Phonetic distances (y-axis) between the dialects in a region and the standard, and the regional speech of each region (x-axis) in the Netherlands and Flanders. The dashed horizontal line is the distance between regional speech and standard. See text for further explanation.

We asked the second question because the conical model predicts that regiolects should be closer to the standard than the base dialects are (and not merely that base dialects are closer to the regiolect than they are to the standard). The conical model of regiolect functioning does not foresee the chance of a speech form functioning regionally that is actually *less* like the standard than the base dialects are. But this is what we see in Groningen and Antwerp. In terms of Auer and Hinskens' (1996) cone, this regional speech has dropped below the base formed by the basilects. We return to this in the discussion.

The case of Groningen is particularly interesting with respect to the second question. As figure 4 shows (top right graph), it turns out that more than 75% of the base dialects are closer to the standard than the regional speech is. This means that most base dialects would be better candidates for facilitating communication. This, we submit, is a clear case of regional speech which serves more as a vehicle of identification than as a means of coordinating communication.

Tying the first two questions together, we note that only one case (in eight) satisfies the conditions set out in the conical model, namely West Flanders. This regional speaker succeeds in producing speech which is closer to the base dialects than the standard is and which occupies an intermediate position (at the 90th percentile) in proximity to the standard (i.e. only about 10 percent of the dialects in West-Flanders are closer to the standard language than to the regional speech). All of the other seven cases violate one of the two predictions of the conical model.

The third question was included as a check on our regional speakers, and it is reassuring to note that they virtually all succeeded in using a version of regional speech that was closer to the base dialects of their own region than to the base dialects of any other. The *Randstad* speaker was the only exception. In his case, the base dialects of North Brabant turned out to be marginally better represented by his speech than those of the *Randstad* itself. This is shown in figure 5. For all the other seven regions the base dialects of the region in question were much closer to the regiolect than any others (not shown graphically). Given that the Dutch *Randstad* and North Brabant variants are quite similar to each other, we are willing to conclude that the regional speakers faithfully represent the speech of their own region. They are not merely adding dialectal coloring from various areas to their speech.

Before closing this presentation of results we would like to present some general observations. First, the distance from the regional speech to the standard increases in more peripheral regions. Thus the distance between standard Dutch and the regional speech of Groningen is larger than the distance

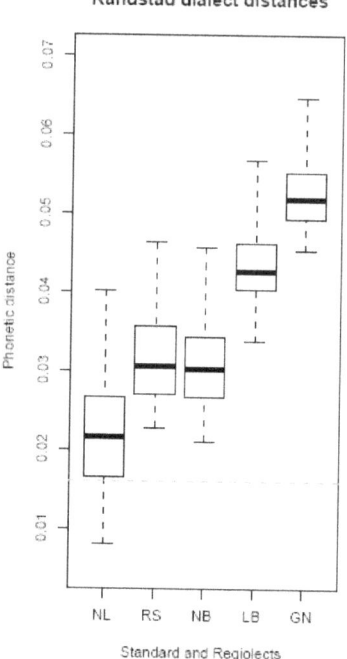

Figure 5. Phonetic distances (y-axis) between the Randstad dialects and the standard (NL), and the regional speech of each region (x-axis) in the Netherlands, viz. Randstad (RS), North Brabant (NB), Limburg (LB) and Groningen (GN). The dashed horizontal line indicates the distance between the Randstad regional speaker and standard Dutch. See text for further explanation.

between the standard and the regional speech of the *Randstad*. The height of the dashed lines rises from left to right in both rows of figure 4, which are ordered from central to peripheral areas. Interestingly, the same *cannot* be said about the distance between the dialects and the standard (leftmost box in each graph). The mean distance in the Netherlandic Dutch dialects does increase, but there is no simple rise in Belgian Dutch dialects.

An alternative view of the regional speech we examined as a general intermediate variety would be that the regiolect might be a personal intermediate variety between the standard and the dialect of each particular speaker. To assess this, we took a closer look at the data, asking whether the regional speech is more similar to the dialect of the place the speaker originates from (when available), than to other dialects. This was not the case, which suggests

Measuring socially motivated pronunciation differences 129

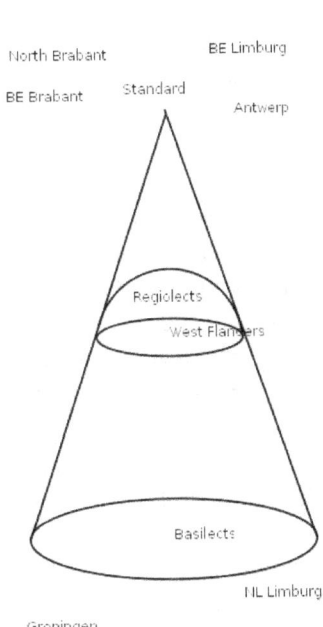

Figure 6. Samples of regional speech with respect to the regiolectal cone. Five of the eight samples were more different from the basilects of their region than the standard, and two differed more from the standard than the basilects did. Only the regional speech of West Flanders succeeded in striking a compromise between its standard language (Belgian Dutch) and its base dialects.

that the regional speech as used in this study is not merely a standardized form of each particular speaker's own dialect. The regional speech might also be conjectured to be an intermediate form between the variety of a large urban center and the standard, but the distances between the dialects of larger cities and the regional speech and standard also did not reveal an influence of this kind.

Figure 6 summarizes the relations between the regional speech samples, the basilects in the various regions and the standard languages. In fact only one sample may be positioned within the Auer-Hinskens cone of regiolects. We discuss this result in the final section.

6.2. Some further observations

We may also compare Belgium and the Netherlands using these measurements. For historical reasons, we expected the Belgian Dutch speech to be more diverse, both socially and geographically, than the Dutch of the Netherlands. In other words we expected the differences between the regional speech and the dialects and the standard language to be larger in Belgium than in the Netherlands, and indeed the mean distance of the Belgian dialects from the Belgian standard is significantly larger than the distance of the Dutch dialects from the Dutch standard ($p < 0.001$), where we add that we did not weight these averages by the populations in the different regions, which we suspect would magnify the difference, since a very large proportion of the Dutch population lives in or near the *Randstad*. Although we did not develop a hypothesis about the relation of the regional speech to the standard, it also turns out that the Dutch regional speech is a bit further from the (Dutch) standard than the Belgian regional speech is (from the Belgian standard), but the sample is too small for significance to be reached. We might conjecture that the function of social identification is more important to the regiolects in the Netherlands than in Belgium, at least in the case of the peripheral regiolects of Groningen and Limburg where the differences are largest. Again, within Belgium the two peripheral regions of Limburg and West Flanders show the largest distances between regional speech and standard. Speakers who live in areas far away from the political and economic centers may feel a greater need to manifest their regional identity than speakers who live closer to these centers.

7. Conclusions, discussion and prospects

In this paper we introduced a formal measure of pronunciation distance to study a sociolinguistic question, viz. the relation of regional speech to standards on the one hand and base dialects on the other. As far as we know this is the first focused sociolinguistic study using a formal measure of pronunciation distance, even though there have been studies which included both social and geographical variables (Leinonen 2010: 7.2, Wieling et al. 2011). Rather than examine a small number of linguistic variables in depth, as is customary in sociolinguistics, we applied an aggregate measure of pronunciation distance, arguing that the strategy of taking a broad view is more appropriate when studying the effects of standardization or "regionalization," where we have good reason to suspect that many changes are occurring at the same time.

We have quantitatively examined the speech of professional regional speakers from the perspective of Auer and Hinskens' (1996) conical model in order to better understand the communicative and social function of regiolects. The conical model predicts that regiolects take an intermediate linguistic position between base dialects and the standard language. By measuring the phonetic distances between local dialects, regional speech and the standard language in Belgium and the Netherlands we hoped to be able to draw conclusions about the relative position of the eight Dutch and Belgian regional forms of speech in relation to the base dialects and standard languages in the same region.

We approached the question from two perspectives. First, we looked at the mean phonetic distances between the base dialects of each area and the corresponding regional speech on the one hand and standard languages on the other. The conical model predicts that the base dialects should be closer to their regional speech than they are to the standard language. However, this prediction was completely incorrect in half of the cases. In four regions the base dialects were closer to the standard than to the regional speech (i.e. the *Randstad*, North Brabant, Belgian Brabant and Belgian Limburg). In a fifth case, Antwerp, there was no significant difference.

This result shows that regional speech of the sort heard on regional radio stations does not always facilitate communication between speakers within a given region, since the speakers might better have used the standard language for this purpose. Regional speech of this sort is also unlikely to facilitate communication between speakers of different regions, as the standard is in general quite sufficient. We interpret this result, therefore, to indicate that regional speech functions at least some of the time to allow speakers to show identification and solidarity with their regions.

Next, we checked the prediction of the model that regional speech is linguistically a step toward the standard, i.e. in an intermediate position between the base dialects and the standard. Given our answer to the first question above, it only makes sense to ask this second question of those varieties where the base dialects are closer to regional speech (than to the standard), i.e. Groningen, Limburg and West Flanders. We had found that the regional speakers in Groningen and in Antwerp used speech closer to the base dialects (than the standard would be), but we observed that the speech of the regional speakers is actually further from the standard. In terms of the conical model, their speech drops below the base of the cone. The main function of this regional speech therefore cannot be extra-regional communication; the function must presumably revolve around social identification.

The position of West Flanders should also be emphasized, as the only region in which the configuration of basilects to regiolect and standard conforms to the conical model.

With respect to the examination of the conical model, we are cautious and do not suggest that it be discarded. Many modern speakers of Dutch have little facility with local dialects but do adopt some local vocabulary and some local coloring in their pronunciation, making their speech indeed intermediate between the standard and local dialects. Acknowledging that one might wish to reserve the term regiolect for this sort of speech, we nonetheless conclude that the dynamics of regional speech are more complex than the conical model foresees. After all the speech of the regional broadcasters is regional speech and is widely recognized as such (even to the point of remuneration). Perhaps it should not be regarded as regiolectal, and in fact it does not satisfy Auer and Hinskens' definition (above), since it is not "intermediate", but it certainly is regional.

We have presented a method to test the relationship between the dialectal, regional and standard forms of a language area quantitatively. We are aware of the fact that a single regional speaker cannot be regarded as representative, in spite of the mitigating circumstance that these are people with professional functions involving regional speech. We anticipate the objection that our examination justifies only conclusions about these radio announcers and how they fulfill their professional role as regional speakers. It is possible that each speaker has his own way of manifesting regional affinity linguistically. We add, however, that we sought, but found no indications that our speakers based their regional speech on their own dialect in particular, nor on the dialect of a major town or city in the vicinity. Nor did we find indications that the speakers use a speech form which could be characterized as "general regional speech" with characteristics from other regions. It is possible that speakers tend to base their choice of speech forms on stereotypes and shibboleths when signaling their regional identity rather than on one particular dialect from the region. Furthermore, it is uncertain how stable the regional speech forms of different speakers from the same region would be in this respect and how stably the various manifestations of a regiolect vary with respect to the standard and to the base dialects, both in individual speakers but especially across speakers.

Auer's (2005) caution that one perhaps should not regard regiolects as varieties was perhaps prescient in view of the results here. Perhaps we should rather regard regional speech as the (situated) varietal performance of a regional identity rather than as a natural koiné. Auer and Hinskens (1996: 6) compare some regional speech to "learner varieties" because of their occasionally "makeshift" nature. Eckert (2001) reminds us how linguistically systematic such matters may be, but in resolutely referring to some linguistic variation as style, she reminds us how personal it also is.

Our discussion would not be complete without some mention of Coupland's (2001) characterization of Welsh-English accents in radio broadcasts as "stylized dialect performances", which is in keeping with our own conclusions. We base our study on measurements involving eight radio broadcasters and more than 300 dialect speakers, while Coupland analyzed a single broadcast involving two speakers, so we extend his work in that respect, and naturally, we focus on a different dialect area. We further add to Coupland's analysis that the pronunciations produced reflect dialect speech rather poorly, tending to exaggerate. Since our data comes from elicited word lists, we do not interpret the exaggerations as part of a performance " 'put on for show' " in a way that listeners would perceive as intended (Coupland 2001: 347, scare quotes in original). We suggest instead that it is simply difficult to adopt generic regional pronunciations, and that listeners appreciate being able to recognize the more exaggerated versions.[7]

Future research should include more speakers in order to be able to draw conclusions about the variability of regiolects. To shed more light on questions of regional speech, we should examine the speech of a number of speakers in each region accompanied by detailed information about the speakers' linguistic backgrounds and their choices of linguistic forms. In view of the possibility that we are dealing here with a matter of situated style, it will be important to set the stage carefully when collecting data. The naturalistic data collection might be accompanied by perception experiments presenting the speech of different regiolect speakers to listeners from the region. The aim of such experiments would be to get an idea of what listeners regard as representative speech for their region, what the linguistic characteristics are of these regiolects, and which attitudes listeners have towards them. In our investigation we have used professional speakers from regional radio stations. Since such speakers are likely to be more aware of how to switch between dialect, regiolect and standard, we collected our data by asking them to read a list of words in the style of speech they used as professional speakers in the region. In future research it is important to find ways to include the regiolectal speech forms of other groups of speakers as well.

Appendix. List of 37 Dutch words used for the pronunciation analysis

GTRP reference nr.	Dutch word	English gloss	Part of speech
379	meid	girl	noun
723	zakken	bags	noun
748	aardig	nice	adjective
784	droog	dry	adjective
791	duur	expensive	adjective
806	goed	good	adjective
816	groot	big	adjective
819	haastig	hasty	adjective
821	hard	hard	adjective
830	hoog	high	adjective
836	juist	correct	adjective
842	kort	short	adjective
881	proper	clean	adjective
898	schoon	clean	adjective
905	simpel	simple	adjective
906	slecht	bad	adjective
935	vreemd	strange	adjective
954	ziek	ill	adjective
965	zwaar	heavy	adjective
1194	gebruiken	use	verb
1267	kopen	buy	verb
1300	lachen	laugh	verb
1313	leunen	lean	verb
1318	liggen	lie	verb
1329	maken	make	verb
1340	mogen	may	verb
1344	noemen	call	verb
1357	rijden	drive	verb
1373	scheren	shave	verb
1381	schrijven	write	verb
1426	spreken	speak	verb
1446	stampen	pound	verb
1473	vallen	fall	verb
1509	vrijen	make love	verb
1527	weten	know	verb
1549	wrijven	rub	verb
1553	zeggen	say	verb

Notes

1. We are grateful to Peter Auer and Frans Hinskens for discussion of this work, also to the Göteborg audience at the workshop *(Comparing) Approaches to Measuring Linguistic Differences*, Oct. 2011. We are further indebted to our partners in the Dutch-Flemish cooperative project "Mutual Comprehensibility of Dutch Dialects", namely Renée van Bezooijen, Dirk Geeraersts, Stef Grondelaers, Roeland van Hout, Leen Impe, Sebastian Kürschner and Dirk Speelman,. We also thank Lotte Thissen for an important reference and finally two anonymous referees.
2. In deference to its speakers' wishes we refer to the language spoken in Flanders as BELGIAN DUTCH. See nl.wikipedia.org/wiki/Nederlands_in_België It is spoken primarily by the Flemish.
3. Haugen (1966) defines four stages of standardization: (1) selection of form, (2) codification of form, (3) elaboration of function and (4) acceptance by the community.
4. Auer's (2005) remark is anticipated by Auer and Hinskens' (1996: 6) observation that "dialectologists and linguists tend to be somewhat rash in assigning the status of a 'variety' to a certain way of speaking".
5. The working assumption is that the prestige of a region increases when the capital city of a country is situated in or near the region.
6. In the case of Brabant the difference is barely significant ($p = 0.016$), and in all other cases the differences are highly significant ($p < 0.001$).
7. Coupland's detailed analysis is to be recommended for its sensitive attention to how subtly Welsh English accent is used in the radio dialogues he examines, in a way that engages issues of regional identity in an entertaining way, and without slipping into an apparent denial of the legitimacy of non-dialectal, unaccented speech.

References

Auer, Peter
    2005   Europe's sociolinguistic unity, or: A typology of European dialect/ standard constellations. In *Perspectives on Variation. Sociolinguistic, Historical, Comparative,* Nicole Delbecque, Johan Van der Auwera and Dirk Geeraerts (eds.), 7–42. Berlin/New York: Mouton de Gruyter.

Auer, Peter and Frans Hinskens
    1996   The convergence and divergence of dialects in Europe. New and not so new developments in an old area. *Sociolinguistica* 10: 1–30.

Campbell, Lyle
    2004   *Historical Linguistics: An Introduction.* Edinburgh: Edinburgh University Press.

Chambers, J. K.
  2003 *Sociolinguistic Theory.* Cambridge: Blackwell.
Chambers, J. K. and Peter Trudgill
  1998 (¹1980) *Dialectology.* Cambridge: Cambridge University Press.
Coetsem, Frans van
  1988 *Loan Phonology and the Two Transfer Types in Language Contact.* Dordrecht: Foris.
Coupland, Nikolas
  2001 Dialect stylization in radio talk. *Language in Society* 30: 345–375.
Eckert, Penelope
  2001 Style and social meaning. In *Style and Sociolinguistic Variation*, Penelope Eckert and John R. Rickford (eds.), 119–126. Cambridge: Cambridge University Press.
Geeraerts, Dirk
  2001 Een zondagspak? Het Nederlands in Vlaanderen: Gedrag, beleid, Attitudes. *Ons Erfdeel* 44: 337–343.
Goeman, Ton and Johan Taeldeman
  1996 Fonologie en morfologie van de Nederlandse dialecten. Een nieuwe materiaalverzameling en twee nieuwe atlasprojecten. *Taal en Tongval* 48 (1): 38–59.
Gooskens, Charlotte and Wilbert Heeringa
  2004 Perceptive evaluation of Levenshtein dialect distance measurements using Norwegian dialect data. *Language Variation and Change* 16 (3): 189–207.
Greenhill, Simon J.
  2011 Levenshtein distances fail to identify language relationships accurately. *Computational Linguistics* 37 (4): 689–698.
Grondelaers, Stefan, Hilde van Aken, Dirk Speelman, and Dirk Geeraerts
  2001 Inhoudswoorden en preposities als standaardiseringsindicatoren. De diachrone en synchrone status van het Belgische Nederlands. *Nederlandse Taalkunde* 6: 179–202.
Gussenhoven, Carlos
  2007 Wat is de beste transcriptie voor het Nederlands? *Nederlandse Taalkunde* 12: 331–350.
Haugen, Einar
  1966 Dialect, language, nation. *American Anthropologist* 68: 922–935.
Hinskens, Frans
  1998 Dialect levelling: a two-dimensional process, *Folia Linguistica*, XXII (1–2) (Peter Auer, guest editor), 35–51.
Hinskens, Frans
  to appear Koineization in the present-day Dutch dialect landscape: postvocalic /r/ and more. In *The Formation of Regiolects in the Low Countries*

(special issue of *Taal en tongval*), Wilbert Heeringa and Gunther de Vogelaer (eds).

Hinskens, Frans, Peter Auer, and Paul Kerswill
    2005   The study of dialect convergence and divergence. Conceptual and methodological considerations. In *Dialect Change: Convergence and Divergence in European Languages,* Peter Auer, Frans Hinskens, and Paul Kerswill (eds.), 1–50. Cambridge: Cambridge University Press.

Hoppenbrouwers, Cor
    1983   Het genus in een Brabants regiolect. *TABU, Bulletin voor Nederlandse Taalkunde* 13: 1–25.

Hoppenbrouwers, Cor
    1990   *Het regiolect: van dialect tot algemeen Nederlands.* Muiderberg: Coutinho.

Howell, Robert B.
    2006   Immigration and koineization: the formation of Early Modern Dutch urban vernaculars. *Transactions of the Philological Society* 104: 207–227.

Howitt, Dennis and Duncan Cramer
    2008   *Introduction to Research Methods in Psychology.* Edinburgh Gate: Prentice Hall.

Impe, Leen, Dirk Geeraerts, and Dirk Speelman
    2008   Mutual intelligibility of standard and regional Dutch language varieties. *International Journal of Humanities and Arts Computing* 2 (1–2): 101–117.

Kerswill, Paul
    2003   Dialect levelling and geographical diffusion in British English. In *Social Dialectology. In Honour of Peter Trudgill,* David Britain and Jenny Cheshire (eds.), 223–243. Amsterdam: Benjamins.

Labov, William
    1972   *Sociolinguistic Patterns.* Philadelphia: University of Pennsylvania Press.

Leinonen, Therese
    2010   An acoustic analysis of vowel pronunciation in Swedish dialects. Ph.D. Diss., University of Groningen.

Levenshtein, Vladimir
    1965   Binary codes capable of correcting deletions, insertions and reversals. *Cybernetics and Control Theory* 10 (8): 707–710. (translation of Левенштейн, В. И.. Двоичные коды с исправлением выпадений, вставок и замещений символов. Доклады Академий Наук СССР 163 (4): 845–848)

Mattheier, Klaus
    1996   Varietätenkonvergenz: Überlegungen zu einem Baustein einer Theorie der Sprachvariation. *Sociolinguistica* 10: 1–31.

Nerbonne, John and Wilbert Heeringa
2009   Measuring dialect differences. In *Language and Space: Theories and Methods*, in series *Handbooks of Linguistics and Communication Science*, Jürgen Erich Schmidt and Peter Auer (eds.), 550–567. Berlin/ New York: Mouton de Gruyter.

Randstadmonitor 2006
2006   Utrecht: Regio Randstad. http://www.rijksoverheid.nl/onderwerpen/ randstad/documenten-en-publicaties/brochures/2007/12/01/randstadmonitor-2006.html

Sanders, Nathan and Steven B. Chin
2009   Phonological distance measures. *Journal of Quantitative Linguistics* 16 (1): 96–114.

Smakman, Dick.
2006   *Standard Dutch in the Netherlands. A sociolinguistic and phonetic description.* Ph.D. dissertation, Radboud University.

Sobrero, Alberto A.
1996   Italianization and variations in the repertoire: the Koinai. *Sociolinguistica* 10: 105–111.

Spruit, Marco René, Wilbert Heeringa, and John Nerbonne
2009   Associations among Linguistic Levels. *Lingua* 119 (11). Spec. issue *The Forests behind the Trees*, John Nerbonne and Franz Manni (eds.).1624–1642.

Streck, Tobias
2012   *Phonologischer Wandel im Konsonantismus der alemannischen Dialekte Baden-Württembergs. Sprachatlasvergleich, Spontansprache und dialektometrische Studien.* Stuttgart: Steiner (Zeitschrift für Dialektologie und Linguistik – Beihefte, Band 148).

Trudgill, Peter
1986   *Dialects in Contact.* Oxford: Blackwell.

Velde, Hans van de
1996   *Variatie en verandering in het gesproken Standaard-Nederlands (1935–1993).* Ph.D. Diss., University of Nijmegen.

Verhoeven, Jo
2005   Belgian Standard Dutch. *Journal of the International Phonetic Association* 35: 243–247.

Wieling, Martijn, Wilbert Heeringa, and John Nerbonne
2007   An aggregate analysis of pronunciation in the Goeman-Taeldeman-van Reenen-Project. *Taal en Tongval* 59: 84–116.

Wieling, Martijn, Eliza Margaretha, and John Nerbonne
2012   Inducing a measure of phonetic similarity from pronunciation variation. *Journal of Phonetics* 40 (2): 307–314.

Wieling, Martijn and John Nerbonne
2011   Measuring Linguistic Variation Commensurably. *Dialectologia*, Special Issue II. 141–162.

Wieling, Martijn, John Nerbonne, and Harald Baayen
    2011   Quantitative Social Dialectology: Explaining Linguistic Variation Geographically and Socially. *PLoS ONE*, 6 (9): e23613. doi:10.1371/journal.pone.0023613

Wieling, Martijn, Jelena Prokić, and John Nerbonne
    2009   Evaluating the pairwise string alignment of pronunciations. In *Language Technology and Resources for Cultural Heritage, Social Sciences, Humanities, and Education* (LaTeCH – SHELT&R 2009) Workshop at the 12th EACL, Lars Borin and Piroska Lendvai (eds.), 26–34. Athens, 30 Mar. 2009.

Distance-based phylogenetic inference algorithms in the subgrouping of Dravidian languages

Taraka Rama and Sudheer Kolachina

1. Introduction[1]

Historical linguistics has as one of its main aims the classification of languages into language families. The internal classification of languages within a language family is known as *subgrouping*. Subgrouping is concerned with the way daughter languages within a single family are related to one another and, therefore, with the branching structure of the family tree (Campbell 2004). In much of the literature on the subject, *shared innovations* are discussed as the only acceptable criteria while establishing subgroups within a language family. Within the framework of lexical diffusion, it has been shown that it is possible to infer subrelations among a set of related languages from the distributional pattern of changed (innovations) versus unchanged (retentions) cognates across these languages even with respect to a single sound change (Krishnamurti 1983).

The origins of quantitative methods in historical linguistics can be traced back to the lexicostatistical methods and glottochronology of Swadesh (1952, 1955). Although Swadesh's methods are criticized to this day as being fraught with untenable assumptions, it is indisputable that his work marks the beginning of a search for alternatives to the traditional comparative method. See McMahon and McMahon (2005) for a historical overview of the use of quantitative methods for language classification. In particular, recent years have seen a rapid increase in interest in the application of phylogenetic inference methods, most of which come from computational biology, to diachronic language data leading to the emergence of a distinct research area, increasingly being referred to as Computational historical linguistics (CHL, henceforth). The basic intuition in such research is that these methods, which were developed to infer (genetic) phylogeny from gene sequences, can do so from language data too, which also consist of sequences. Interestingly, this is not the first time that a cross-pollination of ideas between the fields of biology and linguistics has taken place (Atkinson and Gray 2004).

Phylogenetic inference methods that have been used for estimating linguistic phylogeny in recent CHL literature are either *character-based* or *distance-based*. Character-based methods such as Maximum Parsimony (MP) (Felsenstein 2003) and Bayesian inference (Felsenstein 2003) estimate phylogeny of a set of related languages from character-based data. A *character* can represent any aspect of language evolution: lexical, phonological, morphological or syntactic change. For example, a lexical character encodes information about the presence or absence of a cognate across the languages that are to be subgrouped. Each language is assigned a state with respect to this character based on the presence or absence of that cognate in the language. Two languages would have the same state if and only if the cognate represented by this lexical character is either present or absent in both languages. Similarly, phonological, morphological and syntactic characters encode information about the presence or absence of corresponding types of language change. Thus, in a character-based dataset, each language is represented as a sequence consisting of states of that language with respect to the different characters considered. Distance-based methods such as Unweighted Pair Group Method with Arithmetic means (UPGMA) and Neighbor Joining (NJ) (Felsenstein 2003) estimate linguistic phylogeny from a distance matrix containing pairwise inter-language *phylogenetic distances*. Different measures have been discussed in the literature as estimates of phylogenetic distance between languages. One common practice is to estimate pairwise phylogenetic distance from character-based data as the Hamming distance between character sequences representing languages. All the above methods, whether character-based (MP, Bayesian inference) or distance-based (UPGMA and NJ), assume linguistic phylogeny to be tree-like. However, this assumption is problematic in the context of linguistic areas where shared linguistic traits could also be the result of convergence due to extensive language contact. Some recent works such as Nakhleh et al. (2005), Huson and Bryant (2006) propose the use of phylogenetic networks to address the limitations of the tree model of language evolution. See the tutorial on linguistic phylogeny by Nichols and Warnow (2008) for a comprehensive and detailed discussion about network-based phylogenetic inference methods.

Diachronic datasets used in recent literature on inference of linguistic phylogeny are lexical datasets, usually derived from Swadesh lists. A Swadesh list is a short (of length 40 – 200), culturally universal list of meanings that are supposed to be highly resistant to borrowing. Such lists are most often compiled from etymological dictionaries. A character-based dataset can be obtained from the Swadesh lists by grouping the lexical items corresponding to a meaning slot in different languages into cognate classes based on the cognacy judgments available in the etymological dictionary.

As mentioned previously, languages with cognates belonging to the same cognate class are coded as being in the same state with respect to that lexical character. Similarly, phylogenetic distances required for the application of distance-based phylogenetic inference methods can also be estimated from Swadesh lists. The ASJP project (Brown et al. 2008), a notable recent work on the application of distance-based methods for language classification, estimates inter-language distances as the aggregate sum of the degree of cognateness between pairs of strings in parallel Swadesh lists of two languages, where degree of cognateness is measured using a metric based on Levenshtein distance.[2] In fact, even the traditional lexicostatistical method is a distance-based method that treats the percentage of shared cognates for each language pair as an estimate of the phylogenetic distance between them. It must be noted that while the use of Swadesh lists or rather lexical datasets is quite convenient when etymological dictionaries are available, lexical data is relatively more prone to borrowing compared to datasets containing phonological, morphological or syntactic features.

Over the past few years, phylogenetic inference methods have been applied to data from well-studied large-scale language families such as Indo-European, Austronesian among others to address interesting questions about their time depth (Gray and Atkinson 2003), spatial spread (Holman et al. 2008) and prehistoric migration patterns (Gray et al. 2009). As discussed above, the availability of diachronic datasets in electronic formats – Swadesh lists with cognate judgments, comparative feature datasets and typological databases, is a prerequisite for such studies. The focus of our work in this paper is the Dravidian language family. Although Dravidian languages are one of the few instances of the successful application of the comparative method to reconstruct the proto-language (Campbell 2004), there is very little work on the application of phylogenetic inference methods to these languages. Such an application will be interesting not only to compare the automatically inferred phylogenetic trees against the manually constructed family tree but also to look for possible solutions to unresolved questions about the subgrouping of Dravidian languages. The lack of diachronic datasets is the main hurdle that needs to be overcome to take up such studies. In this paper, we present two new diachronic datasets for Dravidian languages created from existing resources which can be used in different kinds of quantitative studies on these linguistic phylogeny of these languages. We also explore the application of distance-based phylogenetic inference methods to the task of subgrouping Dravidian languages. In particular, we study the performance of this class of methods with respect to a specific subgrouping question discussed in recent literature. In addition to subgrouping, these diachronic datasets can also be used to study possible correlations between the current spatial distribution of these languages and the genetic subrelations among them. The geographical discontiguity of Dravidian languages is an interesting puzzle which, if solved, will open up new directions in the study of the linguistic prehistory of the subcontinent.

The paper is organized as follows. In section 2, we present a few details about Dravidian languages by way of providing the reader with a background about these languages. We briefly review three extant classifications and point out the differences among them. In section 2.3, we describe the specific subgrouping issue of ternary versus binary branching of Proto-Dravidian. Section 3 summarizes previous work on the application of quantitative methods to study the diachrony of Dravidian languages. In section 4, we describe the four diachronic datasets created from existing resources. In section 5, we describe the various distance-based methods used in our experiments, the method used to obtain distance matrices from character-based data and also, the strategy we followed for rooting the unrooted trees returned by the phylogenetic inference methods. In section 6, we present the trees and networks resulting from our experiments. We summarize our findings and conclude in section 7.

2. Dravidian languages

This section is divided into three subsections. In the first subsection, we present some general details about the Dravidian language family by way of providing the readers with a background about these languages. In the next subsection, we briefly review three subgrouping schemes from different sources. In the last subsection, we discuss a specific problem in the subgrouping of Dravidian languages, namely ternary versus binary branching of Proto-Dravidian, which we will attempt to address in our experiments.

2.1. Dravidian language family

The Dravidian language family is the world's fifth largest language family with over 200 million speakers in South Asia (Krishnamurti 2003). The majority of the languages are geographically located in the southern and central parts of the Indian sub-continent with a few scattered pockets in Northern India (Kurux, Malto) and Nepal (Kurux) and a lone population scattered across Pakistan and Afghanistan (Brahui). There are four major languages with long literary, written traditions – Tamil, Malayalam, Kannada and, Telugu. They are written, if at all, using scripts of neighbouring languages.

Krishnamurti (2003) is a compendious work covering various aspects of the Dravidian languages. There exists a voluminous body of literature in the area of Dravidian linguistics owing to the efforts of many scholars. One resource that needs mention for its potential value to research on various aspects of the Dravidian language family is the Dravidian Etymological Dictionary (DEDR)[3] (Burrow and Emeneau 1984).

2.2. Subgrouping of Dravidian languages

In this section, we briefly the describe three main subgrouping schemes for Dravidian languages discussed in the literature.

2.2.1. Krishnamurti (2003)

Figure 1 shows the family tree of the Dravidian languages discussed in Krishnamurti (2003). This tree can be considered as the "gold standard" tree as it is the one widely accepted. However, there still remains some unresolved issues (Krishnamurti 2003) in this classification, such as the following:

- The position of the Nilgiri languages (Toda, Kota, Irula, Badaga and Kurumba) in relation to Tamil and Kannada is not clear.
- The position of Tulu in the family tree is doubtful.
- The placement of Koraga in the subgrouping scheme is undecided.
- The position of Naikri in Central Dravidian subgroup is doubtful.

The above uncertainties are indicated using broken lines in figure 1. It is interesting to note that most of these uncertainties pertain to the South Dravidian I subgroup.

2.2.2. WALS

The *World Atlas of Language Structures* (Haspelmath et al. 2008) provides a two level classification of the Dravidian languages (23 languages) with the following subgroups (in order of geographical contiguity):

- South Dravidian: Badaga, Betta Kurumba, Kannada, Kodava, Kota, Malayalam, Tamil, Tamil (spoken), Toda, and, Tulu
- South-Central Dravidian: Gondi, Konda, Koya, Kui, Kuwi (Kuvi; a name variant), Pengo, and, Telugu
- Central Dravidian: Gadaba, Kolami and Parji
- Northern Dravidian: Brahui, Kurukh and Malto

The WALS classification does not include Irula, Koraga, Naiki and, Ollari (present in Krishnamurti's classification) since, WALS does not include them.

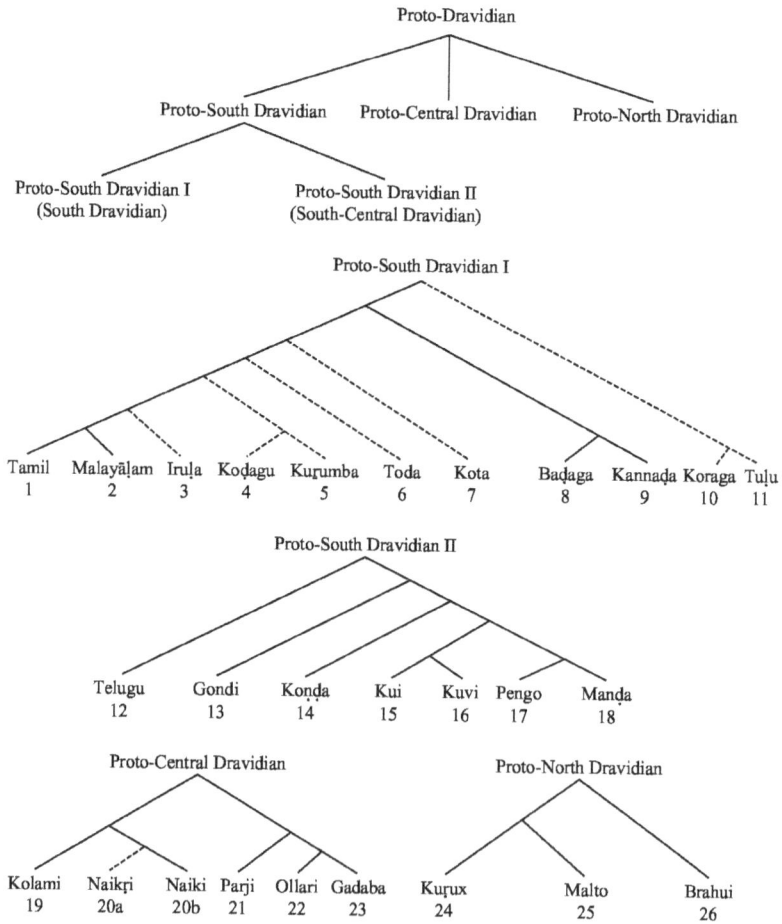

Figure 1. Family tree of Dravidian languages given in Krishnamurti (2003). Broken lines depict uncertain relationships.

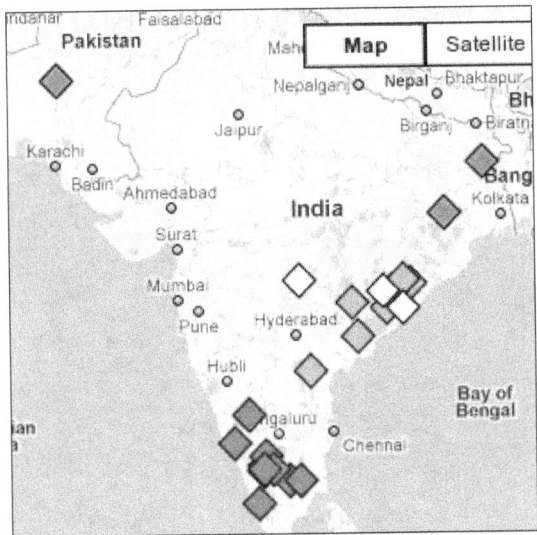

Figure 2. Geographical distribution of Dravidian languages in WALS database. Dark diamonds above the white diamonds are North Dravidian; White diamonds are Central Dravidian; Light-dark diamonds are South-Central Dravidian; The darkest diamonds are South Dravidian.

2.2.3. Ethnologue

Ethnologue (Lewis 2009) lists a far larger number of languages and dialects (85) than WALS or Krishnamurti (2003). Figure 3 displays the Ethnologue classification for only those languages present in the ASJP database.[4] The Ethnologue tree for Dravidian languages shows four subgroups attached to the root of the tree and the highest level subgrouping is unresolved.

Concerning the internal classification within each subgroup:

1. Proto-North Dravidian is polytomous (more than two children).
2. South Dravidian I subgroup's ancestral node is polytomous as well.

We can conclude that the Ethnologue tree is at least not as resolved as the tree given by the comparative method at the highest level subgrouping of the Dravidian language family (Krishnamurti 2003) and that there are quite a number of nodes which are polytomous. The Ethnologue tree shows the same subgroups as the tree given by Krishnamurti (2003). It differs largely in the placement of languages in the SDI subgroup, where the two trees differ in the placement of Koromfe and Kodava in SDI subgroup.

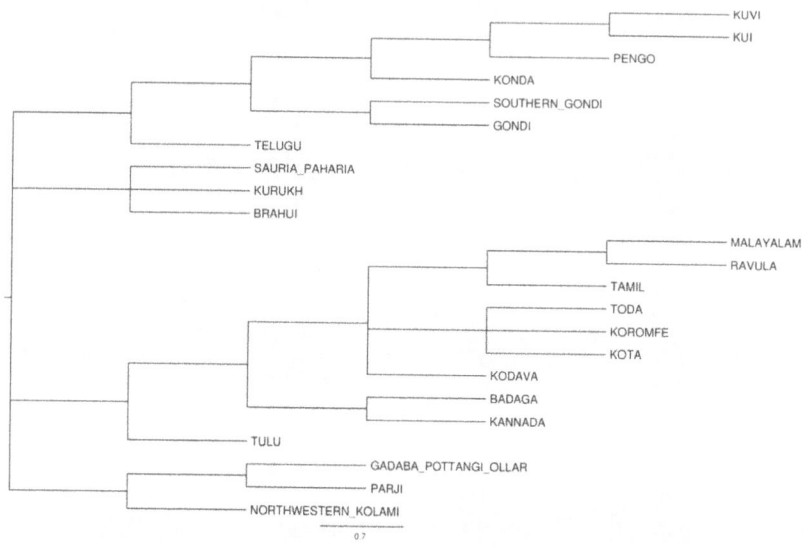

Figure 3. Ethnologue Tree for the Dravidian languages present in ASJP database

2.3. Ternary vs. binary branching

There are two prevailing thoughts about the main subdivision of the Dravidian languages: ternary vs. binary (Krishnamurti 2003). According to the ternary hypothesis, Proto-Dravidian (PD) has three branches: Proto-North Dravidian (ND), Proto-Central Dravidian (CD) and Proto-South Dravidian (SD), which is further split into South Dravidian I (SD I) and South Dravidian II (SD II). This is the subgrouping adopted in Krishnamurti (2003). This subgrouping is established on the basis of isogloss maps constructed using 27 features from comparative phonology and morpho-syntax. An alternate subgrouping option is to have a binary division of Proto-Dravidian into Proto-North Dravidian (ND) and Proto-South-Central Dravidian (SCD). Proto-South-Central Dravidian further splits into Proto-South Dravidian and Proto-Central Dravidian. In this regard, Krishnamurti (2003) notes that although in general a binary division of a speech community is more likely than a ternary, there is scant evidence to set up a common stage of South and Central Dravidian. In this paper, we explore the application of distance-based methods to the datasets described previously in our search for a solution to this subgrouping problem.

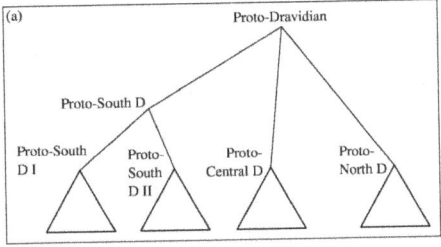

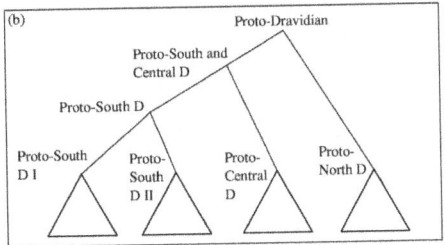

Figure 4. Alternative splits of Proto-Dravidian (Krishnamurti, 2003)

3. Background

The aim of this section is to provide a brief overview of the previous attempts at applying quantitative/computational methods to the internal classification of Dravidian languages.

The first attempt to apply quantitative methods to Dravidian languages was made by Andronov (1964). He applied the method of glottochronology proposed by Swadesh (1952, 1955) to word lists of nineteen Dravidian languages. Although this work is several decades old, it remained largely unnoticed until it was reviewed by Krishnamurti (2003). This early glottochronological study was followed by two other similar lexicostatistical studies: Kameswari (1969) and Namboodiri (1976). All the three works received critical review in Krishnamurti (2003). Krishnamurti's main objection relates to the wide variation in the divergence times predicted by these studies. According to Andronov (1964), the Tamil and Telugu sub-branching took place around 10th century BC, whereas according to Kameswari (1969), it was in 4th century BC to 4th century AD. Krishnamurti (2003) takes this divergence times as an evidence of the unreliability of the glottochronological/lexicostatistic technique.

Further, he also notes that the glottochronological/lexicostatistic approach is incapable of dealing with differing rates of lexical replacement in different languages. For example, Brahui, as a result of heavy borrowing from Balochi and Indo-Aryan languages, has retained only 15 percent of the native lexemes. Due to such a high degree of cognate loss, the glottochronological method estimates that Brahui separated from the rest 5000 BP (5000 years before present), a date which is untenable in the light of other kinds of evidence (Elfenbein 1987).

In addition to these early studies, there are two other interesting applications of computational methods for sub-grouping Dravidian languages before the advent of phylogenetic inference methods from computational biology. These two studies are Krishnamurti (1978) and Krishnamurti et al. (1983). Both these works attempt to show that within the framework of lexical diffusion, data pertaining to just one sound change is sufficient to discover the internal classification of a set of related languages.

Krishnamurti (1978) aims at showing that a single sound change in progress is sufficient for the internal classification of six South-Central Dravidian languages.[5] Krishnamurti (1978) compiles a list of cognate sets from six South-Central Dravidian languages qualified for a particular sound change (apical displacement) using the *DED*.[6] Since the sound change considered was one in progress, in each language, some of the items would have changed while others would have remained unaffected. The number of changed items that a language shares with a sister language is treated as a measure of their "proximity". A multi-dimensional scaling algorithm was applied to a matrix containing such pairwise proximity values (numbers of shared cognates-with-change) for all six languages. The resultant scatter plot makes the following predictions: Kui and Kuvi are closest to each other and similarly, Pengo-Manda form another cluster and Konda is closer than Gondi to the rest. All these predictions are in agreement with the relations obtained from the manually constructed standard tree for this sub-family.

In a sequel to this work, Krishnamurti et al. (1983) apply another interesting quantitative method to a subset of the earlier lexical diffusion data to setup subrelations for the same set of languages. The dataset used in this study contains 63 cognate sets which are all qualified for the apical displacement sound change. This work claims that genetic subrelations can be inferred from the distribution pattern of just one sound change in progress. Their method for doing this can be described briefly as containing the following steps: Encode the status of the sound change in each cognate set (either changed [1] or unchanged [0]) for a language. Enumerate all possible binary branching trees for the six languages. The number of changes required to explain a cognate set is taken to be the score of a tree for that cognate set. The tree with the lowest score (least number of accumulated changes) over all the cognate sets is selected as the best tree explaining the data. Krishnamurti et al. (1983) find that the best tree obtained thus is "identical" to the standard tree manually constructed using the comparative method. It must be noted that had the number of languages been greater than six, the authors would have encountered the tree combinatorial explosion problem. Although the authors claim their approach to be novel, Embleton (1986) notes that this tree-scoring criterion had in fact already been explored in the historical linguistic literature and was being independently rediscovered in this work for the third time.

McMahon and McMahon (2007) note that the general linguistic scenario in South Asia where contact between four language families – Indo-Aryan (Indo-Iranian sub-family of Indo-European family), Sino-Tibetan, Munda (of Austroasiatic) and Dravidian – over several millenia is well-attested and attempt to cast new light on the genetic classification of South Asian languages by applying network building programs rather than phylogenetic tree inference methods. According to the authors, the rationale behind doing this is that in extensive contact situations such as evidenced in South Asia, evolution of languages cannot be tree-like. The tree model is incapable of handling the wide-spread intra-family borrowing which is highly likely in the South Asian context. McMahon and McMahon (2007) create two sets of data the thirty most conservative and the thirty least conservative items for Indo-Aryan languages taken from the older Dyen et al. (1992) database of Indo-European Swadesh lists and apply the Neighbour Network method to each of these datasets. They observe that the resulting networks do not differ significantly, which can be taken to suggest that wide-spread family-internal borrowing affects the most conservative vocabulary items as much as it affects the least conservative ones. The main drawback of this work, in our opinion, is that the datasets used are not large enough for the results to be of general interest. It would be interesting to repeat this study using a larger dataset containing data for more Indo-Aryan languages.

Rama et al. (2009) apply different phylogenetic inference methods such as Maximum Parsimony, UPGMA, Neighbor-joining and Bayesian phylogenetic inference to the datasets of Krishnamurti (1983) to infer the phylogeny of six South-Central Dravidian languages. In this exploratory study, they report the output trees and discuss the similarities and differences with the standard tree. They also point out that the approach discussed in Krishnamurti et al. (1983) is a restricted case of the well-known maximum parsimony method known as Dollo's parsimony.

Kolachina et al. (2010) apply the maximum parsimony method (MP) to address a specific problem pertaining to the subgrouping of Dravidian languages. Krishnamurti (2003) discusses two subgrouping alternatives – one with ternary branching of Proto-Dravidian and another with binary branching, finally adopting the ternary branching alternative for the highest order subgrouping, based on isoglosses of 27 features from comparative phonology, morphology and syntax. Kolachina et al. (2010) convert this feature data into character sequences of 1/0 bits and apply the maximum parsimony method for internal classification. Since MP returns an unrooted tree, they root the output tree using ND as the outgroup. This is done because both the subgrouping alternatives have in common North Dravidian as the outgroup. The authors observe that branch lengths returned by MP do not support a ternary branching at the highest level and thus select the binary branching alternative.

4. Datasets

In this section, we give a brief description of four datasets to be used in our subgrouping experiments. We have created two of these datasets (1 and 2), one based on the DEDR and the other based on Krishnamurti (2003).

- We created a new character-based dataset using the *DEDR*. The *DEDR* is a compilation of 6027 cognate sets for 28 Dravidian languages (29 if Pālu Kurumba and Ālu Kurumba are counted as separate languages)[6] belonging to the Dravidian language family. Each cognate set in DEDR is identified by an entry number. In a few instances, cognate sets share the same entry number. It is not clear why two widely differing cognate sets are listed under the same number. There are 5548 cognate sets with unique entry number. With regard to each pair of cognate sets with the same identification number, we included the first cognate set in our dataset. Further, we also excluded those cognate sets which are probable borrowings from Indo-Aryan to Dravidian. For a cognate set to appear in the database, it is not necessary that the cognate set has corresponding entries in all 28 languages. The language entry consists of the lexical item along with its possible variants and its meaning in that language. It is worth pointing out here that in the *DEDR* cognate sets, the meanings of the corresponding items across individual languages is not necessarily the same. This characteristic feature of our database distinguishes this dataset from the datasets used in previous works on phylogenetic inference (e.g., the well-known IE dataset compiled by Dyen et al. (1992)), where a lexical item has the same meaning across all the languages. Furthermore, doubtful cognate judgments are indicated in DEDR, by a "?", was removed. There are cases similarly, where a cognate can belong to more than one cognate set and is cross-referenced. We also excluded such items from our dataset. The final DEDR based character dataset consists of 4169 characters containing data from 28 Dravidian languages. Each cognate set is represented as a binary character with the presence or absence of a language coded as 1/0. The state 0 for a character in a language could be either due to the real absence of the lexical item in that language or, simply, due to missing data. At this point, there is no way of differentiating between these two possibilities. Our dataset, we refer to as CDR (based on complete DEDR).

- The second database which we built is based on Krishnamurti (2003). Krishnamurti (2003) provides reconstructions for 656 cognate sets in an appendix along with the reconstructed proto-forms. Each reconstruction is given along with its *DEDR* entry number. Here again, as in the case of *DEDR*, the entry numbers are not unique. After removing cognate sets with duplicate entry numbers, the dataset is left with 348 characters each representing a lexical item. This dataset can be used not only to infer linguistic phylogeny but also to evaluate approaches that claim to automate reconstruction of proto-forms. We refer to this as ADR (based on the appendix in Krishnamurti 2003).

- Apart from providing cognate sets and their reconstructed proto-forms, Krishnamurti (2003) also provides a list of phonological, morphological and syntactic features which form the basis of subgrouping discussed in that work (figure 1). Kolachina et al. (2010) encode these features as characters and create a character-based dataset. A character can have one of three states: 1 indicating presence of a feature, 0 indicating absence and ? indicating unknown. It must be noted that character-based datasets 1, 2 and 3 need to be converted into distance matrices in order for distance-based phylogenetic inference methods to be applicable. We convert these character-based datasets to a distance matrix by computing pair-wise length-normalized Hamming distance between the languages represented as character sequences. We refer to this as the Comparative Features database.

- The fourth database is based on Swadesh lists for Dravidian languages from the ASJP database. Estimation of inter-language distances from the Swadesh word lists is another direction in which a number of recent efforts (Serva and Petroni 2008; Holman et al. 2008) have been directed. One such notable effort is the ASJP (Holman et al. 2008) project which estimates inter-language distance as the aggregate sum of the degree of cognateness between pairs of strings in parallel Swadesh lists of two languages; where degree of cognateness is measured using a metric based on Levenshtein distance (See note 1). As part of this effort, a database of Swadesh lists for 4817 languages was compiled and a distance matrix containing all possible pairwise inter-language distances was constructed. The ASJP database contains 40-item Swadesh lists for 23 Dravidian languages. In this work, we explore the ASJP approach too for subgrouping Dravidian languages using inter-language distances obtained from this database.

5. Methods

In this section, we describe two distance-based algorithms (UPGMA and NJ), conversion of character data matrices to distance matrices, significance testing of trees, calculation of ASJP inter-language distances, and a rooting strategy for addressing the specific question of ternary vs. binary split of Proto-Dravidian.

UPGMA is a simple hierarchical clustering algorithm which works in the following fashion. In the first iteration, UPGMA combines the least distant language pair, A and B into a language group AB. Then, UPGMA recomputes the distance between AB and any language C by computing the average of the distance between AC and BC and recreates the distance matrix. The algorithm repeats the above steps of combining the two closest languages or language groups and recomputing the distance matrix until the distance matrix is left with a single language group. UPGMA assumes an evolutionary clock model which states that each unit branch length corresponds to a unit time. UPGMA returns a rooted tree due to the assumption of an evolutionary clock.

NJ is a fast, greedy and heuristic tree building algorithm which yields an unrooted tree. NJ builds the tree by beginning with a star-like phylogeny, where each taxon is connected to a single node, and iteratively computes the branch lengths until the phylogeny is resolved. NJ does not assume an evolutionary clock and returns an unrooted tree. The sum of the branch lengths along the path connecting any two languages in a NJ tree indicates the lexical distance between the two languages and does not represent divergence time between the corresponding pair of languages.[8]

The character matrices are converted into distance matrices before they are input to the UPGMA and NJ implementations in the Splitstree package.[9] Three of the four datasets described in section 3.2 are character-based datasets (character matrices). Each of these character matrices is converted into a distance matrix by computing the pair-wise length-normalized Hamming distance between languages represented as character sequences. Hamming distance, between two character sequences, is defined as the total number of positions at which the corresponding characters differ. This pairwise distance is a length normalized (transformed into a value between 0 and 1) by dividing the distance by the length of a sequence.

Since NJ is a heuristic tree building program, phylogenetic trees obtained through the application of NJ to distance matrices derived from character data matrices have to be tested for statistical significance by running a bootstrap analysis with a large number of iterations. Note that the original character-based data is required to perform the bootstrap analysis. In each bootstrap iteration, a new dataset of the same size as the original character dataset is created through random selection of data points (characters) from the original data. The same character can be drawn more than once which means that some of the columns of the random data matrix can be duplicated.[10] In each bootstrap iteration, the newly created character dataset is converted to a distance matrix and a new NJ tree is inferred from the distance matrix. This process is repeated for 10, 000 iterations yielding a set of 10, 000 trees.

The next step is to get an estimate of the confidence in the phylogenetic analysis returned by NJ. The confidence score of a node in the phylogenetic tree can be estimated as the count of its occurrence in the set of 10, 000 bootstrap trees. This confidence estimate is also known as the *support value* of that node. A support value greater than 95%, for a node, implies a high statistical significance and that the node was not constructed by chance.

Splitstree also assigns another confidence measure to a tree (both NJ and UPGMA trees) which is the *least squares fit* of the tree. This is computed as the sum of the squares of difference between the true distances (from the distance matrix) and the total branch length (from the inferred tree) for a pair of languages. Unlike the bootstrap analysis which assigns a confidence score to each node in the tree, the least squares fit is a general goodness measure of the constructed tree and measures the amount of tree signal in the data. A least squares fit score of 95% implies that the constructed tree explains 95% of the true inter-language distances given by the distance matrix.

UPGMA and NJ are tree building programs and, therefore, impose a tree structure regardless of the underlying structure of the data. However, it is well-known that evolution of languages need not be tree-like, especially in cases of extensive contact situations. As noted earlier, the Dravidian language family is one such situation. In such a situation, a tree structure is not sufficient to display the relationship between languages and a network can be used to display the relations. There are two kinds of networks: *explicit* and *implicit* (Nichols and Warnow 2008). In explicit networks, the borrowing between related languages can be shown using directed dotted lines from one branch to another branch in a tree. In implicit networks, the branches are not resolved when there is a conflict and the language relations are shown by parallel edges or a web-like structure. The parallel edges could be collapsed to obtain a tree structure. Alternatively, the parallel edges could be interpreted as an indication of reticulation in the language group. As Nichols and Warnow (2008) note, the interpretation of phylogenetic networks is an open problem. In our experiments, we use the Neighbor Network program available in the Splitstree package to produce implicit networks.

The ASJP word lists contain entries for a subset of the 200-word Swadesh list. The word lists' composition and length is determined empirically, by Brown et al. (2008). The ASJP database and Krishnamurti's (2003) list of the Dravidian language family differ not only in the number of languages but also use different names for the same language. Our dataset consisting of ASJP lists includes only those languages which could be mapped with DEDR or Krishnamurti (2003) based on similarity of name and the proximity of geographical region of the speakers. This criterion yields an ASJP subset of 20 languages from all the four subgroups and allows for a meaningful comparison with the standard tree. We use the LDND (Levenshtein distance corrected for chance similarity) implementation available on the ASJP website[11] for computing the distance matrix suitable for input to a phylogenetic program (specifically MEGA).[12]

Note that while UPGMA returns a rooted tree, NJ, returns an unrooted tree. A NJ tree needs to be rooted for a meaningful comparison with the standard tree. The issue of rooting the unrooted trees inferred by different phylogenetic inference methods has been the subject of much lively debate in recent literature. Kolachina et al. (2011) treat the North Dravidian (ND) clade as outgroup to root the unrooted phylogenetic trees returned by the Maximum parsimony method since both the subgrouping alternatives for Dravidian evaluated in that work agree upon ND being the first outgroup to diverge (cf. figure 4). In our experiments, we follow the same rooting strategy as Kolachina et al. (2011).

Whenever a tree does not group all the ND languages under a single node, that tree is rooted using only those ND languages which are grouped together. We follow this outgrouping strategy consistently in our experiments. One might argue for a simpler solution by adopting Brahui as the outgroup for rooting the trees. It has to be noted that the choice of Brahui as an outgroup is not without problems since Brahui has undergone substantial lexical replacement. It is also unclear whether Brahui was the first language to diverge in the ND subgroup.

Finally, we describe our procedure for evaluating the trees returned through the application of the above methods. We qualitatively evaluate the NJ and UPGMA tree of each dataset using the minimum compatibility criterion of Nichols and Warnow (2008) – the criterion tells that the constructed phylogenetic tree should return all the established subgroups (all the four major subgroups in Dravidian language family) – in the next section. One might argue for a quantitative evaluation of tree quality by application of a tree distance measure such as Robinson-Fould's distance (Felsenstein 2003) for comparing each NJ and UPGMA tree with the standard tree. However, it has to be kept in mind that the trees returned by the tree building methods such as NJ and UPGMA trees are binary trees whereas the standard tree is not only polytomous but also unresolved in the SD I subgroup. In such a scenario, Robinson-Fould's distance is not really helpful in gauging the quality of the inferred trees.

6. Experiments and results

This section is divided into five subsections. The first subsection gives an analysis of the composition of character-based datasets derived from *DEDR* in terms of number of languages and size of each cognate set (defined below). Each of the remaining four subsections presents and qualitatively evaluates the trees inferred from the application of NJ and UPGMA algorithms to the four datasets.

6.1. Composition of CDR

In this subsection, we analyze the composition of the character-based dataset derived from the CDR.

In the first step, we plot the distribution of cognate size in CDR. The size of a cognate set – henceforth, referred to as cognate set size – is the number of languages attested in that cognate set. We make the following observations about cognate set size:

- The minimum cognate set size is two; the maximum size is twenty-four.
- No cognate set has all the twenty-eight languages from the Dravidian language family.

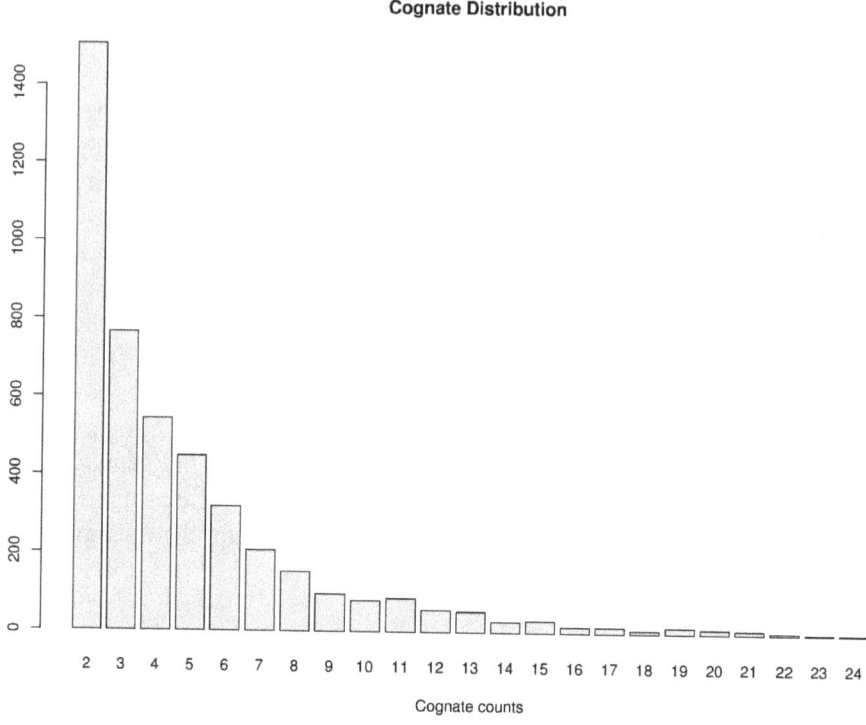

Figure 5. Barplot of the cognate set sizes from DEDR

Figure 5 displays the bar-plot of cognate set sizes for CDR. The figure shows that half of the cognate sets are of size two. The bar-plot suggests that there is an inverse relation between cognate set size and frequency of occurrence, commonly known as Zipf's law. It is not clear if the Zipf's law-like distribution exhibited between cognate set size and frequency of occurrence is an intrinsic property of cognate set size or the effect of cognate set sampling.

We now turn to an examination of the distribution of languages in DEDR-based datasets. Figure 6 displays the dot-plot of number of cognate sets for each language. The dot-plot shows a clear division between literary, to the right, and non-literary languages, to the left. One might argue that this distribution is expected due to the vast amounts of information available on literary languages. We successively removed cognate sets of size ranging from 2 to 6 and observed a similar distribution. We further observe that the same distribution holds for the much smaller ADR dataset. The dot-plots suggest that there is a representational bias towards literary (and semi-literary) languages in DEDR. Irula, Kuruba, Kurumba, and Belari have the least cognate set counts.

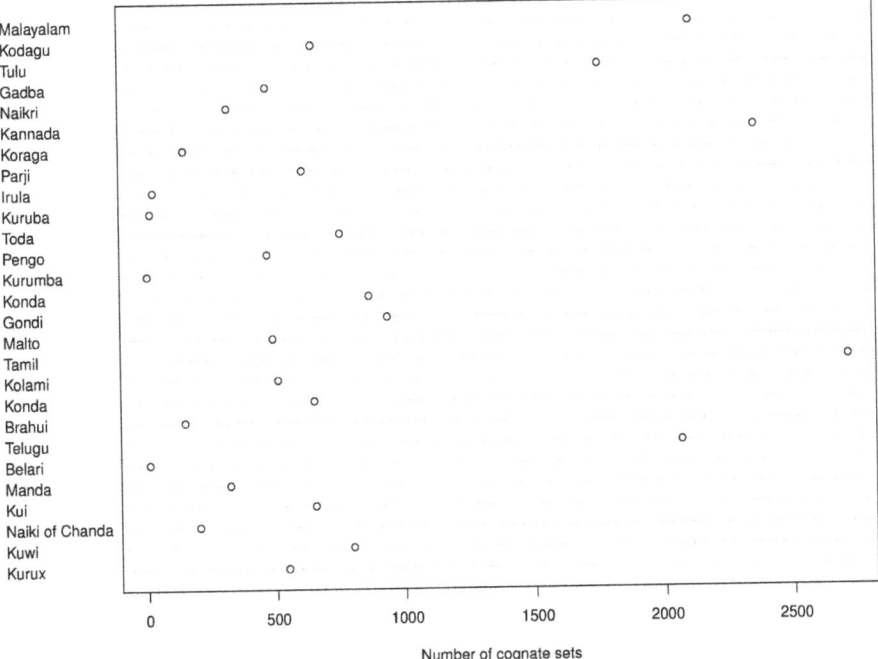

Figure 6. Dotplot of distribution of languages in CDR

Before we proceed to present and describe the trees, we note that each of the trees is a phylogram which provides details not only about the topology but also the branch lengths where branch length represents the amount of linguistic change that took place along the branch.

6.2. CDR

The NJ tree displayed in figure 7 is rooted using Kurukh-Malto as the outgroup. The tree does not return all the major subgroups. The following observations can be made about the internal grouping of the languages.

- The tree returns Tamil-Malayalam.
- The NJ tree groups Toda and Kota together whereas the closeness of Toda and Kota is viewed as suspicious in Krishnamurti (2003), who does not place Toda and Kota together.

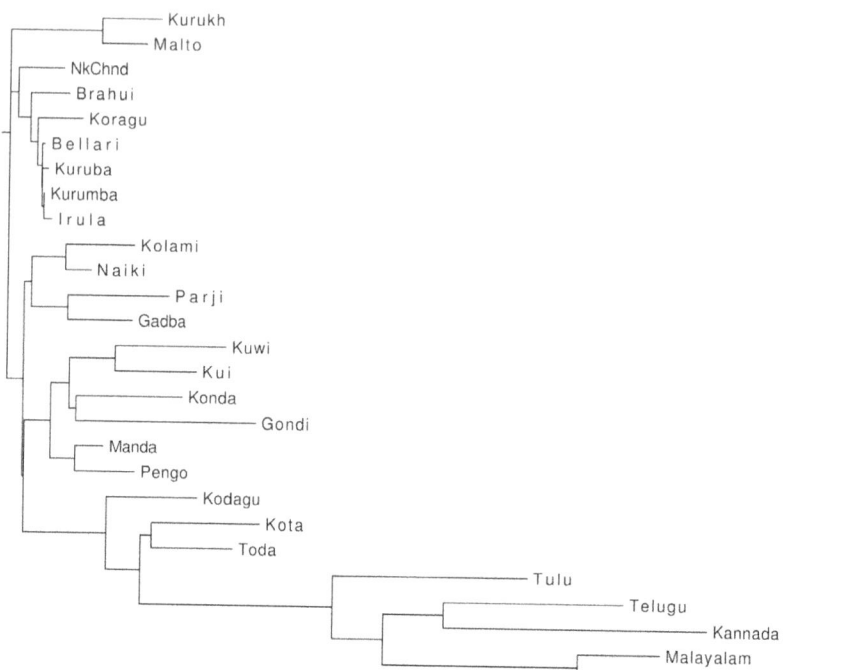

Figure 7. NJ tree rooted using Kurukh-Malto

- The standard tree groups Kodagu with other Nilgiri languages whereas NJ tree classifies Kodagu closer to Toda and Kota.
- All languages in SD II (except for Telugu) are placed under a single node. The internal classification of SD II is not identical to the standard tree. Kui-Kuwi, Pengo-Manda are grouped together just as in the standard tree. Konda and Gondi are incorrectly placed together.
- In CD languages: Kolami-Naikri, Parji-Gadba are placed together. Krishnamurti (2003) groups Naikri with Naiki of Chanda whereas Bhattacharya and Burrow considered Naikri to be a dialect of Kolami.
- The remaining languages: Naiki of Chanda (CD), Brahui (ND), Bellari (SD I), Kurumba (SD I), Kuruba (SD I), Koragu (SD I), and Irula (SD I) belonging to different subgroups are placed under a single node. Of these languages, Irula and Kurumba are Nilgiri languages. All these languages are placed close to the root and the support for the branch connecting these languages to the root is not statistically significant (58.1; figure 17).

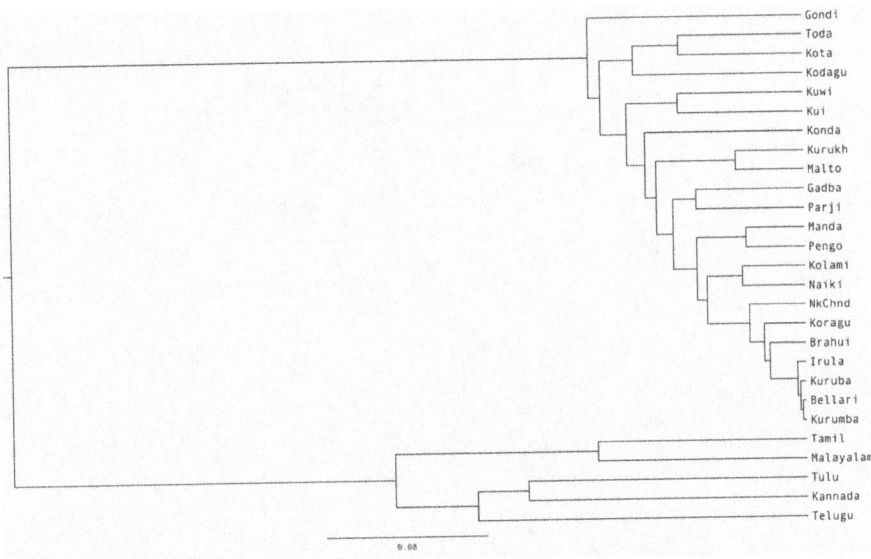

Figure 8. UPGMA tree

- The bootstrapped NJ tree (figure 17) annotated with support value is given in the appendix. The support value suggests that the branch connecting Kurukh-Malto to rest of the tree is well supported. The internal branches connecting the CD languages and SD II languages to the rest of the tree have support values of 34.6 and 71 respectively which are statistically non-significant.
- Finally, the NJ tree shows a ternary branching at the root.

The UPGMA tree (figure 8) does not return any of the major subgroups. The tree mixes languages from the established different subgroups. The tree returns the following language pairs correctly: Toda-Kota, Kui-Kuwi, Kurukh-Malto, Gadba-Parji, Pengo-Manda, Kolami-Naiki, Tamil-Malayalam. Konda and Gondi are neither grouped together nor do they share an immediate common ancestor with the remaining SD II group's languages. The tree groups Kannada with Tulu incorrectly. The tree shows a binary branching at the root.

Since the interpretation of a network is an open question (Nichols and Warnow 2008), we describe the network in figure 9 conservatively. We observe that the literary and non-literary languages are separated by a long

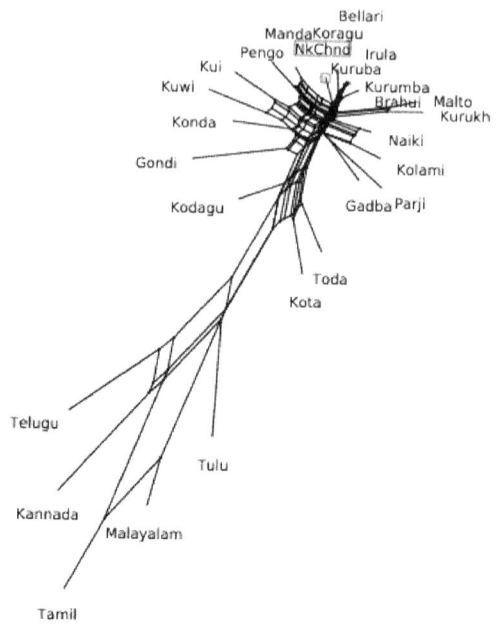

Figure 9. Network derived from CDR dataset

parallel edge. The network returns the Tamil–Malayalam language pair correctly and places Tulu as the most distant group of the literary languages.

Among the non-literary languages:

- Among SD I languages, Toda and Kota are grouped together. The remaining Nilgiri languages (Irula, Kuruba and Kurumba) are grouped together with the non-literary SD I languages. These Nilgiri languages show a highly undecipherable reticulation.
- SD II languages (except Telugu) are grouped to the left hand side of the structure.
- Among CD languages, Naiki-Kolami, Gadba, and Parji are grouped together. These CD languages are placed next to ND languages.
- All the ND languages are placed together on the right hand side of the network.

The subgrouping of Dravidian languages 163

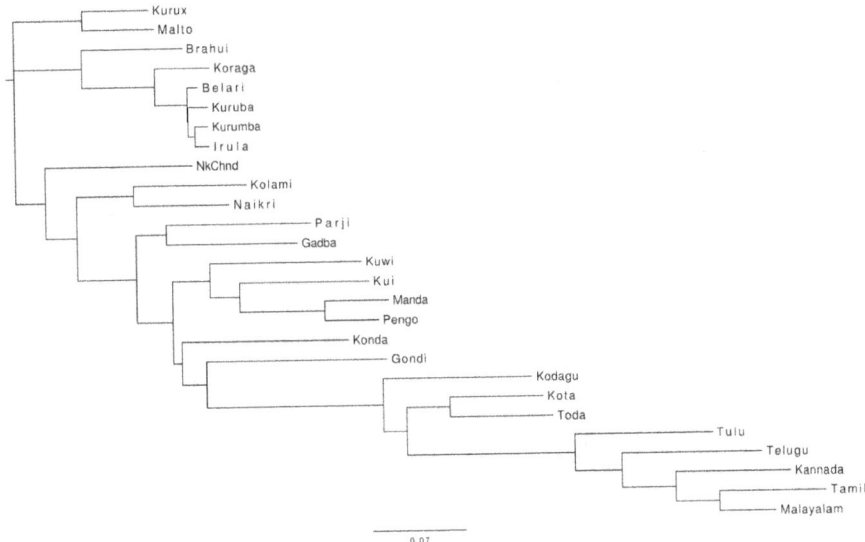

Figure 10. NJ tree rooted using Kurux-Malto

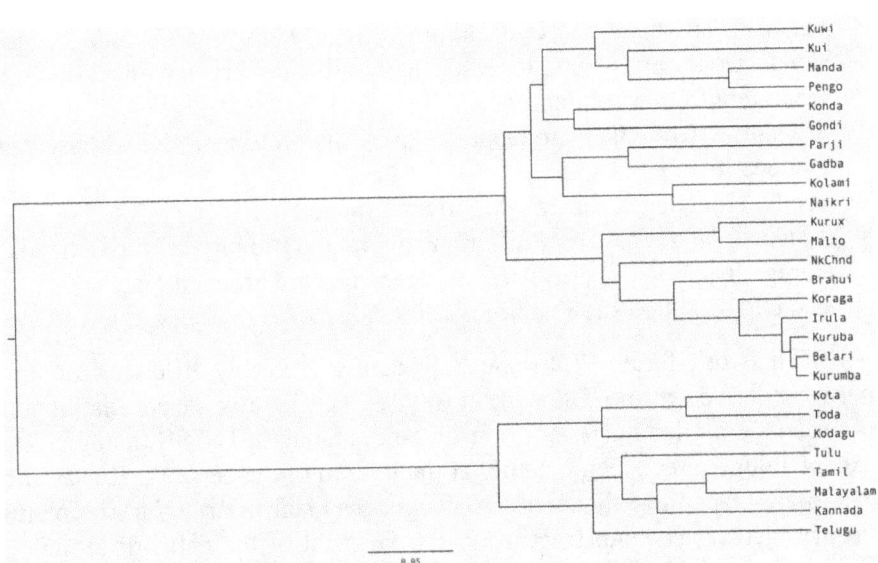

Figure 11. UPGMA tree

6.3. ADR

The NJ tree given in figure 10 is different from the NJ tree from the CDR dataset (figure 7). The tree does not return any of the major subgroups given in the standard tree. The tree differs from figure 7 in the following aspects:

- For the first time, Kannada and Telugu are not placed together. Rather, Telugu is placed apart from Tulu-Tamil-Malayalam-Kannada.
- Kui-Kuwi, Gondi-Konda do not occur together.
- Naiki of Chanda is placed closer to the remaining CD languages (Naikri-Kolami, Parji-Gadba).
- The bootstrapped NJ tree displayed in figure 18, in the appendix, suggests that the internal branches connecting the different language groups are not well supported.

The UPGMA tree (figure 11) does not return all the four established subgroups. Surprisingly, the tree makes fewer mistakes than its NJ counterpart (figure 10) and is closer to the standard tree in internal classification at lower level subgroups. Comparing with the standard tree:

- Three Nilgiri languages – Kota, Toda, Kodagu – are classified under a single node.
- The SD II languages (except Telugu) are grouped together. Manda-Pengo, Konda-Gondi are placed together. Kui and Kuwi are shown to diverge separately from a common node.
- In Central Dravidian languages: Naikri and Naiki of Chanda are not grouped together.
- The ND languages Kurukh-Malto are grouped together.
- As usual, languages from different subgroups, Brahui, Naiki of Chanda, Koraga, Irula, Kuruba, Belari, and Kurumba are grouped together.
- The UPGMA tree shows a binary branching.

The network (figure 12) for the ADR dataset is visibly different from the network derived from CDR dataset (figure 11). There is a clear distinction between literary languages and non-literary languages. The SD II languages, except Telugu, are placed together at the bottom of the network. Kurux and Malto are placed together. The CD languages Gadba-Parji, Naikri-Kolami occur together. The substructure in the far right of the network grouping Belari, Kuruba, Kurumba, Irula, Koraga, and Brahui is highly reticulated. Brahui and Koraga clearly diverge whereas the structure of the remaining four languages is highly unresolved. The network places Naikri-Kolami and Naiki of Chanda next to each other.

The subgrouping of Dravidian languages   165

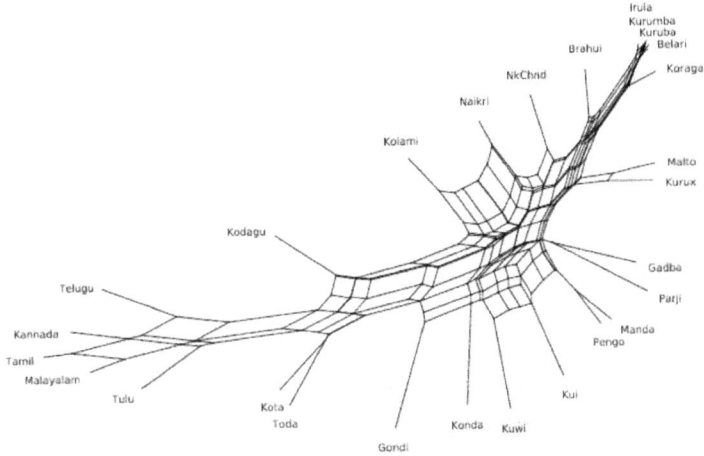

Figure 12. Neighbor Network

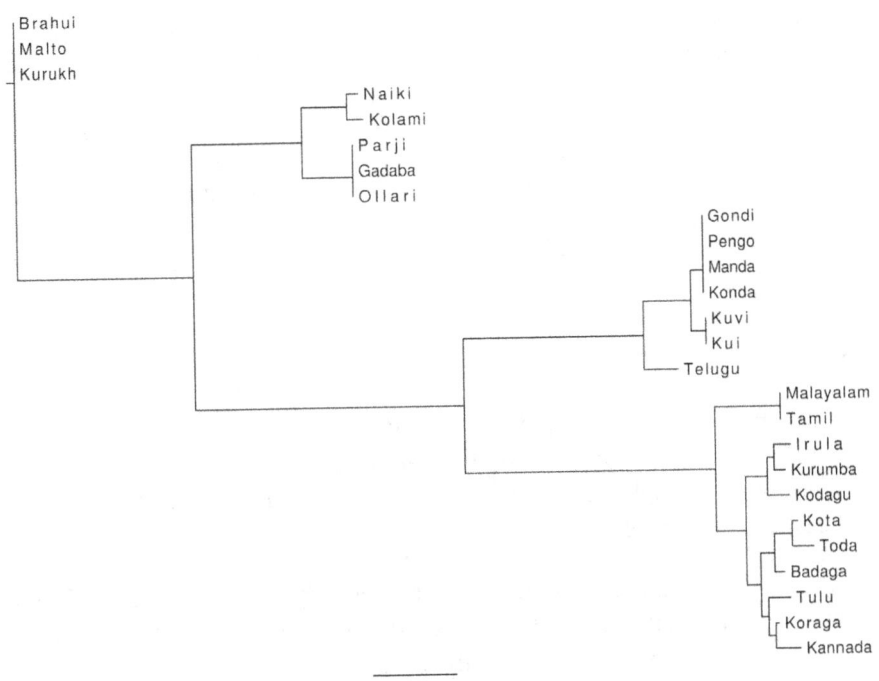

Figure 13. NJ tree using ND as outgroup

6.4. Comparative features

The NJ tree is displayed in figure 13. The tree is rooted using the ND clade as the outgroup. The tree returns all the four subgroups intact. The tree returns the following language groups.

- Among the SD I languages, Tamil-Malayalam, Toda-Kota are placed together. Koraga-Kannada and Tulu are placed together under a single node. The standard tree lists Badaga and Kannada as related whereas the NJ tree places them in different subgroups. Among the Nilgiri languages, Toda-Kota and Irula-Kurumba are grouped together. Kodagu occurs with the Irula-Kurumba language group.
- Telugu is the earliest diverging language in the SD II subgroup. Kui-Kuvi are grouped together. The node depicting Gondi, Pengo, Manda, and Konda is polytomous.
- The dataset treats Naikri and Naiki of Chanda as a single language. All the CD languages are grouped together. The tree classifies Naikri-Kolami under a single node. The Parji-Gadba-Ollari language group's ancestral node is polytomous.
- The tree shows a clear binary split at the root with ND and CD groups placed under one branch and SDI and SDII placed under the other branch.

The UPGMA tree (figure 14) returns all the four subgroups. The UPGMA tree is topologically similar to the NJ tree (figure 13). Thus, we do not describe the internal classification of each subgroup. The tree shows Proto-Dravidian splitting into ND-CD and SD I-SD II. It is interesting to note that this branching structure does not occur as an alternative in figure 4.

6.5. ASJP

In this subsection, we describe the NJ and UPGMA trees inferred from the ASJP distance matrix of 20 Dravidian languages.

The NJ tree, displayed in figure 15, is rooted using Kurukh as outgroup. The NJ tree is unresolved and returns the following language groups.

- Telugu is placed outside the SD II subgroup. The dialects of Gondi (Gondi and Southern Gondi) are placed next to each other and sharing an immediate common ancestor with Konda_1 (Konda).
- The tree groups the CD languages – Parji, Gadba Pottangi Ollari and Northwestern Kolami – with Kota (belonging to the SD I subgroup).

The subgrouping of Dravidian languages   167

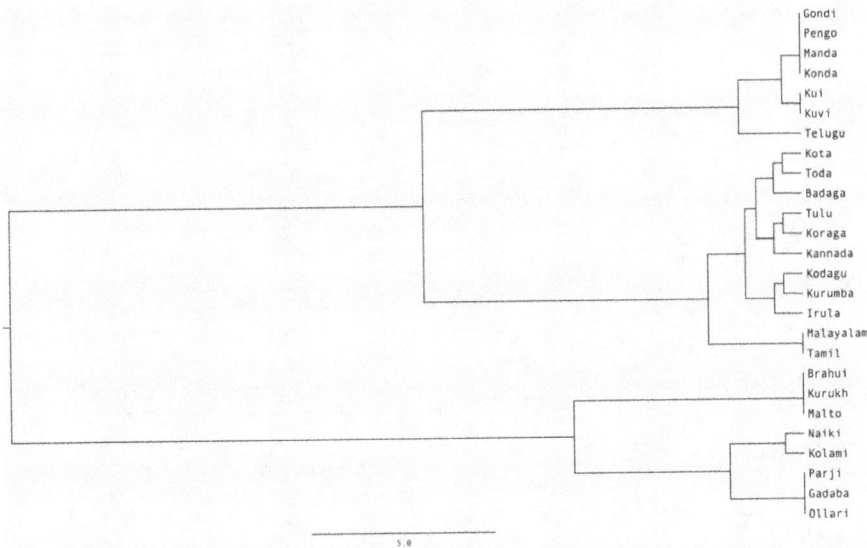

Figure 14. UPGMA tree

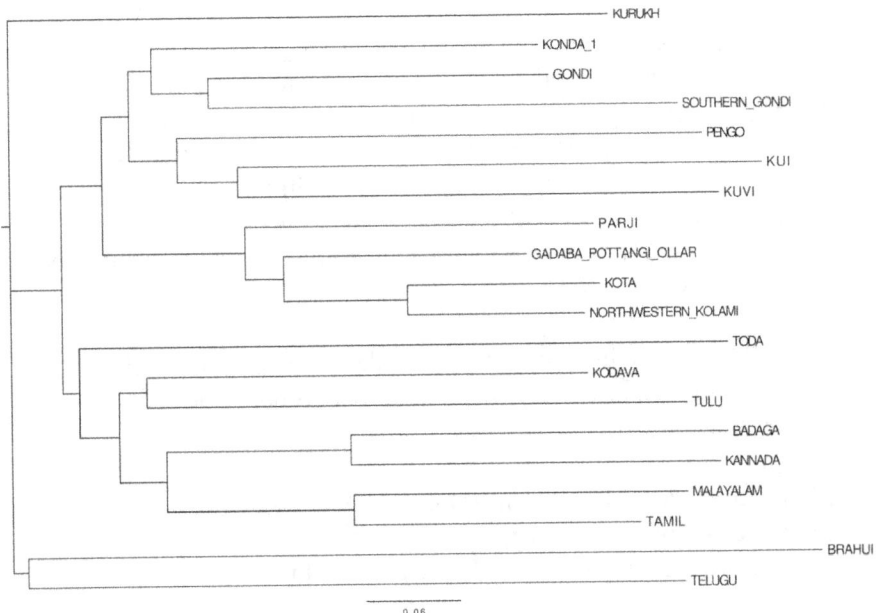

Figure 15. NJ tree rooted using Kurukh as the outgroup

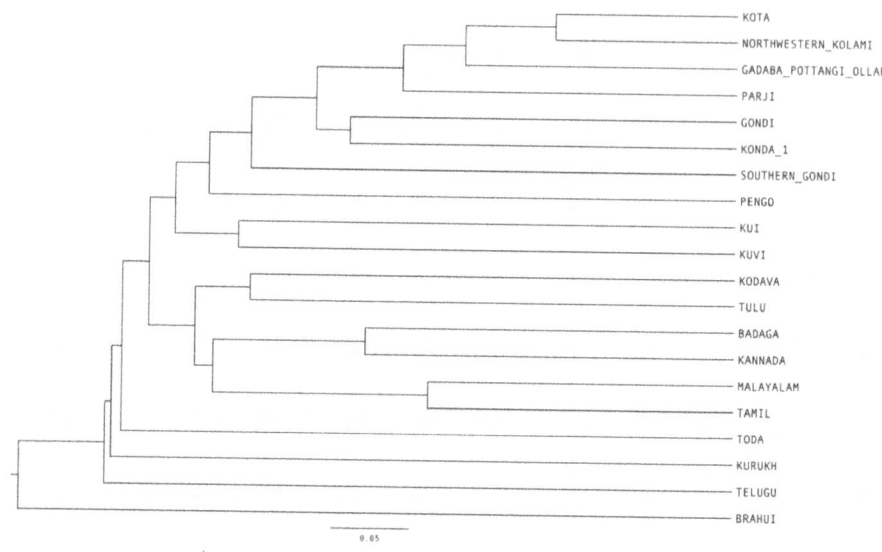

Figure 16. UPGMA tree

- All the SD I languages are placed under a single node. The tree returns the Badaga-Kannada and Tamil-Malayalam language pairs correctly.
- Brahui (a ND language) and Telugu are placed next to each other and are shown to diverge at the outset of the tree. Unlike the other datasets, ADR, CDR or Comparative features, the technique of bootstrapping is not applicable to the ASJP dataset. Hence, the support for the branch joining Brahui-Telugu to the root cannot be determined conclusively.
- The tree shows a ternary branching at the root.

The UPGMA tree inferred from ASJP data is displayed in figure 16. The tree does not return any of the four major subgroups. The tree returns the following language groups correctly:

- SD I: Kannada-Badaga, Tamil-Malayalam.
- SD II: Kui-Kuvi, Konda_1-Gondi.
- The root of the UPGMA tree shows a binary branching.

Table 1 presents the least squares fit (LSF) value for each of the trees described above. The least squares fit is highly significant for the NJ tree in each dataset. The NJ tree beats UPGMA by a large margin in all the datasets except ASJP.

Table 1. Least squares fit for NJ and UPGMA trees for four different datasets

Dataset	NJ	UPGMA
CDR	99.372	65.663
ADR	98.218	68.222
Comp. feat.	99.857	76.818
ASJP	96.857	99.372

7. Conclusion

We have pointed to the relevance of creating new datasets for subgrouping Dravidian languages for the purpose of throwing new light on the prehistory of the Indian subcontinent. We summarized three extant classifications of the Dravidian language family. We created two new diachronic datasets from *DEDR* which can not only be character encoded but also be used for computing lexical and semantic distances among Dravidian languages. The non-literary languages are underrepresented in both the datasets. We summarized two other datasets based on comparative features and Swadesh lists collected from different sources. In this work, we applied two distance methods NJ and UPGMA, and a network method for subgrouping Dravidian languages. The quality of the resolution of subgrouping for each dataset is summarized in table 2.

Table 2. Summary of subgrouping from different datasets

Dataset	Subgrouping resolution
CDR	No
ADR	No
Comp. Feat.	Yes
ASJP	No

The trees inferred using these datasets are unreliable. There is a little resemblance to the standard tree (Krishnamurti 2003). The NJ tree from the ASJP lists gets almost all the subgroups right with the exception of Telugu and North-Dravidian. Although the UPGMA tree has a higher LSF than the NJ tree on the ASJP list, it is much less resolved than the NJ tree. It is unclear why the trees are different for the CDR and ADR datasets when both datasets are derived from DEDR. The language group consisting of Naiki of Chanda, Brahui, Koragu, Belari, Kuruba, Kurumba, and Irula recurs across all the trees based on CDR and ADR. One possible explanation is the under-representation of these languages in CDR and ADR. The support for binary branching at highest level comes from the results on the Comparative features dataset (both NJ and UPGMA trees).

The unreliability of the trees based on NJ and UPGMA points to the need for the application of character-based methods such as Bayesian Inference (Huelsenbeck and Ronquist 2001) and Maximum Parsimony (Felsenstein 2003) to the CDR and ADR datasets for subgrouping the Dravidian languages. There is a need for quantitative work in determining the direction of family-internal borrowing. We conclude that the subgrouping of Dravidian languages is an open problem which requires future work.

Notes

1. We are grateful to Anju Saxena and Lars Borin for the useful comments on the earlier draft of the paper. We thank the reviewer for the highly useful comments in preparing the revised version of the paper.
2. Levenshtein distance is defined as the minimum number of basic edit operations required to convert a string of characters to another string.
3. An electronic version of the dictionary is available online at http://dsal.uchicago.edu/dictionaries/burrow/
4. Paul Huff's program on the ASJP website was used to generate the Ethnologue tree.
5. Konda, Gondi, Kui, Kuvi, Pengo and Manda
6. Dravidian Etymological Dictionary (An earlier version of DEDR).
7. DEDR includes Belari (its name variants, Bellari, Bellary, Belary), but Belari does not appear in Krishnamurti's (2003) classification.
8. Huff and Lonsdale (2011) provide an excellent step-by-step explanation to both UPGMA and NJ algorithms in the context of inferring linguistic phylogeny.
9. Downloadable at http://www.splitstree.org/
10. The tree constructed from a new random matrix might be different from the tree constructed using the original data matrix.
11. http://wwwstaff.eva.mpg.de/~wichmann/ASJP_Distances.zip
12. We use MEGA for the sake of replicability.

The subgrouping of Dravidian languages 171

Appendix

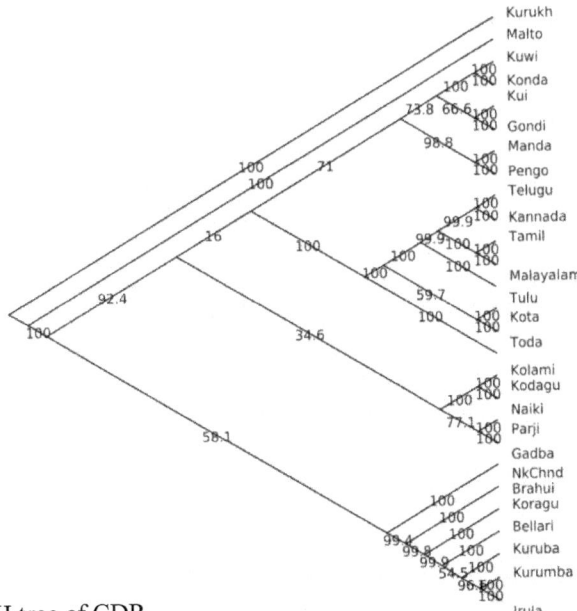

Figure 17. Bootstrapped NJ tree of CDR

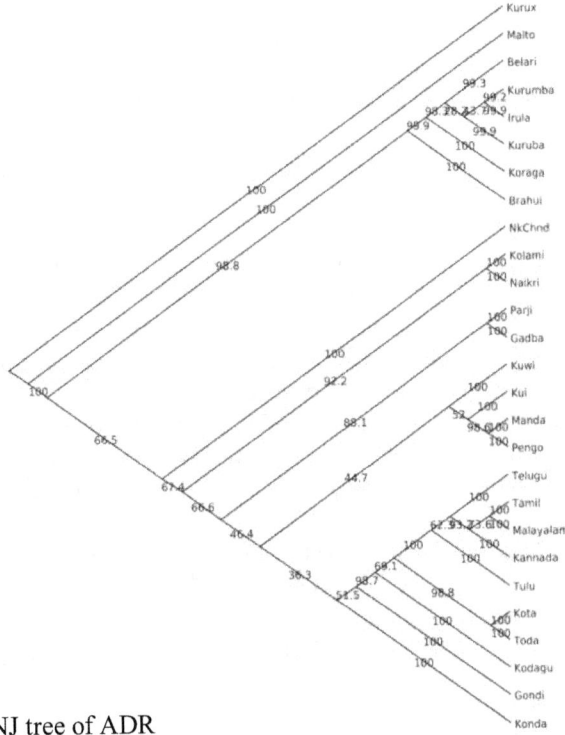

Figure 18. Bootstrapped NJ tree of ADR

References

Andronov, M. S.
  1964   Lexicostatistic analysis of the chronology of disintegration of Proto-Dravidian. *Indo-Iranian Journal* 7 (2): 170–186.
Atkinson, Quentin D. and Russell D. Gray.
  2005   Curious parallels and curious connections: Phylogenetic thinking in biology and historical linguistics. *Systematic Biology* 54 (4): 513–526.
Brown, Cecil H., Eric W. Holman, Søren Wichmann, and Viveka Velupillai
  2008   Automated classification of the world's languages: a description of the method and preliminary results. *STUF – Language Typology and Universals* 61 (4): 285–308.
Burrow, Thomas and Murray B. Emeneau
  1984   *A Dravidian Etymological Dictionary [DEDR]*. Second Edition. Oxford: Clarendon Press.
Campbell, Lyle
  2004   *Historical Linguistics: An Introduction.* Second Edition. MIT Press.
Dyen, Isidore, Joseph B. Kruskal, and Paul Black
  1992   An Indo-European classification: A lexicostatistical experiment. *Transactions of the American Philosophical Society* 82: 1–132.
Elfenbein, J.
  1987   A periplus of the 'Brahui problem'. *Indo-Iranica* 16. 215–233.
Felsenstein, Joseph
  2003   *Inferring Phylogenies.* Sunderland, MA: Sinauer Associates.
Felsenstein, Joseph
  2004   PHYLIP (Phylogeny Inference Package) version 3.6. Distributed by the author. Department of Genetics, University of Washington, Seattle.
Gray, Russell D. and Quentin D. Atkinson
  2003   Language-tree divergence times support the Anatolian theory of Indo-European origin. *Nature* 426: 435–439.
Gray, Russell D., Andrew J. Drummond, and Simon J. Greenhill
  2009   Language phylogenies reveal expansion pulses and pauses in Pacific settlement. *Science* 323: 479–483.
Haspelmath, Martin, Matthew S. Dryer, David Gil, and Bernard Comrie
  2011   Wals online, Munich: Max Planck Digital Library.
Holman, Eric W., Søren Wichmann, Cecil H. Brown, Viveka Velupillai, André Müller, and Dik Bakker
  2008   Explorations in automated language classification. *Folia Linguistica* 42 (3–4): 331–354.
Huelsenbeck, John P. and Fredrik Ronquist
  2001   MRBAYES: Bayesian inference of phylogeny. *Bioinformatics* 17 (8): 754–755.

Huff, Paul and Deryle Lonsdale
    2011   Positing language relationships using ALINE. *Language Dynamics and Change* 1 (1): 128–162.
Huson, Daniel H. and David Bryant
    2006   Application of phylogenetic networks in evolutionary studies. *Molecular Biology and Evolution* 23 (2): 254.
Kameswari, T. M.
    1969   The chronology of Dravidian languages – a lexico-statistic analysis. In Agesthialingom and Kumaraswami Raja (eds.), 269–274.
Kolachina, Sudheer, Taraka Rama, and B. Lakshmi Bai
    2011   Maximum parsimony method in the subgrouping of Dravidian languages. In *Quantitative Investigations in Theoretical Linguistics,* Amir Zeldes, and Anke Lüdeling (eds.), 52–56. Berlin: Humboldt-Universität.
Krishnamurti, Bhadriraju
    1978   Areal and lexical diffusion of sound change: Evidence from Dravidian. *Language* 54 (1): 1–20.
Krishnamurti, Bhadriraju
    2003   *The Dravidian Languages.* Cambridge: Cambridge University Press.
Krishnamurti, Bhadriraju, Lincoln Moses, and Douglas G. Danforth
    1983   Unchanged cognates as a criterion in linguistic subgrouping. *Language* 59 (4): 541–568.
Lewis, M. Paul (ed.)
    2009   *Ethnologue: Languages of the World.* 16th edition. Dallas: SIL International. Online version: http://www.ethnologue.com.
Maddison, Wayne P.
    1993   Missing data versus missing characters in phylogenetic analysis. *Systematic Biology* 42 (4): 576–581.
McMahon, April and Robert McMahon
    2005   *Language Classification by Numbers.* Oxford: Oxford University Press.
McMahon, April and Robert McMahon
    2007   Language families and quantitative methods in South Asia and elsewhere. In *The Evolution and History of Human Populations in South Asia,* Michael D. Petraglia, Bridget Allchin (eds.), 363–384. Netherlands: Springer Press.
Nakhleh, Luay, Donald A. Ringe, Jr., and Tandy Warnow
    2005   Perfect phylogenetic networks: A new methodology for reconstructing the evolutionary history of natural languages. *Language* 81 (2): 382–420.
Namboodiri, E. V. N.
    1976   *Glottochronology (as applied to four Dravidian languages).* Trivandrum: Sangma.
Nichols, Johanna and Tandy Warnow
    2008   Tutorial on computational linguistic phylogeny. *Language and Linguistics Compass* 2 (5): 760–820.

Rama, Taraka, Sudheer Kolachina, and B. Lakshmi Bai
   2009   Quantitative methods for phylogenetic inference in historical linguistics: An experimental case study of South Central Dravidian. *Indian Linguistics* 70.

Ringe, Don, Tandy Warnow, and Ann Taylor
   2002   Indo-European and computational cladistics. *Transactions of the Philological Society* 100 (1): 59–129.

Serva, Maurizio and Filippo Petroni
   2008   Indo-European languages tree by Levenshtein distance. *Europhysics Letters* 81 (6): 68005.

Swadesh, Morris
   1952   Lexico-statistic dating of prehistoric ethnic contacts: with special reference to North American Indians and Eskimos. *Proceedings of the American Philosophical Society* 96 (4): 452–463.

Swadesh, Morris
   1955   Towards greater accuracy in lexicostatistic dating. *International Journal of American Linguistics* 21 (2): 121–137.

Tamura, Koichiro, Joel Dudley, Masatoshi Nei, and Sudhir Kumar
   2007   MEGA4: Molecular Evolutionary Genetics Analysis (MEGA) Software Version 4.0 *Molecular Biology and Evolution* 24 (8): 1596–1599.

Wichmann, Søren
   2010a   Internal language classification. In *The Continuum Companion to Historical Linguistics*, Luraghi, Silvia, and Vit Bubenik (eds.), 70–86. London/New York: Continuum Books.

Wichmann, Søren, Eric W. Holman, Dik Bakker, and Cecil H. Brown
   2010b   Evaluating linguistic distance measures. *Physica A* 389: 3632–3639.

Carving Tibeto-Kanauri by its joints: Using basic vocabulary lists for genetic grouping of languages

Anju Saxena and Lars Borin

1. Introduction[1]

The aim of this paper is to examine the internal subgrouping of the Tibeto-Kanauri languages, a lower-level branch of the Tibeto-Burman (or Sino-Tibetan) language family, using a computational approach applied to empirical primary language data. The procedure which is used here is similar to recent works in dialectometry (e.g., Nerbonne and Heeringa 2009) and lexicostatistics (e.g., Holman et al. 2008) in relying on a completely automatic comparison of the items in the word lists. However, it differs from most of these works (McMahon et al. 2007, Saxena and Borin 2011 and Saxena 2011 being notable exceptions) in its usage of rules tailored to the particular linguistic configuration under investigation, rather than a general method for string comparison. In this respect, it falls somewhere in between traditional lexicostatistics (or glottochronology) – where expert statements are required about the cognacy of items – and these modern approaches – which rely entirely on surface form for determining identity of items – although closer to the latter than the former. The main methodological advantage of our approach is its consistency.

2. Background

There is considerable disagreement over the internal classification of the Tibeto-Burman languages, on all levels of the family tree (see Saxena 2004 and Handel 2008 for summaries of the various proposals). In most such classifications the internal classification of the Tibeto-Kanauri subgroup is not even mentioned.[2] Further, to date there has not been any systematic, comparative linguistic study of these languages, and consequently no systematic basis for examining how the Tibeto-Burman varieties spoken in the Indian Himalayan region relate to one another. This is the aim of this paper. The work presented here is a continuation and extension of an earlier study where only the Tibeto-Burman varieties of Kinnaur were studied (Saxena

2011; Saxena and Borin 2011). Here we will present the results of our new study, where we have compared and contrasted a comparable word-list in seventeen Tibeto-Kanauri language varieties:

1	Sangla (kfk)	7	Poo (nes?)	13	Tinani (lbf)
2	Nichar (kfk?)	8	Kuno (–)	14	Pattani (lae)
3	Kalpa (–)	9	Nàvakat (–)	15	Byangsi (bee)
4	Ropa (–)	10	Tabo (spt)	16	Chaudangsi (cdn)
5	Chitkul (cik)	11	Ladakhi (lbj)	17	Bhramu (brd)
6	Labrang (scu?)	12	Gahri (bfu)		

ISO 639-3 language code assignments follow the *Ethnologue* (Lewis 2009). A question mark indicates that the assignment is uncertain because this particular variety is not mentioned in the Ethnologue, and a minus sign that there is no ISO code for the variety. The order in which the languages are listed here is roughly geographical, from west to east. The same ordering will be used in all tables in this article. All languages except Bhramu are spoken in the Indian Himalayan region. Bhramu is spoken in Nepal. Figure 1 demarcates the Indian Himalayan region on a map of India. The map in figure 2 highlights the Himachal Pradesh, Uttarakhand and Ladakh – the last named in Jammu and Kashmir – regions in India where these languages (except Brahmu) are spoken.[3]

The selection of languages included in this study was restricted by the non-availability of data for many languages. For the same reason, we often were not able to find the equivalents for all entries in the word list even for the languages that are included in this investigation. The data of the following languages are from Anju Saxena's own fieldwork and/or fieldwork conducted in our various projects: Nichar (Ni), Sangla (Sa), Chitkul (Chit), Kalpa (Ka), Kuno (Ku), Labrang (Lab), Poo (Po), Ropa (Ro), Nàvakat (Na) and Tinani (Ti). The data of the remaining languages are from secondary sources.

The data comprise (i) a basic vocabulary list (a revised Swadesh list; Swadesh 1955) for all sites (157 senses); (ii) an extended IDS list (Borin, Comrie and Saxena this volume) for Sangla, Nàvakat, Tabo and Ladakhi (1884 senses); and (iii) selected grammatical constructions. The focus in this paper is on the lexical data from the basic vocabulary list.

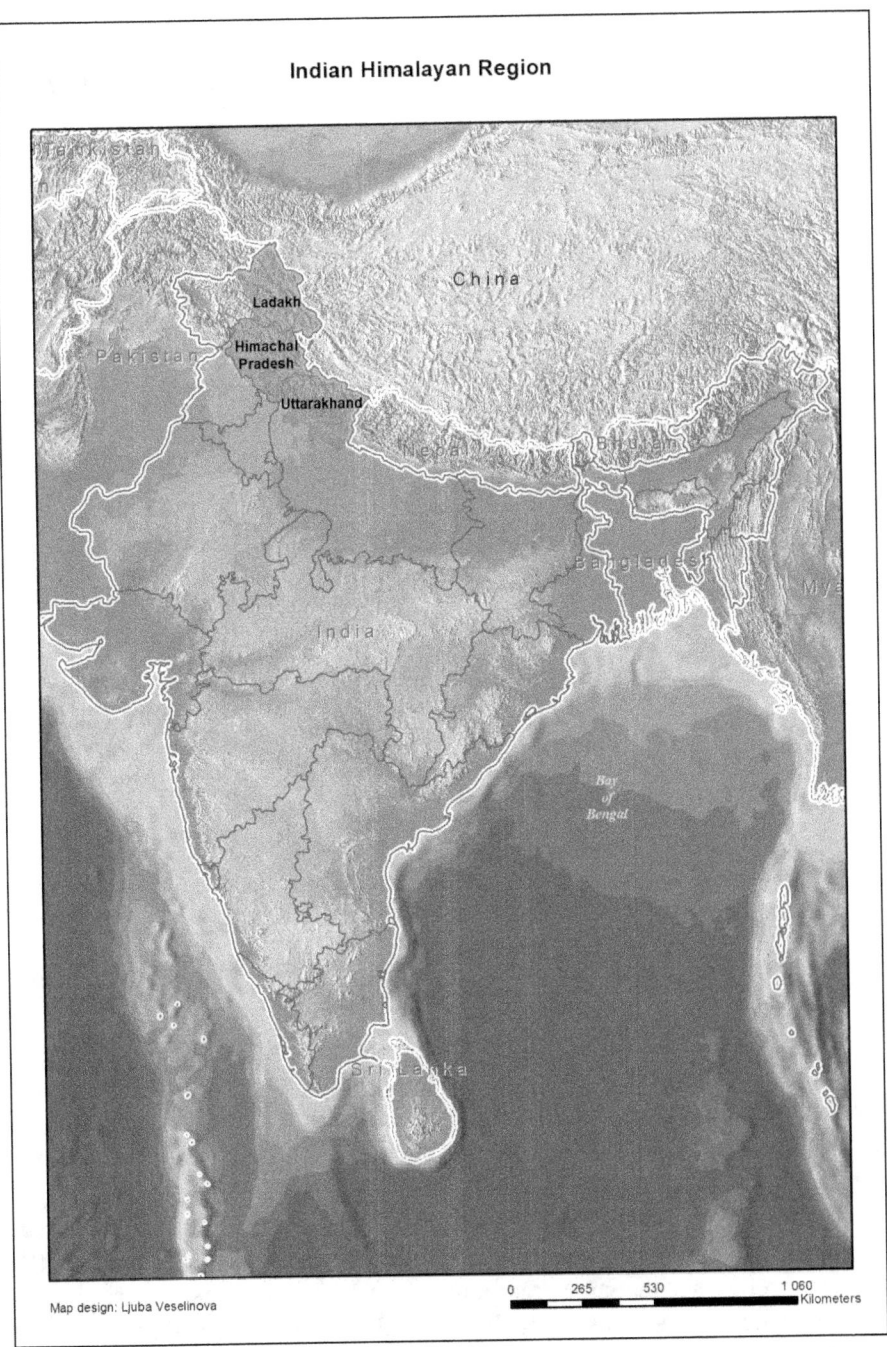

Figure 1. The Indian Himalayan region

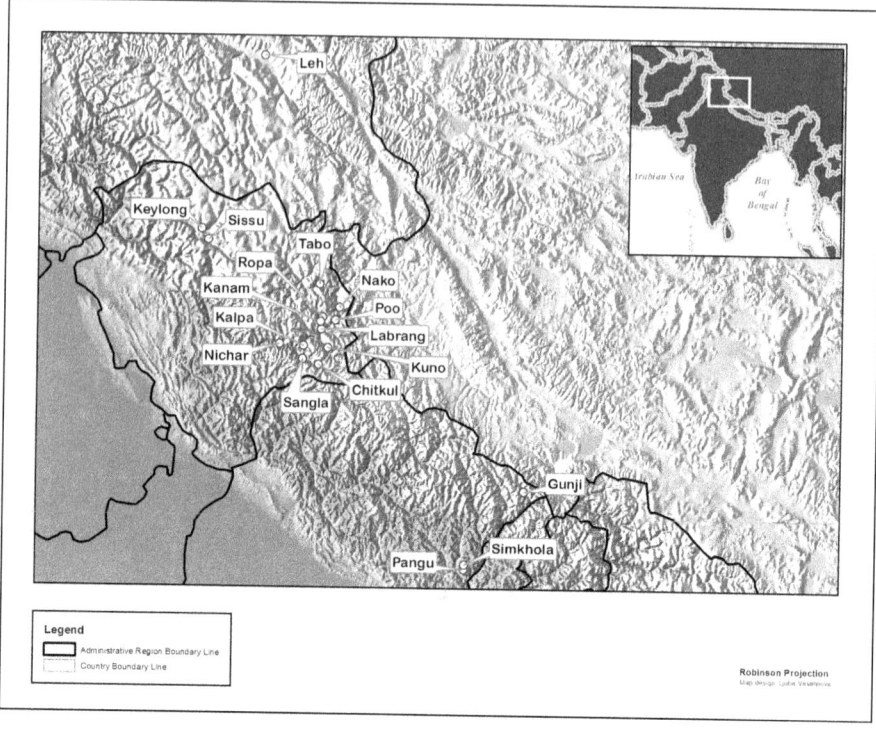

Figure 2. Regions in Himachal Pradesh, Uttarakhand and Kashmir where Tibeto-Kanauri languages are spoken.

3. Method

3.1. Using basic vocabulary lists for genetic grouping of languages

A revised Swadesh list has been the main basis for comparison of the Tibeto-Kanauri language varieties examined here. Using such sense lists presents its own methodological challenges. The fundamental decision in this context is whether a particular sense is represented by the same item (word) in two language varieties.

Here we must first define what we mean by "the same item". In Swadesh-style lexicostatistics, this is normally interpreted as cognacy, i.e., whether the items are reflexes of the same proto-language item. Finer points of (derivational) morphological structure are often disregarded in this context, and only cognacy of roots or stems is important. Even in this case, determining that two items are cognate is far from straightforward and requires expert knowledge, especially if the languages are only distantly related. A classical and oft-cited example is Armenian *erku* 'two', which has developed through a series of regular sound changes from the same Indo-European root which also has yielded English *two*. Another example could be Swedish *i* and Russian *v*, both meaning 'in' and both descended in regular fashion from Proto-Indo-European *$\stackrel{*}{\underset{\circ}{n}}$.

This arguably means that the information about genetic grouping sought by these methods is to a large extent already known by other means, e.g., the classical comparative method. The requisite expert knowledge is a scarce resource, and if we would like to conduct larger-scale genetic linguistic investigations encompassing also poorly documented languages, we need some other way of doing this. When the expert knowledge is available, it serves as a valuable yardstick, a known gold standard against which less knowledge-intensive methods can be judged before being applied to those cases where less is known beforehand.

Large-scale investigations such as that presented by Holman et al. (2008) rely on a mechanical procedure – automatically computed Levenshtein distance (also called edit distance) between strings transcribed using a standardized coarse phonetic transcription – for determining cognacy. This has the advantage of being totally consistent, and the disadvantage of both missing some cognates and misclassifying some non-cognate pairs as cognates. The assumption is that if such a procedure is consistently in agreement with existing expert judgments, it will produce correct results also in the cases where no such judgments exist.

In dialect studies, the judgment of sameness may include also the sound shape and morphological structure of obviously cognate items in the sense of the preceding paragraph. This is the method chosen here when comparing the Tibeto-Kanauri basic vocabulary lists: Certain – but not all – sound correspondences, and certain – but not all – morphological structures, are considered equal for the purpose of comparing lexical items among Tibeto-Kanauri varieties. See below.

Second, an often-made presupposition in Swadesh-style lexicostatistics is that only one word from each language will represent each sense in the list. Sometimes a language has synonymous words for the same sense. Depending on one's definition of synonymy, it will be more or less prevalent in a language, but it may also depend on the particular language itself (Fleck and Voss 2006). In this case, one or more – but not all – synonyms may have cognates in the other varieties under scrutiny.

There may be a word in a language which due to semantic change no longer carries the same meaning as its cognates in related language varieties. A case in point could be German *Fleisch* 'meat, flesh' which is cognate with English *flesh*, and also exhibits a reasonable semantic fit with this item. However, the cognate of these words in a third Germanic language – Swedish – is *fläsk* 'pork, pig meat', whereas the normal Swedish word for 'meat, flesh' would be *kött*. Such cases are legion in languages, but they present us with a methodological problem: Should we provide Swedish *fläsk* for Swadesh list item 29 ('flesh/meat'), or rather the general word *kött*?

In our view the answer to this question must depend on the purpose of the investigation. Traditional genetic linguistics is form-oriented; it will prefer to record that a language has a reflex of a particular original form, disregarding differences in meaning, provided that these can be accounted for by postulating plausible semantic changes.

On the other hand, lexicostatistically and glottochronologically oriented investigations may wish to take account of semantic drift, thus aiming at recording the most appropriate exponent of the sense in the language, i.e., the stylistically most neutral expression that is in active use in the language. Also, with larger-scale investigations involving poorly documented language varieties that the researcher may not know well, this may well be the only feasible alternative. In working with secondary sources and language consultants, presumably we will end up with one or several common expressions of the sense sought, regardless of their genetic relationship to the corresponding expressions in related language varieties.

Often, in this kind of study, sameness is a categorical matter; two items are or are not the same. Sometimes it makes sense to use a similarity measure instead. This has been proposed, e.g., for cases where there is more than one exponent given for a sense, and more than one of these could be cognate to a single item in another language (e.g., Grace 1961). The proposed solution would then be to assign a fractional value as the outcome of this comparison, e.g., 0.5 if there are two exponents, etc. In our investigation, every correspondence gets one point, but multiple correspondences for the same sense still count as only one correspondence. An example will make this clearer. Let us assume that a particular sense is expressed in the following way in four languages (capital letters represent forms/words):

Language 1	Language 2	Language 3	Language 4
A	A, B	A, B	B

In our investigation, we always make pairwise comparisons between language varieties, which will result in comparison tables showing the ratio of same items to total number of items (but with at most one item counted per sense). In this simple example, the correspondence table becomes:

	Lg 2	Lg 3	Lg 4	
Lg 1	1/1 (100%)	1/1 (100%)	0/1 (0%)	Lg 1
	Lg 2	**1/1 (100%)**	1/1 (100%)	Lg 2
		Lg 3	1/1 (100%)	Lg 3

With this way of calculating similarity, languages 2 and 3 are as similar to each other (the boldfaced ratio in the table) as each of them is to language 1 and 4, although languages 2 and 3 share two items in this sense slot. This decision is not completely arbitrary, but not very strongly motivated either. However, it can easily be reconsidered – e.g., if more information becomes available on these language varieties – and the results recalculated. The main point to be made here is that the calculation is completely deterministic and repeatable; anybody can apply it to the same or some other dataset in order to see whether it yields reasonable results.

3.2. Data collection

As has perhaps become clear from the preceding, creating a comparable, systematic, linguistic database is something of a challenge. We have seen that one complicating factor here is that a language can have more than one word for a sense, and it is somewhat fortuitous which alternative or alternatives the language consultant happens to provide. Thus the data presented in the present work cannot be seen as complete. There may exist terms in these languages which have cognates in other languages, but which do not happen to show up in our database. On the other hand, the terms provided by a consultant may say something about terms which are more neutral or more frequent or more basic than the other possible alternative forms which were not provided. Further, it takes a while using the questionnaire before the questionnaire starts working. It evolves as we collect and analyze data, becoming aware of senses which are crucial, but missing in the present version of the questionnaire, thus necessitating a revision of the questionnaire. The first author experienced this again and again in her dialect survey work, and she found herself continuously adding new senses to the questionnaire. So, in practice, the basic word list questionnaire, which is provided in appendix 1, will give readers an idea about the kind of comparable lexical entries we were striving for, but our database in all cases contains many more entries.

In most cases more than one language consultant was used for one variety. Frequently, the data collected was rechecked with other speaker(s) from the same village. We did this as a way to ensure that the information provided by a language consultant reflects the speech of this village, and not an idiosyncrasy of this particular speaker. In almost all cases we did not inform the consultant of one variety what word had been provided for another variety, or what is our hypothesis, instead we let them provide the data for a given entry. This was also a decision we took, as a way not to influence our data or results.

3.3. Comparison methodology: details

The following procedure was used in this investigation:

- After the data collection and initial processing of the data (including normalization of the transcription into IPA),
- a list of observations of relationships among varieties was made.
- This list formed the basis for developing a set of principles for comparing the linguistic correspondences in these Tibeto-Kanauri languages. Their purpose was to determine which segmental differences were non-significant for the purpose of considering items in different varieties as the same.
- The principles were encoded as context-sensitive phonological segment equivalence rules in a small computer program for comparing items fully automatically in order to achieve consistency.
- The equivalence rules were revised after inspection of the result, and the program run again on the data. This process went through a few iterations until the result contained no obvious errors.

The results from the comparison come in the form of two kinds of tables:

- tables of individual word senses and lexical items expressing them, where each language variety gets a numerical index (1–17), and each word sense/ language variety combination is provided with a list of indices showing which varieties share one or more expressions of this sense;
- summary tables, where similarities among all lexical items of a particular grammatical or semantic category (nouns, kinship terms, etc.) are shown as ratios and percentages (see the example in section 3.1 above).

In the present investigation, the following principles were used in comparing word list items among varieties (the following symbols are used below: V: vowel; T: stop; Ø: zero/no segment).

Vowels: The following vowels appear to be in free variation in many of these varieties, and consequently the members of each – semicolon-separated – group are considered equal for the purposes of our comparison, in any position:

a ~ ʌ ~ ɐ ~ ɑ ~ ə; a ~ ʌ ~ ɐ ~ ɑ ~ ɔ;
i ~ ɪ; u ~ ʊ; e ~ ɛ ~ æ; o ~ ɔ; o ~ ø.

Note however that the similarities are not to be construed as transitive: e.g., ə and ɔ do not count as the same.

Vowel length: Long and short vowels are not distinguished for the purposes of the comparison.

Vowel articulation diacritics: IPA diacritics indicating slight modifications in vowel height or frontness are disregarded in the comparison.

Vowel nasalization and phonemic tone: Nasalization is disregarded in the comparison, as is tone (orthographically marked on vowels in the transcription).

Hyphen: Sometimes a word-internal hyphen is used in the transcription to indicate morphological structure. All word-internal hyphens are disregarded in the comparison.

Consonants: The following consonants appear to be in free variation in many of these varieties, and consequently the members of each group are considered equal, in any position:

g ~ ɣ; dʒ ~ ɖʐ ~ ɟ ~ dz ~ z ~ ʒ ~ ʐ ~ ʑ;
p ~ f; ʃ ~ ʂ; tʃ ~ ʈʃ ~ c ~ ɕ ~ tɕ; s ~ ts; ʊ ~ v.

Consonant gemination: Short and long consonants are treated as one and the same, in any position. In the preliminary analysis of the sound systems of these varieties, there has been no indication that geminates are phonemic in any of them.

Prenasalization, labialization and palatalization: Prenasalization, labialization and palatalization of consonants are disregarded in the comparison.

Aspiration: Aspiration of all affricates is disregarded in the comparison.

Sound sequences: The following sequences are treated as equal for the purposes of the comparison, in any position:

ɖr ~ ɖ; ʈr ~ ʈ; V_1jV_2 ~ V_1V_2

Word endings: The following word ending alternants are treated as equal for the purposes of the comparison:

-h ~ -Ø; -ts ~ -Ø; -j ~ -Ø;
-pa ~ -ba ~ -ʋa; -po ~ -bo ~ -ʋo;
-V₁T ~ -V₁

Illustrating with a concrete example, the last item in this list states that word-final stops are counted equal to Ø following a vowel, as there is dialect-internal variation in this respect. Different stops are considered as separate, however. Thus, *ja* counts as the same as both *jag* and *jak*, but the latter two count as different.

Phrases: For terms such as 'older brother', 'younger brother', 'maternal aunt', 'paternal aunt', if the term consists of more than one word, e.g., 'old'+'sister', then the modifier is disregarded; only the noun is used for the comparison.

3.4. Comparison methodology: summary

As already mentioned above, in order to achieve consistency of judgment, the above principles were encoded in a small computer program which was then used to compare items fully automatically. In practice, the principles were initially manually developed and then successively refined by an iterative process where the program was applied to the data and the results subsequently inspected. Typically during such a round we would find that the program had missed some correspondence that should have been found. Because the principles tended to be fairly conservative, the opposite almost never occurred. The great advantage of having automated the application of the principles emerged in these situations, since a revision of the principles made on the basis of one or a few correspondences could be immediately and effortlessly tested on all the data in order to check that it would not introduce errors elsewhere.

This procedure was used in order to establish the principles for a completely automatic comparison of a number of word lists representing the Tibeto-Kanauri varieties under investigation. The results reported in the next section come from this automatic comparison.

4. Results

Because of the limited space, we will illustrate the results of this investigation by focusing our attention on (i) adjectives, (ii) nouns and (iii) total vocabulary.

4.1. Adjectives

Table 1 shows the result of the comparison for some adjectives and table 2 contains the summary result of pairwise comparisons of adjectives between all varieties. In table 1, each language is assigned a numerical index (leftmost column in the table). Each comparison cell then simply lists all indices of items identified as the same by the automatic comparison procedure, in addition to the word or words in the variety in question (e.g., the item 'new' in Poo, Kuno, Nàvakat, Tabo and Ladakhi). In the table, vocabulary items refer to senses and are identified by italicized English words. Swadesh list items are further identified by their Swadesh list number added to the end of the English word and separated from the word by a slash: "bad/186"). Items without this number do not appear in the Swadesh list, but have been added by us. An asterisk ("*") indicates the 40 items identified by Holman et al (2008) as the most stable subset of the Swadesh list ("new/183*"). In the summary tables, a similarity degree of 45% or more is indicated by a grey cell background. This is a heuristic device for highlighting clustering of varieties; no particular significance is attached to this particular 'threshold'.

Some observations can be made concerning the adjectives, based on the data of *all* the languages examined:

1. Sangla, Nichar, Kalpa and Ropa – the "Sangla group" – show a higher degree of similarity, which they do not share with the other languages considered.
2. Chitkul and Labrang, which are also spoken in the Kinnaur region, show more similarities to each other than to the Sangla group.
3. The next group which is formed, based on the similarities in the adjectives considered here, contains Poo, Kuno, Nàvakat, Tabo and Ladakhi – the "Nàvakat group" – with Poo and Nàvakat showing the highest degree of similarity. Note that Poo, Kuno and Nàvakat are spoken in Kinnaur, Tabo in Spiti in the Himachal Pradesh region while Ladakhi is spoken in Ladakh in Jammu and Kashmir.

Table 1. Some adjectives compared across varieties.

	bad/186	black/176	dry/195	new/183*	red/172
[1] Sangla	[1/3] mari	[1/2/3/4] rok	[1] tʃarmu	[1/2/3/4] ɲug; ɲuːg	[1/2/3] ʃʋig
[2] Nichar	[2] maːr	[1/2/3/4] rok	[2/3] tʃarts	[1/2/3/4] ɲuːg	[1/2/3] ʃʋig
[3] Kalpa	[1/3] mari	[1/2/3/4] rɔk	[2/3] tʃarts	[1/2/3/4] ɲu(k)	[1/2/3] ʃʋig
[4] Ropa	[4/6] halam	[1/2/3/4] rɔ(k)	[4] tʃar	[1/2/3/4] ɲu(k)	[4] ʃʋik
[5] Chitkul	[5] maʃəro	[5/6/12] kʰai	[5/6] fɔsi	[5/6/12/13] nui	[5/6/12] maĩ
[6] Labrang	[4/6] halam	[5/6/12] kʰai	[5/6] fɔsi	[5/6/12/13] nui	[5/6/12] maĩ
[7] Poo	[7] akʰe	[7/8/9/10/11] nakpo	[7/8/9/10] kampo	[7/8/9/10/11] soma	[7/8/9/11] marbo
[8] Kuno	[8] tʰʋa	[7/8/9/10/11] nakpo	[7/8/9/10] kambo	[7/8/9/10/11] soma	[7/8/9/11] marbo
[9] Nako	[9/10/11] ŋànba	[7/8/9/10/11] nàkpo	[7/8/9/10] kámpo	[7/8/9/10/11] sóma	[7/8/9/11] márʋo
[10] Tabo	[9/10/11] ŋànpá	[7/8/9/10/11] nàkpó	[7/8/9/10] kámpó, kám	[7/8/9/10/11] sómá	[10] máró
[11] Ladakhi	[9/10/11] ŋanpa, rhtsokpo	[7/8/9/10/11] nakpo	[11] skampo	[7/8/9/10/11] soma	[7/8/9/11] marpo
[12] Gahri	[12] mdrei	[5/6/12] kʰəi	[12] kʰʲui	[5/6/12/13] nui	[5/6/12] məi, maĩ
[13] Tinani	[13] sukpo	[13] rəʷki	[13] kɑrki, kɑrkɪ, tʰiŋ	[5/6/12/13] nui	[13] mɑŋgi
[14] Pattani	[14] kʰərab, mazi	[14] roki	[14] kartʃi	[14] kʰərkoi	[14] çei
[15] Byangsi	[15] jaddɛ	[15] ʋamdɛ	[15] tsʰartɛ	[15] nuːdɛ	[15] maŋdɛ
[16] Chaudangsi	[16] jadə	[16] ʋomdə	[16] cʰərtə	[16] nũdə	[16] məŋdə
[17] Bhramu	[17] məsen	[17] ciliŋ	[17] sukʰkʰa	[17] kaʋoi	[17] pʰəija

Table 2. Adjectives: summary

	Sa	Ni	Ka	Ro	Chit	Lab	Po	Ku	Na	Ta	Lad	Ga	Ti	Pa	Bya	Chau
Bhr	0/13 (0%)	0/13 (0%)	0/13 (0%)	0/13 (0%)	0/13 (0%)	0/13 (0%)	0/13 (0%)	0/13 (0%)	0/13 (0%)	0/11 (0%)	0/12 (0%)	0/13 (0%)	0/12 (0%)	0/13 (0%)	0/11 (0%)	0/10 (0%)
Chau	0/14 (0%)	0/14 (0%)	0/14 (0%)	0/14 (0%)	0/14 (0%)	0/14 (0%)	0/14 (0%)	0/14 (0%)	0/14 (0%)	0/13 (0%)	0/13 (0%)	0/12 (0%)	0/13 (0%)	0/14 (0%)	1/12 (8%)	
Bya	0/15 (0%)	0/15 (0%)	0/15 (0%)	0/15 (0%)	0/15 (0%)	0/15 (0%)	0/15 (0%)	0/15 (0%)	0/15 (0%)	0/13 (0%)	0/14 (0%)	0/13 (0%)	0/15 (0%)	0/15 (0%)		
Pa	0/19 (0%)	0/19 (0%)	0/19 (0%)	0/19 (0%)	0/19 (0%)	1/19 (5%)	1/19 (5%)	0/19 (0%)	0/19 (0%)	0/17 (0%)	0/18 (0%)	3/17 (17%)	3/17 (17%)			
Ti	0/17 (0%)	0/17 (0%)	0/17 (0%)	0/17 (0%)	0/17 (0%)	2/17 (11%)	2/17 (11%)	0/17 (0%)	0/17 (0%)	0/15 (0%)	0/16 (0%)	5/15 (33%)				
Ga	0/17 (0%)	0/17 (0%)	0/17 (0%)	0/17 (0%)	0/17 (0%)	4/17 (23%)	5/17 (29%)	0/17 (0%)	1/17 (5%)	0/15 (0%)	0/16 (0%)					
Lad	1/18 (5%)	0/18 (0%)	0/18 (0%)	0/18 (0%)	1/18 (5%)	1/18 (5%)	1/18 (5%)	10/18 (55%)	11/18 (61%)	7/17 (41%)						
Ta	1/17 (5%)	0/17 (0%)	0/17 (0%)	0/17 (0%)	1/17 (5%)	1/17 (5%)	1/17 (5%)	8/17 (47%)	11/17 (64%)							
Na	1/19 (5%)	0/19 (0%)	0/19 (0%)	0/19 (0%)	1/19 (5%)	1/19 (5%)	1/19 (5%)	14/19 (73%)								
Ku	0/19 (0%)	0/19 (0%)	0/19 (0%)	0/19 (0%)	0/19 (0%)	0/19 (0%)	12/19 (63%)									
Po	1/19 (5%)	0/19 (0%)	0/19 (0%)	0/19 (0%)	1/19 (5%)	1/19 (5%)										
Lab	2/19 (10%)	1/19 (5%)	1/19 (5%)	1/19 (5%)	9/19 (47%)											
Chit	2/19 (10%)	1/19 (5%)	1/19 (5%)	2/19 (10%)												
Ro	11/19 (57%)	10/19 (52%)	12/19 (63%)													
Ka	11/19 (57%)	12/19 (63%)														
Ni	14/19 (73%)															

Table 3. All nouns: summary

	Ni	Ka	Ro	Chit	Lab	Po	Ku	Na	Ta	Lad	Ga	Ti	Pa	Bya	Chau	Bhr
Sa	67/87 (77%)	72/88 (81%)	59/88 (67%)	47/88 (53%)	31/88 (35%)	11/88 (12%)	14/87 (16%)	13/87 (14%)	10/84 (11%)	11/85 (12%)	12/76 (15%)	17/84 (20%)	14/80 (17%)	4/70 (5%)	3/55 (5%)	3/54 (5%)
Ni		61/87 (70%)	49/87 (56%)	38/87 (43%)	26/87 (29%)	10/87 (11%)	12/86 (13%)	12/86 (13%)	9/84 (10%)	10/85 (11%)	11/76 (14%)	16/84 (19%)	13/80 (16%)	4/69 (5%)	3/54 (5%)	2/54 (3%)
Ka			58/88 (65%)	44/88 (50%)	29/88 (32%)	10/88 (11%)	13/87 (14%)	12/87 (13%)	10/84 (11%)	10/85 (11%)	12/76 (15%)	14/84 (16%)	13/80 (16%)	4/70 (5%)	3/55 (5%)	3/54 (5%)
Ro				39/88 (44%)	37/88 (42%)	17/88 (19%)	20/87 (22%)	17/87 (19%)	16/84 (19%)	17/85 (20%)	14/76 (18%)	18/84 (21%)	12/80 (15%)	5/70 (7%)	3/55 (5%)	3/54 (5%)
Chit					28/88 (31%)	11/88 (12%)	13/87 (14%)	12/87 (13%)	10/84 (11%)	9/85 (10%)	13/76 (17%)	17/84 (20%)	16/80 (20%)	6/70 (8%)	6/55 (10%)	3/54 (5%)
Lab						22/88 (25%)	25/87 (28%)	23/87 (26%)	20/84 (23%)	18/85 (21%)	14/76 (18%)	20/84 (23%)	15/80 (18%)	6/70 (8%)	4/55 (7%)	4/54 (7%)
Po							57/87 (65%)	62/87 (71%)	39/84 (46%)	36/85 (42%)	12/76 (15%)	16/84 (19%)	9/80 (11%)	7/70 (10%)	5/55 (9%)	3/54 (5%)
Ku								59/87 (67%)	43/84 (51%)	40/84 (47%)	15/75 (20%)	17/83 (20%)	10/79 (12%)	7/69 (10%)	5/54 (9%)	3/53 (5%)
Na									44/84 (52%)	39/84 (46%)	14/75 (18%)	16/83 (19%)	10/79 (12%)	7/69 (10%)	5/54 (9%)	3/53 (5%)
Ta										44/84 (52%)	16/74 (21%)	15/82 (18%)	10/79 (12%)	5/66 (7%)	4/51 (7%)	3/53 (5%)
Lad											16/75 (21%)	18/83 (21%)	10/80 (12%)	4/67 (5%)	4/52 (7%)	3/54 (5%)
Ga												20/75 (26%)	13/70 (18%)	4/59 (6%)	3/46 (6%)	3/48 (6%)
Ti													28/78 (35%)	4/66 (6%)	2/52 (3%)	3/54 (5%)
Pa														4/63 (6%)	3/52 (5%)	3/52 (5%)
Bya															16/48 (33%)	1/42 (2%)
Chau																0/34 (0%)

Table 4. Total basic vocabulary: summary

	Ka	Ro	Chit	Lab	Po	Ku	Na	Ta	Lad	Ga	Ti	Pa	Bya	Chau	Bhr	
Sa	111/154 (72%)	116/155 (74%)	97/155 (62%)	66/152 (43%)	45/153 (29%)	13/154 (8%)	16/150 (10%)	16/155 (10%)	13/134 (9%)	13/135 (9%)	12/127 (9%)	21/143 (14%)	18/125 (14%)	6/113 (5%)	5/102 (4%)	3/96 (3%)	Sa
Ni		103/153 (67%)	88/153 (57%)	56/151 (37%)	39/151 (25%)	11/153 (7%)	14/149 (9%)	14/153 (9%)	11/133 (8%)	11/134 (8%)	11/127 (8%)	20/142 (14%)	16/124 (12%)	5/112 (4%)	4/101 (3%)	2/95 (2%)	Ni
Ka			101/154 (65%)	65/152 (42%)	42/153 (27%)	11/153 (7%)	15/150 (10%)	14/154 (9%)	12/133 (9%)	11/135 (8%)	12/127 (9%)	18/142 (12%)	16/125 (12%)	6/113 (5%)	5/102 (4%)	3/95 (3%)	Ka
Ro				61/151 (40%)	52/152 (34%)	19/153 (12%)	22/149 (14%)	20/154 (12%)	19/133 (14%)	19/134 (14%)	14/126 (11%)	22/142 (15%)	15/125 (12%)	7/113 (6%)	5/102 (4%)	3/95 (3%)	Ro
Chit					45/150 (30%)	14/152 (9%)	16/149 (10%)	16/151 (10%)	14/132 (10%)	12/134 (8%)	18/126 (14%)	23/140 (16%)	20/124 (16%)	8/113 (7%)	9/101 (8%)	4/94 (4%)	Chit
Lab						26/151 (17%)	31/150 (20%)	28/152 (18%)	25/132 (18%)	23/134 (17%)	20/126 (15%)	26/141 (18%)	18/124 (14%)	6/112 (5%)	4/101 (3%)	4/94 (4%)	Lab
Po							98/150 (65%)	105/153 (68%)	64/133 (48%)	58/134 (43%)	13/127 (10%)	18/142 (12%)	12/124 (9%)	7/113 (6%)	6/101 (5%)	5/95 (5%)	Po
Ku								99/150 (66%)	66/131 (50%)	62/132 (46%)	17/125 (13%)	19/139 (13%)	13/122 (10%)	7/111 (6%)	6/99 (6%)	5/92 (5%)	Ku
Na									74/134 (55%)	62/134 (46%)	16/126 (12%)	18/142 (12%)	13/124 (10%)	7/112 (6%)	6/101 (5%)	5/95 (5%)	Na
Ta										63/133 (47%)	17/112 (15%)	17/129 (13%)	13/122 (10%)	5/99 (5%)	5/86 (5%)	5/93 (5%)	Ta
Lad											17/114 (14%)	19/130 (14%)	12/124 (9%)	4/101 (3%)	5/87 (5%)	5/94 (5%)	Lad
Ga												26/123 (21%)	18/106 (16%)	6/98 (6%)	5/86 (5%)	3/80 (3%)	Ga
Ti													38/121 (31%)	6/108 (5%)	4/95 (4%)	3/94 (3%)	Ti
Pa														6/95 (6%)	5/85 (5%)	3/89 (3%)	Pa
Bya															26/88 (29%)	1/71 (1%)	Bya
Chau																0/64 (0%)	Chau

Table 5. 40 most stable Swadesh items: summary

	Sa	Ni	Ka	Ro	Chit	Lab	Po	Ku	Na	Ta	Lad	Ga	Ti	Pa	Bya	Chau
Bhr	1/24 (4%)	1/24 (4%)	1/24 (4%)	1/24 (4%)	1/24 (4%)	1/24 (4%)	2/24 (8%)	2/24 (8%)	2/24 (8%)	2/24 (8%)	2/24 (8%)	2/24 (8%)	1/21 (4%)	1/24 (4%)	2/23 (8%)	0/19 (0%)
Chau	1/19 (5%)	1/19 (5%)	1/19 (5%)	1/19 (5%)	1/19 (5%)	2/19 (10%)	2/19 (10%)	4/19 (21%)	4/19 (21%)	4/19 (21%)	4/19 (21%)	4/19 (21%)	1/18 (5%)	0/19 (0%)	1/19 (5%)	
Bya	1/20 (5%)	1/20 (5%)	1/20 (5%)	1/20 (5%)	2/20 (10%)	2/20 (10%)	3/20 (15%)	3/20 (15%)	3/20 (15%)	3/20 (15%)	3/20 (15%)	3/20 (15%)	2/20 (10%)	1/19 (5%)	5/17 (29%)	
Pa	5/24 (20%)	4/24 (16%)	4/24 (16%)	4/24 (16%)	7/24 (29%)	4/24 (16%)	3/24 (12%)	3/24 (12%)	3/24 (12%)	3/24 (12%)	3/24 (12%)	3/24 (12%)	3/22 (13%)	9/24 (37%)		
Ti	5/25 (20%)	5/25 (20%)	4/25 (16%)	6/25 (24%)	6/25 (24%)	7/25 (28%)	3/25 (12%)	3/25 (12%)	3/25 (12%)	3/25 (12%)	3/25 (12%)	5/22 (22%)				
Ga	3/22 (13%)	3/22 (13%)	3/22 (13%)	4/22 (18%)	4/22 (18%)	5/22 (22%)	3/22 (13%)	3/22 (13%)	3/22 (13%)	4/22 (18%)	2/22 (9%)					
Lad	3/25 (12%)	3/25 (12%)	3/25 (12%)	3/25 (12%)	4/25 (16%)	13/25 (52%)	13/25 (52%)	13/25 (52%)	16/25 (64%)							
Ta	3/25 (12%)	3/25 (12%)	3/25 (12%)	4/25 (16%)	4/25 (16%)	15/25 (60%)	15/25 (60%)	15/25 (60%)								
Na	3/25 (12%)	3/25 (12%)	3/25 (12%)	4/25 (16%)	4/25 (16%)	5/25 (20%)	21/25 (84%)	19/25 (76%)								
Ku	3/25 (12%)	3/25 (12%)	3/25 (12%)	4/25 (16%)	4/25 (16%)	5/25 (20%)	19/25 (76%)									
Po	3/25 (12%)	3/25 (12%)	3/25 (12%)	4/25 (16%)	4/25 (16%)	5/25 (20%)										
Lab	11/25 (44%)	11/25 (44%)	10/25 (40%)	14/25 (56%)	11/25 (44%)											
Chit	11/25 (44%)	11/25 (44%)	9/25 (36%)	10/25 (40%)												
Ro	20/25 (80%)	19/25 (76%)	18/25 (72%)													
Ka	22/25 (88%)	19/25 (76%)														
Ni	20/25 (80%)															

4. Tabo, Gahri, Tinani and Pattani are spoken in the Lahaul-Spiti region in Himachal Pradesh. The degree of similarity among these languages is, however, rather low – very low when it comes to the comparison of Tabo with Gahri, Tinani and Pattani. Among the latter, Gahri and Tinani are more similar to each other (33%) than they are to Pattani (17%). An interesting observation here is the relatively higher degree of similarity which Gahri and Tinani display with Labrang and Chitkul.
5. Next, Byangsi and Chaudangsi – which are spoken in the Uttarakhand region in India, do not show any similarity to any other language. Even the degree of similarity with each other is very low.
6. Similarly, Bhramu, which is spoken in Nepal, does not show any similarity to any of the other investigated languages with regard to its adjectives.

4.2. Nouns

Table 3 provides a summary comparison of all nouns in the basic word list.

1. In this case, too, we find a high degree of similarity in the Sangla group.
2. Interestingly, Chitkul shows a much higher degree of similarity with the Sangla group here (43–53%), than it did concerning adjectives.
3. Labrang shows the highest degree of similarity with Ropa (42%). Generally speaking, it shows higher degree of similarity with the Sangla group (29–42%) than with any other language in this table.
4. As was the case with adjectives, Poo, Kuno, Nàvakat, Tabo and Ladakhi show a higher degree of similarity to one another (42–71%) than they do to any other language in this table.
5. Once again, Gahri, Tinani and Pattani seem to be a rather heterogeneous group, showing a relatively low degree of similarity to any other language. Unlike with the adjectives, Tinani shows more similarity to Pattani (35%) than to Gahri (26%)
6. Lastly, Byangsi, Chaudangsi and Bhramu do not show any similarity to any other language in this table. Byangsi and Chaudangsi show the highest degree of similarity to each other (33%).

4.3. Total basic vocabulary

A similar pattern emerges when we take into consideration the whole basic vocabulary, shown in table 4. Once again, we find that:

1. Sangla, Nichar, Kalpa and Ropa show a high degree of similarity.
2. Labrang and Chitkul show the highest degree of similarity with the Sangla group, although their degree of similarity with the languages of the Sangla group is relatively lower than among those making up the Sangla group. Further, the degree of shared similarity is higher between Chitkul and the Sangla group, than between Labrang and the Sangla group. The degree of similarity between Chitkul and Labrang is not very high.
3. Poo, Nàvakat, Kuno, Tabo and Ladakhi show a relatively higher degree of similarity among each other – higher than to any other languages in this table.
4. Gahri, Tinani and Pattani show a relatively low degree of similarity, either among themselves or to any other language. Tinani and Pattani are closest to each other.
5. The degree of similarity between Byangsi and Chaudangsi is relatively low when the whole basic vocabulary list is taken into account.
6. As expected, the degree of similarity of Brahmu to the other languages is very low.

4.4. Most stable vocabulary items

Swadesh lists are often used in this kind of lexicostatistical investigation. Holman et al (2008) present a reduced – 40-item – Swadesh list, which they claim represents the globally most stable Swadesh items. In table 5 we present the summary statistics based on this reduced Swadesh list, form which 25 items are present in our basic vocabulary list. Again, the Sangla and Nàvakat groups stand out, although generally similarities are higher among all varieties using this set of words. This is to be expected, since this Swadesh subset was designed for the computation of considerably deeper genetic relationships than the ones among these languages. In fact, it is somewhat surprising that the similarity figures are not higher.

5. Conclusion

Based on the observations made here, the following proposal can be made concerning the internal sub-grouping of the Tibeto-Burman languages of the Indian Himalayas examined here:

1. Sangla, Nichar, Kalpa and Ropa should perhaps be treated as part of one sub-group – the Sangla group. The core members of this group mostly, but not always, show at least 50% similarity with the other members of the group.
2. Bhramu – strictly speaking not a language of the Indian Himalayas, but classified as West Himalayish in the Ethnologue – always stands out as distinct. Thus, it should be treated as a distinct sub-group. This finding is consistent with the results of ongoing work by SIL (Christopher P. Wilde, p.c.) and those of Turin (2004), where Bhramu is placed in the same sub-group as Newari.
3. Byangsi and Chaudangsi to a large extent show a higher degree of similarity. Thus, they should be treated as part of the same group.
4. Ladakhi is generally regarded as belonging to the Western sub-branch of the Tibetan (or Tibetic) branch of the Tibeto-Burman language family, and not the West Himalayish sub-branch. As we have seen earlier, Nàvakat, Poo and Kuno which are spoken in the West Himalayish region, consistently show a higher level of similarity with Ladakhi and Tabo. This strongly suggest these languages should be classified as Tibetan rather than West Himalayish.
5. Concerning the status of Chitkul, Labrang and Gahri:
    a. The degree of similarity between Chitkul and Labrang is neither very high nor very low.
    b. Chitkul – much more than Labrang – shows a relatively higher degree of similarity with the Sangla group than with the Nàvakat group.
    c. The status of Labrang is interesting. It does not show much similarity with either the Sangla group or the Nàvakat group
6. Gahri shows a rather low degree of similarity with any of the other West Himalayish languages, and should, at least at this stage, be placed separately.

To conclude, based on the results presented here, the genetic classification of these Tibeto-Burman languages would be as outlined above. The resulting subgrouping is similar – although not identical – to the classification proposed by Nishi (1990), which in turn is based on that of Shafer (1966).[4]

In this paper, we have made a systematic comparison of seventeen Tibeto-Kanauri languages in order to throw some light on the genetic relationships among these underdescribed linguistic systems. The comparison has focused on the lexicon, which was investigated using an automatic, computational and purely quantitative method inspired by modern work on lexicostatistics and dialectometry, combined with traditional linguistic analysis and reasoning.

This approach has helped to provide some answers and in the process proved its worth. Given that one accepts lexicostatistics using Swadesh-style basic vocabulary lists as producing valid results, the refinement of this method that we have presented here seems to be a step in the direction of making this methodology even more useful for teasing out the relationships among closely related language varieties.

Appendix: Basic word list

Below we reproduce the modified Swadesh list used in our investigation. The list contains 157 items (English words serving as sense identifiers). Swadesh list entries are identified with their Swadesh list numbers, and the 40 items identified by Holman et al (2008) as the most stable subset of the Swadesh list are marked by "*" after the Swadesh number.

1	m.grandfather	17	paternal uncle	33	blood/64*
2	m. grandmother	18	paternal aunt	34	bone/65*
3	p.grandfather	19	head/72	35	butter
4	p. grandmother	20	face	36	cat (f; m)
5	wife/40	21	hair (head)/71*	37	child/39
6	mother/42	22	tail/69	38	cloud/160
7	daughter	23	ear/73*	39	copper
8	older sister	24	eye/74*	40	day/178
9	younger sister	25	nose/75*	41	dog/47*
10	husband/41	26	mouth/76	42	egg/67
11	father/43	27	tooth/77*	43	fire/167*
12	son	28	hand/83*	44	food
13	older brother	29	foot/80	45	forest/52
14	younger brother	30	animal/44	46	fruit/54
15	maternal uncle	31	autumn	47	glacier
16	maternal aunt	32	bird/46	48	goat

49 gold
50 grass/60
51 hen
52 iron
53 lamb
54 leaf/56*
55 man (human)/38
56 man (male)/37
57 meat/63
58 milk
59 moon/148
60 mountain/171*
61 night/177*
62 pond; lake
63 rain/151
64 river/152
65 root/57
66 rope/61
67 salt/155
68 seed/55
69 sheep
70 silver
71 sky/162
72 snake/49
73 snow/164
74 spring (season)
75 star/149*
76 stone/156*
77 sugar
78 summer
79 sun/147*
80 tree/51*
81 village
82 water/150*
83 wind/163
84 winter
85 woman/36

86 yak
87 yak (female)
88 year/179
89 bad/186
90 beautiful
91 big/27
92 black/176
93 cold/181
94 dry/195
95 good/185
96 green/173
97 long/28
98 new/183*
99 old/184
100 red/172
101 round/190
102 small/32
103 straight/189
104 wet/194
105 warm/180
106 white/175
107 yellow/174
108 today
109 yesterday
110 1 day before y.
111 2 days before y.
112 3 days before y.
113 4 days before y.
114 tomorrow
115 1 day after t.
116 2 days after t.
117 3 days after t.
118 4 days after t.
119 one/22*
120 two/23*
121 three/24*
122 four/25

123 five/26
124 six
125 seven
126 eight
127 nine
128 ten
129 twenty
130 thirty
131 thirty-one
132 forty
133 forty-one
134 fifty
135 sixty
136 seventy
137 seventy-one
138 eighty
139 ninety
140 one hundred
141 five hundred
142 one thousand
143 one thousand one
144 who/11
145 what/12
146 where/13
147 when/14
148 how/15
149 1sg/1*
150 2sg +hon/2
151 2sg −hon/2*
152 3sg/3
153 1pl incl/4*
154 1pl excl/4
155 2pl +hon/5
156 2pl −hon/5
157 3pl/6

Carving Tibeto-Kanauri by its joints 195

Notes

1. We would like to thank Anju Saxena's language consultants without whose help this study would have never been possible. We would like to thank especially Mrs. Santosh Negi and Mr. Padam Sagar for their generosity and for their help in practical matters. The research reported on here was supported by the Swedish Research Council (the project *Digital areal linguistics: a lexical view of the Himalayan microarea*/VR dnr 2009–1448).
2. In contrast to most other current classifications, LaPolla (2003) does not recognize Tibeto-Kanauri as a valid genealogical unit, but instead places Tibetic and West Himalayish rather far apart in the Tibeto-Burman family tree (under the higher-level units Bodic and Rung, respectively). This is relevant to our investigation insofar as all the varieties investigated here belong to the traditionally recognized Tibeto-Kanauri (or Tibeto-Kinnauri) lower-level branch of Tibeto-Burman. This is the classification used in the *Ethnologue*, among others. Matisoff (2000) also does not recognize a Tibeto-Kanauri branch, but simply places Tibetic and "the westernmost TB languages of Himachal Pradesh" (Matisoff 2000: 351) together under the higher-order grouping Himalayish (which also encompasses some other TB "linguistic nuclei" of the Himalayan area), without assigning any further internal structure to it. What we are attempting here is to get a clearer picture of the relationships among the languages traditionally classified as Tibeto-Kanauri. However, any results about the relative placements of these varieties with respect to one another must be interpretable within LaPolla's or Matisoff's proposed genealogies, too, if the method is valid.
3. The map indicates the villages where these languages are spoken. A few varieties are spoken over a larger area. Ladakhi, for which we have chosen the Leh variety, is used as a lingua franca in Ladakh, and thus not restricted only to Leh. The same is also the case with Pattani. In other cases, for example, Nàvakat, Kuno and Ropa, the varieties are restricted to the villages indicated in the map (Nàvakat in the Nako village, and the Kuno and Ropa varieties in the villages with the same names). For data from secondary sources (e.g., for Chaudangsi and Byangsi) we indicate the locations mentioned in these sources (Krishan 2001; Sharma 2001). The Bhramu data is from the STEDT online database, where the location of data collection is not mentioned.
4. This subgrouping is in itself not in conflict with that of LaPolla (2003), where Tibeto-Kanauri is not a valid genealogical unit (see footnote 2). On the other hand, the overall results of the comparison are not completely consonant with LaPolla's proposal, since then we would have expected considerably less similarity to obtain between West Himalayish and Tibetic than inside West Himalayish itself, but this is not what we actually find. On the contrary, Sangla Kinnauri (West Himalayish) is generally closer to Ladakhi (Tibetic) than to, e.g., Chaudangsi or Bhramu (both West Himalayish). This matter will have to be left for future research.

References

Fleck, David W. and Robert S. Voss
    2006   On the origin and cultural significance of unusually large synonym sets in some Panoan languages of western Amazonia. *Anthropological Linguistics* 48 (4): 335–368.

Grace, George W.
    1961   Lexicostatistical comparison of six eastern Austronesian languages. *Anthropological Linguistics* 3 (9): 1–22.

Handel, Zev
    2008   What is Sino-Tibetan? Snapshot of a field and a language family in flux. *Language and Linguistics Compass* 2 (3): 422–441.

Holman, Eric. W., Søren Wichmann, Cecil H. Brown, Viveka Velupillai, André Müller, and Dik Bakker
    2008   Explorations in automated lexicostatistics. *Folia Linguistica* 42 (2): 331–354.

Krishan, Shree
    2001   A sketch of Chaudangsi grammar. In Nagano and LaPolla 2001, 401–448.

LaPolla, Randy J.
    2003   Overview of Sino-Tibetan morphosyntax. In *The Sino-Tibetan Languages*, Graham Thurgood, and Randy J. LaPolla (eds.), 22–42. London: Routledge.

Lewis, M. Paul (ed.)
    2009   *Ethnologue: Languages of the World*, 16th edition. Dallas: SIL International. Online version: <http://www.ethnologue.com/>.

Matisoff, James
    2000   On the uselessness of glottochronology for the subgrouping of Tibeto-Burman. In *Time Depth in Historical Linguistics*, Colin Renfrew, April McMahon, and Larry Trask (eds.), 333–371. Cambridge: McDonald Institute for Archaeological Research.

McMahon, April, Paul Heggarty, Robert McMahon, and Warren Maguire
    2007   The sound patterns of Englishes: Representing phonetic similarity. *English Language and Linguistics* 11 (1): 113–142.

Nagano, Yasuhiko and Randy LaPolla (eds.)
    2001   *A Linguistic Approach to Zhangzhung and Related Languages in the Indian Himalayas*. (Senri Ethnological reports 19). Osaka: National Museum of Ethnology.

Nerbonne, John and Wilbert Heeringa
    2009   Measuring dialect differences. In *Language and Space: Theories and Methods*, Jürgen Erich Schmidt, and Peter Auer (eds.), 550–567. Berlin/New York: Mouton De Gruyter.

Nishi, Yoshio
    1990   The distribution and classification of Himalayan languages (Part I). *Kokuritsu minzokugaku hakubutsukan kenkyu hokoku*. (Suita: Kokuritsu minzokugaku hakubutsukan), 15 (1): 265–337. (In Japanese)

Saxena, Anju
    2004   Linguistic synchrony and diachrony on the roof of the world – The study of Himalayan languages. In *Himalayan Languages: Past and Present*, Anju Saxena (ed.), 3–29. Berlin/New York: Mouton de Gruyter.

Saxena, Anju
    2011   Towards empirical classification of Kinnauri varieties. *Proceedings of Conference on Language Documentation & Linguistic Theory 3*, 15–25. School of Oriental and African Studies, University of London.

Saxena, Anju and Lars Borin
    2011   Dialect classification in the Himalayas: a computational approach. *NODALIDA 2011 Conference Proceedings*, 307–310. Riga: NEALT.

Shafer, Robert
    1966   *Introduction to Sino-Tibetan (Part 1)*. Wiesbaden: Otto Harrassowitz.

Sharma, Suhnu Ram
    2001   A sketch of Byangsi grammar. In Nagano and LaPolla 2001, 271–341.

Swadesh, Morris
    1955   Towards greater accuracy in lexicostatistic dating. *International Journal of American Linguistics* 21 (2): 121–137.

Turin, Mark
    2004   Newar-Thangmi lexical correspondences and the linguistic classification of Thangmi. *Journal of Asian and African Studies* 68: 97–120.

The effect of linguistic distance across Indo-European mother tongues on learning Dutch as a second language

Job Schepens, Frans van der Slik and Roeland van Hout

1. Introduction[1]

It is a commonplace to state that learning a mother tongue (L1) is successful in most circumstances, but that learning a second language (L2) returns a less evident result. L2 learners diverge widely in their degree of success in acquiring a new language. The central question here is whether linguistic distance measures between the L1 and L2 are suitable instruments to predict the degree of success in learning an L2. The assumption is that the larger the distance the harder it is to learn another language. Establishing a clear relationship between L2 learning and linguistic distance gives strong support to external validity of the concept of linguistic distance.

Where do language similarities and dissimilarities come from? Looking back in history, one can see how languages diverge and converge. The Austronesian expansion of settlers to unexplored Polynesian islands established divergence step by step, causing new innovations to appear in a clear tree-like fashion (Gray and Jordan 2000). In contrast, in the Russian Empire, language convergence by standardization was a crucial tool for excluding other languages and language variation (Ostler 2003).

Processes of divergence and convergence have led to a complex distribution of many languages over many countries in the world. However, many countries explicitly opt for one single standard language in their language policy. As a consequence of massive migration waves, large groups of adults need to learn the (standard) language of the country of immigration. Tests and exams have been developed to test their L2 proficiency levels. In the Netherlands, for example, most immigrants have to pass the official state exam called "Dutch as a second language".

In a previous study, a substantial amount of between mother tongue variance was explained with a measure of linguistic distance between the L1 and L2 on the basis of 11 West-European languages (Van der Slik 2010). In the present study, we want to deepen our understanding of how barriers in learning an L2 are related to linguistic distances. We do so by expanding the set of L1 languages to all Indo-European languages (35 in our database), spoken in different countries (89 in our database), and by testing two different linguistic distance measures.

Using multilevel models, we decomposed variance in proficiency scores across adult learners of Dutch as a second language into individual (learner characteristics) and contextual (group characteristics) components. The linguistic distance between the mother tongue and the second language (L2) of a learner is a contextual effect that varies according to the degree of difference between a learner's mother tongue and the L2. We have analysed L2 learners' state exams for Dutch speaking proficiency to explain variance in L2 proficiency scores on the basis of two different linguistic distance techniques: the traditional expert-based, historical-comparative method as used in Gray and Atkinson (2003), and the automatic distance based method as applied in the ASJP project (Brown et al. 2005).

We used data from more than 33,000 examinees, speaking 35 different Indo-European languages, originating from 89 different countries. Our main aim was to partial out the impact of linguistic distance on proficiency in speaking Dutch as an L2. The multilevel models that we used incorporated one confounding variable on the contextual level: the quality of the educational system, and five confounding variables on the individual level: gender, educational level, length of residence, age of arrival in the Netherlands, and proficiency in an additional language. We were able to identify robust L1 distance effects, for both of the distance measures we used, and we compared them to the predicted scores obtained in our multilevel analysis. Our conclusion is that differences in second language learning proficiency offer an excellent testing ground not only for validating the concept of linguistic distance itself, but also for comparing the performances of different types of linguistic distance.

The remainder of this introductory section contains a discussion of current approaches in measuring linguistic distances, the effects of linguistic distance on L2 learning, and the approach taken in the present study.

1.1. Approaches to measuring linguistic distance

Recent discoveries in the dynamics of linguistic change disclose lineage dependent structural relationships in the evolution of word order in three large language families (Dunn et al. 2011). By reconstructing language family trees, it was shown that certain states of development are more likely given a previous state of development in a particular language family. The study of Dunn et al. is a recent example of a quantitative diachronic approach in which tree-like phylogenetic models are applied to language variation and change. Phylogenetic analysis uses the finding that linguistic data contain deep historic signals that can be used to date language branching (Crystal 1987).

The treelike model of language evolution can be inferred and reconstructed from lexical (Gray and Atkinson 2003), (morpho-) syntactic/structural (Dunn et al. 2005), or phonological data (Atkinson 2011). Each of these three data types has its own limitations. The lexicostatistical approach, based on the comparative method to estimate cognacy, is an early method for inferring language relatedness; the structural and phonological approaches are fairly recent. Linguistic comparison on the basis of each of these different data types may produce different linguistic distance measures. In this paper we will apply lexical distance measures, although in the near future we intend to expand our research to the phonological and (morpho-) syntactical domains of linguistic distance.

The dominant lexical distance measures are based on the percentage of shared cognates between languages. Cognates are words that historically relate to the same word in a common ancestor language. Cognates can share form and meaning, just like borrowings and accidental form resemblances, which do not have a shared origin. Cognacy can be qualitatively coded, as in the comparative method (Swadesh 1952; Dyen Kruskal, and Black 1992), or as a quantified degree of distance from one form to another (Kessler 1995; Heeringa et al. 2006; McMahon and McMahon 2005). The distance-based method is based on the observation that cognates tend to share their form across languages, although not always in identical form. In the distance based method, string distances between two word forms can be automatically simulated. To exclude borrowing effects on measuring distance as much as possible, both the comparative method and the distance-based method are usually applied to Swadesh lists, (or subsets of Swadesh lists; Brown et al. 2008; Holman et al. 2008), which should sample from basic vocabulary. The percentage of shared cognates, or the average distance between words on the list, generalizes to a measure of linguistic distance between languages.

We used the linguistic distances found in two lexicostatistical studies. The first study (Gray and Atkinson 2003) determined shared cognates on historical-comparative grounds in a binary way, the second study (Holman et al 2008) determined the degree of cognacy of word pairs by computing string distances. Both studies carried out a phylogenetic analysis in order to retrieve the optimal tree-like structure from the distances obtained. In this paper, we refer to the measurements of Gray and Atkinson (2003) as G&A, and to measurements described in Brown et al. (2008) and Holman et al. (2008) as ASJP (the name of the project: the Automated Similarity Judgment Program).

The historical-comparative method entails a judgment process carried out by experts who are able to identify how sounds are preserved or have changed over time. Gray and Atkinson (2003) used expert cognacy judgments from Dyen, Kruskal, and Black (1992) and applied a phylogenetic analysis while imposing certain time-constraints on the tree-like structure. They retrieved the historical signals proportional to evolutionary change, including dates of linguistic innovations.

The similarity measures from the ASJP were computed automatically using a distance based method (Brown et al. 2008). For the distances used in this paper, we used ASJP database version 13 (Wichmann et al. 2011) and software from Holman (2010, 2011) which computes normalized Levenshtein distance measures. Wichmann et al. (2010) evaluated the normalization of Levenshtein distances by word length and average chance similarity.

ASJP-based linguistic distances can either be extracted as the average normalized string edit distance between the Swadesh lists of two languages, or as branch lengths from the resulting phylogenetic tree (the correlation between the two distances is .986). The normalized string edit distance is the Levenshtein distance measure normalized by dividing it by its theoretical maximum (length of longest word). In ASJP, it is additionally corrected for chance similarity by dividing it by the average distance of words not referring to the same concept in that language pair. The measure was developed to be able to distinguish between related and unrelated language pairs. The method and results section describe the differences between the automatic method and the expert-based method after applying them to the Indo-European languages from our dataset.

1.2. Second language learning effects of linguistic distances

The best known predictor for transfer in second language acquisition is the degree of congruence between the source language (L1) and the recipient language (L2) (Jarvis and Pavlenko 2008: 176; Kellerman 1979). This constraint has been labelled "language distance", "typological proximity", "psychotypology" (perceived proximity), or "cross-linguistic similarity". The effect of the mother tongue on second language learning was amply discussed within Contrastive Analysis (Lado 1957; Weinreich 1953; Odlin 1989), but this method was not developed to determine or calculate linguistic distances.

The empirically based model proposed by Chiswick and Miller (1995, 1996, 1999, 2007) poses that language proficiency scores result from the interaction between incentives (motivation, money, labour), exposure (time, lessons), and capacity (education, talent, language background). Recent immigrant studies (Chiswick and Miller 2005; Van Tubergen and Kalmijn 2009) have found support for this model.

An important part of capacity is the effect of linguistic distance from one's mother tongue to a destination language (Espenshade and Fu 1997). Recently, the L2 effect was modelled with multilevel models by incorporating linguistic distance from learner's mother tongues to Dutch on a contextual level (Van der Slik 2010), using linguistic distance measures from McMahon and McMahon (2005). The effect of linguistic distance on second language proficiency of immigrants has been incorporated in only a few other studies, although mostly in a reverse way. In such a reverse approach, immigrant proficiency scores are explained by incorporating measures based on the ease or difficulty American emigrants experience in learning a specific language (Chiswick and Miller 1999, 2005a, 2005b; Van Tubergen and Kalmijn 2009). Such empirically determined differences in second language learning were also used to infer which typological features may be involved in second language leaning (see Cysouw's contribution, page 57 ff. in this volume). This approach, in which the difficulty of learning a foreign language is accounted for is problematic for various reasons. Most importantly, motivation among emigrants is expected to differ for different languages. A measure of linguistic distance from one's mother tongue to Dutch does not suffer from these impairments.

We know of one recent study that relates immigrant's proficiency scores to a quantified measure of linguistic distance (Isphording and Otten 2011) by assuming that linguistic distance varies across migrants coming to Germany. However, we argue that an effect of linguistic distance has to be explained across mother tongues. Neglecting this hierarchical structure leads to an underestimation of standard errors and hence to a potential unjustified rejection of null hypotheses (Snijders and Bosker 1999).

Most sociological and economic studies on language proficiency measure proficiency using self-report. According to Charette and Meng (1994) and Finnie and Meng (2005), this is not a valid way of measuring language proficiency as speakers tend to overestimate or underestimate their proficiency. Immigrants may evaluate their skills relative to those of other immigrants rather than native-level proficiency. Formal assessment by language tests overcomes these shortcomings of self-reports.

In our model, we incorporated quantified linguistic distance measures (G&A, ASJP) to explain the variance in scores on the state exam "Dutch as a Second Language". These measures may explain part of the variation in individual proficiency levels, together with other predictors. Overlap between linguistic and empirical measures may show why a high level of proficiency in Dutch is more easily attainable for some learners than for others on the basis of linguistic differences. In this way, linguistic distance could turn out to be an important but underspecified contextual factor in understanding learning differences in second language acquisition.

Empirical measures of linguistic distance need to take into account other contextual and individual differences that may affect performance on tests of L2 proficiency. This implies that a distinction has to be made between contextual effects such as linguistic distance and quality of schooling in the country of origin on the one hand, and individual effects such as length of residence on the other. Given the many multilingual countries in the world, identifying the effect of linguistic distance implies the necessity of separating on the contextual level the effect of the L1–L2 distance from country effects. For example, the country's estimated schooling quality for immigrants speaking Kurdish as their mother tongue can be the schooling quality of Turkey, Iraq, or of a number of other countries. Beenstock, Chiswick, and Repetto (2000) also made a distinction between languages and country of origin, as they also tested linguistic distance by separating it from national characteristics.

1.3. Present study

In a previous study on the Dutch state exam results, Van der Slik (2010) traced back the overall variation in oral and written proficiency in Dutch to a cognate (McMahon and McMahon 2005) and a genetic (Cavalli-Sforza et al. 1994) measure to establish linguistic distances from eleven Western European languages to Dutch. The genetic linguistic distance, based on genetic differences between populations, explained less variance in language proficiency as compared to the cognate measure of linguistic distance.

In the present study we aim to extend the previous study in several ways. First, we apply two distance measures, the traditional historical-comparative method (G&A) and the more recent gradual, automated measure (ASJP). These two methods allowed us to expand the number of L1 languages from 11 to 35 Indo-European languages in our analyses. We took a larger list of mother tongues to show that a linguistic distance based model is generally applicable to explain second language proficiency in speakers with different mother tongues.

The fact that the Indo-European language family is well-studied and that linguistic distance measures are relatively readily available for this language family is a persuasive argument to include all IE languages present in our dataset. This selection resulted in 35 different languages with speakers from 89 different countries.

We analysed test scores of more than 33,000 learners that took part in the Dutch language exam and we used exam scores from 15 years of immigrant history (1995–2010).

At the individual level of the learner, we used the model of language proficiency used by Chiswick and Miller to distinguish between indicators of capacity (measured by gender, years of daily education), exposure (measured by age of arrival, length of residence), and incentives. Unfortunately, we had no measures on incentives at our disposal. Effects of capacity, exposure, and incentives may differ across learners according to other individual and contextual characteristics. For example, it is has been argued that less memory capacity is available for language learning at a higher age (Ullman 2005). Therefore, learning a more distant target language might be more problematic for older learners, as more cognitive capacity is required than for learning a more similar language. The full disentanglement of such interaction effects is not the focus of this study, but we do hypothesize a pervasive presence of linguistic distance effects in different processes involved in language learning.

Language and country characteristics refer to distinct but related constructs at different contextual levels. Linguistic distance is part of the construct language characteristics. Given that languages are different, a quantified distance measure might explain effects of linguistic differences. Country of origin characteristics may include educational quality amongst others. Given that countries have organized their educational systems in quite different ways, we expect effects of quality of education on second language learning as well. Educational quality is part of the construct country characteristics. We will focus on oral proficiency as the dependent variable.

2. Methods

We analysed test scores of Dutch language proficiency from the State Examination Board of Dutch as a Second Language (NT2), which is based on the Common European Framework of Reference for Languages. The NT2 exam scores were kept comparable over a time period of 16 years (1995 – 2010), with different spacing and structuring of tests each year, using an item response theory model. A proficiency level of 500 or more in all four different proficiency components (reading, writing, listening, speaking) determined exam success. 77.7% of all examinees in our dataset passed the exam at their first attempt. Participants were given the opportunity to register for as many exams as needed to pass all four components, but we took only test scores of first attempts. Participants were given the choice of taking exams specially tailored towards higher education (called STEX II; required for admittance to a Dutch university) or of taking exams for vocational training (called STEX I). Only scores on the STEX II exam were used in this study.

2.1. Sample

We selected all Indo-European languages with more than 30 speakers in our database in order to have a sufficient number to include context characteristics. The number of languages was 35, with 945 speakers per language on average ($SD=1260$). The selected languages were spoken in 89 different countries (at least 20 speakers per language per country, $Mean=376$, $SD=735$). Combining languages and countries resulted in 119 groups, see the appendix. The sample included test scores of 33,066 immigrants with an Indo-European mother tongue over a time frame of 16 years (1995 to 2010). 73% of the participants were women. We only included participants who answered a question on years of daily education in the questionnaire that was given to participants, prior to the start of the exam.

2.2. Dependent variable

Examinees had to perform on different speaking tasks for 30 minutes. Performance was judged according to a formal judgment model on content, correctness, wording, pronunciation, pace, vocabulary, register, coherence, and word order, amongst others. Both the test and a formal judging scheme were jointly developed by two Dutch test battery development institutes. A more detailed discussion of the language test can be found in Van der Slik (2010).

The exams took place at specific exam dates. Until 2005, there were four exam sessions a year, while from 2005 onwards there were 30 sessions per year. To pass the full STEX II exam, participants had to complete tests of listening, reading, speaking, and writing. Participants could choose to do different exams at different exam dates; therefore measurement points are generally not comparable across individuals. Furthermore, some individuals only participated in one, two, or three out of the four exams. Generally, doing the exams required a considerable amount of effort from the learner, both in training, as well as in arranging the different sessions for the four tests.

2.3. Contextual characteristics

We defined the contextual level not only by language but also by country of origin in order to capture the intertwining of language and country characteristics and their cross-classifications.

For linguistic distance as a contextual variable, we computed the distance from the mother tongue of the L2 learners to Dutch. We did so by extracting branch lengths from the phylogenetic trees of Gray and Atkinson (2003) and ASJP (2005) with R (making use of the ape package; Paradis, Claude, and Strimmer 2004) and dedicated ASJP software (see below). In the phylogenetic tree of Gray and Atkinson, branch lengths are based on expert accounts of character substitutions in 200 item word lists, following the comparative method. In the case of language evolution, a character substitution refers to the inferred changes in cognacy status of a word on the Swadesh list. We used two phylogenetic trees in which the length of a branch indicates the amount of evolutionary change between two nodes. A node can either be a leaf of the tree, which is a language as it currently is, or a shared common ancestor between two leaves. The amount of evolutionary change can be considered as a product of time between two nodes and the speed of evolutionary change between those nodes. The sum of branch lengths joining one language to the other (via the most recent common ancestor) represents the amount of evolutionary change between two languages.

We applied software developed by Holman (2010, 2011) and Huff (2010) to the latest version of the ASJP Database (version 13; Wichmann et al. 2011) in order to compute ASJP branch lengths. ASJP measures were extracted for all 35 languages. G&A measures were extracted for 30 languages because they were not available for Kurdish, Bosnian, Pashto, Urdu, and Norwegian. The missing scores were imputed using expectation maximization predicted from ASJP measures. Imputing the missing G&A distances had hardly any influence on their mutual dependency.

Figure 1 shows a scatter plot with both linguistic distance measures on the axes. It shows that differences between distances from Romance, Slavic, or Baltic languages to Dutch are fairly small; hence the graph contains a

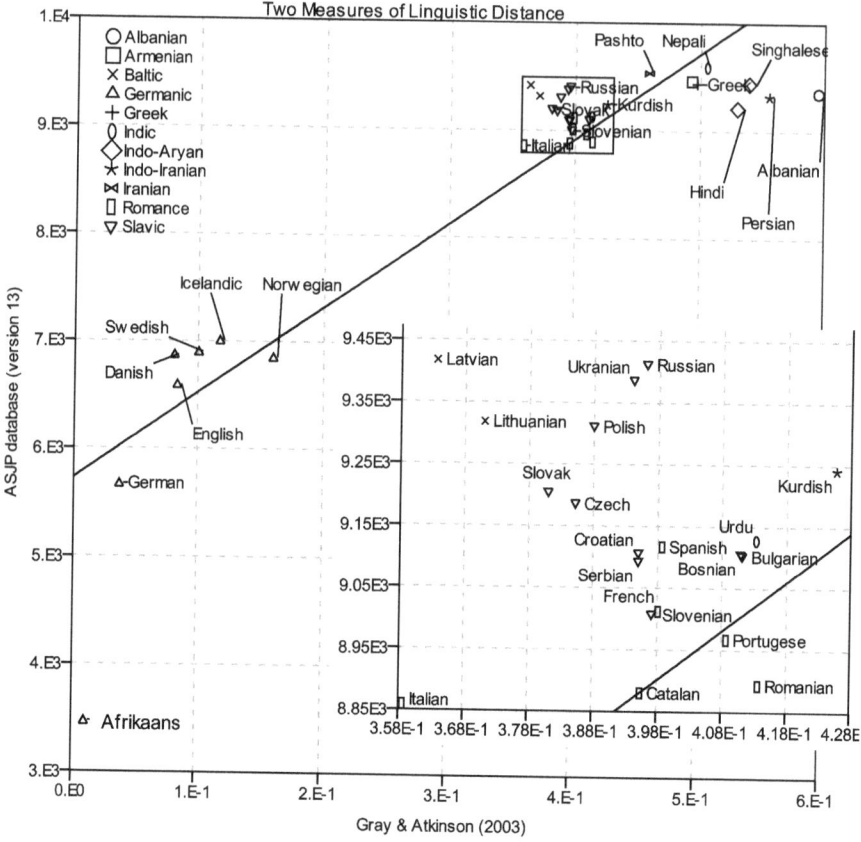

Figure 1. Scatterplot (with a linear regression line) of the two measures of linguistic distance from 34 Indo-European languages to Dutch. Subfamilies are distinguished by using different symbols.

part that zooms in there. The correlation of ASJP with G&A was .90, see figure 1. In terms of phylogenetic differences between both linguistic distance measures, we see that in G&A, the distance between Germanic and non-Germanic languages is 83% of the average distance from non-Germanic languages to Dutch, whereas in ASJP it is 33%. In G&A, the distance from Germanic languages to Dutch is 16% of the average distance from non-Germanic languages to Dutch, whereas in ASJP, it is 67%. In other words, the distance from Germanic languages to Dutch relative to the distance from all other IE languages to Dutch is 2.5 times higher in ASJP than in G&A. Also, we see that the distance between Germanic and other IE languages relative to distances from other IE languages to Dutch is more than 4 times higher in

G&A than in ASJP. Although the correlation between the two measures is high, the underlying deviations from the means differ for relative distances between individual languages as well as between genera. As our results show below, the differences between ASJP and G&A have consequences for the performance of both measures in our regression analyses.

The second contextual level is country of birth. We extracted educational difference measures from the World Bank database. We used gross secondary school enrolment (available for all selected countries) as predictor of educational quality. This variable measures the ratio of total enrolment into secondary education. Secondary education is part of the basic education program that begins with primary education. It offers subject and skill-oriented instruction from specialized teachers. Where available, data from 2006 was used. When 2006 data was not available, earlier data was used. For the former Soviet Union and Yugoslavia, estimates of the current countries were used as based on each learner's mother tongue. Schooling quality correlated -.17 with G&A and -.21 with ASJP.

2.4. Individual characteristics

With respect to the capacity of the learner, we added gender, years of daily education, and a binary indicator whether or not the examinee had already mastered an additional language beforehand. Years of daily education was measured by asking the examinees, prior to taking the exam, to estimate the number of years that they received daytime education. We measured this variable in steps of 5 years. The mean years of daily education was about 13 years. For a more detailed discussion of the variables added, see Van der Slik (2010). Besides adding gender and years of daily education, we added age of arrival and length of residence as measures of exposure.

2.5. Description of the sample

The temporary increases and decreases of specific groups of examinees taking the state exam tend to overlap with historical events, such as the admission of Poland to the European Union and sharpened rules for marriage across EU borders. The five largest language groups represent almost half of the examinees in our dataset (53.3%). The other language group sizes decrease in a logarithmical fashion.

Most of the sample's learner characteristics, such as mean speaking proficiency, were somewhat lower than those in Van der Slik (2010), as we included also non-Western European countries. Average gross enrolment rate and number of countries with a liberal democracy decreased with respect to the larger data set used here.

2.6. Analyses

We first constructed a multilevel model with migrants cross-classified by languages and countries with no predictors added. An analysis of the languages included in our study showed that country characteristics do not necessarily overlap with language characteristics and vice versa. Table 1 exemplifies the Southwest Asian situation in which languages and countries are not uniquely mapped.

Table 1. Cross classification of mother tongue by country of birth in Southwest Asian immigrants. Numbers are based on our dataset. Cells with less than 20 examinees were excluded from the analyses (i.e. reset to zero).

	Kurdish	Farsi	Armenian	Pashto
Iraq	738	0	71	0
Iran	91	2063	45	0
Armenia	0	0	109	0
Afghanistan	0	1252	0	274

To measure the effect parameters of the various determinants we had identified, we added fixed effects to the model step by step. First, the learner characteristics were added to the null model as a baseline model. Then, the contextual determinants were added one by one. Improvement in fit was accepted only when an addition of a new predictor resulted in an improvement of fit of at least a chi-square of 3.84 at p=.05 against 1 degree of freedom on the -2 log-likelihood ratio (-2LL). We will call this the *deviance* between the old and new model. Only when the deviance of the newer model was significantly lower than the deviance of the older model, we checked the direction and size of the individual and contextual effects.

Following Hox (2002) and Heck, Thomas, and Tabata (2010), a cross-classified model of variance components between languages, between countries, and within a language and country together, can be modelled as follows:

$$Y_{i(jk)} = X_{i(jk)} \beta_{0(jk)} + \varepsilon_{i(jk)},$$

where $Y_{i(jk)}$ is the proficiency of learner i within the cross-classification of languages j and countries k; $\beta_{0(jk)}$ is the intercept (overall mean proficiency) of learners for language j in a country k; the residual $\varepsilon_{i(jk)}$ is the deviation of learner ijk's proficiency from the language j in country k mean. The parentheses indicate that classifications are grouped together at the same level. The model assumes equal variance at the learner level, but still allows predictors to cross-level interact with fixed or random effects at the contextual level 2. Furthermore, the model assumes that proficiency varies independently across languages and countries.

The level 2 null model is:

$$\beta_{0(jk)} = \gamma_{00} + u_{0j} + v_{0k},$$

where γ_{00} is the grand mean proficiency of all learners; u_{0j} is the residual error for language j (the contribution of language j averaged over all countries), and v_{0k} is the residual error for country k (the contribution of country k averaged over all languages).

The application of this null model to the speaking proficiency scores results in three variance components, one for each random effect and one for residual variance. The proportion of variance that is due to differences between languages and countries can be estimated with a measure of the dependency between individual learners, called the intra-class correlation.

The between language differences can be estimated by:

$$\frac{\sigma^2_{language}}{\sigma^2_{language} + \sigma^2_{country} + \sigma^2_{\varepsilon}},$$

where the squared sigmas represent the variance components. The measure indicates that 10.6% of the variation in proficiency scores is across languages and 14.2% is across countries. Summing these up (see e.g. Goldstein, 2011), we observe that 24.8% of the total variance can be attributed to country and language as characteristics of groups of learners. Accordingly, the remaining variance at the individual level was estimated at 75.2% of the total variance in proficiency scores (these percentages are underlined in table 2).

In the next section, we will try to explain the reported variance between languages (10.6%). For this purpose, we add fixed level 1 and level 2 explanatory variables to the cross-classified design of languages by countries. The null-model coefficient $\beta_{0(jk)}$ gradually becomes a vector of fixed part coefficients by the addition of more variables to the variable design matrix $X_{i(jk)}$.

Adding one predictor results in:

$$X_{i(jk)}\beta = \beta_0 + \beta_1 x_{1i(jk)} + u_{0j} + v_{0k}$$

where $\beta_1 x_{1i(jk)}$ is the fixed slope defined by a parameter estimate of a predictor variable.

3. Results

In this section, we specify the characteristics of the cross-classified multi-level models that we constructed with learner data cross-classified across home countries and mother tongues. The results show that learner and contextual determinants explain part of the variance in speaking proficiency levels within and between groups.[2] First, we report measures of fit resulting from the addition of a number of fixed predictors to the null model. Second, we report how level 1 and level 2 fixed predictors interact. Third, we compute predicted scores based on fitted parameters and compute the correlation of observed scores with predicted scores instead of raw linguistic distance measures. Fourth, we compare parameter settings for G&A with parameter settings for ASJP.

Table 2 shows how the linguistic distance measures correlated with observed speaking proficiency scores at the individual level, the language level, and at the cross-classified level of language by country. From this table it can already be inferred that speaking proficiency is strongly related to linguistic distance.

Table 2. Correlations of lexical distance measures and speaking proficiency, at the cross-classified level of mother tongues and countries of birth (Co x L1), at the country of birth level (Co), at the mother tongue level (L1), or at the individual learner level (In). N gives the number of cases at the level investigated.

	G&A (L1)	ASJP (L1)	Schooling (Co)	N
Speaking (Co x L1)	–.49	–.49	.67	119
Speaking (L1)	–.77	–.66		35
Speaking (Co)			.66	89
Speaking (In)	–.42	–.40	.32	33,066

Note: All correlations were significant at the .01 level or higher (2-tailed)

3.1. Estimated models

Adding individual determinants resulted in a baseline model that explained part of the variance observed in the null model, as can be seen in table 3. Adding gender, age of arrival, length of residence, years of daily education, and command of an additional language reduced the unexplained variance observed in the null model by 4.3% at the individual level, 3.1% between language variance, and 9.8% between country variance. The deviance measure indicated that the model for speaking fitted better to the data than the null model (a decrease of 1,435.5 in the deviance score, with five parameters added).

Adding contextual determinants resulted in a model that explained most of the remaining contextual variance observed in the baseline model. With respect to country level characteristics, most variance was explained using the World Bank measures of gross secondary school enrolment. The C Model (Country Model) fitted better to the data than the Baseline Model (the −2 log likelihood ratio decreased with 54.5 points against one degree of freedom).

After addition of language level characteristics to the country model, we observed significant effects for both measures of linguistic distance. Models at this step contain country (C) and mother tongue characteristics (C+T Models). Both C+T models fitted better to the data than the C Model, see table 3, because -2log-likelihood ratios decreased with 17.6 (ASJP) points and 26.6 (G&A). Both reductions are significant against 1 degree of freedom ($p<0.05\%$). Because the resulting -2loglikelihood is lower for G&A, we conclude that the G&A model fits better to the data (the critical value for a significant difference is 3.84). The percentage of explained between-language variance rose from 25.3% to 63.7% (ASJP) and to 75.1% (G&A). These differences in explained variance indicated that the G&A based model leaves less variance in the data unexplained.[3]

A multilevel model can allow for the effect of a learner characteristic to vary randomly across languages and countries. Because we are interested in establishing a robust analysis of between-language variation, it is informative to assess whether learner characteristics interact with contextual level characteristics. In this case, we derived from our hypothesis that linguistic distance may enhance the negative effects of age of arrival and length of residence. Hence, we allowed these individual characteristics to interact in a fixed way with the contextual effect of linguistic distance.

We also tested robustness by incorporating a fixed interaction effect between schooling quality and education length, as it is likely that a lower education quality lowers the positive effect of a longer education.

Table 3. Multilevel model parameter estimations for measures of Dutch speaking proficiency (standard errors in parentheses) per mother tongue and country of birth.

	Null Model	Baseline Model	C Model	C+T Model (ASJP)	C+T + I*C/T Model (ASJP)	C+T Model (G&A)	C+T + I * C/T Model (G&A)
Level 1, learner effects (Baseline Model)							
Intercept	522.42³ (2.65)	517.73³ (2.84)	489.87³ (4.07)	533.96³ (10.17)	473.00³ (11.12)	509.97³ (5.07)	496.78³ (5.60)
Female (H1)		5.73³ (.42)	5.70³ (.42)	5.72³ (.41)	5.85³ (.41)	5.71³ (.41)	5.75° (.41)
Age of arrival (H2)		-.71³ (.024)	-.71³ (.024)	-.72³ (.024)	1.84³ (.12)	-.72³ (.024)	.058³ (.045)
Length of residence (H3)		.34³ (.040)	.34³ (.040)	.34³ (.040)	.62² (.22)	.34³ (.040)	.45³ (.076)
Daily education (H4)		2.03³ (.21)	2.03³ (.21)	2.03³ (.21)	-1.17° (.73)	2.03³ (.21)	-.60° (.74)
Additional language (H5)		6.80³ (.51)	6.83³ (.51)	6.86³ (.51)	7.07³ (.51)	6.86³ (.51)	7.08³ (.51)
Level 2, country of birth effects (C Model)							
Educational quality (H6)		—	.34³ (.039)	.34³ (.038)	.21³ (.04)	.33³ (.038)	.22³ (.044)
Level 2, mother tongue effects (C+T Model)							
Linguistic distance (H10)		—	—	-5.16E-03³ (1.08E-03)	3.51E-03² (1.17E-03)	-54.90³ (8.79)	14.32° (9.46)

Cross-level interaction effects (C+T + I*C/T Model)							
Age of arrival (H2) * Linguistic distance (H10)	—	—	—	—	—	-3.15E-04³ (1.50E-05)	-2.56³ (.13)
Length of residence (H3) * Linguistic distance (H10)	—	—	—	—	—	-3.24E-05° (2.60E-05)	-.30° (.21)
Daily education (H4) * Educational quality (H6)	—	—	—	—	—	3.93E-02³ (8.03E-03)	3.34E-02³ (8.08E-03)
Variance components							
Learner	977.51³ (7.65)	935.73³ (7.32)	935.86³ (7.32)	935.96³ (7.33)	921.68³ (7.21)	935.96³ (7.32)	923.21³ (7.22)
Country of birth	184.33³ (34.68)	166.35³ (31.51)	79.07³ (16.30)	76.14³ (15.44)	72.50³ (14.80)	75.48³ (15.10)	71.72³ (14.5)
Mother tongue	137.28² (48.45)	132.98² (46.73)	102.59² (33.01)	49.80² (19.03)	52.33² (19.50)	34.20¹ (13.98)	34.27¹ (13.89)
Measures of fit							
R2Learner	0 (75.2%)	4.3%	4.3%	4.2%	5.7%	4.2%	5.6%
R2Country	0 (14.2%)	9.8%	57.1%	58.7%	60.7%	59.0%	61.1%
R2Language	0 (10.6%)	3.1%	25.3%	63.7%	62.0%	75.1%	75.0%
-2 (log likelihood)	319,076.0	317,640.5	317,586	317,568.4	317,063.9	317,559.4	317,107.4
Correlations of fixed predicted values with proficiency measures							
Mother tongues	0	.32°	.72³	.84³	.84³	.87³	.86³
Learners	0	.24³	.40³	.49³	.50³	.49³	.50³

Legend: Reference categories are Male, Monolingual; effects B; ° $p \geq .05$, ¹ $p < .05$; ² $p < .01$; ³ $p < .001$.

With the addition of these three interactions to the model, we observed a strong overall improvement of model fit. The intercept estimates remained largely the same while the deviance from the data decreased substantially, indicating that the model fitted better to the data with the addition of interaction variables. The models with interaction effects (C+T+I*C/T Models) both fitted significantly better than the C+T Models. The -2loglikelihood decreased with 505.5 (ASJP) and 452.0 (G&A) points against three degrees of freedom. The explained variance only increased marginally between models with and without interaction effects (1.7% for ASJP and .1% for G&A). The interactions of linguistic distance with length of residence and age of arrival were both significant. Adding these interactions to the model shifted the effects of linguistic distance and age of arrival (in the case of G&A) to non-significant. The third interaction between educational quality and years of education was significant in both models. In all, we found that all three learner characteristics significantly interact with contextual characteristics. With respect to education, a longer education generally has less of an effect as educational quality is lower. The interaction might be a kind of effectiveness measure of received education. With respect to age of arrival and length of residence, being older at arrival and residing for a longer period generally influence second language learning more negatively as linguistic distance is greater. These interactions might imply that coping with a greater distance is more difficult at a later age due to decline of cognitive functions, and when being longer but less intensively exposed.

3.2. Fixed predicted scores

The discussion of the variance components suggested that most of the variance across mother tongues could be explained by the fixed effect parameters we fitted to the data. The remaining variance across mother tongues suggests that the model's fixed predicted scores do not completely overlap with observed scores. Here, we inspect this overlap at the level of the mother tongue. The fixed predicted scores can be inferred using the fixed effect parameter estimates. The fixed predicted scores are essentially regression means over the remaining random variance in the model, represented by the variables and their parameters only. These scores can be averaged over languages to inspect predicted differences across mother tongues and assess if they overlap with observed differences.

Mean observed scores and fixed predicted scores are shown in figure 2 for both ASJP (left) and G&A (right). A linear regression line represents the linearity of the model predictions, which we applied for all parameter estimations. The model predictions show in detail how every single unit deviates from the linear regression line, enabling quantitative comparison between models and predictions. The points deviate from the linear fitted line in comparable ways between both models. For example, speakers of Kurdish seem to score far under their predicted score in both models. Speakers of German performed even better than inferred from their favourable parameter settings.

A closer look at both panels also reveals a number of differences between the two different models. We consider a number of differences between both models, and judge the correctness of their claims according to the distance of the prediction to the linear model and the distance with each other. In table 4, we show the ten languages on which both models disagree the most (*model difference*). In figure 2, model difference is represented as the difference in position on the x axis for a language. For example, Albanian has the highest difference on the x axis. The other column in table 4 shows which of the models is more accurate in terms of observed proficiency scores (*difference in fit*). For example, G&A found a better fit for Albanian of 2.77 points because the ASJP based estimation was 5.94 too high, whereas the G&A bases estimation was 3.17 too low. For Afrikaans, the observed score did not provide much evidence for either the one or the other prediction as both models deviate about equally in different directions from the observed score. Summing up all the differences in fit, the G&A model fitted 14.36 points better than the ASJP predictions (average per language of .41). The differences spread about equally across linguistic subgroups.

Table 4. The 10 most different predictions between the ASJP and G&A models. Positive values indicate difference of fit in favour of ASJP, negative values indicate difference in fit in favour of ASJP.

Language	Difference in fit	Model difference
Albanian	2.77	9.11
Afrikaans	−0.81	7.53
Persian	5.12	6.86
Hindi	−6.09	6.09
Danish	4.18	5.92
Singhalese	5.64	5.64
Swedish	5.15	5.15
Icelandic	−4.71	4.71
English	−4.57	4.57
Latvian	3.82	3.82

3.3. Model parameter comparison

We can now take a closer look at both models and inspect their specific parameter settings as depicted in table 3. The predicted values have shown us that the G&A model generally provides better estimates than the ASJP model. An inspection of the model parameters can provide additional information on the nature of these estimates. To do so, we look at estimated effect sizes B, while keeping in mind that the ASJP model explains about 11.5% less variance across mother tongues than the G&A model (75.1 for G&A – 63.7 for ASJP).

G&A and ASJP models behaved differently in terms of their level 1 intercept estimations. Adding interactions reduces this difference to some extent. However, estimated intercept size is not very meaningful for comparing models. In general, individual learner effect estimations were already well established in the baseline model and did not change much by the addition of level 2 predictors to the baseline model. As in Van der Slik (2010), we found an advantage for being female over being male, arriving younger, having resided longer, having daily education for a longer period, and having command over an additional language besides Dutch and the mother tongue. Adding these predictors resulted in a model that is able to account for confounding variables.

With respect to the level of the country of birth, no large differences were found between the models tested. The interaction of daily education with educational quality was constant between the ASJP and G&A models. In both models, the individual effect of daily education became non-significant with the addition of the interaction effect. The proposed meaning of this interaction as a measure of educational effectiveness seems to account for the effect of years of daily education.

With respect to the level of the mother tongue, linguistic distance brought the unexplained between language variance to a minimum. The different effect sizes of ASJP and G&A are difficult to compare because both follow different scales. However, given that all the other variables are identical across models, the difference in variance components and percentages of explained variance indicate that G&A's measure for linguistic distance behaves best in terms of fit to the data.

Altogether, the interaction models incorporated 13 parameters, of which 11 were fixed and 2 were random. Educational quality explained most of the variance across countries of birth. The linguistic distance measures explained most of the variance across mother tongues.

4. Conclusion

We investigated the effects of two linguistic distance measures on the variation in speaking proficiency scores across 30,066 immigrants, having 35 different mother tongues, originating from 89 different countries (resulting in 119 language by country subgroups). We fitted a range of fixed learner level, country level, and language level effects with either the G&A or ASJP linguistic distance measure to the observed scores. Thereafter, we compared estimated model predictions of mean scores by mother tongue against observed means by mother tongue. In this section, we discuss how the multilevel model settings relate to learning effects of linguistic distances in general. We look in more detail at the levels that we analysed, and more specifically at learning difficulty and linguistic distance.

We started the analysis by distinguishing variance components on three levels in the null model. *Intra-unit correlations* indicated that 10.6% of the variation in scores varied across mother tongues, 14.2% varied across countries, and 75.2% varied at the individual level. A cross-classification analysis on the level of country and mother tongue allowed us to distinguish these two effects and to separate the impact of language on the basis of linguistic distances. The effect of distance from the mother tongue to Dutch was consistently found in models with this kind of structural hierarchy.

The final multilevel models incorporated significant individual learner effects (gender and additional language) and cross-level interactions of age of arrival with linguistic distance, length of residence with linguistic distance, and years of daily education with educational quality. The small decline in explained variance when adding interaction effects (63.7 to 62.0 for ASJP, 75.1 to 75.0 for G&A) shows that the interaction slopes explain slightly less variance of the overall between-language variance. In general, the negative interaction effects indicate that being younger and having resided for a shorter period in the host country together results in higher proficiency scores, while being older and having resided in the Netherlands longer results in lower proficiency scores. One explanation of these interactions is that the estimation procedure found a dependence of relatively small distance with relatively young age in the special case of German learners. Incentives, which may or may not be an important category of predictors, might be relatively high in German learners because of a substantial degree of university attendance that is present in this group. However, the effect of linguistic distance keeps its robust and pivotal place in explaining variance between mother tongues across models regardless of the interaction effects that we fitted to the data.

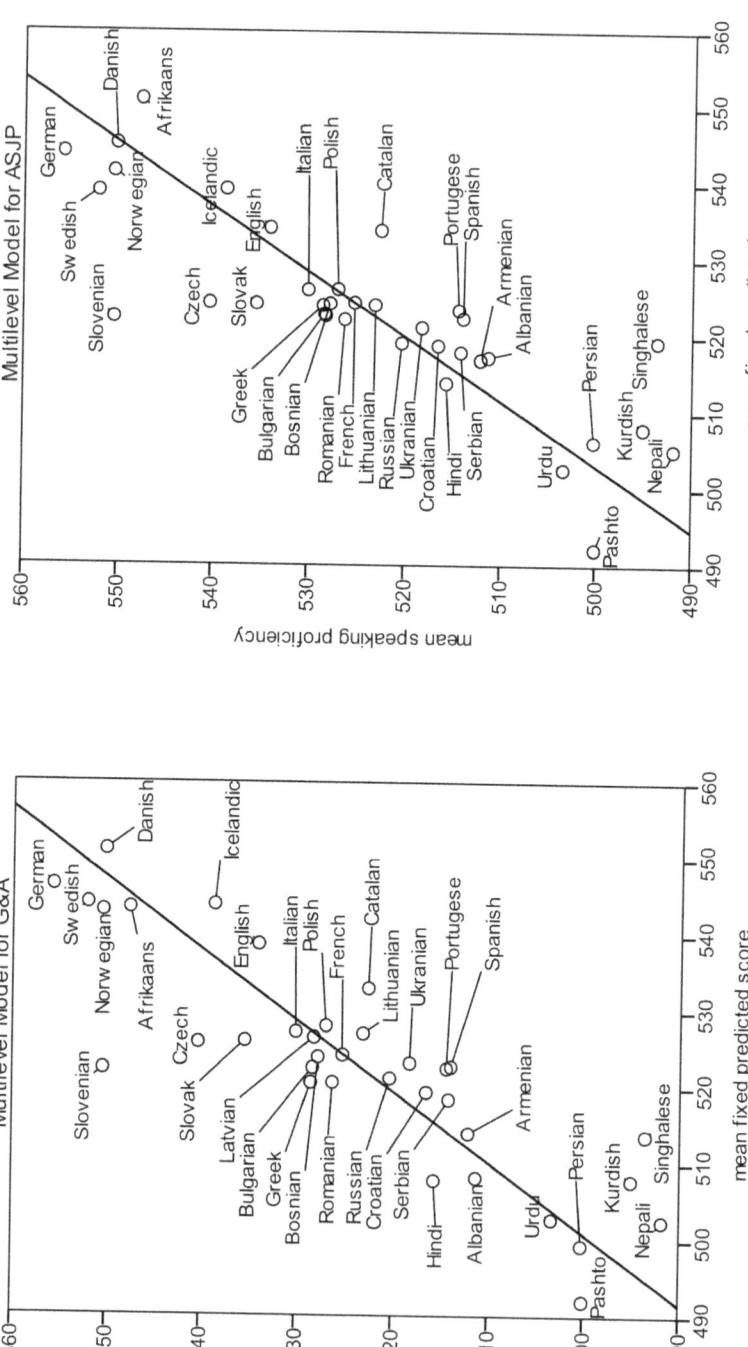

Figure 2. Language level fixed effect part estimates of the multilevel interaction model for speaking proficiency. The left panel shows estimates for G&A measurements; the right panel shows estimates for ASJP measurements. Deviations from the fitted line represent either a higher observed speaking proficiency than predicted speaking proficiency or vice versa.

A significant percentage of variance in speaking proficiency scores could be ascribed to differences in mother tongues (10.6% of the total variance across learners). The lowest observed mean for a mother tongue was observed for Nepali (491.9 points) and the highest one for German (555.8 points), resulting in a difference of 63.9 points on the scoring scale (see figure 2). Because linguistic distance explained most of this variance component between languages, we conclude that linguistic distance nicely predicts general difficulty of learning Dutch as a second language. More specifically, we conclude that learning difficulty gradually increases with a higher linguistic distance. We expect that a deeper understanding of the differences between languages requires a more detailed model of linguistic effects (e.g., by including other linguistic distance measures), and a more complete model of learner effects (e.g., by including linguistic distances of additional L2s, acquired before arriving in the Netherlands). Given that addition of cross-level interactions to the model explained more learner level variance than language level variance, we expect that further modelling of cross-level effects will enhance the model's performance at the learner level, leaving the explained variance between languages more or less intact. The cross-level interaction effect between age of arrival and linguistic distance did not add to the degree of explained variance between languages while it explained a substantial amount of variance between learners within languages.

We have seen that both an automatic and an expert-based linguistic distance measure are appropriate instruments to explain most of the empirically observed between-language variation across learners. The predicted scores were in favour of the G&A distances (better average fit of .41 points per language and a difference in explained variance of more than 10%) than the ASJP distances. Given the differences between the two measures described earlier, this finding suggests that distances from Germanic to Dutch are relatively small and distances from Germanic to other Indo-European languages are relatively large if they are used for explaining the linguistic distance effect in SLA. However, in terms of proficiency scores, both the mean observed and mean predicted proficiency scores develop more gradually than both measures of linguistic distance do. We hope to investigate the role of linguistic distance further by turning the model around. Can we predict the optimized distances from a reversed model? Such a reversed measure may inform us whether empirically determined linguistic distances are distributed differently from phylogenetically determined linguistic distances. Interesting testing cases are, in many respects, the non-Indo-European languages in our database.

We conclude that linguistic distance measures are impressive predictors for explaining average differences in L2 speaking proficiency scores between Indo-European mother tongues (63.7% for ASJP and 75.1% for G&A). This outcome is remarkably robust against more complex models. The correlation between the mean scores of learners of Dutch as an L2 with the distance from their mother tongue to Dutch starts at .66 for ASJP and .77 for G&A. No other variables were included in the computation of these correlations, but these raw correlations support the idea that linguistic distance and L2 learning are related. Incorporating other effects, both on the country level and the learner level, raised the correlations substantially: to .84 for AJSP and .87 for G&A (see table 3). These high correlations provide convincing evidence that linguistic distance is an important factor in SLA. Addition of cross-level interaction effects led to an improvement of fit while the effect size and relative ordering of linguistic differences remained consistent.

Appendix

The following table contains mean speaking scores for the cross-classification of all 35 Indo-European languages by the 89 countries of origin. The table also contains a measure of schooling quality as based on the gross enrolment rate in secondary schools (World Bank 2011), ASJP linguistic distance measurements (based on Brown et al. 2005), G&A linguistic distance measurements (Gray and Atkinson 2003), and a count of the number of individuals in each cross-classification.

Country of Birth	Mother Tongue	Mean Speaking	Schooling Quality	ASJP Distance	G&A Character	Group Size
	SD	20	51	1320	0.16	602
	Mean	522	448	8442	0.33	278
South Africa	Afrikaans	551	466	3458	0.0105	265
Albania	Albanian	512	384	9355	0.5951	111
Yugoslavia	Albanian	505	384	9355	0.5951	162
Armenia	Armenian	505	458	9462	0.4930	109
Azerbaijan	Armenian	509	389	9462	0.4930	42
Iran	Armenian	508	440	9462	0.4930	45
Iraq	Armenian	501	391	9462	0.4930	71
Syria	Armenian	501	423	9462	0.4930	31
Turkey	Armenian	517	454	9462	0.4930	19
USSR	Armenian	512	458	9462	0.4930	265
Bosnia	Bosnian	518	462	9107	0.4109	76

Linguistic distance and Dutch L2 learning 223

Country of Birth	Mother Tongue	Mean Speaking	Schooling Quality	ASJP Distance	G&A Character	Group Size
Bulgaria	Bulgarian	527	432	9104	0.4111	557
Spain	Catalan	525	484	8880	0.3955	65
Croatia	Croatian	543	474	9108	0.3950	58
Yugoslavia	Croatian	515	474	9108	0.3950	382
Czech Rep.	Czech	541	461	9187	0.3852	353
Czechoslovakia	Czech	534	490	9187	0.3852	104
Denmark	Danish	552	499	6862	0.0808	192
Aruba	English	532	477	6586	0.0832	19
Australia	English	541	519	6586	0.0832	174
Cameroon	English	493	359	6586	0.0832	49
Canada	English	543	527	6586	0.0832	173
Germany	English	550	510	6586	0.0832	32
Ghana	English	498	389	6586	0.0832	29
Guyana	English	512	479	6586	0.0832	29
India	English	527	402	6586	0.0832	47
Ireland	English	541	497	6586	0.0832	155
Liberia	English	485	375	6586	0.0832	37
Malaysia	English	534	427	6586	0.0832	24
Netherlands	English	555	519	6586	0.0832	80
New Zealand	English	538	524	6586	0.0832	76
Nigeria	English	499	371	6586	0.0832	71
Philippines	English	525	449	6586	0.0832	22
Sierra Leone	English	499	359	6586	0.0832	20
Singapore	English	539	543	6586	0.0832	39
South Africa	English	541	466	6586	0.0832	219
United Kingdom	English	540	500	6586	0.0832	983
United States	English	539	496	6586	0.0832	795
Zimbabwe	English	537	375	6586	0.0832	24
Algeria	French	520	449	9012	0.3981	32
Belgium	French	533	509	9012	0.3981	98
Burundi	French	497	336	9012	0.3981	23
Cameroon	French	493	359	9012	0.3981	59
Canada	French	530	527	9012	0.3981	40
Congo, Dem.Rep.	French	491	350	9012	0.3981	65
Congo, Rep.	French	495	384	9012	0.3981	61
Cote d'Ivoire	French	496	357	9012	0.3981	35
France	French	531	497	9012	0.3981	936
Morocco	French	514	394	9012	0.3981	42
Netherlands	French	542	519	9012	0.3981	27
Switzerland	French	550	517	9012	0.3981	37
Austria	German	566	487	5664	0.0373	232
Germany	German	558	510	5664	0.0373	4434
Netherlands	German	560	519	5664	0.0373	25

Country of Birth	Mother Tongue	Mean Speaking	Schooling Quality	ASJP Distance	G&A Character	Group Size
Poland	German	550	501	5664	0.0373	18
Switzerland	German	571	517	5664	0.0373	190
Germany	Greek	544	510	9440	0.4974	20
Greece	Greek	529	473	9440	0.4974	271
India	Hindi	507	402	9211	0.5302	92
Suriname	Hindi	530	430	9211	0.5302	38
Iceland	Icelandic	539	501	6995	0.1174	36
Italy	Italian	533	486	8858	0.3586	594
Netherlands	Italian	547	519	8858	0.3586	20
Iran	Kurdish	491	440	9241	0.4257	91
Iraq	Kurdish	492	391	9241	0.4257	738
Syria	Kurdish	487	423	9241	0.4257	63
Turkey	Kurdish	490	454	9241	0.4257	185
Latvia	Latvian	546	487	9417	0.3636	28
USSR	Latvian	525	487	9417	0.3636	39
Lithuania	Lithuanian	520	479	9318	0.3711	77
USSR	Lithuanian	523	479	9318	0.3711	113
Nepal	Nepali	490	389	9592	0.5054	18
Norway	Norwegian	555	500	6843	0.1598	175
Afghanistan	Pashto	498	346	9539	0.4588	274
Afghanistan	Persian	495	346	9322	0.5553	1252
Iran	Persian	497	440	9322	0.5553	2063
Poland	Polish	526	501	9313	0.3880	2608
Angola	Portuguese	501	342	8967	0.4087	114
Brazil	Portuguese	514	401	8967	0.4087	784
Cape Verde	Portuguese	503	425	8967	0.4087	72
Mozambique	Portuguese	521	336	8967	0.4087	26
Portugal	Portuguese	524	490	8967	0.4087	216
Moldova	Romanian	523	458	8893	0.4137	21
Romania	Romanian	525	426	8893	0.4137	929
Azerbaijan	Russian	512	389	9413	0.3961	40
Belarus	Russian	530	471	9413	0.3961	83
Germany	Russian	527	510	9413	0.3961	22
Kazakhstan	Russian	515	398	9413	0.3961	42
Russia	Russian	524	468	9413	0.3961	767
Ukraine	Russian	520	464	9413	0.3961	210
USSR	Russian	520	468	9413	0.3961	2521
Uzbekistan	Russian	517	477	9413	0.3961	26
Bosnia	Serbian	521	462	9094	0.3950	28
Serbia	Serbian	524	442	9094	0.3950	98
Yugoslavia	Serbian	513	442	9094	0.3950	2000
Sri Lanka	Singhalese	495	456	9440	0.5393	37
Czech Rep.	Slovak	537	461	9205	0.3810	220

Country of Birth	Mother Tongue	Mean Speaking	Schooling Quality	ASJP Distance	G&A Character	Group Size
Slovakia	Slovak	529	488	9205	0.3810	95
Yugoslavia	Slovenian	550	499	9009	0.3971	38
Argentina	Spanish	525	396	9117	0.3986	188
Bolivia	Spanish	505	458	9117	0.3986	55
Chile	Spanish	507	439	9117	0.3986	113
Colombia	Spanish	508	399	9117	0.3986	399
Costa Rica	Spanish	528	443	9117	0.3986	37
Cuba	Spanish	507	466	9117	0.3986	100
Dominican Rep.	Spanish	499	425	9117	0.3986	64
Ecuador	Spanish	510	420	9117	0.3986	113
Guatemala	Spanish	518	397	9117	0.3986	38
Mexico	Spanish	513	420	9117	0.3986	293
Nicaragua	Spanish	504	423	9117	0.3986	34
Peru	Spanish	507	368	9117	0.3986	333
Spain	Spanish	524	484	9117	0.3986	799
Uruguay	Spanish	540	427	9117	0.3986	33
Venezuela	Spanish	508	435	9117	0.3986	190
Finland	Swedish	558	544	6890	0.1005	27
Sweden	Swedish	556	495	6890	0.1005	272
Ukraine	Ukrainian	518	464	9387	0.3941	141
USSR	Ukrainian	519	464	9387	0.3941	186
Pakistan	Urdu	499	362	9128	0.4132	109

Notes

1. We would like to thank the secretary of the State Examination of Dutch as a Second Language for providing the learner data used in this study. We also thank Søren Wichmann and Quentin Atkinson for providing linguistic data, and Theo Bongaerts, Martin Becker, Malte Viebahn, and Thordis Neger for comments on an earlier version of this manuscript.
2. We also tested a number of other contextual effects but these were non-significant (ns) and were therefore excluded from the final model. These effects were: writing system (ns), speaker population size (ns), immigrant group size (ns), and whether or not the country had officially been in a continuous state of liberal democracy during the last 20 years (ns). We also tested if scores differed before and after 2005 (ns). After 2005 immigrants were able to fulfil requirements for a residence permit by completing the state exam instead of the usual lower-level naturalization course. Before 2005 this was not allowed. Furthermore, we tested the effect of gross domestic product per capita using data from the CIA (2011). Although this effect was significant ($p<.001$), we excluded it from our final analyses in favour of a simpler model.

3. Adding G&A language level predictors with out country level predictors resulted in R^2 measures of 13.8% (country level), 66.9% (language level), and 4.3% (learner level), implying that language characteristics, and not characteristics of countries, actually explain most of the between-language variance. The predicted scores correlated with .82 (p<.01) at the language level, and with .48 (p<.01) at the individual level. Adding ASJP language level predictors without adding country level predictors resulted in R^2 measures of 11.7% (country level), 48.8 (language level), and 4.3% (individual level). The predicted scores correlated with .73 (p<.01) at the language level, and with .45 (p<.01) at the individual level.

References

Atkinson, Quentin A.
    2011   Phonemic diversity supports a serial founder effect model of language expansion from Africa. *Science* 332: 346–349.
Beenstock, Michael, Barry R. Chiswick, and Gaston L. Repetto
    2001   The Effect of Linguistic Distance and Country of Origin on Immigrant Language Skills: Application to Israel. *International Migration* 39: 33–60.
Brown, Cecil H., Eric W. Holman, Soeren Wichmann, and Viveka Velupillai
    2008   Automated classification of the world's languages: A description of the method and preliminary results. *STUF – Language Typology and Universals* 61: 285–308.
Cavalli-Sforza, L. Luca, Paolo Menozzi, and Alberto Piazza
    1994   *The History and Geography of Human Genes.* Princeton, NJ: Princeton University Press.
Charette, Michael and Ronald Meng
    1994   Explaining language proficiency: objective versus self-assessed measures of literacy. *Economics Letters* 44: 313–321.
Chiswick, Barry R. and Paul W. Miller
    1995   The endogeneity between language and earnings: International analyses. *Journal of Labor Economics* 13: 246–288.
Chiswick, Barry R. and Paul W. Miller
    1996   Ethnic networks and language proficiency among immigrants, *Journal of Population Economics* 9: 19–35.
Chiswick, Barry R. and Paul W. Miller
    1999   Immigration, language and multiculturalism in Australia. *Australian Economic Review* 32: 369–385.
Chiswick, Barry R. and Paul W. Miller
    2005a   Family matters: the role of the family in immigrants' destination language acquisition. *Journal of Population Economics* 18: 631–647.

Chiswick, Barry R. and Paul W. Miller
  2005b   Linguistic distance: A quantitative measure of the distance between English and other languages. *Journal of Multilingual and Multicultural Development* 26: 1–11.
Chiswick, Barry R. and Paul W. Miller
  2007   Modeling immigrants' language skills. In *Immigration*, Chiswick, B.R. (ed.), pp.75–128. (Research in Labor Economics 27.) Bradford: Emerald Group Publishing Limited.
CIA, the World Factbook
  2011   GDP – per capita (PPP) [Data file]. Retrieved from: https://www.cia.gov/library/publications/the-world-factbook/rankorder/2004rank.html on July 9, 2011.
Crystal, David
  1987   *The Cambridge Encyclopaedia of Language*. Cambridge: Cambridge University Press.
Dunn, Michael, Angela Terrill, Ger Reesink, Robert A. Foley, and Stephen C. Levinson
  2005   Structural phylogenetics and the reconstruction of ancient language history. *Science* 309: 2072–2075.
Dunn, Michael, Simon J. Greenhill, Stephen C. Levinson, and Russel D. Gray
  2011   Evolved structure of language shows lineage-specific trends in word-order universals. *Nature* 473: 79–82.
Dyen, Isodore, Joseph B. Kruskal, and Paul Black
  1992   An Indoeuropean classification: A lexicostatistical experiment. *Transactions of the American Philosophical Society* 82, part 5. Data available from http://www.ldc.upenn.edu/
Espenshade, Thomas and Haishan Fu
  1997   An analysis of English-language proficiency among U.S. immigrants. *American Sociological Review* 62: 288–305.
Finnie, Ross and Ronald Meng
  2005   Literacy and labour market outcomes: Self-assessment versus test score measures. *Applied Economics* 37: 1935–1951.
Goldstein, Harvey
  2011   *Multilevel Statistical Models* (4th ed.). UK: Wiley.
Gray, Russel D. and Quentin D. Atkinson
  2003   Language-tree divergence times support the Anatolian theory of Indo-European origin. *Nature* 426: 435–439.
Gray, Russel D. and Fiona M. Jordan
  2000   Language trees support the express-train sequence of Austronesian expansion. *Nature* 405: 1052–1055.
Heck, Ronald H., Scott L. Thomas, and Lynn N. Tabata
  2010   *Multilevel and Longitudinal Modeling with IBM SPSS*. Taylor and Francis.

Heeringa, Wilbert, Peter Kleiweg, Charlotte Gooskens, and John Nerbonne
  2006 Evaluation of string distance algorithms for dialectology. In: J. Nerbonne and E. Hinrichs (eds.), *Linguistic Distances Workshop at the joint conference of the International Committee on Computational Linguistics and the Association for Computational Linguistics*, pp. 51–62. Sydney.
Holman, Eric W. Soeren Wichmann, Cecil H. Brown, Viveka Velupillai, André Müller, and Dik Bakker
  2008 Explorations in automated language classification. *Folia Linguistica* 42: 331–354.
Holman, Eric W.
  2010 Programs for calculating ASJP distance matrices (Version 2.0) [Software]. Available from http://email.eva.mpg.de/~wichmann/software.htm
Holman, Eric W.
  2011 The Newick reader: a program for producing a distance matrix from the branch lengths in a phylogenetic tree in Newick format (version 1.0). Available from http://email.eva.mpg.de/~wichmann/software.htm
Hox, Joop J.
  2002 *Multilevel Analysis: Techniques and Applications* (2nd ed.). UK: Routledge.
Huff, Paul
  2010 Process_asjp: a script for generating subsets of ASJP data (Version .0.1). [Software]. Available from http://email.eva.mpg.de/~wichmann/software.htm
Isphording, Ingo and Sebastian Otten
  2011 Babylonian confusion – linguistic distance and language fluency of immigrants in Germany. *23rd annual EALE Conference*, September 22–24.
Jarvis, Scott and Aneta Pavlenko
  2008 *Cross Linguistic Influence in Language and Cognition*. Routledge: New York
Kellerman, Eric
  1979 Transfer and non-transfer: Where we are now. *Studies in Second Language Acquisition* 2: 37–57.
Kessler, Brett
  1995 Computational dialectology in Irish Gaelic. *Proceedings of the European Association for Computational Linguistics*, pp. 60–67. Dublin.
Lado, Robert
  1957 *Linguistics Across Cultures: Applied Linguistics for Language Teachers*. Ann Arbor, MI: University of Michigan Press.
McMahon, April and Robert McMahon
  2005 *Language Classification by Numbers*. Oxford: Oxford University Press.

Odlin, Terence
    1989   *Language Transfer: Cross-Linguistic Influence in Language Learning.* Cambridge: Cambridge University Press.

Ostler, Nicholas D. M.
    2003   *Empires of the Word: a Language History of the World.* London: HarperCollins.

Paradis, Emmanuel, Julien Claude, and Korbinian Strimmer
    2004   APE: analyses of phylogenetics and evolution in R language. *Bioinformatics 20*: 289–290.

Snijders, Tom and Roel Bosker
    1999   *Multilevel Analysis: An Introduction to Basic and Advanced Multilevel Modeling.* Sage: London.

Swadesh, Morris
    1952   Lexico-statistic dating of prehistoric ethnic contacts: With special reference to North American Indians and Eskimo's. *Proceedings of the American Philosophical Society* 96: 452–463.

Ullman, Michael T.
    2005   A cognitive neuroscience perspective on second language acquisition: The declarative/procedural model. In C. Sanz (ed.). *Mind and context in adult second language acquisition* (pp. 141–178). Washington: Georgetown University Press.

UNESCO, Institute for Statistics
    2011   School enrolment, secondary (% gross) [Data file]. Retrieved from http://data.worldbank.org/indicator/ SE.SEC.ENRR on September 18, 2011.

Van der Slik, Frans W.P.
    2010   The acquisition of Dutch as a second language: The explanative power of cognate and genetic linguistic distance measures for 11 West-European first languages. *Studies in Second Language Acquisition* 32: 401–432.

Van Tubergen, Frank and Matthijs Kalmijn
    2009   A dynamic approach to the determinants of immigrants' language proficiency: The United States, 1980–2000. *International Migration Review* 43: 519–543.

Weinreich, Uriel
    1953   *Languages in Contact: Findings and Problems.* The Hague: Mouton.

Wichmann, Søren, André Müller, Viveka Velupillai, Cecil H. Brown, Eric W. Holman, Pamela Brown, Sebastian Sauppe, Oleg Belyaev, Matthias Urban, Zarina Molochieva, Annkathrin Wett, Dik Bakker, Johann-Mattis List, Dmitry Egorov, Robert Mailhammer, David Beck, and Helen Geyer
    2011   The ASJP Database (version 13) [Data file]. Retrieved from http://email.eva.mpg.de/~wichmann/languages.htm

Using semantically restricted word-lists to investigate relationships among Athapaskan languages

Conor Snoek

1. Introduction[1]

The Athapaskan languages constitute a widespread family historically spoken across western North America, from just below the Arctic Circle to northern Mexico. Internal classification of the languages has proved to be a formidable problem whose solution has been impeded by both a sparseness of data, and a situation of sometimes intense, long-term interaction among speech communities. This has resulted in a pattern more akin to a dialect complex than a genetic family (Krauss and Golla 1981: 68). Previous work on internal classification has been carried out in the traditional manner of lexical, morphosyntactic and phonological comparison and reconstruction (for example in Cook 1981; Kraus and Leer 1981; Dyen and Aberle 1974). While a respectable number of cognate sets have been discovered (see Krauss 2005 for a thorough review), one of the chief hurdles to be overcome has remained the difficulty of finding larger quantities of reliable cognates and conclusively establishing regular correspondences.

In this paper, I present initial work toward a fresh attempt to establish groupings among the Athapaskan languages. Following comments by Krauss and Golla (1981) I apply methods developed within the field of dialectometry to a dataset that, while collected objectively with the aid of a pre-established list, is particularly likely to contain a high number of cognate terms. I propose that working with a list of terms that is semantically restricted holds the advantage of reducing the potential subjective bias of the analyst in establishing meaning equivalence among terms from different languages. The semantic domain I have chosen to work on is that of the parts and fluids of the body. Furthermore, I will demonstrate that a particular semantic domain, namely that of fluids related to the body, presents a better hunting ground in the search for cognates than others, because it is diachronically more stable.

2. Data

The semantic domain chosen as the basis for this research is the human body. Despite minor genetic variation both between and within populations, human bodies are overwhelmingly the same everywhere. Notwithstanding regional geographically bound diseases, humans everywhere need to deal with the same physiologies and anatomies, and the problems and benefits tied to them. The means developed in different linguistic communities, while varied, nonetheless need to be able to refer to the same anatomical components and physiological functions, regardless of the particular cultural environment. The universality of human anatomy and physiology as referents to linguistic expression make the body and its products an excellent referential context within which semantic variation and polysemy can be dealt with in a principled way (see for example Brown 2011 and Brown and Witkowski 1985 for studies of semantic variation among body-part nomenclatures). In particular, the work of Wilkins (1992) has shown how meaning relations and changes in body related nomenclature may be used in comparative and historical linguistic work. Furthermore, it is to be supposed that the importance of the human body does not diminish over time, or with a change of environment brought on by migration or climatic change. This, in principle, makes the terminology relating to the human body and its functions a lexical domain especially suitable for historically oriented comparative research.

As a conceptual domain, the human body is made up of not only those parts whose removal would constitute great loss to the organism, but also those that are dispensed with regularly (such as bodily excretions) or periodically (such as fingernails). These differences in permanence may have lexical ramifications. In this study, body-part terms (such as 'head', 'arm') are compared to terms from two closely related semantic domains: those of ephemera (e.g. 'fingernails', 'warts') and effluvia (e.g. 'blood', 'urine'). Body-part, Effluvia and Ephemera Terms (henceforth BEETs). The human body therefore provides a stable referent against which the semantic equivalence or relatedness of terms is more easily ascertained.

Differences in the semantic sub-domains present a potential source of information which can be exploited for linguistic research. This information can enable the construction of improved lists for the purposes of cognate identification and computationally supported classification of language relationships. For language families like Athapaskan for which no historical records exist dating back more than one hundred years or so, computational methods may provide crucial information that would otherwise remain unattainable. However, for an algorithm to provide relevant clues to linguistic history and relation the data that is fed into them must be linguistically meaningful. It is here that a restricted wordlist approach can be particularly effective differing as it does form more traditional Swadesh-list approaches in that instead of relying on intuitive notions of natural vocabulary, it instead offers a coherent set of terms which by their nature are highly likely to be encoded in every language.

The data for this study were drawn from published sources and field notes (Antoine et al. 1974; Bray 1998; Dogrib Divisional Board of Education 1996; Elford and Elford 1998; Firth 2005; Golla 1996; Hargus 2001; Hargus 2007; Kaska Tribal Council 1997; Jetté and Jones 2000; Phone et al. 2007; de Reuse 2006; Rice 1978; Young and Morgan 1980). The sample is made up of 23 languages and dialects representing the major geographic regions where Athapaskan is spoken. The map in figure 1 shows the major geographic regions that Athapaskan languages are typically divided into: the Northern languages spoken in interior Canada and Alaska, the Pacific Coast groups spoken in Oregon and California and the Apachean groups spoken in Arizona and New Mexico. The sample contained the Alaskan languages Dena'ina, Koyukon, Ahtna and Lower Tanana; Kaska and Northern Tutchone from the Yukon Territory; Gwich'in, Hare, South Slavey, Mountain Slavey, Tłı̨chǫ (Dogrib) and Dene Sųłiné (Chipewyan) from northern Canada; Tsuut'ina (Sarcee) from southern Alberta; Kaska, Sekani, Central Carrier from British Columbia; Hupa and Tututni (Euchre Creek) from the Pacific Coast group; and Navajo, Jicarilla Apache, Western Apache and San Carlos Apache from the Apachean group. This constitutes a broad if not wholly exhaustive sample of the Athapaskan geographic spread.

Regional distributions are used as the predominant means of grouping Athapaskan languages in the literature and form the backbone of the best classification that is presently available (Mithun 1999: 346). While this geographic classification has great merit, a complementary phylogentic grouping is very much a desirable research objective.

BEETs were collected from each language with the aid of a list consisting of 61 terms from three sub-domains: this list included 40 terms denoting body-parts, 12 terms denoting effluvia and 9 terms denoting ephemera. The individual terms are listed in the Appendix I. The sample contained 1083 terms in total. An overview of the number of terms available per language is given in the Appendix II at the end of this paper.

Figure 1. Dark contours demarcate the areas in which Athapaskan languages were traditionally spoken (after Rice 1989).

3. BEET morphology

Morphologically the terms used to denote body parts, effluvia and ephemera in Athapaskan can take one of three forms. There can be either a simple monomorphemic (and frequently monosyllabic) root, a compound of two roots or a more complex nominal typically derived from a verb form. Examples for each are given below: in (1) for a simple monomorphemic root, in (2) for a compound and for a deverbal nominal in (3).

(1) Lower Tanana (Kari 1991)
shath
wart
'Wart'

(2) Western Apache (Bray 1998)
bi-dáá-tú
3SG.POSS-eye-water
'His/her tear(s)'

(3) Tsuut'ina (Starlight and Donovan 2008)
sī-dzá-dá-zūl-à
3SG.POSS-chest- DIS-light- POS
'My lung', literally: 'my light thing inside my chest'

In (3), the morpheme *-dzá-* is combined with a verb stem *-zūl-* meaning 'to be light'. The form also carries a suffix which occurs irregularly, and in a number of forms, across Athapaskan languages as an additional marker of possession. Within Tsuut'ina itself *-dzá-* is not found outside of derived forms and compounds, but cognates can be found in other languages such as Kaska *madzōh* 'my-chest'. This shows that BEETs vary cross-linguistically within Athapaskan as to the form of the morphological encoding.

All three types of morphological construction can occur with prefixes marking the possessor of the BEET in question. In fact, the data collected in the BEET database consists in large part of what Keren Rice has called "dependent nouns" (1989: 167; see Young and Morgan 1980 for a similar discussion for Navajo). In Athapaskan languages, certain kinds of nouns must carry morphological marking indicating the possessor of the object or thing in question. There are several domains for which this holds true, among them the domain of the parts of the body. That is to say, in Athapaskan languages terms denoting parts of the body are typically inalienably possessed.

(4) Hare (Rice 1978)
be-dá?
3SG.POSS-eye
'his/her eye'

(5) Gwıchya Gwich'in (Firth 2005)
shi-gyìn
1SG.POSS-arm
'my arm'

In examples (3) and (4), the possessive prefix indicating person and number attaches to a base consisting of a root morpheme carrying lexical meaning. Within the larger domain of BEETs, however, not all forms are inalienably possessed. Ephemera such as in the case of 'wart' in (1) above, but especially effluvia display variation among the languages as to whether a particular effluvium must be marked for its possessor or not. For example, the term for 'blood' is obligatorily possessed in some languages, such as the term in Kaska in (5) below, but not in others like Dene Sųłiné (6).

(6) Kaska (Kaska Tribal Council 1997)
ma-dal-é'
3SG.POSS-blood-POS
'his/her blood'

(7) Dene Sųłiné (Elford and Elford 1998)
del
blood
'blood'

This distinction in morphological marking can be treated as an indication of the conceptual difference among the items belonging to the three semantic sub-domains. It can therefore be used to test the validity of distinguishing the three subdomains, as will be done in section 4 below. Equally, the difference is morphological complexity, i.e. simple monomorphemic forms vs. compounds and deverbal nominalizations, can be cross-checked against the semantic subdomain in order to ascertain whether there are significant differences.

4. Testing morphological criteria

The variability in the occurrence of the morphological features of BEETs offers the possibility of investigating the potential distinctiveness of each domain. As the obligatory marking of the possessor for body-part terms is a very salient aspect of the grammar, it can be supposed that differences therein indicate a cultural and conceptual distinction of some interest. In the BEET database each item was annotated both for the semantic sub-domain it belonged to, and whether the item required obligatory marking of the possessor. Semantic sub-domain and obligatory marking, or alienability of terms, as it is sometimes referred to in the literature (Chappell and McGregor 1996), could then be cross-examined by counting the number of alienable and inalienable terms for each domain. The resulting contingency table is represented by the bar chart in figure 2, where the light areas indicate the proportion of inalienable terms and the dark area the proportion of alienable terms.

Visual inspection indicates that effluvia and ephemera have a larger proportion of alienable terms. A χ^2-test reveals that these differences are statistically significant at $p < 0.01$ ($\chi^2 = 189.0589$). The directionality of the differences, that is, what contributes to the statistical significance of the χ^2-test and in what way, can be assessed with the help of a function from the polytomous package for the statistical programming environment R (Arppe 2008). Table 1 shows how the cells in the contingency table cross-matching the semantic sub-domains and the morphological category of inalienable possession influence the statistical test.

The plus ('+') indicates that the distribution exemplified by those cells favours a difference in the direction indicated. The minus ('-') indicates that the particular distribution disfavours that variable.

Table 1. Skewing of differences in cross-referencing BEET sub-domains and the morphological complexity of the terms

	Body-Part Terms	Effluvia	Ephemera
inalienable	+	−	−
alienable	−	+	+

From the table above it can be seen that body parts proper are more likely to exhibit obligatory possession (inalienability), while effluvia and ephemera are frequently either non-obligatorily possessed or never inflect for possession at all.

A second variable that can be used as an indicator of the distinctiveness of semantic sub-domains within the larger domain of BEETs is the morphological complexity of the terms themselves. As described in section 3, BEETs can take the form of monomorphemic stems or of derivationally more complex constructions such as compounds and nominalizations. As with the feature of alienability, the number of terms falling into either the complex or simplex categories can be counted and compared across sub-domains. Figure 3 shows these proportions, where effluvia and ephemera tend to favor simplex forms while body-part terms occur proportionally more often as complex derived forms and compounds. The differences are statistically significant in this case too ($p < 0.01$, $\chi^2 = 15.1094$). Inspecting the directionality reveals that body-parts and effluvia most influence the strength of the effect, while ephemera display no directionality at all (as indicated by the zeroes in the relevant cells).

Table 2. Skewing of differences in cross-referencing BEET sub-domains and the morphological complexity of the terms

	Body-Part Terms	Effluvia	Ephemera
simplex	−	+	0
complex	+	−	0

It therefore seems clear that body-part terms behave markedly differently from effluvia and ephemera terms, and that distinguishing among them is justified. The three constitute separate areas within the semantic domain of the human body and its functions. The third, and for a comparative-historical perspective most relevant property of the sub-domains can now be investigated: the differences in the diachronic stability of BEET terms.

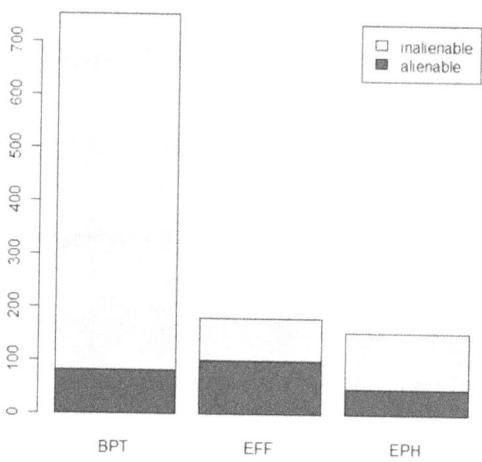

Figure 2. Proportions of alienable and inalienable terms across semantic domains

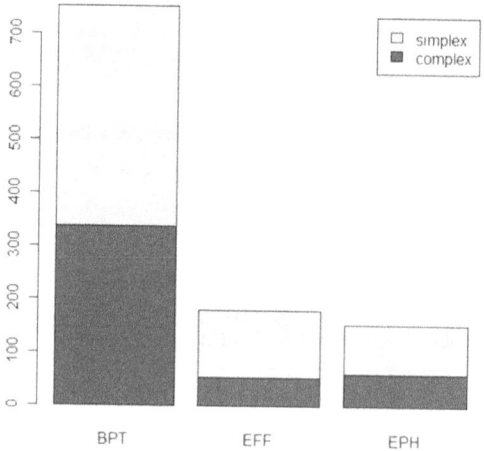

Figure 3. Comparison of morphological complexity (the difference in proportions is significant at *p < 0.01* (χ^2 =15.1094)).

5. Diachronic stability

Having established these semantic domains as being conceptually different in the lexicons of Athapaskan languages, it is possible to ask whether these differences might be exploited in a manner conducive to helping historical linguistic research. Should one of the subdomains contain items which are less likely to be replaced it could make it an opportune place to search for cognates. This is especially important in those cases, such as in comparative Athapaskan research, where data collection can be made difficult through factors such as the wide geographical dispersal of languages, making it difficult for the fieldworker to travel to many destinations, and through language endangerment. Athapaskan languages are no exception to the general trend of language loss present throughout North America and beyond (Krauss 1992: 5). Along with such obvious problems as the absence or rarity of fluent speakers come things such as the availability of the speakers that can still be found, and, frequently, the age of those speakers: the fluent speakers that still exist may be old and may lack the time and energy to devote to intense fieldwork. In such situations it can be highly desirable to have the means to quickly and effectively gather data relevant for comparative work. For these reasons, a reliable and circumscribed list, likely to elicit terms that, with a high probability, have cognates in sister languages can be very useful indeed.

Intuitively, a pattern seemed to emerge in the gathering of the data whereby ephemera and effluvia terms appeared more likely to have cognates in other Athapaskan languages. This intuition then had to be tested by reliable quantitative means. In order to do so each term was compared to a reconstructed Proto-Athapaskan root (as described in Hoijer 1963; Krauss and Leer 1981; Krauss 2005). It could then be ascertained for each term in each language, whether the form in question was a reflex of the ancient form or not. This made it possible to calculate mean rates of retention for each of the terms and the overall mean rate of retention across each particular semantic sub-domain. This results in values which can be compared across all three domains and thereby allows for the estimation of greater relative diachronic stability.

The proportion of cognate terms across the three semantic domains is represented by the mosaic plot in figure 4. Both effluvia and ephemera terms display higher proportions of cognates, as measured by the occurrence of reflexes of the reconstructed Proto-Athapaskan roots. Calculating a Chi-squared test confirms that the difference in distributions is significant (at $p > 0.01$, $\chi^2 = 32.7366$). The proportion of cognates is highest for the effluvia terms. Therefore, there is good reason for paying special attention to the terms of that sub-domain when searching for cognates. Furthermore, computational estimations of language distance can be calculated on smaller data sets with similar results, when those data are known to be reliable repositories of cognate forms. The measurement of language distance will be dealt with in the next section.

6. Measuring language distance on semantically restricted word-lists

The comparison of the semantic sub-domains allows for the construction of dendrograms based on the BEET data. As mentioned in the introduction, the particular situation of the Athapaskan languages would seem to warrant the application of methods from dialectometry. In order to estimate the distances between Athapaskan languages I used the Levenshtein distance, that is, the minimum number of insertions, deletions and substitutions to transform one string into the other (Levenshtein 1969). The algorithm used to calculate the distances between languages is implemented in the *Gabmap* application (Nerbonne et al. 2011).[2] The application, developed to carry out quantitative dialectology, is a highly useful and accessible tool which also draws the dendrograms reproduced below in figures 5 and 6.

Body part, effluvia and ephemera terms from the BEET database were compared and the simple Levenshtein distances were calculated for each pair of orthographic forms. The average Levenshtein distance between two lists of words from two different languages was taken as the distance between the two languages (Heeringa 2004: 145) These averages were then combined into a distance matrix. A cluster dendrogram can be constructed from the matrix. The calculations were carried out through the *Gabmap* web-application mentioned above. The resulting dendrogram is shown in Figure 5.

Because simple clustering has been found to be less than reliable, a technique known as noisy clustering is used (Nerbonne et al. 2011: 17). In order to test for the stability of groupings, clustering is repeated and noise is added. In Figure 6 the small numbers beside the cluster lines indicate the percentage of times that particular cluster re-emerged.

Not all clusters reach a desirable level of reliability. Especially the groups linking languages close to Northern Tutchone and Slavey appear somewhat unstable. On the whole, the dendrogram appears in line with received wisdom even though some placements, in particular the proximity of the Pacific Coast language Tututni to both Northern and Apachean languages, might appear surprising. However, an assessment of the accuracy of this dendrogram (as well as the one in figure 6) is only possible with respect

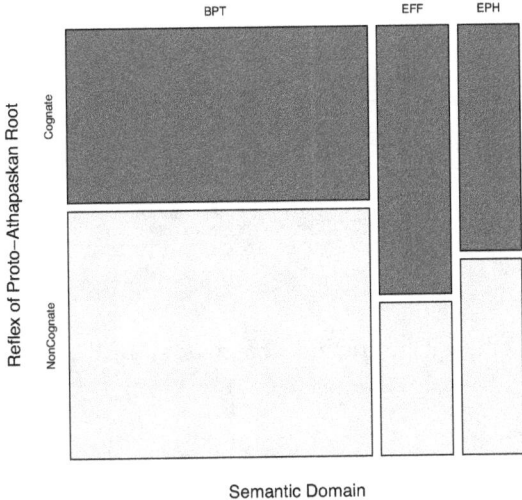

Figure 4. Mosaic plot of the proportions of cognates by semantic sub-domain (BPT = body-part terms, EFF = effluvia, EPH = ephemera).

to the intuitions of experts and the generally held view of Athapaskan language relationships. A rigorous testing of the method requires observing its efficacy when applied to data from language families whose phylogeny is known.[3] Nonetheless, a qualitative assessment of the results is possible.

The comparison of semantic sub-domains carried out above, suggests that it might be possible to work with a smaller dataset if those data have been shown to be reliable. The comparison of diachronic stability among the sub-domains revealed that effluvia terms are more likely to be retained and hence to be cognates. This can be usefully exploited in the calculation of language distance. The dendrogram resulting from the calculation of language proximity based on the effluvia data alone results in some very stable clusterings. From the perspective of regional distance between the locations at which the languages are (or were) spoken both Tututni and Ahtna surface in somewhat unexpected neighborhoods. Rather than then leading the reader to dismiss the methodology out of hand as ineffective in these cases, these relations should be viewed as hypothesis to be investigated further.

Especially for those languages such as Tsuut'ina for which any affiliation is uncertain these placements can provide important clues to be elaborated in further more in-depth study. As such the results presented here are very much stepping stones within the larger project of discovering language relationships within Athapaskan.

242 Conor Snoek

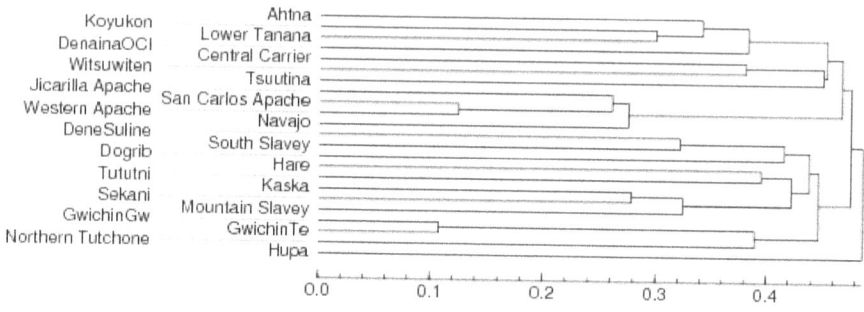

Figure 5. Dendrogram of language proximity based on all BEETs in the sample.

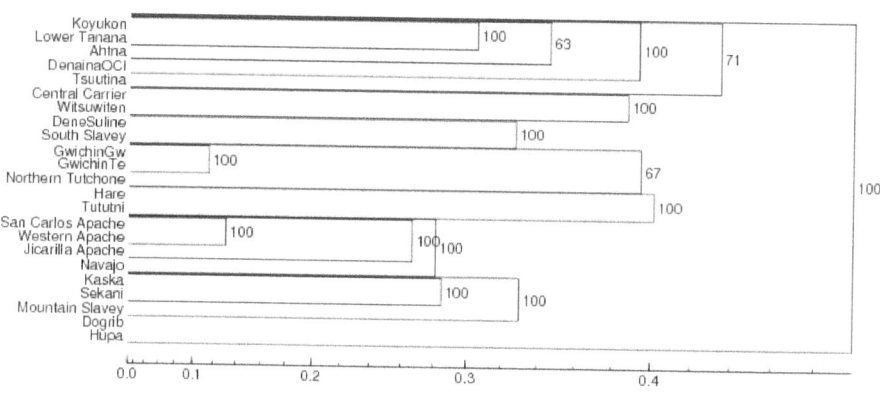

Figure 6. Dendrogram of language proximity based on all BEETs in the sample.

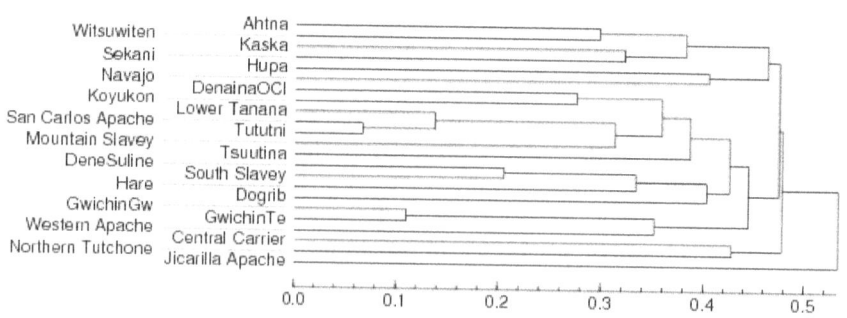

Figure 7. Dendrogram of language proximity based on only effluvia terms.

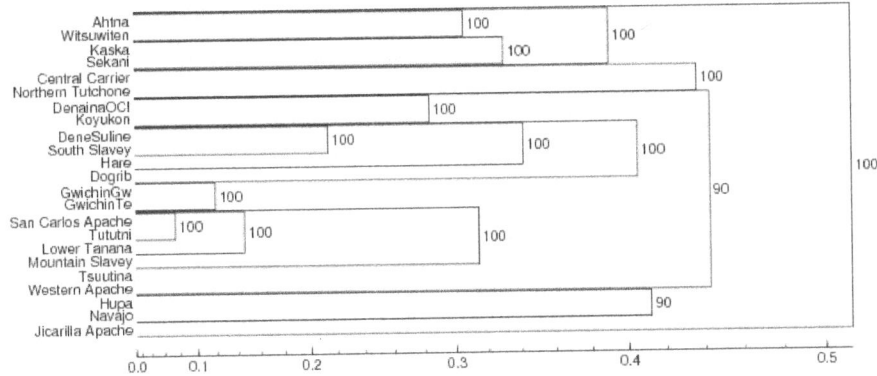

Figure 8. Dendrogram of language proximity based on only effluvia terms.

7. Discussion and conclusion

The cluster dendrograms presented here were based on orthography rather than pronunciations, as would normally be the input for an application such as *Gabmap*. One clear improvement that must be carried out therefore is the gathering of pronunciation data for Athapaskan languages. While this will undoubtedly improve the accuracy of the findings, using orthographies might not be as fatal as could be supposed: Athapaskan orthographies are, in the main, quite close to pronunciations, especially since most have only recently been developed and implemented.

The dendrograms produced here can be a valuable aid in deciphering Athapaskan language prehistory. They are a further step toward a reconstruction of an accurate phylogeny. This latter goal is particularly desirable in light of the renewed interest in the Dene-Yeniseian language hypothesis (Kari and Potter 2010). However, the usefulness of the methodological approach presented here for historical linguistic study will be increased through the testing of the approach on data for which phylogenetics links have already been established with some certainty.

I hope to have shown that gathering data from a semantically restricted domain is a useful and fruitful approach that can be exploited through computational approaches. Beyond Athapaskan linguistics, the domain of the parts of the body has already been found to be a rich lexical domain for comparative work (see for example Matisoff 1978). The application of quantitative methods has, however, been infrequent. This is especially apparent within Athapaskan linguistics itself, which has failed to capitalize on computational power so far, despite the presence of excellent pioneering studies (for example Eddington and Lachler 2006). For a field whose subject of study has proved so difficult and intractable for so long, the rigorous and non-dogmatic application of quantitative methods is sure to bring rich fruit in the future.

Appendix I

Table 3. Body-Part Terms

1.	ankle	11.	finger	21.	liver	31.	shoulder
2.	arm	12.	gums	22.	lungs	32.	shoulder blade
3.	bone	13.	hand	23.	marrow	33.	sinew
4.	breast	14.	head	24.	mouth	34.	testicle(s)
5.	butt	15.	hip	25.	navel	35.	throat
6.	cheek	16.	intestine	26.	neck	36.	thumb
7.	chin	17.	jaw	27.	nipple	37.	toe
8.	ear(s)	18.	kidney(s)	28.	penis	38.	tongue
9.	eye	19.	leg	29.	person/people	39.	vagina
10.	face	20.	lips	30.	ribs	40.	wrist

Table 4. Effluvia

1.	blood	5.	mucus	9.	sweat		
2.	excrement	6.	pus	10.	tear		
3.	fart	7.	saliva	11.	vomit		
4.	gall/bile	8.	snot	12.	urine		

Table 5. Ephemera

1.	wart	4.	hair	7.	teeth		
2.	fat	5.	scab	8.	toenail		
3.	fingernail	6.	scar	9.	umbilical cord		

Appendix II: Number of available items per language

Table 6. Number of available items per language

Language	BEET	Language	BEET
Ahtna	58	Mountain Slavey	40
Central Carrier	56	Navajo	59
Dena'ina	38	Northern Tutchone	54
Dene Sųłiné	53	San Carlos Apache	31
Gwich'in (Gwıchya)	40	Sekani (Fort Ware)	51
Gwich'in (Teetl'ıt)	48	South Slavey (Kátł'odehche)	50
Hare	56	Tłįchǫ	56
Hupa	60	Tsuut'ina	47
Jicarilla Apache	41	Tututni (Euchre Creek)	35
Kaska (Liard)	50	Western Apache	47
Koyukon	56	Witsuwit'en	46
Lower Tanana	11		

Notes

1. I would like to thank Dr. Sally Rice for the many helpful suggestions and comments on this paper.
2. With the kind help of Dr. John Nerbonne and Martijn Wieling, whom I must thank for their excellent tutorial at the Workshop on comparing approaches to measuring linguistic differences at the University of Gothenburg 2011.
3. Thanks to Dr. Grzegorz Kondrak for pointing this out.

References

Antoine, Francesca, Catherine Bird, Agnes Isaac, Nellie Prince, and Sally Sam
    1974   *Central Carrier Bilingual Dictionary.* Fort Saint James (BC): Carrier Linguistic Committee.

Arppe, Antti
    2008   Univariate, bivariate, and multivariate methods in corpus-based lexicography – a study of synonymy. Ph. D. diss., Department of General Linguistics, University of Helsinki.

Bray, Dorothy (ed.)
    1998   *Western Apache-English Dictionary.* Tempe (AZ): Bilingual Press.

Brown, Cecil H.
   2011   Hand and Arm. In *The World Atlas of Language Structures Online*, Matthew S. Dryer, and Martin Haspelmath (eds.), Chapter 29. Munich: Max Planck Digital Library, http://wals.info/chapter/129 (accessed 26 March 2012).

Chappell, Hilary and William McGregor (eds.)
   1996   *The Grammar of Inalienability: a Typological Perspective on Body Part Terms*. Berlin/New York: Mouton de Gruyter.

Cook, Eung-Do and Keren Rice (eds.)
   1989   *Athapaskan Linguistics: Current Perspectives on a Language Family*. Berlin/New York: Mouton de Gruyter.

Dogrib Divisional Board of Education
   1996   *Tłįchǫ Yatiì Enįhtł'è A Dogrib Dictionary*. Rae-Edzo (NWT): Dogrib Divisional Board of Education.

Dyen, Isidor and David F. Aberle
   1974   *Lexical Reconstruction: The Case of the Proto-Athapaskan Kinship System*. London and New York: Cambridge University Press.

Eddington, David and Jordan Lachler
   2006   A computational analysis of Navajo verb stems. *In Empirical and Experimental Methods in Cognitive/Functional Research*, John Newman, and Sally Rice (eds.), 59–72. Stanford: Center for the Study of Language and Information Publications.

Elford, Leon W. and Marjorie Elford
   1998   *Dene (Chipewyan) Dictionary*. Prince Albert: Northern Canada Mission Distributors.

Firth, William G. (ed.)
   2005   *Gwich'in Language Dictionary*. Fort McPherson: Gwich'in Language Centre and Gwich'in Social and Cultural Institute.

Golla, Victor (ed.)
   1996   *Hupa Language Dictionary*. Hoopa: Hoopa Valley Tribal Council.

Hargus, Sharon
   2001   Fort Ware (Kwadeche) Sekani Dictionary: Sekani–English English–Sekani. Unpublished manuscript.

Hargus, Sharon
   2007   *Witsuwit'en Grammar*. Vancouver: The University of British Columbia Press.

Heeringa, Wilbert
   2004   *Measuring Dialect Pronunciation Differences using Levenshtein Distance*. Groningen: Groningen Dissertations in Linguistics 46.

Hoijer, Harry
   1963   The Athapaskan languages. In *Studies in the Athapaskan languages*, Hoijer, Harry (Ed.), 1–29. Berkeley: University of California Press.

Jetté, Jules and Eliza Jones
    2000   *Koyukon Athabaskan Dictionary.* Fairbanks: Alaska Native Language Center.

Kari, James
    2007   *Dena'ina Topical Dictionary.* Fairbanks: Alaskan Native Languages Center.

Kari, James
    1991   *Lower Tanana Athabaskan Listening and Writing Exercises.* Fairbanks: Alaska Native Languages Center.

Kari, James and Ben A. Potter (eds.)
    2010   *The Dene-Yeniseian Connection.* Anthropological Papers of the University of Alaska, Volume 5. Fairbanks: University of Alaska Fairbanks, Department of Anthropology.

Kaska Tribal Council
    1997   *Guzāgi K'úgé': Our language Book: Nouns: Kaska, Mountain Slavey and Sekani.* Whitehorse: Kaska Tribal Council.

Krauss, Michael E.
    1992   The world's languages in crisis. *Language* 68 (1): 4–10.

Krauss, Michael E.
    2005   Athabaskan Tone. In *Athabaskan Prosody,* Keren Rice and Sharon Hargus (eds.). 55–136. Amsterdam: John Benjamins.

Krauss, Michael E. and Jeff Leer
    1981   *Athabaskan, Eyak, and Tlingit sonorants.* Alaska Native Language Center Research Papers Number 5. Fairbanks, AK: University of Alaska, Alaska Native Language Center.

Levenshtein, Vladimir
    1965   Binary codes capable of correcting deletions, insertions and reversals. *Doklady Adademii Nauk SSSR,* 164: 845–848.

Matisoff, James
    1978   *Variational Semantics in Tibeto–Burman: The 'Organic' Approach to Linguistic Comparison.* Occasional Papers of the Wolfenden Society on Tibeto–Burman Linguistics, Volume VI. Philadelphia: Publication of the Institute for the Study of Human Issues.

Mithun, Marianne
    1999   *The Languages of Native North America.* Cambridge: Cambridge University Press.

Monus, Victor (ed.)
    2009   *South Slavey Topical Dictionary Kátł'odehche Dialect.* Forth Smith (NWT): South Slave Divisional Education Council, Northwest Territories.

Nerbonne, John, Rinke Colen, Charlotte Gooskens, Peter Kleiweg & Therese Leinonen
    2011   Gabmap – a web application for dialectology. *Dialectologia* (Special Issue II): 65–89.

Phone, Wilhelmina, Maureen Olson, and Matilda Martinez
    2007   *Dictionary of Jicarilla Apache*. Albuquerque: University of New Mexico.

De Reuse, Willem J.
    2006   *A Practical Grammar of the San Carlos Apache Language*. München: Lincom Europa.

Rice, Keren
    1978   *Hare Dictionary*. Northern Social Research Division, Department of Indian and Northern Affairs.

Rice, Keren
    1989   *A Grammar of Slave*. Berlin/New York: Mouton de Gruyter.

Starlight, Bruce and Gary Donovan
    2004   *Tsuut'ina pedagogical Dictionary*. Calgary.

Wilkins, David P.
    1996   Natural tendencies of semantic change and the search for cognates. In *The Comparative Method Reviewed*, Mark Durie, and Malcolm Ross (eds.). 264–304. Oxford: Oxford University Press.

Witkowski, Stanley R. and Cecil H. Brown
    1985   Climate, clothing and body–part nomenclature. *Ethnology* 24: 197–214.

Young, Robert W. and William Morgan
    1980   *The Navajo Language*. Albuquerque: University of New Mexico Press.

Languages with longer words have more lexical change

Søren Wichmann and Eric W. Holman

1. Introduction: Aims and data[1]

The findings to be presented in this paper were not anticipated, but came about as an unexpected result of looking at how the application of a version of the Levenshtein distance to word lists compares with cognate counting. We were interested in the degree to which the two correlate. The results of this investigation are intrinsically interesting and will be presented in the following section 2, but even more interesting is our finding that differences between counting cognates and measuring the Levenshtein distances vary as a function of average word lengths in the word lists compared. This observation will occupy the remainder of the paper, with section 3 devoted to establishing the statistical significance of the observation across language families, while section 4 establishes the significance within language groups, and section 5 discusses competing explanations. First we briefly explain the specific version of the Levenshtein distance used and the concept of cognate identification.

In numerous previous papers, beginning in Holman et al. (2008a), the present authors as well as other members of the network of scholars participating in the project known as ASJP (or Automated Similarity Judgment Program) have applied a computer-assisted comparison of word lists in order to derive a measure of differences among languages. Our method consists in comparing pairs of words to determine the Levenshtein distance, LD, which is defined as the number of substitutions, insertions, and deletions necessary to transform one word into another. The LD is divided by the length of the longer of the two words compared such that any distance will come to lie in the range 0%–100%. This normalized measure, called LDN,[2] is averaged over all pairs of words referring to the same concept in lists from two given languages. To enhance discrimination between related and unrelated languages, this average LDN is further divided by the average LDN between words referring to different concepts in the different lists, to obtain what we call LDND ('Levenshtein Distance Normalized Divided'). A similarity measure, here called ASJPsim, is defined by subtracting LDND from 100%.

The higher performance of LDND in comparison to LDN for the purpose of classifying languages is supported in Pompei et al. (2011) and Wichmann et al. (2010a), and Huff and Lonsdale (2011) report similar performances of LDND and the more linguistically informed but also much more computer-intensive ALINE algorithm of Kondrak (2000). Greenhill (2011) reports a low performance for LDN (not looking at LDND), but limits the investigation to the specific case of the Austronesian languages.

LDND and ASJPsim have been put to various uses, such as the dating of proto-languages (Holman et al. 2011), the identification of geographical centers of linguistic diversity for the purpose of identifying homelands (Wichmann et al. 2010c), the estimation of the limitations of word list comparisons for identifying deep genealogical relationships (Wichmann et al. 2010b), and the study of the relationship between population sizes and language change rates (Wichmann and Holman 2009). As objective and easily-obtained measures of the difference and similarity between any given pair of languages, LDND and ASJPsim are potentially useful for the investigation of possible correlations between languages and other kinds of data, such as data pertaining to human culture, prehistory, biology, and ecology.

A different method of measuring similarities between languages is that of counting cognates (related words) on a fixed list of lexical concepts. The percentage of concepts for which the words are cognate in two given languages is here called COGNsim. This method was developed within the framework of lexicostatistics (e.g., Swadesh 1955). In more recent years, cognate identification has been used to establish cognate classes as input to character-based phylogenetic methods, and a variety of issues have been explored using such methods, including dating and classification of language groups (Gray and Jordan 2000; Gray and Atkinson 2003), identification of factors that affect speed of lexical change (Pagel et al. 2007; Atkinson et al. 2008), questions of homelands and language expansions (Gray et al. 2009; Walker and Ribeiro 2011), and relationships between the evolution of different cultural traits (cf. Mace and Jordan 2011 for a review). These studies have mostly been carried out in relation to the three largest groups of languages where word lists coded for cognacy are available: Indo-European (Dyen et al. 1992), Austronesian (Greenhill et al. 2008), and Bantu (Bastin et al. 1999).

Identifying a cognate pair of words is not a trivial task. In the ideal situation a full set of sound correspondences is available which will allow the researcher to match up related words correctly, but the prior identification of regular sound correspondences requires hundreds, if not thousands, of sets of word comparisons. Such information is rarely available. Thus, it is more common to resort to some version of what Gudschinsky (1956: 615) calls the "inspection method", which essentially amounts to educated guesses.

The aim of this paper is to compare ASJPsim to COGNsim. ASJPsim is based on the 40 items identified by Holman et al. (2008b) as the most stable in Swadesh's (1955) 100-item lexicostatistical list. This can be compared to COGNsim at two different levels of resolution, depending on the type of data available. Many published studies present matrices of cognate percentages based on Swadesh's 100-item list, his earlier 200-item list (Swadesh 1952) or a modification of one of these.[3] A minority of studies additionally provide word lists where each lexical item is identified as belonging to a given cognate class, thus allowing for a higher resolution of the comparison in the sense that ASJPsim can be compared to judgments of cognacy at the level of words. These comparisons are based on the items in the 40-item ASJP list that are also included in the lists used in the study. For simplicity, all calculations are based on the first synonym listed if the source includes more than one synonym for a concept. Loanwords identified as such in the source are omitted from the calculations.

Table 1 provides an overview of data and sources. These have been found by a search of pertinent literature. Undoubtedly more could be added, but the sample is sufficiently large and has a sufficient spread in terms of geography and genealogies (language families) that it allows us to test the statistical significance of observations made. Language family designations from *Ethnologue* (Lewis 2009) are followed by the abbreviations that we will use in later tables. We follow the sources in naming the different language groups.[4] See the legend after the table for abbreviations of language group names. These names will be used throughout this paper to identify a dataset from a specific source. For instance, in the context of references to data we use "Austronesian" for a small set of languages whose cognate percentages are given in Dyen (1965) rather than for the family as a whole. The appendix shows how we match languages in the sources with word lists in the ASJP database (Wichmann et al. 2012). We additionally provide a checkmark (√) following the reference when word lists encoded for cognate classes were available,[5] and finally we provide the number of languages (N) within each group for which data were available for both COGNsim and ASJPsim. The total number of languages sampled amounts to around 8% of the world's languages by the definition of Lewis (2009). The sample includes 24 families from all world areas, with no major skewing: Africa (3), Eurasia and SE Asia (7), the Pacific (6), North America (3), South America (3), Middle America (2).

Table 1. Overview of sources and the nature of the data

Family	Abb.	Group	Source	N
Afro-Asiatic	AA	Afras	Militarev (2000) √	18
		Cushitic	Bender (1971)	28
		EthSem	Bender (1971)	13
		Omotic	Bender (1971)	21
Altaic	Alt	Turkic	Troike (1969)	6
Australian	Aus	Daly	Tryon (1974)	13
		Iwaidjan	R. Mailhammer (p.c., 2011)	3
		Mayi	Breen (1981)	5
		Paman	Sommer (1976)	3
		WAustr	O'Grady (1966)	7
		WBarkly	Chadwick (1979)	3
		Worrorran	McGregor & Rumsey (2009)	9
Austro-Asiatic	AuA	MonKhm	Peiros (1998) √	16
Austronesian	An	Austr	Dyen (1965)	10
		Malagasy	Vérin et al. (1969)	18
		Melan	Z'Graggen (1969)	6
		Morob	Hooley (1971) √	55
		NHebr	Tryon (1973)	16
		Philip	Llamzon (1976)	72
		Yapen	Anceaux (1961)	18
Carib	Car	Cariban	Villalon (1991)	10
Dravidian	Dra	Dravidian	Andronov (2001)	10
Hmong-Mien	HM	MiaoY	Peiros (1998) √	6
Indo-European	IE	IndEur	Dyen et al. (1992)	55
Japonic	Jap	Japonic	Hattori (1961)	5
Mayan	May	Mayan	C. H. Brown (p.c., 2011) √	30
Macro-Ge	MGe	Ge	Wilbert (1962)	9
Mixe-Zoque	MZ	MiZo	Cysouw et al. (2006) √	10
Na-Dene	NDe	Athap	Hoijer (1956) √	15
Niger-Congo	NC	Atlantic	Sapir (1971)	21
		Benue-Congo	Bennett & Sterk (1977)	22
		Gur	Swadesh et al. (1966)	20
		Kwa	Heine (1968)	13

Family	Abb.	Group	Source	N
Nilo-Saharan	NS	ESud	Thelwall (1981)	12
		NilSah	Bender (1971)	23
		Southern Luo	Blount & Curley (1970)	5
Quechuan	Que	Quechua	Torero (1970)	9
Salishan	Sal	Salish	Swadesh (1950)	21
Sino-Tibetan	ST	Chinese	Xu (1991)	6
		LoloB	Peiros (1998) √	15
		SinTib	Benedict (1976)	7
Tai-Kadai	TK	Kadai	Peiros (1998) √	11
Torricelli	Tor	Kamas	Sanders & Sanders (1980) √	7
Trans-New Guinea	TNG	Angan	Lloyd (1973)	12
		Awyu	Voorhoeve (1968)	6
		Bosavi	Shaw (1986)	22
		Eleman	Brown (1973)	8
		Finisterre	Claasen & McElhanon (1970)	12
		GVDani	Bromley (1967)	7
		GrMad	Z'Graggen (1969)	50
		Huon	McElhanon (1967) √	14
		Kiwaian	Wurm (1973)	8
		Koiarian	Dutton (1969)	6
		Kolopom	Voorhoeve (1968)	3
		Ok	Voorhoeve (1968)	5
		TurKik	Franklin (1973)	4
Uto-Aztecan	UA	Uto-Aztecan	Miller (1984), Cortina-Borja & Valiñas (1989)	26
West Papuan	WP	NHalm	Chlenov (1986)	8
		Yawa	Jones (1986)	6

Legend: Afras: Afrasian; EthSem: Ethiosemitic; WAustr: West Australian; WBarkly: West Barkly; MoKh: Mon-Khmer; Austr: Austronesian; Melan: Melanesian; Morob: Morobe; NHebr: New Hebrides; Philip: Philippines; MiaoY: Miao-Yao; IndEur: Indo-European; MiZo: Mixe-Zoquean; Athap: Athapaskan; ESud: Eastern Sudanic; NilSah: Nilo-Saharan; LoloB: Lolo-Burmese; SinTib: Sino-Tibetan; Kamas: Kamasau; GVDani: Grand Valley Dani; GrMad: Greater Madang; TurKik: Turama-Kikorian; NHalm: North Halmahera.

2. Comparing ASJPsim and COGNsim

The number of data points for ASJPsim and COGNsim for individual language pairs is so large that it is unwieldy for visual inspection. However, to illustrate an interesting tendency in the data we plot language pairs from five different families in figure 1.

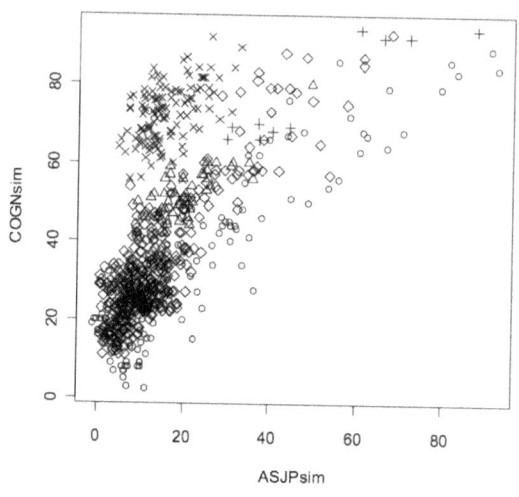

Figure 1. Scatter-plot of COGNsim as a function of ASJPsim for individual language pairs pertaining to five selected families: Australian (o), Uto-Aztecan (◊), Japonic (+), Carib (Δ), Sino-Tibetan (×).

Figure 1 illustrates, for selected data, that different families tend to occupy different regions in a scatter-plot of COGNsim and ASJPsim. For instance, Australian language pairs tend to stay close to the diagonal, whereas Sino-Tibetan language pairs occupy a region where low values for ASJPsim correspond to high values for COGNsim. Language pairs from other families occupy regions in between.

Table 2 provides data on the averages of ASJPsim and COGNsim for all language pairs within each family as well as Pearson's r for the correlation between mASJPsim and mCOGNsim across all language pairs belonging to the family.

Reviewing the second and third columns in table 2 we observe that mCOGNsim, the average cognate similarity within families, is always greater than mASJPsim, the corresponding average ASJP similarity. This is because cognates can be less than 100% similar.

Table 2. Data on mean ASJP similarities and mean cognate similarities

Family	mASJPsim	mCOGNsim	r
AA	12.30	23.13	0.856
Alt	57.84	75.57	0.600
An	23.23	31.80	0.726
AuA	13.82	38.66	0.788
Aus	19.36	32.00	0.886
Car	20.42	52.00	0.765
Dra	23.11	33.13	0.869
HM	10.67	72.36	0.715
IE	9.48	24.05	0.921
Jap	50.70	78.00	0.921
May	29.14	47.82	0.862
MGe	29.31	66.56	0.451
MZ	46.42	66.10	0.806
NC	7.54	31.92	0.741
NDe	19.51	51.83	0.739
NS	6.67	12.53	0.934
Que	54.63	82.43	0.325
Sal	11.79	24.56	0.841
ST	14.62	66.85	0.576
TK	21.69	62.81	0.788
TNG	16.95	31.69	0.836
Tor	63.41	77.52	0.929
UA	14.29	46.83	0.837
WP	49.74	75.21	0.648

In figure 2 we plot the relationship between mCOGNsim and mASJPsim. The dotted line, provided as a point of comparison, intercepts at zero and has a slope of 1. The solid line shows the results of a linear regression, where $r = 0.762$ and $p < 0.0001$. Its slope is 0.93, which is so close to 1 that the intercept, at 25.96%, can be interpreted as the percentage that roughly needs to be added to get from mASJPsim to mCOGNsim. The relatively high r and the low p show that ASJPsim and COGNsim are parallel measures of similarities among languages.[6] However, we observe a cone-shaped distribution of the dots in the chart, with a tremendous amount of variation in mCOGNsim for low values of ASJPsim and an increasingly narrower concentration around the regression line for high values of ASJPsim. This reflects the sort of distribution exemplified in figure 1, where language pairs in different families form clouds in different regions of the chart, except that here (in figure 2) we represent each family as a single data point. In the following section we turn to possible explanations for this variability.

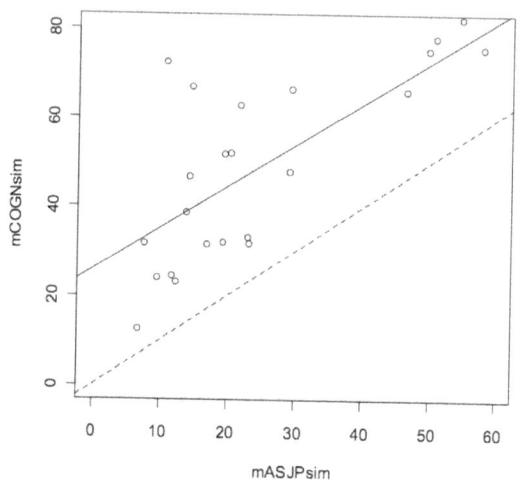

Figure 2. Scatter-plot of mCOGNsim against mASJPsim

3. mCOGNsim vs. mASJPsim in relation to segment inventory size and word length

Given that the relation between ASJPsim and COGNsim is partly a "family matter" we need to somehow capture the relationship across all language pairs pertaining to each family. One way of doing this is simply to take the average of the difference between COGNsim and ASJPsim, which we call mDIFF. Another, more principled approach involves looking at how the two depend on time. Glottochronology (Lees 1953) assumes that the logarithm of COGNsim diminishes in proportion to time, and a similar assumption, supported by evidence from 52 archaeological, historical and epigraphic calibration points, is made for ASJPsim in Holman et al. (2011). Thus, the log of COGNsim should be proportional to the log of ASJPsim. A useful way of characterizing the relation between COGNsim and ASJPsim, then, is to find the average ratio, mRATIO, of log(COGNsim) to log(ASJPsim) across language pairs of a given family.

It could be the case that the size of phonological inventories affects the rate of change in segments. If a language has a relatively large number of segments the phonetic space occupied by each will be relatively small. In this situation a phonetic fluctuation will perhaps more easily cross the phonological boundary of a neighboring segment in the phonetic space, leading to free variation, which may eventually lead to articulatorily driven phonological change. Perceptually driven changes would also seem to occur with a higher probability when the phonetic space is more densely packed, since language users would be more prone to misperceive a sound when phonetically similar sounds constitute part of the inventory. These hypothetical factors translate into the testable prediction that the difference between mASJPsim and mCOGNsim should be positively correlated with the average number of phonological segments found in the group of languages concerned.

While we do not have access to full segment inventories for the languages in our sample, we can use as proxies the number of different segments in the ASJP transcription system (or ASJPcode, cf. Brown et al. 2008) found in the 40-item word lists. In Wichmann et al. (2011) the number of different segments in word lists was used as a proxy for segment inventory sizes in a successful way, inasmuch as we were able to confirm well-known correlations involving segment inventory sizes (Hay and Bauer 2007; Nettle 1995, 1998) using the mean number of segments represented in word lists (mSR).

Another set of hypotheses is that shorter words tend to change faster phonologically than longer ones or that speakers of a language will exchange their words for completely new ones with a relatively high speed when their language contains relatively long words. In both cases, the difference between COGNsim and ASJPsim should be inversely correlated with mean word length, because the rate of loss of COGNsim over time would approach the rate of loss of ASJPsim when words are longer. Now, these are perhaps not the intuitively most plausible hypotheses and we would not have produced them had it not been for the fact that either one or the other is strongly supported by our data. As a measure of word length, we take the first word for each concept in our 40-item lists and average the number of ASJPcode segments (if the translation of the concept is phrasal we still only take the first word). Finally we average the averages within language families to obtain mmWL.

Table 3 contains the data needed to test these different predictions. First we test whether the difference between mASJPsim and mCOGNsim is positively correlated with mSR, and thereby the hypothesis that languages change phonologically faster the more phonemes they have. A linear correlation of mSR and mDIFF indeed shows a positive correlation of $r = .21$, but it is small and non-significant, $p = .32$. As another way of looking at the relationship we can test whether mRATIO, i.e., the mean of the ratios of log(COGNsim) to log(ASJPsim), is negatively correlated with mSR. This is, indeed, the case, but again the correlation is small and non-significant, $r = -.23$, $p = .27$. Thus, judging from the evidence from language family averages, the hypothesis that languages change faster phonologically the more segments they have is not borne out – in spite of the plausible nature of the hypothesis.

We now go on to test whether differences in word length explain the variability in differences between cognate similarities and ASJP similarities across language families. Again referring to table 3 we first correlate mDIFF and mmWL, which yields a solid $r = -.50$, $p = .01$. Again we alternatively test for mRATIO and find that this property is positively correlated with mmWL, $r = .53$, $p < .01$.

Somewhat unexpectedly we have found that, judging by averages across families, lexical replacement increases as a function of word length or, alternatively, phonological change decreases as a function of word length. In contrast, lexical replacement and phonological change are not significantly affected by the sizes of segment inventories.[7] Later in this paper we discuss the competing explanations for the correlations involving word length. But before that, we would like to establish the findings more firmly by looking at the behavior of individual words within language families.

4. Correlations across items within families

We have seen in the previous section that language families with longer words tend to have fewer cognates relative to their overall lexical similarity than do families with shorter words. Does this correlation apply to the words themselves or only to the families? This question can be addressed in the eleven language groups with checkmarks in table 1, for which the sources of the word lists also indicate which words are cognate. With this information it is possible to calculate mASJPsim and mCOGNsim separately for individual items on the ASJP 40-item list, averaged across language pairs in the group. DIFF and RATIO are then defined for each item as mCOGNsim – mASJPsim and log(mCOGNsim)/log(mASJPsim), respectively. One new property of items, mAsimC, is defined as mASJPsim calculated only for those pairs of words identified as cognate. mAsimC indicates the degree of phonological similarity between words that may have undergone phonological change but have not undergone lexical replacement. To ensure representative samples,

Table 3. Data for correlations with numbers of segments and mean word length

Family	mDIFF	mRATIO	mSR	mmWL
AA	10.83	0.644	27.36	4.06
Alt	17.72	0.545	23.83	3.58
An	8.57	0.795	20.65	4.53
AuA	24.84	0.469	25.25	3.65
Aus	12.64	0.686	18.35	5.21
Car	31.58	0.407	19.30	4.68
Dra	10.02	0.746	19.90	3.96
HM	61.69	0.133	28.33	3.29
IE	14.58	0.570	26.80	3.95
Jap	27.30	0.339	20.40	3.79
May	18.68	0.589	24.96	3.66
MGe	37.25	0.353	23.44	3.82
MZ	19.68	0.577	19.50	3.78
NC	24.37	0.436	24.47	3.73
NDe	32.31	0.302	27.93	3.24
NS	5.87	0.775	25.73	3.83
Que	27.80	0.328	21.56	4.41
Sal	12.77	0.641	32.67	5.06
ST	52.23	0.229	27.52	3.37
TK	41.12	0.284	25.00	2.98
TNG	14.75	0.653	20.49	4.27
Tor	14.12	0.573	21.86	4.17
UA	32.54	0.531	20.42	4.42
WP	25.47	0.467	18.29	4.63

Legend: mDIFF: the difference between mASJPsim and mCOGNsim; mRATIO: the mean ratio of log(COGNsim) to log(ASJPsim); mSR: the mean of the number of different phonological segments in the word lists pertaining to the family; mmWL: the average word length within word lists averaged across the languages the family.

all these quantities are calculated only for items that are attested in at least 70% of the languages in the group. Also, mAsimC is defined for an item only if mCOGNsim is above 0%, because otherwise there are no cognate pairs for the item. RATIO is defined only if mCOGNsim is above 0% and mASJPsim is strictly between 0% and 100%, in order to avoid logarithms of nonpositive numbers or division by 0.

Table 4. Correlations within families

Group	mAs	mCs	DIFF	RATIO	mAsimC
Afras	−.359	−.193	−.369	.415	.180
MoKh	−.370	−.326	−.317	.443	−.269
Morob	−.083	.090	−.135	.209	.010
MiaoY	−.092	−.401	.080	−.080	−.462
Mayan	−.569	−.389	−.495	.609	−.016
MiZo	−.409	−.445	−.092	.288	−.376
Athap	−.342	−.259	−.255	.393	−.166
LoloB	−.063	−.402	.154	.091	−.447
Kadai	.038	−.044	.090	−.076	−.140
Kamas	−.368	−.306	−.160	.157	−.004
Huon	−.267	−.519	.100	−.149	−.119
Mean	−.262	−.290	−.127	.209	−.164
t(10)	4.68	5.12	1.95	2.82	2.65

Legend: mAs: mASJPsim; mCs: mCOGNsim

Cases where a concept is translated by a phrase, i.e., two or more words separated by spaces in the data source, rather than by a single word, are treated differently for different purposes. For the estimates of the mean length of words used in previous sections only the first word in a phrase was counted. This seems appropriate when a word list is used as a random sample of words in a language. However, for comparing the way that specific concepts are expressed across concepts and languages, as is done in the present section, the whole phrase is counted. When translations exceed a single word, the properties mASJPsim and mCOGNsim refer to the entire phrase throughout this paper. The data used are provided as an online appendix.

Mean word length is now correlated across lexical concepts with each of the similarity properties defined in the first paragraph of this section. That is, for each of the 40 items pertaining to the ASJP word lists of each language group we determine their average length as well as mASJPsim, mCOGNsim, etc., and then calculate Pearson's r. Table 4 provides the correlations for each of the eleven language groups, ordered as in table 1. The table also gives the mean correlation across groups and the value of Student's t (with 10 degrees of freedom) for testing whether the mean correlation differs from 0.

Most of the individual correlations are weak, possibly because of limited variation within language groups. They are collectively quite consistent across groups, however, producing significant effects ($p < .05$) for all but one measure, namely DIFF. Both measures of similarity, mASJPsim and mCOGNsim, show significantly less similarity when items are represented by longer words than when they are represented by shorter ones. Since similarity is calculated across the same pairs of languages for each item, it follows that time depth is the same across items and therefore that items represented by longer words are less stable through time than items represented by shorter ones. The two relative measures, DIFF and RATIO, are consistent with table 3 in showing less lexical similarity relative to phonological similarity for translational equivalents that have longer words, although this effect is significant only for RATIO. Finally, the significantly negative mean correlation for mAsimC implies that longer words undergo more phonological change even if they are not replaced. It follows that the lower lexical similarity of longer words relative to phonological similarity is a consequence of more lexical change rather than less phonological change. In summary, longer words are more likely to be replaced and more likely to change phonologically if they are not replaced.

The significant negative correlation between word length and stability can be extended to the entire ASJP database. For this purpose, mean word length is calculated for each item in each language family and then averaged across families. Stability is defined as in Holman et al. (2008b), except that their similarity measure is replaced by mASJPsim. More specifically, mASJPsim is first determined for each item in each of the language genera established by Dryer (1989, 2011), who defines genera as the most inclusive groups descended from a common ancestral language spoken within the last 3500 to 4000 years. Then stability is equal to the weighted mean of mASJPsim across genera, with each genus weighted by the square root of the number of language pairs in the genus. The correlation between stability and mean word length across the 40 items in the ASJP list proves to be substantial, $r = -.47$, $p < .01$. The other correlations in table 4 cannot be extended in this way because judgments of cognacy are not available for most language groups.

The negative correlation between word length and stability, whether measured by mASJPsim, mCOGNsim, or mAsimC, can be explained by the finding of Pagel et al. (2007) that frequency of use is positively correlated with stability, given that frequent words tend to be shorter than infrequent ones (Zipf 1935). This explanation, however, does not account for the new observation, replicated both across languages and across items, that short words show less lexical change relative to phonological change.

5. Discussion and conclusion

It is a central concern to historical linguistics to identify causes for language change, and many causes are known to exist. External ones include effects of social stratification, lexical adaptation (the creation of new words for new concepts), borrowing and other effects of language contact, imperfect vertical transmission, etc.; among internal ones we can mention the spread throughout the lexicon of sound changes, analogy, grammaticalization, etc. The introduction of glottochronology widened the search for factors that might affect the *rate* of language change. Examples of such factors would be borrowing or word taboo. To date, however, not a single factor, either external or internal to languages, has been identified which *systematically* affects rates of change. Population size is an example of a proposed external factor influencing the rate of language change which has not stood up to a quantitative scrutiny (Wichmann et al. 2008; Wichmann and Holman 2009). The already-mentioned relation between frequency and stability identified by Pagel et al. (2007) is an example of language-internal factors regulating the rate of change, but does not exemplify a factor that systematically predicts that one language changes faster than another.

Thus, our major finding in this paper, namely that longer words tend to be replaced faster than shorter words both within and across languages, is unique. One implication of the finding is that critics of glottochronology for the first time have a weapon other than case studies to attack the idea that lexical change is regular enough to be a useful tool for dating language divergence. The weapon is rather blunt, however, since the effect of average word length is not overwhelming even if statistically significant, and our work on the ASJP dating technique (Holman et al. 2011) still shows a high degree of regularity in the decay of ASJPsim over time. In fact, the present finding that the effect of word length is stronger for COGNsim than for ASJPsim may explain why some studies of glottochronology report less regular results than do Holman et al. Thus, the 'weapon' may serve practitioners of lexically-based dating techniques better than their critics since it can potentially be used to improve those techniques.

We have not yet addressed possible explanations for our finding, and cannot hope to do so conclusively at this point. One possibly relevant factor is the differing information provided by long and short words for judgments of cognacy. Maybe false cognates are more likely to be accepted for short words. This sort of inaccuracy is less likely to be important if cognacy is inferred by means of regular sound correspondences rather than judged by inspection. Cognitive biases are even more reduced for ASJPsim, which is normalized by word length and calculated automatically.

The other possible explanatory factor is the process of language change itself. Why should speakers of languages that have longer words in their basic vocabulary replace these words more frequently than speakers of languages that have shorter words? The reason is not, for instance, that speakers want to replace longer words with shorter ones, because we draw our observations from the current state of languages, where the ones that have the longer words have replaced *earlier* words faster.

Our tentative hypothesis is that if a language has rich word-formation strategies at its disposal such that many of the words in a language are formed by derivation and compounding, then the words in the language will tend to be longer and also will tend to be replaced more often. An implication is that the creation of complex lexemes is generally preferred over the creation of simplex ones. A problem for testing this hypothesis is that the ASJP word lists are not based on a consistent definition of what a word is. Generally, the word lists simply reflect whatever is given as a translational equivalent for each concept in a particular linguistic source, with the exception that transcribers have stripped off inflectional elements and class markers when their knowledge of the languages allowed them to do so. This is a minor caveat, since the data can be revisited and adjusted for consistency. A more serious problem is that each of the many lexical items used in this study would ideally have to be tagged for its status as simplex, derived, compounded, or phrasal (and maybe other categories, as well as various combinations) in order to provide more substance to our hypothesis. Thus, the further investigation of the proposed relation between differences in word formation strategies and rates of lexical replacement seems to call for a larger, collective effort and several future case studies.

Online appendix: word lists transcribed in ASJPcode with cognate encoding from the literature

The online appendix is available at http://spraakbanken.gu.se/sites/spraakbanken.gu.se/files/cognatedata.zip

The file contains data used in section 4, i.e., ASJP word lists with information on cognacy, mostly drawn from the literature. The format of the data sheet is explained in the file "description.pdf".

Appendix: matching of languages in the lexicostatistical literature with languages represented in the ASJP database used in this study

The data in tables 2–3 were produced by comparing published cognate percentages with ASJPsim for languages that are represented both in the lexicostatistical literature and in the ASJP database (Wichmann et al. 2012), where the latter has been updated to include as many of the languages in the former as possible and, whenever possible, the actual data on which the cognate counts were based. Language groups for which ASJPsim is calculated from the same dataset which was used for counting cognate percentages are identified by a star following the language group name, and when there are but a handful of exceptions where data from other sources have been added, or when data and cognate judgments are from the same author but in different publications, a star is given in parenthesis (note that ASJPsim is based on the reduced, 40-item version of the Swadesh list whereas published cognate percentages are based on other versions or derivatives, as described in section 1 of this paper, so identity of data sources does not mean complete identity of data). When authors providing cognate counts do not provide the word lists used, alternative data sources are used. All sources for ASJP word lists are found at http:// lingweb.eva.mpg.de/asjp/index.php/ASJP. The doculects represented in our database are uniquely identified by their names. In the lists below we provide the language family names (in bold), language group names (in bold italics), references to sources (in parentheses), names of languages in the sources for cognate counts (in normal font), the ISO 639-3 identifier, and the ASJP designation (in capital letters). Exceptions to these patterns are Iwaidjan (Australian) and Mayan, where cognate judgments were made directly in relation to ASJP word lists; thus, only the ISO-code and the ASJP designation are given in these cases. Language names are joined by + in cases where the source gives separate cognate percentages for varieties with the same ISO-code, and these percentages are averaged in the present calculations. In the ASJP database the language designations make use of the underscore characters instead of spaces (e.g., HARARI_2). In this appendix the underscores are replaced by spaces (e.g., HARARI 2) to allow for more line breaks. The information provided in this appendix is intended to ensure replicability of our results.

Afro-Asiatic: *Afrasian** (Militarev 2000): Lebanese Arabic, apc, ARABIC NORTH LEVANTINE; Tigrai, tig, TIGRIGNA; Amharic, amh, AMHARIC 3; Harari, har, HARARI 2; Mehri, gdq, MEHRI 2; Jibbali, shv, SHEHRI; Soqotri, sqt, SOQOTRI 2; Siwa, siz, SIWI; Ghadames, gha, GHADAMES 2; Qabyle, kab, KABYLE; Ahaggar, thv, TAMAHAQ TAHAGGART 2; Zenaga, zen, ZENAGA 2; Hausa, hau, HAUSA 3; Bole, bol, BOLE 2; Beja, bej, BEJA 2; Oromo, hae, EASTERN OROMO 2; Dahalo, dal, DAHALO 2; Kefa, kbr, KEFA 2. *Cushitic** (Bender 1971): Beja, bej, BEJA; Bilen, byn, BILIN 2; Qimant, ahg, KEMANT 2; Xamtanga, xan, XAMTANGA 2; Awngi, awn, AWNGI 2; Hadiyya, hdy, HADIYYA 2; Libido, liq, LIBIDO; Kembata, ktb, KAMBAATA 2; Alaba, alw, ALABA; Sidamo, sid, SIDAMO 2; Derasa, drs, GEDEO 2; Burji, bji, BURJI 2; Afar, aar, AFAR 2; Saho, ssy, SAHO 2; Baiso, bsw, BAISO 2; Arbore, arv, ARBORE 2; Dasenech, dsh, DAASANACH 2; Somali, som, SOMALI 2; Rendille, rel, RENDILLE 2; Mecha, gaz, MECHA OROMO; Borena, gax, BORANA OROMO 2; Qottu, hae, EASTERN OROMO; Konso, kxc, KOMSO 2; Gidole, gdl, GIDOLE 2; N Bussa, dox, BUSSA 2; Gawwada + Gobeze + Werize, gwd, GAWWADA 2; Tsamai, tsb, TSAMAI 2; Iraqw, irk, IRAQW 2. *Ethiosemitic(**) (Bender 1971): Tigre, tig, TIGRE; Tigrinya, tir, TIGRINYA; Amharic, amh, AMHARIC; Argobba, agj, ARGOBBA; Zway, zwa, ZWAY; Walani, stv, WALANI SILTE; Harari, har, HARARI; Gafat, gft, GAFAT; Soddo, gru, SODDO; Mesmes, mys, MESMES 2; Mesqan, mvz, MESQAN; Chaha + Geto, sgw, GETO; Innemor, ior, INNEMOR. *Omotic** (Bender 1971): Dime, dim, DIME; Ari, aiw, ARI; Banna, amf, BANNA; Maji, mdx, MAJI; Sheko, she, SHEKO; Nao, noz, NAO; Southern Mao, myo, SOUTHERN MAO; Shinasha, bwo, SHINASSHA 2; Kefa, kbr, KEFA; Mocha, moy, MOCHA 2; Janjero, jnj, JANJERO; Bencho, bcq, BENCHO; Male, mdy, MALE ETHIOPIA; Basketo, bst, BASKETO; Welamo, wal, WELAMO; Kullo, dwr, KULLO; Dorze, doz, DORZE; Oyda, oyd, OYDA; Kacama, kcx, KACHAMA; Koyra, kqy, KOYRA; Zayse + Zergulla, zay, ZAYSE.

Altaic: *Turkic** (Troike 1969): Turkish, tur, TURKISH 2; Azerbaijani (Azeri), azj, AZERBAIJANI NORTH:2; Karachai, krc, KARACHAY BALKAR; Crimean Tatar, tat, CRIMEAN TATAR; Kazan Tatar, tat, KAZAN TATAR; Misher Tatar, tat, MISHER TATAR.

Australian: *Daly** (Tryon 1974): Mullukmulluk, mpb, MULLUKMULLUK; Yunggor, zml, YUNGGOR; Kamor, xmu, KAMOR; Marithiel, mfr, MARITHIEL; Marityabin, zmj, MARITYABEN; Maridan, zmd, MARIDAN; Maramanadji, zmm, MARAMANADJI; Marengar, zmt, MARENGAR; Ami, amy, AMI; Manda, zma, MANDA; Pungupungu, wdj, PUNGUPUNGU; Wadyginy, wdj, WADJIGINY; Ngangikurr, nam, NGANGIKURRUNGGURR. *Iwaidjan** (Robert Mailhammer p.c., 2011): amg, AMURDAK; ibd, IWAIDJA; mph, MAWNG. *Mayi** (Breen 1981): Ngawun, nxn, NGAWUN; Mayi-Kulan, mnt, MAYKULAN; Mayi-Yapi, mnt, MAYI YAPI; Mayi-Thakurti, mnt, MAYI THAKURTI; Mayi-Kutuna, xmy, MAYAGUDUNA. *Paman* (Sommer 1976): Bariman Gutinhma, zmv, PARIMANKUTINMA; Umbuygamu, umg, UMBUYKAMU; Lamalama, lby, LAMALAMA COASTAL. *West Australian* (O'Grady 1966): Nyungumarda, nna, NYANGUMARTA; Yulbaridja, mpj, YULPARIJA; Warburton Ranges, ntj, NGAANYATJARRA; Pandjima, pnw, PANYTYIMA; Jindjibandi, yij, YINDJIBARNDI;

Ngaluma, nrl, NGALOOMA; Wadjeri, wbv, WAJARRI. *West Barkly* (Chadwick 1979): Wambaya, wmb, WAMBAYA; Djingili, jig, DJINGILI; Gudandji, nji, GUDANJI. *Worrorran*(*) (McGregor and 2009): Wunambal, wub, WUNAMBAL; Gunin Kwini, gww, GUNIN/KWINI; Ngarinyin, ung, NGARINYIN; Unggumi, unp, UNGGUMI; Bunuba, bck, BUNABA; Gooniyandi, gni, GOONIYANDI; Kija, gia, KITJA; Miriwoong, mep, MIRIWUNG; Walmajarri, wmt, WALMAJARRI.

Austro-Asiatic: *Mon-Khmer** (Peiros 1998): Jeh, jeh, JEH; Bahnar, bdq, BAHNAR; Chrau, crw, CHRAU; Kui, kdt, KUI THAILAND; Khmer, khm, KHMER; Semai, sea, SEMAI; Mon, mnw, MON; Nyakur, cbn, NYAKUR; Vietnamese, vie, VIETNAMESE; Ruc, scb, RUC; Wa, wbm, WA; Deang, pce, DEANG; Khmu, kjg, KHMU; Ksinmul, puo, KSINMUL; Khasi, kha, KHASI; Mundari, unr, MUNDARI.

Austronesian: *Austronesian* (Dyen 1965): Banoni, bcm, BANONI; Saposa, sps, TAIOF; Iai, iai, IAAI; Tongan, ton, TONGAN; Tanna, tnn, NORTH TANNA; Fiji, fij, FIJIAN; Zabana, kji, ZABANA; Roviana, rug, ROVIANA; Acira, adz, ADZERA; Yapese, yap, YAPESE. *Malagasy** (Vérin et al. 1969): Betsileo Ambositra, plt, MALAGASY AMBOSITRA; Antaisaka, bjq, MALAGASY ANTAISAKA; Antambahoaka, bjq, MALAGASY ANTAMBAHOAKA; Antankarana, xmw, MALAGASY ANTANKARANA; Bara, bhr, MALAGASY BARA; Betsimisaraka, bmm, MALAGASY BETSIMISARAKA; Betsileo Fianarantsoa, bjq, MALAGASY FIANARANTSOA; Mahafaly, tdx, MALAGASY MAHAFALY; Merina, plt, MALAGASY MERINA; Sakalava 1, skg, MALAGASY SAKALAVA 1; Sakalava 2, skg, MALAGASY SAKALAVA 2; Sihanaka, plt, MALAGASY SIHANAKA; Taimoro, plt, MALAGASY TAIMORO; Antandroy 1, tdx, MALAGASY TANDROY 1; Antandroy 2, tdx, MALAGASY TANDROY 2; Tsimihety, xmw, MALAGASY TSIMIHETY; Vezo, skg, MALAGASY VEZO; Zafisoro, bjq, MALAGASY ZAFISORO. *Melanesian** (Z'Graggen 1969): Manam, mva, MANAM; Sepa, spb, SEPA; Gedaged, gdd, GEDAGED; Bilbil, brz, BILBIL; Takia, tbc, TAKIA; Matukar, mjk, MATUKAR. *Morobe** (Hooley 1971): Wagao, bzh, WAGAU; Mapos, bzh, MAPOS; Manga, kby, MANGA; Patep, ptp, PATEP; Kumaru, ksl, KUMARU; Zenag, zeg, ZENAG; Towangara, goc, TOWANGARA; Sambio, tbx, SAMBIO; Dambi, dac, DAMBI; Piu, pix, PIU; Buasi, val, BUASI; Latep, zeg, LATEP; Dunguntung, mpl, DUNGUNTUNG; Dangal, mcy, DANGAL; Silisili, mpl, SILISILI; Bubwaf, mpl, BUBWAF; Dagin, lbq, DAGIN; Azera, adz, AZERA; Wampar, lbq, WAMPAR; Sirak, srf, SIRAK; Guwot, gve, GUWOT; Duwet, gve, DUWET; Musom, msu, MUSOM; Sukurum, zsu, SUKURUM; Sirasira, zsa, SIRASIRA; Maralango, mcy, MARALANGO; Wampur, waz, WAMPUR; Mari, hob, MARI; Onank, una, ONANK; Yaros, adz, YAROS; Amari, adz, AMARI; Labu, lbu, LABU; Bukaua, buk, BUKAUA; Kela, kcl, KELA; Kaiwa, kbm, KAIWA; Sipoma, sij, SIPOMA; Hote, hot, HOTE; Yamap, ymp, YAMAP; Jabem, jae, JABEM; Tami, tmy, TAMI; Malasanga, mqz, MALASANGA; Gitua, ggt, GITUA; Lukep, apr, LUKEP; Mangap, mna, MANGAP; Barim, bbv, BARIM; Mutu, tuc, MUTU; Tuam, tuc, TUAM; Sio, xsi, SIO; Nengaya, met, NENGAYA; Roinji, roe, ROINJI; Arawe, aaw, ARAWE; Maleu, mgl, MALEU; Nakana, nak, NAKANA; Halia, hla, HALIA; Gedaged, gdd, GEDAGED. *New Hebrides*[*] (Tryon 1973): Toga (Torres), lht, TOGA; Mosina (Banks), msn, MOSINA; Peterara (Maewo), mwo, CENTRAL MAEWO; Nduindui (Aoba), nnd, WEST AMBAE; Sakau (Santo), sku, SAKAO; Malo (Santo), mla, NORTH MALO; Fortsenal (Santo), frt, FORTSENAL; Raga (Pentecost), lml, RAGA; Sa (Pentecost), sax, SA; Dakaka (Ambrym), bpa, DAKAKA BAIAP; Aulua (Malekula), aul, AULUA; Big Nambas (Mal.), nmb, BIG NAMBAS UNMET; Lewo (Epi), lww, LEWO FILAKARA; Nguna (Efate), llp, NORTH EFATE NGUNA; Sie (Erromanga), erg, SIE; Lenakel (Tanna), tnl, LENAKEL LENAUKAS. *Philippines* (Llamzon and Martin 1976): Agta, agt, AGTA; Atta, att, ATTA PAMPLONA; Balangaw, blw, BALANGAW; Batak, bya, BATAK PALAWAN; Bilaan Koronadal, bpr, BILAAN KORONADAL; Bilaan Sarangani, bps, BILAAN SARANGANI; Binukid, bkd, BINUKID; Bontoc, bnc, CENTRAL BONTOC; Dumagat, dgc, DUMAGAT CASIGURAN; Gaddang, gdg, GADDANG; Amganad Ifugao, ifa, IFUGAO AMGANAD; Batad Ifugao, ifb, IFUGAO BATAD; Bayninan Ifugao, ify, IFUGAO BAYNINAN; Ilonggot, ilk, ILONGOT KAKIDUGEN; Inibaloi, ibl, INIBALOI; Isneg, isd, ISNEG; Itbayaten, ivv, ITBAYATEN BATANES ISLANDS; Itneg, itb, ITNEG BINONGAN; Ivatan, ivv, IVATAN BATANES ISLANDS; Kalagan, klg, KALAGAN; Kalinga, knb, KALINGA GUINAANG; Kallahan Kayapa, kak, KALLAHAN KAYAPA PROPER; Kallahan Keleyqiq, ify, KALLAHAN KELEYQIQ IFUGAO; Kankanay, xnn, KANKANAY NORTHERN; Mamanua, mmn, MAMANWA; Ata Manobo, atd, MANOBO ATA; Dibabawon Manobo, mbd, MANOBO DIBABAWON; Ilianen Manobo, mbi, MANOBO ILIANEN; Kalamsig Manobo, mta, MANOBO KALAMANSIG COTABATO; Sarangani Manobo, mbs, MANOBO SARANGANI; Tigwa Manobo, mbt, MANOBO TIGWA; Western Bukidnon Manobo, mbb, MANOBO WESTERN BUKIDNON; Mansaka, msk, MANSAKA; Siasi, sml, SAMAL; Sambal, sbl, SAMBAL BOTOLAN; Sangil, snl, SANGIL SARANGANI ISLANDS; Sangir, sxn, SANGIR; Sindangan Subanon, syb, SUBANUN SINDANGAN; Siocon Subanon, suc, SUBANON SIOCON; Tboli, tbl, TBOLI TAGABILI; Aborlan Tagbanwa, tbw, TAGBANWA ABORLAN; Kalamian tagbanwa, tbk, TAGBANWA KALAMIAN; Tausug, tsg, TAUSUG; Tagalog, tgl, TAGALOG; Cebuano, ceb, CEBUANO; Hiligaynon, hil, HILIGAYNON; Waray, war, WARAY WARAY; Ilocano, ilo, ILOKANO; Bicol, bcl, CENTRAL BICOLANO; Pampango, pam, KAPAMPANGAN; Pangasinan, pag, PANGASINA; Tagakaolo, klg, KALAGAN TAGAKAOLO; Yakan, yka, YAKAN; Sibutu, ssb, SIBUTU SOUTHERN SAMA; Kapul, abx, INABAKNON; Palun Mapun, sjm, MAPUN; Maranao, mrw, MARANAO; Tasaday, mdh, MAGUINDANAO; Kiniray'a, krj, KINARAY-A; Masbateño, msb, MASBATENYO; Sorsogonon, bks, NORTHERN SORSOGON; Butuanon, btw, BUTUANON; Hanunoo, hnn, HANUNOO; Itawes, itv, ITAWIT; Ibanag, ibg, IBANAG; Yogad, yog, YOGAD;

Aklanon, akl, AKLANON; Capiznon, cps, CAPIZNON; Cagayanzillo, cgc, KAGAYANEN; Romblonon, rol, ROMBLOMANON; Tiruray, tiy, TIRURAY; Mandaya, mry, MANDAYAN CARAGA. *Yapen* (Anceaux 1961): Woi, wbw, WOI; Pom, pmo, POM; Marau, alu, MARAU; Ansus, and, ANSUS; Papuma, ppm, PAPUMA; Munggui, mth, MUNGGUI; Serui Laut, seu, SERUI-LAUT; Ambai, amk, AMBAI; Wadapi-Laut, amk, WADAPI LAUT; Wabo, wbb, WABO; Kurudu, kjr, KURUDU; Wandamen, wad, WANDAMEN; Dusner, dsn, DUSNER; Ron, rnn, RON; Biak, bhw, BIAK; Waropen, wrp, WAROPEN; Mor, mhz, MOR; Irarutu, irh, IRARUTU.

Carib: *Cariban* (Villalon 1991): Yabarana, yar, YABARANA; Panare, pbh, ENAPA WOROMAIPU; Pemon + Kamarakoto + Taurepan, aoc, PEMON; Makushi, mbc, MACUSHI; Oayana, way, WAYANA; Carib, car, KALINA; Yukpa, yup, YUKPA; Bakairi, bkq, BAKAIRI; Makiritare, mch, MAQUIRITARI; Hianacoto-Umaua, cbd, CARIJONA.

Dravidian: *Dravidian*^(*) (Andronov 2001): Tamil, tam, TAMIL; Malayalam, mal, MALAYALAM; Kannada, kan, KANNADA; Telugu, tel, TELUGU; Kolami, kfb, NORTHWESTERN KOLAMI; Parji, pci, PARJI; Gondi, ggo, ADILABAD GONDI; Kurukh, kru, KURUKH; Malto, mjt, SAURIA PAHARIA; Brahui, brh, BRAHUI.

Hmong-Mien: *Miao-Yao** (Peiros 1998): Hmu, hea, HMU; Xiangxi Hmong (or Xx), mmr, XIANGXI HMONG; Hmong Njua, hnj, HMONG NJUA; Bunu, bwx, BUNU; She, shx, SHE CHINA; yao, ium, YAO.

Indo-European: *Indo-European* (Dyen et al. 1992): Irish, gle, IRISH GAELIC; Welsh, cym, WELSH; Breton, bre, BRETON; Rumanian, ron, ROMANIAN 2; Vlach, rup, VLACH; Italian, ita, ITALIAN; French, fra, FRENCH; Provençal, frp, ARPITAN; Spanish, spa, SPANISH; Portuguese, por, PORTUGUESE; Catalan, cat, CATALAN; German, deu, STANDARD GERMAN; Dutch, nld, DUTCH; Afrikaans, afr, AFRIKAANS; Flemish, vls, WESTVLAAMS; Frisian, fry, FRISIAN WESTERN; English, eng, ENGLISH; Takitaki, srn, SRANAN TONGO; Swedish, swe, SWEDISH; Danish, dan, DANISH; Riksmal, nob, NORWEGIAN BOKMAAL; Icelandic, isl, ICELANDIC; Faroese, fao, FAROESE; Lithuanian, lit, LITHUANIAN; Latvian, lav, LATVIAN; Lusatian L, dsb, LOWER SORBIAN 2; Lusatian U, hsb, UPPER SORBIAN; Czech, ces, CZECH; Slovak, slk, SLOVAK; Polish, pol, POLISH; Ukrainian, ukr, UKRAINIAN; Byelorusssian, bel, BELARUSIAN; Russian, rus, RUSSIAN; Bulgaria, bul, BULGARIAN; Slovenian, slv, SLOVENIAN; Serbocroatian, srp, SERBOCROATIAN; Singhalese, sin, SINHALA; Kashmiri, kas, KASHMIRI; Lahnda, pnb, WESTERN PANJABI SHAHPUR; Marathi, mar, MARATHI; Gujarati, guj, GUJARATI; Panjabi, pan, PUNJABI MAJHI; Hindi, hin, HINDI; Bengali, ben, BENGALI; Nepali, nep, NEPALI; Ossetic, oss, DIGOR OSSETIAN; Afghan, pbu, NORTHERN PASHTO;

Waziri, pst, BANNU PASHTO; Wakhi, wbl, CENTRAL GOJAL WAKHI; Persian, pes, PERSIAN; Tadzik, tgk, TAJIK; Greek, ell, GREEK; Armenian, hye, WESTERN ARMENIAN; Albanian T, als, ALBANIAN TOSK.

Japonic: *Japonic** (Hattori 1961): Tokyo, jpn, TOKYO JAPANESE; Kyoto, jpn, JAPANESE KYOTO; Naha, ryu, NAHA; Shuri, ryu, SHURI; Yonamine, xug, YONAMINE.

Mayan: *Mayan** (Cecil H. Brown p.c., 2011): CHICOMUCELTEC, cob; SOUTHERN CAKCHIQUEL SAN ANDRES ITZAPA, ckf; jai, JACALTEC; qum, SIPAKAPENSE; kjb, QANJOBAL SANTA EULALIA; toj, TOJOLABAL; usp, USPANTEKO; ctu, CHOL TUMBALA; mhc, MOCHO; poa, POCOMAM EASTERN; quc, CENTRAL QUICHE; kek, EASTERN KEKCHI CAHABON; ixj, IXIL CHAJUL; mop, MOPAN; quv, SACAPULTECO SACAPULAS CENTRO; ttc, TECO TECTITAN; tzj, TZUTUJIL SAN JUAN LA LAGUNA; knj, ACATECO SAN MIGUEL ACATAN; caa, CHORTI; mam, MAM NORTHERN; pob, POQOMCHI WESTERN; tzb, TZELTAL BACHAJON; agu, AGUACATEC; chf, CHONTAL TABASCO; cnm, CHUJ; lac, LACANDON; tzz, ZINACANTAN TZOTZIL; hva, HUASTEC; itz, ITZAJ; yua, MAYA YUCATAN.

Macro-Ge: *Ge* (Wilbert 1962): Apinaye, apn, APINAYE; Creye, xre, KREYE; Canela, ram, APANIEKRA; Craho, xra, KRAHO; Pucobye, gvp, PYKOBJE; Suya, suy, SUYA; Cayapo, txu, KAYAPO; Shavante, xav, XAVANTE; Sherente, xer, XERENTE.

Mixe-Zoque: *Mixe-Zoque** (Cysouw et al. 2006): North Highland Mixe, mto, NORTH HIGHLAND MIXE; South Highland Mixe, mxp, SOUTH HIGHLAND MIXE; Lowland Mixe, mco, LOWLAND MIXE; Sayula Popoluca, pos, SAYULA POPOLUCA; Oluta Popoluca, plo, OLUTA POPOLUCA; Texistepec Zoque, poq, TEXISTEPEC ZOQUE; Soteapan Zoque, poi, SOTEAPAN ZOQUE; Santa Maria Chimalapa Zoque, zoh, MARIA CHIMALAPA; San Miguel Chimalapa Zoque, zoh, MIGUEL CHIMALAPA; Chiapas Zoque, zoc, CHIAPAS ZOQUE;

Na-Dene: *Athapaskan** (Hoijer 1956): Hare, scs, HARE; Chipewyan, chp, CHIPEWYAN; Beaver, bea, BEAVER; Carrier, crx, CARRIER; Kutchin, gwi, KUTCHIN; Sarcee, srs, SARCEE; Galice, gce, GALICE; Kato, ktw, KATO; Mattole, mvb, MATTOLE; Hupa, hup, HUPA 2; Navaho, nav, NAVAHO; San Carlos, apw, SAN CARLOS; Chircahua, apm, CHIRICAHUA; Jicarilla, apj, JICARILLA; Lipan, apl, LIPAN.

Niger-Congo: *Atlantic* (Sapir 1971): Fula, fuc, FULA; Wolof, wol, WOLOF; Serer, srr, SERER SINE; Lehar, cae, LEHAR; Safen, sav, SAFEN; Non, snf, NON; Ndut, ndv, NDUT FALOR; Fogny, dyo, JOLA; Manjaku, mfv, MANJACA CHURO;

Papel, pbo, PAPEL; Balanta, ble, BALANTA; Biafada, bif, BIAFADA; Pajade, pbp, PAJADE; Nalu, naj, NALU; Bijago, bjg, BIJOGO; Temne, tem, TEMNE; Mmani, buy, MMANI; Sherbro, bun, SHERBRO; Krim, krm, KRIM; Kisi, kqs, KISSI; Gola, gol, GOLA. *Benue-Congo* (Bennett and Sterk 1977): Nupe, nup, NUPE; Gade, ged, GADE; Igbira, igb, IGBIRRA; Idoma, idu, IDOMA; Eloyi, afo, ELOYI; Igbo, ibo, IGBO ONITSHA; Igala, igl, IGALA; Yoruba, yor, YORUBA; Ora, ema, EMAI; Bini, bin, EDO; Urhobo, urh, URHOBO; Isoko, iso, ISOKO; Degema, deg, DEGEMA 2; Aten, etx, ITEN; Mambila, mzk, MAMBILA; Tiv, tiv, TIV 2; Tunen, baz, TUNEN; Jarawa, jar, BANKALA; Bobangi, bni, BOBANGI; Nyanja, nya, NYANJA; Kikuyu, kik, GIKUYU; Kwanyama, kua, KWANYAMA. *Gur* (Swadesh et al. 1966): Basal, bud, BASSARI; Konkomba, xon, KONKOMBA 2; Gurma, gux, GOURMANCHEMA; Pilapila, pil, YOM; Naudem, nmz, NAWDM; Buli, bwu, BULI GHANA; Dagbani, dag, DAGBANI; Mampruli, maw, MAMPRULI; Kusal, kus, KUSAL; Hanga, hag, HANGA; Frafra, gur, NINKARE; Moore, mos, MOORE; Dagaari, dga, DAGAARE; Vagala, vag, VAGALA; Sisala, sil, SISAALA TUMULUNG; Kasem, xsm, KASEM; Lamba, las, LAMA; Kabre, kbp, KABIYE; Mambar, myk, MAMARA SENOUFO; Pantera + Fantera, nfr, NAFAARA. *Kwa* (Heine 1968): Twi, aka, TWI ASANTE; Logba, lgq, IKPANA; Adele, ade, ADELE; Lipke, lip, LIKPE; Santroko, snw, SELE; Akpufu, akp, AKPAFU; Lelemi, lef, BUEM LELEMI; Avatime, avn, SIDEME; Nyangbo, nyb, TUTRUGBU; Bowili, bov, TUWULI; Ahlo, ahl, AHLO; Animere, anf, ANIMERE; Ewe, ewe, EWE ADANGBE.

Nilo-Saharan: *Eastern Sudanic* (Thelwall 1981): Meidob, mei, MEIDOB NUBIAN; Debri, dil, DILLING; Dongolawi, kzh, NUBIAN OF DONGOLA; Nobiin, fia, NOBIIN; Gaam, tbi, INGASSANA; Liguri, liu, LOGORIK; Shatt, shj, SHATT; Nyala + Lagowa, daj, NYALA; Sila, dau, SILA; Temein, teq, TEMEIN; Dinka, dik, REK; Shilluk, shk, SHILLUK; *Nilo-Saharan*(*) (Bender 1971): Nuer, nus, NUER; Anyuak, anu, ANYUAK; Shilluk, shk, SHILLUK; Jumjum, jum, JUMJUM; Mabaan, mfz, MABAAN; Burun, bdi, BURUN; Inyangatom, nnj, NYANGATOM 2; Tirma, suq, TIRMA; Mursi, muz, MURSI; Meen, mym, MEEN; Kwegu, xwg, KWEGU; Zilmamu, koe, BAALE; Murle, mur, MURLE; Mesengo, mpe, MESENGO; Nara, nrb, NARA; Ingassana, tbi, INGASSANA; Kunama, kun, KUNAMA; Wetawit, wti, WETAWIT; Uduk, udu, UDUK; C. Koma, xom, CENTRAL KOMA; Langa, lgn, LANGA; N. Koma, kmq, GWAMA; Gumuz, guk, GUMUZ; *Southern Luo** (Blount and Curley 1970): Lango, laj, LANGO; Acholi, ach, ACHOLI 2; Alur, alz, ALUR; Luo, luo, LUO; Shilluk, shk, SHILLUK.

Quechuan: *Quechua* (Torero 1970): Corongo, qwa, YANAC; Caras, qwh, QUECHUA HUAYLAS ANCASH; Tarma, qvn, QUECHUA NORTH JININ; Ferreñafe, quf, INKAWASI; Cajamarca, qvc, CHETILLA; Chachapoyas, quk, QUECHUA CHACHAPOYAS; Ayachuco, quy, QUECHUA AYACUCHO; Cuzco, quz, QUECHUA DE CUSCO; Potosí + Chuquisaca, quh, MARAGUA.

Languages with longer words have more lexical change 271

Salishan: *Salish* (Swadesh 1950): Bella Coola, blc, BELLA COOLA; Comox, coo, SLIAMMON; Seshelt, sec, SECHELT; Fraser + Nanaimo, hur, COWICHAN; Squamish, squ, SQUAMISH; Lkungen + Lummi, str, SALISH STRAITS; Clallam, clm, CLALLAM; Nootsak, nok, NOOKSACK; Twana, twa, TWANA; Cowlitz, cow, COWLITZ; Chehalis + Satsop, cjh, CHEHALIS UPPER; Quinault, qun, QUINAULT; Tillamook, til, TILLAMOOK; Lillooet, lil, LILLOOET; Thompson, thp, THOMPSON; Shuswap, shs, SHUSWAP; Okanagan, oka, OKANAGAN COLVILLE; Spokane, spo, SPOKANE; Kalispel + Pend d'Oreille, fla, KALISPEL-PEND DOREILLE; Columbia, col, COLUMBIA WENATCHI; Coeur d'Alène, crd, COEUR DALENE.

Sino-Tibetan: *Chinese* (Xu 1991): Xiamen, nan, AMOY MINNAN CHINESE; Meixian, hak, HAKKA; Guangzhou, yue, CANTONESE; Changsha, hsn, XIANG; Suzhou, wuu, SUZHOU WU; Beijing, cmn, MANDARIN 2. *Lolo-Burmese** (Peiros 1998): Burmese, mya, BURMESE; Zaiwa, atb, ZAIWA; Achang, can, ACHANG; Nusu, nuf, NUSU; Akha, ahk, AKHA; Biyue, byo, BIYUE; Lahu, lhu, LAHU; Jino, jiu, JINO; Mpi, mpz, MPI; Bisu, bzi, BISU; Xide, iii, XIDE; Dafang, yig, DAFANG; Nanjiang, ywt, NANJIANG; Lisu, lis, LISU; Naxi, nbf, NAXI. *Sino-Tibetan* (Benedict 1976): Burmese, mya, BURMESE; Tibetan, bod, TIBETAN LHASA; Lushai, lus, LUSHAI; Kachin, kac, JINGPHO; Garo, grt, GARO; Mandarin, cmn, MANDARIN 2.

Tai-Kadai: *Kadai** (Peiros 1998): Siamese, tha, SIAMESE; Longzhou, zzj, ZHUANG SOUTHERN; Zhuang, zyb, ZHUANG NORTHERN; Saek, skb, SAEK; Ong Be, onb, ONG BE; Lakkja, lbc, LAKKJA; Mulao, mlm, MULAO; Kam, kmc, SOUTHERN DONG; Maonan, mmd, MAONAN; Sui, swi, SUI.

Torricelli: *Kamasau** (Sanders and Sanders 1980): Tring, kms, TRING; Wau, kms, WAU; Kamasau, kms, KAMASAU; Yibab, kms, YIBAB; Wandomi, kms, WANDOMI; Kenyari, kms, KENYARI; Paruwa, kms, PARUWA; Samap, kms, SAMAP.

Trans-New Guinea: *Angan** (Lloyd 1973): Angaataha, agm, ANGAATAHA; Ankave, aak, ANKAVE; Ampale, apz, AMPALE; Baruya, byr, BARUYA 2; Ivori, ago, IVORI; Kamasa, klp, KAMASA; Kapau, hmt, KAPAU; Kawacha, kcb, KAWACHA; Lohiki, miw, LOHIKI; Menya, mcr, MENYA 2; Simbari, smb, SIMBARI; Yagwoia, ygw, YAGWOIA. *Awyu*[*] (Voorhoeve 1968): Aghu, ahh, AGHU; Kaeti, bwp, KAETI; Pisa, psa, PISA; Syiagha, aws, SIAGHA; Yenimu, awy, YENIMU; Wambon, wms, WAMBON. *Bosavi* (Shaw 1986): Duna, duc, DUNA; Bimin, bhl, BIMIN; Bogaia, boq, BOGAYA; Pare, ppt, PARE; Agala, agl, AGALA; Kubo, jko, KUBO; Samo, smq, SAMO; Bibo, goi, GEBUSI; Honibo, goi, HONIBO; Oibae, goi, OIBAE; Kalamo, kkc, ODOODEE; Bedamini, beo, BEDAMINI; Etoro, etr, ETORO; Onabasulu, onn, ONABASULU; Kaluli, bco, KALULI 2; Sunia, siq, SUNIA; Kasua, khs, KASUA 2; Aimele, ail, AIMELE;

Kamula, xla, KAMULA; Bainapi, dby, DIBIYASO; Namumi, faa, NAMUMI; Bamu, bcf, BAMU 2. **Eleman*** (Brown 1973): Aheave, xeu, AHEAVE; Kaipi, oro, KAIPI; Keuru, xeu, KEURU; Opao, opo, OPAO; Orokolo, oro, OROKOLO 2; Sepoe, tqo, SEPOE; Toaripi, tqo, TOARIPI 2; Uaripi, uar, UARIPI. **Finisterre** (Claasen and McElhanon 1970): Nankina, nnk, NANKINA; Awara, awx, AWARA; Wantoat, wnc, WANTOAT; Nek, nif, NEK; Yabong, ybo, YABONG; Saep, spd, SAEP; Ganglau, ggl, GANGLAU; Kolom, klm, KOLOM; Suroi, ssd, SUROI; Lemio, lei, LEMIO; Usino, urw, USINO; Sinsauru, snz, SINSAURU. **Grand Valley Dani*** (Bromley 1967): Upper Pyramid, dni, UPPER PYRAMID DANI; Pyramid-Wodo, wlw, PYRAMID WODO; Mid-Grand Valley, dnt, MID GRAND VALLEY DANI; Lower Valley Hitigama, dni, HITIGIMA DANI; Lower Valley Tangma, dni, TANGMA DANI; Jalimo Angguruk, yli, ANGGURUK YALI; Kiniageima Amo, wul, KINIAGEIMA. **Greater Madang*** (Z'Graggen 1969): Isebe, igo, ISEBE; Bau, bbd, BAU; Amele, aey, AMELE; Garus, gyb, GARUS; Yoidik, ydk, YOIDIK; Rempi, rmp, REMPI; Garuh, gaw, GARUH; Foran, fad, KAMBA; Mawan, mcz, MAWAN; Utu, utu, UTU; Saruga, sra, SARUGA; Kare, kmf, KARE; Usino, urw, USINO; Sumau, six, SUMAU; Urigina, urg, URIGINA; Korak, koz, KORAK; Waskia, wsk, WASKIA; Malas, mkr, MALAS; Bunabun, buq, BUNABUN; Dimir, dmc, DIMIR; Pay, ped, PAY; Pila, sks, PILA; Saki, sks, SAKI; Tani, pla, TANI; Ulingan, mhl, ULINGAN; Bepour, bie, BEPOUR; Mawak, mjj, MAWAK; Musar, mmi, MUSAR; Wanambre, wnb, WANAMBRE; Wanuma, wnu, WANUMA; Yaben, ybm, YABEN; Parawen, prw, PARAWEN; Amaimon, ali, AMAIMON; Moresada, msx, MORESADA; Ikundun, imi, IKUNDUN; Pondoma, pda, PONDOMA; Wanambre, wnb, WANAMBRE; Katiati, kqa, KATIATI; Osum, omo, OSUM; Atemple, ate, ATEMPLE; Angaua, anh, ANGAUA; Emerum, ena, EMERUM; Musak, mmq, MUSAK; Paynamar, pmr, PAYNAMAR; Kaian, kct, KAIAN; Gamei, gai, GAMEI; Mikarew, msy, MIKAREW MAKARUB; Anor, anj, ANOR; Rao, rao, RAO; Banaro, byz, BANARO. **Huon*** (McElhanon 1967): Kâte, kmg, KATE; Dedua, ded, DEDUA; Mape, mlh, MAPE 2; Hube, kgf, HUBE; Tobo, tbv, TOBO; Kosorong, ksr, KOSORONG; Mindik, bmu, MINDIK; Burum, bmu, BURUM; Ono, ons, ONO; Komba, kpf, KOMBA; Selepet, spl, SELEPET; Timbe, tim, TIMBE; Nabak, naf, NABAK; Momolili, mci, MOMOLILI. **Kiwaian** (Wurm 1973): Wabuda, kmx, WABUDA; Middle Bamu Kiwai, bcf, BAMU; Morigi, mdb, MORIGI; Kerewo, kxz, KEREWO; Urama, kiw, URAMA; Gope, kiw, GOPE; Gibaio, kiw, GIBAIO; Arigibi / Anigibo / Anigibi / Ani, kiw, ANIGIBI. **Koiarian** (Dutton 1969): Koita, kqi, KOITA; Koiari, kbk, KOIARI 2; MtnKoiari, kpx, MOUNTAIN KOIARI; Aomie, aom, AOMIE; Barai, bbb, BARAI; Managalasi, mcq, ESE MANAGALASI. **Kolopom** (Voorhoeve 1968): Kimaghana, kig, KIMAGHAMA; Riantana, ran, RIANTANA; Ndom, nqm, NDOM. **Ok** (Voorhoeve 1968): Asmat, cns, ASMAT CENTRAL; Telefol, tlf, TELEFOL; Kati, yon, NORTH KATI; Aghu, ahh, AGHU; Mombum, mso, MOMBUN; **Turama-Kikorian** (Franklin 1973): Omati, mgx, OMATI; Ikobi, meb, IKOBI; Mena, meb, MENA; Kairi, klq, RUMU.

Uto-Aztecan: *Uto-Aztecan* (Miller 1984, Cortina-Borja and Valiñas 1989): Northern Paiute, pao, NORTHERN PAIUTE; Panamint, par, PANAMINT; Shoshoni, shh, SHOSHONI; Comanche, com, COMANCHE; Kawaiisu, xaw, KAWAIISU; Southern Paiute, ute, SOUTHERN PAIUTE; Ute, ute, UTE 2; Tübatulabal, tub, TUBATULABAL; Cahuilla, chl, CAHUILLA; Cupeno, cup, CUPENO; Luiseno, lui, LUISENO; Hopi, hop, HOPI; Papago, ood, TOHONO OODHAM; Nevome, ood, UPPER PIMA; Northern Tepehuan, ntp, NORTHERN TEPEHUAN; Guarijio, var, WARIHIO; Tarahumara, tar, CENTRAL TARAHUMARA; Opata + Eudeve, opt, OPATA; Mayo, mfy, MAYO; Yaqui, yaq, YAQUI; Tubar, tbu, TUBAR; Huichol, hch, HUICHOL; Cora, crn, EL NAYAR CORA; Tetelcingo Nahuatl, nhg, TETELCINGO NAHUATL; Zacapoaxtla Nahuatl, azz, HIGHLAND PUEBLA NAHUATL; Pipil, ppl, PIPIL.

West Papuan: *North Halmahera* (Chlenov 1986): Loda, loa, LODA; Galela, gbi, GALELA; Tobelo, tlb, TOBELO; Tabaru / Tobaru, tby, TABARU; Pagu / Isam, pgu, PAGU; Madole / Modole, mqo, MADOLE; Sahu, saj, SAHU; Tidore, tvo, TIDORE. *Yawa** (Jones 1986): Tindaret, yva, TINDARET; Ambaidiru, yva, AMBADAIRU; Ariepi, yva, ARIEPI; Sarawandori, yva, SARAWANDORI; Konti Unai, yva, KONTI UNAI; Mariadei, yva, MARIADEI.

Notes

1. We thank Cecil H. Brown and Robert Mailhammer for providing cognate judgments for Mayan and Iwaidjan, respectively. An earlier version of this paper was presented at the ICHL in Osaka, July 2011. We are grateful to Claire Bowern for highly useful comments on that occasion.
2. The normalization leading to LDN is argued by Serva and Petroni (2008) to be absolutely necessary for arriving at good results for language classification. To our knowledge, other types of normalization have not been tested for string comparisons involving languages that are not closely related, analyses having been limited to the field of dialectology (Heeringa 2005). This is a potentially interesting item for future research.
3. This variation in lists would be expected if anything to increase the variability of COGNsim relative to ASJPim, which is always based on the same list. The additional variability would tend to weaken the observed correlations, thus rendering our tests conservative.
4. An exception is the name 'Greater Madang', which we use as a collective term for the following Trans-New Guinea groups included in Z'Graggen (1969): Madang, Isumrud, Kaukombaran, Mawamuan, Pihom, Josephstaal, and Wanang.
5. An exception where we provide cognate judgments ourselves is the Torricelli group Kamasau. This is a set of dialects for which it requires no special expertise

to distinguish cognates from non-cognates. In the case of Mixe-Zoque we used the judgments of Cysouw et al. (2006), but corrected for some typos in that paper.
6. Not surprisingly, the magnitude of the correlation between COGNsim and ASJPsim is greater when both measures are based on the same data set. In the appendix we indicate for each language group whether the data sets for the two measures are the same, almost so, or not. Families containing language groups where the data sets are all the same or almost so include AA, Alt, AuA, Dra, HM, Jap, May, MZ, NDe, TK, and Tor. The average r for these families is .81. Families containing groups where the data sets are all different include Car, IE, MGe, NC, Que, Sal, and UA. The average r for these is .70. The families Aus, NS, ST, TNG, and WP are represented by language groups for which the sources are mixed, some data sets being the same or almost so and some not. Average r for these families is .77.
7. It was observed by a referee that if mmWL correlates significantly with both mDIFF and mRATIO, while mSR does not, then mSR and mmWL perhaps do not correlate significantly, which would run counter to previous observations about an inverse relationship between word length and segment inventory sizes (Nettle 1995, 1998; Wichmann et al. 2011). The data used in the present paper are limited, so differences from the results of Wichmann et al. (2011) with regard to word length and segment inventory size are entirely expected and not particularly telling. The correlation in the present data is $r = -.38$, $p = .07$. These figures depend highly on the small number of data points, as can be seen by an increase in the correlation to $r = -.74$, $p < .0001$ with the removal of a single outlier, Salishan.

References

Anceaux, Johannes Cornelis
    1961   *The Linguistic Situation in the Islands of Yapen, Kurudu, Nau and Miosnum, New Guinea*. Verhandelingen van het Koninklijk Instituut voor Taal-, Land- en Volkenkunde. 'S-Gravenhage: Martinus Nijhoff.
Andronov, Mikhail
    2001   *Dravidian Historical Linguistics*. München: Lincom Europa.
Atkinson, Quentin D., Andrew Meade, Chris Venditti, Simon J. Greenhill, and Mark Pagel
    2008   Languages evolve in punctuational bursts. *Science* 319: 588.
Bastin, Yvonne, A. Coupez, and Michael Mann
    1999   *Continuity and Divergence in the Bantu Languages. Perspectives from a Lexicostatistic Study*. Tervuren: Musée Royal de l'Afrique Centrale.
Bender, M. L.
    1971   The Languages of Ethiopia. *Anthropological Linguistics* 13: 165–288.

Benedict, Paul K.
  1976   Sino-Tibetan: Another look. *Journal of the American Oriental Society* 96: 167–197.
Bennett, Patrick R. and Jan P. Sterk
  1977   South Central Niger-Congo: A reclassification. *Studies in African Linguistics* 8: 241–273.
Blount, Ben and Richard T. Curley
  1970   The Southern Luo languages: A glottochronological reconstruction. *Journal of African Languages* 9: 1–18.
Breen, Gavan
  1981   *The Mayi Languages of the Queensland Gulf Country*. Canberra: Australian Institute of Aboriginal Studies.
Bromley, H. Myron
  1967   The linguistic relationships of Grand Valley Dani: A lexico-statistical classification. *Oceania* 37: 286–308.
Brown, Cecil H., Eric W. Holman, Søren Wichmann, and Viveka Velupillai
  2008   Automated classification of the world's languages: A description of the method and preliminary results. *STUF – Language Typology and Universals* 61: 285–308.
Brown, Herbert A.
  1973   The Eleman language family. In *The Linguistic Situation in the Gulf District and Adjacent Areas, Papua New Guinea*, Franklin, Karl J. (ed.), 281–376. (Pacific Linguistics Series C – N. 26.) Canberra: Australian National University.
Chadwick, Neil
  1979   The West Barkly languages: an outline sketch. In *Australian Linguistic Studies*, Stephen A. Wurm (ed.), 653–711. (Pacific Linguistics, Series C, No. 54.) Canberra: Australian National University.
Chlenov, M. A.
  1986   North Halmahera languages: A problem of internal classification. *Papers in New Guinea Linguistics* 24. Pacific Linguistics, A-70, 39–44. Canberra: Australian National University.
Claassen, Oren R. and Kenneth A. McElhanon
  1970   Languages of the Finisterre Range, New Guinea. Pacific Linguistics A-23: 45–78. Canberra: Australian National University.
Cortina-Borja, Mario and Leopoldo Valiñas C.
  1989   Some remarks on Uto-Aztecan classification. *International Journal of American Linguistics* 55: 214–239.
Cysouw, Michael, Søren Wichmann, and David Kamholz
  2006   A critique of the separation base method for genealogical subgrouping, with data from Mixe-Zoquean. *Journal of Quantitative Linguistics* 13: 225–264.

Dryer, Matthew S.
   1992   The Greenbergian word order correlations. *Language* 68: 81–138.
Dryer, Matthew S.
   2011   Genealogical language list. In *World Atlas of Language Structures Online*, ed. Matthew S. Dryer, and Martin Haspelmath. Munich: Max Planck Digital Library, chapter iv. Available online at http://wals.info/chapter/iv.
Dutton, Thomas Edward
   1969   *The Peopling of Central Papua. Some Preliminary Observations.* Pacific Linguistics, Series B – Monographs, No 9. Canberra: Australian National University.
Dyen, Isidore
   1965   A *Lexicostatistical Classification of the Austronesian Languages.* Supplement to International Journal of American Linguistics, Vol. 31, No. 1. Baltimore: Waverly Press.
Dyen, Isidore, Joseph Kruskal, and Paul Black
   1992   An Indoeuropean classification, a lexicostatistical experiment. *Transactions of the American Philosophical Society* 82.5.
Franklin, Karl J.
   1973   Other language groups in the Gulf district and adjacent areas. In *The Linguistic Situation in the Gulf District and Adjacent Areas, Papua New Guinea*, Karl J. Franklin (ed.), 263–277. (Pacific Linguistics Series C – N. 26.) Canberra: Australian National University.
Gray, Russell D. and Quentin Atkinson
   2003   Language-tree divergence times support the Anatolian theory of Indo-European origins. *Nature* 426: 435–439.
Gray, Russell D., Alexei J. Drummond, and Simon J. Greenhill
   2009   Language phylogenies reveal expansion pulses and pauses in Pacific settlement. *Science* 323: 479–483.
Gray, Russell D. and Fiona M. Jordan
   2000   Language trees support the express-train sequence of Austronesian expansion. *Nature* 405: 1052–1055.
Greenhill, Simon J.
   2011   Levenshtein distances fail to identify language relationships accurately. *Computational Linguistics.* doi: 10.1162/COLI_a_00073.
Greenhill, Simon J., Robert Blust, and Russell D. Gray
   2008   The Austronesian Basic Vocabulary Database: From bioinformatics to lexomics. *Evolutionary Bioinformatics* 4: 271–283
Gudschinsky, Sarah
   1956   The ABCs of lexicostatistics (glottochronology). *Word* 12: 175–210.
Hattori, Shiro
   1961   A glottochronological study on three Okinawan dialects. *International Journal of American Linguistics* 27: 52–62.

Hay, Jennifer and Laurie Bauer
  2007 Phoneme inventory size and population size. *Language* 83: 388–400.
Heeringa, Wilbert
  2004 Measuring dialect pronunciation differences using Levenshtein distance. Ph.D. diss., Rijksuniversiteit Groningen.
Heine, Bernd
  1968 *Die Verbreitung und Gliederung der Togorestsprachen.* Berlin: Dietrich Reimer.
Hoijer, Harry
  1956 The chronology of the Athapaskan languages. *International Journal of American Linguistics* 22: 219–232.
Holman, Eric W., Cecil H. Brown, Søren Wichmann, André Müller, Viveka Velupillai, Harald Hammarström, Sebastian Sauppe, Hagen Jung, Dik Bakker, Pamela Brown, Oleg Belyaev, Matthias Urban, Robert Mailhammer, Johann-Mattis List, and Dmitry Egorov
  2011 Automated dating of the world's language families based on lexical similarity. *Current Anthropology* 52: 841–875.
Holman, Eric W., Søren Wichmann, Cecil H. Brown, Viveka Velupillai, André Müller, and Dik Bakker
  2008a Advances in automated language classification. In *Quantitative Investigations in Theoretical Linguistics*, Antti Arppe, Kaius Sinnemäki, and Urpu Nikanne (eds.), 40–43. Helsinki: University of Helsinki.
Holman, Eric W., Søren Wichmann, Cecil H. Brown, Viveka Velupillai, André Müller, Pamela Brown, and Dik Bakker
  2008b Explorations in automated language classification. *Folia Linguistica* 42: 331–354.
Hooley, Bruce A.
  1971 Austronesian languages of the Morobe District, Papua New Guinea. *Oceanic Linguistics* 10: 79–151.
Huff, Paul and Deryle Lonsdale
  2011 Positing language relationships using ALINE. *Language Dyna-mics and Change* 1: 128–162.
Jones, Larry B.
  1986 The dialects of Yawa. *Papers in New Guinea Linguistics* 25. Pacific Linguistics, A-74, 31–68. Canberra: Australian National University.
Kondrak, Grzegorz
  2000 A new algorithm for the alignment of phonetic sequences. *Proceedings of the First Meeting of the North American Chapter of the Association for Computational Linguistics*, 288–295.
Lees, Robert B.
  1953 The basis of glottochronology. *Language* 29: 113–127.

Lewis, M. Paul (ed.)
  2009   *Ethnologue. Languages of the World*. 16th ed. Dallas: SIL International. Online version: http://www.ethnologue.com.
Llamzon, Teodoro and Teresita Martin
  1976   A subgrouping of 100 Philippine languages. In *South-East Asian Linguistic Studies*, Vol. 2, Nguyen Dang Liem (ed.), 141–172. (Pacific Linguistics, Series C, No. 42.) Canberra: Australian National University.
Lloyd, Richard G.
  1973   The Angan language family. In: *The Linguistic Situation in the Gulf District and Adjacent Areas, Papua New Guinea*, Karl J. Franklin (ed.), 31–110. (Pacific Linguistics Series C – N. 26.) Canberra: Australian National University.
Mace, Ruth and Fiona M. Jordan
  2011   Macro-evolutionary studies of cultural diversity: A review of empirical studies of cultural transmission and cultural adaptation. *Philosophical Transactions of the Royal Society B* 366: 402–411.
McElhanon, Kenneth A.
  1967   Preliminary observations on Huon Peninsula languages. *Oceanic Linguistics* 6: 1–45.
McGregor, William B. and Alan Rumsey
  2009   *Worrorran Revisited: The Case for Genetic Relations among Languages of the Northern Kimberley Region of Western Australia*. (Pacific Linguistics.) Canberra: Australian National University.
Militarev, Alexander
  2000   Towards the chronology of Afrasian (Afroasiatic) and its daughter families. In *Time Depth in Historical Linguistics*, Vol. 1, Colin Renfrew, April McMahon, and Larry Trask (eds.), 267–307. Cambridge: McDonald Institute for Archaeological Research.
Miller, Wick R.
  1984   The classification of the Uto-Aztecan languages based on lexical evidence. *International Journal of American Linguistics* 50: 1–24.
Nettle, Daniel
  1995   Segmental inventory size, word length, and communicative efficiency. *Linguistics* 33: 359–367.
Nettle, Daniel
  1998   Coevolution of phonology and the lexicon in twelve languages of West Africa. *Journal of Quantitative Linguistics* 5: 240–245.
O'Grady, Geoffrey N.
  1966   Proto-Ngayarda phonology. *Oceanic Linguistics* 5: 71–130.
Pagel, Mark, Quentin D. Atkinson, and Andrew Meade
  2007   Frequency of word-use predicts rates of lexical evolution throughout Indo-European history. *Nature* 449: 717–720.

Peiros, Ilya
  1998   *Comparative Linguistics in Southeast Asia.* (Pacific Linguistics Series C, 142.) Canberra: Australian National University.
Pompei, Simone, Vittorio Loreto, and Francesca Tria
  2011   On the accuracy of language trees. *PLoS One* 6.6, e20109.
Sanders, Joy and Arden G. Sanders
  1980   Dialect Survey of the Kamasau Language. *Papers in New Guinea Linguistics*, No. 20. (Pacific Linguistics Series A, No. 56.) Canberra: Australian National University.
Sapir, J. David
  1971   West Atlantic: An inventory of the languages, their noun class systems and consonant alternation. In *Current Trends in Linguistics*, Vol. 7: *Linguistics in Sub-Saharan Africa*, Thomas A. Sebeok (ed.), 45–112. The Hague: Mouton.
Serva, Maurizio and Filippo Petroni
  2008   Indo-European languages tree by Levenshtein distance. *EuroPhysics Letters* 8: 68005.
Shaw, R. Daniel
  1986   The Bosavi language family. *Papers in New Guinea Linguistics* 24: 45–76. (Pacific Linguistics A-70). Canberra: Australian National University.
Sommer, Bruce A.
  1976   Umbuygamu: The classification of a Cape York Peninsular language. *Papers in Australian Linguistics* 10: 13–31. (Pacific Linguistics Series A, No. 47.) Canberra: Australian National University.
Swadesh, Mauricio and Evangelina Arana, with John T. Bendor-Samuel and W. A. A. Wilson
  1966   A preliminary glottochronology of Gur languages. *Journal of West African Languages* 3: 27–65.
Swadesh, Morris
  1950   Salish internal relationships. *International Journal of American Linguistics* 16: 157–167.
Swadesh, Morris
  1952   Lexico-statistic dating of prehistoric ethnic contacts. *Proceedings of the American Philosophical Society* 96: 452–463.
Swadesh, Morris
  1955   Towards greater accuracy in lexicostatistic dating. *International Journal of American Linguistics* 21: 121–137.
Thelwall, Robin
  1981   Lexicostatistical subgrouping and lexical reconstruction of the Daju group. In *Nilo-Saharan: Proceedings of the First Nilo-Saharan Linguistics Colloquium, Leiden, September 8–10, 1980*, Thilo C. Schadeberg and M. Lionel Bender (eds.), 167–184. Dordrecht: Foris Publications.

Torero, Alfredo
 1970   Lingüística e historia de la sociedad andina. *Anales Científicos de la Universidad Agraria* 8: 231–264.
Troike, Rudolph C.
 1969   The glottochronology of six Turkic languages. *International Journal of American Linguistics* 35: 183–191.
Tryon, Darrell T.
 1973   Linguistic subgrouping in the New Hebrides: A preliminary approach. *Oceanic Linguistics* 12: 303–351.
Tryon, Darrell T.
 1974   *Daly Family Languages, Australia.* (Pacific Linguistics Series C, No. 32.) Canberra: Australian National University.
Vérin, Pierre, Conrad P. Kottak, and Peter Gorlin
 1969   The glottochronology of Malagasy speech communities. *Oceanic Linguistics* 8: 26–83.
Villalón, María Eugenia
 1991   A spatial model of lexical relationships among fourteen Cariban varieties. In *Language Change in South American Indian Languages*, Mary Ritchie Key (ed.), 54–94. Philadelphia: University of Pennsylvania Press.
Voorhoeve, C. L.
 1968   The Central and South New Guinea Phylum. In *Papers in New Guinea Linguistics*, No. 8, C. L. Voorhoeve, Karl J. Franklin, and G. Scott (eds.), 1–17. (Pacific Linguistics, Series A – No. 16.) Canberra: Australian National University.
Walker, Robert S. and Lincoln A. Ribeiro
 2011   Bayesian phylogeography of the Arawak expansion in lowland South America. *Proceedings of the Royal Society B.* doi: 10.1098/rspb.2010.2579.
Wichmann, Søren and Eric W. Holman
 2009   Population size and rates of language change. *Human Biology* 81: 259–274.
Wichmann, Søren, Eric W. Holman, Dik Bakker, and Cecil H. Brown
 2010a Evaluating linguistic distance measures. *Physica A* 389: 3632–3639.
Wichmann, Søren, Eric W. Holman, André Müller, Viveka Velupillai, Johann-Mattis List, Oleg Belyaev, Matthias Urban, and Dik Bakker
 2010b Glottochronology as a heuristic for genealogical language relationships. *Journal of Quantitative Linguistics* 17: 303–316.
Wichmann, Søren, André Müller, and Viveka Velupillai
 2010c Homelands of the world's language families: A quantitative approach. *Diachronica* 27 (2): 247–276.

Wichmann, Søren, André Müller, Viveka Velupillai, Annkathrin Wett, Cecil H. Brown, Zarina Molochieva, Julia Bishoffberger, Eric W. Holman, Sebastian Sauppe, Pamela Brown, Dik Bakker, Johann-Mattis List, Dmitry Egorov, Oleg Belyaev, Matthias Urban, Harald Hammarström, Agustina Carrizo, Robert Mailhammer, Helen Geyer, David Beck, Evgenia Korovina, Pattie Epps, Pilar Valenzuela, and Anthony Grant
    2012   The ASJP database (version 15). http://email.eva.mpg.de/ ~wichmann/languages.htm.

Wichmann, Søren, Taraka Rama, and Eric W. Holman
    2011   Phonological diversity, word length, and population sizes across languages: The ASJP evidence. *Linguistic Typology* 15: 177–197.

Wichmann, Søren, Dietrich Stauffer, Christian Schulze, and Eric W. Holman
    2008   Do language change rates depend on population size? *Advances in Complex Systems* 11: 357–369.

Wilbert, Johannes
    1962   *Material lingüístico ye*. Caracas: Editorial Sucre.

Wurm, Stephen A.
    1973   The Kiwaian language family. In *The Linguistic Situation in the Gulf District and Adjacent Areas, Papua New Guinea*, Karl J. Franklin (ed.), 217–260. (Pacific Linguistics Series C – N. 26.) Canberra: Australian National University.

Xu, Tongjiang (Hsu tong chiang)
    1991   *Lishi yuyanxue* [Historical linguistics]. Beijing: Shangwu Yingshuguan.

Z'Graggen, John Anton
    1969   Classificatory and typological studies in languages of the Western Madang district, New Guinea. Ph.D. Diss., Australian National University.

Zipf, George K.
    1935   *Psycho-Biology of Language*. Boston, MA.: Houghton Mifflin.

Methods and tools

The Intercontinental Dictionary Series – a rich and principled database for language comparison

Lars Borin, Bernard Comrie and Anju Saxena

> *Nomina si nescis perit cognitio rerum*
> 'If you know not the names of things, the knowledge of things themselves perishes'
> (Sir Edward Coke, *The First Part of the Institutes of the Laws of England, or, a Commentary upon Littleton.* ~1628)

1. The Intercontinental Dictionary Series[1]

1.1. Background and motivation

The lexicon of a language is perhaps its most salient characteristic and the most obvious expression of the connection that language bears to the world. The lexicon also reflects the genetic affiliations of the language and its contact history, and it can be used to elucidate language change, both in meaning and in grammar. Lexical data from many languages collectively are the object of study of the branch of linguistics known as lexical typology, where the limits of the lexical diversity of human languages are investigated (Koptjevskaja-Tamm 2012). Linguistic studies drawing on this diversity are labor-intensive and logistically difficult, because of the amount and quality of data that are required and because the data sources are scattered over diverse institutions in the world and published in dozens of languages and scripts. There is need of a database where one can find comparable material to formulate hypotheses and test and validate those theories. For example, theories on intercontinental connections have been proposed on the basis of the distribution of 'sweet potato' and yet there is no single source, where words with this meaning can be found in many languages. Good quantitative and statistical studies are almost impossible to do now in non-Western languages.

The *Intercontinental Dictionary Series* (IDS)[2] is an attempt to address some of these difficulties. The IDS is an international collaboration for establishing a database where lexical material from a broad range of languages is organized in such a way as to provide a solid quantitative base for a scientific approach to language analysis and comparisons (see also section 2 below). Historical studies, comparative, and theoretical linguistic research can be based on this documentation. The IDS will provide the research tools necessary for expanding studies such as phonological theory, word formation, language change, lexical distribution, sound symbolism and onomatopoeia, classification, and other ideas that have to do with history of people and migrations. The languages available in IDS are interesting also in the context of language technology, potentially addressing recent concerns about the language-independence of the basic research methodology in this field (Bender 2011).

IDS is a long term cooperative project that involves linguists all over the world. It is a pioneering effort that contributes to preserving information on the little-known and "non-prestigious" languages of the world, many of which are becoming extinct. The project brings together data on the languages of the world, in a way that gives equal importance to all languages.

The originator of the IDS was the late Mary Ritchie Key at the University of California, Irvine. The idea for a work such as the IDS came to her in 1975 while studying the semantic grouping in the cognate sets established in comparative studies. This was followed by pilot projects using comparative data of recognized language families. Scholars were contacted who were chosen for their interests in cross-cultural research and for their skills and willingness to give time and thought to the objectives of the dictionary series. In 1984, an award from the University of California, Irvine Faculty Research Committee to launch the IDS set the series on its way. Bernard Comrie (Max Planck Institute for Evolutionary Anthropology, Leipzig) is the current project leader of IDS and the general editor of the series.

1.2. Structure, technical implementation and status

Comparative work in Indo-European (IE) has been carried on over 200 years, and excellent research tools have been produced. Specifically, a model for IDS is *A dictionary of selected synonyms in the principal Indo-European languages* (Buck 1949). This 1500-page dictionary is organized in a thesaurus-like topical outline of 22 chapters. The outline has been adapted for the IDS, with the numbering system generally maintained. Buck's dictionary contains approximately 1,200 potential entries. The IDS adaptation contains 1,310 entries. The entries are identified using English words as labels, but they are intended to represent word senses, expressing concepts falling roughly into the following categories:

(1) universal concepts finding expression in most human languages ('arm', 'speak', 'dry', etc.; but cf. Goddard 2001);
(2) concepts related to certain geographical or environmental phenomena: 'earthquake', 'tide', 'parrot', etc.;
(3) cultural concepts: 'mead', 'tattoo', 'cobbler', etc.

Even though the English words used for sense labels come with particular parts of speech (in English), the corresponding item in the described language may well have a different part of speech.

Naturally, not all concepts from groups (2) and (3) will be found in all the languages. In some cases, it may be important to add extra concepts to represent information relevant to a particular language group or a region. Therefore, in the process of data collection, the list of word senses will be expanded, but under no circumstances will the senses be lost from the master list. If the corresponding concept does not find lexical expression in a particular language, the entry will simply remain blank. The reason for this strict rule is quite clear: by adding senses, the main body of the databases is still kept compatible, while deleting senses may create databases which are no longer compatible.

The format of IDS lends itself exceptionally well to the use of the computer. The IDS data is currently stored in a simple machine-readable format which is posted on the internet under an open license, providing unlimited access to IDS data for scholars from all over the world, who are thus able to use the dictionaries for further research.

The final outcome of the project will be an electronic database representing the entire range of human languages. It will bring together information on languages of the world published in dozens of different languages and scripts and scattered in hundreds of publications and manuscripts, which are often not available to the linguistic community.

At present 215 IDS lists are available for online browsing and downloading at the main IDS website (see figure 1). The IDS is developed in cooperation and complementation with other research projects, and additional lists have been collected in such projects. The Loanword Typology project (LWT; Haspelmath and Tadmor 2009) has added 31 new languages out of a total of 41 languages investigated in the project on the basis of (somewhat extended) IDS lists,[3] and the Digital areal linguistics project described in section 3 below will contribute another 15 languages, all from South Asia.

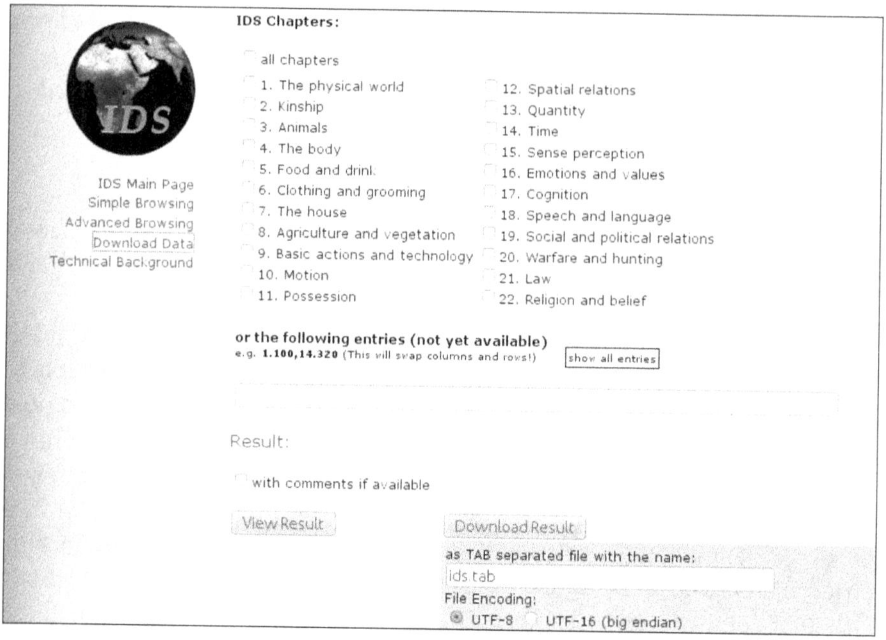

Figure 1. The IDS website.

2. The IDS – not just another Swadesh list

2.1. Basic vocabularies in linguistics

The notion of "basic" or "core" vocabulary is construed in various ways, depending on the branch of linguistics involved, and ultimately determined by the purpose for which such vocabularies are constructed. The notion of basic vocabulary has been understood at least in the following ways in various branches of linguistics:

(1) in applied linguistics, the vocabulary appearing first in L1 acquisition, and the vocabulary most useful or "central" in L2 learning;
(2) in corpus linguistics, the most frequent words over a broad range of text types;
(3) in lexical typology, a set of meanings with universal or near-universal lexicalization (e.g., Goddard 2001, 2012);
(4) in contact linguistics, lexical items resistant to borrowing (Haspelmath and Tadmor 2009);

(5) in genetic linguistics, a set of items highly resistant to lexical replacement. In particular, the basic vocabulary lists of this kind now known as *Swadesh lists*, first proposed in the late 1940s by Morris Swadesh (1948, 1950, 1952, 1955), have found a multitude of uses in linguistics and occasionally outside it.

In fact, there may be very little overlap between even very small basic vocabularies composed for these different purposes (Borin 2012). Since basic vocabularies are generally designed for one – fairly narrow – kind of use, this should perhaps not come as a surprise.

A common characteristic of many of these basic vocabularies is that they are small, especially those used in comparative studies (types 3–5 above). In the particular case of the Swadesh list, it has actually grown smaller over the years. From an original size of about 200 items (Swadesh 1952), it was soon pared down to the widely used 100-item version by the elimination of items judged to be not universal enough or not fully arbitrary (e.g., onomatopoetic or sound-symbolic), etc. (Swadesh 1955). The most recent version of the Swadesh list, the ASJP list (Holman et al. 2008), holds only 28–40 items.

2.2. The IDS list – empiricism strikes back

Where does the IDS fit into this picture? We noted above that basic vocabulary lists tend to be short, especially those used in comparative studies, where an important aim is to cover a broad spectrum of languages. This has at least the following (interrelated) corollaries.

The incremental effort required to add a language to the database is small. Let us compare the IDS and ASJP in this regard. While the preparation of IDS lists for South Asian languages (see section 3 below) has required on average one person-month of work per list, an ASJP list takes less than a day to prepare. The twenty-odd languages covered in Buck's original dictionary required about the same number of years from the start of the project (announced by Buck 1929) until the eventual publication of the dictionary (Buck 1949), but then Buck also included a wealth of detailed etymological material. From this follows that a project like ASJP can rely mainly on volunteer work, whereas this is much harder in the case of IDS. There is obviously a tension here between breadth and depth of coverage. The ASJP project, like much typological work (e.g., WALS: Haspelmath et al. 2005, 2008; Dryer and Haspelmath 2011), aims for breadth at the expense of depth. It covers a significant fraction of the world's languages (5,751 lists in version 15 of ASJP).

With a very small selection of items there is a risk that the list may fail to fulfill its (narrow) purpose. Here, the initial basis for choosing which items to include becomes crucial. Ideally, any list should be assembled using the full lexicons of all included languages as the sampling frame. As far as we can see, none of the popular extant basic vocabularies lives up to this ideal, with the possible exception of the Natural Semantic Metalanguage (NSM; Goddard 2012), a basic vocabulary belonging in category 3 according to the classification in the previous section. For instance, both the ASJP list (Holman et al. 2008) and the Leipzig-Jakarta list of basic vocabulary resulting from the LWT project (Tadmor 2009) are based on much smaller, judgment-based sampling frames. The ASJP list is made up of the most stable items from the 100-item Swadesh list, and the Leipzig-Jakarta list is made up of the 100 items most resistant to borrowing from the slightly extended IDS list used in the LWT project. In both cases it is probably fair to say that the original selection of items was made "by a combination of intuition and experience following certain guidelines" which characterized Swadesh's work (Oswalt 1971: 422). For the predecessor of IDS, Buck (1929, 1949) does not explicitly state the criteria for which items should be included, beyond the goal to "work out a tentative and skeleton dictionary covering a limited number, perhaps a thousand, of representative groups of synonyms in the principal IE languages" (Buck 1929: 216). Thus, in both cases, we have no hard empirical evidence that the ASJP list and Leipzig-Jakarta list comprise the optimal selection of items in their respective categories. There may be a better 100-item Swadesh list or a better 1460-item LWT/IDS list. The overlap between the 100-item Swadesh list and the (100-item) Leipzig-Jakarta list is only 62% (Tadmor 2009: 73) and only about a third of the 42 NSM items listed by Goddard (2001) are present in either of these two lists (Borin 2012). This indicates that there is still much to be found out about basic vocabularies.

Size does matter, however. If the selection principles have been more or less similar, we can be fairly certain that the LWT/IDS list will be a much better basis for all kinds of linguistic investigations than the Swadesh lists, simply because it provides a sufficiently broader empirical base. It is about an order of magnitude larger than the ASJP list, which is significant, since many linguistic phenomena obey a power distribution known as *Zipf's law* (Zipf 1949), one practical consequence of which is that data requirements increase exponentially as we wish to investigate increasingly rare linguistic phenomena.[4] At the other end, is there some point below which language data just will not be useful for comparative purposes, when it will not be possible to say interesting (and true!) things about it? Apparently the ASJP list with its 28–40 items can be used to investigate many interesting aspects of genetic linguistics and language change, such as: the incidence of sound symbolism in certain basic vocabulary items (Wichmann, Holman, and Brown 2010), the probable locations of language family homelands (Wichmann, Müller, and Velupillai 2010), and the relationship between word length and rate of lexical change (Wichmann and Holman this volume). However, most details of the language systems remain hidden when using 28–40 central vocabulary items from each language, and nothing else.

A relevant comparison in this connection could be the vocabulary needed for communicating in a foreign language. The ASJP vocabulary is on a par with that found in many tourist guide phrase lists, typically a column or two of words and short phrases, which everyone knows is sufficient only for displaying good intentions to native speakers, but hardly for any kind of real communication to be possible. The IDS in turn provides a vocabulary comparable in size to that defined for the Common European Framework of Reference (CEFR) A1 level, the lowest communicative proficiency level in a foreign language in this framework (around 1,500 items; Milton 2009: 186). At the A1 level, the learners should be capable of the following (COE 2012):

> Can understand and use familiar everyday expressions and very basic phrases aimed at the satisfaction of needs of a concrete type.
> Can introduce him/herself and others and can ask and answer questions about personal details such as where he/she lives, people he/she knows and things he/she has.
> Can interact in a simple way provided the other person talks slowly and clearly and is prepared to help.

A basic premise of the IDS endeavor is that a vocabulary of a size which is capable of supporting linguistic activities at this quite impressive level of sophistication also will enable equally impressive broad comparative linguistic studies.

3. Using the IDS in linguistic research: An example from South Asia

The *Digital areal linguistics* project[5] is a collaboration with the IDS project, and responsible for the Himalayan languages in the larger IDS project. One aim of this project is to create a database of comparable lexical items in a number of representative Himalayan languages and other South Asian languages, adhering to the IDS scheme. The data collection phase of the project is largely completed, although some of the lexical lists still remain to be finalized for publication.[6] This database is now being used in pursuit of the main project aim, that of investigating the linguistic situation in the Indian Himalayas, and for evaluating some of the claims about South Asian areal traits found in the linguistic literature.

Since the publication of Emeneau 1956, South Asia has been considered a prototypical linguistic area in the literature on areal linguistics. However, systematic investigations of this claim have been few (e.g., Masica 1976) and somewhat spotty, mostly relying on data from the major Indo-Aryan and Dravidian languages, but more rarely the other language families of South Asia. The picture of which areal phenomena are characteristic of South Asia, as well as their geographical extent, is actually far from clear (Thomason 2000). Ebert (2006), in a survey of the field, notes that languages of the Himalayan region are rarely taken into account in areal linguistic studies on South Asia. In the Himalayan region a number of Tibeto-Burman (TB) and lesser-known Indo-Aryan (IA) languages are spoken. Any conclusion on South Asia as a linguistic area is premature if languages of this vast region are not included.

Further, even though some areal features have been attributed to South Asia, scattered observations in the literature show both that not all features are represented in all language families in some subareas and that there may be "microareas" within South Asia. One such microarea is arguably the Himalayan region (Bickel 2004, 2008; Bickel and Nichols 2009; Saxena 2006), where a long history of language contact and multilingualism has led to convergence on many linguistic levels between the two genetically unrelated language families of the area (TB and IA).

Long-standing contact between different language families, as well as among different subbranches of the same language family (for example, within the Tibeto-Burman language family) in the Himalayan region has resulted in intense lexical and grammatical borrowing. For languages where we do not have historical data, it is hard, or sometimes impossible, to distinguish similarities between languages due to common heritage from those due to contact in such cases. Based on the lexical data (IDS lists) collected in the project, along with grammatical and cultural data collected by Anju Saxena in another project and the information available in secondary sources, we are conducting a systematic comparative study of the lexical domain (phonology, morphology and lexical semantics), as well as selected morpho-syntactic constructions – which lie at the root of areal linguistics (Thomason and Kaufman 1988; Heine and Kuteva 2005; Matras and Sakel 2007) – with a goal to investigate the areal hypothesis.

The first results of the study have been published, using reduced versions of the IDS lists (Saxena and Borin 2011, this volume) and a monograph on the linguistic situation of Kinnaur is under preparation by Anju Saxena, where full IDS lists are used in a number of comparative investigations of two TB and one IA language local to the region (Saxena forthc.).

4. Conclusion and future prospects

4.1. Extending the IDS database

The compilation of one single IDS list is a non-trivial undertaking, requiring a work effort amounting to about one person-month. Achieving similar coverage for the IDS to that of ASJP in terms of number of languages – close to 6,000 in the ASJP – would require an effort corresponding to more than 400 person-years. Even if the effort could be reduced to, say, one week per language – which does not seem likely, given the quality requirements that we would like to put on the IDS data – we are still looking at more than 100 person-years of work. Thus, even though the IDS database will continue to grow, its growth is likely to be quite slow, if it is to rely mainly on initiatives like the Loanword Typology project or the Digital areal linguistics project described above.

An emerging alternative means of linguistic data collection which is being experimented with extensively in the computational linguistics community is *crowdsourcing*, i.e., large-scale voluntary collaborative efforts by the public (or in some cases by experts), a model pioneered by Wikipedia (Gurevych and Wolf 2010; Munro et al. 2010). In recent years, computational linguists have begun to make extensive use of a commercial extension of the original crowdsourcing idea, Amazon's *Mechanical Turk*,[7] where users can register for crowdsourcing work where they are paid small amounts of money for performing limited tasks referred to as "human intelligence tasks" (HITs), e.g., linguistic classification or annotation tasks (Callison-Burch and Dredze 2010). The results are somewhat ambiguous, both with regard to quality (Gillick and Liu 2010) – in part because the means for ascertaining the level of expertise of individual contributors are still nonexistent or very rudimentary – and with regard to ethics (Fort, Adda, and Cohen 2011).

Some form of crowdsourcing could be an alternative for extending the IDS database in a way that will not require an impossible budget. The Wiktionary is a crowdsourcing dictionary project hosted by the WikiMedia Foundation. Because of its broad coverage in terms of content and number of languages it is one of the most popular collaboratively created language resources in the natural language processing research community (Zesch, Müller, and Gurevych 2008).[8]

Table 1. Wiktionary languages with at least 1,460 entries and not present in IDS or LWT.

Afrikaans	14,993	Macedonian	2,288
Asturian	11,394	Malay	1,460
Belarusian	2,282	Malayalam	101,982
Bosnian	2,933	Min Nan	6,260
Burmese	114,891	Norwegian (Bokmål)	127,598
Cambodian	2,616	Norwegian (Nynorsk)	4,460
Corsican	2,028	Occitan	22,128
Croatian	20,858	Pashto	4,081
Esperanto	25,560	Sicilian	16,671
Fijian	10,887	Serbian	15,949
Galician	32,366	Slovak	1,513
Georgian	5,318	Slovenian	7,130
Hebrew	11,419	Tagalog	13,001
Icelandic	21,080	Tatar	7,037
Ido	194,893	Turkish	281,020
Interlingua	1,800	Turkmen	4,378
Kashubian	1,495	Ukrainian	30,780
Kazakh	3,813	Upper Sorbian	3,896
Kirghiz	3,374	Urdu	13,071
Korean	340,351	Volapük	23,544
Kurdish	54,147	Walloon	7,340
Lao	60,674	West Frisian	13,160
Limburgian	95,519	Wolof	2,693
Luxembourgish	4,970		

At the time of writing, there were wiktionaries for 171 languages available at the Wiktionary website, with highly varying degrees of coverage. Existing wiktionaries could be used as a foundation for a collaborative effort on extending the IDS database. If we require that in order to be useful as a starting point for this, a wiktionary should have at least as many entries as the LWT master list,[9] we end up with 96 languages having from 1,460 (Malay) to 2,975,173 (English) "good" entries (in the terminology used on the main Wiktionary site). In this group there are 47 languages which are not yet represented in IDS or LWT (see table 1). Out of these 47 languages, three – Bosnian, Croatian and Serbian – represent recent political splits of Serbo-Croatian, which is present in IDS. The LWT database has an entry for Indonesian (Malay), while the label Malay in Wiktionary is assumed to refer to the Malaysian variety. In both cases we may note that IDS already has several instances where more than one dialect or variety of a language are present in the database. The list also contains wiktionaries for some constructed languages (Esperanto, Ido, Interlingua and Volapük). There is no reason to exclude these from the IDS, given that users can easily make an active selection of languages from the database.

Many wiktionaries are linked to the English Wiktionary on the lemma or sense level, so that the procedure for creating initial lists for the chosen languages would use the English word sense labels of the IDS list in order to collect candidate entries, possibly complemented by synonyms supplied by the English WordNet (Fellbaum 1998) in order to maximize coverage. Wiktionaries are only semi-structured, and to boot with a slightly different structure for each language edition, so this step entails a fair amount of work (Navarro et al. 2009; Gurevych and Wolf 2010: 1079ff; McCrae, Montiel-Ponsoda, and Cimiano 2012). Once this is accomplished, however, there will be a set of seed IDS lists which can be posted on the web and all interested parties can be invited to correct or contribute entries. The logical next step would then be to allow volunteers to add new languages.

4.2. Ensuring the future of the IDS database

Areal and typological linguists traditionally work with secondary language data, i.e. dictionaries and descriptive grammars. In the last few years, these disciplines have moved into the computer age, compiling large databases of selected linguistic features for many languages (see, e.g., Dryer and Haspelmath 2011; Everaert, Musgrave, and Dimitriadis 2009; Greenhill, Blust, and Gray 2008; Haspelmath et al. 2005, 2008; Haspelmath and Tadmor 2009; Lewis and Xia 2010; Nerbonne 1998). The computer now gives us the potential for tying together these linguistic databases (see, e.g., Chiarcos, Nordhoff, and Hellman 2012), but not without a conscious effort.

However, although linguists have started collecting typological and other data in digital databases, data standardization beyond the confines of a single project has rarely been an issue, neither with regard to storage format nor with regard to the data categories and their labels, which means that the data are not interoperable in practice. There is also often no way of unambiguously referring to a particular data item, e.g., a lexical entry, which is a prerequisite for working with distributed datasets, a need that linguists increasingly are becoming aware of. Increasing numbers of linguists have understood the methodological necessity of sharing their underlying research data freely (Liberman 2012), asking only to be cited as the originators of the data (e.g., LWT, WALS, ASJP, and IDS itself). However, even in this day and age, there is a clear dividing line in the linguistic research community between this attitude and one that unfortunately still seems to predominate, where the base data are not made accessible at all or made accessible only online, through a search interface, which severely limits the kinds of interaction a researcher can have with the data. For several of the data collection initiatives mentioned above (e.g., Everaert, Musgrave, and Dimitriadis 2009; Greenhill, Blust, and Gray 2008; Lewis and Xia 2010), there are no indications in publications or on the corresponding websites that the base data would be available for downloading and republishable under the same conditions as the original data.

In the IDS project we fully recognize the importance of standard data formats and content models for real comparison to be possible, and the usefulness of so-called "open content", i.e. (in this case) data that are freely accessible as a whole (and not only browsable through a web interface), modifiable and republishable under the same conditions as the original data (in the computer software world, this is known as "open source" – Borin, Forsberg, and Lönngren 2008; Borin, Saxena, and Veselinova 2009; Saxena et al. 2008). The goal is for all IDS lists to be published online under an open content license using widely recognized standard formats, e.g., the ISO standard LMF (Lexical Markup Framework; ISO 2008; see also Aristar-Dry et al. 2012) and a stable convention for identifying and cross-referencing lexical items. In this way, we aim to ensure that the IDS will not end up in a "data graveyard", but remain fully accessible and usable to future generations of linguists.

Notes

1. In this article we make use of some introductory text on the IDS prepared by the late Mary Ritchie Key.
2. The Intercontinental Dictionary Series is available for browsing and downloading at http://lingweb.eva.mpg.de/ids/.
3. The database from the LWT project is available for browsing and downloading at http://wold.livingsources.org/. The LWT master list includes all IDS senses, but adds a further 150 senses – most of them under two new topic headings – taking the total up to 1,460 items subdivided into 24 categories.

4. At the next order of magnitude – about 64,000 items – we find full-size reference dictionaries as are available only for comparatively few languages.
5. The project *Digital areal linguistics: a lexical view of the Himalayan microarea* is funded by the Swedish Research Council (project no. 2009–1448). See http://spraakbanken.gu.se/eng/research/digital-areal-linguistics.
6. Those word lists that have been published can be browsed and downloaded at http://spraakbanken.gu.se/eng/research/digital-areal-linguistics/word-lists. Generally, these lists aspire to go beyond the IDS list to cover the 1,460 senses of the LWT master list. The lists will also be available from the main IDS website.
7. See http://www.mturk.com.
8. Of course, wiktionary languages are generally such where there exists a tradition of writing, which excludes the vast majority of the world's languages.
9. This lower bound is logically determined – a wiktionary with fewer entries could never provide a full IDS list – and not meant to be realistic. We do not know how big a wiktionary has to be in order to provide, say, 75% of an IDS list, but it is likely that several thousands of entries are required for this.

References

Aristar-Dry, Helen, Sebastian Drude, Menzo Windhouwer, Jost Gippert, and Irina Nevskaya
    2012   Rendering endangered lexicons interoperable through standards harmonization: The RELISH project. *Proceedings of LREC 2012*, 766–770. Istanbul: ELRA.

Bender, Emily M.
    2011   On achieving and evaluating language-independence in NLP. *Linguistic Issues in Language Technology* 6 (3). http://elanguage.net/journals/lilt/article/view/2624

Bickel, Balthasar
    2004   The syntax of experiencers in the Himalayas. In *Nonnominative Subjects*, Peri Bhaskararao, and K.V. Subbarao (eds.), 25–59. Amsterdam: John Benjamins.

Bickel, Balthasar
    2008   Verb agreement and epistemic marking: A typological journey from the Himalayas to the Caucasus. In *Chomoangma, Demawend und Kasbek. Festchrift für Roland Bielmeier zu seinen 65. Geburstag*, Brigitte Huber, Marianne Volkart, and Paul Widmer (eds.), 1–14. Halle: International Institute of Tibetan and Buddhist Studies.

Bickel, Balthasar and Johanna Nichols
    2009   The geography of case. In *The Oxford Handbook of Case*, Andrej Malchukov, and Andrew Spencer (eds.), 479–493. Oxford: Oxford University Press.

Borin, Lars
2012 Core vocabulary: A useful but mystical concept in some kinds of linguistics. In *Shall we Play the Festschrift Game? Essays on the Occasion of Lauri Carlson's 60th Birthday*, Diana Santos, Krister Lindén, and Wanjiku Ng'ang'a (eds.), 53–65. Berlin: Springer.

Borin, Lars, Markus Forsberg, and Lennart Lönngren
2008 The hunting of the BLARK – SALDO, a freely available lexical database for Swedish language technology. In *Resourceful Language Technology. Festschrift in Honor of Anna Sågvall Hein*, Joakim Nivre, Mats Dahllöf, and Beáta Megyesi (eds.), 21–32. Acta Universitatis Upsaliensis: Studia Linguistica Upsaliensia 7.

Borin, Lars, Anju Saxena, and Ljuba Veselinova
2009 GIS and OWL in documentation of ethnobiological terms in the Himalayas. Presentation at the *Colloquium on methods and case studies in geographically-referenced language documentation*, at the *1st International Conference on Language Documentation and Conservation (ICLDC)*, Honolulu, 13th March, 2009.

Buck, Carl Darling
1929 Words for world, earth and land, sun. *Language* 5 (4): 215–227.

Buck, Carl Darling
1949 *A dictionary of Selected Synonyms in the Principal Indo-European Languages. A Contribution to the History of Ideas.* Chicago: University of Chicago Press.

Callison-Burch, Chris and Mark Dredze
2010 Creating speech and language data with Amazon's Mechanical Turk. *Proceedings of the NAACL HLT 2010 Workshop on Creating Speech and Language Data with Amazon's Mechanical Turk*, 1–12. Los Angeles: ACL.

Chiarcos, Christian, Sebastian Nordhoff, and Sebastian Hellman (eds.)
2012 *Linked data in linguistics: Representing and connecting language data and language metadata.* Berlin: Springer.

COE
2012 *Common European Framework of Reference for Languages: Learning, Teaching, Assessment (CEFR).* Council of Europe. http://www.coe.int/t/dg4/linguistic/Cadre1_en.asp. Accessed 25th June 2012.

Dryer, Matthew S. and Martin Haspelmath (eds.)
2011 *The World Atlas of Language Structures Online.* Second ed. Munich: Max Planck Digital Library. http://wals.info/

Ebert, Karen
2006 South Asia as a linguistic area. In *Encyclopedia of Languages and Linguistics*, 2nd ed., Keith Brown (ed.). Oxford: Elsevier.

Emeneau, Murray
1956 India as a linguistic area. *Language* 32: 3–16.

Everaert, Martin, Simon Musgrave, and Alexis Dimitriadis (eds.)
    2009   *The Use of Databases in Cross-Linguistic Studies.* Berlin/New York: Mouton de Gruyter.

Fellbaum, Christiane (ed.)
    1998   *WordNet: An Electronic Lexical Database.* Cambridge, Massachusetts: MIT Press.

Fort, Karën, Gilles Adda, and K. Bretonnel Cohen
    2011   Amazon Mechanical Turk: Gold mine or coal mine? *Computational Linguistics* 37 (2): 413–420.

Gillick, Dan and Yang Liu
    2010   Non-expert evaluation of summarization systems is risky. *Proceedings of the NAACL HLT 2010 Workshop on Creating Speech and Language Data with Amazon's Mechanical Turk*, 148–151. Los Angeles: ACL.

Goddard, Cliff
    2001   Lexico-semantic universals: A critical overview. *Linguistic Typology* 5: 1–65.

Goddard, Cliff
    2012   Semantic primes, semantic molecules, semantic templates: Key concepts in the NSM approach to lexical typology. *Linguistics* 50 (3): 711–743.

Greenhill, Simon J., Robert Blust, and Russell D. Gray
    2008   The Austronesian basic vocabulary database: From bioinformatics to lexomics. *Evolutionary Bioinformatics* 2008 (4): 271–283.

Gurevych, Iryna and Elisabeth Wolf
    2010   Expert-built and collaboratively constructed lexical semantic resources. *Language and Linguistics Compass* 4 (11): 1074–1090.

Haspelmath, Martin, Matthew S. Dryer, David Gil, and Bernard Comrie (eds.)
    2005   *The World Atlas of Language Structures.* Oxford: Oxford University Press.

Haspelmath, Martin, Matthew S. Dryer, David Gil, and Bernard Comrie (eds.)
    2008   *The World Atlas of Language Structures Online.* Munich: Max Planck Digital Library. http://2008.wals.info/

Haspelmath, Martin and Uri Tadmor (eds)
    2009   *Loanwords in the World's Languages: A Comparative Handbook.* Berlin/New York: Mouton de Gruyter

Heine, Bernd and Tania Kuteva
    2005   *Language Contact and Grammatical Change.* Cambridge: Cambridge University Press.

Holman, Eric W., Søren Wichmann, Cecil H. Brown, Viveka Velupillai, André Müller, and Dik Bakker
    2008   Explorations in automated language classification. *Folia Linguistica* 42: 331–354.

ISO
    2008   Language resource management – Lexical Markup Framework. ISO 24613. Geneva: ISO.

Koptjevskaja-Tamm, Maria
    2012   New directions in lexical typology. *Linguistics* 50 (3): 373–394.

Lewis, William D. and Fei Xia
    2010   Developing ODIN: A multilingual repository of annotated language data for hundreds of the world's languages. *Literary and Linguistic Computing* 25 (3): 303–319.

Liberman, Mark
    2012   Big inaccessible data. Posted on *Language Log*, 4th June, 2012. http://languagelog.ldc.upenn.edu/nll/?p=3999. Accessed 19th June, 2012.

Masica, Colin P.
    1976   *Defining a Linguistic Area: South Asia*. Chicago: University of Chicago Press.

Matras, Yaron and Jeanette Sakel (eds.)
    2007   *Grammatical Borrowing in Cross-Linguistic Perspective*. Berlin/New York: Mouton de Gruyter.

McCrae, John, Elena Montiel-Ponsoda, and Philipp Cimiano
    2012   Integrating WordNet and Wiktionary with *lemon*. In *Linked Data in Linguistics*, Christian Chiarcos, Sebastian Nordhoff, and Sebastian Hellman (eds.), 25–34. Berlin: Springer.

Milton, James
    2009   *Measuring Second Language Vocabulary Acquisition*. Bristol: Multilingual Matters.

Munro, Robert, Steven Bethard, Victor Kuperman, Vicky Tzuyin Lai, Robin Melnick, Christopher Potts, Tyler Schnoebelen, and Harry Tily
    2010   Crowdsourcing and language studies: The new generation of linguistic data. *Proceedings of the NAACL HLT 2010 Workshop on Creating Speech and Language Data with Amazon's Mechanical Turk*, 122–130. Los Angeles: ACL.

Navarro, Emmanuel, Franck Sajous, Bruno Gaume, Laurent Prévot, Shu-Kai Hsieh, Tzu-Yi Kuo, Pierre Magistry, and Chu-Ren Huang
    2009   Wiktionary and NLP: Improving synonymy networks. *Proceedings of the 2009 Workshop on the People's Web Meets NLP, ACL-IJCNLP 2009*, 19–27. Suntec, Singapore: ACL and AFNLP.

Nerbonne, John (ed.)
    1998   *Linguistic Databases*. CSLI Lecture Notes, Vol. 77. Stanford: CSLI.

Oswalt, Robert L.
    1971   Towards the construction of a standard lexicostatistic list. *Anthropological Linguistics* 13 (9): 421–434.

Saxena, Anju
    2006   It takes two to tango: Linguistic and cultural (co)variation in digital documentation. In *Language and Cultural Contact: Digital Docu-*

Saxena, Anju
    forthc. *mentation*, vol. 3, Peter Austin (ed.), 181–195. London: The Hans Rausing Endangered Languages Project.
    forthc. The linguistic landscape of Kinnaur.

Saxena, Anju and Lars Borin
    2011 Dialect classification in the Himalayas: a computational approach. *NODALIDA 2011 Conference Proceedings*, 307–310. Riga: NEALT.

Saxena, Anju, Lars Borin, Ljuba Veselinova, and Santosh Negi
    2008 GIS supported language documentation of the Himalayas. Workshop on language documentation and language description. The 23rd Scandinavian Conference of Linguistics. Uppsala University, 30 Sept – 1 Oct 2008.

Swadesh, Morris
    1948 The time value of linguistic diversity. Paper presented at the *Viking Fund Supper Conference for Anthropologists*, 12th March, 1948. (Abstract in part: Swadesh 1952: 454.)

Swadesh, Morris
    1950 Salish internal relationships. *International Journal of American Linguistics* 16 (4): 157–167.

Swadesh, Morris
    1952 Lexico-statistic dating of prehistoric ethnic contacts: with special reference to North American Indians and Eskimos. *Proceedings of the American Philosophical Society* 96 (4): 452–463.

Swadesh, Morris
    1955 Towards greater accuracy in lexicostatistic dating. *International Journal of American Linguistics* 21 (2): 121–137.

Tadmor, Uri
    2009 Loanwords in the world's languages: Findings and results. In *Loanwords in the World's Languages: A Comparative Handbook*, Martin Haspelmath, and Uri Tadmor (eds), 55–75. Berlin/New York: Mouton de Gruyter

Thomason, Sarah Grey
    2000 Linguistic areas and language history. In *Languages in Contact*, Dicky G. Gilbers, John Nerbonne, and Jos Schaeken (eds.), 311–327. Amsterdam: Rodopi.

Thomason, Sarah Grey, and Terrence Kaufman
    1988 *Language Contact, Creolization and Genetic Linguistics*. Berkeley: University of California Press.

Wichmann, Søren, Eric W. Holman, and Cecil H. Brown
    2010 Sound symbolism in basic vocabulary. *Entropy* 12 (4): 844–858.

Wichmann, Søren, André Müller, and Viveka Velupillai
    2010 Homelands of the world's language families: A quantitative approach. *Diachronica* 27 (2): 247–276.

Zesch, Torsten, Christof Müller, and Iryna Gurevych
   2008   Extracting lexical semantic knowledge from Wikipedia and Wiktionary. *Proceedings of LREC 2008*, 1646–1652. Marrakech: ELRA.

Zipf, George Kingsley
   1949   *Human Behavior and the Principle of Least Effort*. Cambridge, MA: Addison-Wesley.

Towards automated language classification: A clustering approach

Armin Buch, David Erschler, Gerhard Jäger and Andrei Lupas

1. Introduction

In this paper, we discuss advantages of clustering approaches to automated language classification, describe distance measures used for this purpose, and present results of several proof-of-concept experiments. We advocate the use of probability based distances – those that take into account the distribution of relevant features across the language sample in question.

Tree-building algorithms have become a popular tool in computer-aided historical linguistics to discover and visualize large-scale patterns among large groups of languages. The technique crucially uses similarity measures, see, for instance, MacMahon and MacMahon (2005), Forster and Renfrew (2006) and Nichols and Warnow (2008).

While being powerful tools, tree-building (usually termed *phylogenetic* in bioinformatics) algorithms have a few disadvantages. This is well-known in bioinformatics, and perhaps even more pressing in linguistic applications. To start with, phylogenetic algorithms are designed to discover tree-like signals. Non-tree shaped structures (due to lateral transfer, parallel or convergent evolution, or chance) are systematically misinterpreted. Furthermore, phylogenies (i.e. trees produced by such algorithms) lose resolution in the deep nodes as the number of sequences increases, because branching decisions are always taken hierarchically from the leaves to the root and therefore the effects of contradicting data accumulate as the computation progresses towards the root. Also, phylogenies become more inaccurate with the number of sequences because the multiple alignments on which they are based accumulate errors. The likelihood of including incorrect alignments which distort the topology of the tree, increases, and highly divergent sequences are shuffled to the root of the tree where they are artificially joined into a basal clade, i.e. a constituent close to the root of the tree. Furthermore, at each branching decision, tree-building algorithms exclude contradicting data, which thus becomes irrevocably lost. Clustering algorithms are free from this drawback. Last but not least, in phylogenetic analyses the time needed to find the optimal tree increases exponentially with the number of sequences,[1] so that trees of more than a few thousand sequences become computationally prohibitive.

Frickey and Lupas (2004) devised the software package CLANS (CLuster ANalysis of Sequences) that visualizes similarities between data points by projecting them onto a low-dimensional (2d or 3d) cluster map. Using a force-directed graph layout algorithm, groups of similar data points form clusters that are easy to identify visually or via standard clustering methods. Cluster maps do not suffer from the above-mentioned problems. In particular, errors do not accumulate but cancel out each other, and the computational complexity is not worse than quadratic (Fruchtermann and Reingold 1991). CLANS has been applied successfully to the analysis of phylogenetic relationships between protein sequences and other biological characteristics of organisms.

It is obviously possible to feed appropriately encoded linguistic data into clustering software. However, it is not clear *a priori* to which extent clustering methods are applicable in linguistics and how useful they are for research.

We argue that this kind of technique would indeed be useful and illustrate it with a number of proof-of-concept experiments. We show that, when based on lexical data, our technique essentially reproduces the classically known relationships between Indo-European languages. On the other hand, applying the procedure to morphosyntactic features does not provide anything remotely approaching a genetic classification, as expected. Furthermore, we argue that CLANS allows to better visualize results than SplitsTree (Huson and Bryant 2006) an application that has become very common in the field (Nichols and Warnow 2008).

From the very outset, we should stress the point that findings procured from CLANS clusterings are statistical by their nature. That is to say, the larger a cluster is, and the more connections does the algorithm produce for it, the more significant are the findings.

In bioinformatics, a very large amount of input data is granted, given the very large number of proteins in living organisms and the length of protein sequences. In linguistics, assembling a database that would be amenable to meaningful statistical processing is a much more challenging task. We used three readily available databases: the database of Gray and Atkinson[2] (2003) on Indo-European languages, which is based on the well-known database of Dyen, Kruskal, and Black (1992), further on to be called the DKB database; the morphosyntactic feature database from WALS (Haspelmath et al. 2008) and the Automated Language Classification Database of Wichmann et al.,[3] further on to be called the ASJP database.

The paper is organized as follows: In section 2, we describe main features of CLANS software and comment on the key technical ingredient: similarity or distance matrices. Then we proceed to examine a number of test cases. In section 3, we explore binary feature based distances. The datasets in question are the DKB database and a subsample of WALS. Using the latter sample, we compare the results of CLANS with a network produced by SplitsTree. In section 4, we investigate a measure of language similarity based on distances between words. We show that the findings for Indo-European languages are in a good agreement with the traditional classification. In section 6, we investigate language distances based on unsupervised alignment of parallel texts. Section 7 concludes.

2. Introducing CLANS

CLANS is an implementation of the Fruchterman–Reingold (1991) graph layout algorithm. It has been designed for discovering similarities between protein sequences.

> Sequences are represented by vertices in the graph, BLAST/PSIBLAST high scoring segment pairs (HSPs) are shown as edges connecting vertices and provide attractive forces proportional to the negative logarithm of the HSP's P-value. To keep all sequences from collapsing onto one point, a mild repulsive force is placed between all vertices. After random placement in either two-dimensional or three-dimensional space, the vertices are moved iteratively according to the force vectors resulting from all pairwise interactions until the overall vertex movement becomes negligible. While this approach, coupled with random placement, causes non-deterministic behavior, similar sequences or sequence groups reproducibly come to lie close together after a few iterations thus generating similar, although non-identical graphs for different runs. (Frickey and Lupas 2004)

It is the reproducibility of the overall picture that makes the outcomes of CLANS clustering reliable.

P-values, the usual input data for CLANS, measure the probability that a similarity between two sequences is due to chance. The more non-trivial a similarity is, i.e. the closer the sequences are, the lower gets the p-value. Therefore, p-values can be thought of as measures of distance. In principle, the program is able to operate with any distance-like measure.

3. Binary feature based distances

3.1. Hamming distance

The most straightforward approach to the measurement of distances between languages is to posit a number of binary parameters for each language. The state of any language would then be ideally described by a binary vector, and the Hamming distance between the vectors can be considered as a distance between the respective languages. The downside is that in all known realizations of this idea, parameters have to be set manually.

An immediate technical problem is that it is almost always the case that for some languages, the values of some of the parameters are missing: they could be either unknown (due to a gap in a wordlist or a grammatical description), or non-defined altogether. (For instance, it is meaningless to discuss the locus of complementizer placement in a language that does not use complementizers at all.)

One way to circumvent this problem is to normalize the Hamming distance $H(L',L'')$ between a pair of languages, L' and L'', by the overall number of parameters N. Then the normalized distance will be

$$h(L',L'') = \frac{H(L',L'')}{N}$$

We applied this distance to cognation judgments that are built into the DKB database. This is a natural step to take, because it is essentially cognation judgments that underlie classifications in traditional historical linguistics. In this case, the vectors consists of words from the DKB database, the distance between two words is taken to be zero if they are labelled as cognate in the database, and 1 otherwise.

The picture for Indo-European languages we obtained (see fig. 1) reproduces the classically known one in a reasonably satisfactory manner: All subgroups of Indo-European that are presented in the database by sufficiently many varieties (these are Albanian, Germanic, Greek, Indo-Aryan, Iranian, Romance, and Slavic), are realized as separate clusters; moreover, Indo-Aryan and Iranian, two subbranches of the Indo-Iranian branch, end up sufficiently close on the map.

3.2. Feature distribution across a language sample as the source of distances

A frequently explored alternative to cognation judgments is morphosyntactic features [see, among others, Dunn et al. (2008), Dunn (2009), Langobardi and Guardiano (2009), and Greenhill et al. (2011)]. It is thus natural to test our technique against this source of distance.

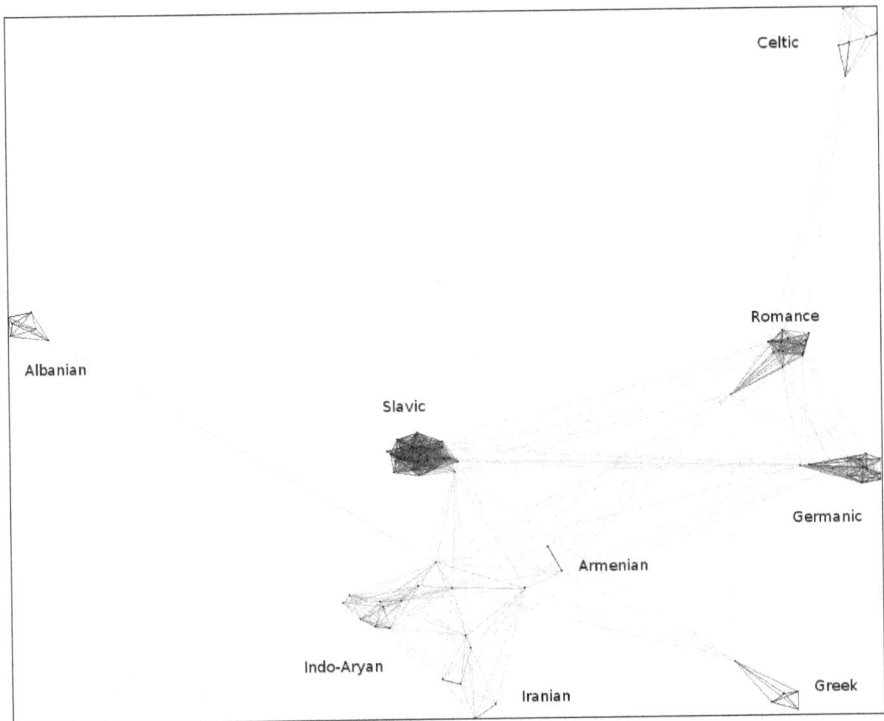

Figure 1. Clustering of the DKB database.

For 133 languages that contain sufficiently many feature values in WALS, we computed a pairwise similarity matrix. The similarity of two languages is defined as the sum of weights of all WALS features where both languages have defined but different values. The weight $w(f)$ of a feature f is defined as the mutual information between the value of this feature and the language family affiliation (as listed in the WALS database) of the languages in question. Intuitively, mutual information resembles the correlation between two random variables.

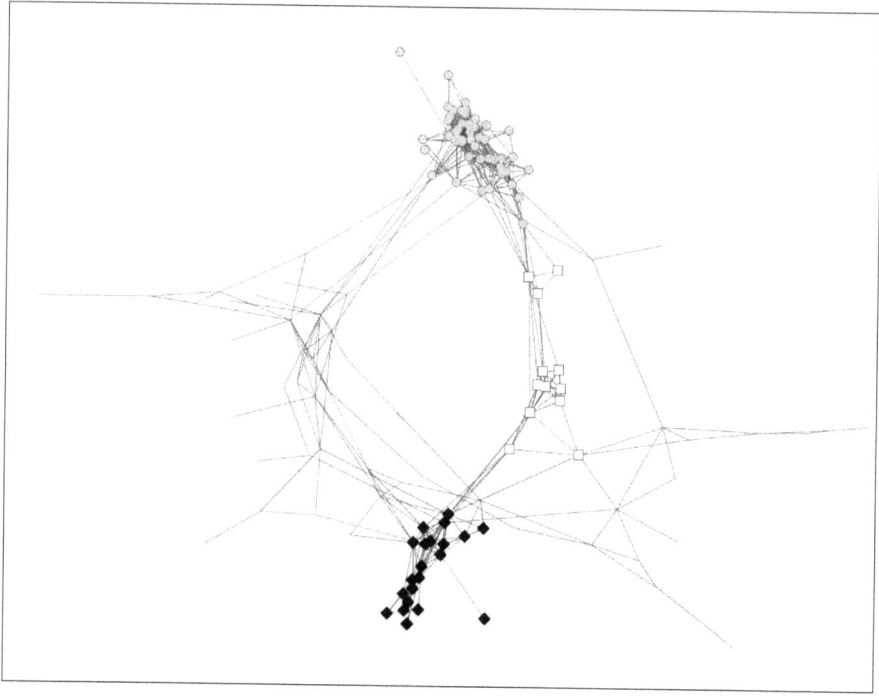

Figure 2. CLANS clustering of WALS.

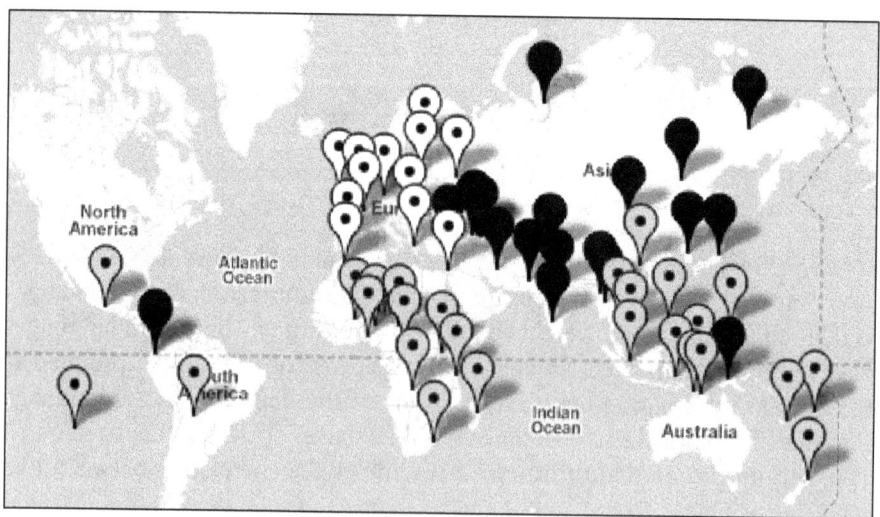

Figure 3. Geography of the language sample.

In this way, features which contain much information about the genetic affiliation of languages receive a high weight (and vice versa). By doing so, we hoped to extract a deep genetic signal from the WALS data.

The resulting cluster map (see fig. 2) shows a circular structure. There are two large clusters of languages at opposite sides of the circle (shown in gray and black), and a third, smaller cluster (shown in white) in between.

The other languages are arranged somewhere on the circle between these three regions without forming distinct groups. The map on fig. 3 shows the geographic distribution of respective languages (the colors on the map match the colors on fig. 2).[2]

A manual inspection of this outcome reveals that this cluster map captures a strong typological and a somewhat weaker areal signal, but no usable information about genetic affiliations. The cluster shown in grey contains languages with head-initial basic word order (SVO or VSO), small phoneme inventories, and lack of case marking. The black cluster, on the other hand, is characterized by head-final word order, nominative-accusative alignment both for pronouns and full NPs, a large number of cases (mostly more than 6) and predominant dependent marking. Figure 2 shows that these groupings are neither genetically nor areally motivated.

That perfectly well agrees with the findings of Greenhill et al. (2011) and Donohue et al. (2011): The distribution of morphosyntactic features does not sufficiently well reflect genetic relationships between languages.

It should be stressed that this conclusion does not mean that morphosyntactic features of proto-languages are not amenable for reconstruction – it only means that (a) the possible depth of reconstruction is less than that for words and (b) the inventory of morphosyntactic features is much more restricted than that of possible words, and therefore morphosyntactic features are more prone to chance coincidences.

3.3. Comparing CLANS with SplitsTree

In this subsection, we use WALS data to argue for advantages of CLANS clustering. Given that the use of SplitsTree has become a near-standard in the field, it is worth comparing its output with that of CLANS. Besides computational advantages, already mentioned in the introduction, we contend that CLANS pictures better visualize findings. To illustrate this point, we present here the network created with SplitsTree for WALS features, see figure 3. We submit that the SplitsTree network brings out the patterns that are inherent in the WALS data much less clearly.

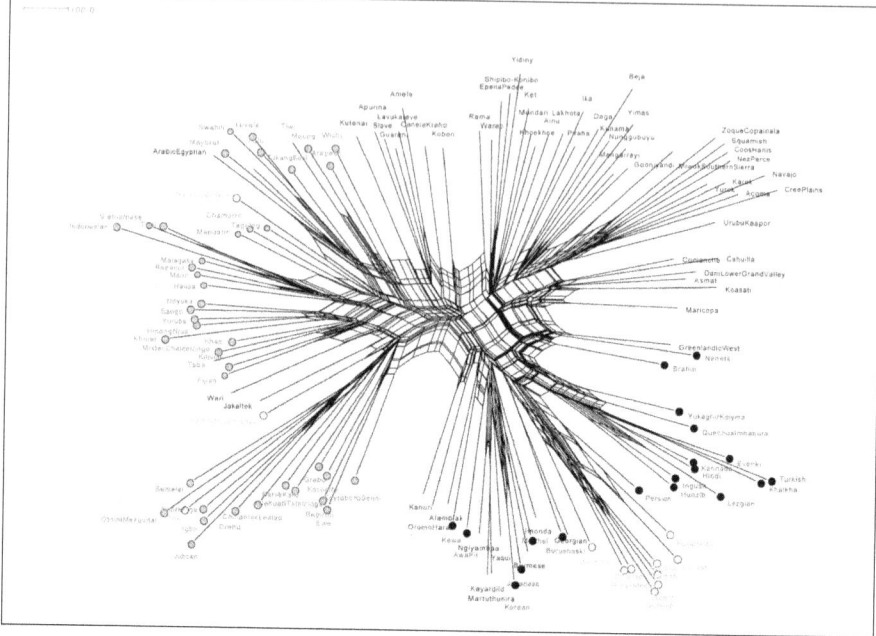

Figure 4. SplitsTree network for the WALS data

4. Word similarity based measures

For any method of automated classification to be of practical interest to researchers, it has to be applicable to large datasets from little studied languages. Consequently, cognation judgments cannot be built in into the databases. Additionally, given the difficulty of assembling any sufficiently large database, it is virtually unavoidable that such methods must work with word lists – this is the only type of data that is relatively easy to collect. Therefore, the task of defining a distance between languages gets reduced to defining a distance between word lists.

It is intuitively clear that, first, any distance between wordlists should be based on pairwise distances between words with the same meaning, and, second, it should somehow take into account the average distance between a random pair of words from the two lists.

In this section, we implement this intuition and apply the resulting similarity measure to Indo-European languages from the ASJP database. The latter includes 40 basic meanings from the Swadesh list for each language, see details in Wichmann et al. (2010: 3633).

4.1. Constructing the similarity matrix

4.1.1. Levenshtein distance

A basic ingredient for this matrix is the Levenshtein distance. Recall that the Levenshtein distance is defined in the following way. Given an alphabet A, consider two finite strings, s_1 and s_2, of symbols from this alphabet. The following operations are permitted: replace a symbol of s_2 by another one, delete a symbol of s_2; add a symbol to s_2. The distance is $L(s_1, s_2)$ defined as the minimal number of such operations necessary to create s_1 from s_2. The Levenshtein distance has been applied to language classification problems in a number of works, see, among others, Petroni and Serva (2010) and Wichmann et al. (2010).

For example, if the alphabet consists of letters a and b, then $L(a, a)=0$; $L(a, b)=1$, because we have to replace a by b in the second word, and $L(ab, ba)=2$, we have, for instance, to delete the first b in ba and then add b to the right of a, and it is impossible to achieve the result by only one operation.

4.1.2. Preparing data

Now, lists of 40 meanings are accumulated for all languages of the sample – if a word list for a particular language contains more items, they are excluded from further consideration. (However, even these shorter 40-word lists sometimes contain gaps.)

Now, all vowels are treated as a single class; all consonants are collapsed into four classes: non-nasal labials and labiodentals (b, p, f, v, w); nasals (m, n); velars and uvulars (g, k, x, к, etc.), the rest of the consonants are collapsed into one more class.

4.1.3. Computation of similarity

For each pair of languages, L' and L'', only the meanings present in both lists are kept. Let M denote the number of remaining meanings. For each remaining pair of words v_i and w_j, the Levenshtein distance $L(v_i, w_j)$ is computed – disregarding whether or not the two words correspond to the same meaning. The similarity $\sigma(v_i, w_j)$ is then defined in the following manner:

$$\sigma(v_i, w_j) = \frac{2(max(length(v_i), length(w_j)) - L(v_i, w_j))}{length(v_i) + length(w_j)}$$

Thus, the similarity is 1 if the words are identical and 0 if they are totally different.

Now consider the similarity value $\sigma_I = \sigma(v_i, w_i)$ for a specific potential cognate pair v_i, w_i. (Now these are two words with the same meaning!) By itself, this value is not very telling. What we want to estimate is how likely it is for a random pair of words from the two languages to have the same (or higher) similarity value. We estimate this probability p_i as the number of pairs with the similarity greater or equal to σ_I, divided by the overall number of pairs.

$$p_i = \frac{|\{j | \sigma_j \geq \sigma_i\}|}{M^2}$$

The lower the value of p_i is, the higher is the chance that the similarity between v_i and w_i is non-accidental. Assuming that similarities among different pairs of potential cognates are independent, we take the product of p_i's for all meanings out of the 40 for which we have data. Let P denote this product.

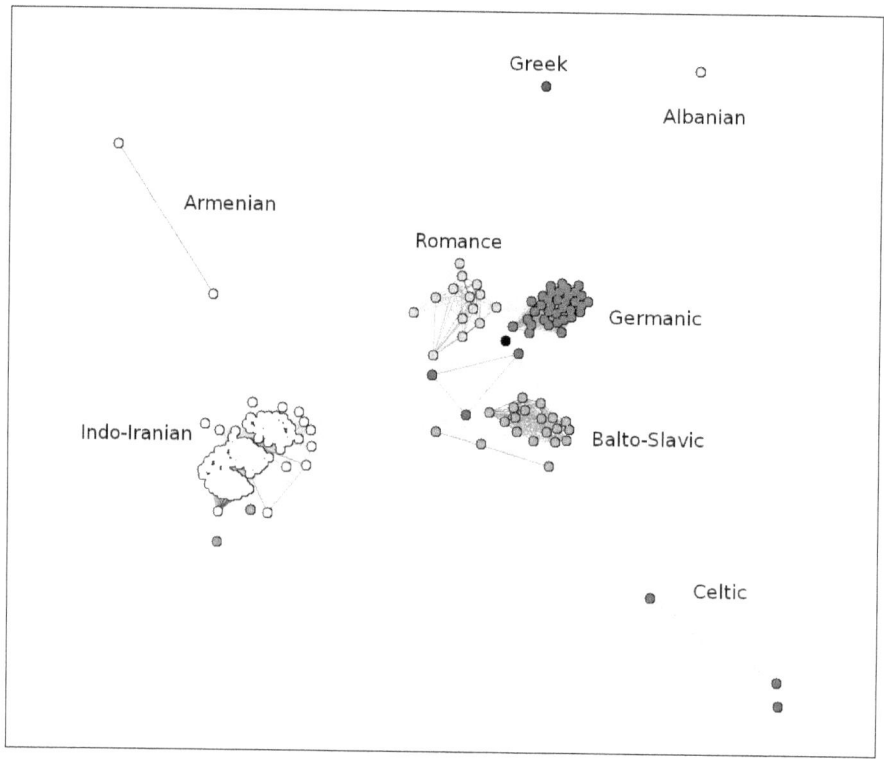

Figure 5. Indo-European language cluster with respect to the Word Similarity measure

Now, we define the similarity $S_{L'L''}$ between L' and L'' as $-log(P)$ (the minus sign renders the term positive). The values $S_{L'L''}$ serve as the input for CLANS.

The method we use might look suspiciously similar to Greenberg's (1987) "mass comparison", justly criticized by many authors; for a detailed discussion and reference see, for example, Campbell and Poser (2008). The crucial difference between our approach and Greenberg's mass comparison is that, unlike in Greenberg's work, the similarity between words is established by an algorithm and not by a human. Furthermore, in our procedure, we have much better control over the semantic similarity of potential cognates. That makes results considerably more reproducible (as long as the same initial dataset is used.)

5. Exploring syntactic similarity

We have shown earlier that "hand-made" discrete morphosyntactic distances are not very promising in language classification. However, it does not rule out a possibility that there exist more natural hidden parameters.

We try a data-oriented approach here. The relevant data for syntactic comparisons are multi-lingual parallel corpora. There, the structure of sentences can be indirectly compared by automatically aligning the sentences word-by-word. These alignments give rise to several similarity measures.

A shortage of input data is an issue here, but for the languages with sufficient data we obtain reasonable similarities. While this cannot exceed previous knowledge about language relationships at the present time and state of the data collected, it does prove the viability of this fully unsupervized method.

5.1. The Bible as a parallel corpus

Having a single text translated into many languages has advantages over a set of bilingual corpora instantiating each language pair: It maximizes the comparability of language pairs, and it reduces the amount of data needed. There is a single text standing out for its translations into many languages, and also for its given alignment of sentences (more accurately, verses) and its faithfulness of translation: The Bible. Among its disadvantages are unnatural word orderings due to an overly close replication of, say, the Latin Vulgate's syntax, and archaic language.

Syntactically annotated parallel corpora would be preferable in this endeavor. However, there is little hope of finding such for a reasonable selection of languages. Automatically parsing the corpus is not an option either, because for many languages there are no parsers available. We therefore devise a method to obtain a similarity measure in an unsupervised manner.

The Bible has been considered as a source of parallel texts before. The University of Maryland Parallel Corpus Project (Resnik et al. 1999). created a corpus of 13 Bible translations. Their project was unfortunately discontinued; only 3 versions agree in verse counts, and many contain artifacts of the automatic processing (parse errors etc.). We enlarged the corpus by translations from several online resources.[4]

Most corpora required at least some (if not considerable) manual corrections. We removed comments and anything else that did not belong to the main text. In the original digitization, there were unrecognized verse/line breaks as well as falsely recognized ones (e.g. at numbers) and numerous other mistakes, which we corrected where possible, but we are fully aware that many errors remain.

Our final corpus format consists of one line per verse, indexed by a shorthand for the book, the chapter, and the verse:

GEN.1.1 In the beginning God created the heaven and the earth.

We chose this format for ease of processing. The encoding is utf-8.

Currently our corpus comprises 46 complete (Old and New Testament) Bible translations in 37 languages, where "complete" means that they contain the same number of verses (31102), yet a few lines still might be empty. Diverging verse numberings in the raw versions obtained from the web resources might also be due to more severe annotation errors. We have checked divergences manually and hope that the remaining errors will be insignificant in comparison to the overall corpus size.

The languages are: Albanian, Arabic (Afroasiatic, Semitic), Bulgarian, Cebuano (Austronesian; Philippines), Chinese, Czech, Danish, Dutch, English, Esperanto, French, German, Haitian Creole, Hindi, Hmar (Tibeto-Burman; India), Hungarian (Uralic), Indonesian (Austronesian), Italian, Kannada (Dravidian; India), Korean, Lithuanian, Malagasy (Austronesian; Madagascar), Maori (Austronesian; New Zealand), Hebrew (Afroasiatic, Semitic), Norwegian, Persian, Portuguese, Romanian, Russian, Somali (Afroasiatic, Cushitic), Spanish, Tagalog (Austronesian; Philippines), Tamil (Dravidian; India and Sri Lanka), Telugu (Dravidian; India), Thai (Tai-Kadai), Ukrainian, and Xhosa (Niger-Congo, Bantu; South Africa).

Some languages are represented several times in the corpus: English with 7 translations; German and Spanish with 2 each. These data allow us to study intra-language variation. See 5.4.2 for a discussion.

5.2. Constructing the similarity matrix

We now propose a method to evaluate the similarity of languages based on unannotated parallel corpora, with the assumption that they are already aligned on the sentence level. This method exhibits the following properties:

- Applicability to any language. This excludes the use of parsers, and even of taggers, because they need to be trained on annotated data. It also rules out the application of language-specific linguistic knowledge.
- Full automatization. As similarities need to be computed for any pair of languages, any manual step would have to be repeated prohibitively often.
- Evaluation of syntactic properties. In spite of the lack of annotation, the method reflects similarity on a structural level, insofar as the structure is reflected in the surface word order.

If a source sentence and a target sentence are translations of each other, we may expect that they will contain words being translations of each other. (In this particular case, this applies to verses and not to sentences.) However, a word-by-word translation is ungrammatical in most cases. The word order differs between languages. Also, the translation of a single word in the source language may consist of more than one word in the target language.

Still, there are algorithms from Natural Language Processing that automatically identify pairs of corresponding words in parallel texts with reasonable accuracy, even in the absence of prior information about the languages involved. The similarity between two texts can then be quantified as the degree to which the linear order of corresponding words differ. Averaging over several parallel texts gives us a measure of the similarity of two languages.

It seems reasonable to expect that related languages have a similar syntax, and therefore a similar word order. In short, we want to define syntactic similarity as closeness to a word-by-word translation.

Here we abstract over lexical choice. It does not matter how a word is translated, only whether it has a counterpart at all, and whether this counterpart appears in a different position in the target sentence. Hence the measure will only be structural, not lexical.

5.2.1. Alignments

We compute word-to-word alignments using GIZA++ (Och and Ney 2003). It takes as input two corpora aligned by sentences. We prepared our corpus by stripping off all punctuation and converting it to lower case (where applicable). Whitespace delimits words, however, it is sparsely used in languages such as Kannada. For Chinese, we tokenized the text into single characters. Via many-to-one mappings, GIZA++ is supposed to be able to also capture diverging usages of word boundaries. Empty sentences are skipped by GIZA++ automatically. GIZA++ outputs some probability tables, and, mainly, the alignment file.

There, words in the source sentence are implicitly labeled 1, ... n_s, where n_s is its length. These numbers reappear with the words in the target sentence; they denote the translation relation. The words in the target sentence are each labeled with zero, one, or more indices, but every index is used at most once. So, there are many-to-one translations, one-to-one translations, and insertions, respectively. However, GIZA++ is unable to identify one-to-many translations. To find these, one can reverse the source and the target languages, and aggregate the information into a symmetric alignment.

The remaining numbers are assigned to a NULL word, representing deletions.

For the interested reader, we provide some actual alignments. Consider the following example (Genesis 1:3) with Spanish (Reina-Valera translation) as source, (1a), and English (American Standard Version) as target, (1b). GIZA++ output is represented in (1c).

(1) a. y   dijo Dios sea   la   luz   y   fué   la   luz
        and   said God   let.be DEF light and was   DEF light

  b. and God said let there be light and there was light

  c. NULL ({ 5 9 }) and ({ 1 }) god ({ 3 }) said ({ 2 }) let ({ }) there ({ }) be ({ 4 }) light ({ 6 }) and ({ 7 }) there ({ }) was ({ 8 }) light ({ 10 })

With English, (1b), as the source and Spanish, (1c), as the target, GIZA++ finds a similar, yet not identical solution.

(2)   NULL ({ 5 9 }) y ({ 1 }) dijo ({ 3 }) dios ({ 2 }) sea ({ 4 6 }) la ({ }) luz ({ 7 }) y ({ 8 }) fué ({ 10 }) la ({ }) luz ({ 11 })

NULL serves as an anchor for all non-alignable words, representing deletions. Being not aligned either is due to a structural difference between the two languages or to inconclusive evidence for GIZA++'s algorithm. For instance, the article *la* is not aligned, because in this construction English treats light as a mass noun, so there is no article. In other cases, articles are aligned non-consistently because of a wide range of possible articles in one language and only one definite article (the) in English: there, GIZA++ misses what a human annotator would have accepted as equivalence.[5]

On the other hand, the English sentence features some words without a counterpart in the Spanish sentence: *let there be* is constructed differently there. *sea* is mapped to *let* and *be* in the second example. But GIZA++ does not identify this one-to-many relation, (3) is impossible by design.

(3) Let{4} there{} be{4}

5.2.2. Symmetric alignments

In the example sentence, the alignment differed in the two translation directions. While there are also (many) examples of symmetric alignment, asymmetry is the predominant case. However, a measure of similarity needs to be symmetric by definition. It is easier to define a symmetric measure on a symmetric alignment. Also, for some language pairs, it appears that GIZA++ finds one direction much easier than the other. The two alignments could inform each other, yielding better alignments. For these two reasons we will symmetrize the alignments.

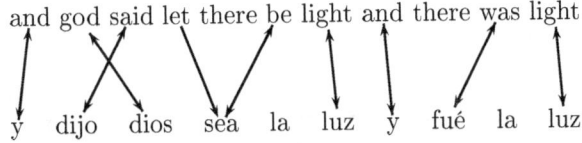

Figure 6. English-Spanish alignment.

The difference in the English-Spanish example (1a-b) was inevitable, because the inverse of 'sea ({ 4 6 })' is 'let ({ 4 }) be ({ 4 })', which is impossible by design. This can be overcome easily by adding the missing link, fig. 6.

The situation is not always that simple. Consider the same verse in Cebuano and Danish, fig. 7. This example exhibits insufficient information for the conjunctions, as is often the case with non-content words. Adding the reverse links does not compete with other alignments, and therefore improves the solution. On the contrary, adding the reverse direction for *dina→lys* clashes with *blev→dina*. Arguably, the best solution is to delete the former link, and to symmetrize the latter, fig. 8.

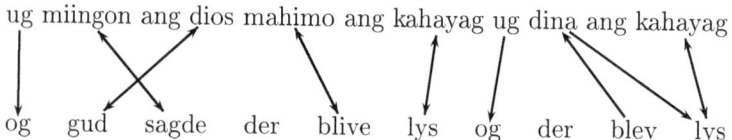

Figure 7. Cebuano-Danish alignment.

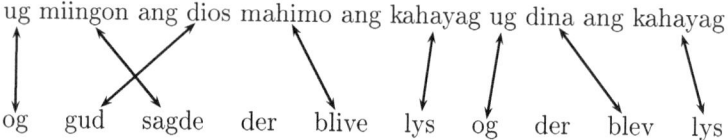

Figure 8. Symmetrized Cebuano-Danish alignment.

In the general case, alignments are less clean, and there will be no immediate symmetrization which also corrects all alignment errors. See Genesis 1:2 in Malagasy and Esperanto, fig. 9.

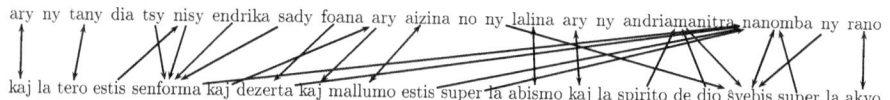

Figure 9. Malagasy-Esperanto alignment.

We would like to achieve symmetrization nonetheless, and therefore devise a general strategy. If two words are mutually linked, or not linked at all, no action needs to be taken, as this is already symmetric. Every unidirectional link is either to be deleted or to be turned into a bidirectional one. A simple criterion shall decide: Keep the link if and only if it is the only one to connect (at least) one of the words involved. This minimizes unaligned as well as multiply aligned words, which is meant to capture the intuition that one-to-one alignments are linguistically desirable (as also underlies GIZA++). It leads to the above mentioned correction of the Cebuano-

Danish example. For the other example, the result is much less chaotic and linguistically more sound, fig. 10.

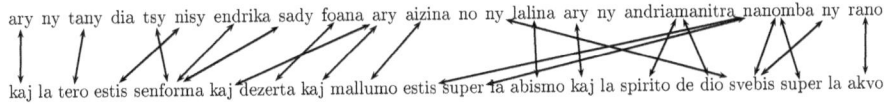

Figure 10. Symmetrized Malagasy-Esperanto alignment.

In the latter example, a certain notion of transitivity is violated because both instances of *ny* do not connect with *super* although indirectly they are connected (disregarding the fact that this alignment is linguistically undesired; as usual, GIZA++ has difficulties with articles). Other criteria when to keep a link and when to delete it might resolve this situation (and others) differently. For the present purposes, the one described above suffices.

5.3. Constructing the similarity matrix

Maximal similarity is achieved by a non-crossing, one-to-one alignment of words. This is a rare occurrence, but it does happen in about 0.05% of cases.

For any possible measure, any alignment deviating from this ideal situation has to receive a lower similarity value. In the general case, an alignment is a permutation including insertions and deletions.

In the following, we consider two types of alignment measures. First, there are feature-based measures (section 4.3.1). They count subsequences or other properties shared by the two sentences. Typically, they are partial and often also local: they look at only a subset of the possible subsequences, say, subsequences bounded by a certain length. For these reasons, they are computationally efficient, yet they do not allow an interpretation of how one sentence would need to be re-ordered and modified in order to obtain its translation. This is addressed by the second type of similarity measure we are considering: Levenshtein distance measures (section 5.3.2). They define a set of operations admissible to transform a sentence into another one. The minimal number of operations necessary then is the distance between two sentences, and distances can be converted into similarities.

For any measure, we take the average over all sentences as the overall similarity of two languages.

5.3.1. A feature-based measure

Let sentence similarity be defined as the number of shared bigrams, normalized by sentence length (minus 1).[6] Consider the above symmetric Malagasy-Esperanto example, fig. 10, in the notation of GIZA++, with Esperanto as the target, and without the actual words:

(4) ({ 1 }) ({ }) ({ 3 }) ({ 6 }) ({ 5,7,8 }) ({ 10 }) ({ 9 }) ({ 10 })
({ 11 }) ({ 18 }) ({ 18 }) ({ }) ({ 14 }) ({ 15 }) ({ }) ({ 17 })
({ }) ({ 17 }) ({ 13,18,19 }) ({ 18 }) ({ }) ({ 20 })

Count a shared bigram whenever two subsequent words in the target language appear in the same order as in the source language. The third and fourth word, aligned to words 3 and 6, respectively, are an example. We will skip non-aligned words. This has the effect that for example the first and third word form a bigram, which otherwise would be interrupted by the non-aligned article in both languages. Therefore the measure is one of permutation, and only indirectly one of insertions and deletions; they only come into play as missed chances of shared bigrams.

For multiply aligned words, evaluate the last alignment of the first and the first alignment of the last. Hence, ({ 6 }) ({ 5,7,8 }) is not a shared bigram, but ({ 5,7,8 }) ({ 10 }) is.

Altogether, there are 9 shared bigrams in 22 words in the example. The alignment similarity is computed as 9/(22–1)=0.429. 1 is subtracted from the sentence length because there are n-1 shared bigrams in a perfectly aligned sentence pair (see above). The reverse similarity (Malagasy as the target) is 14/(20–1)=0.739, which goes to show that feature-based measures will (possibly) yield different values depending on the direction, which means that they will also work on asymmetric alignments. In the strict sense then, this is not a similarity measure. It could be turned into one by taking the average of the two distances.

5.3.2. Levenshtein distance

Assume that the source sentence is numbered 1 to x_s, where x_s is its length. Then the target sentence is obtained by the following operations:

- Deletion: Leaving a source word un-aligned.
- Insertion: The reverse of deletion, introducing an un-aligned word in the target language.

- Split: Mapping one source word to many target words.
- Merge: The reverse of split, mapping many words to one in the target.
- Move: Displacing a word.

The order of operations is nearly arbitrary, yet we want to restrict merges to adjacent words, so (certain) moves have to happen beforehand.

There exists a wealth of edit and permutation distances (Deza and Deza 2009: ch. 11), yet there is none capturing splits and merges. They could be modelled as insertions and deletions of the surplus words, but this does not reflect the nature of the alignment: First, it could not serve as a description of the translation process. Second, there is no way to assign different weights to multi-word translations and real insertions. Third, discontinuous translations, e.g. ({ 5,7,8 }) in (4) will not be considered any more complex than continuous ones. For these reasons, we opt to treat splits and merges as primary operations, just as insertions and deletions. For similar reasons, a move should not be considered a combination of a deletion (in one place) and an insertion (in the other place). This motivates the need for 5 operations.

For the sake of transparency, we will only consider symmetric alignments, obtained as outlined above (section 5.2.2). The operations are symmetric, so the measure is symmetric. Deletions and insertions, as well as merges and splits, can be treated alike: they are simply counted, and incur a unit cost of 1. The more problematic case is move. Coming from both sides of the translation, having performed all other four operations, we are left with a permutation problem. The above example reduces to (5a) as a permutation of (5b):

(5) a. 3, 6, 5, 7, 8, 10a, 9, 10b, 11, 18a, 18b, 14, 15, 17a, 17b, 3, 18c, 9, 18d, 20
  b. 1, 3, 5, 6, 7, 8, 9, 10a, 10b, 11, 13, 14, 15, 17a, 17b, 18a, 18b, 18c, 18d, 19, 20

The number of moves necessary is defined by the Ulam metric (see Deza and Deza 2009: 212). Each move also incurs a unit cost. Together with the other operations, this is our definition of Levenshtein distance for alignments. It is normalized for combined sentence length (i.e. divided by length(source) + length(target)), and subtracted from 1 in order to turn it into a similarity measure.[7]

5.4. Results

We clustered the 37 languages[8] with CLANS and inspected the results manually. There are differences between the results using each of the two similarity measures, but none of them appear noteworthy.

Initial results closely resemble known language relationships. The Dravidian languages (Tamil, Telugu, Kannada) form a tight cluster, which curiously accommodates the otherwise isolate Korean as an outlier. Hebrew and Arabic (both Semitic; with Xhosa as a curious outlier), Danish and Norwegian, Cebuano and Tagalog (both Central Philippine), as well as Russian and Ukrainian feature close relations, see fig. 11 and 12.

Resulting from the data sample European (Western Indo-European) languages form the core cluster. Other language families are represented by only a few, one, or no data points at all. The Germanic languages exhibit a western (German, Dutch) and a northern (Danish, Norwegian) subgroup, connected via Esperanto to the Romance languages: Spanish, Portuguese, French with Romanian as an outlier, and Italian, which is the best connection for Albanian. Because of the geographic proximity this is an interesting point for further research.[9]

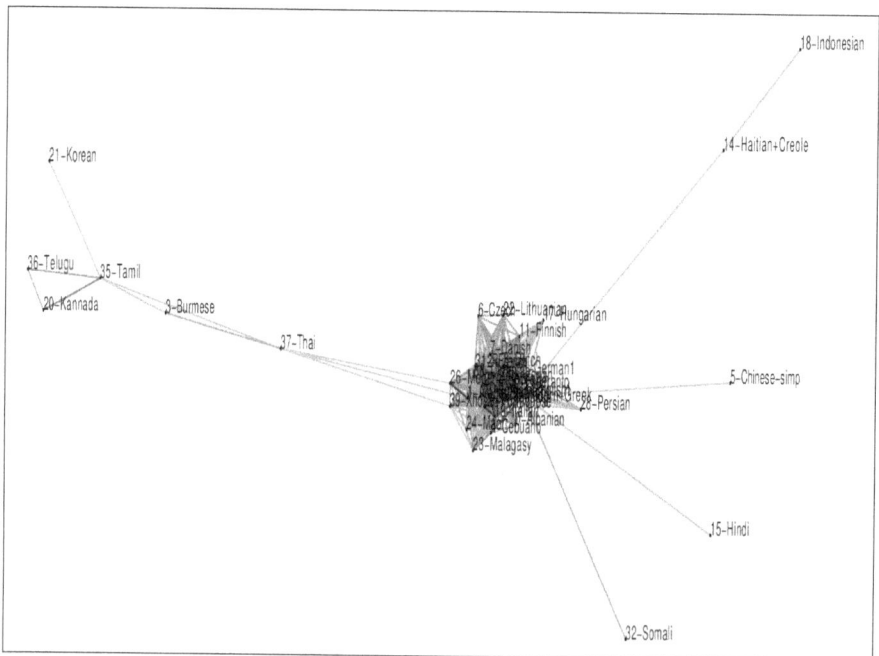

Figure 11. Clustering of Bible translations: Overall picture

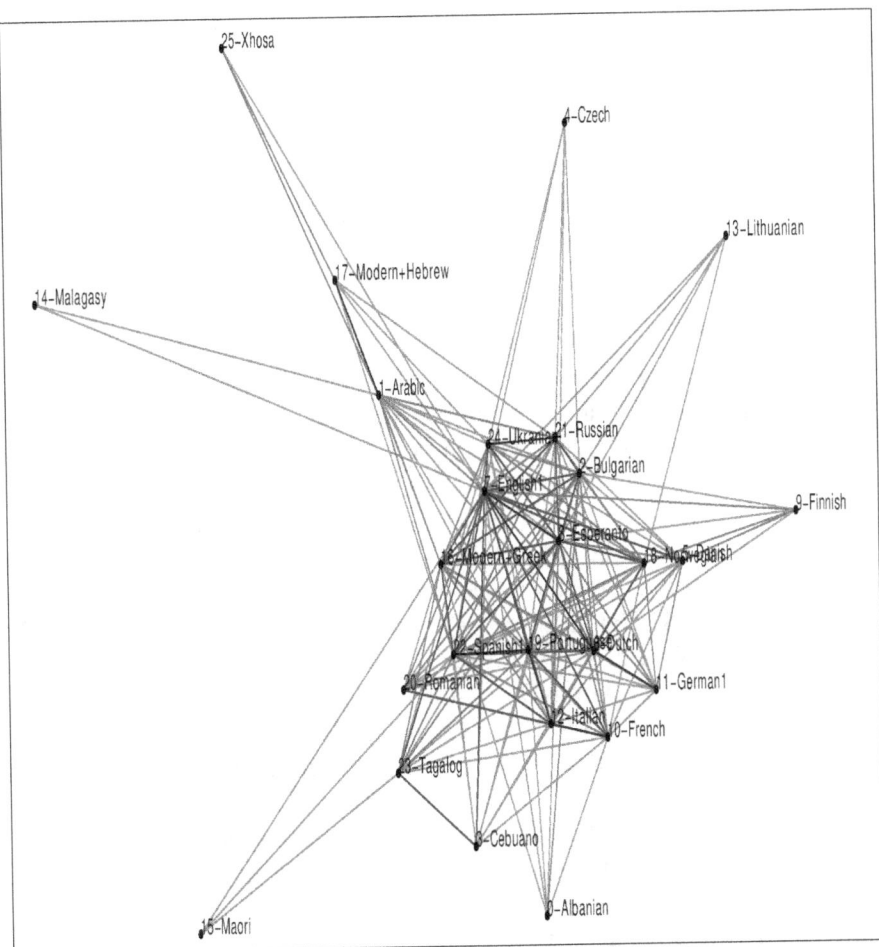

Figure 12. Clustering of Bible translations: Main cluster

These western European languages further connect to the group of Slavic languages, which are more loosely inter-connected. The remaining languages either appear as isolates or as near-isolates with no conclusive connections. A larger Malayo-Polynesian group (the two Central Philippine languages plus Maori, Indonesian, and Malagasy) cannot be established.

English plays a literally central role. It lies in the middle of the above mentioned European groups. Many languages are only kept within the core cluster because they enjoy a strong link to English. This is true of at least Persian, Maori, Chinese, Somali, Hindi, and Indonesian. We suspect these translations might be based on an English one (or maybe on the Latin

Vulgate, to which the English translation is very close). In the case of Maori, it is reasonable to assume that the translator was a native speaker of English. In order to clean up the picture, we additionally clustered all languages except English. In this run, for example, Cebuano and Tagalog separate from the core of European languages well before, say, the Slavic languages.

5.4.1. Intra- versus inter-language variation

Language duplicates were excluded from the above reported experiments. In another clustering, we specifically looked at intra-language variation. The lowest similarity value for two English translations (Levenshtein distance measure) is 0.78, while it goes as high as 0.99 (King James Version vs. Webster's Revised King James Version). Despite this internal variation, English forms a tight cluster, with the most diverging versions as outliers. The cutoff in CLANS can safely be set higher; these two do not need to be directly connected. 0.8 is a reasonable value, because the two German and Spanish versions rate at 0.82 and 0.85, respectively. These values are otherwise only reached by Arabic and Hebrew (0.82) and Norwegian and Danish (0.80). Some other language pairs (Dutch-English, Esperanto-English) exceed or get close to the threshold of 0.78, but only in comparison with outliers of the English group. Overall, there will be a lower similarity between, say, Dutch and English.

Other significant similarities are Dutch-German and Spanish-Portuguese (0.78 each, considering the better match of the languages with two versions available), and other closely related languages. Similarities below 0.8 are fairly evenly distributed, with no apparent gaps. Altogether there is small overlap between the similarities of identical and closely related languages, so the method cannot always keep them apart. It comes as no surprise that Danish and Norwegian, notably Bokmål and not Nynorsk, and considering the conservative language used in Bible translations, cannot be kept apart on a syntactic level more than needs to be allowed for as intra-language variation. The method proves to be reasonable in the sense that intra-language variation is smaller than inter-language variation,[10] and the inevitable border cases are interpretable as such.

Comparing the outcomes of this experiment with the one treated in section 3.2, we may tentatively conclude that the raw data based method described in this section yields somewhat better results than ones using manually encoded morphosyntactic data. With more and more texts being digitalized with increasing quality, it can be reasonably expected that, in a near future, one will be able to assemble aligned Bible corpora for a significantly larger number of languages, thus allowing to apply our method for real language classification problems.

6. Conclusion

In this paper, we have argued for the introduction of a clustering approach into the study of language relationships. Potentially, it might be able to take into account both phylogenetic and contact-induced signals.

It goes without saying that the approach advocated here is called to supplement, and not supplant, the classical techniques of historical linguistics. We consider it as a source of hints for historical linguists as to which path of inquiry might be worth pursuing.

We have shown that using CLANS allows to roughly reproduce known genetic units. This can be achieved with a relatively small amount of manual curation.

Furthermore, we have argued that although the use of traditional "overt" morphosyntactic features does not allow to even remotely reproduce known genetic classification, a promising alternative comes from automated text alignment. Unfortunately, creating a sufficiently representative aligned corpus remains prohibitively effort-consuming.

Clustering approaches are particularly efficient at analyzing large sets of data. If the dream of large scale language classification is ever to come true, the comparison of huge amounts of data is an inevitable step. We hope that clustering approaches will play a significant role in this endeavor.

Notes

1. An exception is the Neighbor Joining Method (Saitou and Nei 1986), which is cubic in the number of points. However, trees it produces are considered less accurate.
2. We thank the authors for sharing their database with us.
3. We thank Soeren Wichmann for sharing the database with us.
4. http://www.biblegateway.com/versions/; http://www.jesus.org.uk/bible.
   Although all translations were freely available on the internet (for personal use, at least), they all needed post-processing. Given that redistributing altered versions of potentially copyrighted material might be problematic, we have not made our corpus public.

5. GIZA++ can be provided with word class information to improve alignments, but even then it does not directly discover grammatical rules.
6. When the sentence length equals one, we can posit that the function equals 1. The number of such sentences in the corpus is so low, that it does not affect any conclusions.
7. There are alternative possibilities here.
8. Those with several instances were represented by a single translation, in order to reduce the (quadratic) computational effort.
9. Unfortunately, the source (http://www.biblegateway.com/versions/index.php?action=getVersionInfo&vid=1) does not say anything about the origin of this translation.
10. The small sample does not allow for testing for significance.

References

Campbell, Lyle and William J. Poser
    2008   *Language Classification: History and Method*. Cambridge: Cambridge University Press.

Deza, Michel Marie and Elena Deza
    2009   Encyclopedia of Distances. Berlin et al.: Springer.

Donohue, Mark, Simon Musgrave, Bronwen Whitting, and Søren Wichmann
    2011   Typological feature analysis models linguistic geography. *Language* 87 (2): 369–383.

Dunn, Michael
    2009   Contact and phylogeny in Island Melanesia. *Lingua* 11 (11), 1664–1678.

Dunn, Michael, Stephen C. Levinson, Eva Lindström, Ger Reesink, and Angela Terrill
    2008   Structural phylogeny in historical linguistics: Methodological explorations applied in Island Melanesia. *Language* 84 (4): 710–759.

Dyen, Isidore, Joseph B. Kruskal, and Paul Black
    1992   An Indoeuropean Classification: A Lexicostatistical Experiment. *Transactions of the American Philosophical Society. New Series* 82 (5).

Forster, Peter and Colin Renfrew (eds.)
    2006   *Phylogenetic methods and the prehistory of languages*. Cambridge: McDonald Institute for Archaeological Research.

Frickey, Tancred and Andrei Lupas
    2004   Clans: a java application for visualizing protein families based on pairwise similarity. *Bioinformatics* 20 (18): 3702–3704.

Fruchterman, Thomas M. J., and Edward M. Reingold
    1991   Graph Drawing by Force-Directed Placement. *Software – Practice & Experience* (Wiley) 21 (11): 1129–1164.

Gray, Russell D. and Quentin D. Atkinson
    2003   Language-tree divergence times support the Anatolian theory of Indo-European origin. *Nature* 426: 435–439.

Greenberg, Joseph
    1987   *Language in the Americas*. Stanford: Stanford University Press.
Greenhill, Simon, Quentin D. Atkinson, Andrew Meade, and Russel D. Gray
    2011   The shape and tempo of language evolution. *Proceedings of the Royal Society*. Series B. 278: 474–479.
Haspelmath, Martin, Matthew S. Dryer, David Gil, and Bernard Comrie (eds.)
    2008   *The World Atlas of Language Structures Online*. Munich: Max Planck Digital Library.
Huson, Daniel and David Bryant
    2006   Application of Phylogenetic Networks in Evolutionary Studies. *Molecular biology and evolution* 23 (2): 254–267
Langobardi, Giuseppe and Christina Guardiano
    2009   Evidence for syntax as a signal of historical relatedness. *Lingua* 119 (11): 1679–1706.
Nichols, Johanna and Tandy Warnow
    2008   Tutorial on Computational Linguistic Phylogeny. *Language and Linguistics Compass* 2 (5): 760–820.
Och, Franz Josef and Hermann Ney
    2003   A Systematic Comparison of Various Statistical Alignment Models. *Computational Linguistics* 29 (1): 19–51.
Petroni, Philippo and Maurizio Serva
    2010   Measures of lexical distance between languages. *Physica A: Statistical Mechanics and its Applications* 389 (11): 2280–2283.
Resnik, Philip, Mari Broman Olsen, and Mona Diab
    1999   The Bible as a Parallel Corpus: Annotating the 'Book of 2000 Tongues', *Computers and the Humanities* 33 (1–2), pp. 129–153.
Saitou, Naruya and Masatoshi Nei
    1987   The neighbor-joining method: A new method for reconstructing phylogenetic trees. *Molecular biology and evolution* 4 (4): 406–425.
Wichmann, Søren, Eric W. Holman, Dik Bakker, Cecil H. Brown
    2010   Evaluating linguistic distance measures. *Physica* A 389: 3632–3639.

Dependency-sensitive typological distance

Harald Hammarström and Loretta O'Connor

1. Introduction

Increasing amounts of data in machine readable form are becoming available for the study of linguistic typology, especially with the appearance of WALS.[1] Most such databases come in the form of a matrix of languages and features, where each language, for each feature, is given a value from a discrete set of possible values. If we fix a particular ordering of the list of features, we may denote a language X with its feature vector $L_X = [v_1, ..., v_n]$, meaning that it has value v_i for feature F_i. Similarly, we may use $L_X[i]$ to denote the feature value v_i of feature F_i in language X.

For a variety of purposes, researchers make use of a distance measure between two languages (cf. Chiswick and Miller 2004; Cysouw 2007; Holman et al. 2007; Dahl 2008; Polyakov et al. 2009; Wichmann and Holman 2010) that says how similar two languages are from 0.0 (identical) to 1.0

$$G(L_X, L_Y) = \frac{\#_{i \in DEF(L_X, L_Y)} L_X[i] \neq L_Y[i]}{|DEF(L_X, L_Y)|}$$

(totally different). Traditionally, such a distance measure has taken the form of the Gower coefficient (also known as relative Hamming distance):

Where $DEF(L_X, L_Y) = \{i | L_X[i]$ and $L_Y[i]$ are defined$\}$, i.e., the set of features which are defined for both languages (since, in general, there may be missing values). The Gower coefficient simply counts the number of features where the languages have a different value, divided by the total number of features compared. Therefore, using the Gower coefficient makes sense if the features are all independent and of equal weight. These assumptions appear to be largely well-founded if the features in question indicate, for example, the presence/absence of a lexical cognate for a particular meaning. However, in the case of typological features, many functional dependencies have been established (Dryer 1992) and linguists have intuitions about many further dependencies.

In this paper, we will develop two kinds of dependency-sensitive distance metrics.[2] The first captures the idea that if it can be shown that one feature can be (partly) predicted by another, then the predictable feature should be (partly) "discounted". This strategy tackles dependencies between features as a whole, not between specific values of features. The second dependency-sensitive metric addresses the significance of similarities between specific values of features. Globally, a specific combination of values may be very predictable, or, on the other end of the scale, a combination of values may be extremely unusual. Accordingly, when comparing two specific languages, scores may be weighted as to whether they share something predictable or something quirky.

The dependency-sensitive metrics will be illustrated on a dataset of typological features for Chibchan and neighboring languages developed by Constenla Umaña (1991). The database is dense (almost all features are defined for almost all languages) and published (thus publicly available). We are interested in potential differences the metrics may give as regards the classification of these particular languages. On the one hand, it could be that removing the dependencies merely has the effect of concentrating the distances uniformly across the languages. On the other hand, there could be drastic effects involving particular pairs of languages. A pair of languages that looked very similar when inflated by dependencies might become as distant as random languages when the dependencies are removed. Alternatively, two languages that do not share an impressive number of features may share them in such an unusual, "quirky" way (within this data sample) that the dependency value-sensitive metric singles out that pair of languages for, e.g., a borrowing scenario or a genealogical relation to explain the quirk.

2. The Isthmo-Colombian Area dataset

The Isthmo-Colombian Area dataset used in the present paper represents languages of Central America and the northwest corner of South America. We extracted the information for 34 languages from Constenla Umaña (1991) and added one more language, Damana, using sources (Williams 1993; Trillos Amaya 2005) that appeared after Constenla Umaña's compilation. The dataset consists of a total of 35 languages and 81 structural features, where all features are defined for all languages except for Damana, in which two feature values are undefined. Fifteen of the languages are Chibchan, with smaller representations from nine other families plus three isolates. More languages belonging to each family are attested, but they are either outside the geographic sphere of interest or are insufficiently documented to be included.

The 35 languages in question are listed in table 1 (in bold, with ISO codes) and mapped in figure 1.

Table 1. Languages in the Isthmo-Colombian Area dataset: names and classifications are adapted from the following sources: Chibchan (Constenla Umaña 2012), Guajiro (Captain 2005), Quiché (Campbell 1997), Barbacoan (Adelaar and Muysken 2004: 141–151), Chocoan (Aguirre Licht 2006), Quechua (Cerrón-Palomino 2003) and Misumalpan (Pineda 2005).

Chibchan
    Core Chibchan
        Isthmic
            Eastern Isthmic
                Guaymiic
                    Movere [gym]
                    Bocotá [sab]
            Kuna
                Cuna [cuk]
            Western Isthmic
                Viceitic
                    Bribri [bzd]
                    Cabécar [cjp]
                Boruca [brn]
                Teribe [tfr]
        Magdalenic
            Northern Magdalenic
                Arhuacic
                    Eastern-Southern Arhuacic
                        Bintucua [arh]
                        Eastern Arhuacic
                          Damana [mbp]
                  Cágaba [kog]
            Southern Magdalenic
                Chibcha
                    Chibcha [chb]
                Tunebo
                    Central Tunebo [tuf]
        Votic
            Guatuso [gut]
            Rama [rma]
    Paya [pay]

Chocoan
    Embera
        Atrato
            Katio
                Katío [cto]
                Sambú [emp]
    Woun Meu
        Huaunana [noa]
Paez
    Páez [pbb]
Cofan
    Cofán [con]
Arawak
    Arawak
        Maipuran
            Northern Maipuran
                Lokono-Guajiro
                    Guajiro [guc]
Barbacoan
    Cayapa-Colorado
        Cayapa [cbi]
        Colorado [cof]
    Coconucan
        Guambiano [gum]
    Unclassified Barbacoan
        Awa-Cuaiquer [kwi]
Jicaquean
    Jicaque [jic]
Kamsa
    Camsá [kbh]
Lencan
    Lenca [iso-code missing]
Mayan
    Yucatecan-Core Mayan
        Core Mayan
            Quichean-Mamean
                Greater Quichean
                    Poqom-Quichean
                      Core Quichean
                        Quiche-Achi
                          K'iche' [quc]

```
Misumalpan
    Sumalpan
        Matagalpan
            **Cacaopera [ccr]**
        Sumo-Mayangna
            **Sumo [sum]**
            **Ulua [sum]**
    **Mískito [miq]**
Quechuan
    Quechua II
        Quechua II.B
            **Imbabura Highland/Lowland Napo Quichua [qvi/qvo]**
Xincan
    **Xinca-Guazacapan [iso-code missing]**
```

Non-trivial identifications based on Constenla Umaña's sources (1991: 190–192) are:

Constenla Name	Variety	ISO 639-3
Lenca	Lenca of El Salvador	–
Quechua	Amalgam of Imbabura Quechua and Lowland Napo Quechua	[qvi] and [qvo]
Xinca	Xinca of Guazacapán	–
Quiche	Central Quiché	[quc]
Cuna	San Blas Kuna	[cuk]
Tunebo	Central Tunebo	[tuf]

The ISO 639-3 codes for Xincan and Lencan languages are erroneous in that they lump together all varieties of each as one language. Both families are divergent enough to constitute families of different languages (Campbell 1997). Since the codes are thereby indeterminate, we chose not to use them at all. Note that Sumo and Ulua are distinguished by Constenla but considered the same language in ISO 639-3.

There are reasons why the Isthmo-Colombian Area dataset is of more than casual interest for the present experiment. The languages are spoken on and around the land bridge that unites the two American continents. Once considered an ever-changing transit region for people and goods moving between powerful civilizations north and south, the region has recently

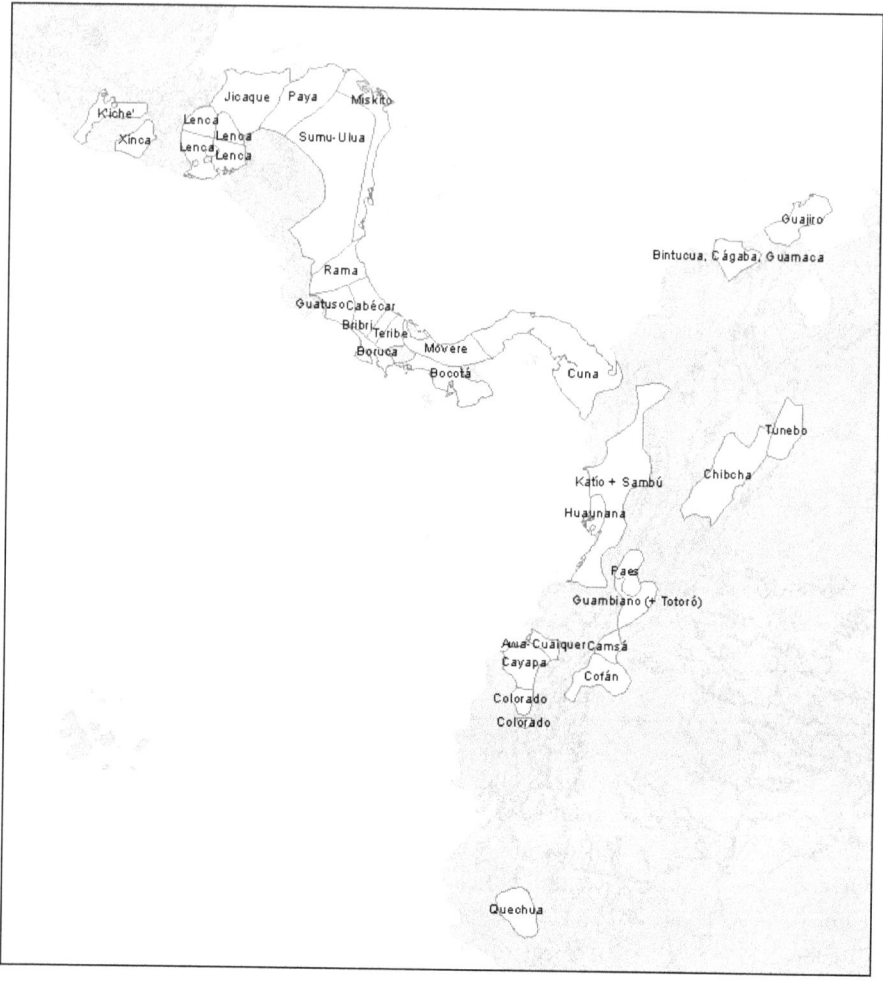

Figure 1. Locations of languages in the Isthmo-Colombian Area dataset (language polygons from Eriksen 2011: 12–15).

come to be recognized as the site of long-time settlement by small, sedentary groups (Quesada 2007: 22–26 and references therein). This suggests long-term interaction *in situ* between particular groups of speakers and increases the likelihood of shared changes through language contact with each other and with common visitor groups. In addition, historical linguistics has seen a meshwork of genealogical proposals involving the Chibchan, Chocoan, Barbacoan, and Paezan languages present in this dataset (see Adelaar and Muysken [2004: 22–34, 36–38, 41–45] for relevant discussion) and overlapping proposals of areal relationship that include three regional linguistic subareas for the entire dataset (Constenla Umaña 1991: 121–131) and a two-way division between Chibchan languages of Central America and those of Colombia (Quesada 2007: 44–45). Human genetics research with present-day speakers suggests clear differences between Chibchan and Chocoan populations of the Isthmus (Kolman and Berminghan 1997) and indicates different networks of possible relationship between and among the two regional groupings of Chibchan languages, Emberá, Guajiro, and Quiché (Melton et al. 2007). Any or all such historical events might yield pairs of languages with salient (dis)similarity involving feature dependencies.

The list of 81 features is given in the appendix. It consists of 42 morphosyntactic features (e.g. Is there VO order in transitive clauses? Is there a distinction between inclusive and exclusive for personal pronouns?) and 39 phonological features (e.g. Is there a nasality contrast for vowels? Is there an aspiration contrast for plosives?). All features are binary, although the methods employed in the present paper do not require them to be binary. (Features do, however, need to be discrete-valued).

3. Computational approaches to dependencies

There are good reasons to expect that abstract grammatical features of language should show functional dependencies, even when features are logically independent. Grammatical features may (partly) overlap in function, and constraints on communicative efficiency may favor certain configurations of features and functions over others. For example, case-marking and strict constituent order may be both used to signal who did what to whom in a basic declarative clause. It is logically possible to use both (and indeed, some languages do), but it is nevertheless conceivable that there is some pressure from communicative principles that causes the redundancy to go away (Sinnemäki 2010). Perspectives in the linguistic literature vary on the types of dependencies present in language and particularly on the motivations for dependencies: explanations range from "nativist", i.e., inborn constraints on grammar (e.g. Chomsky 1981), to constraints from cognition, social interaction and/or efficient communication (cf. papers in Christiansen et al. 2009).

For the purposes of this paper, it makes no difference whether functional dependencies are innate or environmental in origin. In either case, dependencies that come from (hypothetical) communicative principles or (hypothetical) inborn constraints must:

a. be universal (in the sense of being common to all natural languages), since by definition natural languages are used for communication between humans, and,

b. concern the whole feature in question (not just some particular values), since all values of a feature have the same domain, and the hypothesized dependencies stem from overlapping domains.

Universal dependencies are not the *only* factors shaping the features landscape – random, areal and genealogical effects can, in fact, overshadow those that come from universal principles (Dunn et al. 2011). Universal dependencies (in the view taken in this paper) exist if (and only if) there are non-random dependencies in the languages of the world that cannot be explained areally or genealogically. Because of overshadowing effects, they do not have to be present in every (sub-)trajectory of history as long as they appear more often than random.

3.1. Factoring out feature dependencies

Assuming here that universal dependencies exist and that we are given a large and balanced enough sample of languages and their features, how can we find and factor out the dependencies?

One possibility would be to apply Principal Component Analysis (PCA) to the language-feature matrix (Pearson 1901). In essence, PCA breaks a given matrix with column dependencies into a smaller matrix without column dependencies which account for as much of the variability in the data as possible. The constraints are a) on the number of components (the number of new uncorrelated columns), b) that the new columns have to be linear combinations of the old ones, and c) that the new columns have to be independent. PCA would seem to be a well-suited technique for the data we have at hand except there is no natural way to know the appropriate number of components. Presumably, this number would vary across different datasets of linguistic features, and giving one number of components for all datasets seems arbitrary. Therefore we choose not to use PCA as a general approach to factoring out dependencies between linguistic features.

Another possibility,[3] which also has the advantage of being more easily interpretable to linguists, is as follows. Dependencies can be captured as (probabilistic) implications from n features to one other feature. We will make the simplifying assumption that the essential implications are where $n=1$ (the extension to other values of n is relatively straightforward). We first go through the matrix to collect all such implications, creating a dependency graph. The dependency graph has features as nodes, and directed edges between the nodes reflect the implications. Potentially, every feature depends on every other feature to some degree, including circular dependencies, so it is not obvious how to go from a dependency graph between features to a distance metric. We then assume that the core dependencies can be captured by the Chu-Liu tree (Chu and Liu 1965) of the dependency graph. The Chu-Liu algorithm creates a maximum spanning tree of a directed graph, meaning it keeps the single strongest incoming dependency for each feature, and it removes epiphenomenal and circular dependencies. Now, using the Chu-Liu tree, we can modify the Gower coefficient to get a dependency-weighted distance metric. Essentially, instead of scoring 0 or 1 we score an amount proportional to how predictable the feature is. A more detailed description follows.

3.1.1. Finding feature implications

A general method for quantifying the predictive relationship of one frequency distribution from another which has the same domain (in this case, languages) is to calculate how much of the entropy (measure of uncertainty) of one variable can be predicted from knowing the other. This technique has already been used in linguistics by Bickel (2010) and, in a specialized form, by Daumé and Campbell (2007). Formally, for two features A and B we quantify 'A predicts B' as follows:

$$A \rightarrow B = MI(A,B)/H(B)$$

where $MI(A,B)=H(A)+H(B)-H(A,B)$ is the mutual information of A and B, and $H(B)$ is the Shannon entropy[4] of B.

A toy example is shown in table 2. Intuitively speaking, we can say that F_1 is some help in predicting F_2 (if F_1 is 1 then guess 'a'; if F_1 is 0 then guess 'b' or 'c' but not 'a'), that predicting F_1 from F_2 is easier, but that F_1 is no help at all in predicting F_3.

Table 2. Toy example of languages, features, and feature implication calculations.

	F_1	F_2	F_3	F_4
L_1	1	a	1	a
L_2	1	a	0	b
L_3	1	a	1	?
L_4	1	b	0	?
L_5	0	b	1	?
L_6	0	b	0	?
L_7	0	c	1	?
L_8	0	c	0	?
$H(A)$	1.00	1.56	1.00	0.81

		P(A, B)			MI(A,B)	MI(A,B)/H(B) →	
$F_1 \rightarrow F_2$	$P(1,a)=3/8$	$P(1,b)=1/8$	$P(0,b)=2/8$	$P(0,c)=2/8$	0.65	0.65/1.56	0.41
$F_2 \rightarrow F_1$	$P(1,a)=3/8$	$P(1,b)=1/8$	$P(0,b)=2/8$	$P(0,c)=2/8$	0.65	0.65/1.00	0.65
$F_1 \rightarrow F_3$	$P(0,0)=2/8$	$P(0,1)=2/8$	$P(1,0)=2/8$	$P(1,1)=2/8$	0.00	0.00/1.00	0.00

These intuitions are reflected accordingly in the spelled-out calculations of table 2. A final note concerns missing values: they are treated as distinct separate values, erring on the safe side (example F4 in table 2); otherwise, sparse data might exhibit strong random correlations.

Applied to all pairs of features in the Isthmo-Colombian Area dataset, some sample implications are shown in table 3.

Table 3. Some sample feature implications from the Isthmo-Colombian Area dataset.

Rank	Implication	Strength
1	13 → 12	1.000
649	39 → 67	0.180
1297	77 → 71	0.113
1945	37 → 6	0.079
2593	50 → 19	0.055
3241	14 → 27	0.037
3889	54 → 45	0.026
4537	38 → 29	0.015
5185	10 → 47	0.005
5833	28 → 42	0.000

3.1.2. Feature implication distillation

When checking statistical implications between all pairs of features this way, one risks finding epiphenomenal implications. For example, if A predicts B and B predicts C then we will also find that A predicts C, but this information is redundant if we already know the underlying first two implications. Bickel (2010) suggests removing the weakest dependency in all such chains, which is sufficient for a number of purposes. In our case, we are interested in creating a transparent similarity metric and need a slightly stronger method of purging, keeping only the strongest implications in chains and allowing maximally one (strongest) predictor for a feature. In other words, from the complete dependency graph, we compute the maximal directed spanning tree, also known as the Chu-Liu tree (Chu and Liu 1965). For the definition and proof of correctness of the Chu-Liu algorithm, the reader is referred to the more accessible treatment by Georgiadis (2003). Figure 2 shows the Chu-Liu tree for the Isthmo-Colombian Area dataset. The sum "predictability" in the tree is 35.02 (out of a total of 81 features). This can be taken to mean that approximately 35.02/81≈43.2% of the feature mass is redundant.

Figure 2. The maximal directed spanning tree (or Chu-Liu tree) for the Isthmo-Colombian Area dataset. (The one edge reaching feature 66 with value 0.0 has been graphically removed, but is strictly speaking part of the tree.)

3.1.3. A dependency-sensitive distance

Using the Chu-Liu tree, we can modify the Gower coefficient to get a dependency-weighted distance metric:

$$G_d(X,Y) = \frac{\sum_{i \in DEF(L_X,L_Y) \text{ and } L_X[i] \neq L_Y[i]} 1.0 - W(i)}{\sum_{i \in DEF(L_X,L_Y)} 1.0 - W(i)}$$

where $W(A)$ is the weight of the incoming edge predicting A (or 0.0 if there is no such edge). As with the Gower coefficient, only features for which both languages have a value are considered. For each feature, instead of a penalty of 1 for mismatches, we penalize the appropriate amount as to how predictable the feature in question is. The mismatch score is then relativized as to the maximum amount of penalty possible.

In the toy example of table 2, L_2 and L_3 differ only as to feature F_3 out of three features for which both are defined, so their (unmodified) Gower coefficient would be $G(L_2,L_3) = 1/3 \approx 0.33$. The Chu-Liu tree for the toy example in table 2 is $F_2 \rightarrow F_1 \approx 0.66$, $F_2 \rightarrow F_4 \approx 0.44$, $F_4 \rightarrow F_3 \approx 0.25$, so $W(1) \approx 0.66$, $W(2)=0.0$, $W(3) \approx 0.25$ and $W(4) \approx 0.44$. Thus the dependency-sensitive modified Gower coefficient for L_2 and L_3 is $G_d(L_2,L_3) = (1-0.25)/(1-0.66 + 1-0.00 + 1-0.25) \approx 0.75/2.09 \approx 0.36$.

3.2. Feature dependencies and quirky values

The dependency-sensitive distance metric G_d as described, eliminates redundancy between features as a whole. It does *not* differentiate between common and uncommon feature *value* constellations as a result of feature dependencies.

To see the difference, consider the following analogy. Suppose there are creatures which have legs and arms. Some functional pressure, such as access to fruits in tall trees, favors tall creatures over short, and as a result nearly all creatures are tall. Suppose further that the creatures who are tall tend to have both long legs and long arms (as opposed to their having only long arms or only long legs), perhaps because the growth hormone in the creature is the same for both arms and legs. In this world, we will find a correlation between long arms and long legs, and the dependency-sensitive distance metric would tell us that, because of this, the distance between short and tall creatures is on the order of one unit (legs or arms) rather than two units (legs plus arms). The distance metric would also, as designed, show that if we find two short creatures they are just as alike as if we find two tall creatures – in both cases, the distance is zero – even though, because of the functional pressure, finding two short creatures is very unusual. What this illustrates is that, given functional pressure, one might also want to distinguish, already within the distance metric itself, between significant (dis) similarity and insignificant (dis)similarity. For example, if we find two short creatures, or some other unusual constellation such as two creatures both with short legs and long arms, it would be much more likely that they share a common history than it would be for two creatures who share the usual constellation of features. This intuition has surfaced in linguistics under the name 'shared quirk' (Gensler 2003), or in other words, a match against the preference of a dependency.

Potential quirks are all constellations of feature values. In the present study we will restrict ourselves to unary and binary quirks, in other words, feature value constellations involving one or two variables. The quirkiness of a feature constellation (here, a binary constellation) can be defined as:

$$Q(f_i = u, f_j = v) = \frac{\text{The number of languages with values } f_i = u \text{ and } f_j = v}{\text{Total number of languages with } f_i \text{ and } f_j \text{ defined}}$$

It is relatively straightforward to enumerate potential unary and binary quirks and, when comparing two languages, score their matches proportionately to their quirkiness. Again, we make a modified version of the Gower coefficient (the binary case):

$$G_q^2(X,Y) = 1.0 \frac{\sum_{i<j \in DEF(L_x,L_y) \text{ and } L_x[i]=L_y[i] \text{ and } L_x[j]=L_y[j]} 1.0 - Q(i = L_x[i], j = L_x[j])}{|\{(i,j) | i < j \in DEF(L_x,L_y)\}|}$$

Again, let us look at the toy example of table 2. As to unary quirks, L_2 and L_3 match their values for features $F_1 = 1$ and $F_2 = a$. $Q(f_1 = 1) = 4/8$ and $Q(f_2 = a_2) = 3/8$, so their distance based on unary quirks is $1.0 - (1 - 4/8 + 1 - 3/8)/3 \approx 0.71$. As to binary quirks, the only match between the two languages is $G_q^2(L_2,L_3) = Q(f_1 = 1, f_2 = a_2) = 3/8$, so their distance based on unary quirks is $G_q^1(L_2,L_3) = 1.0 - (1 - 3/8)/(3!/1!2!) \approx 0.79$. (Counting both unary and binary quirks at the same time yields $1.0 - (1 - 4/8 + 1 - 3/8 + 1 - 3/8)/(3+3) \approx 0.71$.)

The quirk-based measure is strictly speaking not a distance measure because $G_q(X, X)$ is not necessarily 0: whether it is 0 or not depends on how *significant* the feature values of X are.

4. Experimental results

We are now ready to apply the new metrics to the Isthmo-Colombian Area dataset to see if there are language pairs that behave drastically differently. In all experiments, we use the Isthmo-Colombian Area dataset itself to extract dependencies and quirkiness rates. Ideally, we would use a large enough world-wide database with the same features, but such a database is not available for most of the features as defined in the Isthmo-Colombian Area dataset. Also, ideally, the dataset used for extracting dependencies and quirkiness rates should be genealogically and areally stratified to make sure that any skewed rates are the result of universal dependencies rather than historical relationships. The experiments reported here are relative to the assumption that the Isthmo-Colombian Area dataset as a whole contains sufficient evidence for universal dependencies.

We first look at the G_d-distances versus the traditional Gower coefficient (G). As an orientation, table 4 shows the top-5 and bottom-5 distances before (G) and after (G_d) dependency. As those distances suggest, in general the differences are slight, both in the actual values and in their relative rank.

Table 4. The top-5 and bottom-5 language pairs in terms of unmodified G-distance and the dependency-sensitive G_d-distance.

Rank	G		G_d	
1	Ulua-Sumo	0.00	Ulua-Sumo	0.00
2	Sumo-Misquito	0.01	Sumo-Misquito	0.02
3	Ulua-Misquito	0.01	Ulua-Misquito	0.02
4	Cabecar-Bribri	0.04	Cabecar-Bribri	0.05
5	Sambu-Catio	0.05	Sambu-Catio	0.07
...	...	...	...	...
591	Quiche-Bocota	0.58	Quiche-Bocota	0.54
592	Quiche-Cabecar	0.58	Xinca-Cabecar	0.55
593	Xinca-Cabecar	0.58	Xinca-Teribe	0.56
594	Teribe-Quiche	0.59	Teribe-Quiche	0.57
595	Quiche-Movere	0.60	Quiche-Movere	0.59

Table 5 shows the pairs whose distances change the most as dependencies are factored out.

Table 5. Language pairs that became more distant (left) or became closer (right) as a result of applying the dependency-sensitive Gower coefficient.

	G_d-G	G	G_d		G_d-G	G	G_d
Sambu-Cayapa	0.10	0.38	0.48	Quiche-Lenca	-0.08	0.36	0.28
Paya-Bintucua	0.09	0.26	0.35	Quiche-Cayapa	-0.07	0.43	0.36
Paya-Cagaba	0.09	0.22	0.31	Quiche-Paez	-0.06	0.49	0.43
Ulua-Paez	0.09	0.36	0.45	Quiche-Cuna	-0.06	0.41	0.35
Sumo-Paez	0.09	0.36	0.45	Quiche-Boruca	-0.06	0.47	0.41
Cuna-Boruca	0.09	0.26	0.35	Xinca-Camsa	-0.06	0.36	0.30
Paya-Muisca	0.09	0.25	0.33	Xinca-Cofan	-0.06	0.44	0.39
Paez-Bintucua	0.09	0.41	0.49	Quiche-Huaunana	-0.06	0.46	0.40
Huaunana-Boruca	0.08	0.23	0.32	Xinca-Boruca	-0.06	0.44	0.39
Paez-Misquito	0.08	0.35	0.43	Quiche-Colorado	-0.05	0.43	0.38

The pairs that become more distant include Paya, a Chibchan language of Honduras, now more distant from three Chibchan languages of Colombia; Chocoan languages Sambú and Huaunana, now more distant from a Barbacoan and a Chibchan neighbor, respectively, and Paez, now more distant from a genealogically heterogeneous group of languages. The pairs that become closer involve the two northernmost languages in the sample, Xinca and Quiché, each now closer to a large number of languages.

To get a feeling for the relative contribution of these changes, Neighbor-Joining trees (Saitou and Nei 1987) for the two distance matrices are shown in the leftmost columns of figure 3.[5]

Comparing the first two trees we see that Xinca and Quiché, as a result of having become closer to many other languages, cease to group together exclusively and move one short step up the tree along with their immediate neighbors. There is, however, little appreciable difference between the trees overall.

The high level of dependency in the feature set as a whole (recall the 43% estimate above) constitutes strong evidence that the dependency-induced inflation is uniformly distributed in the dataset. If this were to prove typical of feature sets in typology in general, there would be little need to consider feature dependencies in typological comparison.

Next we turn to applications of the quirkiness-sensitive metric. It is not meaningful to compare the quirk-based distances directly to the G and G_d since quirk-based distances count significant value-matches and the others do not, but there may be interesting relative effects between trees generated by the quirk- vs. non-quirk-based distances. Table 6 shows the top-5 and bottom-5 language pairs, comparing unmodified distances to distances based on unary and binary quirks.

Table 6. The top-5 and bottom-5 language pairs in terms of G-distance (unmodified Gower) and G_q-distances (modified for unary quirks and binary quirks).

Rank	G		G_q^1		G_q^2	
1	Ulua-Sumo	0.00	Cabecar-Bribri	0.49	Cabecar-Bribri	0.48
2	Sumo-Misquito	0.01	Ulua-Sumo	0.53	Ulua-Sumo	0.53
3	Ulua-Misquito	0.01	Sumo-Misquito	0.55	Sumo-Misquito	0.54
4	Cabecar-Bribri	0.04	Ulua-Misquito	0.55	Ulua-Misquito	0.54
5	Sambu-Catio	0.05	Sambu-Catio	0.58	Sambu-Catio	0.58
...	...		...			
591	Quiche-Bocota	0.58	Xinca-Cabecar	0.93	Xinca-Cabecar	0.93
592	Quiche-Cabecar	0.58	Xinca-Teribe	0.93	Xinca-Teribe	0.93
593	Xinca-Cabecar	0.58	Quiche-Bocota	0.93	Quiche-Bocota	0.93
593	Teribe-Quiche	0.59	Quiche-Movere	0.94	Quiche-Movere	0.94
595	Quiche-Movere	0.60	Teribe-Quiche	0.94	Teribe-Quiche	0.94

Ulua-Sumo – the pair that shares every feature – is no longer the pair with the smallest distance in the quirkiness-sensitive distances, as what the Cabecar-Bribri pair shares is more significant. In general, as in the earlier tests, differences among language pairs are slight; nevertheless, there may still be specific pairs with drastic relative changes.

To check this, we again compute Neighbor-Joining trees (Saitou and Nei 1987) for the quirk-distances, shown in the rightmost trees in figure 3, and comb the outcome trees for reshuffled languages. There is very little difference compared to trees already commented on; in fact, the unary-quirk tree (third column) and the dependency-sensitive tree (second column) are topologically identical. A clear trend in the case of the binary-quirk distance (tree shown in fourth column) is that differences between all or any of the languages are de-emphasized, which presumably reflects that most quirks are not shared (a situation that dilutes the impact of any few that are shared). If this were to prove typical of feature sets in typology in general, quirks would be either insignificant details when it comes to typological profiles, or they would need to be projected on a different scale (artificially enhanced?) to have ramifications.

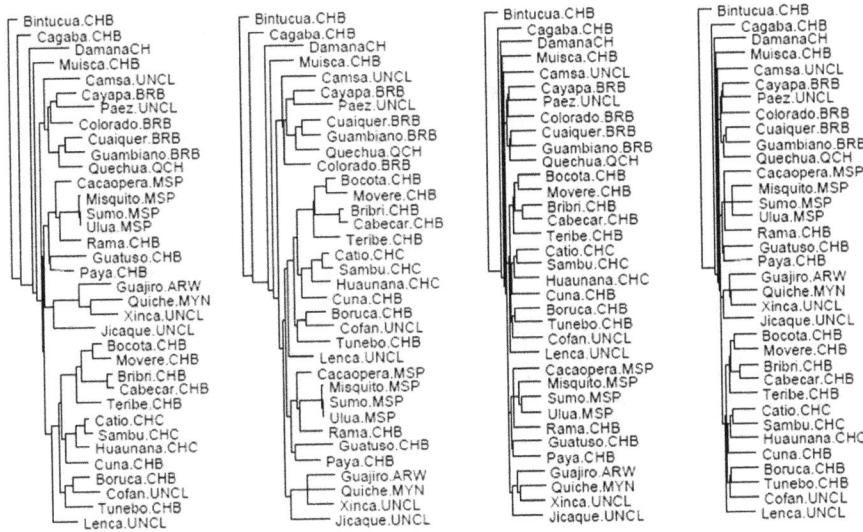

Figure 3. Neighbor-Joining trees based on distances calculated with the normal Gower coefficient G (far left), the modified dependency-sensitive Gower coefficient G_d (mid-left), the unary quirk-based distance G_q^1 (mid-right) and the binary quirk-based distance G_q^2 (far right). All have been arbitrarily rooted with Bintucua as the outlier.

5. Discussion and conclusions

In this paper we have presented two approaches to factoring out functional dependencies from datasets of typological features for natural languages. We first addressed the *presence of dependencies* among features and eliminated these in a dependency-sensitive version of the distance metric. The second approach considered distance with respect to the *value of features* in a modified metric that addressed the relative quirkiness of the features shared by a pair of languages. Both dependency-sensitive metrics make the assumption that the dependencies are of low order (binary or unary) in order to get a tractable approximation of arbitrary-order dependencies

Experiments on a dataset of Chibchan and neighboring languages revealed numerous dependencies between features. However, the impact of this dependency was found to be minimal for typological comparison between languages. When comparing any two languages, there was little difference between blind and dependency-sensitive distance metrics.

There is still the possibility that striking dependency-related effects between certain languages do exist, but on a more micro-level than the full typological profiles of the languages question. To test something in this direction, we re-ran the modified algorithms against the two meaningful subsets in the original 81-feature database: one data matrix with 42 morphosyntactic features, and a second data matrix with 39 phonological features. While there were a few changes using the dependency-sensitive metrics, these changes were as minor as those reported for the full typological profiles, and no valuable insights at all were gained from the quirkiness-sensitive measures.

Thus our final result is that dependencies inhabit the language-feature matrix of the Isthmo-Colombian Area uniformly and not as surprising contingencies between particular geographical neighbors or particular pairs of unrelated languages.

Acknowledgements

The authors are grateful to Michael Dunn and Annemarie Verkerk for digitizing the Constenla Isthmo-Colombian Area data and translating the list of features, and to Devdatt Dubhashi and Vinay Jethava for discussion and literature pointers regarding computational approaches to feature dependencies. We thank Pieter Muysken and Bernard Comrie for comments on an earlier draft; Muysken, Comrie, Mily Crevels, and Östen Dahl for comments on the final version, and the participants of the October 2011 Approaches to Measuring Linguistic Difference workshop at University of Gothenburg for useful discussion and suggestions. The usual disclaimers apply. This study was conducted with support from ERC Advanced Grant 230310 'Traces of Contact'.

Appendix: The set of typological features of the Isthmo-Colombian Area dataset, adapted from Constenla Umaña (1991: 88–120, 179–185).

1 Is there VO order in transitive clauses?
2 Is there VS (verb-agent) order in transitive clauses?
3 Is there OS (patient-agent) order in transitive sentences?
4 Is there VS (S may be agent or object) order in intransitive sentences?
5 Is the order of adpositions and nouns as follows: preposition – noun?
6 Is the order of adpositions and nouns as follows: noun – postposition or noun – case suffixes?

7	Is the order of the noun that is possessed and the noun that indicates the possessor (the genitive) N – Gen?
8	Is the order of the noun that is possessed and the noun that indicates the possessor (the genitive) Gen – N?
9	Is the order of the adjective and the noun A – N?
10	Is the order of the adjective and the noun N – A?
11	Is the order is numerals with respect to the indefinite nominal phrase Num – N?
12	Is the order of the demonstrative and the noun Dem – N?
13	Is the order of the demonstrative and the noun N – Dem?
14	Is the order of the interrogative word and the clause obligatorily question word – clause (i.e., are question words positioned initially)?
15	Is there a passive voice (only consider whether the language has a passive voice when it is possible to include a nominal phrase which indicates the semantic agent in the passive clause)?
16	Is there an anti-passive?
17	Is there an distinction between inclusive and exclusive for personal pronouns?
18	Is there an opposition between masculine and feminine personal pronouns?
19	Is there an opposition between formal and informal personal pronouns?
20	Is it the case that a negational element, which may be a particle or a prefix, constantly and obligatorily precedes the declarative clause?
21	Is it the case that a negational element, which may be a particle or a suffix, constantly and obligatorily follows the declarative clause?
22	Is there a morpheme that marks genitive case in inalienable possession?
23	Is there a morpheme that marks genitive case in alienable possession?
24	Is there a morpheme that marks accusative case?
25	Does the language have a case system that distinguishes between the agent of an intransitive action verb and the patient of intransitive process verbs?
26	Does the language have a case system that does not distinguish between the agent or patient of an intransitive verb and the patient of an transitive verb?
27	Are non-verbal predicates inflected for tense, aspect or person?
28	Are there gender oppositions (animate/inanimate, masculine/feminine or both) expressed in the inflection of any major word class (generally on verbs, on adjectives, or both types of word classes)?
29	Are there inflectional prefixes?
30	Is there inflection expressed with or marked through replacement of segmental or non-segmental phonemes?
31	Are there prefixes which indicate (grammatical) person?
32	Are there suffixes which indicate (grammatical) person?
33	Is there inflection for indicating the (grammatical) person of the possessor on the noun (personal possessive inflection)?

34	Is there inflection for indicating the (grammatical) person on intransitive verbs?
35	Is there inflection for indicating the (grammatical) person of the agent on transitive verbs?
36	Is there inflection for indicating the (grammatical) person of the object on the transitive verb?
37	Are there prefixes to indicate tense or aspect?
38	Are there suffixes to indicate tense or aspect?
39	Are there directional elements attached to the verb?
40	Is there a distinction in the shape of (all or some) nouns for possessed/non-possessed?
41	Are there numeral classifiers?
42	Is there definite marking distinct from demonstratives?
43	Is there an opposition between high plus mid vowels versus front vowels?
44	Is there an opposition between high plus mid vowels versus back vowels?
45	Is there a rounding contrast for non-front (central or back) vowels of the same height?
46	Is there a open/closed contrast for vowels of the same height and the same 'series'?
47	Is there a nasality contrast for vowels?
48	Is there a quantity contrast for vowels?
49	Are there tonal contrasts?
50	Is there a non-labial glottalized occlusive?
51	Is there a labial glottalized occlusive?
52	Is there at least one implosive?
53	Is there an aspiration contrast for occlusives?
54	Is there a phonemic condition for the glottal occlusive?
55	Is there a phoneme /p/ (simple, bilabial, voiceless occlusive)?
56	Is there one or more uvular occlusive phoneme?
57	Is there at least one obstruent phoneme (occlusive or fricative) which is labial and voiced or weak/lenis?
58	Is there at least one obstruent phoneme (occlusive or fricative) which is dental or alveolar and voiced or weak/lenis?
59	Is there at least one obstruent phoneme (occlusive or fricative) which is velar and voiced or weak/lenis?
60	Is there at least one fricative phoneme that is hissing and voiced or weak/lenis?
61	Is there a sonority or lenition contrast for affricates?
62	Is there a glottalization contrast for affricates?
63	Is there an aspiration contrast for affricates?
64	Is there at least one alveolar affricate?

65	Is there at least one prepalatal affricate?
66	Is there a lateral affricate?
67	Is there at least one retroflex affricate?
68	Is there a voiceless labial fricative phoneme (/ɸ/ or /f/)?
69	Is there a voiceless prepalatal fricative phoneme (/ʃ/)?
70	Is there a voiceless retroflex fricative phoneme (/ʂ/)?
71	Is there a voiceless lateral fricative phoneme (/ɬ/)?
72	Are there the consonantal nasal phonemes bilabial /m/ and alveolar /n/?
73	Is there a mediopalatal nasal phoneme (/ɲ /)?
74	Is there a velar nasal phoneme /ŋ/?
75	Are there voiceless nasal phones as realizations of nasal phonemes before /h/ or before sequences of nasal phonemes with /h/?
76	Are there word initial consonant clusters that consist of consist of one nasal and another consonant?
77	Is there a voiced lateral approximant (/l/)?
78	Is there a voiced mediopalatal approximant /ʎ/?
79	Is there a simple central vibrant phoneme /ɾ/?
80	Is there a simple lateral vibrant phoneme /ɺ/?
81	Is there a multiple vibrant phoneme /r/?

Notes

1. Available online at http://wals.info accessed 1 June 2011.
2. The other assumption underlying the use of the Gower coefficient – that fully independent features should carry equal weight when calculating distance – is not explored in this paper.
3. Though there is a fair amount of work in the field of structured data prediction (cf. Getoor and Taskar 2007) we are not aware of any previous work that develops modified distance measures based on feature dependencies.
4. $H(B) = -\sum P(b_i) \log P(b_i)$ where P is the underlying probability/frequency distribution for the values b_i of feature B.
5. We are not concerned here with the validity of these trees for historical linguistics in the region – the interest is whether there is rearrangement of some kind in the distance-based clustering.

References

Adelaar, Willem F. H. and Pieter C. Muysken
2004   *The Languages of the Andes* (Cambridge Language Surveys). Cambridge: Cambridge University Press.

Aguirre Licht, Daniel
2006   Choco Languages. In Keith Brown (ed.), *Encyclopedia of Language and Linguistics,* Volume 2, 367–381. 2d ed. Amsterdam: Elsevier.

Bickel, Balthasar
2010   Capturing particulars and universals in clause linkage: a multivariate analysis. In Isabelle Bril (ed.), *Clause-hierarchy and clause-linking: the syntax and pragmatics interface,* 51–101. Amsterdam: John Benjamins.

Campbell, Lyle
1997   *American Indian Languages: the Historical Linguistics of Native America.* Oxford: Oxford University Press.

Captain, David
2005   Proto Lokono-Guajiro. *Revista Latinoamericana de Estudios Etnolingüísticos* 10: 137–172.

Cerrón-Palomino, Rodolfo
2003   *Lingüística quechua* (Monumenta Lingüística Andina 10). 2d ed. Cuzco: Centro de Estudios Regionales Andinos "Bartolomé de las Casas".

Chiswick, Barry R. and Paul W. Miller
2004   Linguistic Distance: A Quantitative Measure of the Distance Between English and Other Languages. Institute for the Study of Labor (IZA DP No. 1246). Bonn: IZA.

Christiansen, Morten H, Chris Collins, and Shimon Edelman (eds)
2009   *Language Universals.* Oxford: Oxford University Press.

Chomsky, Noam
1981   *Lectures on Government and Binding.* Dordrecht: Foris Publications.

Chu, Yoeng-Jin and Tseng-Hong Liu
1965   On the Shortest Arborescence of a Directed Graph. *Scientia Sinica* 4: 1396–1400.

Constenla Umaña, Adolfo
1991   *Las lenguas del área intermedia: introducción a su estudio areal.* San José: Universidad de Costa Rica.

Constenla Umaña, Adolfo
2012   Chibchan languages. In Lyle Campbell and Verónica Grondona (eds.), *The Indigenous Languages of South America: A Comprehensive Guide* (The World of Linguistics 2), 391–440. Berlin/New York: De Gruyter Mouton.

Cysouw, Michael
    2007   New Approaches to Cluster Analysis of Typological Indices. In Reinhard Köhler and Peter Grzybek (eds.), *Exact Methods in the Study of Language and Text*, 61–76. Berlin/New York: Mouton de Gruyter.
Dahl, Östen
    2008   An exercise in *a posteriori* sampling. *Sprachtypologie und Universalienforschung* 61(3): 208–220.
Daumé, Hal III and Lyle Campbell
    2007   A Bayesian Model for Discovering Typological Implications. In *Proceedings of the 45th Annual Meeting of the Association of Computational Linguistics*, 65–72. Prague: Assn for Computational Linguistics.
Dryer, Matthew S.
    1992   The Greenbergian Word Order Correlations. *Language* 68(1): 81–138.
Dunn, Michael, Simon J. Greenhill, Stephen C. Levinson, and Russell D. Gray
    2011   Evolved structure of language shows lineage-specific trends in word-order universals. *Nature* 473: 79–82.
Eriksen, Love
    2011   *Nature and Culture in Prehistoric Amazonia. Using G.I.S. to reconstruct ancient ethnogenetic processes from archaeology, linguistics, geography, and ethnohistory.* Lund: Lund Studies in Human Ecology 12.
Gensler, Orin D.
    2003   Shared quirks: a methodology for "non-orthodox" historical linguistics. Paper presented to the 17th International Conference of Historical Linguistics, Prague, 29 July.
Georgiadis, Leonidas
    2003   Arborescence optimization problems solvable by Edmonds' algorithm. *Theoretical Computer Science* 71: 233–240.
Getoor, Lise and Ben Taskar
    2007   Introduction. In Lise Getoor and Ben Taskar (eds.), *Introduction to Statistical Relational Learning* (Adaptive Computation and Machine Learning), 1–11. MIT Press.
Holman, Eric W., Christian Schulze, Dietrich Stauffer, and Søren Wichmann
    2007   On the relation between structural diversity and geographical distance among languages: Observations and computer simulations. *Linguistic Typology* 11(2): 395–423.
Kolman, Connie J. and Eldridge Bermingham
    1997   Mitochondrial and Nuclear DNA Diversity in the Chocó and Chibcha Amerinds of Panamá. *Genetics Society of America* 147: 1289–1302.
Melton, P. E., I. Briceño, A. Gomez, E. J. Devor, J. E. Bernal, and M. Crawford
    2007   Biological Relationship Between Central and South American Chibchan Speaking Populations: Evidence from mtDNA. *American Journal of Physical Anthropology* 133: 753–770.

Pearson, Karl
 1901 On Lines and Planes of Closest Fit to Systems of Points in Space. *Philosophical Magazine* 2(6): 559–572.
Pineda, Baron
 2005 Miskito and Misumalpan Languages. In Philipp Strazny (ed.), *Encyclopedia of linguistics* volume 2, 693–695. New York: Fitzroy Dearborn.
Polyakov, Vladimir N., Valery D. Solovyev, Søren Wichmann, and Oleg Belyaev
 2009 Using WALS and Jazyki Mira. *Linguistic Typology* 13: 137–167.
Quesada, J. Diego
 2007 *The Chibchan Languages*. Cartago: Editorial Tecnológica de Costa Rica.
Saitou, Naruya and Masatoshi Nei
 1987 The neighbor-joining method: A new method for reconstructing phylogenetic trees. *Molecular Biology and Evolution* 4: 406–425.
Sinnemäki, Kaius
 2010 Word order in zero-marking languages. *Studies in Language* 34(4): 869–912.
Trillos Amaya, Maria
 2005 *Lenguas Chibchas de la Sierra Nevada de Santa María: Una Perspectiva Histórico-Comparativa*. Bogotá: Universidad de los Andes.
Wichmann, Søren and Eric W. Holman
 2010 Pairwise comparisons of typological profiles. In Jan Wohlgemuth and Michael Cysouw (eds.), *Rethinking Universals: How rarities affect linguistic theory* (Empirical Approaches to Language Typology 45), 241–254. Berlin/New York: De Gruyter Mouton.
Williams, Cindy
 1993 A grammar sketch of Dəmənа. University of North Dakota MA thesis.

Degrees of semantic control in measuring aggregated lexical distances

Kris Heylen and Tom Ruette

1. Introduction

The goal of the current study is to show how aggregated lexical variation can be studied by means of corpus-based techniques, which differ in their amount of semantic control. In the current variationist field, one finds many studies of phonological or morphological variation on the basis of corpora.[1] Remarkably at first sight, though, studies of lexical variation in corpora are rare, especially in comparison with dialectology, where the study of lexical variation is part of the main research goal. In contrast to the other corpus-based variationist studies, however, the dialectological account of lexical variation is very much restricted to elicited data, as stored in well-known dialect atlases. Therefore, the current study sets out to show how this void of corpus-based studies of lexical variation can be filled, while taking into account possible issues with lexical semantic complexity.

In the introduction to the paper, we would like to point out two things. First, we will explain why there is a plethora of studies on phonological and morphological variation and a scarcity of studies on lexical variation. Second, we will shed a different light on what can be understood under lexical variation from a corpus-linguistic point of view.

1.1. The stigma of lexical variation

The stigmatization of studies on lexical variation can partially be attributed to the well-debated article of Lavandera (1977). Before we give a brief account of its criticism, the context of the first generation variationist studies must be sketched. After William Labov performed his famous New York City experiment (Labov 1966), a methodological consensus in the form of the *Principle of Accountability* (Labov 1972) was established that the only valid sociolinguistic variable consisted of a set of variants that do the same "thing" (Chambers and Trudgill 1980: 91). This is obviously a functional-semantic restriction on what may be considered to be a sociolinguistic variable. With this in mind, the Lavandera critique is sparked off by an article of Sankoff (1972), in which she extends the Labovian phonological variable to a syntactic variable. The simple conceptual jump of Sankoff (1972) that if allophones may constitute a variable, two seemingly identical syntactic alternants may do so too, is problematic: where the Labovian work correlates the choice between "meaningless" variants and a socio-stylistic distribution of the options, Sankoff tries to link a socio-stylistic distribution of options to the choice between variants that are constrained in usage: e.g. she finds that the choice for "que"-deletion in Montreal French is not socio-stylistically motivated, but rather syntactic. Lavandera's criticism zooms in on this point, and proposes that only semantically equivalent options may constitute a variable, thus effectively excluding every linguistic phenomenon, except morpho-phonological variables.

It is now clear why the study of lexical variation is so problematic in the sociolinguistic field – perhaps even more problematic than syntactic variation. The main issue is that a lexical sociolinguistic variable is allowed to consist only of words that are equivalent in all perspectives, i.e. meaning, except for their socio-stylistic distribution. For words, this is a (quasi) impossible task. The meaning of words is highly contextual, even highly individual, and – according to the latest Cognitive Linguistic insights in lexical semantics (Geeraerts 2010) – completely encyclopedic (Taylor 1989: Chapter 5). From the point-of-view of Lavandera, therefore, lexical variation can simply not be studied in a sociolinguistic way. Interestingly enough, this is also one of the reasons why dialectology refrains from corpus-based studies. Instead, dialectologists have elicited lexical preferences from their subjects by using questionnaires or naming tasks, to keep strict control on the meaning component. In order to gain even more control, dialectologists primarily elicited concrete notions, which can be shown to the subject, or can be described in sufficient detail.

In the current study, we argue in favor of a non-elicited approach to lexical variation: a large-scale corpus study of aggregated lexical variation. The idea of aggregation is central here. Whereas typical variationist studies zoom in on the socio-stylistic distribution of a single variable, we will aggregate the variational patterns of many lexical variables, as is common in dialectometry (Goebl 1982, Grieve et al. 2011). Although we lose detail in the behavior of individual variables, we do gain an insight in the overall variational patterns that play in the lexicon. Moreover, because we combine the patterns of many variables, subtle meaning differences between the variants of a single variable – which were the reason for Lavandera (1977) to abolish non-phonological variation – are averaged out, and become less important. Now, optimistically speaking, only the problem of finding a large set of lexical alternation variables remains. For this we will employ a (semi-)automatic way of modeling semantics in corpora: on the one hand, we want to identify concepts and lexical variants that can refer to them. On the other hand, we want to check whether lexemes refer to the same concept across varieties and not to another one.

1.2. What is lexical variation?

Although the previous paragraph dealt exclusively with the sociolinguistic notion of lexical variation, we would like to show two more approaches to lexical variation, which can be found in the literature. These methods differ from the variationist approach because they assign a different value to what we will call "semantic control" in the variable. In total, we distinguish three types of lexical variation: the use of different lexemes, the use of different lexemes to express the same thing (cf. alternation variables), and the different uses of a single lexeme. In what follows, we assume that we are looking at the lexical variation between two subcorpora.

1.2.1. The use of different lexemes

A very straightforward way of looking at lexical variation is merely the observation that two subcorpora use different words. Although the two subcorpora might have considerable overlap in the lexical types, the frequency distribution of these types might point towards a difference between the subcorpora. Most famously, this approach has been put to work by the work of Douglas Biber (Biber 1988, 1995, Biber and Barbieri 2007). In his seminal 1988 book, Biber compared the frequency distribution of certain words, e.g. first person pronouns, across texts from different registers, and showed how frequency distributions turned out to be correlated to the register. From a semantic point-of-view, this is the most uncontrolled approach, and only applicable – for these purposes – to function words (because they are the only kind of words that are frequent enough in small corpora to be quantitatively analyzed). Nevertheless, it is a very popular and widespread method, at the basis of many applications such as authorship attribution and document classification.

1.2.2. The use of different lexemes to express the same thing

The second approach is derived from the variationist view on linguistic variation, ignoring the warning words of Lavandera (1977). It is claimed that lexical variation exists in the options that language users have to name a certain concept. This type of lexical variation is historically – in a European pre-structuralist tradition – known as onomasiological variation. Just as Labov (1978) suggests in his reply to Lavandera, we adopt a slightly relaxed attitude: perhaps it is true that the options are not exactly identical in their meaning at all levels, but it is not unthinkable that these lexical options are substitutable in many cases. This appeal to common sense is also present in a more recent paper by Edmonds and Hirst (2002).

1.2.3. The different uses of a lexeme

A third and last possible way of defining lexical variation is different from the previous two approaches, because it does not compare (orthographically) different lexemes, but looks at the different uses of a single lexeme. Words may have different meanings[2] depending on the context. The most obvious and extreme example is of course polysemy. On a more subtle level, and with relation to the variationist perspective of this paper, we might find that a certain word is used to express A in one situation, but B in another situation, with A and B only slightly different. As an example, the word *ketel* is used to refer to all sorts of pots in Limburgian (Dutch) dialects, whereas its use is far more restricted in the other Dutch dialects, where it refers to an old-fashioned, round metal container typically suspended over an open fire. This type of lexical variation has been extensively studied by Justyna Robinson (e.g. Robinson 2010), and can be grasped under the label semasiological variation.

On the basis of these three notions of lexical variation, we will calculate the lexical distance between subcorpora. The underlying idea is that a low amount of variation implies a small lexical distance. How exactly we will quantify this distance is explained below. To figure out the influence of semantic control on lexical distance measurements, we perform a corpus-based study of three registers in two national varieties of Dutch. The results show how different the outcomes of the semantically controlled measurements are: the approaches do not really agree with each other. The conclusion of the paper will be that a combination of two specific approaches might be the most trustworthy solution.

The remainder of this paper consists of section 2 in which the compilation and structure of the corpus is described. Section 3 introduces the Semantic Vector Space model, which we will take as a starting point for studying lexical variation in the three ways that were described above. The actual lexical variables that we will be using to measure the lexical distance between the subcorpora of our corpus are introduced in section 4. Section 6 then overviews the results of these three different ways of controlling the semantics of lexical distance measurements, and results are discussed in the final section.

2. Corpus

Our corpus consists of texts that were gathered from Usenet posts, popular newspapers, quality newspapers and official government announcements (legalese). For each of these text types, we have texts written by people from the Netherlands and from Belgium (To avoid confusion over the adjective Dutch, we will use Netherlandic to refer to Dutch as spoken in the Netherlands). Moreover, we only gathered texts that were published between 1999 and 2004. As we will measure the distances between the parts of this corpus by counting lexical items, every subcorpus needs to be big enough to supply reliable frequencies. Table 1 gives an overview of the sizes of the subcorpora. With almost 2 billion words, we can be quite certain that the frequencies for the lexical items in the corpus are representative of their actual usage.

Table 1. Overview of subcorpora and their sizes in words

	Usenet	Popular news	Quality news	Legalese	Total
BE	22 million	905 million	373 million	70 million	1.4 billion
NL	26 million	126 million	161 million	115 million	428 million
Total	48 million	1 billion	499 million	185 million	1.8 billion

However, word derivations or inflections could also introduce an error in the frequency counts. This can be solved by not just counting the occurrences, but to count the root form, possibly controlled by the part-of-speech. For that reason, all texts in the corpus were automatically lemmatized and annotated for part-of-speech by the current state-of-the-art dependency parser for Dutch, which is Alpino (Bouma et al. 2001). A further cause of mistakes in the frequency counts may be due to polysemy of the lexical items. How we have dealt with that problem in the current study – and how we will deal with it in further research – is explained in Section 4.

The actual texts of the corpus were either downloaded from the internet – Usenet and legalese – or obtained from the publishers – the popular and quality newspapers. The newspapers were requested and processed by the University of Twente and Groningen for the Netherlandic material, and by the University of Leuven for the Belgian material. The Usenet articles were downloaded from the Usenet archive online at Google Groups[3] by means of a series of Python scripts which removed meta-information (e.g. headers) and duplicated content (e.g. quotes). The legalese consists of the downloaded texts from the "Staatsblad" in Belgium[4] and The Netherlands[5]. All the Usenet and legalese texts were downloaded during 2010 and 2011. The corpus is not freely available due to copyright restrictions, but anybody is free to request and download the same materials.

3. Semantic Vector Space models

The three types of lexical variation from the introduction can now be formulated in corpus linguistic terms: (1) the subcorpora use different lexemes. (2) the subcorpora use different lexemes for the same concept. (3) the subcorpora use the same lexemes differently, i.e. with a different meaning. For the large-scale corpus-based operationalization of these three approaches and the level of semantic control they require, we turn to a statistical approach developed in Computational Linguistics. There, so-called Semantic Vector Spaces (SVS's) have become the mainstay of processing semantics in large corpora. These models capture semantics in terms of frequency distributions of words over documents and of words co-occurring with other words. They have been applied to a wide variety of computational linguistic tasks – from Information Retrieval (Baeza-Yates and Ribeiro-Neto 1999) and Question answering (van der Plas et al. 2010) to automated essay scoring (Landauer and Dumais, 1997) or the modeling of human behavior in psycholinguistic experiments (Lowe and McDonald 2000). In recent years, Semantic Vector Spaces have also seen applications in more traditional domains of linguistics like diachronic lexical studies (Sagi et al. 2009), or, as in our case, the study of lexical variation (Peirsman et al. 2010).

Broadly speaking, Semantic Vector Spaces can be used to model two types of semantics: text semantics and word semantics. Each type of semantics comes with its own specific SVS implementation (see Turney and Pantel 2010 for a general overview). In this paper we will use both a text-oriented

SVS, for our analysis of the first type of lexical variation, and a word-oriented SVS, for the other two types.

SVS models for text semantics try to capture the semantic content of documents by recording which words occur in each document and how often. Documents that contain the same words and with similar frequencies are then said to have the same semantic content. In practice, these models construct a so-called term-by-document matrix, in which each document is assigned a vector that captures the frequency distribution over all words in a given vocabulary (i.e. the terms in SVS parlance). Usually, the vocabulary is restricted to words that are of interest to a certain domain. In our case, we will restrict the vocabulary to the set of lexical items that forms the basis of comparison for our 3 types of measuring lexical variation (see section 4) For the vector comparison, SVS's use a geometrical metaphor (hence Spaces): the term-by-document frequencies can be seen as co-ordinates defining a point in a high-dimensional term space. Points (documents) closer together in the space contain the same terms and are said to be semantically more related. The resulting document distances can then be used to classify or cluster the documents. We will therefore call this type of SVS the document classification approach and we will use it to operationalize our first type of lexical variation. By constructing a word-by-subcorpus matrix, we will measure to what extent our regionally and stylistically stratified subcorpora use the same words (see section 5.1).

Let us now turn to the SVS models for word semantics. They are also based on a frequency distribution matrix but instead of the semantics of documents, the focus lies on the semantics of the words. To model word semantics, these SVS's record the co-occurrence frequencies of a set of target words with a large set of context words. The hypothesis is that words occurring in similar contexts, i.e. that are surrounded by the same context words, will have a similar meaning. For example, the semantic similarity of *clinic* and *hospital* can be induced from the fact they both co-occur with words like *doctor, nurse, operation, treatment*, etc. In practice, most models define context as the words occurring in a given window around the target words. In this study we set the window to 5 words to the left and right. As in most models, we work with a restricted vocabulary of possible context words: we used the 4000 most frequent words, excluding the top 30, which were all function words. The raw co-occurrence frequencies were weighted with Point Wise Mutual information to increase the weight of more informative words, i.e. those that co-occur only with a limited set of (semantically related) target words. Using the same geometrical metaphor as before, the target words then become the points in a high dimensional space of context words. Target words are close together in the space if they share relatively high co-occurrence frequencies with the same context words and therefore they are likely to be semantically similar. Following SVS standards, the cosine was used as a proximity measure. Computing the cosine similarity between all pairs of target word vectors results in a target-word-by-target-word similarity matrix.

A word-based Semantic Vector Space will be the input for the operationalization of the two other types of lexical variation in our study. First, the word-by-word similarity matrix can be subjected to a cluster analysis that groups the target words into sets of near-synonyms, i.e. lexemes referring to the same "thing". In our onomasiological measurement of lexical variation, we can then analyze whether the subcorpora differ with respect to their lexical choices, given the concepts. Secondly, we can construct target word vectors for each subcorpus separately and then calculate the similarity between the vectors. This will tell us for each target word whether it is used in the same contexts and with the same meaning in the different subcorpora. In our semasiological measurement of lexical variation, we can then assess to what extent the subcorpora tend to use lexemes differently, i.e. with a different meaning. In the next section, we will specify which target words we will use as the lexical variables in our variation study.

4. Variable set

In most studies that aggregate a number of linguistic variables to analyze underlying variational dimensions, the variable set is usually limited. In dialectometry, most studies aggregate the variables that are available in dialect atlases. In sociolectometric research (e.g. Geeraerts et al. 1999, Soares da Silva 2010), lexical variable from random lexical fields were chosen. And in stylometric studies, a collection of so-called functional variables is gathered from grammars and stylebooks.

Although quite similar in method and approach, there is a difference in research question between dialectometric or stylometric studies and sociolectometric studies. Whereas dialect- and stylistic research sets out to point out a specific regional or functional difference between certain language varieties, our study does not presuppose a variational dimension. In other words, we do not have an a priori dimension of variation that we want to point out, but rather, we want to discover these dimensions bottom-up. Therefore, in our study, it would be wrong to analyze a dataset that is biased towards a certain pattern.

This is exactly why previous (lexical) sociolectometric studies have limited themselves to the analysis of two (or a small number of) lexical fields. It is manually feasible to get a representative, or even an exhaustive list of concepts that belong to the same lexical field, and for this limited number of concepts it is possible to find most or all the words that can refer to each one of these concepts. As such, there is no variational pattern pre-programmed in this set of variables under investigation. The only way to discover a certain pattern is by investigating how the items in the variables are distributed over subcorpora that differ along the dimension under investigation.

However, the manual collection of variables in this approach makes it unscalable to a study that has the ambition to investigate the variational patterns of the lexicon in general. Given that the vocabulary is vast, only a tiny portion and a very specific part of the lexicon is analyzed when the variable set is collected manually. Ideally, the variable set should consist of a set of words that is representative for a sizeable part of the vocabulary, and such a quantity of variables should be gathered in an automatic and bottom-up way.

So, what exactly is the task that we give to this automatic approach? We want (a) to find words that refer to the same concept, and (b) to find a large number of concepts that come from different parts of the vocabulary. The first part ensures that our variable set contains (onomasiological) lexical variation, the second part takes care of the representativity of the feature set. Here, the word-based Semantic Vector Space model outlined in the previous section comes into play.

The word-by-word similarity matrix is submitted to a clustering algorithm known as Clustering by Committee (CBC) (Pantel and Lin 2002). CBC was designed to describe each sense of a target word by means of a cluster of words that are semantically closely related to the sense of the target word under consideration. One phase of the algorithm consists of finding clusters of semantically related words, so-called committees, and the outcome of this phase seems to comply roughly with our desired feature set. Because the underlying method is (still) somewhat imprecise, we will manually filter out those committees that are representative of a single concept – cf. step (a) of the task. With relation to step (b) of the task, we can point out that CBC is completely frequency related, and thus there is a bias in the retrieved clusters towards frequent concepts. Nonetheless, these concepts come from diverse lexical fields.

There are 476 variants (lexemes), contained in 218 variables (concepts), that were manually retained from the automatically generated alternation variables. We restricted the variants to nouns only, because Vector Space Models appear to be most successful for referential items. In table 2, a selection of variables is presented. The two other types of lexical variation require a less strict variable selection: in principle, the document classification approach would have allowed to analyze frequency differences between subcorpora for all lexemes, and in the semasiological approach, we could have compared target word vectors between subcorpora for a much larger selection of lexemes. However, our explicit aim is to compare the three approaches to lexical variation, so that we restricted ourselves to the same selection of 476 lexemes in all approaches.

Table 2. Example variables

CONCEPT	Items
MANNER	wijze, manier
GENOCIDE	volk_moord, genocide
POLL	peiling, opiniepeiling
MARIHUANA	cannabis, marihuana
PUTSCH	staatsgreep, coup
MENINGITIS	hersenvliesontsteking, meningitis
DEMONSTRATOR	demonstrant, betoger
AIRPORT	vliegveld, luchthaven
COLDNESS	koude, kou
TORTURE	marteling, foltering
VICTORY	zege, overwinning
HOMOSEXUAL	homo, homoseksueel
SAXOPHONE	sax, saxofoon
INTERNETPROVIDER	provider, internetprovider, internetaanbieder
AIRCONDITIONING	airconditioning, airco
RELIGION	religie, godsdienst
THE OTHER SIDE	overkant, overzijde
EXPLOSION	explosie, ontploffing
RESTROOM	toilet, wc
INJURY	kwetsuur, letsel
BLAST	windstoot, ruk_wind
LAST MINUTE	nippertje, valreep
XENOPHOBIA	vreemdeling_haat, xenofobie
PASSER-BY	voorbijganger, passant
AIR STRIKE	luchtaanval, bombardement
FIGHTING SPIRIT	vechtlust, strijdlust
GOVERNMENT FORCES	regeringsleger, regeringstroepen
CAR	auto, wagen
PROFIT FORECAST	winst_verwachting, winst_prognose

5. Degrees of semantic control

In this section, we arrive at the heart of our research goal: what is the influence of different degrees of semantic control on an aggregated study of lexical variation. More specifically, we compare an approach with no semantic control at all (Section 5.1) to two approaches that apply a different type of semantic control: an approach that accounts for the difference in usage of a single word (semasiological approach, Section 5.2), and an approach that accounts for the differences in naming a concept with a different word (onomasiological approach, Section 5.3).

5.1. Document classification

The first approach is based on a straightforward document classification algorithm and refrains from any semantic control, cf. the first type of SVS introduced above. Technically speaking, the frequencies of the features in a subcorpus constitute an identifying vector for the subcorpus, and the similarity between two subcorpora is measured by means of the cosine similarity metric. This metric measures the cosine of the (hyperdimensional) angle between two vectors: if the cosine is close to 1, the angle between the two vectors is small, and the two subcorpora are considered to be very similar. The cosine metric applied to two subcorpora V_1 and V_2, on the basis of their identifying vectors $\vec{x}$ and $\vec{y}$ is formally described in equation 1.

$$\cos(V_1, V_2) = \cos(\vec{x}, \vec{y}) = 1 - \frac{\vec{x} \cdot \vec{y}}{|\vec{x}||\vec{y}|} = \frac{\sum_{i=1}^{n} x_i y_i}{\sum_{i=1}^{n} x_i^2 \sum_{i=1}^{n} y_i^2} \quad (1)$$

Because the cosine metric merely works with the (raw) frequencies of the input features and does not take into account that there are groups of features that are semantically related, we call this a non-semantically controlled approach. This is the most rudimentary approach, and from its typical application in document classification, we know that it should primarily pick up on referential or content-related differences between the subcorpora.

Calculating the similarity between all pairs of subcorpora that we have available yields a similarity matrix. This similarity matrix can easily be converted to a dissimilarity matrix, by subtracting it from 1. The resulting distance matrix can be visualized by means of Multidimensional Scaling (MDS). In figure 1 and figure 2, one can find the two- and three-dimensional solutions of the non-metric MDS implementation isoMDS in the statistical program R, with the MASS package loaded.

The two-dimensional solution shows a strong group of Belgian and Netherlandic newspapers, except for the Belgian popular newspapers. The two national varieties of Usenet also practically overlap. Dominating the first (horizontal) dimension, we find the Belgian and Netherlandic legalese subcorpora, on the right side of the plot. The second (vertical) dimension is not very pronounced: it seems largely to set apart the Usenet subcorpora. Because of this unclear dimension, and despite the already very low stress value, we calculate a three-dimensional solution in figure 2, to see if this clears up dimension 2.

The three-dimensional solution preserves the distinction between legalese and the other subcorpora on dimension 1, and it confirms the idea that dimension two sets apart Usenet. The third dimension, which is admittedly also not very pronounced, now seems to separate the Netherlandic and Belgian subcorpora. The Netherlandic subcorpora are consistently "lower" than the Belgian subcorpora.

5.2. Semasiological approach

In the semasiological approach, we take each of the 476 lexemes in our variable set and construct a word-based SVS with a separate target word vector for each subcorpus. Calculating the cosine similarity between the vectors results in a distance matrix between subcorpora. Subcorpora are similar if they tend to use a particular lexeme in the same way, i.e. in the same contexts and with the same meaning. They are different if they use the lexeme with a different meaning. Aggregating over all lexemes, we can assess to what extent the subcorpora show variation in word usage and word meaning in general. Given the lexemes L_1 to L_m, then the global dissimilarity D between two subcorpora V_1 and V_2 on the basis of R up to L_m can be calculated as:

$$D_{\cos}(V_1, V_2) = \sum_{i=1}^{m} D_{\cos, L_i}(V_1, V_2) \qquad (2)$$

Looking at the MDS solution for subcorpus distance matrix, we see that the semasiological approach immediately promotes the national distinction in the variable set. The two-dimensional visualization should be interpreted

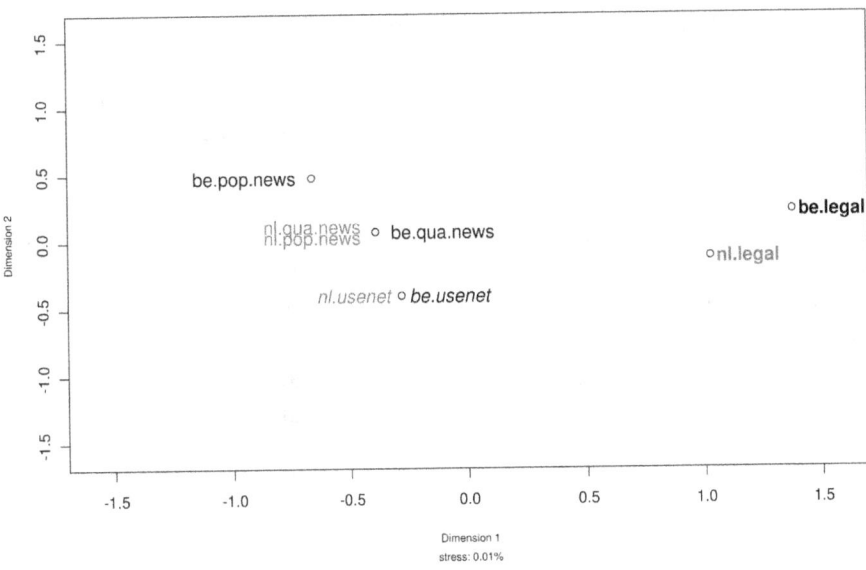

Figure 1. 2D Multidimensional Scaling visualization of lexical distances, without semantic control

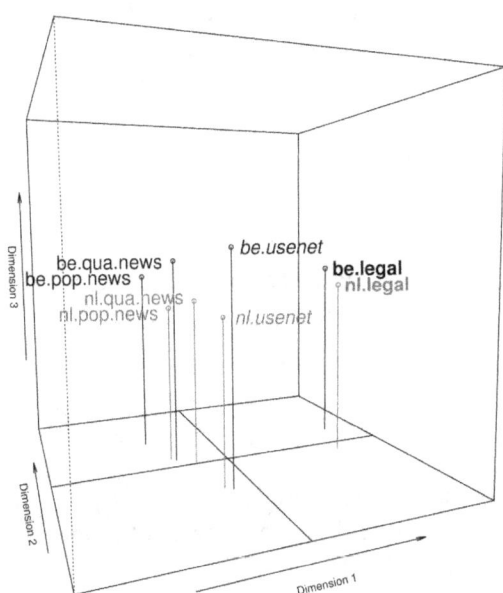

Figure 2. 3D Multidimensional Scaling visualization of lexical distances, without semantic control

as follows: especially in Usenet and legalese, a word is not used the same way in Belgium and The Netherlands. Remarkably, all the newspapers do agree on how to use a certain word. This might point out that the deviating behavior of Usenet and legalese has to do with their specificity and technicality.

The three dimensional solution changes the order of the dimensions. This is not impossible in a non-metric MDS solution, but it would be in a Principal Components and Coordinates Analysis. The non-metric iterative algorithm keeps improving the configuration, irrespective of the dimensions, until an optimal fit is found. This may influence the order of the dimensions. Dimension 1 now distinguishes the newspapers from Usenet and legalese, and dimension 2 distinguishes legalese from Usenet. It is only at dimension 3 that the country distinction – so obvious in the two-dimensional solution – reveals itself.

5.3. Onomasiological approach

Finally, we arrive at the onomasiological approach. Here, the distance metric is informed about the groups of semantic related input features by means of recalculating the frequency of a single feature relative to the sum of the frequencies of the semantic group to which it belongs. As such, the distance metric is sensitive to lexical variation as could be measured as the well-known sociolinguistic alternation variable[6].

Given two subcorpora V_1 and V_2, a group of semantically related words L and x_1 to x_n the exhaustive list of words in L, then we refer to the absolute frequency F of the usage of x_i for L in V_j with:[6]

$$F_{V_j, L}(x_i) \qquad (3)$$

Subsequently, we introduce the relative frequency:

$$R_{V_j, L}(x_i) = \frac{F_{V_j, L}(x_i)}{\sum_{k=1}^{n} F_{V_j, L}(x_k)} \qquad (4)$$

Now we can define the (City-Block) distance $D_{CB, L}$ between V_1 and V_2 on the basis of W as follows (the division by two is for normalization, mapping the results to the interval [0,1]):

$$D_{CB, L}(V_1, V_2) = \frac{1}{2} \sum_{i=1}^{n} |R_{V_1, L}(x_i) - R_{V_2, L}(x_i)| \qquad (5)$$

Degrees of semantic control in measuring aggregated lexical distances 367

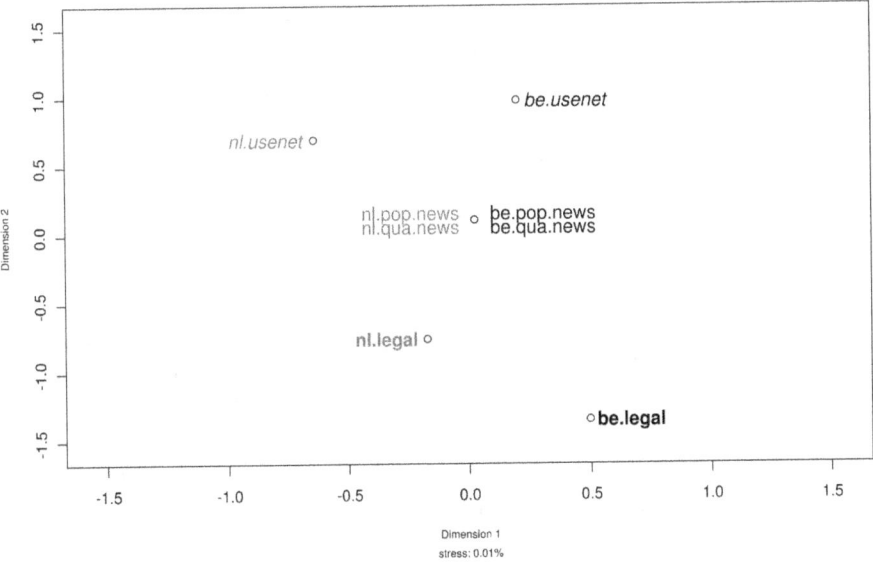

Figure 3. 2D Multidimensional Scaling visualization of lexical distances, with semasiological control

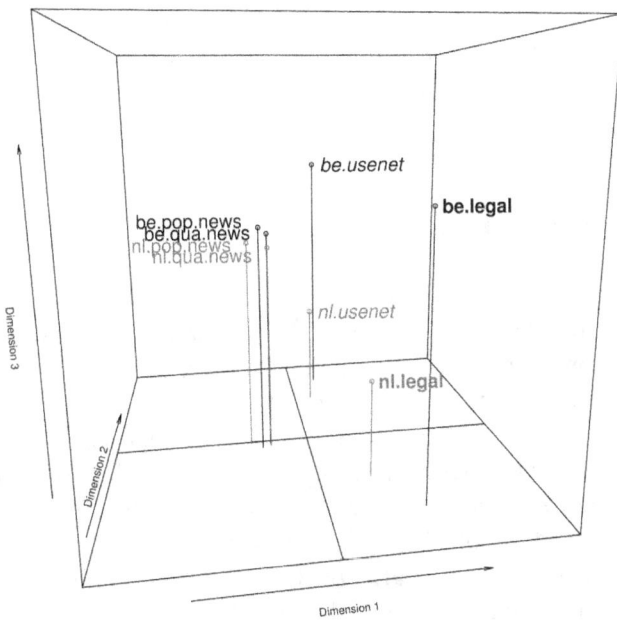

Figure 4. 3D Multidimensional Scaling visualization of lexical distances, with semasiological control

To calculate the dissimilarity between subcorpora on the basis of many groups of semantically related words, we just sum the dissimilarities for the individual groups. In other words, given a set of groups L_1 to L_m, then the global dissimilarity D between two subcorpora V_1 and V_2 on the basis of L_1 up to L_m can be calculated as:

$$D_{CB}(V_1, V_2) = \sum_{i=1}^{m} (D_{L_i}(V_1, V_2) W(L_i)) \qquad (6)$$

The W in the formula is a weighting factor. We use weights to ensure that groups of words which have a relatively higher frequency (summed over the size of the two subcorpora that are being compared[7]) also have a greater impact on the distance measurement. In other words, in the case of a weighted calculation, semantic groups that are more common in everyday life and language are treated as more important.

In figure 5, we see again the distinction between the legalese and the rest of the subcorpora, but this time, the grouping of the subcorpora is extremely tight. Therefore, a three-dimensional solution in figure 6 might reveal some more variation in the patterning of the subcorpora.

Indeed, the first dimension still singles out the legalese subcorpora, but now, the second dimension puts the Belgian subcorpora at the front, and the Netherlandic subcorpora at the back. The third dimension seems to pull down the Usenet subcorpora, distinguishing them from the newspapers and legalese.

6. General discussion

In the above experiment, we have compared three ways of measuring the lexical distance between subcorpora. The first approach neglected any kind of semantic control of the lexical input features. Figure 2 shows how this document classification approach separates – as expected – most distinctively the registers: dimension 1 singles out the legalese, and dimension 2 splits Usenet from newspaper articles. It is only at the third dimension that a very weak country distinction, most obvious in the Usenet material, props up.

The second and the third approach presented two different perspectives on semantic control of lexical variation. On the one hand, the difference in use of an individual word across the different subcorpora was used as the basis for a semasiological distance metric. This showed (figure 3) that on average there is a national pattern in words that are used differently. However, this

Degrees of semantic control in measuring aggregated lexical distances 369

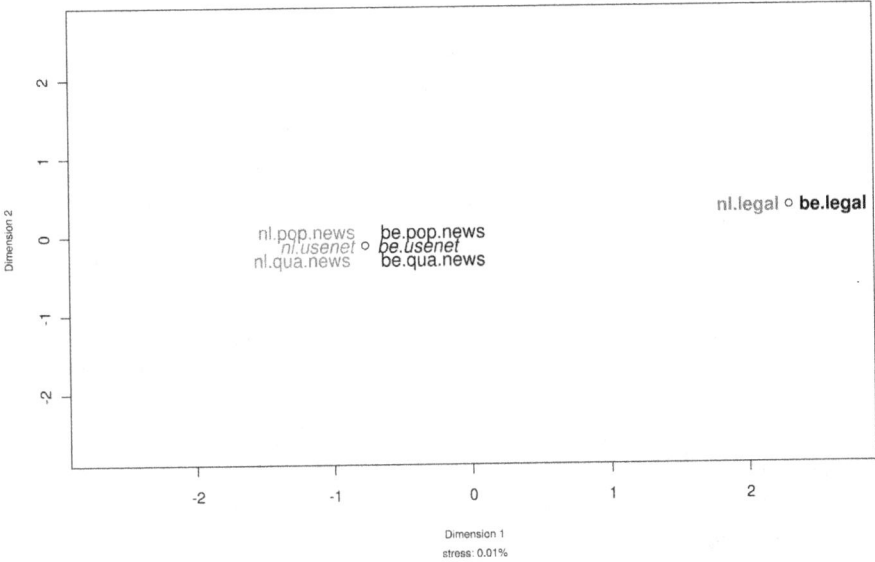

Figure 5. 2D Multidimensional Scaling visualization of lexical distances, with onomasiological control

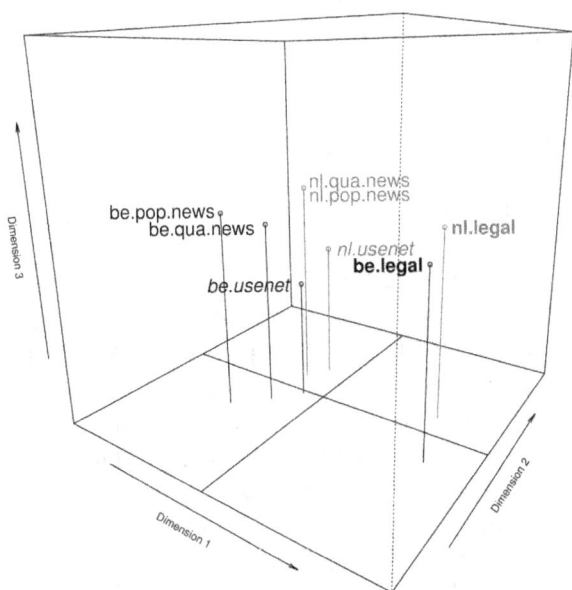

Figure 6. 3D Multidimensional Scaling visualization of lexical distances, with onomasiological control

national pattern is not homogeneous across the three registers that are present in our corpus. The newspaper articles show surprisingly similar use of words, whereas the more specific subcorpora of legalese and Usenet drift apart.

On the other hand, the choice of a specific word for expressing a certain concept was the basis for the onomasiological distance metric. Figure 6 shows how neatly legalese is split off decisively, how then second the national distinction becomes clear, and how finally the Usenet subcorpora are separated. And all these distinctions are due to the fact that another word is used to refer to a concept.

There are two main conclusions to be drawn here. First, we have pointed out that semantic control (or the lack thereof) has a profound influence on the outcome of an aggregated study of lexical variation. Although the three approaches agree on the special position of legalese, it is unclear how the variational dimensions relate to each other after that. At least, the three approaches do not agree with each other, although every single approach is valid in its own right.

Second, assuming that we discard the approach without any semantic control whatsoever – because one can hardly call its input lexical variation –, an approach that combines both the semasiological and onomasiological control is probably needed. The semasiological approach comes first to identify which words are actually comparable across the subcorpora: if a certain word is used completely differently in Belgium than in The Netherlands, it makes no sense to use it in the onomasiological approach. Indeed, the onomasiological approach assumes that the words in the variable are interchangeable, but a word with a large semasiological range does not comply with that expectation.

Of course, in an ideal situation, this boils down to a scrutiny of every single observation to verify whether the occurrence is relevant. This is obviously not feasible for a large-scale corpus-based study with thousands of observations. However, recent developments in the SVS domain are able to model the usage-based meaning of a single token, and will allow us in future studies to evaluate and correct the accurateness of the frequency counts.

Finally, we want to point out that the current study proposes a method to get a bird's eye view of whether there is any interesting lexical variation between different varieties of a language. The next logical step is to pinpoint this variation and look at individual variables (concepts and words) that contribute to overall lexical divergence between varieties. Quantitative methods, like Individual Difference Scaling, allow an insight in the behavior of individual variables within an overall variational structure, and they will be the focus of our future research.

Notes

1. That is, if a corpus is taken to be a naturalistic sample of language use.
2. The link between meaning and use will be discussed below.
3. http://groups.google.com
4. http://www.ejustics.just.fgov.be/cgi/welcome.pl
5. https://www.officielebekendmakingen.nl/staatsblad
6. The following introduction to the City-Block distance method is based on Speelman et al. 2003.
7. The size of the two subcorpora is not the actual number of words in the two subcorpora but the sum of all profiles in these two subcorpora.

References

Baeza-Yates, Ricardo and Berthier Ribeiro-Neto
    1999   *Modern Information Retrieval*. ACM Press / Addison-Wesley.

Biber, Douglas
    1988   *Variation across Speech and Writing*. Cambridge: Cambridge University Press.

Biber, Douglas
    1995   *Dimensions of Register Variation: A Cross-Linguistic Comparison*. Cambridge: Cambridge University Press.

Biber, Douglas and Federica Barbieri
    2007   Lexical bundles in university spoken and written registers. *English for Specific Purposes* 26 (3): 263–286.

Bouma, Gerlof, Gertjan van Noord, and Rob Malouf
    2001   Alpino: Wide-coverage computational analysis of Dutch. In *Computational Linguistics in the Netherlands 2000*, W. Daelemans, K. Sima'an, J. Veenstra, and J. Zavrel (eds.), 45–59. Amsterdam: Rodolpi.

Chambers, Jack and Peter Trudgill
    1980   *Dialectology*. Cambridge: Cambridge University Press.

Edmonds, Philip and Graeme Hirst
    2002   Near-synonymy and lexical choice. *Computational Linguistics* 28 (2): 105–144.

Geeraerts, Dirk
    2010   *Theories of Lexical Semantics*. Berlin/New York: De Gruyter Mouton.

Geeraerts, Dirk, Stefan Grondelaers, and Dirk Speelman
    1999   *Convergentie en divergentie in de Nederlandse woordenschat. Een onderzoek naar kleding- en voetbaltermen*. Amsterdam: Meertens Instituut.

Goebl, Hans
    1982   *Dialektometrie: Prinzipien und Methoden des Einsatzes der numerischen Taxonomie im Bereich der Dialektgeographie*. Wien: Oesterreichische Akademie der Wissenschaften.

Grieve, Jack, Dirk Speelman, and Dirk Geeraerts
  2011   A statistical method for the identification and aggregation of regional linguistic variation. *Language Variation and Change* 23: 193–221.
Labov, William
  1966   *The Social Stratification of English in New York City.* Center for Applied Linguistics.
Labov, William
  1972   Some principles of linguistic methodology. *Language in Society* 1 (1), 97–120.
Labov, William
  1978   Where does the linguistic variable stop? A response to Beatriz Lavandera. *Working Papers in Sociolinguistics* 44: 5–22.
Landauer, T. and S. Dumais
  1997   A solution to Plato's problem: The Latent Semantic Analysis theory of acquisition, induction and representation of knowledge. *Psychological Review* 104: 411–240.
Lavandera, Beatriz
  1977   Where does the sociolinguistic variable stop? *Working Papers in Sociolinguistics* 40: 6–24.
Lowe, Will and Scott McDonald
  2000   The direct route: Mediated priming in semantic space. *Proceedings of the 22nd Annual Conference of the Cognitive Science Society*, 675–680.
Pantel, Patrick and Dekang Lin
  2002   Discovering word senses from text. *Proceedings of the 8th ACM SIGKDD International Conference on Knowledge Discovery and Data Mining (KDD 2002)*, 613–619.
Peirsman, Yves, Dirk Geeraerts, and Dirk Speelman
  2010   The automatic identification of lexical variation between language varieties. *Natural Language Engineering* 16 (4): 469–491.
Robinson, Justyna
  2010   Awesome insights into semantic variation. In *Advances in Cognitive Sociolinguistics,* Dirk Geeraerts, Gitte Kristiansen, and Yves Peirsman (eds.), Berlin/New York: De Gruyter Mouton.
Sagi, Eyal, Stefan Kaufmann, and Brady Clark
  2009   Semantic density analysis: Comparing word meaning across time and phonetic space. *Proceedings of the Workshop on Geometrical Models of Natural Language Semantics*, 104–111. Athens: Association for Computational Linguistics.
Sankoff, Gillian
  1972   Above and beyond phonology in variable rules. In *New Ways of Analyzing Variation in English*, R. Shuy, and C. Bailey (eds.), Washington, D.C.: Georgetown University Press.

Soares da Silva, Augusto
    2010   Measuring and parameterizing lexical convergence and divergence between European and Brazilian Portuguese. In *Advances in Cognitive Sociolinguistics*, Dirk Geeraerts, Gitte Kristiansen, and Yves Peirsman (eds.), Berlin/New York: De Gruyter Mouton.

Speelman, Dirk, Stefan Grondelaers, and Dirk Geeraerts
    2003   Profile-based linguistic uniformity as a generic method for comparing language varieties. *Computers and the Humanities* 37: 317–337.

Taylor, John R.
    1989   *Linguistic Categorization: Prototypes in Linguistic Theory*. Oxford: Clarendon Press.

Turney, Peter and Patrick Pantel
    2010   From frequency to meaning: vector space models of semantics. *Journal of Artificial Intelligence Research* 37: 141–188.

van der Plas, Lonneke, Gosse Bouma, and Jori Mur
    2010   Automatic acquisition of lexico-semantic knowledge for QA. In *Ontologies and Lexical Resources for Natural Language Processing*, Chu-Ren Huang, Nicoletta Calzolari, Aldo Gangemi, Allessandro Lenci, Allesandro Oltramari, and Laurent Prevot (eds.), 271–287. Cambridge: Cambridge University Press.

Word similarity, cognation, and translational equivalence

Grzegorz Kondrak

1. Introduction[1]

The focus of this presentation is the following observation: *words that are phonetically similar across different languages are more likely to be mutual translations*. This phenomenon has been exploited in the past to improve various tasks in Natural Language Processing (NLP). However, to the best of my knowledge, the proposition has never been explicitly stated or justified.

The term *mutual translations* should be understood here as words that can be used to express the same meaning. In particular, words that correspond to each other on two sides of a sentence in a bilingual corpus (*bitext*) are considered translations, as well as words that are used to define each other in a bilingual dictionary.

Even though the term *phonetic similarity* is used in the above formulation, phonetic similarity is usually reflected in orthographic similarity. If the languages use different scripts, orthographic similarity can be emulated by mapping one script to another, or converting both scripts to a more universal transcription, such as the International Phonetic Alphabet (IPA). Even if the mapping is imperfect, much of the similarity will be preserved. In this presentation, however, I focus on the written forms of the words.

The fact that similar words are more likely to be translations has been utilized in various tasks within Statistical Machine Translation (SMT), such as word alignment, sentence alignment, inducing translation models, and generating translation lexicons. Another application is automatic acquisition of transliterations (transliteration mining).

The publications that utilize the principle rarely if ever articulate it or explain it. In the first part of this presentation, I discuss the reasons behind the principle, which include the prevalence of cognates, loanwords, technical terms, and proper names. In the second part, I analyze the results of comparisons between French and English that provide insights into the issue of word similarity.

2. Definitions

In this section, I propose several definitions, accompanied by rationale and examples from French and English, respectively.

Cognates are word pairs in related languages that derive directly from the same word in the ancestor language. Because of gradual phonetic and semantic changes over long periods of time, cognates may no longer look similar and have quite different meanings. E.g., *pére / father, chef / head*.

Loanwords (also called *lexical borrowings*) are words that have been transferred form one language to another at some point of time, such as the word *reconnaissance* in English. The languages involved in the transfer need not be related.

Names are designations of persons, organizations, and places. They are normally not found in dictionaries. In English, and many other languages, names usually start with a capital letter. Names are rarely translated into other languages; instead, they are either copied verbatim, or transliterated on the basis of their pronunciation.

Unrelated words (as opposed to **related**) belong to neither of the previous three categories. Their forms cannot be traced to any common origin. However, they can be mutual translations.

False friends (*faux amis*) are pairs of words across languages that look or sound similar but have different meanings. In many cases, the similarity is purely accidental, e.g. *main* 'hand', but some false friends are cognates that have undergone semantic shifts, e.g. French *suave* 'sweet'.

True friends (*vrais amis*) are words that look or sound similar *and* are mutual translations. The words with identical spelling are called *homographs*. Aside from cognates and loanwords, true friends can be traced to nursery terms, onomatopoeia, and even accidental similarity.

Partial friends are similar words that have the same meaning in some, but not all, contexts. They are either true or false friends depending on the context. For example, *facteur* in French signifies not only 'factor' but also 'mailman'.

3. Theoretical view

We can classify cross-language word pairs according to the following three criteria: common origin, semantic similarity, and similarity of form (either phonetic or orthographic).

The three criteria vary in terms of the subjectivity and granularity. The first criterion is binary: words either have the same origin or not. The ones that do include cognates, loanwords, as well as names. In most cases, this can be established objectively. The other two criteria involve similarity, which is usually a subjective notion, and falls on a spectrum ranging from total synonymy to nothing in common. Here, I map semantic similarity onto a binary notion of *translatability*, which can be approximated by a bilingual dictionary look-up.

In order to convert form similarity into binary relation, I employ two imperfect projections: *identity* and *thresholding*. Identity is not subjective, but encompasses only a small subset of word pairs that are clearly similar. Thresholding, on the other hand, involves an arbitrary choice of a similarity measure and a threshold, which results in a relation that only partly correlates with human judgment. However, even human annotators would undoubtedly have difficulty with sharp demarcation of similar vs. dissimilar words.

The application of the above three criteria to the classification of cross-lingual word pairs produces eight categories listed in table 1, with Spanish-English examples.

Machine translation specialists, who aim at exploiting form similarity to find translations, are mainly interested in true friends, which correspond to categories (1) and (3). The difference between these two classes in immaterial for them. However, they need to avoid false friends, which are covered by categories (5) and (7).

Table 1. Classification of cross-lingual word pairs.

	Criteria			Example	
	Translations	Related	Similar	Spanish	English
1	+	+	+	sal 'salt'	salt
2	+	+	−	pie 'foot'	foot
3	+	−	+	mucho 'much'	much
4	+	−	−	sangre 'blood'	blood
5	−	+	+	muerte 'death'	murder
6	−	+	−	carbon 'coal'	hearth
7	−	−	+	flor 'flower'	floor
8	−	−	−	fruto 'fruit'	door

For historical linguists, on the other hand, who are interested primarily in identifying cognates, category (3) is the treacherous one. Fortunately, it contains few pairs, for it is unusual for unrelated words to converge in both form and meaning. However, distinguishing between cognates and loanwords is often difficult. Regular sound correspondences are helpful for this purpose.

Closely related languages, such as Spanish and Italian, contain numerous cognates, most of which fall into category (1). The more remote the relationship, the greater fraction of cognates falls into categories (2), (5), and (6).

Figure 1 shows the situation in a schematic way. The points on the graph represent pairs of words from two related languages. The black points denote cognates, while the white points denote unrelated words. The two axes correspond to the semantic and phonetic similarity. The pairs that are on the vertical axis have identical meanings (*synonyms*), while the pairs on the horizontal axis are identical in form (*homonyms*). The origin point of the graph is reserved for pairs that have exactly the same form *and* meaning.

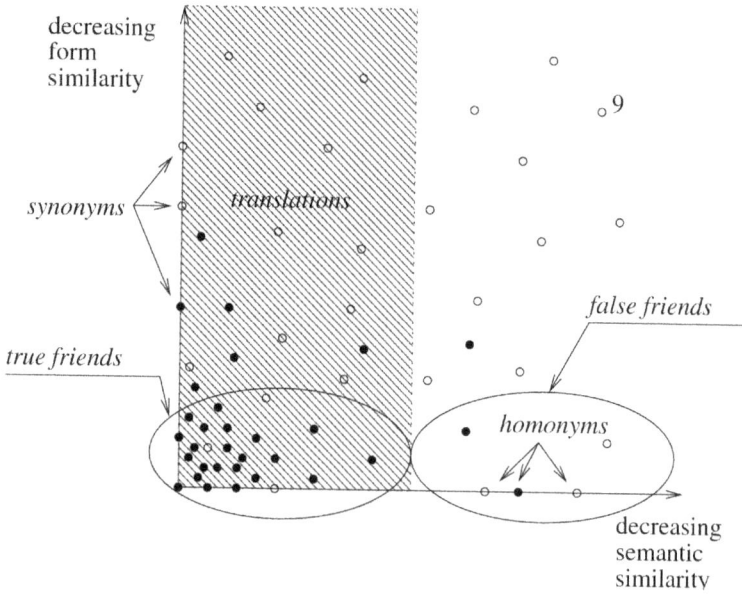

Figure 1. A schematic depiction of the set of cross-lingual word pairs.

The distribution of the unrelated words is shown as fairly uniform. Cognates, on the other hand, are clustered mostly in the vicinity of the plot origin. At the very moment of a language split, all word pairs are considered to be at the origin point. With time, cognates undergo phonetic and semantic changes that slowly cause them to disperse further and further away from the origin. Loanwords also start their existence in the vicinity of the origin point, but may move away from it. Names, on the other hand, tend to remain at the origin point.

4. Empirical analysis

In this section, I investigate the distribution of similar French-English word pairs in two resources: a dictionary and a bitext. The objective is to provide some empirical evidence for the observation stated in the introduction.

4.1. Preliminaries

In order to compute concrete statistics, we need to make a clear distinction between names and other words. This is not always straightforward (e.g., *Greek*). I adopt the following rule of thumb: a name must be capitalized and must not be listed in a standard dictionary.

The algorithm for deciding whether two morphologically complex words are related is slightly more complicated. The focus here is on the roots of the words, without paying much attention to affixes. If the roots are related, the words are considered related. In the case of compounds, one common root is sufficient.

A simple string similarity measure can be used to emulate the notion of orthographic similarity. The Longest Common Subsequence Ratio (LCSR) of two strings is defined as the length of their longest common subsequence normalized by the length of the longer string. It returns a value between 0 (no similarity) and 1 (identity).

4.2. Dictionary entries

The starting point of the analysis presented in this section is an automatically generated phrase translation table containing about eighty thousand French-English phrase pairs, such as *anneau de caoutchouc / rubber ring*. I limit my analysis to 8012 entries that map single French words to single English words. I manually annotated a randomly-selected sample of 1000 entries as either *related* or *unrelated*. Surprisingly, the related pairs are more frequent in the sample: 636 vs. 364. Of the related pairs, 140 are homographs, e.g. *horizontal*.

In the Cartesian product of the 1000 entries, which is composed of one million pair, there are 141 homographs, of which 140 are the translations mentioned above. All homograph translations are related words.[2] They consist mostly of words of Latin origin (e.g. *constellation*), but also quite a few direct loanwords (e.g. *folklore, chalet, cousin*), as well as words from other languages (e.g. *eldorado*). The one non-translational pair (*but* 'target') are unrelated false friends. Another pair that are almost identical, differing only by a single diacritic involves the French word to curé 'parson', which evolved from the same Latin root as English *cure*. In this relatively small sample, all but one of the homographs across French and English are mutual translations.

Using the same Cartesian product approach, I identified 1097 homographs in a larger set of 8012 entries. 1016 (92.6%) of them correspond to two sides of the same dictionary entry. This means that homographs are over ten times more likely to be mutual translations than not, even under the assumption that all remaining pairs are false friends. Note that the set is likely to contain most of the common words in both languages.

I analyzed the remaining 81 homographs that occur in separate dictionary entries. The set contains 53 (65%) related and 28 unrelated pairs. The latter category is entirely composed of false friends. Many are function words from one language paired with a content word from another languages, e.g. *car* 'because', *or* 'gold'. Some pairs originate from different Latin words, e.g. *court* 'short', with the French and English words derived from *curtus* and *cohort*, respectively.

Most of the 53 related pairs are words of Latin origin. Some of them are partial friends, e.g. *inexcusable*, which is translated as 'unpardonable'. A few pairs are clearly false friends, e.g. *concussion* 'embezzlement'. The majority of the pairs, however, are at various stages of semantic shifts, with partly overlapping meanings, such as *index*. A number of pairs contain words that belong to different parts of speech, such as *absorbent*, which is a verbal form in French, but a noun in English. In addition, there are some modern loanwords, such as *film* and *attaché*, which are partial friends.

The average length of the homographs measured in letters is 7.5 for related homographs, but only 4.1 for accidental homographs. This is because the latter are more likely to be short words. The longer the homographs, the more likely they are to be mutual translations.

The average similarity of translations in the 1000-entry sample according to the LCSR measure is 0.619. The corresponding values for the subset of related translations and unrelated translations are 0.815 and 0.276, respectively. Interestingly, the latter value is substantially larger than the average similarity of random pairs of French-English words, which is approximately 0.235 (ignoring diacritics). This shows that even disregarding directly related translations, translatability and similarity are not completely independent. The reasons behind the apparent correlation are discussed in section 5.

4.3. Bitext alignment links

The resource that underlies the analysis in this section is the Blinker corpus (Melamed 1998), a word-aligned French-English bitext composed of 250 Bible verses (non-continuous). It contains 7510 English word tokens and 8191 French word tokens. The alignment links that associate words across two sides of the bitext are quite accurate. The total number of links is 10097.

I classified all 967 related word pairs in the corresponding sentences of the Blinker corpus as cognates (10%), loanwords (47%), and proper names (43%).[3] The cognates are words that go back all the way to Proto-Indo-European. Apart from numerals, these include words which have changed dramatically over the five thousand years, such as *coeur / heart* and *oeil / eye*.[4]

The number of pairs that are related and at the same time linked (aligned) in the bitext is 386 (40%). The remaining 60% of related pairs are not explicitly linked because they do not correspond to each other in the translated sentences, but the majority of them are mutual translations in the dictionary sense. For example, sentence #227 contains the word *division* three times on both sides of the bitext, inducing nine cross-lingual pairs, but only three of them are actually linked as corresponding translations.

If we disregard function words, all 174 instances of the homographs are related words. The majority of such pairs are names, but there are also many common words, such as *province* and *temple*. A few short function words, such as *a* and *on* are identical false friends, but these can be filtered by employing relatively small lists of function words. The closest an unrelated pair of content words comes to identity is French *cent* 'hundred' and English *sent*.[5]

We can try to binarize the subjective and continuous notion of form similarity by thresholding the LCSR measure st 0.66. In Blinker, 660 pairs exceed that threshold, out of which 631 (96%) are related. The set of 29 false friends includes accidental similarities across different parts of speech (*temple / remplie* 'full'), names (*Izharites / Amramites*), and shared affixes (*desolations / dévastations*).

In comparison, 92% of pairs in an independent list of 326 French-English false friends (Inkpen, Frunza, and Kondrak 2005) exceed the threshold of 0.66, which confirms that this thresholding approach is effective at identifying a great majority of words that are perceived as similar.

5. Discussion

The results in section 4.2 suggest that unrelated translations exhibit greater similarity than random bilingual pairs, which seems to contradict the Saussurean principle of the arbitrariness of the linguistic sign. In order to confirm this observation, I performed another experiment using eight lists of 200 basic words in phonetic notation compiled by (Kessler 2001), which henceforth I refer to as *Kessler's set*. The lists represent Albanian, English, French, German, Latin, Hawaiian, Navajo, and Turkish. All cognates and borrowings are carefully annotated in the data. In Kessler's set, the average LCSR similarity value for 5029 unrelated translations is 0.142, whereas the corresponding value for over one million of pairs of words belonging to different languages is 0.129.

Another, independent confirmation of the phenomenon is provided by Wichmann et al. (2010). After analyzing the lists of 40 basic words across over ten thousand pairs of unrelated language families from different hemispheres, the authors found that the words for the same concept are slightly more similar to each other than are the words for different concepts. They attribute the difference to sound symbolism, which is further investigated in Wichmann, Holman and Brown (2010).

Here, I propose a different explanation of the phenomenon. My intention is not to deny the influence of sound symbolism, which is clearly a factor, but to suggest another reason for the observed divergence. I posit the correlation between the following word characteristics: translatability, frequency, length, and similarity. Below, I consider these in order.

The key observation is that mutual translations are on average closer in terms of their length than random words. Let us define the *length ratio* of two words as the length of the shorter word divided by the length of the longer word. The length ratio is always a value between 0 and 1. In the set of 1000 French-English word pairs described in section 4.2, the average length ratio of unrelated translations is 0.758, as opposed to the average length ratio of 0.704 of random pairs of French-English words. Similarly, in Kessler's set, the corresponding values are 0.717 and 0.692.

In general, pairs of words with smaller average length difference also exhibit higher average LCSR similarity value. The mathematical explanation is that the length of the shorter word is the upper bound for the length of the longest common subsequence, which constitutes the numerator in the LCSR formula. Therefore, the greater the difference in length between the two words, the lower is the upper bound of the LCSR value. This agrees with the intuition that the similarity of length contributes to the overall similarity of words.

What could be the underlying reason of the fact that translations tend to differ less in length than non-translations? One possibility is that words that are mutual translations have similar frequency. Intuitively, translations refer to the same semantic concept, which tends to be expressed with similar frequency across languages. In order to confirm this intuition, I collected the frequencies of all words in the French-English set described in section 4.2. The English word frequencies were taken from the CELEX database (Bayen et al. 1996), while the French frequencies were computed from *Le Monde Diplomatique* text corpus. The total number of word tokens in either resource are around 15 million. It turns out that the translation pairs in our dictionary data set exhibit a positive correlation of 0.573 with respect to the negative logarithm of their frequencies. On the other hand, the correlation for word pairs that are not mutual translations is close to zero. These numbers strongly support the observation that there is a connection between translatability and frequency.

Finally, it is well known that there is a connection between word frequency and length (Zipf 1936). For example, Piantadosi et al. (2011) calculate the correlation values between 0.1 and 0.4 for each of eleven European languages including both French and English. This completes the chain of reasoning that provides an explanation for the phenomenon which has been observed in the experiments; namely, that one reason of the greater similarity of translations is their similar frequency, which in turn is reflected in their similar length. This is a hypothesis that can be tested in the future on sets containing more languages and more concepts.

6. Conclusion

In this presentation, I have provided a theoretical justification and some empirical evidence for the observation that form similarity is positively correlated with translational equivalence. Data from a bilingual dictionary and an aligned bilingual corpus show that translation pairs tend to be similar, and that similar pairs tend to be translations. An interesting consequence of this bias is that electronic dictionaries and automatically generated bitext alignment links can be used for the purpose of evaluating word similarity measures (Kondrak 2005), and that cognate detection can improve machine translation quality (Kondrak 2003). In addition, I proposed a novel explanation of the word similarity divergence between mutual translations and random pairs of words. These are just a few examples of how computational linguists, lexicographers, and statistical language processing engineers can benefit from paying attention to each other's research.

Notes

1. I am grateful to Lars Borin and Anju Saxena for their suggestion to investigate the observation that unrelated translations exhibit greater similarity than random word pairs. Comments made by John Nerbonne and Søren Wichmann during the 2011 workshop in Gothenburg were very helpful as well. This research was supported by the Natural Sciences and Engineering Research Council of Canada.
2. Unrelated homograph translations do exist, but those that can't be attributed to child language (e.g. *mama* 'mother') or onomatopoeia (e.g. *miau* 'meow') are extremely rare. One example is the word *bad*, which has the same meaning in English and Persian, but apparently no common origin.
3. The lists of pairs are available on request.
4. A list of over a hundred French-English cognate pairs that are still mutual translations is available at http://www.cs.ualberta.ca/~kondrak.
5. LeBlanc and Seguin (1987) identified 23,160 French-English cognate pairs, including 6,447 homographs, across two general-purpose dictionaries, each containing around 70,000 words.

References

Baayen, Harald, Richard Piepenbrock, and Leon Gulikers
   1996   *The CELEX2 lexical database.*
Inkpen, Diana, Oana Frunza, and Grzegorz Kondrak
   2005   Automatic Identification of Cognates and False Friends in French and English. *Proceedings of the International Conference on Recent Advances in Natural Language Processing,* 251–257.
Kessler, Brett
   2001   *The Significance of Word Lists.* Stanford: CSLI Publications.

Kondrak, Grzegorz
 2003 Cognates can improve statistical translation models. *Proceedings of Human Language Technology Conference of the North American Chapter of the Association for Computational Linguistics*, 46–48.

Kondrak, Grzegorz
 2005 Cognates and word alignment in bitexts. *Proceedings of the Tenth Machine Translation Summit*, 305–312.

LeBlanc, Raymond and Robert Seguin
 1987 Homographes et parographes dans l'enseignement de la langue seconde. *8th AILA World Congress*.

Melamed, Dan
 1998 Manual annotation of translational equivalence: The Blinker Project. IRCS #98-07. University of Pennsylvania.

Piantadosi, Steven T., Harry Tily, and Edward Gibson
 2011 Word lengths are optimized for efficient communication. *Proceeding of the National Academy of Sciences of the USA* 108 (9): 3825–3826.

Wichmann, Søren, Eric W. Holman, and Cecil H. Brown
 2010 Sound symbolism in basic vocabulary. *Entropy* 12 (4): 844–858.

Wichmann, Søren, Eric W. Holman, André Müller, Viveka Velupillai, Johann-Mattis List, Oleg Belyaev, Matthias Urban, and Dik Bakker
 2010 Glottochronology as a heuristic for genealogical language Relationships. *Journal of Quantitative Linguistics* 17 (4): 303–316.

Zipf, George
 1936 *The Psychobiology of Language*. London: Routledge.

Comparing linguistic systems of categorisation

William B. McGregor

1. Introduction

A variety of more or less good quantitative measures for genetic distances between languages have been developed over the past few decades or so.[1] This paper addresses the question of whether it is possible to devise sensible measures of the distances between constructions. Is it possible, that is, to devise measures that provide useful information about grammatical constructions in a set of languages, such as how typologically similar they are, and whether they might be diachronically related? And if so, how do these measures work, and why?

In this paper I address these questions in relation to a verbal construction widespread in the languages of northern Australia. I refer to the *compound verb construction* (CVC),[2] a structure that sometimes goes under the rubric *complex predicate* (e.g. Amberber et al. 2010). This construction is a binomial expression prototypically involving the pairing of an *uninflecting verb* (UV) – often referred to as a *coverb* or *preverb* – and an *inflecting verb* (IV) which takes verbal inflections for categories such as tense, mood, aspect, as well as (in some languages) person and number information concerning the subject and object of the clause.

The main point of the paper is that we can get a handle on the question of measuring constructional distance through examination of habitual collocations of UVs and IVs in the various languages. These collocations are in essence lexical, and more or less non-predictable (although they are typically motivated). They – or at least some of them – tend to show a fairly high degree of resilience over time, evidently because of their basis in habitual usage; thus the collocational patterns retain key diachronic information. The genetic signal is more stable in these patterns than it is in structural properties of the CVC, which like typological features generally, are more susceptible to change, and provide less reliable diachronic signals.

The paper is organised as follows. In §2 I provide some necessary background to the question of comparison of CVCs in Australian languages by briefly overviewing its structure and the ways this has been approached and described in the literature. Following this, in §3, I address the main concern of the paper, quantitative methods for comparing constructions, for measuring the distance between constructions across languages. The paper winds up in §4 with a summary and conclusions.

2. CVCs in northern Australian languages

2.1. Basic properties of CVCs

As mentioned in §1, CVCs typically involve the collocation of a UV and an IV. The UV provides the major component of lexical meaning while the IV discharges more grammatical functions and serves as the locus for the representation of grammatical categories. One qualification that must be mentioned from the outset is that most languages with CVCs permit lexemes from other parts of speech, in particular nominals and adverbials, to occur in the position usually occupied by a UV. In this paper I use the term UV somewhat loosely to refer to any lexeme that occurs in this position in a CVC, regardless of its part of speech membership.

In CVCs in the majority of languages the UV immediately precedes the IV, as in the Nyulnyul example (1), where *kurd* 'hide' is the UV and -J ~ -D 'say' is the IV. There are just a few exceptional languages in which the normal order is for the UV to follow the IV (some Daly River languages such as Ngan'gityemerri – Reid 2003, 2011: 102–103), and in some languages both orders are permissible, though one is usually significantly more frequent than the other. UVs usually don't occur freely without an IV, although in certain restricted environments they sometimes do – e.g. in non-finite clauses or imperatives. Regardless of the number of IVs in the language, it is typically the case that up to a score of them may collocate with UVs, although usually only half of this number does so productively. The sizes of the collocation sets of UVs within a language typically vary from a few to a few hundred.[3]

(1) Nyulnyul
   bin wamb yiil jin   kurd i-n-d-in
   this man dog 3MIN.OBL hide 3NOM-CM-say-PRS
   'This man's dog is hiding.'

Most languages permit IVs to occur alone, i.e. without a UV, in what I refer to as the simple verb construction (SVC), which consists of just an inflected form of an IV, as shown by example (2). The number of IVs a language has varies quite considerably, from around ten to a few hundred.

So also does the number of IVs that can occur in SVCs: in Nyulnyulan languages, all usually do – and they form largish classes of eighty or so to almost three hundred members; by contrast, in Bunuba just one, -MA 'say, do' can occur in a SVC – all others are restricted to occurrence in CVCs.[4]

(2) Nyulnyul
    irr-in   *i-li-rr-j-jan*
    3AUG.CRD-ERG   3NOM-IRR-AUG-say-1MIN.OBL
    'They might say to me.' or 'They might tell me.'

The compound verb construction serves as locus for a system of verb – and correspondingly event – classification in which the IV categorises the UV (Schultze-Berndt 2000; McGregor 2002), assigning it to one of a set of categories that normally number around a dozen or so. These categories are not disjoint, and in the typical northern Australian language with such a system of verb classification each UV usually collocates with between one and seven IVs. The collocations contrast semantically, and examination of the entire set of contrasts reveals something about the semantic basis of the verb classification system.

2.2. Comparisons of CVCs in northern Australian languages

As already mentioned, the verb classifying CVC is spread over a wide geographical area in northern Australia – see figure 1 – and over many lineages, including: Nyulnyulan, Worrorran, Bunuban, Jarrakan, Daly River families, and Pama-Nyungan. On the face of it, it looks like a good case could be made for areal diffusion of the system, and in this connection a number of Australianists have addressed the question of comparability of the constructions. Almost without exception the comparisons have been based exclusively on formal characteristics,[5] and classifying subtypes of CVCs are not rigorously separated from other types CVC. This is the case, for instance, in Dixon (2002: 186–196); Bowern (2008), amongst many others.

Dixon (2002: 187–197) uses the following fairly standard and unexceptional set of purely formal characteristics in his comparison of the verbal constructions of Australian languages: number of IVs; number of UVs; occurrence dependence/independence of IVs and UVs; degree of fusion of prefixes with IVs and/or CVCs; fusion of UV and IV (i.e. number of phonological and grammatical words they comprise); and relative token frequency of CVCs vs. SVCs. These features he employs in a broad typology of verbal

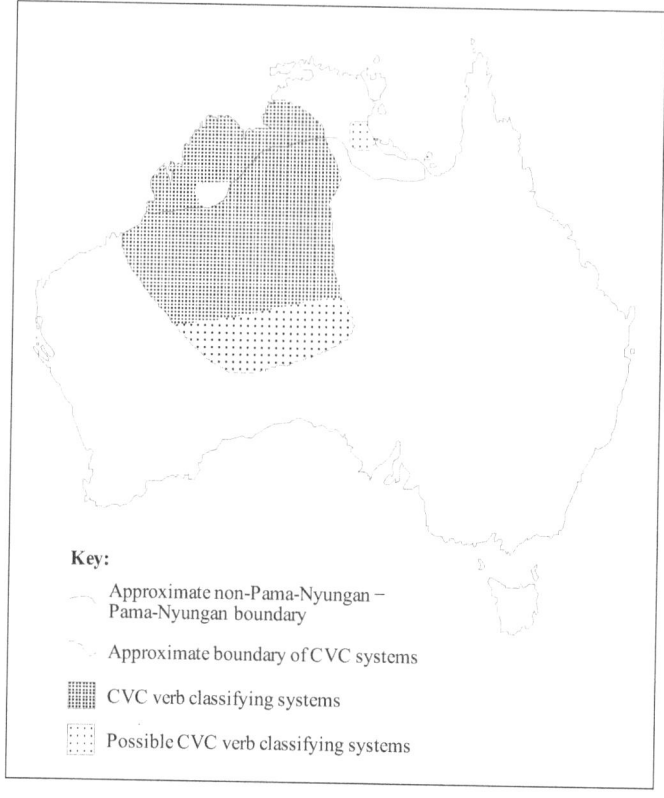

Figure 1. Approximate distribution of CVC verb classifying systems in Australia (source McGregor 2002: 26)

constructions in Australian Aboriginal languages. According to this scheme there are seven distinct types of verbal construction that are, he avers, areally spread across the continent and enter into cycles of grammaticalisation (Dixon 2002: 198–200).

Among the numerous problems with Dixon's approach and resulting typology, two are particularly pertinent to the present paper.

First, no motivation is provided for the types identified: that is to say, the types are identified on purely etic grounds according to a set of features that may or may not be emically significant; and no attempt is made to demonstrate emic status. The result is not a typology of constructions understood as linguistic signs (e.g. Goldberg 1995; McGregor 1997), but merely of expression types. Moreover, each of Dixon's types is divided into a range of subtypes that are again not shown to be anything more than etic.

These subtypes Dixon identifies systematically with his areal subgroups for the Australian continent. Unfortunately, the reality is not nearly so neat, and careful examination reveals that the compound verb systems in some of the languages in his areal subgroups fall well outside of the subtypes he associates with those groups; in some instances they even fall outside of the higher order types he identifies.

Second, similarities in verbal construction types arise only, in the scheme of Dixon (2002), via diffusion and independent grammaticalisation on the basis of diffused constructions. There is no place for genetic retention of constructions or parts of constructions (except within single languages).

To be sure, I concur with Dixon (2002) that the Australian continent represents one single very large verbal construction sprachbund (see e.g. McGregor 2002, forthcoming-a). However, there is also reason to believe that a certain amount of temporal layering can be teased out, permitting a distinction to be drawn not just in the lexicon of the languages between cognates and borrowings, but also in constructions between retentions from a proto-language and subsequent borrowings and innovations.

Furthermore, I also agree that there are different types of verbal construction in Australian languages, although these need to be established on the evidence of formal and semantic correlations (as per e.g. construction grammar and semiotic grammar). For instance, it is evident that CVCs and SVCs are distinct constructionally from one another, both within and across languages. Moreover, CVCs themselves to not represent a single construction type; as observed in McGregor (2002: 301–307) (see also Bowern 2008), a small number of different constructions share expression in forms involving the pairing of UVs and IVs. A proper subset of CVCs is the verb classifying construction. The present paper accordingly restricts attention to that particular category of constructions, ensuring that that which is compared and quantified is really comparable (and not, for example, apples and fingernails).

I would argue that the formal features that Dixon and others – myself included (see next subsection) – have uses. In particular, they can be used intuitively to gain some conceptualisation of the ways in which CVCs are cross-linguistically similar or dissimilar, and indeed, how similar or dissimilar they might be. Thus, if we restrict attention to the verb classifying types of CVC, what emerges from comparison of formal features is not a partitioning of subtypes that forms an emic typology of CVCs, but rather a scale of gradation (see also next section), which might perhaps be refined into a distance measure.

McGregor (2002, forthcoming-b); McGregor and Rumsey (2009) suggest that it is possible to compare CVC systems of verb classification in ways that are revealing both diachronically in that they permit one to distinguish retentions from borrowings, and synchronically in that they reveal typological similarity and/or dissimilarity. Three primary dimensions are relevant to such comparisons: (a) formal properties of the CVC, such as discussed above; (b) system-level semantics, including the number of verbal categories distinguished, and their coded and inferred meanings; and (c) category membership in terms of the UV types that constitute them. These dimensions were examined largely qualitatively in McGregor (2002: 149–205); in this paper I attempt to show how some of them can be refined and construed as quantitative methods.

3. Measures of similarity and dissimilarity

The primary motivation for developing a means of system comparison in McGregor (2002) was to gain an understanding of the diversity across verb classification systems on the one hand, and to determine whether this correlated with areal and/or genetic diversity on the other. Subsequently, the problem – how can grammatical and/or lexical systems and constructions be compared and contrasted? – emerged as worthy of attention in and of itself. In this section I first briefly overview the main formal and semantic features employed in the comparisons; then I turn to discuss three type-level phenomena that lend themselves well to quantitative measures, and that show an interesting genetic signal.

3.1. Formal features

The following formal features are deployed in the broad comparison of classifying CVCs in northern Australian languages in McGregor (2002: 149–152):

- Status: how many phonological and/or grammatical words does the CVC comprise?
- Order: what is the normal order of UV and IV? Is it free or fixed, and if fixed which order do they come in?
- Types: do other types of verbal compound exist in the language?
- Number of categories: how many categories are distinguished in the language? That is, what is the number of IVs occurring in classifying CVCs?
- Number of IVs: what is the total number of IVs in the language?

- Frequency: how frequent are CVCs in the expression of lexical verbal meanings? What is the ratio of CVCs to SVCs according to dictionary count?
- Category overlap: how much overlap exists in the categories? That is, what fractions of UVs collocate with different IVs?

Figure 2 displays graphically the comparison amongst the languages according to these seven formal characteristics. There are evident differences between the intermediate points and endpoints for the features in this diagram in terms of the degree of apparent grammaticalisation. It is impossible to align each of the feature scales according to an increasing degree of grammaticalisation, and doing so for each feature separately would result in different orderings for the languages. On the other hand, there are some correlations amongst the features; they clearly do not vary independently. Thus, as observed in McGregor (2002: 151), no linear scale can do justice to the facts, and it is impossible invoke a simple measure of linear distance between CVCs in the languages on the basis of the distance measured on a single dimension. It is not, however, my purpose in this paper to propose or critique any measure of formal similarity.

Another observation that emerges from figure 2 is that, as already observed, contra Dixon (2002: 188–197), distinct types of CVCs do not fall out on the basis of formal features. The types he identifies clearly merge into one another, and are not distinct and separated from one another; moreover, there is not a perfect alignment between genetic lineages and formal features; at best the association is probabilistic. Observe, for instance, the clear differences among the features for Nyulnyulan languages. The inter-language differences amongst the CVCs are evidently scalar rather than discrete in nature, and – one guesses – correlate with degree of grammaticalisation for each feature separately.

Other formal features might be taken into account, such as for instance size of the UV class and its distinctiveness (i.e. how frequently lexemes of other parts of speech are permitted to collocate with IVs in CVCs). And in addition to comparison of numbers of IVs that may occur in CVCs one might take into account which IVs are employed.

3.2. Semantic features

Semantic features of CVCs are even more difficult to integrate in an enlightening way into a comparison of systems, and here I mention for completeness –

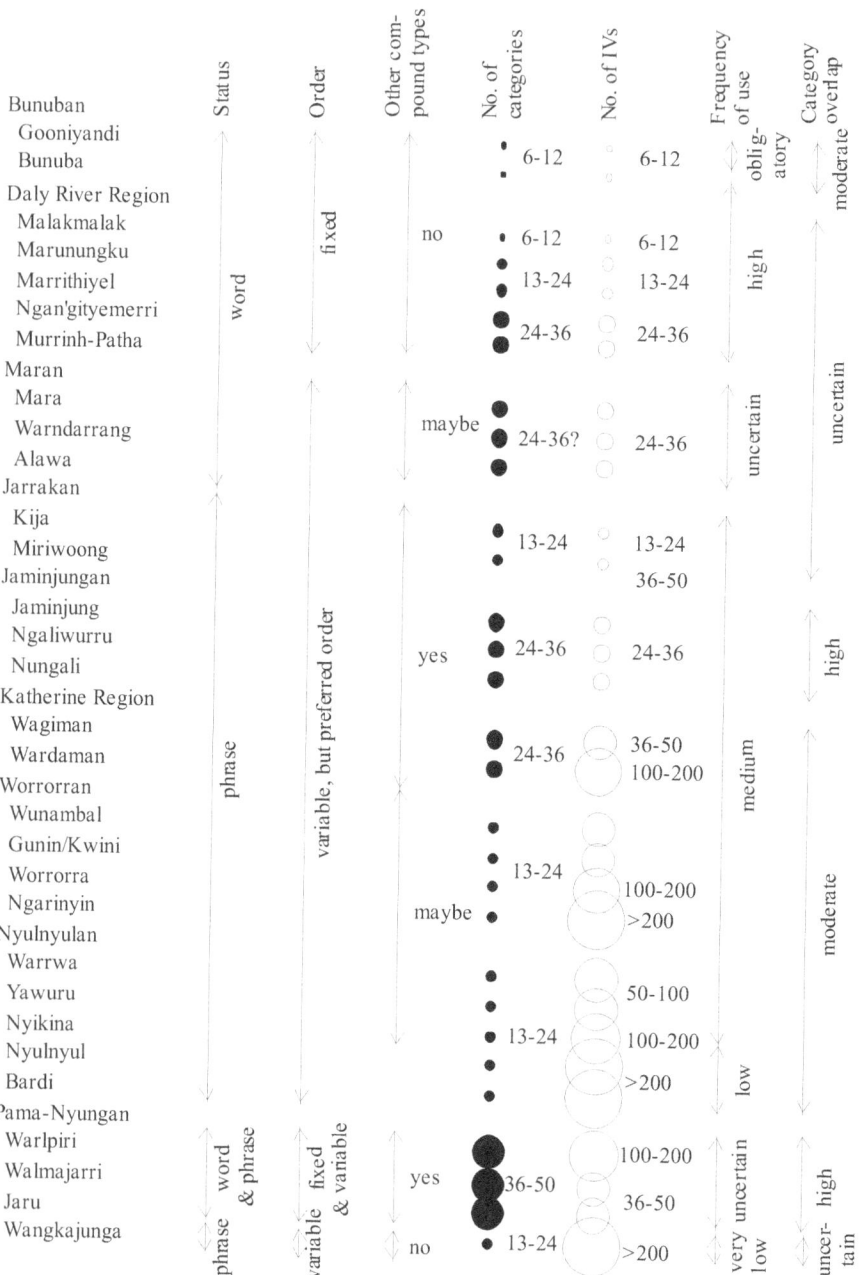

Figure 2. Cross-linguistic comparison of CVCs according to formal features (McGregor 2002: 150)

and to provide the reader with a clearer idea of the nature of the classification systems – a few very broad comparative observations.

Just as gender and animacy are semantic dimensions habitually deployed in nominal classification systems, systems of verb classification habitually deploy three recurrent general features (see McGregor 2002: 29–34):

- Aktionsart – typically the telicity contrast of telic vs. atelic; this feature is relevant to the event-type itself specified by the CVC, and not to the situation type denoted by the clause (thus *go* would be classified as telic, regardless of whether or not it occurs in a telic clause with a point of achievement, as in *she went to the shop*);
- Valency – number of inherent participants or arguments associated with a verb; again this is a lexical and/or constructional feature that correlates imperfectly with clausal transitivity;
- Vectorial configuration – by which I refer to an abstract configuration of action vectors that are relevant to a schematic representation of the semantics of the category. For instance, figure 3 depicts the vectorial configuration for the category marked by the IV -R 'poke' in Nyulnyul: events assigned to this category share one of the depicted actional configurations, (a)–(c): effectively, there is point contact between an agent and something else in the event.

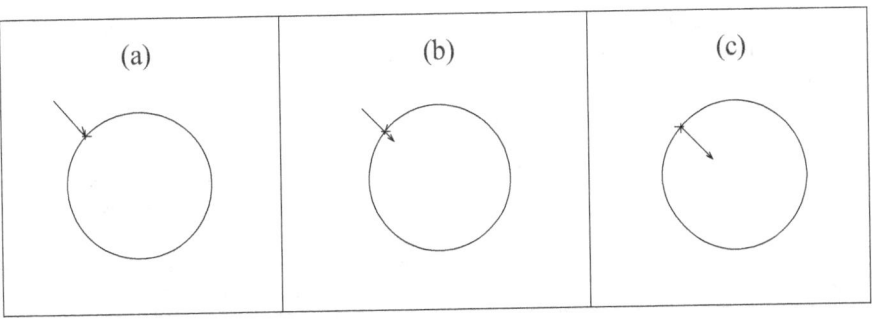

Figure 3. Vectorial configuration for -R 'poke' category in Nyulnyul (source: McGregor 2012: 479)

To give some idea of the extent of semantic similarities and dissimilarities found among the languages, consider the data presented in table 1, which shows characterisations of the semantics of the major verbal categories in three languages, two Nyulnyulan (Nyulnyul and Warrwa) and one Bunuban (Gooniyandi), based on information contained in McGregor (1990, 2002,

2012). In this tabulation categories in the three languages that appear in the same row correspond most closely semantically. There is one notable exception, namely the second last row, on which the neutral reflexive/reciprocal category of Nyulnyul and Warrwa are associated with the accomplishment reflexive/reciprocal category of Gooniyandi. In reality, of course, the Nyulnyul and Warrwa categories correspond to both reflexive/reciprocal categories of Gooniyandi; this situation is not, however, easy to display on a two dimensional table.

Table 1. Semantics of major verbal categories in three Kimberley languages

Nyulnyul	**Warrwa**	**Gooniyandi**
Atelic		*Extendible*
-N 'be' [stative]	-NI ~ -WANI 'be' [stative]	+I 'be' [stative; motion; activity progresses over time]
-JID 'go' [activity progresses over time]	-ARNDA 'go' [activity progresses over time]	
-KAL 'wander' [action not uniquely directed towards a specific goal]		
-K 'carry' [move something to a new location by constantly applied force]	-KA 'carry' [move something to a new location by constantly applied force]	+A 'carry' [continued activity that extends to some entity]
		+ARNI$_2$ 'carry-self' [reflexive/reciprocal action]
Telic		*Accomplishment*
-R 'poke' [action taking place in a straight line, impacting on something at a point]		+ARNI$_1$ 'emerge' [motion with contact at a point]
	-NKA 'hit' [impact violently on something]	+BINI 'hit' [action on a straight line connecting with something]

Nyulnyul	Warrwa	Gooniyandi
Telic		*Accomplishment*
-W 'give' [action directed outwards from actor, making contact with something]	-WA ~ -ø 'give' [action directed outwards from actor, making contact with something]	
-M 'put' [induce something to enter new state, condition, or location]	-MA 'put' [induce something to enter new state, condition, or location]	
-NY 'get' [acquire or achieve an entity or condition by active means]	-ANDI 'get' [acquire or achieve an entity or condition by active means]	+DI 'catch' [establish contact with something]
	-NGARA 'become' [inchoative]	+BINDI 'become, get' [inchoative]
		+ANI 'fall' [happening befalling something; inchoative]
	± Telic	+ARRI 'throw' [placement of object into state or trajectory]
		+BIRLI 'consume' [use up completely]
-BARNJ 'exchange' [reflexive/reciprocal action]	-BANYJI 'exchange' [reflexive/reciprocal action]	+MARNI 'say-self' [reflexive/reciprocal action]
-J 'say, do' [dynamic activity]	-JI 'say, do' [dynamic activity]	+MI 'say, do' [effective action]

Perusal of the table reveals that the Nyulnyul and Warrwa systems share more with one another semantically than either does with the Gooniyandi system. In most cases the specifications for corresponding categories in Nyulnyul and Warrwa are either identical or almost identical, whereas many of the Gooniyandi categories differ fairly substantially. For instance, the specifications of the 'carry' category in the two Nyulnyulan languages are virtually identical, but very different to the specification of the corresponding category in Gooniyandi, which is a much more generic one. And in the final row one sees that the category marked by the 'say, do' verb is more generic in the two Nyulnyulan languages than in Gooniyandi, where the action must be more than merely dynamic – it must be telic (i.e. an accomplishment).

One further notable feature revealed by table 1 is that Nyulnyul and Warrwa categories show neutralisation of Aktionsart (the telicity contrast) in two categories, whereas Gooniyandi shows no neutralisation on this dimension.

Again, it is not a concern of this paper to propose measures of the semantic distances amongst the corresponding categories, or indeed the overall semantic distances between the three verbal categorising systems. The above information is intended merely to give an idea of the semantic basis for the typical verb classification system of a northern Australian language. Interestingly, these features appear to be relevant more generally to verb classification systems in the world's languages (e.g. McGregor 2002: 289), and may well represent the verbal counterparts of features such as gender and animacy that are cross-linguistically generally relevant to systems of nominal categorisation.

3.3. Lexical type features

We now turn to the third dimension of comparison, the level of lexical types, where our concern is not so much the general formal and semantic features, but more the peculiarities of the CVCs in terms of the lexical items they involve. In other words, we turn focus away from the recurrent generic properties that characterise the CVC as a grammatical construction towards the more individual and less general ones that constitute the CVC as an emergent phenomenon involving two sets of lexical items, UVs and IVs. It seems reasonable to presume that these pairings will give us a handle on greater time depth than the grammatical properties of the construction itself, granted the reasonable hypothesis that the collocational pairings predate the rise of the CVC as a verb classifying construction.

Relevant dimensions of such a comparison are:

- Relative size of the categories defined by the IVs – i.e. the size of the collocating UV sets for each corresponding IV;
- Comparability of the categories – the degree of likeness and/or dissimilarity of the collocating UV sets; and

Comparing linguistic systems of categorisation 399

– Shared versus language particular UV-IV collocations

In the following subsections we take each of these dimensions in turn, and suggest some possible measures of their degrees of similarity and dissimilarity.

3.3.1. Relative category size

Perhaps the most obvious and crudest measure of similarity is the relative sizes of corresponding categories – that is, how productive each is relative to the corresponding category in the other language. Put in another way, this concerns the differential relative numbers of UVs that collocate with corresponding IVs, the proportion of the entire set of UV-IV collocates that involve each of the IVs.

Two remarks are in order before we proceed with the comparison. First, our concern must be with relative rather than absolute numbers since it is necessary to control for the absolute number of UVs attested in each language, which numbers differ quite markedly. Second, to make a sensible cross-linguistic comparison we need to not just compare relative category sizes in our languages, but also to do this in relation to categories that correspond across the languages. Clearly two languages could show very similar category divisions while the categories that are comparable in terms of their relative sizes might not correspond in any other way. For instance, to return to Nyulnyul and Gooniyandi, it could be that the categories carved up the UV space in comparable ways numerically, but that the matching categories do not correspond to the matching categories as set out in table 1. In such circumstances we would clearly not want a similarity measure to show close proximity of the CVC systems. The category correspondences we use will of course be according to the semantics of the categories, as per table 1, and not in terms of (presumed) cognacy or phonological similarity of the marking IVs.

Table 2 below shows the relative sizes of corresponding collocate sets in four languages, three Nyulnyulan (Bardi, Nyulnyul, Warrwa) and one Bunuban (Gooniyandi).

Table 2. Comparison of relative sizes of corresponding categories in four Kimberley languages

Bardi		Nyulnyul		Warrwa		Gooniyandi	
-JOO 'say, do'	31%	-J 'say, do'	33%	-JI 'say, do'	30%	-MI 'say, do'	13%
-(I)NYA 'pick up'	10%	-NY 'get, catch'	13%	-ANDI 'get, fetch'	5%	-DI 'catch'	9%
-MA 'put'	20%	-M 'put'	13%	-MA 'put'	11%		
ø ~ -WA 'give'	9%	-W 'give'	11%	-ø ~ -WA 'give'	8%		
-KA 'carry'	4%	-K 'carry'	6%	-KA 'carry'	3%	-A 'carry'	27%
-JIIDI 'go'	4%	-JID 'go'	4%	-ARNDA 'go'	8%		
-BANJI 'exchange'	1%	-BARNJ 'exchange'	4%	-BANYJI 'exchange'	6%	-ARNI$_2$ 'carry self'	3%
						-MARNI 'say to self'	2%
-NI 'sit, be'	2%	-N 'be'	3%	-NI ~ -NGA 'be'	12%	-I 'be'	17%
-KAL 'wander'	3%	-KAL 'wander'	2%				
-BOO 'poke'	2%	-R 'poke'	0.5%			-ARNI$_1$ 'emerge'	2%
-BI 'hit'	1%			-NKA 'hit'	2%	-BINI 'hit'	7%
				-NGARA 'become'	6%	-BINDI ' become'	6%
						-ANI 'fall'	9%
						-ARRI 'throw'	5%
						-BIRLI 'consume'	0.4%

The distributional patterns are brought out more clearly in the bar graph display of figure 4, and the line-graph display of figure 5, both of which are organised according to decreasing relative category size in Bardi. (Corresponding categories are glossed according to their most common senses, not according to the Bardi sense.) These displays reveal quite clearly that the categories in each language overall follow a Zipfian distribution. Furthermore, this distribution is quite comparable across the three Nyulnyulan languages, which, as shown by figure 5, follow curves that are overall quite similar, but differ significantly from the Gooniyandi curve. Indeed, the curves for Bardi and Nyulnyul are barely distinguishable over most of their extent. The curve for Warrwa is somewhat different, though it is overall still quite close to the other two Nyulnyulan languages, particularly for the first five categories. It shows, however, some tendencies towards the curve for Gooniyandi. One guesses that this is a result of areal influence, the traditional region for Warrwa being located adjacent to that for Bunuba, an immediate western neighbour of Gooniyandi and its only known genetic relative, a language that has a CVC verb classifying system that is very close to that of Gooniyandi.

Based on the display of figure 5, it is suggested that a reasonable measure of the differences in relative category "sizes" in two languages is in terms of the sum of the distances between the points for each corresponding IV, i.e. each pair of IVs in a vertical line. Each individual distance is obviously the differences in percentages across each corresponding category. This should be the absolute value of the difference, rather than the signed value, since what is of interest is the variation, not which direction it goes in. Thus the distance measure would be:

(3) $$\sum_{k=0}^{n} |P_k - Q_k|$$

where P_k represents the percentage for category number k in one language (P), Q_k the percentage for the corresponding k'th category in the other language (Q), and k ranges across the total number of compared categories

With this measure we can compute the distance between each pair of languages, obtaining the results shown in table 3. This measure is in agreement with expectations from the previous graphs, and confirms that the Bardi and Nyulnyul systems are very similar, the Warrwa system somewhat different, and the Gooniyandi system more markedly different. Furthermore, this distance measure agrees well with the genetic picture: Bardi, Nyulnyul and Warrwa are members of the two branches of one lineage, while Gooniyandi is a member of a distinct lineage.

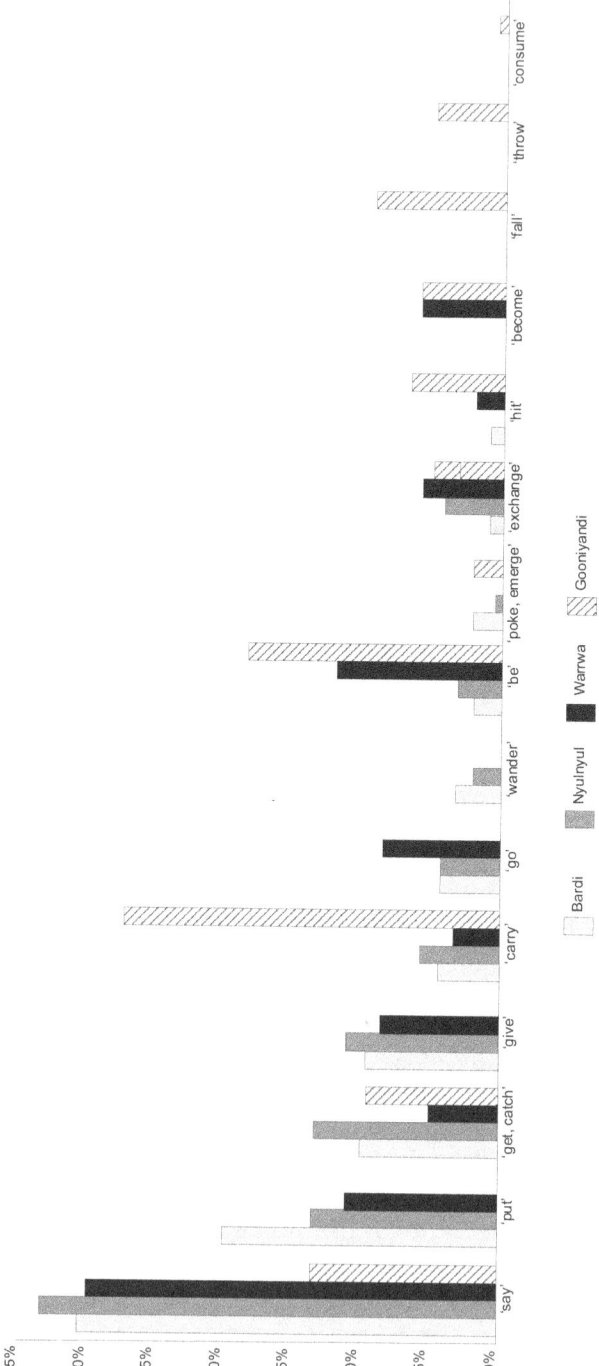

Figure 4. Bar graph of relative sizes of verbal categories in four languages

Comparing linguistic systems of categorisation 403

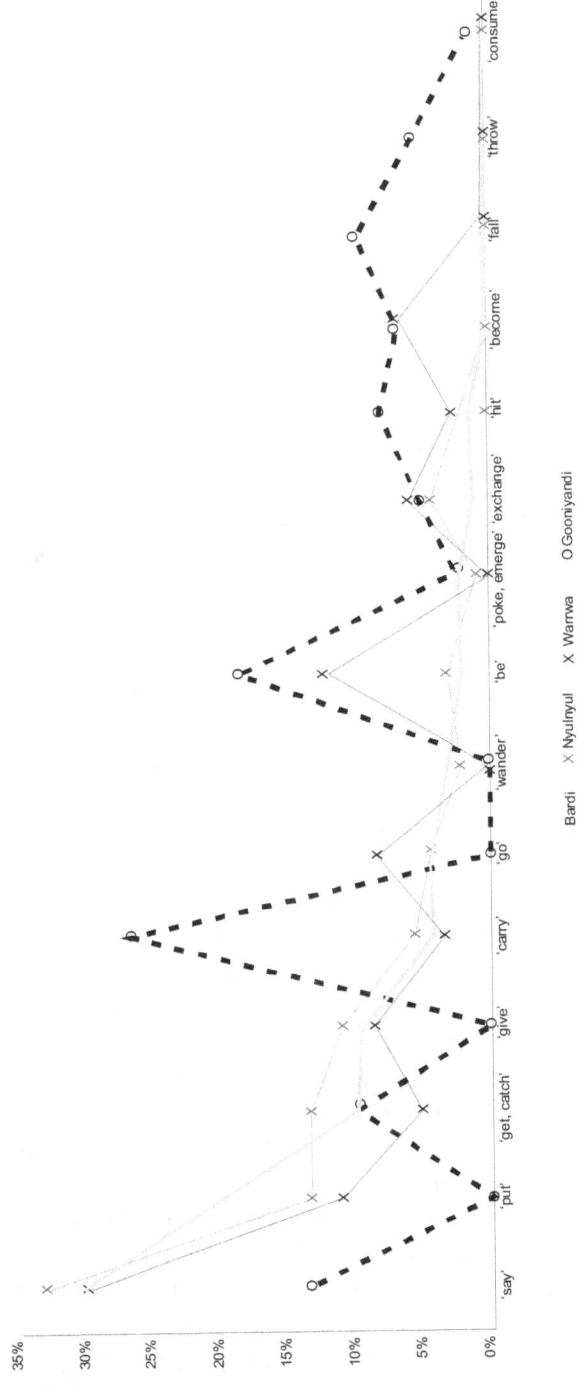

Figure 5. Line graph of relative sizes of verbal categories in four languages

Table 3. Relative distances between the constructions in the four languages in terms of their relative sizes

	Bardi	**Nyulnyul**	**Warrwa**
Nyulnyul	23.5		
Warrwa	44	43.5	
Gooniyandi	122.4	121	103.4

3.3.2. Shared UV-IV collocations

McGregor and Rumsey (2009) and McGregor (forthcoming-b) argue that it is possible to reconstruct certain characteristics of the verbal constructions of proto-Worrorran and proto-Nyulnyulan respectively through comparison of the collocations of UVs with IVs in the modern languages. Such a comparison, of course, must be founded on a viable means of identifying both UVs and IVs across the languages in the comparison sets. For IVs, it is reasonable to make the identification as per the previous section, that is, roughly according to the broad semantics of the category they mark. Similarly, for UVs the identification is also based on meaning, UVs in different languages being identified which represent the nearest synonyms. Both operations of identification are of course fraught with difficulties, and involve in many instances fairly arbitrary decisions given our present inadequate knowledge concerning the semantics and pragmatics of the lexical and other items involved in the construction.

Comparison of the collocation sets of the two verbal classes reveals that between languages within the two families there is considerably more agreement in terms of the IVs that habitually associate with UVs showing particular meanings than there is among languages of different lineages (see e.g. McGregor and Rumsey 2009: 66–67). Indeed, it seems plausible to reconstruct UV-IV pairings in the proto-language on the basis of repeated pairings in the modern languages. The case for considering pairings to be reflexes of proto-pairings is strongest in three circumstances (McGregor and Rumsey 2009; McGregor forthcoming-b). First, if the collocations are restricted to fairly basic meanings involving cognate UVs, the likelihood of borrowing of collocations is expected to be reduced.[6] Second, particular importance is assigned to pairings that are relatively unpredictable or unexpected and are not repeated in neighbouring families. For instance, the 'cut' and 'dig' UVs of the Worrorran languages Worrorra, Ngarinyin and Wunambal collocate with the 'hit' IV; these collocations are not, however, attested in nearby non-Worrorran languages (McGregor and Rumsey 2009: 57, 60–61). If borrowing was involved, it was almost certainly within Worrorran, and the fact that the UVs can be traced back to proto-Worrorran argues against this. The third circumstance is where the collocating IVs correspond (according to the above considerations) but are either not cognate or have an exceptional lexical meaning. For instance, reflexes of Proto-Nyulnyulan *jub 'cut' in Warrwa and Nyikina collocate with -ANDI 'get' but with the reflexes of non-cognate *-NYA 'get' in other Nyulnyulan languages, suggesting that the proto-language collocation was with the latter IV, and that when it was replaced by –ANDI 'get', the replacement was in all of its uses. On the other hand, some UVs that collocate with the Bardi IV –R 'kill lice' – e.g. reflexes of *kiny 'choke, strangle' – correspond to collocations involving -RA ~ -R 'poke, spear' in various other Nyulnyulan languages. The Bardi collocations are almost certainly reflexes of proto-collocations involving the 'poke, spear' IV that have not disappeared even though the IV (in its lexical use in SVCs) has undergone considerable lexical-semantic change. In short, the situation is not nearly as messy and irregular for Nyulnyulan languages as suggested in Bowern (2008).

As an alternative to this style of qualitative analysis of the collocational evidence, we could compare the collocations quantitatively to get a handle on the degree of similarity of the CVCs. Such a quantitative measure would involve comparison of each pair of languages in terms of the relative proportions of shared and different collocations of UVs with IVs for a set of basic verbal meanings.

To show how such a measure might be elaborated, I draw on the data employed in my reconstruction of proto-Nyulnyulan CVCs in McGregor (forthcoming-b). This involved a comparative examination of the complete attested sets of IVs in four Nyulnyulan languages that pair with each of 27 UVs reconstructable to proto-Nyulnyulan.[7] Table 4 provides a tabulation of a subset of the collocations, namely for six of the UVs. Each row of the table represents a distinct IV collocation, or (in a few cases) an IV that occurs in an SVC. Cells in a row that are coloured in grey indicate shared collocations.

Table 4. Collocations of cognate UVs with IVs in four Nyulnyulan languages

	Gloss	Warrwa	Yawuru	Nyulnyul	Bardi
A	'be alive'	nunjaya+WANI 'be'	nunja+NI 'be'	ninyj+N 'be'	
				~ +KAL 'wander'	ninyj+KAL 'wander'
		~ +NGARA 'become'			
				~ +J 'say'	
				~ +JARR-JARR 'stand'	
B	'angry'	bili+MA 'put'	bili+MA 'put'		
		~ +NGARA 'become'	~ +NGARA 'become'		
			~ -gaja+JU 'say'	bil+J 'say'	bili+JOO 'say'
		~ +NI 'be'			
			~ +NGARI 'leave'		
C	'blow'	buu+MA 'put'	buu+MA 'put'	buu+M 'put'	boo+MA 'put' ('blow away')
			~ +JU 'say'	~ +J 'say'	
		~ -kay+ WANI 'be'			
D	'call out'	kawu+JI 'say'	kaw+JU 'say'	kaw+J 'say'	kaw+JOO 'say'
			~ +MA 'put'	~ +M 'put'	
		~ +BANJI 'exchange'			
				[-LIRRMI]	

	Gloss	Warrwa	Yawuru	Nyulnyul	Bardi
E	'carry on shoulder'	*kurndu*+KA 'carry'	*kundu*+KA 'carry'	*kurnd*+K 'carry'	*kurnd*+K 'carry'
				~ +N 'be'	~ +N 'be'
				~ +NY 'get'	
		~ +JI 'say'			
					[-MOONG-GARA]
F	'choke'		*kiny*+NY 'get'	*kiny*+NY 'get'	*kiny*+NY 'get'
			~ +R 'poke'	~ +R 'poke'	~ +R 'kill lice'
		kiny+WA 'give'		~ +W 'give'	
			~ +JU 'say'		
			kinykiny+NYA 'get'		
				kinykiny+J 'say'	
				~ +BARNJ 'exchange'	
					[-MINGGI]

Beginning with set A, 'be alive', we have for Warrwa and Yawuru 1 shared UV-IV collocation, and 1 UV-IV collocation that is not shared; for Warrwa and Nyulnyul there is 1 shared and 4 different ones. If this procedure is carried out for each pair of languages and for all of the UV-IV collocations attested, we get the data shown in table 5, where the first figure in each cell indicates number of shared collocations, the second the number of different collocations, and the % figure indicates the percentage of shared collocates.

Table 5. Comparison of four Nyulnyulan languages in terms of shared and different UV-IV collocations

	Warrwa	**Yawuru**	**Nyulnyul**
Yawuru	24/52; 32%		
Nyulnyul	23/68; 25%	34/53; 39%	
Bardi	15/61; 19%	23/54; 30%	34/47; 42%

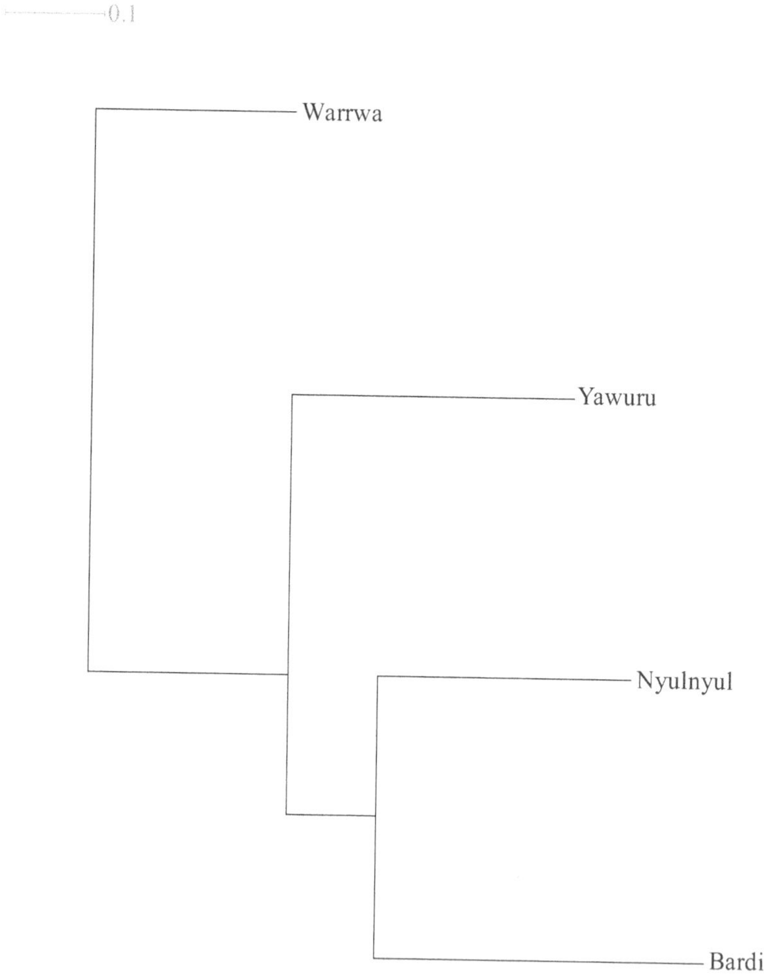

Figure 6. Phylogenetic tree representation of similarities amongst the UV-IV pairings in four Nyulnyulan languages

The percentage similarities between each pair of languages can be readily converted into a measure of the relative distance between the two languages in terms of UV-IV collocations, to which hierarchical cluster analysis techniques can be applied. Figure 6 shows the relationship in terms of a standard phylogenetic tree, created with SplitsTree4 (Huson and Bryant 2006).

To test the viability of this line of approach a little further, I performed the same statistical measures on the comparative tables of collocations set up in McGregor and Rumsey (2009: 57–63) for 9 Kimberley languages belonging to four distinct lineages, Nyulnyulan, Jarrakan, Bunuban, and Worrorran; to these I added one more Nyulnyulan languages, Nyulnyul. The collocation sets were not the same as those used for Nyulnyulan languages, since many of the reconstructed UVs for proto-Nyulnyulan are not represented in the available corpora for the other languages. Instead, we selected 10 basic verbal meanings and compared and contrasted their expression in each of the languages (McGregor and Rumsey 2009). The basic verbal meanings were:

'climb'
'cry, weep'
'cut'
'die'
'dig'
'eat'
'hear'
'see'
'sit'
'stand'

A table like table 4 was set up for these basic meanings in the 10 languages (abbreviations in the table: Ww – Warrwa; Nk – Nyikina; NN – Nyulnyul; Bd – Bardi; Mw – Miriwoong; Kj – Kija; Bb – Bunuba; Wr – Worrorra; Ng – Ngarinyin; Wl – Wunumbal), from which table 6 was constructed according to the model of table 5, showing the similarities and differences amongst the modes of expression of the above meanings in each pair of languages. A number of these basic meanings were expressed in some languages in the form of SVCs; these were excluded from the comparison, since we are concerned only with CVC expression.

Employing the same hierarchical cluster analysis algorithm as previously, we get the phylogenetic tree as shown in figure 7. Interestingly, collocational patterns in the four Nyulnyulan languages do not show a strong tendency to group together against the other languages. We return to this point below (§4).

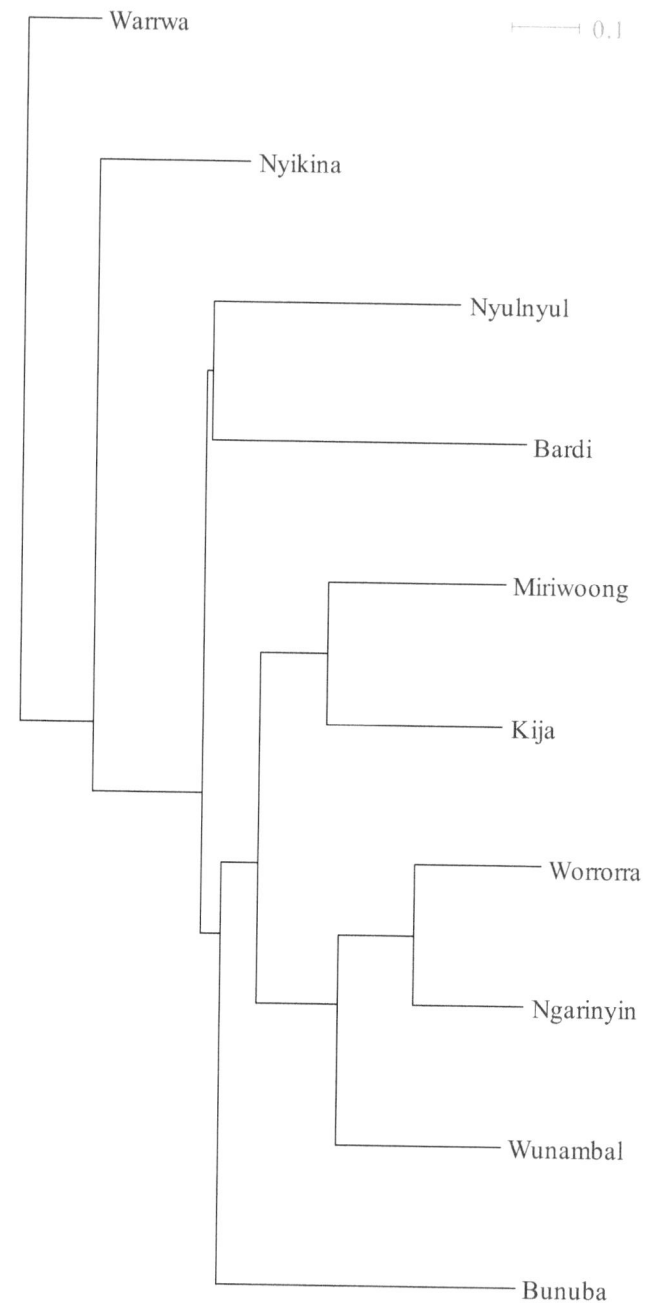

Figure 7. Phylogenetic tree representation of similarities amongst the UV-IV pairings in 10 Kimberley languages

Table 6. Comparison of the 10 languages in terms of shared and different UV-IV collocations

	Ww	Nk	NN	Bd	Mw	Kj	Bb	Wr	Ng
Nk	10/8; 56%								
NN	6/16; 27%	4/16; 20%							
Bd	3/20; 13%	4/18; 18%	3/15; 17%						
Mw	6/26; 19%	7/21; 25%	3/28; 11%	3/29; 9%					
Kj	7/27; 19%	7/23; 23%	6/27; 22%	2/34; 6%	11/12; 48%				
Bb	4/24; 14%	3/24; 11%	4/21; 19%	1/25; 4%	4/22; 15%	3/28; 10%			
Wr	4/28; 13%	3/25; 11%	3/26; 12%	1/30; 3%	6/23; 21%	5/27; 16%	4/16; 20%		
Ng	5/30; 14%	3/30; 9%	3/28; 11%	2/30; 6%	8/22; 27%	6/26; 19%	3/21; 13%	13/7; 65%	
Wl	7/26; 21%	5/27; 16%	4/29; 14%	2/25; 7%	7/19; 27%	10/20; 33%	3/22; 12%	8/12; 40%	13/11; 54%

3.3.3. Category comparability

A little less crude than measuring the relative sizes of corresponding categories across the languages is to examine how much the corresponding categories have in common with one another. That is, the question is how much overlap do matching categories show across the languages in terms of their extensions, the UVs that are assigned to them. In terms of collocational patterns the problem is to determine for each shared UV in a pair of languages which IVs in the respective languages collocate with each one separately, and then for the entire set of UVs in each language, how frequent the resulting IV associations are. Here again a shared UV is interpreted as a UV in one language that is roughly synonymous with a UV in the other language, so that the two UVs serve as approximate translation equivalents.

There are some very real difficulties with this line of attack on the problem of category comparison. A significant problem is that different UV-IV collocations code different meanings, so that a match between UV-IV pairs across two languages established in this way need not necessarily be significant. To clarify this problem, consider the UVs meaning 'eat' in Gooniyandi and Ngarinyin. The Gooniyandi verb is *ngab-* (verbs in this language correspond to UVs in the other languages), which collocates with +A 'carry', +I 'be', and +BIRLI 'consume'. The Ngarinyin UV *minjarl* 'eat' is attested with -YI 'be' and -WU 'hit'. Here for convenience I have glossed the verbal classifiers or IVs etymologically; these glosses should not be taken seriously. There are six IV correspondences between the two languages: each of the three Gooniyandi classifiers +A 'carry', +I 'be', and +BIRLI 'consume' correspond with both Ngarinyin IVs -YI 'be' and -WU 'hit'. But of these at least three – namely +A 'carry' with -YI 'be', +I 'be' with -WU 'hit', and +BIRLI 'consume' with -YI 'be' – are bogus correspondences: the members of each pair differ in transitivity, and do not represent genuine category overlaps. Clearly we should control not just for the UV but also for the UV-IV pairing, making sure that what we count as correspondence 'hits' are synonymous on both dimensions. Unfortunately, however, to do this would impose an extremely heavy burden on the coding process, and in order to perform it in a reasonable amount of time I have opted to ignore this problem, and simply compare and contrast collocations uncontrolled for UV-IV meaning. That is to say, I have controlled for just UV meanings, ignoring the meanings of the collocations. What this means in practice is that the sizes of the overlaps as measured in this section are likely to be somewhat larger than they are in reality.

McGregor (2002: 171–205) undertakes in an extensive comparison of the verb classification systems of Gooniyandi and Nyulnyul, including a comparison according to category extensions. An initial tack on this comparison was intended to provide an intuitive conceptualisation of the degree of similarity of the two systems. What was done was to set up a Venn diagram representing the categories in one language and overlay on it a Venn diagram for the categories in the other language. The result is shown in figure 8. The box itself is divided into smaller unfilled rectangles representing each of the Gooniyandi categories according to their relative size. For simplicity, the overlaps among the categories are not shown: the resulting figure would be too complicated to be conceptually useful.[8] Over this basic diagram has been overlain a number of more complex shapes each with a fill-pattern; these represent categories in Nyulnyul. The latter shapes overlap with the rectangles of the Gooniyandi Venn diagram, showing category overlaps. For instance, the Nyulnyul -J 'say, do' category overlaps with the Gooniyandi

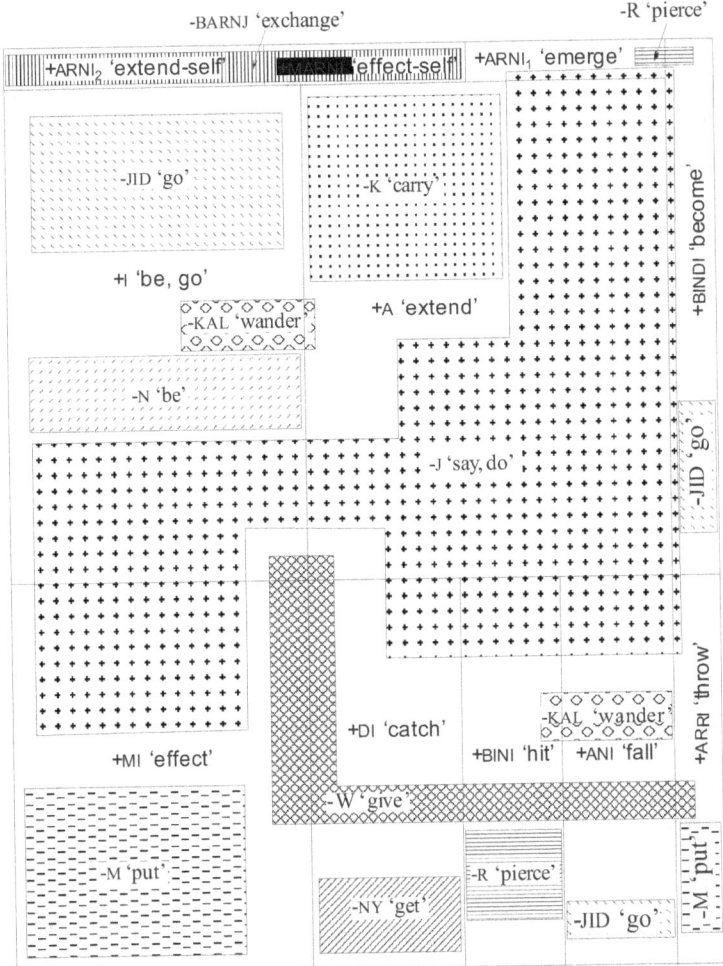

Figure 8. Schematic Venn diagram comparison of Gooniyandi and Nyulnyul verb categories

categories marked by the classifiers +A 'carry', +I 'be', +MI 'say, do', +DI 'catch', +BINI 'hit', +ANI 'fall', and +ARNI₁ 'emerge'. The relative sizes of the depicted overlaps approximately represent the sizes of the overlap of the corresponding categories. (In this figure, as usual, the Gooniyandi categories are glossed according to their gross approximate meanings, not etymologically.) Also represented in this depiction is the fact that the CVC in Nyulnyul covers a proper subset of verbal or event meanings, whereas the verbal construction in Gooniyandi covers the entirety of such meanings.

Figure 9 provides an alternative visual representation of the situation, using lines to link corresponding categories. Unbroken lines indicate correspondences that are manifested in a fair number of instances, while broken lines indicate rare correspondences instantiated by just a few pairs. Where only one or two correspondences are attested these are not shown.

This representation suggests a very crude measure of system similarity could be made on the basis of the ratio of attested IV correspondences to possible correspondences. The smaller the ratio, the more alike the systems would be expected to be. For instance, there are 110 possible pairings of IVs between Gooniyandi and Nyulnyul, since each of the 11 IVs of Gooniyandi can correspond to a maximum of 10 IVs in Nyulnyul. If every IV of Gooniyandi corresponded to just one IV of Nyulnyul we would obviously have a very good category correspondence, and a ratio of 11:110, i.e. 0.10. By contrast, if each category of Gooniyandi corresponded to each and every category of Nyulnyul we would have a ratio of 1.0, the maximum value. The actual value lies in between these two extremes: 30 pairings are attested, of which 20 (two thirds of them) are "major" – i.e. are instanced a fair number of times (i.e. more than three or four times). That is, 0.27 of possible pairings are attested, whilst 0.18 of possible pairings are "major".

These values might be taken as measures of the distance between the two languages in terms of the dimension of category overlap. However, there are at least three serious problems with this measure.

First, it does not factor in the overlaps of categories within the two languages: as already mentioned IVs collocate with between 1 and 7 UVs. These overlaps are generally not large, and cluster analysis shows that despite them, the categories themselves are relatively distinct from one another: they show no more than about 0.1 level of similarity (see McGregor 2002: 46–48).

Second, the measure does not take into account the correspondences of IVs already established on the basis of semantics. That is to say, the same distance will be assigned regardless of which particular IVs are associated with one another. Clearly this is not a good circumstance. If the associations of Gooniyandi +I 'be' and +A 'carry' in figure 9 were to be switched, ideally this should be reflected in a larger measured distance between the languages.

Third, the measure does not accord sufficient attention to the relative strengths of the correspondences. According to one measure, all of the correspondences are treated as equally weighted, while the other merely excludes correspondences that are weak and manifested only occasionally.

Let us begin with the third problem, as it is amenable to fairly obvious quantificational treatment. Clearly some sort of weighting needs to be assigned to each of the pairings. One way of doing this is as follows. Let us

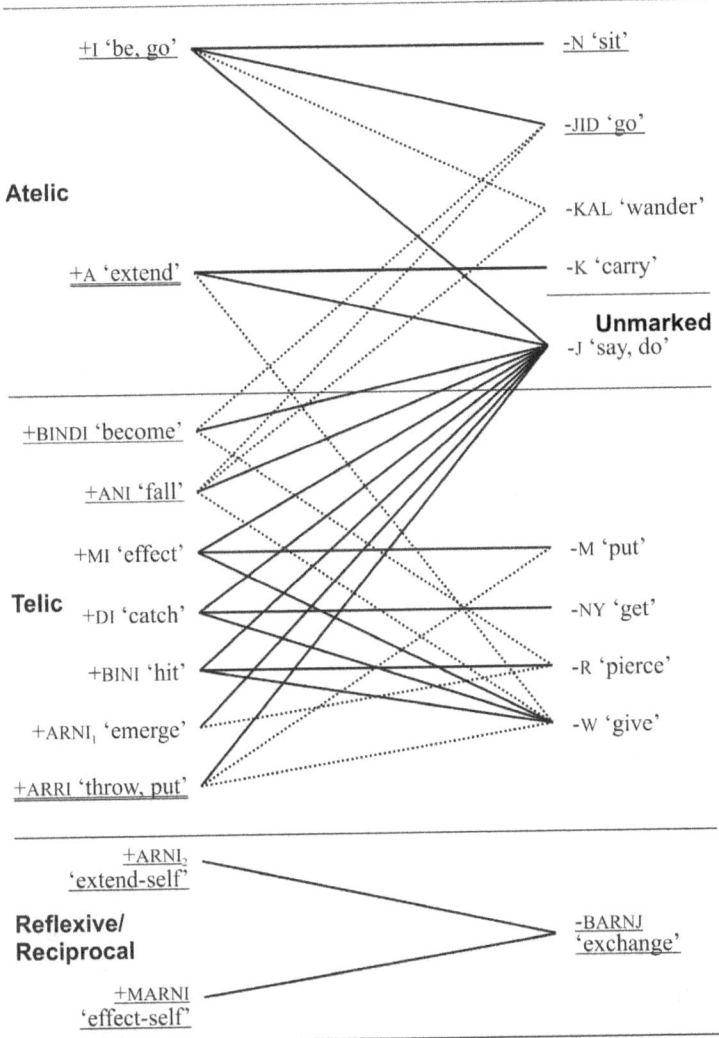

Figure 9. An alternative schematic comparison of Gooniyandi and Nyulnyul verbal categories

begin with the simpler problem of assigning a measure of distance between two categories in the languages. It seems reasonable to presume that in the random case we would have each of the 10 pairings of Nyulnyul IVs for Gooniyandi +I 'be' as equiprobable, i.e. a probability of 0.1 can be assigned to each. By contrast, at the opposite extreme is the perfect and fully deterministic case in which a single pairing exists for the Gooniyandi IV. Our problem then boils down to one of devising a measure that compares the attested correlations with the random situation on the one hand, and fully deterministic one on the other, and places the actual somewhere in between these extremes.

Unfortunately the actual collocational data on which the preceding two diagrams are based has been long lost.[9] So I instead exemplify the discussion with more recently compiled collocational pairings between two Nyulnyulan languages, Nyulnyul and Warrwa. This data set does not, unfortunately, cover all of the IVs. For illustrative purposes we consider just one category, that marked by -M (Nyulnyul) ~ -MA (Warrwa) 'put' [induce something to enter a new state, condition, or location]. Figure 10 shows the correspondences between these two IVs in each language and IVs that collocate with the same UVs. The percentages shown are the percentage of the union of the two corresponding collocate sets that are constituted by the intersection of the collocate sets – i.e. that which is common to them.

A reasonable measure of the difference between the two categories in Nyulnyul and Warrwa would be according to how these IV correlations (which correspond to category correlations) differ from a fully random distribution in which each correlation is equally likely. Following from the earlier comparison of §3.3.1, we would measure the distance of each attested value from the predicted value for each (IV_{NN}, IV_{Ww}) pair, where, obviously enough, the subscripts indicate IVs in the two languages. There are 100 distinct dyads (IV_{NN}, IV_{Ww}). If each dyad is equally likely then it has a probability of 0.01: that is, we would expect if there was a random distribution to find that each pairing shared 0.01 (1%) of the collocations. Such a circumstance would obviously coincide with maximum distance between the constructions: complete chaos in the correspondences between the categories.

Of the hundred dyads, 19 involve the corresponding 'put' IVs in either or both languages. The expected (random) and actual values of the percentage correspondences are shown in figure 11. In this graph the IV dyads are labelled for simplicity by number, according to the ordinal position of the IV in figure 10, numbering from top downwards.

Using the formula $\sum_{k=0}^{n} |P_k - Q_k|$ we can calculate the distance of the actual distribution from random distribution. The calculated value for 'put' is 97. The maximum possible value occurs when there is a single IV_{NN} to IV_{Ww} correspondence at 100%; the measured distance from random in this case is 117. A reasonable measure of the distance between the corresponding categories in Nyulnyul and Warrwa is suggested to be the difference between these two values, 20 in this instance. The distance for an entirely random set of correlations would be 117, since the above formula gives a

Comparing linguistic systems of categorisation 417

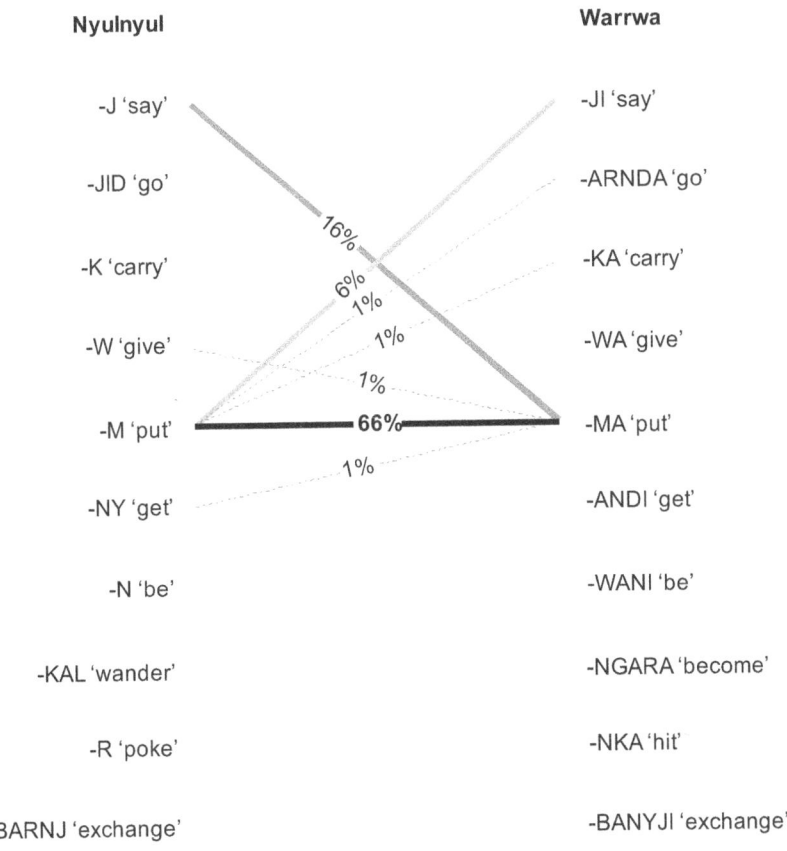

Figure 10. Correspondences of collocate sets for 'put' categories in Nyulnyul and Warrwa

value of 0. On the other hand, the distance between e.g. 'put' and itself in Nyulnyul would be 0, as one would hope.

To get an overall measure of the distance between the constructions in Nyulnyul and Warrwa according to this collocational dimension one simply performs these calculations on the entire set of 100 dyads, subtracting from the maximum value of 1170 to obtain the distance between CVCs in the two languages.

Another way of dealing with the same data is to use cluster analysis. One could set up correspondence tables for the categories of Nyulnyul and Warrwa in a 10 by 10 matrix. The portion for our data set (in terms of shared percentages calculated as per above) is shown in table 7. From the completely

Figure 11. Bar graph showing difference between actual and random proportions of shared collocations for the 'put' IV in Nyulnyul and Warrwa

filled-out tabulation one could derive a tree diagram showing the proximity amongst the corresponding categories.

Table 7. Partial table of correspondences between the verbal categories of Nyulnyul and Warrwa

		Nyulnyul									
		-J	-JID	-K	-W	-M	-NY	-N	-KAL	-R	-BARNJ
Warrwa	-JI					6					
	-ARNDA					1					
	-KA					1					
	-WA					0					
	-MA	16	0	0	1	66	1	0	0	0	0
	-ANDI					1					
	-WANI					0					
	-NGARA					0					
	-NKA					0					
	-BANYJI					0					

The second difficulty mentioned above concerned the possibility that there may be a mismatch between the best correspondences according to collocations and according to the semantics of the categories. My knowledge of the two languages suggests that this is not a serious difficulty: in other words, according to my intuitions about the languages, I believe that the other categories will correlate in a way comparable to the 'put' category. The strongest associations will be between categories marked by correlating IVs. For the 'carry' category evidence suggests a somewhat stronger association, while for the 'go' category it is somewhat weaker.

Nevertheless, it would seem advisable to factor in this feature, which might be more of a concern in other pairs of languages, such as for instance Nyulnyul and Gooniyandi. What might reasonably be done is to measure the actual correspondences not just against the random one, but also the perfect correspondence between IVs that we previously identified as corresponding. That is to say, we use the same measure to give a value of the distance of the actual situation from the perfect correspondence which would be for a 100% overlap between corresponding categories. In the case of the Nyulnyul –M 'put' category the ideal would be a 100% correspondence with the

Warrwa –MA 'put' category, with 0% for all of the other possible correlating pairs. Using the above measure, the distance from this ideal would be 62, as against the random situation, which would show the value 108.

How this factor is best incorporated into the distance measure remains unclear to me; so also does it remain puzzling how to take into account the overlaps of the categories within each language.

3.3.4. Final remarks

The three features deployed in the measures proposed in the previous subsections are significant in that they relate to what is more or less unpredictable in the constructions: as observed in McGregor (1990: 572, 2002: 35–37) predictability of IV given UV is fairly poor, though there is a high degree of motivation – that is, few collocations are exceptional in the sense that they go against the general semantic principles. Put in another way, while predictability is fairly low, there are few surprises in the actual collocations, which are normally amenable to explanation. Once known, they can be accounted for semantically; there are few surprises in the shape of completely incongruous pairings (cf. however McGregor 2002: 83–85).

Significantly, the collocations are founded ultimately on usage, on collocations of UVs and IVs that have become increasingly entrenched in the languages. The CVC in particular is a construction that is not just characterised by the grammatical relations that obtain between its component units. It also shows strong lexical peculiarities, a fact that is hardly surprising given that one of the primary functions of the northern Australian systems of verb classification is lexical, the creation of lexical items (McGregor 2002; Schultze-Berndt 2000, 2006). What we have seen in the preceding three subsections is that strong signals of similarity are discernible in the collocational data for some language pairs (e.g. Nyulnyul and Warrwa), while they are far weaker for other pairs (e.g. Nyulnyul and Gooniyandi). The signals of similarity can plausibly be traced to three sources:

- retention from a proto-language;
- independent innovation;
- borrowing.

There are of course other collocational features that might be expected to provide us with quantifiable differences amongst CVCs in different languages. One obvious one concerns the relative proportions of UVs that collocate with 1, 2, ... IVs. For instance, the differences between Gooniyandi and Nyulnyul are apparent in the data presented in table 8: a somewhat larger percentage of UVs in Gooniyandi are promiscuous. Indeed, the difference between the two languages is statistically significant: the χ^2-test gives a *p*-value of 0.015.[10]

Table 8. Comparison of two languages in terms of degree of promiscuity of UVs

	1	2	3	4	5	6	7
Gooniyandi	366 (70%)	94 (18%)	47 (9%)	10 (2%)	5 (1%)	1 (0.2%)	0 (0%)
Nyulnyul	429 (78%)	77 (14%)	28 (5%)	17 (3%)	6 (1%)	0 (0%)	2 (0.4%)

A reasonable measure of the distance between the constructions according to the relative degrees of promiscuity of UVs might be proposed along the lines of the measure proposed in §3.3.1. However, such a measure would presumably indicate differences in the degrees of grammaticalisation of the constructions in the languages, not differences that could be plausibly attributed to either retentions from a proto-language or to borrowings. This supposition is based on the reasonable expectation that there will be a greater proportion of multiple categorisations in more entrenched systems, as supported by the Gooniyandi and Nyulnyul data in table 8. Other features of the constructions strongly attest to the greater entrenchment of the Gooniyandi system.

6. Conclusions

The three quantitative measures discussed in §3.3 show promise of results that will be in good accord with the findings of the comparative method, and lexicostatistical investigations. That is to say, the degree of relatedness of the CVCs as constructions amongst languages shows evidence of replicating the genetic relatedness of the languages themselves, established by independent means.[11] This can be seen by comparing figure 7 above with figure 12, which shows a phylogenetic tree for a selection of Kimberley languages based on lexical resemblance rates. Unfortunately two of the above languages, Bardi and Nyulnyul, were not included in the previous investigation, though evidence from a similar lexical investigation reveals that these two languages

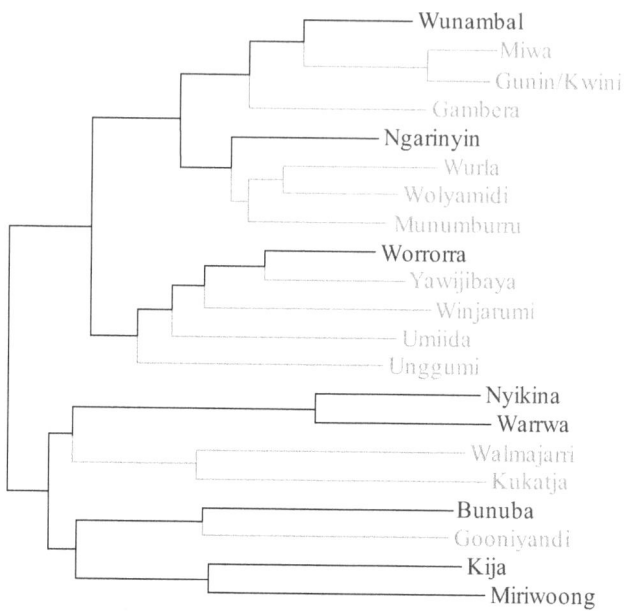

Figure 12. Relations among some Kimberley languages based on a lexicostatistical analysis, after McGregor and Rumsey (2009: 14)

pattern together in a larger group including Nyikina and Warrwa as against the other languages in this table (Stokes and McGregor 2003: 37).

The suggestive homologies of the trees representing the constructions and the language relations add further evidence in support of the genetic relatedness of the Nyulnyulan, Bunuban, and Worrorran languages. On the other hand, they do not strengthen the case for genetic relations amongst the families themselves: although similarities amongst the languages are revealed, they are not very close.

It seems from the evidence adduced in this paper that UV-IV collocations once established may remain relatively stable over time, thus accounting for the greater proportion of shared collocations that are found in modern languages that are members of a single family with respect to languages that are not (closely) genetically related. It is plausible that the picture may be muddied by later borrowed and innovated collocations. Given that the make-up of the Warrwa categories seems to be somewhat intermediate between that for Nyulnyul and Bardi and that for Gooniyandi, one wonders whether the larger proportion of different collocations found in Warrwa may not be accounted for as calques on Gooniyandi collocations. It seems likely that some collocational patterns are comparable with core lexical items in terms of their diachronic behaviour, and rather more resilient to change than many typological features (e.g. word order patterns, alignment patterns, etc.), which, as is well known, do not usually remain particularly stable within lineages. Indeed, the signal from collocational patterns can evidently outlive the CVC construction itself, as is clearly the case in Gooniyandi, and may well be the case more widely across the continent, if (as suggested in McGregor forthcoming-a; see also Merlan 1979) the prototypical verbal structure of Pama-Nyungan languages is a highly grammaticalised version of an earlier CVC. Thus the collocational signal may survive the typological characteristics of the verbal construction.

Not everything is plain sailing, however. As figure 7 indicates, the four Nyulnyulan languages do not cluster together in terms of their UV-IV collocational patterns; indeed, it even shows a split within the Eastern Nyulnyulan group. Why does this anomaly exist? There are a number of possible explanations. For one thing, it could be that the data set is too small – 10 lexemes and around 60 collocate sets may be too small a corpus to draw reliable inferences from. Another possibility is that the actual choice of meanings is not optimal. However, figure 6 reveals that even with a larger set of verbal meanings, and cognate UVs, Warrwa is still problematic. My guess is that Warrwa is indeed problematic due to extensive contact with neighbouring non-Nyulnyulan languages. What could be done to test this possible factor is to include both Yawuru and Nyikina in the set of languages, and see if they pattern alike.

The measures outlined in §3.3 lend themselves to ready adaptation to other grammatical domains of classification. As suggested in McGregor (2002), grammatical classification is by definition constituted by two systems of lexical and/or grammatical elements in collocation. Nominal classification systems – including noun class systems – involve collocations of nominals and some morpheme (in the simplest cases, an agreement morpheme) that normally occurs elsewhere than on the nominal. It is not difficult to see how the above measures can be modified to measure the distances between nominal classification systems. McGregor (2008); McGregor and Rumsey (2009: 50–51) argue that the noun class system of modern Worrorran languages can be traced back to a classification (perhaps class) system of proto-Worrorran. This proto-system can be reconstructed to some degree by application of the comparative method. Key aspects of the argument of this paper are based on unusual categorisations, i.e. unusual collocations of nominal and class-markers. The situation appears ripe for the application of quantitative methods geared to determining the distance between the systems in the various languages of the family.

A more general question lying behind this paper is: how can grammatical constructions be compared in quantitative terms,[12] how can sensible measures of their degrees of similarity and/or distance be devised that incorporate not just measures of collocational similarity, but also measures of formal and semantic similarity. Devising such measures is a daunting task, though the results are potentially of considerable significance. In both linguistic typology and descriptive linguistics we employ labels for categories and constructions like ergative, accusative, irrealis, and so forth, largely because the phenomena we are dealing with look sufficiently similar to one another, and/or perhaps to a presumed ideal type. The result is that it is not always certain that we are comparing the same types of entities, that the typologies are indeed of comparable phenomena (for instance, to what extent is it viable to compare the part of speech verb of a pair of languages), or that the descriptions are not misrepresenting the phenomena to be described. Possession of a quantitative distance measure would be advantageous, though of course it would not tell us everything we would want to know about the relatedness of the phenomena.

Finally, a comment is in order on the limitations of the present paper. My purpose has been to provide some evidence that it is possible to devise distance measures to quantify the degree of similarity and difference between instances of a generic construction type cross-linguistically. I have given brief accounts of some measures that appear to do the job in a manner that is revealing of the historical relations amongst the constructions. They are obviously in need of further refinement before they can be regarded as viable measures.

Notes

1. This is a revised version of a presentation to the *Workshop on comparing approaches to measuring linguistic differences*, University of Gothenburg, 24–25 October 2011. I am grateful to the organisers for the invitation to talk at this workshop; this has forced me to pursue some lines of thought that I would not otherwise have followed up. Thanks also to the anonymous referees for some useful comments.
2. In this paper I employ the terminology and abbreviations of McGregor (2002), since in my opinion they are the most appropriate to the construction; at the same time I recognise the potential of confusion for those working in other traditions, where the terms and abbreviations mean something quite different.
3. Example sentences are laid out according to the Leipzig Glossing Rules, using the recommended abbreviations. For the reader's convenience the full list of

abbreviations follows: AUG – augmented number; CM – conjugation marker; ERG – ergative; IRR – irrealis; MIN – minimal number; NOM – nominative; OBL – oblique; and PRS – present tense. The first three numerals indicate the three person categories. Other abbreviations used in the paper are: CVC – compound verb construction; IV – inflecting verb; SVC – simple verb construction; and UV – inflecting verb. Following a convention I have adopted in other publications on the topic, IV forms are cited in capitals, as are the verbal classifiers of Gooniyandi. In the latter language the classifier is preceded by a plus sign (+) rather than a hyphen, indicating that the morpheme boundary before this item is one over which particular morphophonemic processes operate.

4. Here I identify as the same those IVs that show the same morphological paradigms regardless of whether they occur in a CVC or in an SVC. See McGregor (2010) for arguments and discussion of this point.

5. To be sure, there are a few exceptions. As will be seen below, McGregor (2002) deploys a variety of dimensions in his system comparisons. Nicolas (1998: 324–350) and Knight (2004) undertake comparisons according to semantics, and do pairwise comparisons of the sets of UVs constituting categories identified as comparable (because the marking IVs are cognate). Knight's comparison works fairly well, largely because of the close similarity of the two languages (Bunuba and Gooniyandi); Nicolas' comparison (of two languages from different lineages, Bunuba and Bardi) ends up as rather unenlightening, a morass of detail in which it is difficult to see the forest for the trees.

6. Of course there is a downside to this focus on basic meanings in that in most languages some of the basic meanings are expressed solely by IVs in SVCs. Fortunately, the set of such IVs is usually no more than a dozen to a score. Moreover, there is usually a reasonable degree of intra-lineage agreement as to whether the meaning is expressed by an SVC or a CVC.

7. Along with the 27 cognate UVs were also included non-cognate UVs expressing the same meanings. The reason for this slight relaxation on the requirement of cognacy is that replacement presumably need not necessarily affect the UV-IV collocations – conceivably either UV or IV might be replaced by an innovation without affecting the collocation.

8. In any event, the degree of overlap amongst the Gooniyandi categories is not very large: in most cases it is less than a tenth (McGregor 2002: 46), with a highest value of 12%.

9. It was compiled over a decade ago using the time-honoured method of pencil and paper; only the results were saved.

10. The final two columns were ignored since the values are too small.

11. This is not, of course, to suggest that all measures of constructional distance are likely to reveal results in accordance with the genetic relatedness of the languages. As already mentioned, the fourth measure, alluded to in §3.3.4, the degree of promiscuity of UVs, is unlikely to be relevant to linguistic genetics, and is much more likely to correlate with the degree of entrenchment of the verbal systems than to reflect anything of the proto-construction or proto-system.

12. In fact, development of useful means of comparison in any terms, qualitative or quantitative, is called for, as observed in McGregor (2002: 396) in relation to systems of grammatical classification.

References

Amberber, Mengistu, Brett Baker, and Mark Harvey (eds.)
    2010   *Complex predicate formation: cross-linguistic perspectives on event structure*. Cambridge: Cambridge University Press.

Bowern, Claire
    2008   The reconstruction of Nyulnyulan complex predication. *Diachronica* 25 (2): 186–212.

Dixon, Robert M.W.
    2002   *Australian languages: their nature and development*. Cambridge: Cambridge University Press.

Goldberg, Adele E.
    1995   *Constructions: a construction grammar approach to argument structure*. Chicago and London: University of Chicago Press.

Huson, Daniel H. and David Bryant
    2006   Application of phylogenetic networks in evolutionary studies. *Molecular Biology and Evolution* 23 (2): 254–267.

Knight, Emily
    2004   Aspects of Bunuba grammar and semantics. MA (Hons.) thesis, Armidale, University of New England.

McGregor, William B.
    1990   *A functional grammar of Gooniyandi*. Amsterdam: John Benjamins.

McGregor, William B.
    1997   *Semiotic grammar*. Oxford: Clarendon Press.

McGregor, William B.
    2002   *Verb classification in Australian languages*. Berlin/New York: Mouton de Gruyter.

McGregor, William B.
    2008   The origin of noun classes in Worrorran languages. In *Morphology and language history: in honour of Harold Koch*, Claire Bowern, Bethwyn Evans, and Luisa Miceli (eds.), 185–200. Amsterdam/Philadelphia: John Benjamins.

McGregor, William B.
    2010   'The 'say, do' verb in Nyulnyul, Warrwa, and other Nyulnyulan languages is monosemic.' Unpublished manuscript.

McGregor, William B.
    2012   *The Nyulnyul language of Dampier Land, Western Australia*. Canberra: Pacific Linguistics.

McGregor, William B.
forthc. a Grammaticalisation of verbs as temporal and modal markers in Australian languages. To appear in [Title not known], Folke Josephson and Ingmar Söhrman (eds.). Amsterdam/Philadelphia: John Benjamins.

McGregor, William B.
forthc. b The history of verb classification in Nyulnyulan languages. To appear in *The diachrony of classification systems*, William B. McGregor, and Søren Wichmann (eds.). Amsterdam/Philadelphia: John Benjamins.

McGregor, William B. and Alan L. Rumsey
2009 *Worrorran revisited: the case for genetic relations among languages of the Northern Kimberley region of Western Australia*. Canberra: Pacific Linguistics.

Merlan, Francesca
1979 On the prehistory of some Australian verbs. *Oceanic Linguistics* 18 (1): 33–112.

Nicolas, Edith
1998 Etude du système verbal du bardi, langue du nord-ouest australien, avec une présentation contrastive du système bunuba. PhD thesis, Université Paris VII, Denis Diderot.

Reid, Nicholas J.
2003 Phrasal verb to synthetic verb: recorded morphosyntactic change in Ngan'gityemerri. In *The non-Pama-Nyungan languages of northern Australia: comparative studies of the continent's most linguistically complex region*, Nicholas Evans (ed.), 95–123. Canberra: Pacific Linguistics.

Reid, Nicholas J.
2011 *Ngan'gityemerri: a language of the Daly River region, Northern Territory of Australia*. Munich: Lincom Europa.

Schultze-Berndt, Eva
2000 Simple and complex verbs in Jaminjung: a study of event categorisation in an Australian language. PhD thesis, Catholic University of Nijmegen.

Schultze-Berndt, Eva
2006 Taking a closer look at function verbs: lexicon, grammar, or both? In *Catching language: the standing challenge of grammar writing*, Felix K. Ameka, Alan Dench, and Nicholas Evans (eds.), 359–391. Berlin/New York: Mouton de Gruyter.

Stokes, Bronwyn and William B. McGregor
2003 Classification and subclassification of the Nyulnyulan languages. In *The non-Pama-Nyungan languages of northern Australia: comparative studies of the continent's most linguistically complex region*, Nicholas Evans (ed.), 29–74. Canberra: Pacific Linguistics.

Black box approaches to genealogical classification and their shortcomings

Jelena Prokić and Steven Moran

1. Introduction

In the past 20 years, the application of quantitative methods in historical linguistics has received a lot of attention. Traditional historical linguistics relies on the comparative method in order to determine the genealogical relatedness of languages. More recent quantitative approaches attempt to automate this process, either by developing computational tools that complement the comparative method (Steiner et al. 2010) or by applying fully automatized methods that take into account very limited or no linguistic knowledge, e.g. the Levenshtein approach. The Levenshtein method has been extensively used in dialectometry to measure the distances between various dialects (Kessler 1995; Heeringa 2004; Nerbonne 1996). It has also been frequently used to analyze the relatedness between languages, such as Indo-European (Serva and Petroni 2008; Blanchard et al. 2010), Austronesian (Petroni and Serva 2008), and a very large sample of 3002 languages (Holman 2010). In this paper we will examine the performance of the Levenshtein distance against n-gram models and a zipping approach by applying these methods to the same set of language data.

The success of the Levenshtein method is typically evaluated by visually inspecting and comparing the obtained genealogical divisions against already well-established groupings found in the linguistics literature. It has been shown that the Levenshtein method is successful in recovering main languages groups, which for example in the case of Indo-European language family, means that it is able to correctly classify languages into Germanic, Slavic or Romance groups. In a recent analysis of the Austronesian languages by means of Levenshtein distance (Greenhill 2011), the obtained results were evaluated using a more exact method than by visually inspecting the recovered groups. Greenhill (2011) extracted language triplets and compared their subgroupings against those provided by the Ethnologue (Lewis 2009). The possible subgroupings of any three languages included the following: (1) language A is more similar to language B than C, (2) A is more similar to C than B, (3) B is more similar to C than A, or (4) A, B and C are equally similar. The comparison of two classifications has shown that the accuracy of the Levenshtein method in languages classification reaches only up to 65%. Furthermore, it has been observed that the accuracy of Levenshtein classification decreases rapidly with phylogenetic distance.

Although the Levenshtein algorithm takes into account very little linguistic knowledge about the segments being compared, those in favor of this approach stress that it gives reasonable results, that it can be computed quickly, and that it can easily be applied to large amounts of data. In this paper, we apply Levenshtein's algorithm to sixty-nine indigenous South American languages, and look into more detail what this algorithm is actually measuring and how meaningful are the groups it obtains. We also analyze the same data set using two very simple techniques: an n-gram model and a gzip file compression method. Both of these methods are very simple and require no linguistic knowledge about the data being analyzed. The n-gram method measures the number of overlapping segments, i.e. in our case unigrams and bigrams of phones in words, without regard to the position of the grams. This approach has been applied by Huffman (2003) to the task of language classification. Gzip is a file compression method based on the Lempel-Ziv algorithm (Ziv and Lempel 1978) that searches for the longest common substring between strings. It has been used by Benedetto (2002) to classify 50 Indo-European languages into genetic groups. We show that there is no significant difference in the performances of these three techniques and that they are only partially successful in finding major language groups. None of these approaches reveals linguistic processes that are responsible for the differences found between the languages. The lack of a language model makes any of these black box approaches unsuitable for the investigation of deep phylogenetic relationships between language varieties. We argue that more linguistically-aware methods, or hybrid methods that use black box approaches coupled with linguistic knowledge, should minimally produce linguistic output that is useful for historical linguists, who remain the front runners in revealing deep genealogical relations between languages.

2. Methods

In this section we give a short introduction to the three methods that we use to measure the distances between languages: the Levenshtein method, the n-gram model and the zipping approach.

2.1. Levenshtein distance

Levenshtein distance is a metric used to measure the distances between two strings; it was first introduced by Levenshtein (1966). It represents the smallest number of edit operations (insertions, deletions or substitutions) needed to transform one string into the other. At the same time, it aligns the two strings, as illustrated in figure 1, which presents the alignment of pronunciations of the word for 'tree' in two Tucanoan languages, Siriano and Wanano.

$$j\ u\ k\ i\ g\ i$$
$$j\ u\ k\ i\ k\ i$$

Figure 1. Alignment of two pronunciations of the word for 'tree'

The aligned strings differ only in position 5, where [g] in Siriano corresponds to [k] in Wanano. The absolute distance between these two strings is 1 since they differ in only one position. There are several variants of the Levenshtein approach, but the most important ones are the normalized approach and phone string comparison. In order to discard the influence of the lengths of the strings being compared, Levenshtein distance can be normalized by dividing it by the length of the longer string (Serva 2007) or by the length of the alignment (Heeringa 2004). In our example in figure 1, both normalization methods would give a distance of 1/6. In the phone string comparison approach, the compared segments are represented as a bundle of features, which allows for a more refined comparison. Since [k] and [g] are both velar plosives, voiceless and voiced respectively, the distance between these two segments can be set to 1/3 instead of 1.[1] If the strings that are being compared are cognate forms that differ in only few segments, then the Levenshtein approach lets us get very accurate alignments. The aligned segments [k] and [g] in our example, thus share the same origin in a hypothetical protoform. However, when comparing languages that are more distantly related, the words become less similar in their surface forms and this makes the applications of the Levenshtein method for their comparison less appropriate.

2.2. N-gram analysis

An n-gram is a subsequence of n consecutive items from a given sequence. The size of n can range from 1 (unigrams) to the length of the string in question. N-gram models have been applied to language comparison by Huffman

(2003) and Hoppenbrouwers and Hoppenbrouwers (2001) used frequency of single phones to compare dialect varieties of Dutch. In this paper, we compare the frequency of unigrams and bigrams in order to classify languages in our data set into genetic groups. The method is very simple and the only linguistic knowledge that it requires as input is the information on how to split words into phones. Unlike in the Levenshtein approach, no alignment of the word is involved. The similarity between two words is calculated as the number of shared unigrams or bigrams divided by the length of the longer word. The two words for 'tree' from figure 1 contain the following unigrams, shown in table 1.

Table 1. Two pronunciations of word 'tree' and their phone frequencies

	j	u	k	ɨ	g
jukigɨ	1	1	1	2	1
jukɨkɨ	1	1	2	2	0

The similarity between these two strings is 5/6 because they share 5 unigrams, i.e. phones: [j], [u], [k] and two times [ɨ]. This method produces a similarity metric between two strings. However, in order to get a distance matrix, similarities are converted into distances by subtracting them from 1. The distance matrix is used to calculate the genetic similarity of the languages under investigation.

2.3. Zipping

File compressors (aka zippers) are algorithms designed to encode a file in such a way that it uses fewer bits than the original and thus compresses its file size. One of the best-known data compression algorithms is the Lempel-Ziv algorithm (Ziv and Lempel 1978), which is used in many public domain compressors, such as *zip* and *gzip*. This algorithm works by searching for the duplicate strings in a file, i.e. longest common substrings, and recoding them into smaller strings. In files with many repeated patterns, there are more recoded strings and the compression rate is greater. Benedetto (2002) presents some of the possibilities of applying this algorithm for language recognition and authorship attribution. The distance between two texts A and B in two different languages is estimated by merging texts from two languages and measuring their compression rates. The more similar two texts are, then the higher the compression.[2]

For our approach, we use Normalized Compression Distance (NCD), as presented in Cilibrasi (2004), to measure the distance between two languages:

$$NCD(x,y) = (C(xy) - \min\{C(x),C(y)\})/\max(C(x),C(y))$$

C(xy) is the compressed size of the concatenated texts x and y. C(x) is the compressed size of x. And C(y) is the compressed size of y. To calculate the distance between each of the languages in our data set, we used the publicly available *gzip* compressor.

3. Data set

We tested each black box method on a set of sixty-nine indigenous South American languages extracted from Huber and Reed (1992). The data set consists of 366 word wordlists, based on a list developed by Morris Swadesh and John Rowe.[3] These wordlists were collected for indigenous languages spoken in Columbia. Huber and Reed (1992) classify these languages into 12 language families, most of which are commonly accepted (*ibid* p. V): Chocó, Chibcha, Barbacoa, Kamsá, Quechua, Arawak, Tucano, Carib, Guahibo, Macú-Puinave, Sáliba-Piaroa and Witoto.[4] The number of languages in different groups varies from only one (Kamsá and Quechua) to nineteen (Tucano). We investigate in detail the Tucano language family because it is comprised of the largest number of languages in our data set, and it is well attested in the literature (Campbell 1997; Kaufman 2007; Lewis 2009). According to these three sources, the Tucano language family can be divided into the Western, Eastern and Central Tucanoan branches. Figure 2 illustrates the classification of the Tucanoan languages in Huber and Reed as given in the Ethnologue (Lewis 2009).

According to this classification, the Eastern group can be further divided into Central and Northern, while the Western group is comprised of the Northern, Southern and Tanimuca groups. We use this classification to estimate the performance of the three black box methods.

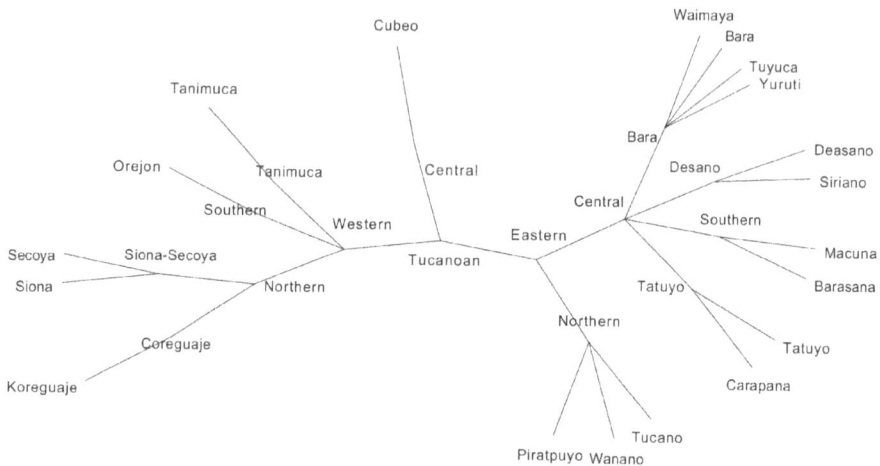

Figure 2. The Tucanoan family tree (Lewis 2009)

4. Results

Distances between the sixty-nine languages in our sample were calculated by means of Levenshtein distance, the amount of shared unigrams and bigrams, and by applying a zipping technique. All distances were analyzed using neighbor-net, as implemented in SplitsTree (Huson and Bryant 2006). Figure 3 shows the neighbor-net of all sixty-nine languages compared, using the Levenshtein algorithm.

The shape of the net in figure 3 is star-like with a very poorly marked hierarchical structure. The only three clearly distinguishable groups are the Chocó, Guahibo and Tucano language families. The rest of the families found in Huber and Reed (1992) can be identified, but the separation between various language groups is not very clear. This may be due to a separate evolution of these languages or it may mark a very weak phylogenetic signal. In figure 4, the same neighbor-net is shown after removing the Chocó, Guahibo and Tucano language families. Witoto and Arawak language families become more distinguishable, but the star-shape is still dominant.

Neighbor-nets of distance matrices obtained using unigram and bigram analyses are shown in figures 5 and 6 respectively. Both networks show high resemblance with the network based on Levenshtein distance. All 12 language families from Huber and Reed (1992) can be identified, with the

Black box approaches to genealogical classification 435

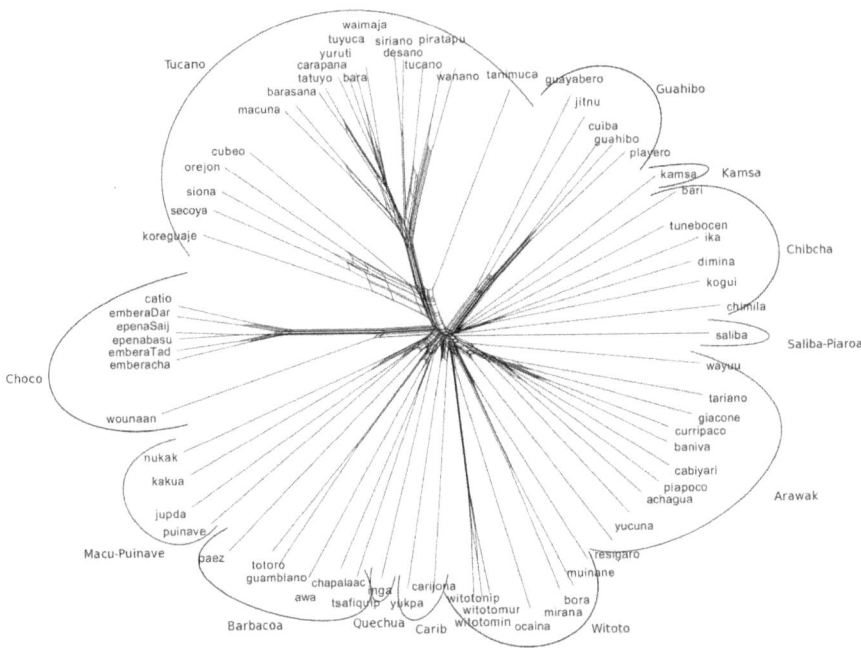

Figure 3. Neighbor-net of the sixty-nine languages compared using the Levenshtein algorithm

Chocó, Guahibo and Tucano families being the only three clearly distinguishable from the others. The rest of the network is star-shaped, which is especially visible in the network based on the bigram analysis. Although more simple than the Levenshtein algorithm, these two techniques give the same results with regard to the language classification on our data set.

In the next step, we analyzed the data by zipping the files as described in section 2.3 and measuring the difference in the compression rates. The results are shown in figure 7. Compared to the classification given in Huber and Reed (1992), some of the languages are misclassified. However, even using this very simple technique, it is possible to identify all language families. The Witoto family is clearly identified, unlike in the other two methods.

Regarding the classification task, the Levenshtein and n-gram models gave very similar results. They show very little hierarchical structure, with the Chocó, Guahibo and Tucano families being the only three exceptions. What makes these three language families different is that their word forms show, on average, much less variation if compared to the other language

436 *Jelena Prokić and Steven Moran*

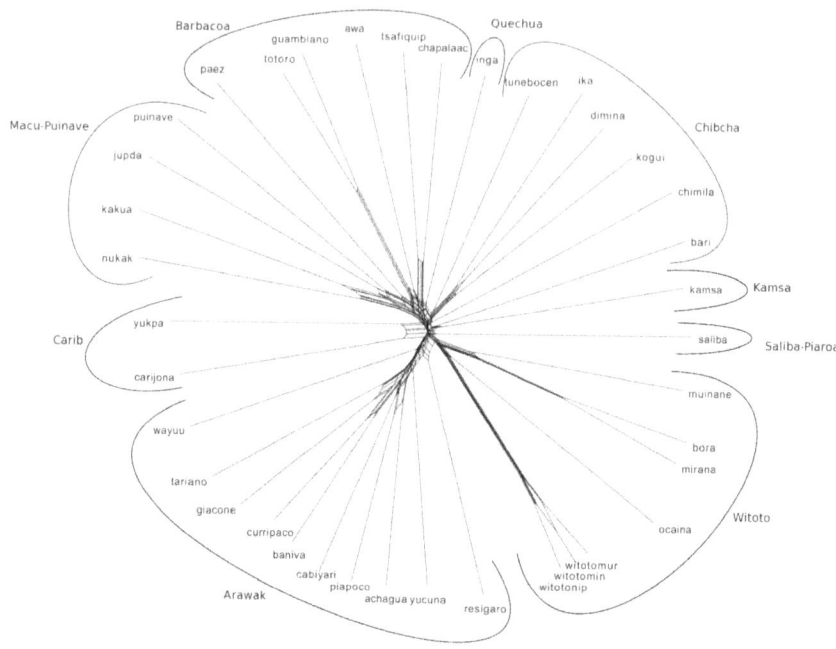

Figure 4. Neighbor-net presented in figure 3 after removing Chocó, Guahibo and Tucano language families

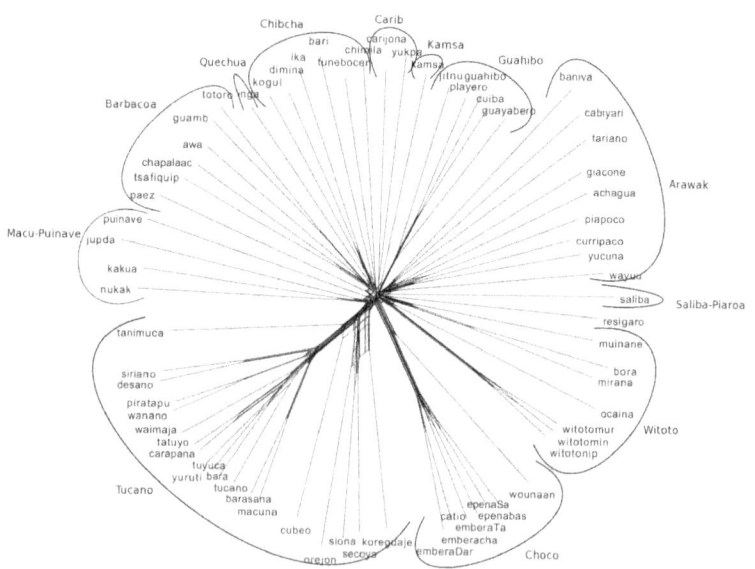

Figure 5. Neighbor-net of the 69 languages compared using the average number of shared unigrams

Black box approaches to genealogical classification 437

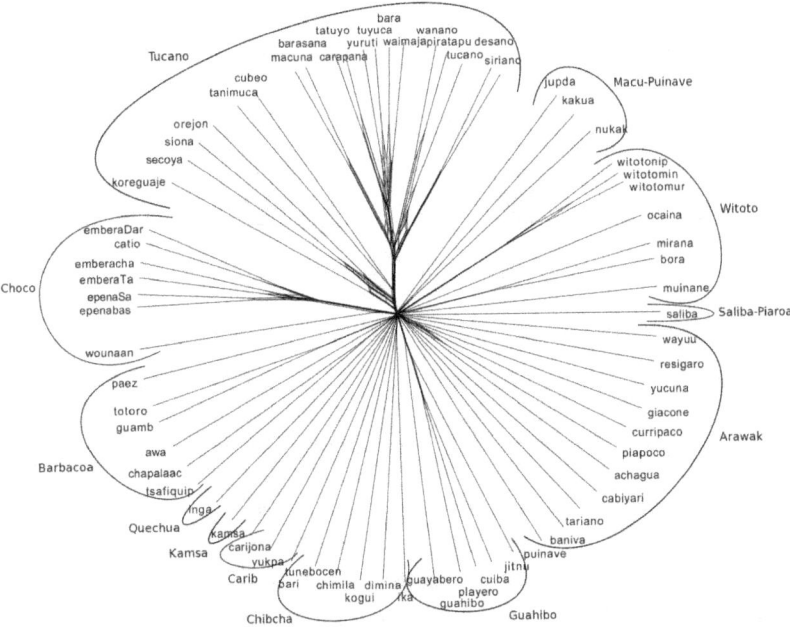

Figure 6. Neighbor-net of the sixty-nine languages compared using the average number of shared bigrams

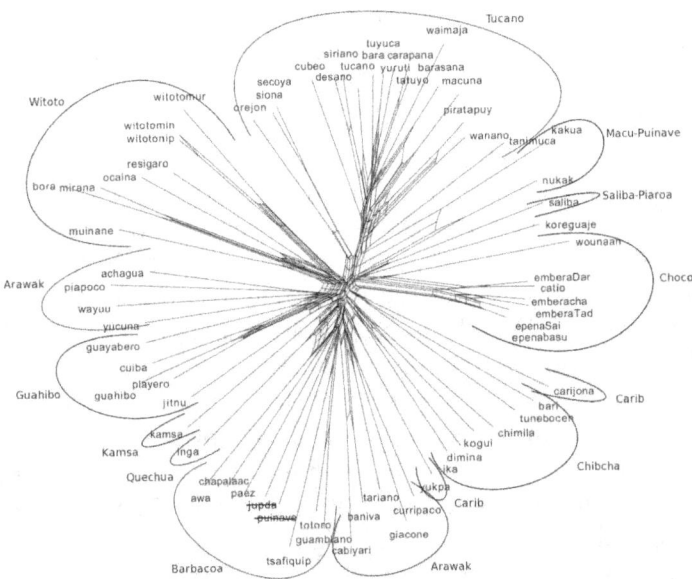

Figure 7. Neighbor-net of the sixty-nine languages compared using the zipping method

families in the data set. Table 2 shows the pronunciation of the word 'leg' in the Chocó, Tucano and Chibcha language families.

Table 2. Pronunciation of the word 'leg' in Chocó, Tucano and Chibcha

Chocó	Tucano	Chibcha
hĩrũ	jẽkã́ɨ̃	ʥúʔkwɨ
hẽ́rũ	jĩtʃɨkɨ	kə́ldə
hĩ́rũ	jĩka	kɨna
hĩ́rã́	jĩkɨ́	kátto
hĩ́rũ	jĩkã̃	bidiinə

Unlike Chocó and Tucano, for languages where the word forms are very different, no internal structure is recovered. We discuss the reasons for the poor performance on remotely related languages in section 5. None of the tested methods gave any information on the relatedness between languages on the macro-family level.

We also checked the performance of the three algorithms on the Tucano languages solely by excluding non-Tucano languages from our analyses. The classification of the Tucano languages given in Ethnologue is given in figure 1. Neighbor-net based on the Levenshtein distances is shown in figure 8.

Although the neighbor-net method correctly reveals a major Eastern-Central-Western split and correctly groups languages at a very low-level in the net, it does not get the precise dividing line correct. For example, the following language pairs are grouped together: Siriano and Desano, Carapana and Tatuyo, and Macuna and Barasana.[5] However, Siriano and Desano are not grouped with the rest of the Central languages of the Eastern group. Tanimuca is classified as Central Tucanoan rather than Western Tucanoan. The net accords with the Ethnologue classification at the very high level (the split of the Tucanoan into Eastern, Central and Western) and at the very low level, but groupings at the intermediate level show differences. In figures 9 and 10, the analyses of the distances obtained by applying unigram and bigram methods to our data set are given. Both networks show the same structure as the network based on the Levenshtein distances. The network based on the zipping technique is presented in figure 11. The Eastern-Western split is less prominent and two languages, Tucano and Waimaja, are misclassified when compared to the Ethnologue's classification. Most of the lower level groupings can still be identified.

Our analyses show that even in the case where language varieties exhibit relatively small variation, the Levenshtein method is successful only in identifying major splits. However, even more simple and less 'linguistically' informative methods are also able to detect the same major groups in the data. Identification of the subgroups is equally problematic for all three tested methods.

5. Discussion

The comparison of three methods evaluated in this paper shows that there is no significant difference in performance of the Levenshtein and n-gram approaches. Although Levenshtein involves alignments of the strings compared and takes into account the ordering of the segments, the classifications obtained show no improvement over the classifications based on simple phone frequency counts. The zipping method is able to identify main language divisions, but in both analyses (all data and the Tucano subset) it was less accurate than the Levenshtein and n-gram methods. Furthermore, relations between the families at the macro-family level were not retrieved by any of the methods. In order to discover these deep phylogenetic relationships, information about the cognacy of words and their regular sound correspondences is necessary. None of the methods we tested are able to distinguish between cognate and non-cognate words. By applying Levenshtein or n-gram methods on the non-cognate words, we get information on the chance similarity between the words. The fact that two non-cognate words share a certain number of phones does not reflect any genealogical relationship between them. The chance that two languages use non-cognate words to denote the same or similar meaning grows with the phylogenetic distance and black box approaches become unreliable tools for detecting the relationships between the languages.

If compared words are cognates whose surface forms differ in more than only one or two elements, which is often the case with the dialect data, then black box methods are often too simplistic to be able to correctly detect the phylogenetic signal. If we look at the pronunciations of the word 'drink' in Tucano and Siriano, it becomes clear that the black box approaches are overestimating the distance.

Tucano: s ĩ ʔ r ĩ j ã
Siriano: – i ʔ r í k a

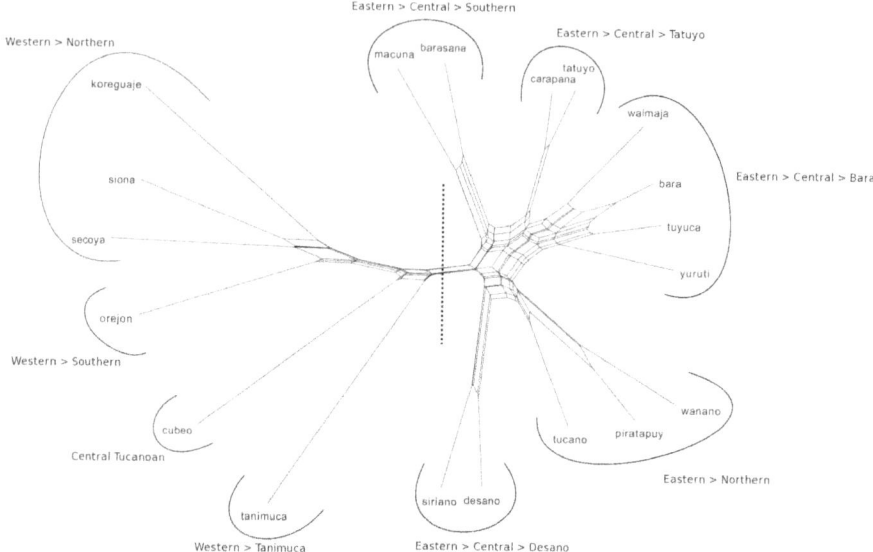

Figure 8. Classification of Tucanoan languages based on Levenshtein distance

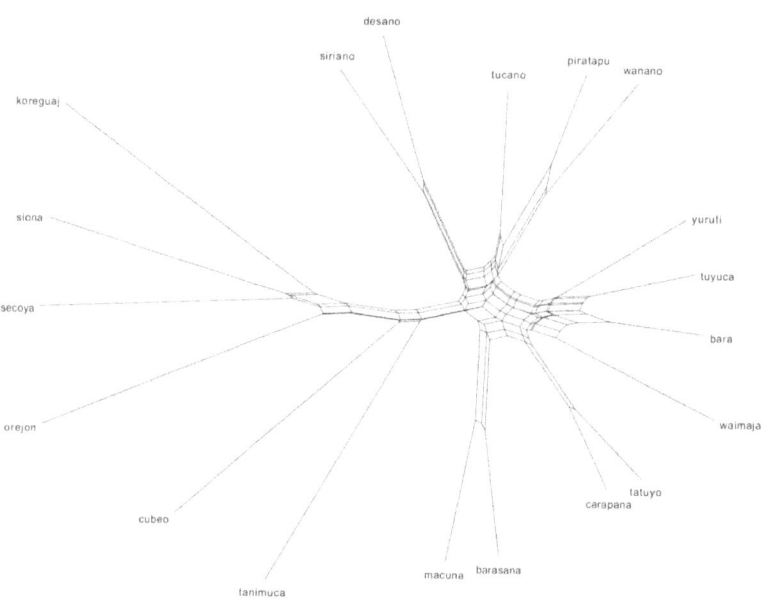

Figure 9. Classification of Tucanoan languages based on the average number of shared unigrams.

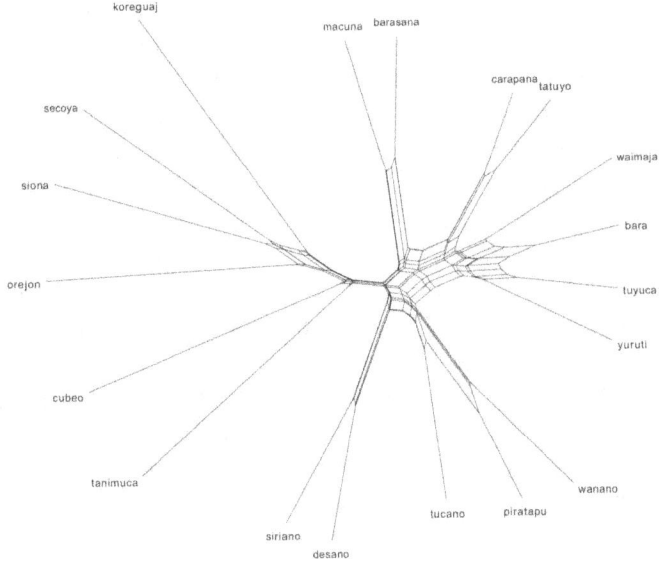

Figure 10. Classification of Tucanoan languages based on the average number of shared bigrams

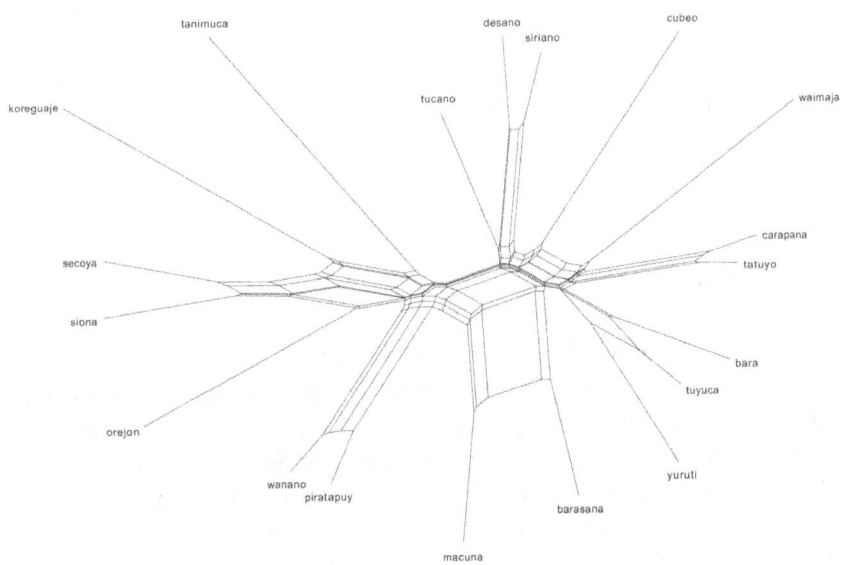

Figure 11. Classification of Tucanoan languages based on the zipping method

Using the Levenshtein or unigram methods, the distance between these two strings is 5/7, since the only two matching phones are [ʔ] and [r]. If phones are evaluated binarily, i.e. they are either the same or are different, then the differences at the suprasegmental level, as well as secondary phonation types (e.g. nasalization, length, etc.) are weighted too heavily. Therefore, approaches to genetic classification need to go beyond the segment level and need to handle phylogenetic signals at the level of features. A feature system that is language data dependent would thus allow genetic classification approaches to handle issues of divergent but related sound changes, e.g. two related languages that expanded their number of vowels where the first uses nasalization and the second raises vowels.

Phylogenetic approaches need transparent models that explain the evolution of changes in languages and how they relate. These processes should explain how one phone changes into another and should capture changes at the level of phonemic systems. The argument that black box approaches give pretty good results is misleading. Black box approaches, as we have shown on a lesser-studied group of languages, do not give good results. They may trivially capture the higher-level groupings, but beyond those we cannot actually make any claims of genetic relatedness at the deeper genetic levels. Nor do these methods provide any additional information that is useful to historical linguists, e.g. regular sound correspondences, a list of recurrent sound changes, the probability of one change into another, a description of the trigging environments of change, probable cognates, etc. Black box approaches that simply count and align segments do not catch these processes. What is needed is a probabilistic model of language change that describes the relatedness of languages and discharges linguistically-relevant data about these processes.

6. Conclusion

In this paper, we applied three black box approaches, namely Levenshtein distance, two n-gram models and a zipping method, to a data set of sixty-nine South American languages that represent a lesser-studied language family. All three approaches use segment counts and statistics and do not leverage additional linguistic knowledge. We show that these three approaches produce roughly equivalent results, i.e. they capture high-level genetic groups, but fail to discover deep genetic classifications and splits. When these black box methods are used on sets of languages whose genetic classification has not been previously described by historical linguists, how can one claim anything beyond possible high-level splits?

Appendix: Languages and their genealogical affiliation according to Huber and Reed (1992)

Achagua	Arawak	Playero	Guahibo
Baniva	Arawak	Guayabero	Guahibo
Cabiyarí	Arawak	Kamsá	Kamsá
Curripaco	Arawak	Jupda	Macú-Puinave
Giacone	Arawak	Kakua	Macú-Puinave
Piapoco	Arawak	Nukak	Macú-Puinave
Tariano	Arawak	Puinave	Macú-Puinave
Wayuu	Arawak	Inga	Quechua
Yucuna	Arawak	Sáliba	Sáliba-Piaroa
Resígaro	Arawak	Bará	Tucano
Awa	Barbacoa	Barasana	Tucano
Cha'palaachi	Barbacoa	Carapana	Tucano
Guambiano	Barbacoa	Cubeo	Tucano
Páez	Barbacoa	Desano	Tucano
Totoró	Barbacoa	Koreguaje	Tucano
Tsafiqui pila	Barbacoa	Macuna	Tucano
Carijona	Carib	Orejón	Tucano
Yukpa	Carib	Piratapuyo	Tucano
Barí	Chibcha	Secoya	Tucano
Chimila	Chibcha	Siona	Tucano
Dɨmina	Chibcha	Siriano	Tucano
Ika	Chibcha	Tanimuca	Tucano
Kogui	Chibcha	Tatuyo	Tucano
Tunebo	Chibcha	Tucano	Tucano
Tunebo Central	Chibcha	Tuyuca	Tucano
Catío	Chocó	Waimaja	Tucano
Embera Chamí	Chocó	Wanano	Tucano
Embera Darién	Chocó	Yurutí	Tucano
Embera Tadó	Chocó	Bora	Witoto
Epena Basurudó	Chocó	Miraña	Witoto
Epena Saija	Chocó	Muinane	Witoto
Wounaan	Chocó	Ocaina	Witoto
Cuiba	Guahibo	Witoto Minica	Witoto
Guahibo	Guahibo	Witoto Murui	Witoto
Jitnu	Guahibo	Witoto Nɨpode	Witoto

Notes

1. Heeringa (2004) provides a detailed explanation of how to apply the Levenshtein method.
2. For a detailed explanation on how to estimate the distance, see Benedetto (2002).
3. An explanation on the wordlist collection can be found in Huber and Reed (1992).
4. We provide the full list of languages and their classifications in the appendix. Throughout this paper, we use the language names provided by Huber and Reed.
5. According to Campbell (1997), these language pairs are actually dialects.

References

Blanchard, Philippe, Filippo Petroni, Maurizio Serva, and Dimitri Volchenkov
    2010   Geometric representations of language taxonomies. *Computer Speech and Language* 25 (3): 679–699.
Benedetto, Dario, Emanuele Caglioti, and Vittorio Loreto
    2002   Language trees and zipping. *Physical Review Letters* 88 (4): 048702.
Campbell, Lyle
    1997   *American Indian Languages: The Historical Linguistics of Native America*. Oxford: Oxford University Press.
Cilibrasi, Rudi and Paul M.B. Vitanyi
    2005   Clustering by compression. *IEEE Transactions on Information Theory* 51 (4): 1523–1545.
Greenhill, Simon
    2011   Levenshtein distances fail to identify language relationships accurately. *Computational Linguistics* 37 (4): 689–698.
Heeringa, Wilbert
    2004   Measuring dialect pronunciation differences using Levenshtein distance. Ph.D. diss, University of Groningen.
Holman, Eric W.
    2010   Do languages originate and become extinct at constant rates? *Diachronica* 27 (2): 214–225.
Huber, Randal Q. and Robert B. Reed
    1992   *Vocabulario comparativo: Palabras selectas de lenguas indígenas de Colombia (Comparative vocabulary: Selected words in indigenous languages of Colombia)*. Bogota: Instituto Lingüístico de Verano.
Huson, Daniel H. and David Bryant
    2006   Application of phylogenetic networks in evolutionary studies. *Molecular Biology and Evolution* 23 (2): 254–267.

Huffman, Stephen M.
  2003 The Genetic classification of languages by n-gram analysis: a computational technique. Ph.D. diss, Georgetown University.
Kaufman, Terrence
  2007 *Atlas of the World's Languages*. 2d ed. London, New York: Routledge.
Kessler, Brett
  1995 Computational dialectology in Irish Gaelic. In *Proceedings of the EACL*.
Levenshtein, Vladimir
  1966 Binary codes capable of correcting deletions, insertions and reversals. *Doklady Akademii Nauk SSSR* 163: 845–848.
Lewis, M. Paul (ed.)
  2009 *Ethnologue: Languages of the World*. 16 ed. Online: http://www.ethnologue.com.
Nerbonne, John, Wilbert Heeringa, Eric van den Hout, Peter van de Kooi, Simone Otten, and Willem van de Vis
  1996 Phonetic distances between Dutch dialects. In *CLIN VI: Proceedings of the Sixth CLIN Meeting*, G. Durieux, W. Daelemans, and S. Gillis (eds.), 185–202.
Petroni, Filippo and Maurizio Serva
  2008 Language distance and tree reconstruction. *Journal of Statistical Mechanics: Theory and Experiment*. 2008: P08012.
Serva, Maurizio and Filippo Petroni
  2008 Indo-european languages tree by Levenshtein distance. *Europhysics Letters* 81 (6): 68005.
Steiner, Lydia, Peter F. Stadler, and Michael Cysouw
  2011 A pipeline for computational historical linguistics. *Language Dynamics and Change* 1 (1): 89–127.
Ziv, Jacob and Abraham Lempel
  1978 Compression of individual sequences via variable-rate coding. *IEEE Transactions on Information Theory* 24 (5): 530–536.

Semantic typologies by means of network analysis of bilingual dictionaries

Ineta Sejane and Steffen Eger

1. Introduction

Similarities and relationships between languages have fascinated linguists at least since the rigorous advance in comparative language studies in the late 18th and early 19th centuries by scholars such as Jacob Grimm (1785–1863), Rasmus Rask (1787–1832), Franz Bopp (1791–1867), Karl Verner (1846–1896), and others. Their initial focus was mainly on phonological resemblances and implied language lineage; much later research also concentrated on morphological and syntactic genealogy – especially noteworthy here is the work of Joseph H. Greenberg (1915–2001). Contrarily, lexical semantic typology has only recently become the focus of linguistic studies, e.g. Koch (2001), possibly due to the vagueness and sheer size of the object under investigation, namely, the lexica of all human languages.

Methodologically, a popular approach for contrasting structural aspects of language, especially of phonology and morphology, has been the *comparative method,* which aims at differentiating languages on a feature-by-feature basis. Hereby, word lists have usually played an important role. For example, the Swadesh lists of comparable basic vocabulary (cf. Swadesh 1952; Strazny 2000) of world languages, proposed around the middle of the 20th century, were designed to explore phonological similarities of words with about the same meaning, thus aiming at recovering genetic relationships between languages. The comparative method was also the basis for inducing the well-known genealogical language family tree(s), still in development since the first advent in the 19th century. The newest, 16th edition of *Ethnologue: Languages of the World* counts as many as 7,358 living languages organized in such language trees (cf. Lewis 2009). A more recent hierarchy is the genealogical language list to be found in WALS (World Atlas of Language Structures) comprising 2,678 languages, subdivided in 510 genera and 212 families (cf. Dryer and Haspelmath 2011). Computational approaches that are based on similar principles as the comparative method include, for example, methods from computational linguistic phylogeny (cf. Nichols and Warnow 2008).

In contrast, investigations into lexical semantic similarities between languages are usually – but not exclusively – based upon the concept of a *network* comprising linguistic entities such as words and semantic relations between these entities such as synonymy, hypernymy, etc. Semantic or concept networks for languages have been pioneered in the WordNet (cf. Fellbaum 1998) and EuroWordNet projects (cf. Vossen 1999). A whole research strand in computational linguistics uses such word networks to determine semantic similarity between words in the same language (e.g. Resnik 1995; Jiang and Conrath 1997) or across languages (e.g. Hassan and Mihalcea 2009; Eger and Sejane 2010). More ambitiously, Mehler, Pustylnikov, and Diewald (2011) and in part Gaume, Duvignau, and Vanhove (2008) (at least indirectly) exploit language networks to induce semantic typologies in analogy to the classical (phonological or morphological) genealogies based on the comparative method.

Two aspects are noteworthy here. First, the application of networks to the problem of semantics is particularly appealing because network analysis and its mathematical foundation, graph theory, are rather novel and "hot" areas of study, intensively developed only in the second half of the 20th century, and with a large and an ever-increasing number of applications in the natural and social sciences since the end of the 1990s (for an overview of the role of networks in e.g. social economics, see Benhabib, Bisin, and Jackson 2010). Secondly, due to the novelty of semantic typologies, little seems to be known as to the extent to which such typologies should be in congruence with typologies derived from phonological or morphological features. Although, clearly, both kinds of classification systems should be correlated, we nonetheless believe in the sovereignty of each. Using one to evaluate the other may be helpful, but it may not be forgotten that results that indicate a divergence of both may be the most interesting if they can be rationalized on linguistic, areal, cultural, or other grounds.

In the current work, we set out to propose a novel method to determine lexical semantic similarity between two languages; such a measure can then easily be extended to inducing a semantic typology. Our method rests on bilingual dictionaries and a selected reference language in which semantic spaces of different languages can be coded. Moreover, our method lends itself to producing numerical values indicating semantic closeness between languages, but can also be used to explicitly outline semantic fields in which languages or language families differ.

This paper is structured as follows. In section 2, we more extensively survey three approaches that are closely related to our own. In section 3, we define and explicate the mathematical notions from network analysis upon which our methodology relies. Section 4 details our approach. Before presenting our results in section 6, we describe our data – open-source bilingual dictionaries for 36 different languages – in section 5. We discuss our results in section 7, and conclude in section 8.

2. Related work

In this section, we briefly survey the three approaches for measuring lexical semantic similarity of natural languages most closely related to our own work. Two of them are based on language networks (Mehler, Gaume); one relies on the curvature of translation histograms (Cooper).

Cooper (2005) investigates the curvature of the function N(s) counting the number of words with s senses in a general monolingual dictionary. He observes that these functions resemble near-exponential functions and are always concave in logarithmic scale. Extending this observation, Cooper (2008) proposes a method for contrasting semantic spaces of different languages using bilingual dictionaries. He suggests that the curvature of the function log(NT(t)) (NT(t) being the number of words with t translations in a bilingual dictionary) indicates relative semantic similarity between two languages. For languages with strong etymological connections, *convexity* – the measure of curvature introduced by Cooper (2008) – is negative; for distant languages it is positive. He applies his approach to measure proximity of semantic spaces between such languages as French-X (X being Catalan, English, Spanish, Italian, Basque, Dutch, Russian, Portuguese, Arabic, Hungarian), Spanish-X, and English-X, using hypotheses about the similarity of languages as seen from the point of view of historical linguistics like language contact and borrowings as a criterion of validity. His results seem to be in accordance with these theoretical predictions. It may be noteworthy that Cooper (2008) measures convexity from a random sample of just approximately 1000 single-term lemmata, which seems to yield reliable estimates, as he indicates.

A peculiarity of Cooper's (2008) approach is that his results may depend heavily on the translation direction. This holds true for i.a. the language pairs analytical language (e.g. English) – fusional language (e.g. Hungarian, Finnish). For example, for the direction fusional language – English, Cooper's convexity is close to zero in his sample, implying supposed semantic closeness, while for the direction English – fusional language it is highly positive, which indicates large semantic distance between these languages, as expected. His approach can, furthermore, be criticized for providing only gradable information about the *degree* of semantic relatedness between two languages without specifying *how* or *in which respect* semantic fields differ. Additionally, it remains to be validated how well his methodology can cope with larger classes of languages and how robust his computations are when different types of dictionaries are consulted.[1] Nonetheless, his approach is elegant in the sense that it is based upon simple calculations applied to a small set of easily accessible data; for comparative linguistics it could be useful in validating existing hypotheses about semantic language typologies or generating new ones.

Mehler, Pustylnikov, and Diewald (2011) analyze conceptual networks derived from the Wikipedia topic classification systems for different languages, considering solely structural properties of these resources, similar to Cooper's (2008) approach, without referring e.g. to the names and values of the categories of their networks. They claim to test a variant of the Sapir-Whorf hypothesis, which, generally speaking, states that a language shapes perception and cognition of its speakers, by comparing their calculated hierarchizations of the concept networks to "classical" genealogical language trees.

Since concepts represent meaning, an analysis of conceptual networks is certainly insightful also for our problem of semantic typologies. However, Mehler, Pustylnikov, and Diewald's (2011) methodology partly differs from the approach pursued in our work. Apart from technical differences[2], Mehler, Pustylnikov, and Diewald (2011) also rely upon a given classification system against which to measure the performance of their method. This theory-driven top-down approach contrasts with our data-driven bottom-up approach; in particular, networks based upon conceptual or semantic relationships may indeed differ from networks derived from morphological or phonological relationships, upon which genealogical trees are based. Postulating presumed congruencies or trying to harmonize one network type with another, as done in Mehler, Pustylnikov, and Diewald (2011), may mask these differences[3].

As opposed to the first two approaches, which take into account only structural properties of language data, **Gaume**, Fabienne, and Bernard (2006) and Gaume, Duvignau, and Vanhove (2008) also consider the actual contents of their data. They work primarily with monolingual and synonym dictionaries and propose different visualization methods so as to make their dictionary analysis results more accessible for different linguistic tasks. Conceptually, they work with probability distributions based on Markov processes analogous to those used in PageRank computations (Brin and Page 1998) to compare network vertices (for a definition, see below), e.g. single words or network *cliques*, that is, fully connected synonym groups (Gaume, Fabienne, and Bernard 2006; for cliques, see Ploux and Ji 2003).

As regards cross-lingual semantic similarity, Gaume, Duvignau, and Vanhove (2008) propose comparing distances between word pairs such as *meat/animal, child/fruit, door/mouth* in several monolingual dictionaries in order to categorize the associated languages. This approach has, to our knowledge, not been realized so far but could certainly be of value for semantic typology.

3. Networks and network analysis

A network (or graph) $G=(V,E)$ is a mathematical structure consisting of a finite set of objects V, called *vertices*, and a binary relation E on V. We call an element $e \in E$ an *edge* of the network G. If the relation E is symmetric, i.e., uEv implies vEu for all $u,v \in V$, then we call the network *undirected*, otherwise we call it *directed*. We call two vertices of a network *connected* if there is a sequence of edges leading from one to the other (a *path*). A *connected* component of a network is a connected subgraph (any two vertices are connected) not connected to any other vertices.

To illustrate, a network might consist of cities as vertex set V, with an edge between any two cities if, say, there is a railway connecting them; this would most likely be an undirected network since if a train goes from city A to city B, it should go from city B to city A as well (for an example, see figure 1, right). An instance of a directed network could be a social relationship network made up of people (the vertices), with an edge between any two people u and v if and only if u likes v; certainly, liking someone does not necessarily entail reciprocity. In linguistics, network vertices are often words, or *concepts* (see e.g. Fellbaum 1998; Ferrer i Cancho and Solé 2001; Batagelj, Mrvar, and Zaveršnik 2002; Motter et al. 2002; Steyvers and Tenenbaum 2004; Abramov and Lokot 2011, whose vertices are morphemes and parts of speech, and many others), and edges may represent various types of relationships between these words or concepts. For example, there might be an edge between two words if they follow each other in a sentence (cf. Ferrer i Cancho and Solé 2001); if one appears in the definition of the other (cf. Motter et al. 2002), and so on.

A special kind of network is a *bipartite graph* where the vertex set V is made up of two disjoint, non-empty subsets such that edges are only allowed between the two vertex subsets, but not within each of them. In linguistics, a network induced by a bilingual dictionary has this property (for an example, see figure 1, left).

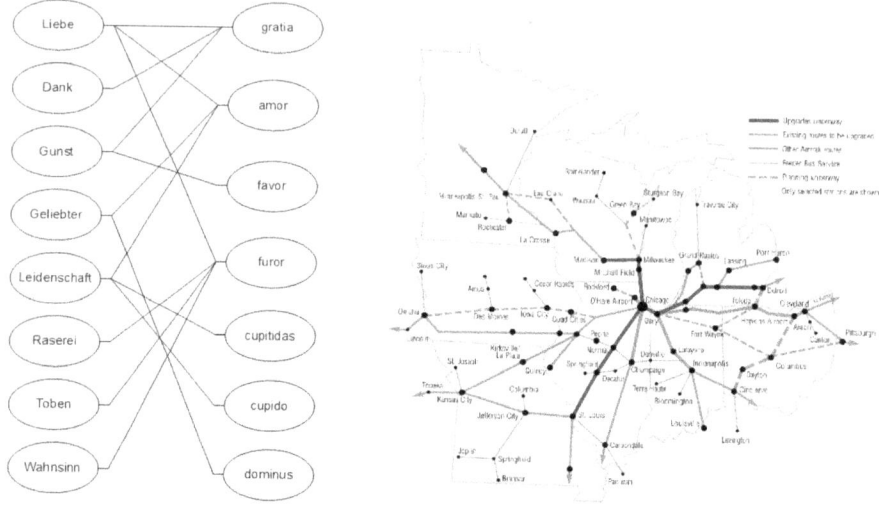

Figure 1. A bipartite graph induced by a bilingual dictionary (adapted from Eger and Sejane 2010). Right: A network of cities and railway connections between them (reprinted from http://www.urbanophile.com/2009/02/15/chicago-reconnectingthe-hinterland-part-1b-high-speed-rail/)

Apart from the above defined ordinary networks, the literature on graphs has introduced several generalizations such as *multigraphs*, in which two vertices can be connected by more than one edge, possibly of different kinds; *hypergraphs*, in which edges can connect more than two vertices; and *weighted graphs*, where weights (e.g. positive real numbers) are associated with vertices and/or edges.

To analyze complex networks in an abstract manner, a multitude of measures on graphs have been proposed such as the number of vertices; the number of edges; the diameter of the network, defined as the maximum over all shortest distances – where the shortest distance between two (connected) vertices is the length of the shortest path connecting them; the density of the network, defined as the number of edges of the network divided by the maximal number of edges. More recent measures on graphs include graph entropy via information functionals defined on network vertices (cf. Dehmer 2008).

Three very important measures that have been extensively investigated in the last two decades are the average path length, i.e., the mean shortest distance between two vertices, averaged over all pairs of vertices; the degree distribution, which gives the probability that a vertex has k, k=1,2,3,..., neighbors, where a neighbor of a vertex u is any vertex v such that there exists

Table 1. Real-world networks and their statistical properties (reprinted from Wang and Chen 2003 with the author's permission)

Table 1.
Small-world pattern and scale-free property of several real networks. Each network has the number of nodes N, the clustering coefficient C, the average path length L and the degree exponent γ of the power-law degree distribution. The WWW and metabolic network are described by directed graphs.

Network	Size	Clustering coefficient	Average path length	Degree exponent
Internet, domain level [13]	32711	0.24	3.56	2.1
Internet, router level [13]	228298	0.03	9.51	2.1
WWW [14]	153127	0.11	3.1	$\gamma_{in} = 2.1$ $\gamma_{out} = 2.45$
E-mail [15]	56969	0.03	4.95	1.81
Software [16]	1376	0.06	6.39	2.5
Electronic circuits [17]	329	0.34	3.17	2.5
Language [18]	460902	0.437	2.67	2.7
Movie actors [5, 7]	225226	0.79	3.65	2.3
Math. co-authorship [19]	70975	0.59	9.50	2.5
Food web [20, 21]	154	0.15	3.40	1.13
Metabolic system [22]	778	–	3.2	$\gamma_{in} = \gamma_{out} = 2.2$

an edge between u and v; and the clustering coefficient (Watts and Strogatz 1998), which indicates how well the neighbors of a vertex are connected, on average. It has been repeatedly shown (see, for example, the survey of Wang and Chen 2003) that many *real-world networks* are characterized by the following parameter settings for the last three measures:

- They have a short average path length, that is, any two vertices are just a short distance away from each other;
- Their degree distribution follows a Power law, $P(k) \sim k^{-a}$, where a is a positive real number. This distribution means that a few vertices (sometimes called *hubs*) have very many neighbors, whereas most vertices have just a few neighbors. Networks with such a degree distribution are also called *scale-free* networks;
- They have comparatively high clustering coefficients, which means that the neighbors of a vertex are usually also neighbors of each other (as one might expect, for instance, for a friendship network).

Networks with a high clustering coefficient and short average path length are said to satisfy the *small world property* (Watts and Strogatz 1998). On the contrary, *random graphs*, where vertices are randomly connected (cf. Erdös and Rényi 1959), have short average distances but low clustering. In table 1, some typical real-world networks and some of their statistical properties are depicted.

4. Methodological approach

Our approach is based on the idea that the bipartite graph induced by a bilingual dictionary represents a network of lexical semantic relationships between the two languages under investigation. Intuitively, the closer two words are in this network – where closeness is measured e.g. in terms of shortest distances – the more semantically similar they should be. If there is a distance of one between two words (this implies that the two words are from different languages), then one word is the translation of the other and the two must be considered – more or less – equivalents in their respective languages. If there is a distance of two between two words (this implies that the two words are from the same language), then there is a common word in the other language such that both words are translations of this word, from which we should be able to conclude that both words are, again, semantically very similar to each other. This reasoning can of course be extended to arbitrary distances between two words and we would expect the degree of similarity between them to decrease as the length of the shortest path increases (for a discussion and analysis of this, cf. Eger and Sejane 2010; see also Wunderlich 1980; Dyvik 2003; Priss and Old 2005).

Now, assume that we have three languages A,B,C and two bilingual dictionaries mapping between them, with language A involved twice (serving as a reference language or a *tertium comparationis* or *interlingua*), i.e., there is a bilingual dictionary mapping from A to B, A – B, and one mapping from A to C, A – C. By deleting language B words in the bipartite graph A – B (and language C words in A – C) and reconnecting edges such that two words in language A are directly connected if and only if they have a mutual translation in language B or C, respectively, one obtains two distinct lexical semantic representations, both encoded in language A. To illustrate, consider figures 2 and 3, where we show an extract (focusing on the network around the word *man/Mann* (German)/*vir* (Latin) of the bipartite graph for the language pair German-Latin (retrieved from http://www.auxilium-online.net) and a similar graph for the language pair German-English (retrieved from http://dict.leo.org), together with the transformed monolingual networks as described above.

Considering the two networks in the German language (in the remainder we will usually speak of representations *in* the reference language as representations *of* the reference language) derived in this way, we note the following: The length of the shortest path between *Mann* 'man' and *Frau* 'woman' in the network derived from the German-English bilingual dictionary is 3, proceeding (among other possibilities) from *Mann* through

Semantic typologies by means of network analysis of bilingual dictionaries 455

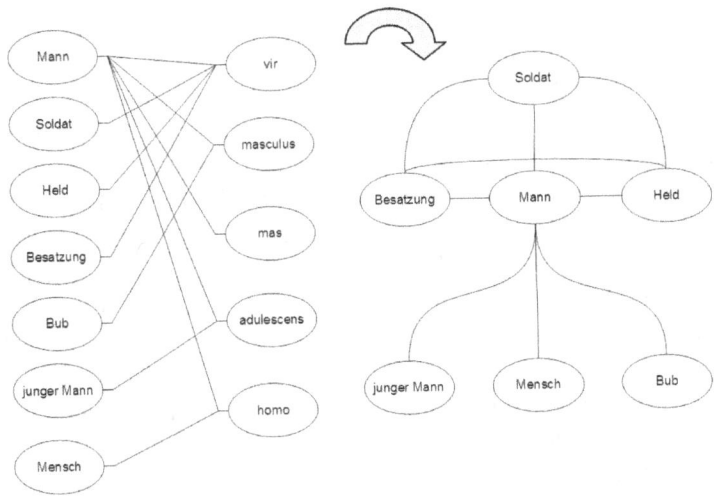

Figure 2. Bipartite graph German-Latin induced by corresponding bilingual dictionary and transformed monolingual network for the language German. Please note for this and the following representations of networks that the arrangement of nodes is arbitrary, except, of course, for the edges between them.

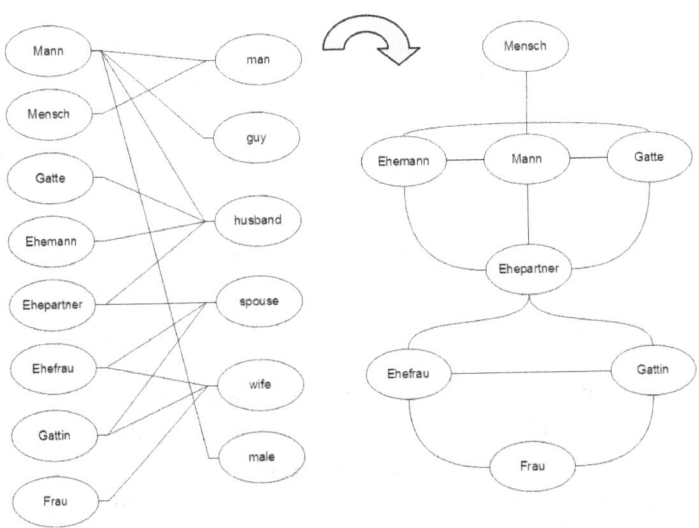

Figure 3. Bipartite graph German-English induced by corresponding bilingual dictionary and transformed monolingual network of German

Ehe-partner 'spouse' and *Ehefrau* 'wife' to *Frau*, while there is no path between *Mann* and *Frau* in the network derived from the German-Latin dictionary. Contrarily, in the latter network, we find paths between *Mann* and *Held* 'hero' or between *Mann* and *Soldat* 'soldier', none of which exists in the former network. But there are also similarities. In the German-English bipartite graph, the actual distance between *Mann* and *Mensch* 'human being' is 2, namely *Mann – man – Mensch,* just as in the German-Latin graph via *Mann – homo – Mensch*. Thus, it seems that, if German is represented via a German-English dictionary, (slightly) different semantic associations are invoked than if German is represented via a German-Latin dictionary. Since the German influence is held fixed in both cases, these differences – and similarities – should be due to different – and similar – segmentations of lexical semantic space in the English and Latin languages.

Extending this reasoning to N languages, where N is at least 2, our approach is to use bilingual dictionaries mapping between a common reference language R and each of the N languages in order to obtain N different semantic network representations of R (which we call *versions*) as described above. More formally, the i-th network representation of R, i=1,...,N, is a graph $G_i=(V_i, E_i)$ consisting of a vertex set V_i of all words of the language R contained in the bilingual dictionary T_i mapping from R to the i-th language, and an edge set E_i, where

$$E_i = \{\{u,v\}: u \in V_i, v \in V_i, u \neq v, \exists w (u T_i w, w T_i v)\} \quad,$$

where we use the notation $aT_i b$ to denote that a is a translation of b in T_i. The choice of the reference language R should thereby be arbitrary.

Our hypothesis is then that the different segmentations of lexical semantic space of different natural languages will be mirrored in the N different network versions obtained in this manner. The networks of languages with similar segmentations of lexical semantic space should be similar to each other, while the networks of languages with very different segmentations should also be very different, so that we should be able to detect and identify these differences and similarities and potentially also group languages according to their division of semantic space.[4]

An advantage of our approach is that we are not only able to analyze the N network versions of the reference language R in an abstract and global manner, e.g. by comparing abstract network statistics such as degree distribution and average path length for the different graphs. Since vertices are comparable across the different network versions and have a consistent and unique interpretation, it is also possible to identify differences on a local vertex level, which allows for a more fine-grained analysis.

Contrarily, a limiting factor of our method could be for example the misleading connections invoked as a result of *homonymy*, i.e., the agreement of forms of two words with very different meanings. For example, using a German-English dictionary one might arrive at a path *Herbst* 'autumn' – *fall* – *Sturz* 'collapse', indicating a presumed close relationship between German *Herbst* and German *Sturz*; likewise, when using an English-German dictionary, one might obtain dubious semantic associations such as *wage* – *Gehalt* (neuter 'contents', masc. 'wage') – *contents* or *page* – *Seite* ('page' and 'side') – *side*. While we ignore this problem currently, we note that many bilingual dictionaries differentiate between cases of homonymy and polysemy so that this issue could possibly be resolved e.g. by marking the different variants of the homonymous word.

Another facet of semantics that our current approach fails to grasp but which might be interesting for language comparisons is one-to-many or few-to-many relationships between two languages. For example, the European Saami people are said to have hundreds of different lexemes corresponding to one English word *snow* (cf. Magga 2006). This phenomenon would go unnoticed in our current approach to modeling lexical semantic spaces across different languages. However, one way to resolve this could be to introduce weighted graphs, where an edge in the monolingual graph between words u and v receives a weight $d(u,v)$ in proportion to the number of ways there are in the bilingual bipartite graph to reach u from v (this may include self-loops). For example, we could set

$$d(u,v) = |\{w : uTw, wTv\}| \ .$$

To summarize, the rationale behind our approach is the language-dependent polysemy of single words which – via the translation relation – entails language-specific structural relationships (e.g. connected components) in such language networks as discussed above. We illustrate this with a few more examples: Latin has a word, *lingua*, with two corresponding words in English, *language* and *tongue* , i.e. 'the organ necessary to articulate language'; very similar words with (nearly) identical meanings exist in French, *langue*, Italian, *lingua*, Spanish, *lengua*, Portuguese, *língua*, and Catalan, *llengua*. Thus, if English or, say, German (which is in this case better suited for illustrative purposes) is represented via any of these languages, an association – and in the network, an edge – between *Zunge* 'tongue' and *Sprache* 'language' is established. This association is not present when German is represented via Dutch (*Zunge* and *Sprache* have no common translation) or Chinese. In the latter case, another association is invoked: *huà* 'language' corresponds to *Strich* 'streak' or *Bild* 'picture'. Furthermore, Russian *свет*

[svet] translates into *world* and *light*; Latin *disciplina* into *education* and *school*, i.e., 'the institution that conveys education'; French *temps*, Spanish *tiempo*, but also Latvian *laiks* into *time* and *weather*; French *bœuf*, Italian *manzo* correspond to both *cow* and *beef*, i.e., 'meat of the respective animal'. Finally, ancient Greek κόσμος [*kósmos*] has a huge associated semantic field potentially not present in many other languages.

We hold that the above-described network approach is able to identify and quantify shared semantic spaces across languages and is thus able to induce a typology of lexical semantic associations.

5. Data

For this study we use open-source universal bilingual dictionaries from the project *dicts.info* (http://www.dicts.info/uddl.php [accessed February–September 2011]). This database comprises 36 languages so that it constitutes a large, freely available resource of comparable bilingual dictionaries.

However, as these particular dictionaries are largely compiled automatically from different digital sources, they, firstly, differ in their respective sizes and, secondly, lack the quality standards of printed and/or revised bilingual dictionaries. As will be seen, these shortcomings limit the quality of the results obtainable by approaches to determining semantic similarity, including our own approach. Nonetheless, such data, in particular, are quite typical for languages that are not well recorded and researched, as many of the world's languages still are, so that this dataset would apparently represent a suitable testbed for language typology.

6. Results

In this section, we first analyze the networks derived from the bilingual dictionaries mentioned in the previous section in an abstract manner, by determining statistical properties derived from the graph measures discussed in section 3. Afterwards, we compare them on a content level, by referring to the values or names of vertices, i.e., to the specific words represented by vertices. This analysis is the basis for finally investigating different segmentations of lexical semantic space across languages.

In the current study, we choose English as the reference language because it is then – for the scientific interpreter – easier to understand the values of network vertices but, as mentioned, we consider the choice of the reference language in general to be arbitrary, which could be an issue for further experimental research. Moreover, we focus on words with the word class noun as is common practice in (computational) semantic similarity research since nouns form the largest, homogeneous group of the lexicon with a frequently precise meaning even without context. The investigation of cross-lingual semantic space for other word classes is left for future research.

6.1. Abstract statistical network properties

For our analysis, we obtained 35 network versions of the English language by considering bilingual dictionaries English-X for the languages X listed in table 2 and applying the techniques described in section 4 to them. Table 2 summarizes statistical properties of these 35 networks. From this, we see that our networks are quite heterogeneous, ranging from just 886 word vertices in the Vietnamese version of English to 2125 words in the Russian version. Nevertheless, all graphs are comparably dense (with an average density of

Table 2. The 35 network versions of English and their statistical properties

ISO 639-1	language	#nodes	#edges	#conn. comp.	diameter	density	av. path length	clust. coeff.	max. degree
ar	Arabic	2079	3429	673	9	0.002	2.333	0.899	19
bg	Bulgarian	1415	2091	531	5	0.002	1.312	0.949	17
ca	Catalan	1703	2725	584	6	0.002	1.696	0.912	19
zh	Chinese	2043	3406	670	8	0.002	2.313	0.877	30
hr	Croatian	1678	2695	575	6	0.002	1.730	0.919	19
cs	Czech	2125	3956	637	9	0.002	2.879	0.877	20
da	Danish	2000	3303	653	8	0.002	2.022	0.898	19
nl	Dutch	2091	3505	659	7	0.002	2.079	0.880	19
eo	Esperanto	1953	3080	654	7	0.002	1.963	0.891	20
fi	Finnish	2066	3613	648	10	0.002	2.658	0.892	20
fr	French	2112	3654	660	10	0.002	2.718	0.882	22
de	German	2124	3897	632	8	0.002	2.797	0.862	23
el	Greek	1958	3170	652	10	0.002	2.536	0.899	18
he	Hebrew	1580	2362	580	8	0.002	1.783	0.935	19
hi	Hindi	1399	2019	521	4	0.002	1.340	0.933	17
hu	Hungarian	1999	3297	646	8	0.002	2.308	0.893	19
id	Indonesian	1986	3290	646	8	0.002	1.900	0.901	17
it	Italian	2098	3483	671	7	0.002	1.943	0.892	19
ja	Japanese	2049	3338	674	6	0.002	1.835	0.899	19
ko	Korean	1918	3149	622	7	0.002	2.065	0.896	19
la	Latin	1708	3133	535	12	0.002	3.677	0.896	22
lt	Lithuanian	1934	3266	638	6	0.002	1.629	0.911	17
mt	Maltese	1754	3151	584	7	0.002	1.833	0.908	24
nb	Norwegian_bokmal	1880	2934	640	6	0.002	1.798	0.914	19
pl	Polish	2076	3487	664	6	0.002	1.938	0.884	21
pt	Portuguese	2067	3496	669	7	0.002	2.102	0.899	21
ro	Romanian	1957	3179	657	8	0.002	1.952	0.908	19
ru	Russian	2125	3867	649	14	0.002	3.885	0.877	24
sr	Serbian	1042	1401	421	5	0.003	1.207	0.965	19
sk	Slovak	2087	3421	654	6	0.002	1.985	0.880	22
es	Spanish	2125	5649	537	14	0.003	5.568	0.780	42
sv	Swedish	2044	3309	659	8	0.002	2.019	0.886	19
th	Thai	943	1307	369	3	0.003	1.127	0.968	17
tr	Turkish	2015	3594	622	15	0.002	4.189	0.887	20
vi	Vietnamese	886	1303	339	3	0.003	1.166	0.965	17

Table 3. LCCs of network versions of English and their statistical properties

ISO 639-1	language	#nodes	#edges	#conn. comp.	diameter	density	av. path length	clust. coeff.	max. degree
ar	Arabic	49	113	1	9	0.096	4.184	0.632	13
bg	Bulgarian	22	70	1	5	0.303	2.307	0.871	12
ca	Catalan	34	169	1	5	0.301	2.524	0.904	19
zh	Chinese	70	371	1	6	0.154	2.819	0.859	30
hr	Croatian	37	89	1	6	0.134	2.971	0.572	14
cs	Czech	78	216	1	9	0.072	4.575	0.658	16
da	Danish	40	116	1	6	0.149	3.040	0.811	13
nl	Dutch	44	141	1	7	0.149	3.023	0.746	16
eo	Esperanto	45	111	1	7	0.112	3.210	0.664	15
fi	Finnish	69	228	1	8	0.097	3.547	0.726	18
fr	French	70	191	1	10	0.079	4.233	0.692	16
de	German	82	244	1	8	0.073	3.702	0.696	16
el	Greek	75	213	1	10	0.077	4.109	0.688	18
he	Hebrew	48	153	1	8	0.136	3.088	0.738	19
hi	Hindi	22	129	1	4	0.558	1.567	0.949	17
hu	Hungarian	60	152	1	8	0.086	3.810	0.669	12
id	Indonesian	37	107	1	6	0.161	2.917	0.801	13
it	Italian	40	113	1	5	0.145	2.863	0.700	15
ja	Japanese	37	88	1	6	0.132	3.132	0.667	12
ko	Korean	49	118	1	7	0.100	3.206	0.592	15
la	Latin	111	348	1	12	0.057	5.187	0.706	22
lt	Lithuanian	33	112	1	5	0.212	2.409	0.761	17
mt	Maltese	43	132	1	7	0.146	3.401	0.765	12
nb	Norwegian_bokmal	33	167	1	5	0.316	2.502	0.918	19
pl	Polish	41	112	1	6	0.137	3.101	0.688	13
pt	Portuguese	56	195	1	7	0.127	3.391	0.863	21
ro	Romanian	38	135	1	5	0.192	2.872	0.819	18
ru	Russian	121	499	1	14	0.069	5.563	0.826	24
sr	Serbian	22	133	1	3	0.576	1.554	0.935	19
sk	Slovak	44	106	1	6	0.112	3.358	0.672	12
es	Spanish	410	1935	1	14	0.023	5.883	0.689	42
sv	Swedish	44	107	1	6	0.113	3.123	0.632	14
th	Thai	18	123	1	2	0.804	1.196	0.982	17
tr	Turkish	133	345	1	15	0.039	5.812	0.643	18
vi	Vietnamese	18	123	1	2	0.804	1.196	0.982	17

0.002) and have short average path lengths, ranging from 1.312 for Bulgarian to 5.568 for Spanish, with a mean value of just 2.236. Clustering coefficients are extremely high, averaging over 0.90. The column *#connected components* is insightful. Obviously, our dictionary networks are composed of many small, disconnected subgraphs. In fact, most words in our networks are single words, without any connection to other words; on average, this concerns around 35% of all words in any of the 35 versions of English. A further 25% of all words are located in a connected component of size two and only about 7% of all words are within clusters of more than six words. That is to say, our networks are very sparsely connected, which leads to high clustering coefficients and short average path lengths. To illustrate, the average shortest path length in a connected component of size two is exactly 1.

Semantic typologies by means of network analysis of bilingual dictionaries 461

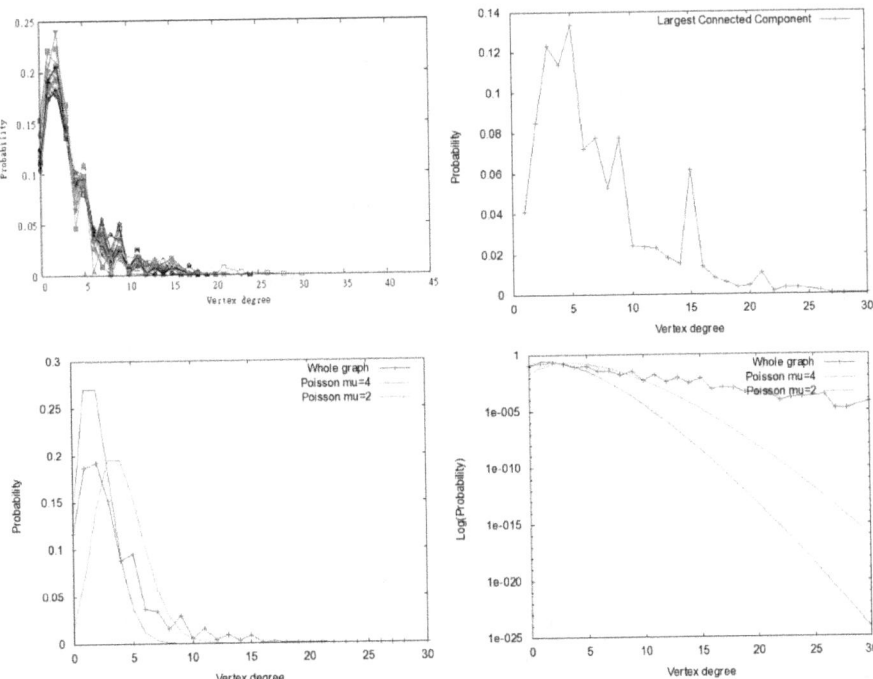

Figure 4. Vertex degree distributions. Top left: All 35 network versions. Top right: LCC, average over networks. Bottom left: Average over networks and Poisson approximations. Bottom right: Logscale of bottom left

In order to compensate for this distorting effect, table 3 focuses on the largest connected component (LCC) of each network version of English. There, we can see that the average path lengths are in fact longer (mean value of 3.29) and the clustering coefficients are lower (mean value of 0.757), although still quite high. As discussed in section 3, short distances between vertices and relatively high clustering coefficients are typical for many real-world graphs and are the defining characteristics of small-world networks.

Finally, we look at the vertex degree distributions of our network versions of English, see figure 4. First, we note that these do not follow Power law distributions as is characteristic of many real-world networks. This does not even change when just focusing on the LCCs (top right figure). What characterizes our vertex degree distributions instead is that they resemble Poisson distributions for small values of vertex degrees k (see bottom left and bottom right figures) – Poisson distributions are typical for Erdös-Rényi random networks (cf. Bollobás 2003) – with some probability mass relocated from small k's to larger k's. Indeed, the bottom right figure shows that our vertex degree distribution P(k) attaches significantly more probability mass to large degrees than a Poisson distribution would do that coincides with P(k) for small values of k. Non-negligible probability for large values of k, in turn, is characteristic of Power law distributions.

Thus, similar to the finding of Motter et al. (2002), who postulated a shift between an exponential and a Power law regime for networks representing monolingual dictionaries, we might conjecture that our vertex degree distributions – derived from bilingual dictionaries – are likewise characterized by a regime shift; for small k, P(k) seems to follow a Poisson distribution, while for larger k, P(k) seems to follow a Power law distribution. More empirical data (on larger bilingual dictionaries) would be helpful in investigating this hypothesis.

6.2. Segmentations of lexical semantic space

In this subsection, we analyze how the different languages contained in our database can be grouped according to their segmentations of lexical semantic space. A crucial question thereby is how to measure distances between our 35 network versions of English. As can be imagined, there are a multitude of different and rationalizable ways to specify such distance measures. To propose one, we want to make use of the fact that vertices in our networks are comparable across languages provided that all bilingual dictionaries have the same entries for the reference language. Thus, one idea would be to use the intersection of English words across the 35 different bilingual dictionaries English-X and to delete all other vertices and the edges associated with them from the respective networks. The problem here is that the resulting intersection of words is very small (comprising only 435 units), since some of our dictionaries are very small.

Hence, we decided to use a subset of languages with a preferably large common English vocabulary. Table 4 shows the 22 languages out of the 35 that we have decided upon; the size of their joint vocabulary is 935, a number which we considered still acceptable.[5] In these 22 network versions of English, we deleted all vertices not contained in the common vocabulary of the 22 languages and the associated edges.[6]

Now, let A and B be two networks with identical vertices (same number of vertices and same label for each vertex), as in our case. Let v be one of these vertices. This vertex could for example be represented by the vectors of shortest distances to all other vertices in networks A and B. Then the distance between vertex v in network A and network B could be specified as the differ-

Semantic typologies by means of network analysis of bilingual dictionaries 463

Table 4. 22 selected network versions of English with common vertex set of size 935

ISO 639-1	language	#nodes	#edges	#conn. comp.	diameter	density	av. path length	clust. coeff.	max. degree
ar	Arabic	935	1330	362	6	0.003	1.523	0.954	19
ca	Catalan	935	1345	371	4	0.003	1.275	0.964	19
zh	Chinese	935	1360	365	5	0.003	1.651	0.940	19
cs	Czech	935	1400	358	7	0.003	1.675	0.945	19
da	Danish	935	1323	367	5	0.003	1.361	0.951	19
nl	Dutch	935	1328	365	4	0.003	1.279	0.951	19
fi	Finnish	935	1369	364	5	0.003	1.361	0.960	19
fr	French	935	1331	367	4	0.003	1.347	0.946	20
de	German	935	1376	360	5	0.003	1.508	0.937	19
hu	Hungarian	935	1344	359	4	0.003	1.383	0.948	19
it	Italian	935	1341	368	4	0.003	1.291	0.957	19
ja	Japanese	935	1377	372	4	0.003	1.269	0.965	19
nb	Norwegian_bokmal	935	1306	373	5	0.003	1.372	0.952	19
pl	Polish	935	1353	362	4	0.003	1.350	0.945	19
pt	Portuguese	935	1325	369	4	0.003	1.296	0.953	19
ro	Romanian	935	1312	369	4	0.003	1.222	0.961	19
ru	Russian	935	1402	352	7	0.003	1.674	0.953	19
sr	Serbian	935	1271	383	4	0.003	1.177	0.968	19
sk	Slovak	935	1309	371	4	0.003	1.281	0.954	19
es	Spanish	935	1706	327	8	0.004	2.212	0.907	25
sv	Swedish	935	1328	365	5	0.003	1.367	0.947	19
tr	Turkish	935	1382	356	5	0.003	1.532	0.942	19

ence between the two vectors associated with v in A and B (for example, by applying the Euclidean vector norm to the difference between these two vectors). The difference between network A and network B could then be defined as the average difference over all such vector representations of common vertices. However, shortest distance may not be the most valuable information to use in this case (cf. Gaume, Fabienne, and Bernard 2006, Gaume, Duvignau, and Vanhove 2008, Gaume et al. 2008). In the two networks A and B, v could have an identical shortest distance to another vertex w, but the network topology between v and w might still be considerably dissimilar in networks A and B. For instance, there might be five different paths of equal shortest length between v and w in network A and just one such path in network B. Therefore, we decided to represent each vertex v in network A (and network B) by the probability distribution that, if starting from this vertex v, one might reach any of the other vertices in network A (and network B) after a prespecified number of time steps T, where in each time step one may pass from vertex v to any of its neighbors with equal probability.[7] Thus, to each vertex v in the networks A and B, we associate vectors v(A) and v(B) – representing the above mentioned probability distributions with T fixed[8] – of dimension of the number of vertices in network A and B and then define the distance between networks A and B as

$$dist(A,B) = 1/|V| \sum_{v \in V} \|v(A) - v(B)\|,$$

where V is the common vertex set of networks A and B, $|V|$ denotes its size and $\|.\|$ denotes the standard Euclidean norm.

To investigate results deducible from the so-defined distance measure on language networks, we apply clustering algorithms to the entailed distance matrix. Figure 5 shows a dendrogram, a tree diagram visualizing the categorizations produced by hierarchical clustering[9].

We note the following. The Spanish language has supposedly a huge semantic distance to all other languages in our database, which may be explained by reference to the statistical network properties shown in tables 2 and 4. The Spanish network obviously has many more edges between words than any other network version of English; we conjecture that this might just be an idiosyncrasy of our dictionaries; see below for a discussion. A next observation is that Swedish and Danish are supposedly semantically very close as well as the language group Portuguese, French, Italian, Catalan (Dutch and Polish being at a decisive distance to this group). These findings are consistent over different parametrizations of the clustering algorithm (e.g. different clustering metrics such as complete linkage, Ward's method, etc.). The remaining language groupings shown in the dendrogram are not confirmed by algorithmic variations of the clustering procedure; these comprise the group Russian – Czech – German and the larger group consisting of

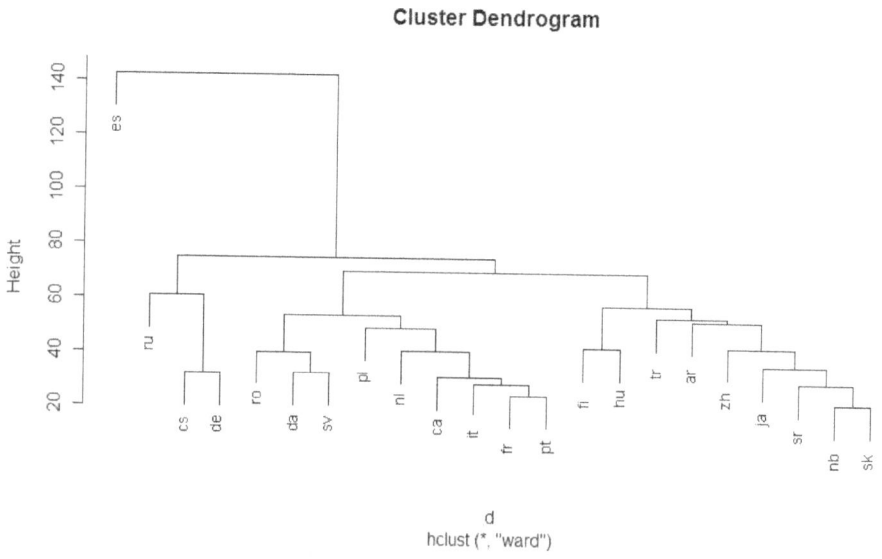

Figure 5. Cluster dendrogram for 22 network versions of English. Lan-guages are abbreviated according to ISO 629-1, see table 4

Norwegian, Slovakian, Serbian, Japanese, Chinese, Arabic, Turkish, Finnish, and Hungarian.

To further investigate the relationships between the Romance languages Catalan, French, Italian, Portuguese, and Spanish, we show in table 5 the languages closest to each of these five languages in terms of absolute distances (and not applying a clustering approach). We see that in all cases, the Romance languages have short distances to each other; Spanish, while being remote from all other languages, still has French, Portuguese and Catalan as its closest semantic partners, with Italian also considerably close. In table 6,

Table 5. Romance languages and their closest semantic partners

Catalan		French		Italian		Portuguese		Spanish	
Norwegian	25.3007	Portuguese	24.7941	Portuguese	26.6807	French	24.7941	French	78.9131
Portuguese	27.8339	Italian	28.7565	French	28.7565	Italian	26.6807	Portuguese	85.5382
French	29.8679	Catalan	29.8679	Catalan	31.4428	Norwegian	27.6748	Catalan	87.2117
Japanese	31.3349	Norwegian	32.5264	Norwegian	34.2465	Catalan	27.8339	German	88.8150
Italian	31.4428	Slovakian	34.6032	Slovakian	35.1883	Dutch	29.9250	Slovakian	89.9539
Danish	32.8654	Danish	35.7209	Danish	36.1929	Slovakian	30.0460	Italian	90.8511
Serbian	33.3570	Japanese	38.2831	Romanian	37.7830	Danish	34.4361	Norwegian	91.3154
Polish	33.4678	Dutch	40.0166	Japanese	38.4899	Japanese	34.8830	Japanese	93.0941
Slovakian	34.1565	Romanian	40.3072	Dutch	38.9243	Romanian	37.1570	Dutch	94.2190
Dutch	35.5748	Swedish	41.1101	Serbian	40.7918	German	37.2996	Danish	96.4415
Finnish	36.4243	Chinese	42.6576	Swedish	43.0163	Polish	37.3042	Arabic	96.5826
Swedish	38.8273	Serbian	42.9863	Finnish	43.1344	Swedish	37.7181	Chinese	96.6399
Chinese	39.6909	German	44.3813	German	45.9067	Finnish	37.8654	Czech	97.4170
Hungarian	40.1763	Polish	45.1632	Chinese	45.9145	Serbian	38.4221	Polish	97.9113
German	40.4225	Hungarian	46.1931	Polish	46.2678	Czech	44.0928	Turkish	98.4799
Romanian	41.0417	Finnish	46.8970	Hungarian	47.0784	Chinese	45.0220	Swedish	98.5375
Turkish	43.8777	Czech	48.5890	Arabic	51.3805	Hungarian	45.8068	Serbian	100.9077
Arabic	45.8613	Arabic	49.7164	Turkish	52.0790	Arabic	46.5975	Hungarian	101.9807
Czech	47.0202	Turkish	51.1400	Czech	52.5966	Turkish	48.4277	Finnish	102.8491
Russian	54.3030	Russian	54.3979	Russian	55.9426	Russian	49.6876	Romanian	103.3453
Spanish	87.2117	Spanish	78.9131	Spanish	90.8511	Spanish	85.5382	Russian	112.7717

Table 6. Germanic languages and their closest semantic partners

Danish		Dutch		German		Norwegian		Swedish	
Norwegian	27.6779	Portuguese	29.9250	Norwegian	32.0666	Slovakian	22.4427	Danish	32.4682
Slovakian	32.0333	Norwegian	31.6406	Czech	32.1229	Catalan	25.3007	Norwegian	32.5633
Swedish	32.4682	Slovakian	31.8317	Slovakian	36.7106	Serbian	27.2520	Portuguese	37.7181
Catalan	32.0333	Danish	35.1088	Portuguese	37.2996	Portuguese	27.6748	Slovakian	37.7635
Portuguese	34.4361	Catalan	35.5748	Danish	37.4890	Danish	27.6779	Catalan	38.8273
Dutch	35.1088	Italian	38.9243	Swedish	39.2860	Japanese	28.8052	Romanian	39.0762
French	35.7209	Japanese	39.1766	Catalan	40.4225	Dutch	31.6406	German	39.2860
Italian	36.1929	French	40.0166	French	43.3813	German	32.0666	French	41.1101
Romanian	37.4466	Finnish	42.9707	Japanese	44.4294	French	32.5264	Serbian	42.6364
German	37.4890	Serbian	43.9035	Chinese	45.1289	Swedish	32.5633	Italian	43.0163
Japanese	40.6173	Swedish	45.5835	Dutch	45.5925	Italian	34.2465	Portuguese	44.5177
Czech	41.1415	German	45.5925	Italian	45.9067	Chinese	35.7667	Dutch	45.5835
Serbian	41.1520	Turkish	45.7011	Serbian	48.1261	Polish	37.1990	Czech	46.8794
Finnish	42.1586	Polish	47.6502	Polish	51.2117	Finnish	37.3401	Chinese	47.0292
Polish	43.7208	Romanian	48.7252	Turkish	52.0507	Czech	37.5628	Finnish	49.6700
Turkish	46.7753	Arabic	50.3108	Arabic	53.2377	Romanian	40.1583	Japanese	52.8877
Chinese	47.5663	Chinese	50.4824	Romanian	55.7574	Turkish	40.2859	Arabic	55.0579
Russian	48.7996	Czech	51.1727	Finnish	56.3291	Arabic	42.3544	Hungarian	58.4784
Arabic	51.2741	Hungarian	51.7303	Hungarian	57.8047	Hungarian	42.9484	Turkish	59.2570
Hungarian	51.8377	Russian	58.3361	Russian	61.8422	Russian	50.7306	Russian	60.8316
Spanish	96.4415	Spanish	94.2190	Spanish	88.8150	Spanish	91.3154	Spanish	98.5375

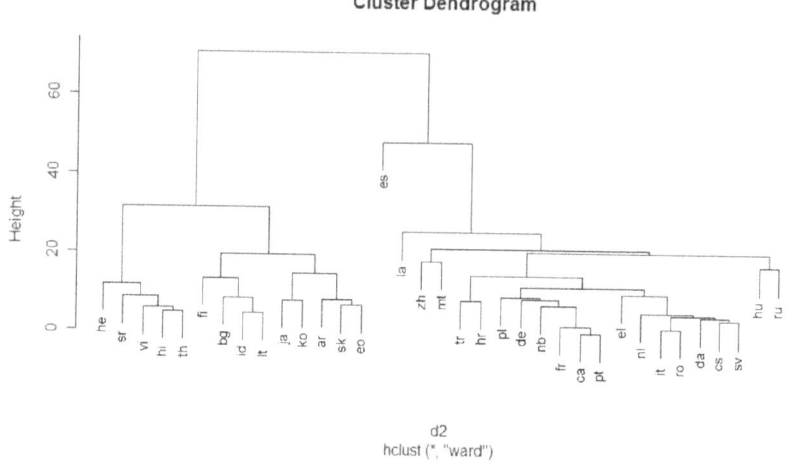

Figure 6. Cluster dendrogram using all 35 network versions of English; for language codes see table 2 or 3

we present similar results for the Germanic languages Danish, Dutch, German, Norwegian, and Swedish.

Next, we also give an analysis using all 35 versions of the English language (cf. figure 6). Although the dendrogram shows some workable results (e.g. clustering of French – Catalan – Portuguese, Italian – Romanian, Danish – Swedish, Japanese – Korean, and Vietnamese – Thai – Hindi), we believe that the subset of just 435 common words is too small for conducting an adequate analysis and reaching definitive conclusions.

6.2.1. Word pairs

Gaume, Duvignau, and Vanhove (2008) suggest contrasting languages by the respective semantic distance they assign to linguistically selected word pairs. Our approach lends itself to pursuing such an analysis. Table 7 displays the semantic distances computed in our framework for the word pairs *door – mouth, house – family,* and *meat – animal,* for each of the 22 languages discussed above. The result shows that in these cases, unfortunately, we cannot satisfactorily compare languages. Rather, it seems that the 22 languages would coincide in their semantic distances assigned to the word pairs *door – mouth* and *meat – animal*. For the word pair *house –family,*

Table 7. Word pairs and their distances in 22 network versions

	door-mouth	house-family	meat-animal
Arabic	0.5001	0.0969	0.4724
Catalan	0.5001	0.0884	0.4726
Chinese	0.5001	0.0970	0.4728
Czech	0.5001	0.0786	0.4722
Danish	0.5001	0.0970	0.4724
Dutch	0.5001	0.5813	0.4728
Finnish	0.5001	0.5813	0.4704
French	0.5001	0.0884	0.4704
German	0.5001	0.0892	0.4726
Hungarian	0.5001	0.0884	0.4724
Italian	0.5001	0.0884	0.4726
Japanese	0.5001	0.5813	0.4726
Norwegian	0.5001	0.5081	0.4726
Polish	0.5001	0.0884	0.4728
Portuguese	0.5001	0.0884	0.4726
Romanian	0.5001	0.0884	0.4728
Russian	0.5001	0.0884	0.4719
Serbian	0.5001	1.1558	0.4733
Slovak	0.5001	0.5813	0.4728
Spanish	0.6709	0.0884	0.3882
Swedish	0.5001	0.0969	0.4728
Turkish	0.5001	0.0969	0.4703

we see small differences, but a typological interpretation of these appears rather difficult.

6.2.2. A comparison: Cooper's approach

In order to compare our results to those obtained by other methods for determining lexical semantic similarities on the same dataset, we implemented Cooper's (2008) idea of inspecting the curvature of the function NT(t) that counts the number of words in a bilingual dictionary with t translations, see table 8. On Cooper's own dataset, he reaches the following results for French and Spanish: Semantically closest partners in decreasing order of closeness are Spanish, Catalan, Portuguese, Italian, English, Basque, Dutch, Russian, German, Hungarian, Arabic for French; and Catalan, French, Portuguese, Italian, Dutch, English, Basque for Spanish. Both results appear to agree with our own rankings shown in table 5. However, when applying Cooper's method to our data, the outcome differs quite substantially from these common findings. This gives us an indication that our dataset has some shortcomings that make the implementation of our task difficult, but that our approach nonetheless generates valuable results, even on this deficient data basis. The next section discusses this.

Table 8. Language distances for French and Spanish via Cooper's (2008) approach – with different random subsets of words, and nouns vs. all words – in decreasing order of semantic closeness

French-X, nouns, 1000		French-X, all, 5000		X-French, nouns, 1000	
Catalan	-0.0444	Catalan	-0.0594	English	-0.0707
Spanish	-0.0278	Dutch	-0.0383	Vietnamese	-0.0422
Dutch	-0.0248	Spanish	-0.0236	Russian	-0.0319
German	-0.0133	German	-0.0126	Romanian	-0.0265
Italian	-0.0127	Portuguese	-0.0055	Arabic	-0.0251
Hungarian	-0.0119	Italian	-0.0006	Finnish	-0.0243
Portuguese	-0.0076	Hungarian	-0.0003	German	-0.0202
Arabic	0.0012	Arabic	0.0028	Korean	-0.0197
English	0.0223	English	0.0052	Slovak	-0.0169
Russian	0.0255	Russian	0.0199	Maltese	-0.0152
				Polish	-0.0139
X-Spanish, nouns, 1000				Turkish	-0.0126
Italian	-0.0283			Chinese	-0.0106
French	-0.0278			Spanish	-0.0101
Dutch	-0.0269			Czech	-0.0099
Arabic	-0.0265			Latin	-0.0089
Portuguese	-0.0238			Lithuanian	-0.0089
English	-0.0202			Croatian	-0.0054
Catalan	-0.0170			Greek	-0.0042
				Japanese	-0.0019
X-Spanish, all, 5000				Esperanto	-0.0016
Arabic	-0.0341			Dutch	-0.0005
Dutch	-0.0297			Indonesian	0.0029
Italian	-0.0254			Norwegian	0.0053
French	-0.0236			Portuguese	0.0064
English	-0.0178			Hungarian	0.0084
Portuguese	-0.0160			Hebrew	0.0091
Catalan	-0.0138			Serbian	0.0108
				Danish	0.0108
				Catalan	0.0110
				Swedish	0.0170
				Hindi	0.0209
				Thai	0.0222
				Bulgarian	0.0267
				Italian	0.0313

7. Discussion

The results presented in the previous section are both encouraging and (partly) disappointing; disappointing because we were not able to delineate linguistically coherent semantic spaces on a large scale. In particular, our approach did not detect semantic boundaries encompassing, say, the Slavic language group (however, as mentioned, due to areal, historical, cultural, etc. reasons, lexical semantic typologies might differ substantially from morphophonological classifications); likewise, Chinese could not be consistently classified other than being some sort of unstable outlier within our data set, and so on. On the other hand, we were able to semantically group the Romance languages in a manner corroborated by similar research endeavors (cf. Cooper 2008). Moreover, some further semantic groupings can easily be justified linguistically such as the similarity between Swedish and Danish as well as that between Japanese and Korean. Could these classifications be due to mere chance? We estimate the probability of having solely the Romance languages clustered together by mere chance as an event of probability at most 2×10^{-5} [10], so that we would reject the null hypothesis of chance by all standard confidence levels.

The reason why our approach was not able to detect further linguistically coherent semantic boundaries may be explained by referring to Cooper's results on our data set. Cooper (2008) states that general-purpose dictionaries are essential for his method to work reliably and we might add that, obviously, these general-purpose dictionaries should satisfy certain quality standards. While a bilingual dictionary is always a subjective endeavor of the lexicologist editing it (or by whatever other means it has been compiled), our dictionaries additionally suffer from the fact that their semi-automatic generation has obviously been deficient. For example, each word has only very few translations, less than we would expect in any dictionary of approved quality. To illustrate, the English-German dictionary has as translations for *tongue* two entries (*Zunge, natürliche Sprache*), while the online dictionary http://dict.leo.org has at least 21 translations for the named English word. Moreover, due to unobservable factors, some languages (such as, prominently, Spanish) seem to have acquired a different topological network structure than the majority of languages, which leads to their classification as statistical outliers. Due to these weaknesses of our data base (this includes also its size, since on average less than 2000 nouns per language must certainly be considered a rather small vocabulary), our method cannot identify many interesting polysemous associations across languages and, therefore, some crucial differences between inter-language lexical semantic fields are not accounted for. However, given that we are still able, unlike apparently Cooper's method, to coherently discriminate between some language families even with the shortcomings of our data is, to us, a strong indication of the potential usefulness, rationality, and adequacy of our methodological approach.

8. Conclusion

In this work, we have presented a methodological framework for determining lexical semantic typologies of natural languages. This rests upon the idea of generating semantic networks of different languages in a common reference language (the *tertium comparationis* or *interlingua*) via bilingual dictionaries so that the resulting network versions of the reference language can be directly compared and arranged into a typology of shared semantic spaces.

Thereby, several technical details have been left for further experimental research, such as how to best determine distances between network versions of the reference language (note that we have just proposed *one* implementation out of a continuum of conceivable possibilities) and which types of classes of lexical entities are particularly suited to or required for performing such an analysis; merely considering the lexical semantic space of nouns, as we have done, may be too restrictive for a general typology. In addition, it must be emphasized that our method evidently does not presuppose human edited bilingual dictionaries but could rely on any knowledge source capable of outlining lexical semantic relationships between languages, such as (statistical) machine translation systems derived from parallel corpora; see for example Rama and Borin (2011), who determine phonologically based typologies via word translations obtained from the Moses machine translation system (Koehn et al. 2007).

We believe that our methods are superior to alternative approaches that do not take the semantic web of words in different languages into account. The best way to confirm this claim would be use of high-quality bilingual dictionaries on which to apply our methodological framework. This would also potentially allow uncovering, on a large scale, particular lexical fields in which different languages (or language families) have idiosyncratic associations and conceptualizations, from which new cross-lingual semantic insights can be expected.

Notes

1. Cooper (2008) addresses this problem himself, stating that different (kinds of) bilingual dictionaries may lead to different conclusions about the relatedness of languages, in his framework. Moreover, it seems to be problematic that his convexity values are always close to zero, in agreement with the visual impression that his translation histograms may in fact be straight lines in log scale, without (or with just random) convex or concave curvature. Cutting the histograms off at the (arbitrary) value of 9 additionally seems to weaken the case for his approach.

2. Mehler, Pustylnikov, and Diewald (2011) report F-scores on the training data, which leads, unsurprisingly, to excellent classification results; these may be misleading, however, since the criterion of the generalization value of a theory is usually the test data. Pathological cases excluded, it is always possible to over-fit one's training data to obtain 100% accuracy results.
3. For example, the fact that Hungarian clustered together with Romanian, which surprised the authors, may be the kind of finding we would expect to be one of the goals of such a typological classification.
4. As an objection to our approach one might argue that it might be more efficient or straightforward to generate semantic networks in individual languages (as was the goal of the EuroWordNet project) and then to apply a knowledge source like bilingual dictionaries to map vertices of these networks to a common interlingua. One should not, however, forget that the cost of generating these individual semantic networks may be significantly higher than the cost of solely consulting bilingual dictionaries, an original source of linguistic relations, to name just one problematic aspect of this idea, from the point of view of technical realization.
5. Recall that Cooper (2008) uses just around 1000 words for his investigations.
6. This may have disadvantages; for example, given two different networks A and B and two distinct vertices u and v, u and v might be connected in A via a path going through another vertex w, but u and v might be disconnected in B. If vertex w and his associated edges are deleted, this difference is nullified.
7. For a technical discussion of this stochastic random walk process, see Brin and Page (1998); Gaume, Fabienne, and Bernard (2006), etc.
8. We choose the value T=4, in accordance with Gaume, Fabienne, and Bernard's (2006) rule of thumb to choose T between L and 2L, where L is the average shortest path length.
9. We use the R program hclust to produce the hierarchical clustering and the dendrogram.
10. Let s(n,k) be the Stirling number of the second kind. Then we estimate the probability of the named event (5 languages correctly clustered out of 22) as $\sum_{k=1}^{17} s(17,k) / \sum_{k=1}^{22} s(22,k) = 1.8.. \times 10^{-5}$.

References

Abramov, Olga and Tatiana Lokot
    2011   Typology by means of language networks. Applying information theoretic measures to morphological derivation networks. In *Towards an Information Theory of Complex Networks: Statistical Methods and Applications*, 321–346. Boston: Birkhäuser.

Batagelj, Vladimir, Andrej Mrvar, and Matjaz Zaveršnik
  2002   Network analysis of dictionaries. In *Jezikovne Tehnologije / Language Technologies*, 135–142. Ljubljana.
Benhabib, Jess, Alberto Bisin, and Matthew O. Jackson (eds.)
  2010   *Handbook of Social Economics*. Vol. 1A. Amsterdam: North-Holland.
Bollobás, Béla
  2003   Mathematical results on scale-free random graphs. In *Handbook of Graphs and Networks*: From the Genome to the Internet, 1–37. Wiley.
Brin, Sergei and Lawrence Page
  1998   The anatomy of a large-scale hypertextual web search engine. In *Proceedings of the Seventh International World-Wide Web Conference (WWW 1998)*, 107–117. Amsterdam: Elsevier Science Publishers B.V.
Cooper, Martin C.
  2005   A mathematical model of historical semantics and the grouping of word meanings into concepts. *Computational Linguistics* 31 (2): 227–248.
Cooper, Martin C.
  2008   Measuring the semantic distance between languages from a statistical analysis of bilingual dictionaries. *Journal of Quantitative Linguistics* 15 (1): 1–33.
Dehmer, Matthias
  2008   Information processing in complex networks: Graph entropy and information functionals. *Applied Mathematics and Computation* 201: 82–94.
Dryer, Matthew S. and Martin Haspelmath (eds.)
  2011   *The World Atlas of Language Structures Online*. Munich: Max Planck Digital Library. http://wals.info/languoid/genealogy [Accessed Sept. 2011].
Dyvik, Helge
  2003   *Translations as a Semantic Knowledge Source*. http://www.hf.uib.no/i/LiLi/SLF/Dyvik/transknow.pdf [Accessed Jan. 2012].
Eger, Steffen and Ineta Sejane
  2010   Computing semantic similarity from bilingual dictionaries. In *Statistical Analysis of Textual Data. Proceedings of the 10th International Conference Journées d'Analyse statistique des Données Textuelles 9–11 June 2010 – Sapienza University of Rome*, 1217–1225.
Erdös, Paul and Alfréd Rényi
  1959   On random graphs I. *Publicationes Mathematicae Debrecen* 5: 290–297.
Fellbaum, Christiane (ed.)
  1998   *WordNet. An Electronic Lexical Database*. Massachusetts: MIT Press.
Ferrer i Cancho, Ramon and Ricardo V. Solé
  2001   The small world of human language. *Proceedings of The Royal Society of London. Series B, Biological Sciences* 268 (1482), 2261–2265.

Gaume, Bruno, Venant Fabienne, and Victorri Bernard
    2006   Hierarchy in lexical organisation of natural languages. In *Hierarchy in Natural and Social Sciences*, 121–142. Dordrecht: Springer.

Gaume, Bruno, Karine Duvignau, and Martine Vanhove
    2008   Semantic associations and confluences in paradigmatic networks. In *From Polysemy to Semantic Change: Towards a Typology of Lexical Semantic Associations*, 233–267. Amsterdam: John Benjamins.

Gaume, Bruno, Karine Duvignau, Laurent Prevot, and Yann Desalle
    2008   Toward a cognitive organization for electronic dictionaries, the case for semantic proxemy. In *22nd International Conference on Computational Linguistics. Proceedings of the Workshop on Cognitive Aspects of the Lexicon*, 86–93.

Hassan, Samer and Rada Mihalcea
    2009   Cross-lingual semantic relatedness using encyclopedic knowledge. In *Proceedings of Conference on Empirical Methods in Natural Language Processing (EMNLP)*, 1192–1201.

Jiang, Jay J. and David W. Conrath
    1997   Semantic similarity based on corpus statistics and lexical taxonomy. In *Proceedings of the 10th International Conference on Research in Computational Linguistics (ROCLING X)*, 19–33.

Koch, Peter
    2001   Lexical typology from a cognitive and linguistic point of view. In *Language Typology and Language Universals,* Martin Haspelmath, Ekkehard König, Wulf Oesterreicher, and Wolfgang Raible (eds.), 1142–1178. Berlin/New York: Mouton de Gruyter.

Koehn, Philipp, Hieu Hoang, Alexandra Birch, Chris Callison-Burch, Marcello Federico, Nicola Bertoldi, Brooke Cowan, Wade Shen, Christine Moran, Richard Zens, Chris Dyer, Ondrej Bojar, Alexandra Constantin, and Evan Herbst
    2007   Moses: Open Source Toolkit for Statistical Machine Translation. In *Proceedings of the ACL 2007 Demo and Poster Sessions*, 177–180.

Lewis, M. Paul (ed.)
    2009   *Ethnologue: Languages of the World*, 16th edition. Dallas, Tex.: SIL International. http://www.ethnologue.com/family_index.asp [Accessed Aug. 2011].

Magga, Ole Henrik
    2006   Diversity in Saami terminology for reindeer, snow, and ice. *International Social Science Journal* 58 (187): 25–34.

Mehler, Alexander, Olga Pustylnikov, and Nils Diewald
    2011   Geography of Social Ontologies: Testing a Variant of the Sapir-Whorf Hypothesis in the Context of Wikipedia. *Computer Speech and Language* 25: 716–740.

Motter, Adilson E., Alessandro P. S. de Moura, Ying-Cheng Lai, and Partha Dasgupta
 2002 Topology of the conceptual network of language. *Physical Review E* 65 (6): 065102.

Nichols, Johanna and Tandy Warnow
 2008 Tutorial on Computational Linguistic Phylogeny. *Language and Linguistics Compass* 2 (5): 760–820.

Ploux, Sabine and Hyungsuk Ji
 2003 A Model for Matching Semantic Maps Between Languages (French / English, English / French). *Computational Linguistics* 9 (2): 55–178.

Priss, Uta and L. John Old
 2005 Conceptual Exploration of Semantic Mirrors. In *Formal Concept Analysis: Third International Conference, ICFCA 2005*. Bernhard Ganter, and Robert Godin (eds.), 21–32. Berlin: Springer.

Rama, Taraka and Lars Borin
 2011 Estimating language relationships from a parallel corpus. A study of the Europarl corpus. In *NEALT Proceedings Series (NODALIDA 2011 Conference Proceedings)*, 161–167.

Resnik, Philip
 1995 Using information content to evaluate semantic similarity in a taxonomy. In *IJCAI-1995 Proceedings of the 14th International Joint Conference on Artificial Intelligence*, 448–453.

Steyvers, Mark and Joshua B. Tenenbaum
 2005 The Large-Scale Structure of Semantic Networks: Statistical Analyses and a Model of Semantic Growth. *Cognitive Science* 29: 41–78.

Strazny, Philipp
 2000 *Morris Swadesh: Critical Essay*. http://strazny.com/writing/swadesh/ [Accessed Sept. 2011].

Swadesh, Morris
 1952 Lexico-statistical dating of prehistoric ethnic contacts: With special reference to North American Indians and Eskimos. *Proceedings of the American Philosophical Society* 96: 452–463.

Vossen, Piek (ed.)
 1999 *EuroWordNet: A Multilingual Database with Lexical Semantic Networks*. Dordrecht: Kluwer.

Wang, Xiao F. and Guanrong Chen
 2003 Complex Networks: Small-World, Scale-Free and Beyond. *Circuits and Systems Magazine, IEEE* 3 (1): 6–20.

Watts, Duncan J. and Steven Strogatz
 1998 Collective dynamics of 'small-world' networks. *Nature* 393 (6684): 440–442.

Wunderlich, Dieter
 1980 *Arbeitsbuch Semantik*. Königstein im Taunus: Athenaeum.

Measuring morphosemantic language distance in parallel texts

Bernhard Wälchli and Ruprecht von Waldenfels

1. Introduction

Every language categorizes meanings into different form classes.[1] In this paper we want to measure how much languages differ in their *morphosemantic* patterns (their pairings of form and meaning). The form classes considered here are word forms. Word forms conflate lexical and morphosyntactic structure. However, since we are concerned here with the overall similarity of languages, there is no need to keep grammar and lexicon apart, which makes word forms highly useful units for cross-linguistic comparison. In our approach semantic functions are accessed indirectly by the distribution of word forms in massively parallel texts (i.e., translations of the same text into many languages, see Cysouw and Wälchli 2007). Differences in patterns of word form distribution across languages are not indicators of "semantic distance"; the measures do not directly address meaning, but rather the distribution of meaning across word forms in what are assumed to be translationally equivalent text segments. A more appropriate term for the kind of measure wanted here is therefore *morphosemantic distance*.[2]

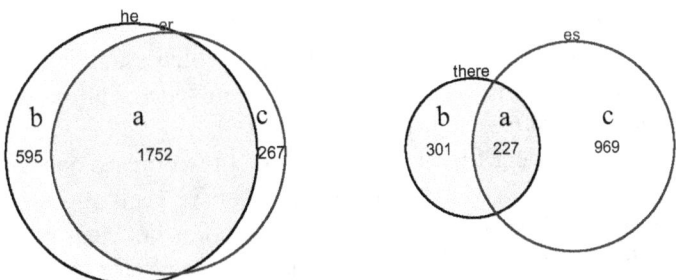

Figure 1. Distributional overlap of two English and German pairs of forms.

The basic rationale of the approach is as follows: It is assumed that forms with most similar distributions across parallel texts also have similar meanings. It is further assumed that the degree of overlap in distributions of the most similar forms in a language pair is a measure of the functional similarity of forms. Consider figure 1 with the English and German word form pairs *he* : *er* and *there* : *es*. English *he* occurs in 2319 verses of the New Testament (American Standard translation) and German *er* in 2014 (Luther). There is a large intersection of 1752 verses, testifying to the highly similar use of the two forms across the two languages. This is a consequence of strong structural similarity in pronouns. Both English and German (a) make a number distinction in third person personal pronouns, (b) have a gender distinction, (c) distinguish non-oblique and oblique forms, and (d) are non-pro drop languages with obligatory use of subjects. However, degree of congruence in use is not constant in a language pair. The English form *there* happens not to be highly congruent with any German word form in the text considered. The best match is *es* 'it' due to the parallel use in existential constructions.

Rather than letting our intuition decide what the best kind of overlap is in Venn diagrams as in figure 1 we can use established collocation measures (see Manning and Schütze 1999: 151–189 for a survey).[3]

The example makes it clear that difference in meanings as addressed here can only be considered in concrete texts; that is, in performance rather than competence. It is hence important to emphasize that a text in a language is not necessarily representative of a language as a whole. Actually, we can address languages in linguistics only in the form of *doculects* (attested language material that can be referred to). The kinds of doculects needed in the present approach are very specific; they must be directly comparable on the level of language use. Of course, it would be desirable to have a balanced corpus with many different genres and samples of spoken and written modality, but there is no balanced massively parallel corpus which is suitable for world-wide cross-linguistic comparison. For this reason we have to resort to available massively parallel texts, which essentially means the New Testament as the sole reasonable option, in spite of all its well-known shortcomings for linguistic purposes.

Figure 1 makes clear that it is not sufficient to compare only one pair of categories to measure language distance; rather we need an index of many pairs to assess the average difference. However, it is not clear what kinds of categories should be used. Possible options are lexemes (or lemmata), grammatical morphemes (grams) or constructions or word forms.

Word forms have the advantage that they are directly accessible in texts without further analysis. If we would like to compare just the most widely used languages for which taggers are available, we could even use lemmata, with the disadvantage that different taggers in different languages do not always make the same decisions. Word forms have the advantage that they conflate grammatical and lexical information, often in highly idiosyncratic ways. To take an example, the Swedish word form *barn* 'child[INDEF: SG/PL]' is grammatically restricted in use in that it does not occur in most definite singular contexts[4] (where we find *barnet*) or definite plural contexts (*barnen*), but *barn* conflates the indefinite singular and plural uses, which is characteristic for many neuter gender nouns in Swedish. If we also take into account that definiteness markers are distributed quite differently across languages this gives *barn* a rather idiosyncratic distribution where it is highly unlikely that any other language would have a form that is very similar in extension, unless it is a closely related language such as Norwegian or Danish. At the same time *barn* is lexically specific in its distribution; for instance, in that it differs from Tagalog in that the two meanings 'child as a relative (son or daughter)' – Tagalog *anak* – and 'child as a young human being' – Tagalog *bata* – are conflated in the same lexeme.

The disadvantage of using word forms is that we cannot isolate the more abstract grammatical and lexical differences in their pure form. We never get at any grammatical or lexical features as they are used in typological investigations. Lexical and grammatical differences are measured only indirectly and there is no simple way to isolate the grammatical or lexical component in the distance. However, if the language distance as a whole is to be measured, there is no need to keep lexicon and grammar apart.

The aim of the approach at hand is to have a synchronic language distance measure that is based entirely on morphosemantic similarity. As in typology, it is possible to compare any pair of languages, not only genealogically related languages as in historical comparative linguistics. However, the morphosemantic similarity distance measure is not independent of linguistic genealogy, since genealogically related languages, especially closely related languages, are expected to be more similar on average than unrelated languages. It requires a considerable amount of divergence to wash away all traces of similarity of genealogically related languages. Even though one might expect language contacts (areality) to be an equally strong factor as genealogy it has to be taken into account that genealogically unrelated contact languages are highly dissimilar from the outset and it takes a large amount of convergence for them to become significantly similar. Known genealogical relationships, along with known areal relationships (to a lesser extent), can thus be used to evaluate the performance of a synchronic language distance measure. Put differently, a synchronic language distance measure needs historical linguistics to be established, not the other way round. What is measured is largely the same thing as the suspected *bias* in linguistic typology that typological sampling aims at minimizing (see section 5 for using this method for sampling).

In an earlier version (Wälchli 2011) it has been argued that measuring morphosemantic distance is typology. There are obvious parallels to typology: the world-wide scope and the synchronic approach. However, there are also crucial differences. The morphosemantic distance measure is based on pair-wise comparison of languages. In this respect it is similar to *contrastive linguistics* (the structural comparison of pairs of languages) rather than typology. The difference with respect to traditional contrastive linguistics is that the approach is massively contrastive. It is not just one language compared to one other language, but all possible pairs of languages in a sample of *n* languages are compared to each other. While the approach is thus, like typology, massively cross-linguistic, it differs from typology in that it exclusively relies on the pair-wise comparison of languages. It follows that one crucial property of virtually all modern typological studies is missing: cross-linguistic features. The present approach never identifies or uses any kind of typological features. Rather, the cross-linguistic comparison is always pair-specific, measuring one language with the language-particular categories of another language.

At the end of this section let us shortly state some of the crucial assumptions of the present approach. Word forms are highly comprehensive structural units of language since they conflate both lexical and grammatical structure. Distribution of word forms is an important aspect of language structure which is largely lost in reference grammars and dictionaries, but can be easily accessed in texts. Texts are hence a very efficient form of representing language structure. Parallel texts provide a shortcut to meaning in the sense that measuring distribution can be an indirect way of measuring meaning (see also Wälchli 2012). Morphosemantic language distance can be measured by the direct pair-wise cross-linguistic comparison of word forms; detours via typological features are not necessary.

2. The measures

The basis for the language distance algorithm is *glossing,* understood here as a shorthand for *word form with word form glossing* with *one-to-one correspondences*. Glossing is different from word alignment which is used in computational linguistics in training corpora for machine translation (Och and Ney 2003). Alignment links equivalent forms of a concrete passage in different language versions of a parallel text. Only those forms that are actually used in the parallel passage are available for alignment, and one and the same word form can be aligned with different forms of the second language depending on context. In glossing, as understood here, a target form is always glossed with exactly one equivalent, which will certainly not yield a good translation in a whole text; rather, it is the extreme form of a literal translation where the original word forms (the expression form) are replaced by word forms from another language, while their distribution (the morphosemantic structure) is retained. This is an automatic kind of *relexification* (Muysken 1981) which is very simplistic, especially because it ignores parts of speech (glosses need not have the same word class as target forms). The word forms of a language are simply exchanged with the best corresponding matches from another language whereas the distribution and order of the original word forms is maintained.

Table 1 presents an example. Here, a French translation of the Gospel (the target doculect, *td*) is glossed using an English translation (the glossing doculect, *gd*). The gloss for each word form in the French target doculect is determined by searching the English glossing doculect for those word forms that best match the distribution of the word form to be glossed. The quality of a match is defined by certain standard collocation measures. Table 1 shows the results for three such measures: Dice, log-likelihood and t-score (see, e.g., Wälchli 2011; Manning and Schütze 1999: 151–189; Cysouw et al. 2007; Dahl 2007 for more details).

None of these measures are optimal, but it is easy to see that the three measures tend to yield the same results if there is a really good structural match between target and glossing language. The results only differ (boldface in table 1) where English does not provide a good match for the French forms. In some cases, this is because there is more than one good match due to homonymy in French (*vit* is both 'live:PRS3SG = liveth' and 'see:PV:PST3SG = saw', and *les* is both 'DEF:PL = the' and '3PL.ACC = them'). Other cases represent collocation errors: French *l'* is the form of the singular definite article before vowels and *esprit* 'spirit' happens to be the most frequent noun beginning with a vowel in the N.T. Therefore, these word forms have a very similar distribution in the compared texts and can be easily mixed up. The result achieved by this method is thus highly dependent on the concrete text chosen.

For measuring linguistic distance we are interested not in the glosses themselves, but in the quality of the glossing as reflected in the collocation measures. Table 2 exemplifies this with a list of the ten most frequent Modern English forms in the Gospel according to Mark and their best correspondents in four other languages.

Table 1. Forced one-to-one glossing: French Mark 1:10 glossed with English.

Tokens	Form	Jaccard/Dice	Log-likelihood	T-Score
692	au	**in**	**midst**	**midst**
18	moment	**cherubim/mercy-seat**	**time**	**time**
257	où	where	where	where
2603	il	he	he	he
7	sortait	**proceedeth/sharp**	**sword**	**out**
4397	de	of	of	of
2024	l'	**the**	**spirit**	**spirit**
63	eau	water	water	water
2603	il	he	he	he
69	vit	**liveth**	saw	saw
2322	les	**the**	**them**	**them**
85	cieux	heavens	heaven	heaven
723	s'	**he**	**sat**	**he**
10	ouvrir	open	open	open
4843	et	and	and	and
2024	l'	**the**	**spirit**	**spirit**
328	esprit	spirit	spirit	spirit
16	descendre	**descending**	**down**	**down**
577	sur	upon	upon	upon
1316	lui	him	him	him
618	comme	as	as	as
871	une	a	a	a
4	colombe	dove	dove	dove

Early Modern English (as represented in the King James Authorized Version Bible, for which the American Standard edition has been used) is clearly the doculect most similar morphosemantically to Modern English in seven of the ten forms. The Dice coefficient, measuring the amount of dissimilarity, is high only in the case of the pairs *to : unto* and *you : ye*. This reflects differences in the grammatical structure of the two doculects due to language change. The strong overall similarity between the two English doculects is summarized in a low *Average Congruence* value. Average Congruence (AC) is an index of the congruence values $d(w,m)$ averaged over the k most frequent word forms w in the target doculect td and their best correspondents m in the glossing doculect gd determined according to different possible collocation measures used for ranking.

$$\text{(1)} \quad AC(td, gd) = \frac{\sum_{n=1}^{k} d(w_n, m)}{k}$$

Table 2. Dice coefficients for best glosses to most frequent English forms in Mark in four other doculects.

English *tl*	English EM		German		Finnish		Vietnamese	
the	the	0.021	**und**	**0.233**	ja	0.358	**người**	**0.463**
and	and	0.191	und	0.193	ja	0.178	và	0.418
to	unto	0.31	zu	0.309	ja	0.447	rằng	0.454
he	he	0.031	er	0.136	hän	0.331	ngài	0.305
him	him	0.03	ihm	0.348	ja	0.486	ngài	0.428
of	of	0.104	**und**	**0.517**	ja	0.554	**người**	**0.559**
they	they	0.064	sie	0.207	he	0.295	ngài	0.598
them	them	0.07	ihnen	0.216	heille	0.537	**phán**	**0.556**
you	ye	0.416	ihr	0.453	te	0.509	người	0.156
in	in	0.074	in	0.576	ja	0.656	trong	0.519
AC automatic		0.131		0.319		0.435		0.445
AC manual		0.131		0.382		0.582		?

The AC value is correct to the extent that the ranking measure finds the correct gloss. If the gloss is not correct, the value chosen is too low. Examples for incorrect glosses are German *und* 'and' for English *the* and *of*. The best correct match for *the* in German would actually be *die* (plural and feminine singular nominative-accusative of the definite article) at 0.484. The best match for English *of* would be German *des* at 0.580. Thus, the difference between English and German is actually larger than automatic AC tells us. For $k=10$ in Mark it is at 0.382 when done manually, not at 0.319. All incorrect glosses in table 2 are marked in boldface. Now the number of incorrect glosses is not distributed equally across language pairs. As we have seen already in the discussion of French–English in table 2 above, best candidates for glosses tend to be wrong glosses if there aren't any good matches; put differently, where the two doculects compared differ considerably in language structure. In other words, there are few errors in doculect pairs with low morphosemantic distance and there are many errors in doculect pairs with high morphosemantic distance. This causes a systematic error in the AC measure if the value is calculated automatically: the more distant the doculects in a pair the more likely AC is to be too low. The consequence is that AC when measured automatically underestimates the difference between similar pairs and dissimilar pairs of doculects. Put differently, the ranking order between similar and dissimilar pairs is correct, but the amplitude of the difference shrinks. Another way to put this is that language difference *is* measured despite the systematic error but not with the maximal efficiency factor.[5]

Comparing English and Finnish shows that there are great difficulties in finding correspondences if the doculects compared greatly differ in their morphological typology. Finnish has cases instead of the prepositions *to*, *of* and *in*. If there are no good correspondences, Dice tends to give a default form with a comparable range of frequency (here *ja* 'and') as best match.

The more distant two doculects are morphosematically, the more difficult it becomes to determine the correct gloss. In Vietnamese the definite article corresponds to a classifier (it has been argued that classifiers in Vietnamese and other South-East Asian languages, such as Hmong, can express definiteness; Bisang 1993). A major problem is that it is unclear whether Vietnamese has any pronouns. The forms used in similar functions are dependent on the social relationship between persons. This has the consequence that best equivalents to pronouns in Vietnamese cannot be defined globally, but only in particular situations. It happens to be the case in the Bible that the best match with English *he* and *him* is *ngài*, the form used to refer to deities and highly respectable persons. In texts where there are no deities or respectable persons, there would be a different equivalent. As an equivalent for *you*, however, we have Vietnamese *người* which is used to address inferiors. This example shows that best equivalents cannot be defined in any abstract way; they are always dependent on a concrete discourse universe which is different in different texts. Accordingly, morphosemantic structure cannot be considered in abstraction of concrete texts. Glosses which are certainly wrong are *rằng* 'quotative particle' for *to* and *phán* 'say, order' for *them*. They result from collocations: *them* frequently occurs where inferior persons are told something by a respectable person, which is why it patterns best in this text with *phán* 'say, order'.

In Wälchli (2011) four families of values have been defined for measuring morphosemantic distance based on one-to-one word form glossing: (i) Average Congruence (AC; see above), (ii) Average Distance (AD), (iii) Set of Best Equivalents (SBC) and (iv) Set Difference (SD).

(i) In Average Congruence (AC) – introduced above – Dice is used to compute an Average Congruence value of the *n* best matches. The ranking (finding the best match) is done using one of three collocation measures: Dice (AC-D), log-likelihood (AC-L), or t-score (AC-T).

(ii) Average Difference (AD) is similar to AC, but rather than taking the value for the best gloss, it measures the difference between the congruence values for the best and the second-best correspondents. The morphosemantic similarity is deemed higher the larger the difference between best and second best candidates is. Unlike AC, Average Difference is based on local glossing rather than global glossing. Local glossing is similar to word alignment (see above): only those word forms are available as glosses which occur in the same verse, but their collocation values are calculated on the basis of the whole text (see Cysouw et al. 2007).

The algorithm glosses all forms with the correspondents which have the best and second best Dice value available and averages over the differences between them:

$$(2) \quad AD(td, gd) = \frac{\sum_{n=1}^{k} 1 - (congr(d_{2ndbest}) - congr(d_{best}))}{k}$$

(iii) Set of Best Candidates (SBC): If two languages are fully congruent morphosemantically, a correspondent will be the best match for no more than one form, it will be unique. Therefore, the set of word forms to be glossed and the set of word forms used for glossing is ideally identical in size. Conversely, the smaller the set of word forms used for glossing, the less isomorphism between the two languages.

This relation can be used as a distance measure: SBC(td, gd)= 1−(t/k) with t defined as the number of word form types used as glosses for k target language forms. Thus, SBC with k=10 for the doculects in table 2 in respect to the Modern English doculect is determined by counting the number of types used in glossing: Early Modern English 10 (SBC 0.0), German 8 (SBC 0.2), Finnish 5 (SBC 0.5) and Vietnamese 6 (SBC 0.4). SBC can be determined with different collocation measures (SBC-D/L/T).

(iv) *Set Difference* (SD) is a meta-measure profiting from the different results of different ranking measures in cases of weak matching between target form and best correspondents. It is simply the ratio of forms where different ranking measures yield different best correspondents. There are different set difference measures depending on the ranking measures considered. SD-DL considers just the different results between Dice and log-likelihood while SD-DLT also takes t-score into account.

AC and AD are indices with much less data reduction than SBC and SD. They have the advantage that they can be tested for statistical significance using the Wilcoxon test. In Wälchli (2011) it is shown that AC and AD actually perform better than SBC for measuring language distance.

In determining AC, AD, SBC and SD, not all word forms of a text are taken. Rare forms are excluded for the following reasons: (a) rare forms have no characteristic distribution and hence their degree of congruence cannot be measured accurately; (b) since finding the best candidate relies on evidence from distribution, automatic glossing is not ideal for rare forms; and (c) frequent forms are arguably more representative for the structure of a language than rare forms.

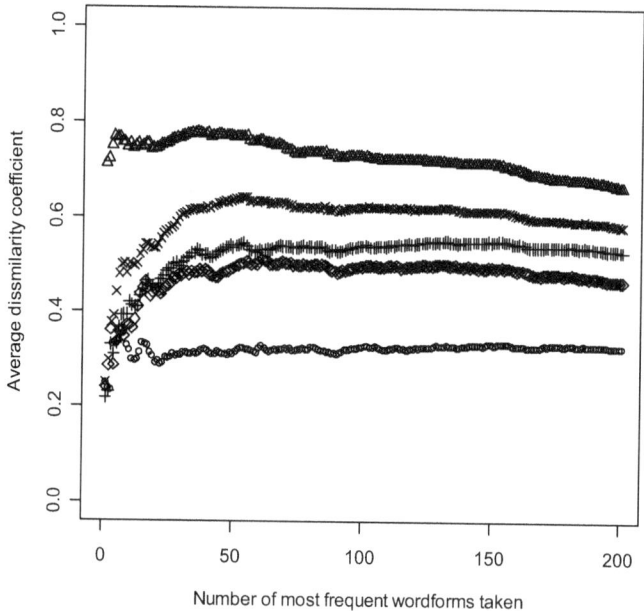

Figure 2. Average Congruence (AC-D) with increasing k (number of most frequent word forms averaged over) for Polish Mark paired with from bottom to top Czech, Ukrainian, English, Finnish, and West Greenlandic.

However, it is not obvious where we should draw the line between frequent and rare forms. The more forms there are, the smaller is the effect of single outliers, thus ten is probably too few. But does it matter whether we take 100 or 200 forms? This is an empirical question. If the ranking order of doculect pairs remains largely the same with a lower and a higher value for k, then the lower k value is as good as the higher one. Figure 2 shows the development of the average dissimilarity coefficient with increasing number of frequent forms *k* taken for Polish Mark paired with five doculects which are from bottom (best match) to top: Czech, Ukrainian, English, Finnish, and West Greenlandic. For these five doculect pairs the ranking order would remain the same from 25 to 200. However, the exact shape of the graphs is far from being predictable. What is important for our purpose is that the measure is generally quite robust for any *k* above 50, so that setting *k* to 100 or 200 (depending on the size of the text considered) is not a bad choice. What is important is that *k* is the same for all pairs of doculects investigated.

Finally, it is important to keep in mind that the doculect pair A:B will not yield the same results as the pair B:A. This is because all measures are calculated in relation to the set of *k* most frequent forms in the target language; this set will be different for each language (except for the case of identical morphosemantic structure). In order to obtain a true distance matrix, the average of the pairs A:B and B:A is taken for all distance measures described above.

3. Testing the method

Developing typological measures with computational methods is a difficult undertaking. Typologists are interested in new results. Obtaining the same kind of results that we know already from other investigations is uninteresting. Computational linguists, however, are interested in assessing the accuracy of results obtained with new algorithms and testing new methods using data where the desired outcome is known but hidden ("gold standards"). This presupposes that the results are already established (at least partly). To convince both typologists and computational linguists, results must be both novel and verifiable, and this is difficult to achieve. As somebody in the workshop has put it, most results of measuring language distance are either all wrong or are just what we already knew before. What would be a really good result then? It would have to be better than what we know already, but it would have to correspond partly to our expectations. Let us call the previous results or our intuitive expectations Model A, and the new results Model B. Model B cannot be better than Model A if it is completely different from Model A (unless our expectations were completely wrong) and it cannot be better if it is identical. Model B can only be better if it can convince us that some of our expectations were wrong or imprecise (and ideally explain why).

Table 3. Sample (60 doculects, 14 families, 26 genera). Frames: pairs expected to show exclusive splits.

Indo-European	Germanic	English, Middle English, Dutch, Afrikaans, German, Low Saxon, Icelandic, Swedish, Danish, Norwegian (Bokmål)
	Romance	Spanish, Portuguese, French, Italian, Romanian Latin
	Greek	Greek (Cl.)
	Albanian	Albanian
	Slavic	Polish, Czech, Ukrainian, Croatian
	Baltic	Lithuanian, Latvian
	Indic	Hindi, Vlax Romani
Uralic	Finnic	Finnish, Northern Saami
	Ugric	Hungarian
Turkic	Turkic	Turkish
Basque	Basque	Basque
Niger-Congo	N. Atlantic	Wolof, Adamawa Ful
	Bantoid	Swahili, Zulu, Xhosa
Sino-Tibetan	Chinese	Mandarin
Austro-Asiatic	Viet-Muong	Vietnamese
Austronesian	Sundic	Indonesian, Javanese
	Meso-Philippine	Tagalog, Cebuano
	Oceanic	Maori, Hawaiian
West Papuan	N. Halmaheran	Tobelo
Creoles	Creoles	Kriol (Australian), Haitian Creole
Eskimo-Aleut	Eskimo-Aleut	West Greenlandic
Mayan	Mayan	Tz'utujil (Eastern), Tz'utujil (Western), Cakchiquel (Central), Cakchiquel (East)
Uto-Aztecan	Aztecan	Nahuatl (Tetelcingo), Nahuatl (N. Puebla)
Oto-Manguean	Otomian	Otomí (Mezquital), Otomí (Tenango)
	Zapotecan	Zapotec (Ozolotepec), Zapotec (Quioquitani)
	Chinantecan	Chinantec (Sochiapan), Chinantec (Lealao)

An excellent example of a successful Model B is the historical comparative method with regular sound correspondences. Finding cognates starts with identifying similar forms with similar meanings which are potential cognates. Using regular sound correspondences will often yield the same result as pure similarity judgments, but it allows us to find cognates that are intuitively dissimilar and to prove that some pairs of similar words are not cognates.

Making progress in assessing genealogical distance by using computer-aided similarity judgments is quite difficult given the high standards set by the comparative method. However, in measuring synchronic morphosemantic language distance, there is no good method yet and our intuitions are very limited. All we know is that genealogically closely related languages and neighboring languages in close contact are likely to be morphosemantically similar. For testing a language distance measure it is therefore most useful to assemble a language sample with a strong bias, containing many pairs where we expect significant exclusive similarity of pairs of languages, that is, pairs of languages that we expect to be significantly more similar to each other than to any other language in the sample.

The investigation reported here uses a sample of 60 doculects with 23 expected exclusive pairs (frames in table 3).[6] Most hypotheses about exclusive splits are genealogical as is obvious from the presentation in table 3. A few are areal within genera. Danish is closer to Swedish genealogically than to Norwegian, but (Bokmål) Norwegian has been heavily influenced by Danish. The same holds for Low Saxon, strongly influenced by German, but genealogically probably closer to Dutch. Mandarin and Vietnamese are known to share many features due to language contact although they are from two different families. Latin and Classical Greek had much areal contact and these are the only two ancient Indo-European languages in the sample. The pair Haitian Creole and Kriol is neither genealogical nor areal, but Creoles are often expected to be similar in structure.

Now the desirable result – morphosemantic language distance – if it can be measured at all, is probably only one of several factors that will have an influence on the effective result. The extent to which the method is useful will depend on whether what we want to measure is a strong signal in comparison to the other factors that are likely to play a role. The following factors may be expected to play a certain role:

- *Noise*: The doculects differ from each other in completely arbitrary ways.
- *Systematic error*: The result is not accidental, but reflects some kinds of regularities that are an artifact of the method.
- *Graphemic error and corrupted texts*: The result reflects differences in the particular shape the texts are written in, e.g., regarding similarity of orthographies, consistency in spelling and the like rather than language

structure. The Middle English text, for instance, has less consistent orthography than Early Modern English.
- *Interference caused by translation history*: Translated texts are perhaps generally different from original texts ("universals of translation", see Mauranen and Kujamäki 2004) and the result might reflect different translation strategies or textual histories; for example, if some Mesoamerican languages cluster with Spanish, this is probably due to the role of the Spanish text in the translation of the Bible into these languages rather than to similarities in their structure.
- *Features of morphological typology*: It may be that some general typological factors, such as degree of synthesis of a language, play a certain role. This might mean, for instance, that morphosemantic similarities are discovered only if languages have a similar degree of morphological synthesis. In that case, pairs such as Latin and Italian are not expected to cluster.
- *True dissimilarities of the languages sampled*: The measures have access to real differences in language structure and give us direct access to the morphosemantic structure of languages.

Table 4 gives a small portion of the distance matrix for the result for AC-L. Numbers in boldface concern the absolute lowest AC-L distance value for each language (in respect to the full set of 60 languages). The table suggests that at least these four pairs of doculects are exclusive; that is, the languages in each of these four pairs are more similar to each other than to any other language in the sample.

Table 4. Part of the distance matrix for AC in N.T. with k=200.

	ENG	ENM	AFR	NLD	DAN	NOB	SPA	POR
English	0	**0.376**	0.411	0.427	0.43	0.452	0.461	0.483
Midd. Engl.	**0.376**	0	0.469	0.464	0.483	0.504	0.459	0.511
Afrikaans	0.411	0.469	0	**0.396**	0.465	0.469	0.481	0.501
Dutch	0.427	0.464	**0.396**	0	0.461	0.492	0.469	0.509
Danish	0.43	0.483	0.465	0.461	0	**0.242**	0.514	0.54
Norwegian	0.452	0.504	0.469	0.492	**0.242**	0	0.535	0.565
Spanish	0.461	0.459	0.481	0.469	0.514	0.535	0	**0.333**
Portuguese	0.483	0.511	0.501	0.509	0.54	0.565	**0.333**	0

However, comparing the index values does not tell us whether this similarity is statistically significant. To check this, the Wilcoxon test[7] is used for testing whether the k values summed up in AC are significantly smaller in the pair with the lowest AC value than in all other pairs involving one of the two languages in the pair. Table 5 summarizes the results for the three measures that proved to be best in terms of statistical significance – AC-L, AC-T, and AD – which all yield similar results. One, two or three stars means that the expected doculect is significantly most similar to the other language of the pair at a significance level of at least 0.05, 0.01 or 0.001, respectively. If the value is not significant, but the expected language is closest, the p-value is given. For instance, Dutch is significantly most similar to Afrikaans at the 0.05 significance level, but Afrikaans is most similar to Dutch only as a tendency, but not significantly. If another doculect than the expected one is most similar, this doculect is mentioned. Thus, French (not Hindi) is most similar to Vlax Romani, but not significantly so, and English (not Romani) is most similar to Hindi (but not significantly). After all it is not so strange that the two Indic languages Hindi and Vlax Romani are not exclusively most similar, since they are spoken in very different areas. The pairs where our expectations have been wrong are marked boldface; the pairs which are not reciprocally most similar in a significant manner are given in italics.

AD performs slightly better than the AC measures. Of the 23 supposed pairs, 12 are significant splits and two additional pairs are significant at least in one direction. For all three measures, 17 of the 23 pairs are most similar as a tendency (but not always significantly so). This is strong evidence that AC and AD actually measure true dissimilarities of the languages sampled rather than anything else. Of course, the pair Latin–Greek could also be interpreted as due to textual history (the Latin Vulgate translation is known to be rather literal), but this does not hold for all the other pairs. Furthermore, textual history is never the dominant factor. It may play a role as an additional factor if the structure of the languages in the pair is highly similar. However, there is one other factor that plays a dominant role: morphological typology. The morphosemantic language distance measures will fail to discover exclusive similarities if the languages in the pair exhibit considerably different levels of morphological synthesis. This holds for the pair Wolof and Ful, which are both Northern Atlantic languages, but Wolof is much more analytic than Ful, which is why Ful groups most closely with another Niger-Congo language with a similar degree of synthesis (Swahili, but not significantly closest). In some other cases we have simply overestimated the similarity of two doculects. It is probably not terribly astonishing after all that Australian Kriol and Haitian Kriol are not significantly most similar since they have different lexifier languages, are spoken in very different parts of the world, and also have very different substrates. Mandarin and Vietnamese are said to be very similar due to areal contact, but the two languages are not genealogically related. Indonesian (which is based on Malay) seems not to be exclusively close to Javanese (perhaps due to the higher degree of synthesis of Javanese) and one of the two Chinantec languages in the sample seems rather to be morphosemantically close to a Zapotec language (both Chinantec and Zapotec belong to the same language family Oto-Manguean).

Table 5. Evidence for significant exclusive pairs in the sample on the basis of four morphosemantic measures with k=200 for the whole N.T. (Wilcoxon test).

Language pair	AC-L	AC-T	AD
English/Middle English	*/***	*/***	*/***
Dutch/Afrikaans	*/0.25	*/0.24	*/0.13
German/Low Saxon	0.92/0.11	0.93/0.11	0.25/0.10
Danish/Norwegian	***/***	***/***	***/***
Spanish/Portuguese	***/***	***/***	***/***
Latin/Classical Greek	***/***	***/***	***/***
Czech/Polish	***/***	***/***	***/***
Latvian/Lithuanian	0.61/0.09	0.69/0.12	0.09/*
Vlax Romani/Hindi	French/English	French/English	French/English
Finnish/Northern Saami	***/***	***/***	***/***
Wolof/Ful (Adamawa)	Hawaiian/Swah.	Afrikaans/Swah.	Maori/Swahili
Zulu/Xhosa	***/***	***/***	***/***
Mandarin/Vietnamese	0.17/Hawai.	0.44/Hawai.	Hawai./Hawai.
Indonesian/Javanese	Afrikaans/0.06	Afrikaans/0.13	Afrikaans/0.10
Tagalog/Cebuano	**/***	*/***	***/***
Maori/Hawaiian	***/***	***/***	**/*
Kriol/Haitian	0.17/Vietn.	0.18/Vietn.	0.42/Hawai.
E./Western Tz'utujil	***/***	***/***	***/***
Central/East Cakchiquel	***/***	***/***	***/***
Tetelc./N. P. Nahuatl	0.22/***	0.24/***	*/***
Mezq./Tenango Otomi	0.32/**	0.31/*	*/**
Ozolot./Quio. Zapotec	***/***	**/***	**/***
Soch./Lealao Chinantec	ZapOzolt/0.68	ZapOzolt/0.41	ZapOzolt/0.11

***/**/* 0.001/0.01/0.5 significance levels. If not significant, the *p*-value of the Wilcoxon test is given if the best match is the expected doculect. If the best match is another doculect, the name of that doculect is given.

The results in table 5 show us that there are considerable differences between the 23 pairs. The measures discussed here allow us to rank the pairs. We can measure with more accuracy what we knew before and some parts of what we believed we knew before turn out to be wrong.

It cannot be concluded from table 5 that the more significant pairs are morphosemantically more similar to one another than the non- or less significant pairs. Whether significance can be established depends on which other doculects there are in the sample. It is more difficult to establish significance between German and Low Saxon than between Zulu and Xhosa, because there are as many as ten Germanic languages in the sample but only three Bantu languages. Actually, the AC-L value for the pair German–Low Saxon at 0.42 is lower than that for the pair Zulu–Xhosa 0.48. This suggests that the pair German–Low Saxon is more similar morphosemantically than the pair Zulu–Xhosa. The pair Finnish–Northern Saami could probably not have been established as an exclusive split if there were another Finnic or Saami language in the sample.

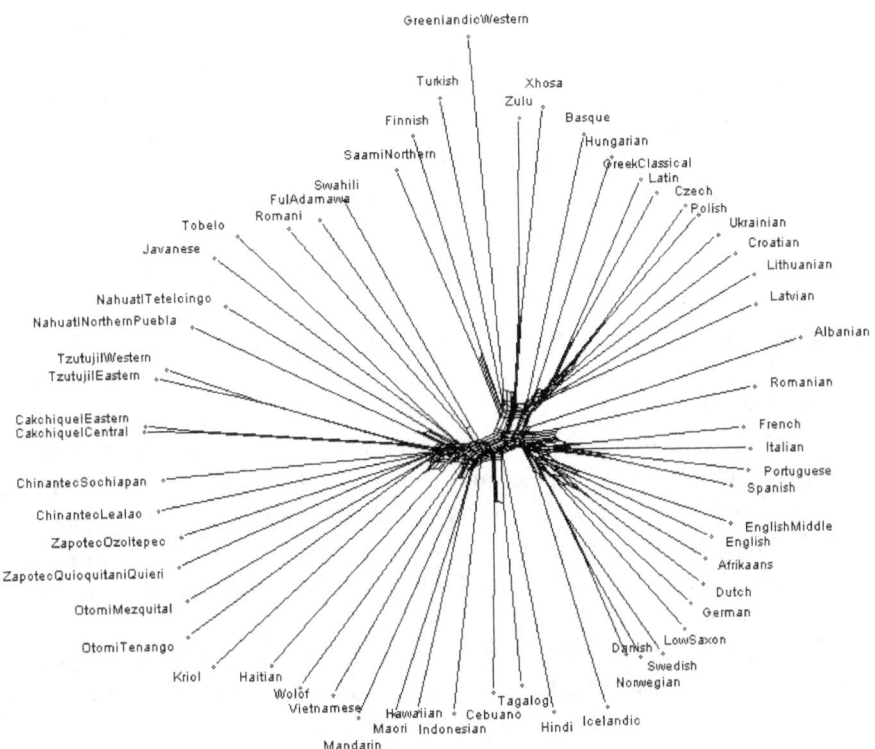

Figure 3. Neighbor-net of language distance measured with AC-L in 60 doculects.

Once it has been shown that the method measures what it is designed for, and to a large extent even in a significant manner, the next step is to visualize the whole data matrix with a powerful visualization tool. Neighbor-net (Huson and Bryant 2006; multiple unrooted trees originally developed in bioinformatics for testing how good the best single tree fits the data) proves to be more useful than multi-dimensional scaling [MDS], because the former shows exclusive splits and because the data set is so diverse that the two first dimensions in MDS contain only a small proportion of the information.

The neighbor-net arranges all items such that the shortest distance by connecting lines between any two items reflects the distance in the data matrix. Thus, the two versions of Cakchiquel with a long shared tail are much closer than the two Chinantec versions. The neighbor-net shows many genealogical genera (clockwise: Slavic, Baltic, Romance, Germanic, the three Austronesian genera, Otomi, Zapotec, Chinantec, Mayan, Nahuatl, and Finnic–Saami). All the Mesoamerican languages cluster to the left. At the same time, morphological typology plays a major role. The most synthetic doculects cluster around twelve o'clock (Greenlandic, Zulu and Xhosa, Turkish) and the most analytic languages around seven o'clock (Creoles, Vietnamese, Oceanic, Otomí). However, another important result is the high amount of diversity. This is shown by the long individual tails of most doculects in figure 3. Note that the intersection is already given much emphasis by using Dice rather than Jaccard as a congruence measure. A workshop participant recommended taking the power of ten of the distance matrix to minimize the diversity effect to obtain a nicer graph, but the high diversity is not simply an artifact of the method.[8] Traditional feature typology with its immense data reduction with highly diverse constructions often assigned to the same type has accustomed linguists to a highly selective and distorted view of language distance. Languages are more different from one another than the average linguist believes.

In fact, scaling down the distance by raising the matrix to a higher power strongly reinforces the factor of morphological typology. Many minor genealogically motivated clusters disappear and only the general typological signal of degree of synthesis is left: all doculects end up being arranged in a scale from West Greenlandic to Kriol. A more useful approach for downscaling is to subtract a constant.

We may conclude that the method proves to be useful at least for one parallel text. Let us now consider whether this holds true also for another text.

4. Using other parallel texts

Another way of investigating the interplay of factors described above is by varying the textual basis. This allows us to assess the impact of specific texts and genres and to evaluate the robustness of the method. The present section describes experiments with texts taken from ParaSol, a "Parallel Corpus of Slavic and Other Languages" (Waldenfels 2006, 2011).[9]

Multilingual texts need to be aligned before they can be used for morphosemantic measurements, i.e., it is has to be determined which portions of the texts are equivalent to each other across languages. The Bible is not only unique in the vast number of translations; it is also exceptional (together with other texts from antiquity) in that it is, by virtue of chapter and verse numbering, effectively hand-aligned. Most massively multilingual parallel corpora, such as ParaSol, employ automatic alignment.[10]

Since the measurements of morphosemantic similarity discussed above are based on the distribution of word forms in equivalent text sections, the quality of alignment has a direct impact on their quality: if the alignment is incorrect, correspondences are random rather than systematic and noise is introduced into the result. This means that any features that are detrimental to alignment quality will also lead to a deterioration of the similarity measures. Since automatic alignment always involves a certain error rate, sentence alignment quality thus needs to be added as a further entry to the list of factors influencing the result of our measurements.

Furthermore, the process of sentence alignment is not independent from morphosemantic similarity. Algorithms for alignment crucially rely on similarities in the shape and distribution of word forms as well as in the length of sentences in order to determine correspondences between the texts. Therefore, morphosemantic differences tend to affect alignment, which in turn affects measurements of morphosemantics. We may thus expect dissimilar morphosemantics to have a disproportionate effect on the measurement if alignment is done automatically. Note that understanding the effects of alignment is important since they relate to what we do with the texts, rather than to properties of the texts themselves.

ParaSol uses *hunalign* (Varga et al. 2005) for sentence alignment. Its algorithm works in a two-step-process. Taking a bitext as input, it uses a comparison of sentence length to construct a first alignment. The basic idea is that short sentences tend to correspond to short sentences and long sentences to long sentences; this is exploited in a statistical model which can also incorporate additional cues from an existing dictionary (in ParaSol, this option is not used). Once this first alignment is ready, the distribution of word forms in those sentences that fit best in length are used to build a co-occurrence dictionary similar to what is used as input for the morphosemantic measurements described above. The corpus is then aligned a second time using both the length and lexical co-occurrence information constructed in the first phase.

In ParaSol, texts are aligned on a one-to-one basis. This means that, unlike Bible verses, the way texts are segmented into aligned chunks varies from pair to pair. Table 6 illustrates this point. Here, two Russian sentences align to two sentences in English, but to a single sentence in Italian. This has the advantage that alignment is as fine-grained as possible.

Table 6. Aligned text with conflicting segmentation in ParaSol.

Russian	Italian	English
Smirno stojat'.$_1$	Devi stare sull'attenti,$_1$ hai capito, o vuoi ancora una botta?$_2$	Stand at attention.$_1$
Ty ponjal menja ili udarit' tebja?$_2$		Do you understand me, or do I hit you?$_2$

Table 7. Aligned text with conflicting segmentation resolved by repetition.

Russian	Italian	English
Smirno stojat'.$_1$	Devi stare sull'attenti,$_1$ hai capito, o vuoi ancora una botta?$_2$	Stand at attention.$_1$
Ty ponjal menja ili udarit' tebja?$_2$	Devi stare sull'attenti,$_1$ hai capito, o vuoi ancora una botta?$_2$	Do you understand me, or do I hit you?$_2$

For the present comparison this alignment was transformed to a format most compatible to the table-like alignment of the Bible in terms of verses. The original text (in this case, the Russian version) was taken as a starting point in an alignment format where the original sentences are stored in a table-like fashion with all of their equivalents appearing on the same line. Segmentation is thus, like in the Bible, not dependent on the language pair considered. However, this approach leads to cases of forced one-to-one alignment as illustrated in table 7 where exact correspondence results from the repetition of material.[11] This does not change the number of co-occurrences in comparison to pair-wise alignment (the Italian word form *capito* is still counted as co-occurring once with each word form in the two Russian and English sentences).

In order to limit the distortion resulting from this and from overly large erroneous alignments, aligned segments larger than ten tokens were used only if they were smaller than three times the size of the sentence in the original. This effectively removed an average of 4% of the segments in the aligned corpora.

Let us now turn to the actual comparison. Due to limitations of space, we restrict ourselves to the text with most translations in the corpus: the Russian classic *Master i Margarita* by Mikhail Bulgakov in 28 versions. Beside Slavic languages, which are the focus of ParaSol, many other languages are included in the corpus; however, the set of languages is, aside from its Slavic core, essentially opportunistic. Figure 4 shows a neighbor-net graph based on the morphosemantic distances between the Bulgakov doculects measured with Average Congruence.

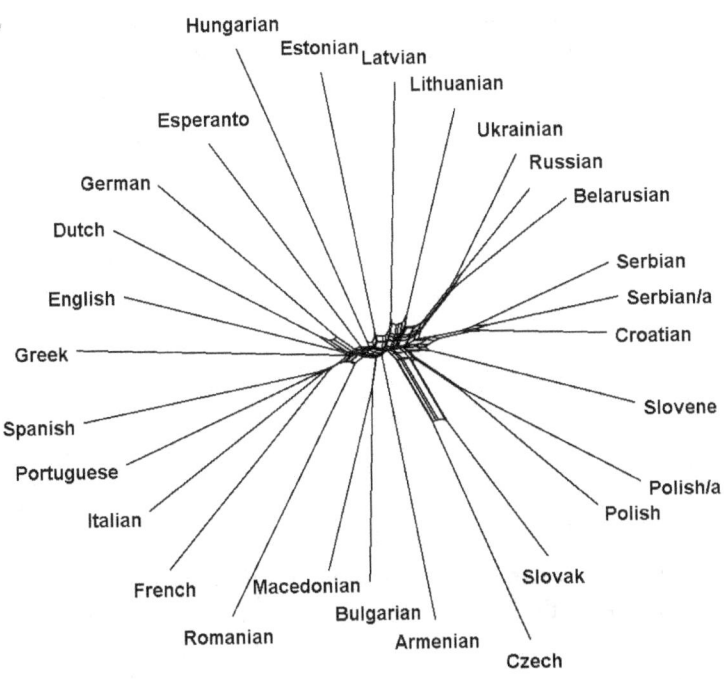

Figure 4. Neighbor-net of doculect distance measured with AC-L in 28 versions of Bulgakov's *Master i Margarita*. Multiple translations labeled with /a.

As in the case of the Bible corpus, the doculects cluster in terms of genealogical units (clockwise: Finno-Ugric, Baltic, Slavic, Romance and Germanic). Greek, Armenian, and Esperanto, which do not fit into any genus, are outliers. The ordering inside and between genera is likewise largely not arbitrary. The East Slavic versions Ukrainian, Belarusian and Russian are as close as the three translations in Serbian/Croatian, the translations into the very closely related Czech and Slovak, or the two alternative translations into Polish. Bulgarian and Macedonian stand out in Slavic, as does Romanian in Romance: both deviate from the prototype of these genera in several respects, e.g., in a clitic second position definite article. The proximity of Bulgarian and Romanian at the periphery of their genera in turn is plausible given their typological and areal relatedness. A similar case can be made for Baltic, which is, as a genus, closely related to Slavic and grouped next to it. The position of Latvian next to the Finno-Ugric language Estonian is plausible in light of intensive contacts between the two languages. On a whole, there seems to be a right to left cline for (nominal) morphological complexity. Taken together, the graph reflects genealogical, structural and areal relatedness fairly well.

To what extent are these results and the results attained with the Bible corpus comparable? Figure 5 presents two neighbor-net graphs constructed on the subset of languages that are common to both the Bible and the Bulgakov corpus as discussed above.

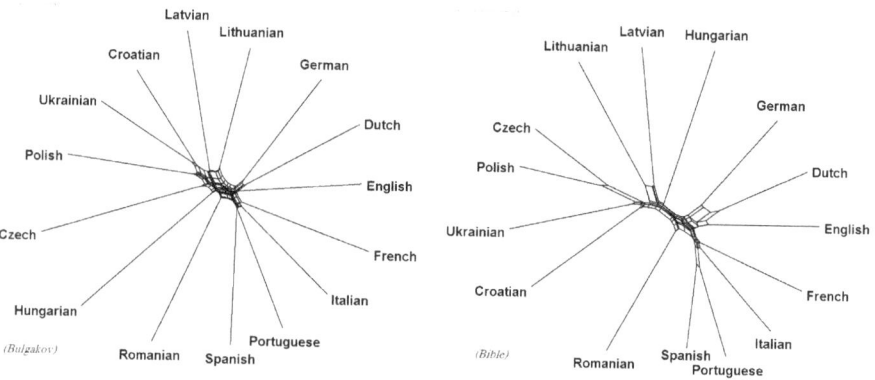

Figure 5. Neighbor-net graphs of 15 versions of Bulgakov's Master i Margarita (left graph) and the N.T. (right graph) as measured with AC-L.

The graphs are remarkably similar. Generally, there is more detail, that is, less noise in the Bible corpus, which is at least partly an effect of less perfect alignment of the Bulgakov corpus. With the exception of Finno-Ugric, represented by Hungarian, the genera are represented in an identical order: Germanic and Romance to the right, Slavic and Baltic to the left. Genera seem to be distributed into two groups according to their morphological complexity. The internal make-up of Germanic and Romance is virtually identical down to the details. Differences mainly concern the relative order inside Slavic and Baltic. The two West Slavic languages Polish and Czech are much closer in the Bible corpus than in the Bulgakov corpus, but in both cases, they are grouped together. The remaining two Slavic languages, Croatian and Ukrainian, are likewise grouped together, but the order of the groups inside Slavic are different. In Baltic, the order of Latvian and Lithuanian is not the same in both graphs. The position of Hungarian seems to be the most important single difference between the two data sets.

While more research into different text types and registers is clearly necessary, this first comparison of two texts suggests that the impact of varying the textual basis may in fact be surprisingly insignificant.[12]

5. Applying the language distance measure: Sampling as an example

One application of the morphosemantic language distance measure is *typological sampling* – "how to choose a representative set of languages for a typological investigation" (Dahl 2008: 208). In contrast to convenience samples – sets of languages that are most easily accessible to the investigator – variety sampling (Rijkhoff and Bakker 1998) aims at reflecting the diversity of human languages in an optimal way. Most literature on typological sampling focuses on determining maximally diverse samples from the global population. For such a purpose parallel texts are not really useful since parallel texts are not available for the full set of languages of the world. However, our focus here is different; the aim is to determine a maximally diverse sample of m doculects out of any group of n doculects in a parallel text corpus. This means, our approach is to find a *relatively* diverse sample (however diverse the original sample is). Relative diversity sampling can theoretically be applied equally well to a set of dialects of the same languages as to a world-wide set of languages. Diversity sampling as defined here is simply the reduction of a given set of n doculects to a smaller set of m doculects (covering as much structural diversity as possible). Homogeneity sampling is defined analogously: finding those m of n doculects which exhibit minimal structural diversity.

Most variety sampling techniques are *a priori*: they are based on assumed biasing factors. There is a general consensus that genealogical relationship and, to a lesser extent, areal neighborhood are the crucial biasing factors; hence, *a priori* sampling techniques tend to minimize genealogical (and, to a lesser extent, areal) bias. An *a posteriori* sampling approach, based on the WALS data, is Dahl (2008). Disregarding genealogical and areal factors, Dahl selects a 101 language sample out of the 222 languages with most data points in WALS on the basis of observed typological diversity. The present approach is similar in that it is based on observed structural diversity and disregards the expected genealogical and areal bias (it is thus not *a priori*). However, the structural diversity is measured automatically (and indirectly) without any need of typological feature investigations (it is thus not *a posteriori* either).

The distance matrix of languages – we take the one computed with AC-D in the N.T. sample as input, but any other one could be taken – is the input for identifying the relative diversity or homogeneity sample. The most obvious solution is to try all subsamples with m doculects and take the one with the highest matrix sum. This gives us, for instance, Albanian, Kriol, and West Greenlandic as the set of the three most diverse doculects and Swedish, Danish, and Norwegian as the set of the three most homogeneous doculects. For four doculects, we get the most diverse set Albanian, Turkish, Kriol, and West Greenlandic and the most homogeneous set Spanish, Portuguese, French, and Italian. However, with $n=60$ finding the ideal set of m languages is no trivial task, for 3 of 60 there are already 1,770 possibilities, for 4 of 60 34,220, and for 5 of 60 5,461,512 possibilities. Rather than trying out all possible samples a more convenient approach is to determine the most similar pair of languages in the sample and eliminate the language that is more similar to the set of remaining languages. This procedure is repeated stepwise until the number of doculects has been reduced to a maximally diverse set of m languages.[13]

Since we know that genealogical relationship is the strongest factor for structural bias, the sampling method can be used also as an evaluation of the structural diversity measure. Starting with a genealogically biased set of n doculects, we expect doculects from the same genera and families to be eliminated before doculects from different genera and families. This would confirm that we have actually measured something that reflects genealogical units as a consequence of structural diversity, since the algorithm has no access to genealogical data.[14]

Table 8 gives a portion of the results of such an elimination process. We start with 60 doculects in languages from 14 families and 26 genera. (Creoles are counted as one family and one genus here.) The first doculect eliminated is Central Cakchiquel because it is in the most similar doculect pair together with Eastern Cakchiquel. This is an intra-genus elimination; hence the number of genera does not diminish. The first genus eliminated is Greek (Classical Greek eliminated by Polish) with a remaining sample size of 39. Put differently, while reducing the sample by one third we do not lose a single genus.

Table 8. Stepwise reduction of the 60 doculects to 0 doculects while maintaining maximal structural diversity.

Sample size	No of Families	No of Genera	Language eliminated	Language eliminating	Value in eliminating pair
59	14	26	CakchiquelCentral	CakchiquelEastern	0.1215
58	14	26	Danish	Norwegian	0.2421
57	14	26	TzutujilWestern	TzutujilEastern	0.2489
56	14	26	Spanish	Portuguese	0.3305
...					
40	14	26	SaamiNorthern	Finnish	0.5123
39	14	25	GreekClassical	Polish	0.5162
...					
34	14	25	ZapotecOzoltepec	ZapotecQuioqu.	0.5653
33	14	24	Cebuano	Maori	0.5653
...					
29	14	22	LowSaxon	Icelandic	0.5822
28	13	21	Vietnamese	Mandarin	0.5873
...					
17	13	16	ZapotecQuioqu.	ChinantecLealao	0.6466
16	12	15	Tobelo	Javanese	0.6480
15	11	14	NahuatlNorthPuebla	ChinantecLealao	0.6520
14	11	14	Swahili	Romani	0.6543
13	11	13	Wolof	Mandarin	0.6561
12	11	12	ChinantecLealao	CakchiquelEastern	0.6659
11	10	11	Basque	Albanian	0.6690
10	9	10	CakchiquelEastern	OtomiTenango	0.6726
9	8	9	OtomiTenango	Kriol	0.6762
8	7	8	Finnish	Turkish	0.6813
7	6	7	Mandarin	Javanese	0.6870
6	5	6	Javanese	Kriol	0.6948
5	5	5	Romani	Kriol	0.7008
4	4	4	Xhosa	Albanian	0.7160
3	3	3	Turkish	Albanian	0.7391
2	2	2	Albanian	Kriol	0.7790
1	1	1	Kriol	GreenlandicWestern	0.8489
0	0	0	GreenlandicWestern		dna

The first family eliminated is Austroasiatic (Vietnamese eliminated by Mandarin) with a remaining sample size of 28. This is well in line with Dahl's [2008] findings that Mainland South East Asia shows exceptional areal convergence, even though Mandarin is not literally a language of Southeast Asia, and is typologically something of an outlier with respect to the area). Certainly degree of synthesis plays a role here. Analytic languages tend to be more similar on average. The second family disappears with a sample size of 16. The last ten doculects remaining are from ten genera and nine families, only Indo-European (Albanian and Romani) is represented twice.

If the same approach is applied to the $n=26$ Indo-European languages in the sample, the eight last remaining doculects cover all seven genera, only Indic is represented twice with Hindi and Romani.

The results are promising given that the distance matrix is sensitive not only to true language distance, but also idiosyncrasies in translations. The algorithm tends to keep the strongest outliers whatever the reason is that they are outliers.[15] That West Greenlandic is last might actually be due to the fact that many verses are missing and that Australian Kriol is second last might be due to the fact that this is a rather free translation.

If the same method is applied to the 28 Bulgakov doculects (with AC-L), the nine genera – for convenience we treat Esperanto as a genus here – are represented in the eleven doculects removed last (listed ordered with the last remaining language first): Hungarian, Czech, Greek, Romanian, Polish/a, Esperanto, French, Armenian, Estonian, Latvian, and Dutch. The result is not fully corresponding to genealogical expectations. Slavic is represented twice, probably due to an exceptionally free translation into Czech. In the case of Romance, however, where Romanian is quite distant from the four other Romance doculects, there is reason to believe that this reflects linguistic facts rather than freedom of translation.

Other obvious potential applications of the language similarity measure that cannot be discussed here due to space restrictions are: (a) testing the existence of *Sprachbunds* (strict linguistic areas with exclusive morphosemantic similarity),[16] (b) testing the relevance of language similarity in second language acquisition, (c) measuring the degree of idiosyncrasy of translations (free vs. literary translation), and (d) investigating language distance across different text types (genres, styles, modalities, etc.).

A further argument for the relevance of measuring degrees of morphosemantic language distance is that it plays a role in the automatic extraction of typological features from parallel texts. For instance, if the degree of prefixing and suffixing is measured in parallel text automatically starting with the lemmata of one trigger language (Wälchli 2012, forthc), different degrees of morphosemantic similarities will manifest themselves as different levels of recall for different languages, and methods must be developed to overcome the effect. In this respect, morphosemantic language distance is a nuisance with a very real effect.

6. Conclusions and outlook

Morphosemantic distance measuring is a more obvious target for computational approaches than genealogical distance measuring, since there is no good manual alternative. For genealogical distance measuring there is an excellent non-computational way to do it: the classical comparative method. In this paper various measures for morphosemantic language distance have been discussed that are applicable for parallel texts. In morphosemantic distance measuring, distance is dissimilarity in comparable texts and this is what computational applications have powerful means to compute. Good results can be achieved with quite simple algorithms such as discussed here. Probably, much better results can be obtained with refined measurements.

For many synchronic applications, such as assessing bias in typological studies, morphosemantic language distance is actually a better method than measuring diachronic genealogical distance. But, morphosemantic language distance measures show a high degree of correlation with genealogical distance which are (a) important for establishing morphosemantic language distance measures and (b) can be useful for studying unusually radical diachronic changes such as when languages change their morphological type. Comparing how genealogy relates to morphosemantic distance is a new methodological challenge for historical-comparative linguistics.

Comparing morphosemantic distance is very flexible, since it can be applied in world-wide diversity samples, in language families or in linguistic areas (or any mixture of the three). There is no need to eliminate typological bias *a priori*, since measuring morphosemantic distance is actually measuring typological bias.

Finally, morphosemantic language distance measures are also important for showing that feature typology has no monopoly over unrestricted massive cross-linguistic comparison. Pair-wise language comparison may be an equally effective tool when practiced in a more efficient fashion than in traditional contrastive linguistics.

Notes

1. We are extremely grateful to Deborah Edwards for many suggestions for better formulations. The following persons have contributed many valuable suggestions to earlier versions of this work: Thomas Mayer, Östen Dahl, Ján Mačutek, Gabriel Altmann, Reinhard Köhler, and Emmerich Kelih. We would like to thank three anonymous reviewers for many useful comments and the editors for a highly inspiring conference.
2. We tried to term this "distance in inner form" (Wälchli 2011) or endomorphic distance, but we have to surrender to the unanimous phalanx of colleagues who all agree with Leopold (1929: 260) that this term made famous by Humboldt (1836: 91) should be "relegated to the museum of linguistic antiquities".
3. The simplest two measures are the Jaccard-coefficient – in the example for $he : er - a/(a+b+c)=0.81$ – and the Dice-coefficient: $2a/(2a+b+c)=0.67$. In both measures 1.0 is maximal similarity and 0.0 is maximal dissimilarity. The two measures are equivalent in the sense that they are monotonically related to each other (Kaufman and Rousseuw 1990: 26), which means they will always yield the same ranking order, but Dice gives more weight to the intersection.
4. The distribution is actually even more idiosyncratic since some definite contexts, e.g. when a relative clause follows (*det barn som* 'that child which'), require the absence of the definite marking.
5. The approach taken here does not try to maximize the efficiency factor. This might be a useful undertaking once the general principle of measuring morphosemantic language distance has been established. There are several obvious ways in which the efficiency factor can be improved. One is effectively restricting the number of available candidates for glosses by reducing the search space from whole verses to smaller word windows (e.g., Dahl 2007).
6. A large number of Bible translations are freely available on the internet. Since we would like to encourage colleagues to further develop the methodology with any set of texts, we do not find it useful to make available the exact set of texts used here. The Mesoamerican texts have been taken from www.scriptureearth.com.
7. The Wilcoxon test does not presuppose normal distribution since the t-test and the values summed up in the AC index are actually not normally distributed as has been verified with the Shapiro-Wilk test. We are grateful to Ján Mačutek for statistical advice.
8. Of course, it must be taken into account that we compare translation doculects, not languages. The diverse result thus reflects the variability as a sum of the translation component and the effective language difference component plus a certain random variation. Since our investigation shows that the languages are grouped according to how we would expect them to group in terms of language difference rather than according to literal and free translations, the language component must be stronger. Hence it is reasonable to conclude that a large amount of the diversity derives from structural differences and is not an artefact of translation.

9. See parasol.unibe.ch and korpus.uni-r.de/ParaSol. This corpus is available to registered users for querying via a web interface; however, for copyright reasons the full texts can only be used in-house.
10. There are, however, examples to the contrary; the Czech *intercorp* project and Adrian Barentsen's ASPAC corpus, e.g., are to a great extent manually aligned.
11. The same procedure is applied in the Bible texts if a translation unites several verses into one verse group.
12. There is no space here to discuss the results from translations of Umberto Eco's *Il nome della rosa* in ParaSol pointing in the same direction.
13. The procedure described is similar to *k*-means clustering; see, e.g., Kaufman and Rousseeuw (1990), but our aim is not partitioning.
14. "Structural" encompasses both lexical and grammatical here. The two components cannot be easily distinguished. A possibility for measuring only lexical diversity would be to use lemmatized text as input. However, this would require that the texts in all languages are lemmatized exactly according to the same principles.
15. It is generally true for variety sampling in typology that outliers are favored. The difference with variety sampling based on parallel texts is that not only structural extravagancy but also translational extravagancy plays a role.
16. In the current sample the best *Sprachbunds* are actually areally defined subsections of genealogical units, such as Romance without Romanian or Northern Germanic without Icelandic, or Latin and Classical Greek.

References

Bisang, Walther
    1993   Classifiers, quantifiers and class nouns in Hmong. *Studies in Language* 17 (1): 1–51.

Cysouw, Michael, Chris Biemann, and Matthias Ongyerth
    2007   Using Strong's Numbers in the Bible to test an automatic alignment of parallel texts. *STUF Language Typology and Universals* 60 (2): 158–171.

Cysouw, Michael and Bernhard Wälchli
    2007   Parallel Texts. Using translational equivalents in linguistic typology. *STUF Language Typology and Universals* 60 (2): 95–99.

Dahl, Östen
    2007   From questionnaires to parallel corpora in typology. *STUF Language Typology and Universals* 60 (2): 172–181.

Dahl, Östen
    2008   An exercise in a posteriori language sampling. *STUF Language Typology and Universals* 61 (3): 208–220.

Humboldt, Wilhelm von
   1836   *Über die Verschiedenheit des menschlichen Sprachbaues und ihren Einfluss auf die geistige Entwickelung des Menschengeschlechts.* Berlin: Königliche Akademie der Wissenschaften.

Huson, D.H. and D. Bryant
   2006   Application of Phylogenetic Networks in Evolutionary Studies. *Molecular Biology and Evolution* 23 (2): 254–267.

Kaufman, Leonard and Peter J. Rousseeuw
   1990   *Finding Groups in Data. An introduction to cluster analysis.* Hoboken, NJ: Wiley.

Leopold, W.
   1929   Inner form. *Language* 5 (4): 254–260.

Manning, Christopher D., and Hinrich Schütze
   1999   *Foundations of Statistical Natural Language Processing.* Cambridge, Mass: MIT Press.

Mauranen, Anna and Pekka Kujamäki (eds.)
   2004   *Translation Universals. Do they exist?* Amsterdam: Benjamins.

Muysken, Pieter
   1981   Halfway between Spanish and Quechua: The case for relexification. In *Historicity and Variation in Creole Studies*, A. Highfield and A. Valdman (eds.), 52–78. Ann Arbor: Karoma.

Och, Franz Josef and Hermann Ney
   2003   A systematic comparison of various statistical alignment models. *Computational Linguistics* 29 (1): 19–51.

Rijkhoff, Jan and Dik Bakker
   1998   Language sampling. *Linguistic Typology* 2 (3): 263–314.

Varga, Dániel, Péter Halácsy, András Kornai, Viktor Nagy, László Németh, and Viktor Trón
   2005   Parallel corpora for medium density languages. In *Proceedings of the RANLP 2005,* 590–596.

Wälchli, Bernhard
   2011   *Quantifying Inner Form. A study in morphosematics.* Arbeitspapiere 46. Institut für Sprachwissenschaft. Bern: Universität Bern. http://www.isw.unibe.ch/unibe/philhist/isw/content/e4229/e4355/e6592/e6593/Arbeitspapier-46_ger.pdf

Wälchli, Bernhard
   2012   Indirect measurement in morphological typology. In *Methods in Contemporary Linguistics,* Andrea Ender, Adrian Leemann, and Bernhard Wälchli (eds.). Berlin/Boston: De Gruyter Mouton.

Wälchli, Bernhard
   forthc.   Algorithmic typology and going from known to similar unknown categories within and across languages. In *Aggregating Dialectology, Typology and Register Analysis: Linguistic Variation in Text and Speech*, Benedikt Szmrecsanyi and Bernhard Wälchli (eds.). Berlin/Boston: De Gruyter Mouton.

von Waldenfels, Ruprecht
    2006   Compiling a parallel corpus of Slavic languages. Text strategies, tools and the question of lemmatization in alignment. In *Beiträge der Europäischen Slavistischen Linguistik (POLYSLAV) 9*, Bernhard Brehmer, Vladislava Ždanova, and Rafał Zimny (eds.), 123–138. München: Sagner.

von Waldenfels, Ruprecht
    2011   Recent developments in ParaSol: Breadth for depth and XSLT based web concordancing with CWB. In *Natural Language Processing, Multilinguality. Proceedings of Slovko 2011, Modra, Slovakia, 20–21 October 2011*, Daniela Majchráková and Radovan Garabík (eds.), 156–162. Bratislava: Tribun EU.

Information-theoretic modeling of etymological sound change

Hannes Wettig, Javad Nouri, Kirill Reshetnikov and Roman Yangarber

1. Introduction[1]

This paper introduces several models for investigating and evaluating etymological data. Our main point of departure is *alignment* of etymological data. Specifically, given a raw set of etymological data, we first aim to find the "best" alignment at the sound or symbol level. The reason for this focus is given in section 1.1. Sets of etymological data are found in digital etymological databases, such as ones we use for the Uralic language family. A database is typically organized into *cognate sets*; all elements within a cognate set are posited (by the database creators) to be derived from a common origin. The origin is some word-form in the ancestral language.

Computational etymology encompasses several problems, including: discovery of sets of cognates – genetically related words; determination of genetic relations among groups of languages, based on linguistic data; discovering regular sound correspondences across languages in a given language family; and reconstruction, either diachronic – i.e., reconstruction of proto-forms for a hypothetical ancestor language, from which the word-forms found in the observed languages derive, or synchronic – i.e., of word forms that are missing from existing languages.

Computational methods can provide valuable tools for the etymological community. The methods can be judged by how well they model certain aspects of etymology, and by whether the automatic analysis produces results that match theories established by manual analysis.

In our work, we do not attempt at the problem of discovering cognates; this problem is addressed, e.g., by Bouchard-Côté et al. (2007: 887–896), Kondrak (2004: 44–59), Kessler (2001). We begin instead with a set of etymological data (or more than one such set) for a language family as given. The data sets may be different, or even conflicting. We focus on the principle of *recurrent sound correspondence*, as in much of the literature, including the mentioned work, Kondrak (2002: 488–494), Kondrak

(2003: 432–443), and others. As we develop our alignment models at the sound or symbol level, in the process of evaluation of these models, we also arrive at modeling relationships among entire languages within the family. Construction of phylogenies is studied extensively by, e.g., Nakhleh, Ringe and Warnow (2005: 382–420), Ringe, Warnow, and Taylor (2002: 59–129), Barbançon et al. (2009: 887–896). This work differs from ours in that it operates on manually pre-compiled sets of *characters*, which capture divergent features of languages within the family, whereas we operate at the level of sounds within words and cognate sets. Other related work is further mentioned in the body of the paper.

1.1. Motivation

While etymological datasets, containing cognate sets, are readily available, the alignment at the sound level between two or more word forms in a cognate set is almost never given explicitly. Instead, one finds general rules of derivation, from parent language to daughter languages, in linguistic handbooks. The handbook, in turn, typically provides a handful of examples of the application of each rule, at best also mentioning how pervasive the rule is, i.e., whether there are exceptions — examples that contradict the rule. The actual alignment for most related forms in the database, is therefore, implicit in these rules.

This creates several immediate problems. First, the user of the database is left to his/her own devices to determine precisely how any two or more words in a cognate set are related — what are the rules of derivation that give rise to the observed forms? By this we mean a full sound-by-sound accounting of relationships in the observed word forms, without exceptions — without leaving any sound unexplained.

Secondly, the presented word forms may contain morphological material that is etymologically unrelated. Some databases give "dictionary" forms, which usually contain extraneous morphological affixes, and thereby obscure which sub-part of a given word form stands in etymological relationship with other members in the cognate set, and which do not. While some affixes may be "obvious to the naked eye", many are not. To complicate matters further, it is common that many obscure — or ossified — elements, are present in some of the observed languages (probably those that are phylogenetically closer), but absent in others.

Most seriously, the posited rules are usually insufficient to explain the totality of the observed data: this is due to the complex nature of the underlying derivation processes, which limits the ability of database creators to capture the regularities in full, and to make them explicit as rules. The rules have "exceptions", which are not mentioned (or acknowledged) in the handbooks – leaving "holes" in the explanation, and calling into question the quality of the data, as well as the quality of the rules.

In fact, rules given in handbooks are usually idealized abstractions, covering only the common examples of relationship, and providing the basis on which further etymological analysis is to be built. In actuality the rules apply cleanly only in the simplest and most straightforward examples, while in much of the data the rules begin to "leak": they have unexplained exceptions, or fail to hold altogether.

While some amount of exceptions or failure may be insufficient grounds to dismiss a rule, it does suggest strongly that modeling the rules deterministically is not the correct approach. The deterministic approach is too simplistic, it is suited only for artificially simplified, "toy" scenarios; it is not capable of accounting for the "exceptional" cases, and thus distorts the true picture. Thus, we arrive at the conclusion that probabilistic modeling is a more appropriate approach to representing etymological rules and correspondences. By this we mean that whenever we speak of a rule, we should assign a score (a probability) of how well it is supported by the observed data.

It is traditional to mark "dubious" etymologies in etymological dictionaries and handbooks with one or more "?" marks. Doubt arises typically either from a weak semantic link, or a violation of expected phonetic regularity (or some of both). The database creators may try to provide the basis and references to scholarly works, to explain what features of a given posited relationship make it doubtful. However, from a strictly quantitative point of view, this is thoroughly unsatisfactory. We would prefer to know exactly to what extent a form is dubious, in probabilistic terms.

Finally, a serious problem in manually constructed etymological data sets is the potential for bias of the human etymologist. Bias may arise for many reasons; for example, at the time when a certain relationship is posited, relevant data may be unknown or unavailable, or may be available but ignored.

A central idea behind our automatic analysis is to use all data available at present, and to extract the rules of correspondence directly from the data. Thus we allow the data and only the data to directly determine what rules underlie it, rather than relying on externally supplied (and possibly biased) rules to explain the data, which may or may not be supported by the data. This approach will provide us a means of measuring the quality of the etymological data sets in terms of their internal consistency – a dataset that is more consistent should receive a higher score. We seek methods that analyze the data automatically in an unsupervised fashion. The question is whether a complete description of the correspondences can be discovered automatically, directly from raw etymological data – the cognate sets within the language family. Another way to state the question is: what alignment rules are "inherently encoded" in a given dataset (the *corpus*) itself. At present, our aim is to analyze given etymological datasets, rather than to construct new ones from scratch.

We should mention, that our models at present operate at the phonetic level only, they leave the semantics, and semantic judgements of the database creators, unquestioned. While other work, e.g., by Kondrak (2004: 44–59), has attempted to approach semantics by computational means as well, our models build upon the fundamental unit of the given cognate set.

Since one of our main goals is to devise automatic methods for aligning the data that are as objective as possible, the models make no *a priori* assumptions, and do not rely on "universal" principles – e.g., no preference for vowel-vowel or consonant-consonant alignments.

Several approaches to etymological alignment that have emerged over the last decade are mentioned in section 2. We formalize the problem of alignment in section 3, give the technical details about our models in sections 4–6. We present our results in section 7, and discuss their implications and next steps in section 8.

2. Data

We use two large-scale digital Uralic etymological resources. *Suomen Sanojen Alkuperä* (SSA), 'The Origin of Finnish Words', is a Finnish etymological dictionary, see Itkonen and Kulonen (2000). The StarLing Uralic database, described by Starostin (2000: 223–265), originally based on Rédei (1988–1991), differs from SSA in several respects. StarLing has about 2000 Uralic cognate sets, compared with over 5000 in SSA. SSA has thousands of cognate sets with entries in languages from the Balto-Finnic branch, which are most closely related to Finnish; StarLing provides data only for Finnish and Estonian from this branch. The data in StarLing is more evenly distributed over the Uralic family, because it is not Finnish-centric, like SSA – every cognate set in SSA contains a member from Finnish. StarLing also contains a reconstructed form for each cogset, which is useful for testing algorithms that perform reconstruction. Most importantly, for our models, SSA gives "dictionary" forms of words, which may contain extraneous morphological material, whereas much of the StarLing data is stemmed –

i.e., extraneous morphological material (mostly suffixes, in Uralic, such as the infinitive markers in verbs) has been removed, revealing the stem of the word only. Although the stemming is not perfectly consistent, it is present to a large extent. Both resources explicitly mark dubious etymologies (by one or more "?" marks). One traditional arrangement of the Uralic languages is shown in Figure 1, adapted from Anttila (1989).

The Uralic language family has not been studied by computational means previously. We investigate the Uralic datasets by modeling various etymological processes. The method in Kondrak (2002: 488–494) learns one-to-one regular sound correspondences between pairs of related languages in the data. The method in Kondrak (2003: 432–443) finds attested complex (one-to-many) correspondences. These models operate on one language pair at a time; also, they do not model the contexts of the sound changes, while most etymological changes are conditioned on context. The MCMC-based model proposed by Bouchard-Côté et al. (2007: 887–896) explicitly aims to model the context of changes, and operates on more than a pair of languages. In testing this method, we found that the running time did not scale well when the number of languages was above three.

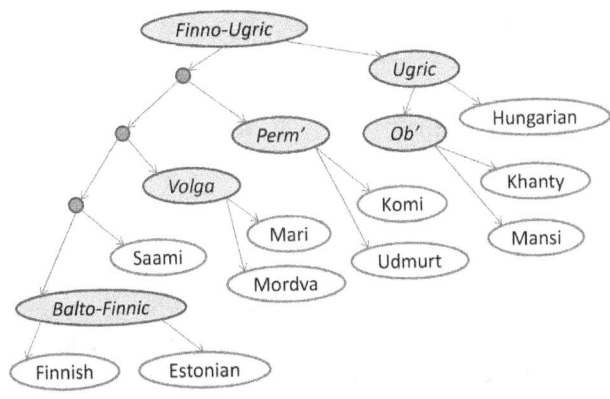

Figure 1. Finno-Ugric branch of the Uralic language family

3. Aligning pairs of words

We begin with pairwise alignment: aligning pairs of words, from two related languages in our data set. For each word pair, the task of alignment means finding which symbols correspond. Some symbols may align with themselves, while others may have undergone changes over the time when the two related languages have been evolving separately. The simplest form of such alignment at the symbol level is a pair $(\sigma:\tau) \in \Sigma \times T$, a single symbol σ from the *source alphabet* Σ with a symbol τ from the *target alphabet* T. We denote the sizes of the alphabets by $|\Sigma|$ and $|T|$.[2]

Clearly, with this type of 1×1 alignment alone we cannot align a source word $\vec{\sigma}$ of length $|\vec{\sigma}|$ with a target word $\vec{\tau}$ of a different length $|\vec{\sigma}| \neq |\vec{\tau}|$.[3] To model also *insertions* and *deletions*, we augment both alphabets with the empty symbol, denoted by a dot, and denote the augmented alphabets by $\Sigma_{\bullet}$ and $T_{\bullet}$. We can now align word pairs such as *vuosi – al* (meaning 'year' in Finnish and Khanty), for example, as any of:

```
v u o s i       v u o s i       v u o . s i
| | | | |       | | | | |       | | | | | |
a l . . .       . . a l .       . a . l . .
```

The alignment on the right, e.g., then consists of the pairs of symbols: (v:.), (u:a), (o:.), (.:l), (s:.), (i:.).

4. The baseline model

We wish to encode these aligned pairs as compactly as possible, following the Minimum Description Length Principle (MDL), see e.g. Grünwald (2007), Rissanen (1978: 465–471). MDL is a formalization of Occam's Razor, which says that we can describe (i.e., write down, or "transmit in a message, from a sending party to a receiving party") our entire data as compactly as possible if and only if we can discover as much *regularity* as possible in the data. Regularity translates into rules, which are short, and which enable us to describe (or explain) large amounts of the data, thus yielding savings in the total length of the message, which we call the *code*. Given a data corpus of N word pairs, $D = \{(\vec{\sigma}_1, \vec{\tau}_1), \ldots, (\vec{\sigma}_N, \vec{\tau}_N)\}$ we first align each word pair $(\vec{\sigma}_i, \vec{\tau}_i)$, and then use the alignment to "transmit" the data, by simply listing the sequence of the pairwise symbol alignments.[3] In order for the code to be uniquely decodable, we also need to encode the word boundaries. This can be done by transmitting a special symbol, #, that we use only at the end of a word. Thus, we transmit objects, or *events*, e, in the event space E – which is in this case:

$$E = \Sigma_{\bullet} \times T_{\bullet} \cup \{(\#:\#)\}$$

Information theory tells us that the total message length is closely related to the entropy of the probability distribution of the events. If our model is not aware of much regularity in the data, the probabilities of all possible events will be about the same, giving high entropy and high code length (cost). If, however, the model is aware of the regularities in the data, then some events will be much more probable than others, lowering the entropy and the cost.

We choose a particular code length, the one given by the Bayesian marginal likelihood, or prequential coding, see e.g., Kontkanen, Myllymäki, and Tirri (1996), which gives the total cost as in equation (1):

$$L_{base}(D) = -\sum_{e \in E} \log\Gamma(c(e) + \alpha(e)) + \sum_{e \in E} \log\Gamma(\alpha(e)) \\ + \log\Gamma\left[\sum_{e \in E}(c(e) + \alpha(e))\right] - \log\Gamma\left[\sum_{e \in E}\alpha(e)\right] \quad (1)$$

Here D is the *aligned* corpus, including the inferred alignments, which we call the *"complete data"*, as opposed to the raw, unaligned (observed) data. The count $c(e)$ is the number of times the event e occurs in a complete alignment of the corpus. In particular, $c(\#:\#) = N$ occurs exactly as many times as there are word pairs.

This cost function captures our intuition exactly – if counts $c(e)$ are large for only a few of the alignment events, then we have learned what kinds of alignments are likely for this language pair, and the value of the cost function will be low. If all counts are about equal, then we have learned little about the pattern of correspondence of sounds between the two languages, and the cost function will be high. This cost function has low value if the counts are skewed: if only some of the counts are large, and all the rest are very small or zero.

The alignment counts are maintained in a corpus-global *count matrix M*, where $M(i,j) = c(i:j)$. The terms $\alpha(e)$ are the (so-called Dirichlet) priors on the events. In the baseline algorithm, we set $\alpha(e)=1$ for all e – the so-called uniform prior, which does not favor any distribution over E *a priori*. (Note, this choice of prior causes the second summation in equation 1 to become zero.)

The baseline algorithm is as follows: Initially, we align the corpus randomly. Then we *re-align* the corpus, one word-pair at a time, greedily minimizing the total cost in eq. (1) using Dynamic Programming. To re-align a word pair, we remove the contribution of its current alignment from the global count matrix, then re-align the word pair using the procedure below, then add the re-aligned events back to the global count matrix. Re-alignment continues until convergence.

Re-alignment procedure: to align source word $\vec{\sigma}$ consisting of symbols $\vec{\sigma}=[\sigma_1...\sigma_n]$, $\vec{\sigma} \in \Sigma^*$ with target word $\vec{\tau}=[\tau_1...\tau_m]$. We use Dynamic Programming to fill the matrix V, e.g., top-to-bottom, left-to-right.[4] We note that the alignments are atomic, meaning that the symbols are not analyzed – in terms of their phonetic features – and are treated by the baseline algorithm as atoms. In particular, the model has no *a priori* notion of similarity – or even identity – of symbols across the languages!

Every possible alignment of $\vec{\sigma}$ and $\vec{\tau}$ corresponds to exactly one path through this matrix: starting with cost equal to 0 in the top-left cell, moving only downward or rightward, and terminating in the bottom-right cell. In this Viterbi-like Dynamic Programming matrix, every cell corresponds to a partially completed alignment: reaching cell (i,j) means having read off i symbols of the source word and j symbols of the target. Each cell $V(i,j)$ – marked X in figure 2 – stores the cost of the *most probable* path so far: the most probable way to have scanned $\vec{\sigma}$ through symbol σ_i and $\vec{\tau}$ through τ_j:

$$V(i,j) = \min \begin{cases} V(i, j-1) & + L(.:\tau_j) \\ V(i-1, j) & + L(\sigma_i :.) \\ V(i-1, j-1) & + L(\sigma_i :\tau_j) \end{cases} \quad (2)$$

Each term $V(\cdot,\cdot)$ has been computed earlier by the Dynamic Programming; the term $L(\cdot)$ – the cost of aligning the two symbols – is a parameter of the model,[5] computed in equation (3). The parameter $L(e)$, or $P(e)$, for every observed event e, is computed from the *change* in the total code-length – the change that corresponds to the cost of adding the new event e to the set of previously observed events E:

$$L(e) = \Delta_e L = L(E \cup \{e\}) - L(E)$$

$$P(e) = 2^{-\Delta_e L} = \frac{2^{-L(E \cup \{e\})}}{2^{-L(E)}} \quad (3)$$

Combining eqs. **(1)** and **(3)** gives the probability:

$$P(e) = \frac{c(e) + \alpha(e)}{\sum_{e'}(c(e') + \alpha(e'))} \quad (4)$$

This has an intuitive interpretation, with the probability being *approximately* the fraction of times that event e has occurred, out of the complete set of events.

The cost of the most probable *complete* alignment of the two words will be stored in the bottom-right cell, $V(n,m)$, marked ■.

	—	τ_1	...	τ_{j-1}	τ_j	...	τ_m
—	0						
σ_1							
...							
σ_{i-1}							
σ_i					X		
...							
σ_n							■

Figure 2. Dynamic programming matrix V, to search for the most probable alignment

4.1. The two-part code

The baseline model revealed two problems. First, it easily gets stuck in local optima, and second, it produces many events with very low counts (occurring only once or twice). To address the first problem we use simulated annealing with a sufficiently slow cooling schedule. This yields a reduction in the cost, and a better – more sparse – alignment count matrix.

The second problem is more substantial. Starting from a common ancestor language, the number of changes that occurred in either language should be small. This does not imply that we expect many self-alignments, but we do expect *sparse* data – that only a small proportion of all *possible* events in E will actually ever occur.

We incorporate this notion into the model by means of a two-part code. First we encode which events have occurred/have been observed: we send (a) the number of events with non-zero counts – this costs $\log(|E|+1)$ bits – and (b) specifically which subset $E^+ \subset E$ of the events have non-zero counts in $\log\binom{|E|}{|E^+|}$ bits. This first part of the code is called the codebook. Given the codebook, we transmit the complete data, E^+, using Bayesian marginal likelihood. The code length becomes:

$$L_{tpc}(D) = \log(|E|+1) + \log\binom{|E|}{|E^+|}$$

$$-\sum_{e \in E^+} \log\Gamma(c(e)+1) + \log\Gamma\left(\sum_{e \in E^+}(c(e)+1)\right) - \log\Gamma(|E^+|) \quad (5)$$

where E^+ denotes the set of events with non-zero counts, and we have set all $\alpha(e)$'s to one. Optimizing the above function with simulated annealing yields much better alignments.

4.2. Aligning multiple symbols

Multiple symbols are aligned in Bouchard-Côté et al. (2007: 887–896), Kondrak (2003: 432–443). For example, Estonian and Finnish have frequent geminated consonants, which correspond to single symbols/sounds in other languages; diphthongs may align with single vowels; etc. We extend the baseline model to a 2×2 model, to allow correspondences of up to two symbols on both the source and the target side. Whereas previously, only events of kinds $\{(\sigma:.), (.:\tau), (\sigma:\tau)\}$ were modeled, now we extend the set of admissible kinds of events, or correspondences to:

$$K = \begin{cases} & (\sigma:.), \quad (\sigma\sigma':.), \\ (.:\tau), & (\sigma:\tau), \quad (\sigma\sigma':\tau), \\ (.:\tau\tau'), & (\sigma:\tau\tau'), \quad (\sigma\sigma':\tau\tau'), \\ & \qquad\qquad (\#:\#) \end{cases} \quad (6)$$

We do not expect the different kinds to be distributed similarly, so we encode the occurrences of all event kinds separately in the codebook of the two-part code:

$$L_{mult} = L(CB) + L(Data \mid CB) \quad (7)$$

$$L(CB) = \sum_{k \in K} \left[\log(N_k + 1) + \log\binom{N_k}{N_k^+} \right] \quad (8)$$

$$L(D \mid CB) = -\sum_{e \in E^+} \log\Gamma[c(e)+1] + \log\Gamma\left[\sum_{e \in E^+}(c(e)+1)\right] - \log\Gamma(|E^+|) \quad (9)$$

where N_k is the number of possible different events of kind k, N_k^+ the corresponding number of such events actually observed in the alignment, with $\Sigma_k N_k^+ \equiv |E^+|$. Note, that for the kind $k=(\#{:}\#)$, N_k^+ is always 1 (because there is at least one word pair, this event is always observed).

Then, the parameters $P(e)$, for every observed event e, are again computed from the *change* in the code-length, eq. (3). But now, e may be of a kind that has been already observed previously – and is already in the codebook – or it may be of a new kind. Eq. (4) gives the formula for probability when $c(e) > 0$ – if $e \in E^+$, – whereas

$$P(e) = \frac{1}{\sum_{e'} c(e') + |E^+|} \cdot \frac{|E^+|}{\sum_{e'} c(e') + |E^+| + 1} \cdot \frac{N_k^+ + 1}{N_k - N_k^+} \qquad (10)$$

when $e \notin E^+$, and e is of kind k. If the event e has been already observed, the value of $P(e)$ is computed by substituting equation (9) into eq. (3) – yielding eq. (4); if this is the first time e is observed, $P(e)$ is computed by substituting *both* eq. (9) and eq. (8) into eq. (3), since then the codebook also changes – yielding eq. (10).

5. Three- and higher-dimensional alignment

The baseline models align languages pairwise. These models allow us to learn 1–1 correspondences in the language family. This is easily extended to *any* number of languages. The model of Bouchard-Côté et al. (2007: 887–896) also aligns more than two languages at a time.

We extend the 2-D model to three dimensions as follows. We align symbols in a 1–1 fashion, as in the 2-D baseline. A three-dimensional alignment is a triplet of symbols $(\sigma{:}\tau{:}\xi) \in \Sigma_. \times T_. \times \Xi_.$. For example, the words meaning 'nine' in Finnish, Estonian and Mordva, can be aligned simultaneously as:

```
y . h d e k s ä n
| | | | | | | | |
ü . h . e k s a .
| | | | | | | | |
v e χ . . k s a .
```

In 3-D alignment, the input data contains all examples where words *in at least two* languages are present[6] – i.e., a word may be missing from one of the languages, (which allows us to utilize more of the data). Thus we have two types of examples: *complete* – where all three words present (as 'nine' above), and *incomplete* – containing words in only two languages. For example, for *haamu* : – : *čama* – meaning "ghost" in Finnish and Mordva – the cognate Estonian word is missing.

We next extend the 2-D count matrix and the 2-D Viterbi matrices to three dimensions. The 3-D Viterbi matrix is directly analogous to the 2-D version. For the alignment counts in 3-D, we handle complete and incomplete examples separately.

Our "marginal" or "pairwise" 3-D model aligns three languages simultaneously, using three marginal 2-D matrices, each storing a pairwise 2-D alignment. The marginal matrices for three languages are denoted $M_{\Sigma T}$, $M_{\Sigma \Xi}$ and $M_{T \Xi}$. The algorithm optimizes the total cost of the complete data, which is defined as the *sum* of the three 2-D costs obtained from applying prequential coding to the marginal count matrices

When computing the cost for event $e = (\sigma, \tau, \xi)$, we consider complete and incomplete examples separately. In "incomplete" examples, we use the counts from the corresponding marginal matrix directly. E.g., for event count $c(e)$, where $e = (\sigma, -, \xi)$, and "–" denotes the missing word, the event count is given by: $M_{\Sigma \Xi}(\sigma, \xi)$, and the cost of each alignment is computed as in the baseline model, directly in two dimensions.

In case when the data triplet is complete – fully observed – the alignment cost is computed as the sum of the pairwise 2-D costs, given by three marginal alignment count matrices:[7]

$$L(\sigma : \tau : \xi) = L_{\Sigma T}(\sigma : \tau) + L_{\Sigma \Xi}(\sigma : \xi) + L_{T \Xi}(\tau : \xi) \tag{11}$$

The cost of each pairwise alignment is computed using prequential two-part coding, as in sec. 4.1. Note that when we register a complete alignment (σ, τ, ξ), we register it in *each* of the base matrices – we increment each of the marginal counts: $M_{\Sigma T}(\sigma, \tau)$, $M_{\Sigma \Xi}(\sigma, \xi)$, and $M_{T \Xi}(\tau, \xi)$.

To calculate the transition costs in the Viterbi algorithm, we also have two cases, complete and incomplete. For incomplete examples, we perform Viterbi in 2-D, using the costs directly from the corresponding marginal matrix, equation (5).

3-D Viterbi: the re-alignment phase for complete examples in 3-D is a direct analogue of the 2-D alignment – in the (i,j) plane – in eq. (2), extended to the third dimension, k. The Viterbi cell $V(\sigma_i, \tau_j, \xi_k)$ – the cost of the most probable path leading to the cell (i, j, k) – is calculated by Dynamic Programming, using the symbol-alignment costs $L(\sigma:\tau:\xi)$. In addition to the three source cells as in eq. (2), in plane k, there are four additional source cells from the previous plane, $k-1$.

6. Context model with phonetic features

We next present a model that takes the context, or *environment*, into account in alignment modeling. In this model, sounds and environments are coded as vectors of phonetic features. Rather than aligning symbols, we align the *features* of the symbols. Each alignment is aware of its context.

Features: Each symbol participating in an alignment has a *Type* feature, with possible values: K (consonant), V (vowel), dot, and #. All consonants and vowels then have 4 features, 2–6 values each:

Contexts: A model admits a fixed, finite set of *candidate contexts*. A context is a triplet (L, P, F), where L is either source or target level, P is one of the positions – relative to the current position – that the model may query, e.g., as listed in figure 3, and F is one of the possible features found at that position.

		Consonant articulation
M	Manner	plosive, fricative, glide, ...
P	Place	labial, dental, ..., velar
X	Voiced	−, +
S	Secondary articulation	−, affricate, aspirate, ...
		Vowel articulation
V	Vertical	high – low
H	Horizontal	front – back
R	Rounding	−, +
L	Length	1 – 5

I	itself, *possibly dot*
$-P$	previous position (excluding self), *possibly dot*
$-S$	previous non-dot symbol (excluding self)
$-K$	previous consonant
$-V$	previous vowel
$+S$	previous or self non-dot symbol
$+K$	previous or self consonant
$+V$	previous or self vowel

Figure 3. A set of phonetic features (above), and a set of positions – relative to position currently being coded – which the Context Model can query

Building decision trees: The model consists of a set of decision trees, *one tree for each feature and for each level*. This is done similarly to standard approaches to training decision trees. We code the features in a fixed, predetermined order, and source level before target level.

We now define the cost function for a given alignment of the complete data. Suppose a source consonant symbol σ is being coded on the source level. We have five trees (one per consonant feature, plus the Type feature) on source level that will be used in turn to code this symbol σ; each tree defines the cost for coding its own *feature* at its level. We add together these costs, to obtain the total cost of the given symbol σ. These 5 feature trees allow us to code all possible consonant symbols. Before we can compute the cost of the proposed alignment, (+:−), from the tree of feature X, we need to build the full tree.

We now go through the process of building the tree for feature X (i.e., voicedness), for the source level, (*NB*: we will need do the same for all other features, on both levels, as well). We build this tree as follows. First, we collect all instances of consonant symbols on the source level in the aligned data, and gather the values of feature X, and build an initial count vector; suppose it is:

X:	+	−
	1001	1002

This vector is stored at the *root* node of the tree; the cost of this node is computed by coding the vector prequentially, as before, using eq. (1), so that the cost is lowest when the two numbers are as uneven as possible.

Next, we try to split this node, by finding such a context that if we query that context, it will help us reduce the entropy in this count vector. We check all possible candidate contexts, (L, P, F), in turn, and choose the best one, as follows. There is a finite set of candidate contexts we will consider, or query. Each candidate refers to a symbol found on the source (σ) or the target (τ) level, at some relative position P, and to one of that symbol's features F. This yields approximately: 2 levels × 8 contexts × 5 features ≈ 80 candidates to query. We will condition the split at this node on all possible values of F. For each candidate, we try to split on its feature, and build the resulting alignment count vectors for every possible feature value.

Suppose one candidate is $(\sigma, -V, H)$ – which says: look up the preceding vowel on the source level, and query its H-feature – and suppose the H-feature has just two values, for simpicity: high/low. The vector at the root node would then split into two vectors, conditioned on the value of H, e.g.:

X | H = low:	+	−	X | H = high:	+	−
	1000	1		1	1001

This would likely be a very good split, since it reduces the entropy in both branches almost to zero. The criterion that guides the choice of the best candidate to use for splitting a node is the sum *code length* of the resulting split vectors.

We go through all candidates exhaustively, and greedily choose the one that yields the greatest reduction in cost. We proceed recursively down the tree, trying to split nodes, and stop when the total tree cost stops decreasing. The split itself costs some bits to code: 1 bit to code the fact that there is a split (1) vs. no split (0); if we do split, then we also encode which of the fixed number of candidates was chosen: $\approx \log 80$ bits. This completes the tree for feature X on level σ. We build trees all the other features and levels similarly, from the current alignment of the complete data.

Turning to our alignment of a pair of words, to code the alignment of the symbol pair (σ, τ), we first code σ, then τ – feature by feature in order, so later features can query features that have already been coded.

When we code feature X of σ, each node in the source-X tree holds a distribution over the values of X. Which one of the nodes/distributions do we use? Starting from the root, the tree structure tells us precisely which path to follow – based on, and completely determined by, the preceding context seen so far – based on some nearby position (say, $-V$, in the example above) and one of its features (say, H) – the tree tells us to query that feature's values; and so on, down to a leaf. For an example and discussion of an actual context decision tree learned by the model, see figure 6.

At all times we are interested only in the code length for the *complete* data, which is the sum of the costs of the count vectors at the *leaves* of all trees, coded prequentially. As previously, the change in the total code length induced by adding an event to the data defines the cost of this event.

We augment the set of possible values at every node with two additional special branches: use a branch labeled $\neq$, meaning that the queried symbol is of the wrong type or a dot – e.g., if the context tries to query previous symbol's feature M, but that symbol is a vowel; we use special feature value #, to mean that the query ran past the beginning of the word.

With the cost thus defined, we can use the Viterbi procedure for a aligning a word-pair just as we did in the 1–1 (context-free) models.

7. Evaluation and results

One way to evaluate the presented models thoroughly would require a gold-standard aligned corpus; the models produce alignments, which would be compared to expected alignments. Given a gold-standard, we could measure performance quantitatively, e.g., in terms of accuracy. However, no gold-standard alignment for the Uralic data currently exists, and building one would be very costly and slow. However, we can use other methods to evaluate the performance of the models.

Alignment: We can perform a qualitative evaluation, by checking how many correct sound correspondences a model finds – by inspecting the final alignment of the corpus and the count matrix. For example, a matrix for a 2-D, 1×1 baseline model alignment of Finnish-Estonian is shown in figure 4. The size of each ball is proportional to the number of alignments in the corpus of the corresponding symbols.

Finnish and Estonian are closely related, and the alignment shows a close correspondence – the model finds the "diagonal," i.e., most sounds correspond to "themselves." It is crucial to note that this model has no *a priori* knowledge about the nature of the symbols, e.g., that Finnish *a* is identical, or has any relation, to Estonian *a*. The languages are coded separately, and may have different alphabets – as they do in general (we use transcribed data).

The plot shows many Finnish-Estonian correspondences – as we find in handbooks, e.g., Lytkin (1973), Sinor (1997). For example, *ä* ~ *ä* and *ä* ~ *a* about evenly – reflecting the rule that original front vowels (*ä*) become back (*a*) in non-first syllables in Estonian. Word-final vowels *a*, *i*, *ä*, preserved in Finnish are often deleted in Estonian; etc. These rules can be observed directly in the count matrix, and in the aligned corpus.

Compression: In figure 5, we compare the models against standard data compressors, Gzip and Bzip, tested on over 3200 Finnish-Estonian word pairs from SSA. Gzip and Bzip compress data by finding regularities in it (frequent substrings). This comparison is a "sanity check": we would like to confirm whether our models find more regularity in the data than would an off-the-shelf data compressor, that has no knowledge that the words in the data are etymologically related. Of course, our models know that they should align pairs of consecutive lines. This test shows that learning about the "vertical" correspondences achieves much better compression rates – allows the models to extract greater regularity from the data.

Language distance: We can use alignment cost to measure inter-language distances. If we align all languages in StarLing pairwise using one

Information-theoretic modeling of etymological sound change 523

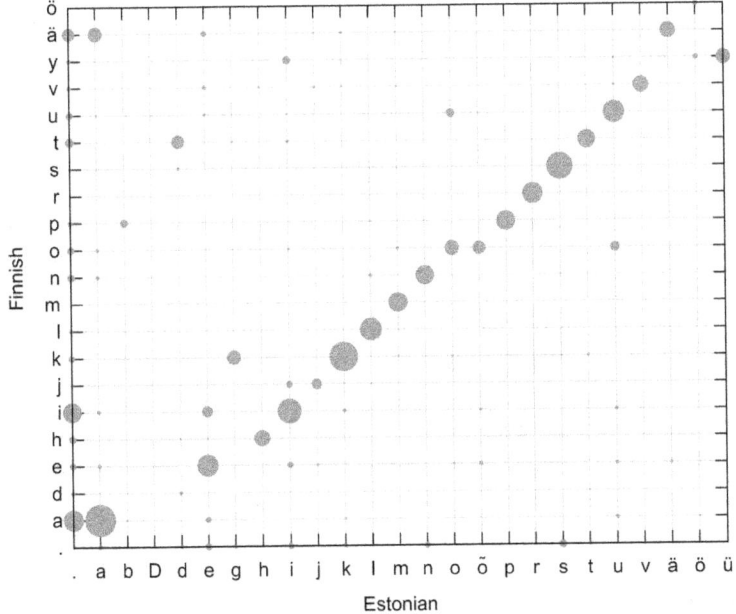

Figure 4. Count matrix using the two-part code

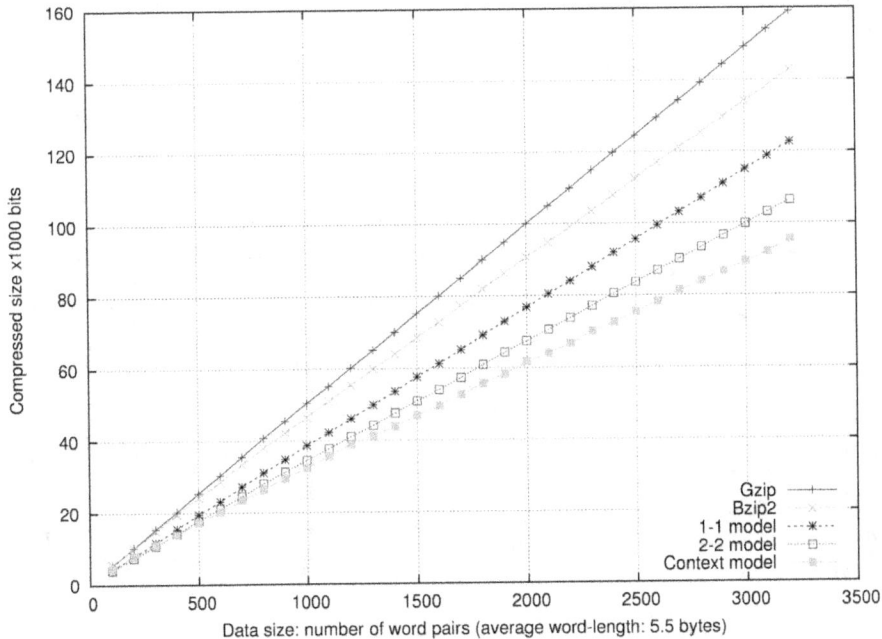

Figure 5. Comparison of compression power

of our models, we can then measure the *Normalized Compression Distance*, (NCD), introduced by Cilibrasi and Vitanyi (2005: 1523–1545):

$$NCD(a,b) = \frac{C(a,b) - \min(C(a), C(b))}{\max(C(a), C(b))}$$

where $0 < NCD < 1$, and $C(a,b)$ is the compression cost – i.e., the cost of the complete aligned data for languages *a* and *b*.[8] NCD normalizes the pairwise costs so that the language distances can be compared. They can also be used to construct phylogenetic trees, as explained below, in the section on *Imputation*. The pairwise NCDs for Finno-Ugric are shown in table 1. Even the simple 1×1 baseline model shows patterns that mirror the relationships in the tree in figure 1. For example, the score for each *sister language* pair, shown in bold, is the smallest entry in its row and column. Although the distances are not perfect for all languages, they confirm that the model is able to compress better – find *more regularity* in the data – between languages that are more closely related.

Rules of correspondence: One our main goals is to model rules of correspondence among languages. We can evaluate the models based on how good they are at discovering rules. In figure 4, the baseline model finds that Fin. *u* ~ Est. *u*, but sometimes *u* ~ *o* – this entropy is not explained further by this model. However, the more complex 2×2 model identifies the cause exactly – by discovering that Finnish diphthongs *uo, yö, ie* correspond to Estonian long vowels *oo, öö, ee*, which covers (i.e., explains!) all instances of (*u* : *o*).

Table 1. Normalized compression costs for Finno-Ugric data in StarLing data.

	fin	khn	kom	man	mar	mrd	saa	udm	ugr
est	**.37**	.70	.70	.71	.70	.66	.58	.73	.77
fin		.73	.69	.75	.69	.63	.58	.69	.77
khn			.67	**.63**	.70	.71	.66	.71	.76
kom				.67	.65	.67	.70	**.41**	.70
man					.67	.71	.77	.68	.75
mar						.64	.67	.67	.73
mrd							.64	.70	.72
saa								.68	.76
udm									.75

Another source of entropy in figure 4 is the alignment of $t \sim t/d$, $p \sim p/b$, and $k \sim k/g$. This is due to the rule of *voicing of word-medial plosives* in Estonian. This rule could be expressed in terms of Two-level Morphology, see Koskenniemi (1983) as: a voiceless plosive in Finnish, *may correspond to voiced in Estonian, if not word-initial*.[9] This rule cannot be captured by the 2×2 model. The context model finds this rule, shown in figure 6. The figure shows only the relevant part of the tree. This tree codes the *Target-level* (i.e., Estonian) *Voiced* consonant feature. In each node, the counts of corresponding feature values are shown in brackets.

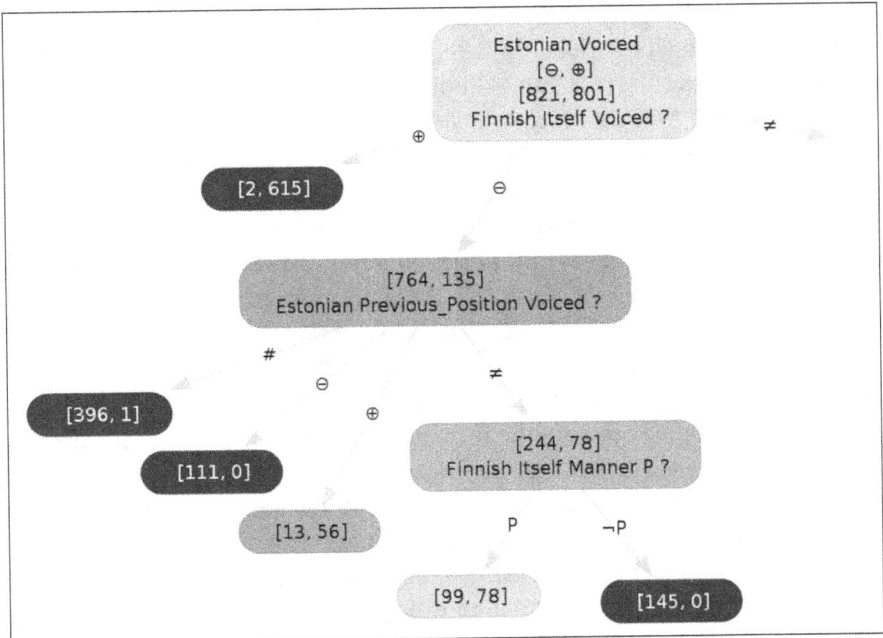

Figure 6. Rule for medial voicing of plosives in Estonian.

In the root node – without knowing anything about the environment – there is almost complete uncertainty (i.e., high entropy) about the value of *Voiced* feature of an Estonian consonant: 821 voiceless to 801 voiced in our data. Nodes where the balance is about even have higher entropy, where the balance is skewed – lower entropy. The query in the root node tells us to check the context *Finnish Itself Voiced* for the best clue about whether the current Estonian consonant is voiced or not. Tracing the options down left to right from the root, we obtain the rules. The leftmost branch says, if the Finnish is voiced (⊕), then the Estonian is almost certainly voiced as well — 2 voiceless to 615 voiced in this case. If the Finnish is voiceless (*Finnish Itself Voiced* =⊖), it says voicing *may occur*, but only in the red nodes — i.e., only if preceded by a voiced consonant on Estonian level (the branch marked by ⊕), or — if previous position is *not a consonant* (the ≠ branch indicates that the candidate's query does not apply: i.e., the sound found in that position is not a consonant) — it can be voiced only if the corresponding Finnish is a plosive (*P*). The blue nodes in this branch say that if this condition is not satisfied, the Estonian consonant almost certainly remains voiceless.

The context models discover numerous complex rules for different language pairs. For example, the rule that initial Finnish *k* "changes" (corresponds) to *h* in Hungarian, if it is followed by a back vowel; the correspondence between Komi trills and Udmurt sibilants; etc.

Imputation: We introduce a novel test of the quality of the models, by using them to *impute* unseen data, as follows. For a given model, and a language pair (L_1, L_2) — e.g., (Finnish, Estonian) — hold out one word pair, and train the model on the remaining data. Then show the model the hidden Finnish word and let it guess the corresponding Estonian. Imputation can be done for all models with a simple dynamic programming algorithm, similar to the Viterbi-like search used during training. Formally, given the hidden Finnish string, the imputation procedure selects from all possible Estonian strings the most probable Estonian string under the model.[10] Lastly, we compute an edit distance between the imputed string and the true withheld Estonian word (e.g., the Levenshtein distance). If we repeat this procedure for all word pairs in the (L_1, L_2) data set, sum the edit distances, and normalize by the total size of the (true) L_2 data, we obtain the Normalized Edit Distance $NED(L_1|L_2, M)$ between L_1 and L_2, under model M.

Although compression cost is the ultimate test of the model's quality, NED has a more intuitive interpretation than comparing costs. For example, if $NED(L_1|L_2, M) < NED(L_1|L_2, M')$, then it is difficult to argue that M is "worse" than M' — it has learned more about the regularities between L_1 and L_2, it knows more about L_2 given L_1. A comparison of imputation power, in terms of NED, of the context vs. the baseline model, on 10·9 language pairs, is shown in figure 7, (each segment connects a pair of languages *a* and *b*, where for one of the points the source is *a*, and for the other point the source is *b*).

The context model, which has much lower cost than the baseline, almost always has lower NED. This also yields an important insight: it is an indication that optimizing the model cost is a good approach — the models do *not* optimize NED directly, and yet their cost correlates strongly with NED, which is a simple and intuitive measure of the model's quality.

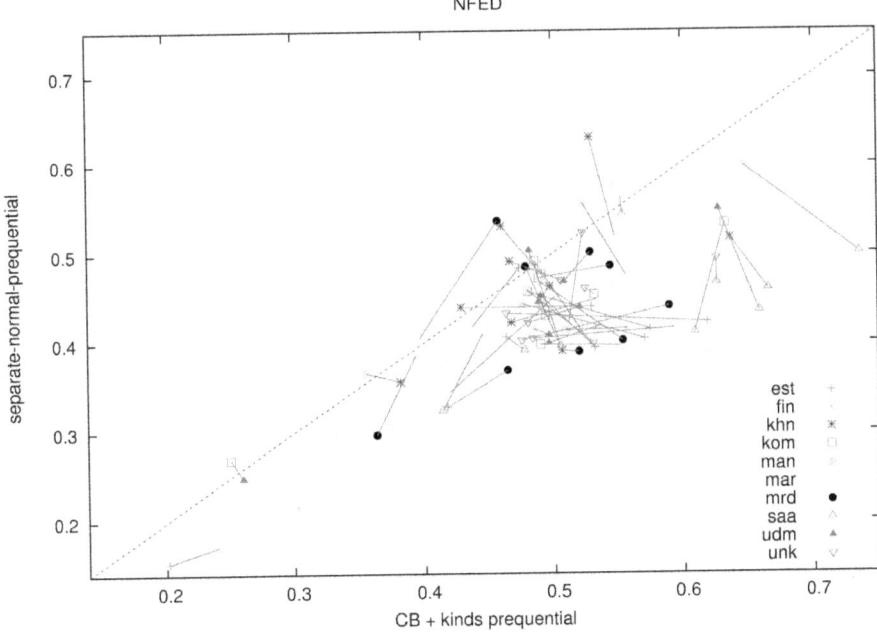

Figure 7. Comparison of NED for pairwise alignments of all language pairs of the baseline 1–1 model (X-axis) vs. the context model (Y-axis)

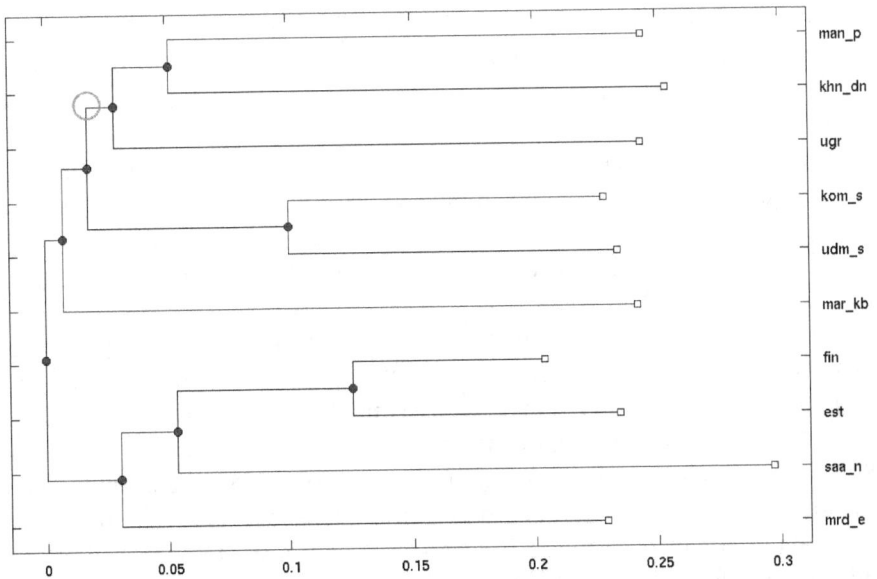

Figure 8. A phylogenetic tree induced by imputation and normalized edit distances

NED also provides yet another inter-language distance measure, as does NCD. The distances can be used to make inferences about how far the languages are from each other; they can be fed into algorithms for drawing phylogenetic trees. The pairwise NEDs from figure 7 can be used as input to the NeighborJoin algorithm, to construct a phylogenetic tree based on these distances. The resulting tree, shown in figure 8 is very close to the "gold-standard" tree in figure 1. Note that NeighborJoin produces *un-rooted* trees – it is not able to identify a root, and the root of the tree in the figure is selected via an arbitrary heuristic. In fact, the root may be placed at any point in the graph. Placing the root at the location circled in red, makes this tree coincide almost completely with the tree in figure 1. The main difference is that Mari and Mordva are not joined together. We should note that there is no unanimous agreement on a "correct" phylogeny for Finno-Ugric, and some mainstream theories do not posit the existence of a "Volgaic" branch. It is most crucial to note that the tree was drawn based on the language distances, which were obtained from models that were trained *only on the raw cognate data*, with no prior assumptions, no selection of characters, or information about how the languages are related.

8. Discussion and current work

We have presented a baseline 1–1 model, extended it to align multiple symbols, to multiple dimensions, and to take into account the context with phonetic features. We have evaluated the models by examining the alignments and the rules of correspondence that they discover, and by measuring compression cost, language distances, and imputation power. The key point is that the models take only an etymological data set as input, and require no further linguistic assumptions of any kind. In this regard, they are as objective as possible, given the data. The data set itself, of course, may be highly subjective and questionable.

However, the objectivity of the models given the data now opens new possibilities for comparing entire data sets. For example, we can begin to compare the Finnish and Estonian datasets in SSA vs. StarLing, although the data sets have quite different characteristics, e.g., different size – 3200 vs. 800 word pairs, respectively – and the comparison is done impartially, relying solely on the given data. Another direct consequence of the presented methods is that they enable us to quantify uncertainty of entries in the corpus of etymological data. For example, for a given entry x in language L_1, we can compute exactly the probability that x would be imputed by any of our models, trained on all the remaining data from L_1 plus any other set of languages in the family. This can be applied equally to any entry, in particular to entries marked dubious by the database creators.

The methods proposed here are *not* intended to replace traditional methods of etymological analysis. We are addressing only some aspects of the wider problem of etymology. However, we believe that the methods provide a basis for further research and exploration of etymological datasets. In particular, we can use them to approach the question of comparison of "competing" etymological datasets. The cost of an optimal alignment obtained over a given data set serves as a measure of its internal consistency.

We are currently working to combine the context with 3- and higher-dimensional models, and to extend these models to perform diachronic imputation, i.e., reconstruction of proto-forms.

Notes

1. Acknowledgements: We are grateful to Suvi Hiltunen and Arto Vihavainen for their contributions to the implementation of the algorithms. We thank Teemu Roos for numerous helpful comments and suggestions. This research was supported by the Uralink Project of the Academy of Finland, and the ALGODAN Center of Excellence of the Academy of Finland.
2. We refer to "source" and "target" language for convenience only – our models are symmetric, as will become apparent.
3. We use the arrow above to denote words, as vectors of symbols.
4. In figure 2, the left column and the top row store the costs for symbol deletions at the beginning of the source and the target word, respectively.
5. To be precise we should speak of predictive probabilities rather than parameters. Model parameters are normally fixed values, which we believe to represent a "true" distribution, whereas in this model, the parameters are not known/computed explicitly at any point. Bayesian predictive probabilities are not fixed, and change all the time, but are fully known at any point during the coding of the data, by both encoder and decoder.
6. This was true by definition in the baseline 2-D algorithm.
7. Note that this results in an *incomplete code*, since every symbol is coded twice, but that does not affect the learning.
8. *C(a)* is a monolingual "alignment" of a language with itself – which is a very naïve model, since the 1×1 model is then able to model only the symbol frequencies independently of their context.
9. In fact, phonetically, in modern spoken Estonian, the consonants that are written using the symbols *b,d,g* are not strictly speaking voiced, but that is a finer point, we use this rule in a simplified sense, for illustration of the principle.

10. For the 1–1 and 2–2 models, imputation is exact: we can compute the actual most probable Estonian string. For the context models, we have to use a heuristic search, keeping for each prefix of the Finnish word, the N best guesses at the corresponding Estonian prefix (with N = 100, for example).
11. There are alternative approaches to constructing phylogenies, e.g., Vitanyi and Cilibrasi's CompLearn.

References

Anttila, Raimo
  1989 *Historical and Comparative Linguistics.* New York: John Benjamins.
Barbançon, François G., Tandy Warnow, Don Ringe, Steven Evans, and Luay Nakhleh
  2009 An experimental study comparing linguistic phylogenetic reconstruction methods. In *Proceedings of the Conference on Languages and Genes.*
Bouchard-Côté, Alexandre, Percy Liang, Thomas Griffiths, and Dan Klein
  2007 A probabilistic approach to diachronic phonology. In *Proceedings of the Joint Conference on Empirical Methods in Natural Language Processing and Computational Natural Language Learning* (EMNLP–CoNLL).
Cilibrasi, Rudi and Paul M. B. Vitanyi
  2005 Clustering by compression. *IEEE Transactions on Information Theory* 51 (4): 1523–1545.
Grünwald, Peter
  2007 *The Minimum Description Length Principle.* MIT Press.
Itkonen, Erkki and Ulla-Maija Kulonen
  2000 *Suomen sanojen alkuperä* [The Origin of Finnish Words]. Helsinki, Finland: Suomalaisen Kirjallisuuden Seura.
Kessler, Brett
  2001 *The Significance of Word Lists.* Stanford, CA: CSLI Publications..
Kondrak, Grzegorz
  2004 Combining evidence in cognate identification. In *Proceedings of the Seventeenth Canadian Conference on Artificial Intelligence* (Canadian AI 2004).
Kondrak, Grzegorz
  2003 Identifying complex sound correspondences in bilingual wordlists. In *Computational Linguistics and Intelligent Text Processing* (CICLing 2003).
Kondrak, Grzegorz
  2002 Determining recurrent sound correspondences by inducing translation models. In *Proceedings of COLING: the 19th International Conference on Computational Linguistics.*

Kontkanen, Petri, Petri Myllymäki, and Henry Tirri
    1996   Constructing bayesian finite mixture models by the EM algorithm. *ESPRIT Working Group on Neural and Computational Learning* (NeuroCOLT).

Koskenniemi, Kimmo
    1983   Two-level morphology: A general computational model for word-form recognition and production. PhD thesis, University of Helsinki.

Lytkin, Vasilij I., Klara E. Majtinskaja, and Károly Rédei
    1974–76   *Osnovy finno-ugorskogo jazykoznanija* [Foundations of Finno-Ugric linguistics]. Vol. 1–3. Moscow: Nauka.

Nakhleh, Luay, Don Ringe, and Tandy Warnow
    2005   Perfect phylogenetic networks: A new methodology for reconstructing the evolutionary history of natural languages. *Language* 81 (2): 382–420.

Rédei, Károly
    1988–91   *Uralisches etymologisches Wörterbuch*. Wiesbaden: Harrassowitz.

Ringe, Don, Tandy Warnow, and Ann Taylor
    2002   Indo-european and computational cladistics. *Transactions of the Philological Society* 100 (1): 59–129.

Rissanen, Jorma
    1978   Modeling by shortest data description. *Automatica* 14 (5): 465–471.

Sinor, Denis
    1997   *The Uralic Languages: Description, History and Foreign Influences (Handbook of Uralic Studies Volume 1)*. Leiden: Brill Academic Publishers.

Starostin, Sergei A.
    2000   Comparative-historical linguistics and lexicostatistics. In *Time Depth in Historical Linguistics,* Colin Renfrew, April McMahon, and Larry Trask (eds.), Volume 1: 223–265. Cambridge: The McDonald Institute for Archaeological Research.

Index

ADR dataset, 158, 164, 170
Afrasian, 253, 264
Afro-Asiatic, 252, 264, 314
Albanian, 60, 75, 217, 222, 269, 306, 314, 322, 382, 486, 498–500
alignment (of sequences), 11, 121, 303, 305, 313, 316–321, 325, 326, 375, 381, 384, 431, 432, 439, 478, 483, 493–496, 507, 508, 510–522, 525, 527–529
    see also *sentence alignment, word alignment*
Altaic, 252, 265
Anatolian, 13, 84–86, 88–92, 94–99
Angan, 253, 267, 271
Arawakan, 12, 29–32, 37, 40, 41, 44, 46–51, 53, 332, 433, 434, 443
archaism, 84, 85, 95, 99
areal linguistics, 5, 6, 17, 33, 43–46, 49, 52, 83, 90, 196, 287, 291–295, 297, 309, 335, 336, 342, 389–392, 401, 448, 468, 477, 487, 490, 496, 498, 500, 503
    see also *contact linguistics, diffusion, language contact, linguistic area, Sprachbund*
ASJP list, 15, 156, 169, 170, 251, 261, 289, 290
    see also *basic meaning, basic vocabulary, core vocabulary, Intercontinental Dictionary Series, Leipzig-Jakarta list, lexicostatistical list, Natural Semantic Metalanguage, Swadesh list, universal concept, word list*
Athapaskan, 14, 231–235, 239–241, 243, 244, 253, 269
Atlantic, 252, 269, 486, 489
Australian languages, 387–389, 391, 392
Austro-Asiatic, 151, 252, 266, 486, 500
Austronesian, 77, 143, 199, 250–253, 266, 314, 429, 486, 492

Automated Similarity Judgment Program, see *ASJP list*
Awyu, 253, 271

Balto-Slavic, 98
Bantu, 77, 90, 250, 314, 491
Barbacoan, 331, 332, 334, 343, 433, 443
base dialect, 108–114, 116, 117, 119, 123–125, 127, 129–132
    see also *basilect*
basic meaning, 310, 404, 409, 425
    see also *ASJP list, basic vocabulary, core vocabulary, Intercontinental Dictionary Series, Leipzig-Jakarta list, lexicostatistical list, Natural Semantic Metalanguage, Swadesh list, universal concept, word list*
basic vocabulary, 7–9, 13, 15, 17, 18, 41, 46, 133, 149, 153, 156, 175, 176, 178, 179, 181, 182, 184, 189, 191, 192, 194, 201, 207, 249–251, 257–260, 263, 264, 288–291, 297, 310, 311, 382, 447
    see also *ASJP list, basic meaning, core vocabulary, Intercontinental Dictionary Series, Leipzig-Jakarta list, lexicostatistical list, Natural Semantic Metalanguage, Swadesh list, universal concept, word list*
basilect, 108, 123, 125, 127, 129, 132
    see also *base dialect*
Basque, 52, 449, 467, 486, 499
BEET, 232–238, 240, 242, 245
    see also *body-part term, effluvia, ephemera*
Benue-Congo, 252, 270
bigram, 17, 320, 430, 432, 434, 435, 437, 438, 441
    see also *n-gram model, unigram*

bilingual dictionary, 7, 17, 375, 377, 383, 447–449, 451, 452, 454–459, 462, 467, 469–471
see also *dictionary*
bitext, 375, 379, 381, 384, 493
see also *parallel corpus, parallel text, translation corpus*
black box (method), 19, 429, 430, 433, 439, 442
Body-part, Effluvia and Ephemera Term, see *BEET*
body-part term, 232, 236–238, 241, 244
see also *BEET, effluvia, ephemera*
borrowing, 33, 41, 44, 48, 53, 89, 99, 112, 142, 143, 150–152, 156, 170, 201, 262, 288, 290, 292, 330, 376, 382, 391, 392, 404, 405, 420–422, 449
see also *lexical borrowing, loan, loanword*
Bosavi, 253, 271
Bunuban, 389, 395, 399, 409, 422

Cariban, 40, 252, 254, 268, 433, 443
case alignment, 43–45, 53, 58, 69, 74, 309, 423
CDR dataset, 162, 164
Celtic, 85, 86, 91, 92, 98, 99
Central American languages, 330, 331, 333, 334, 338, 339, 342, 346
character (in cladistics), 9, 13, 19, 83, 141–144, 152–155, 157, 169, 170, 222–225, 250, 508, 528
character-based method, 13, 83, 141, 142, 152–155, 157, 170, 250
see also *cladistics, cladogram, dendrogram, distance-based method, genetic classification, genetic difference, genetic similarity, genus, language family, lineage, linguistic phylogeny, phylogenetic difference, phylogeny, phylum, subgrouping*
Chibchan, 330, 331, 334, 335, 343, 345
Chinese, 64, 66, 70, 253, 271, 314, 316, 323, 457, 465, 468, 486

Chocoan, 331, 332, 334, 335, 343, 433–436, 438, 443
city-block distance, 371
cladistics, 46, 83, 99
see also *character-based method, cladistics, cladogram, dendrogram, distance-based method, genetic classification, genetic difference, genetic similarity, genus, language family, lineage, linguistic phylogeny, phylogenetic difference, phylogeny, phylum, subgrouping*
cladogram, 32, 38, 41
see also *character-based method, cladistics, dendrogram, distance-based method, genetic classification, genetic difference, genetic similarity, genus, language family, lineage, linguistic phylogeny, phylogenetic difference, phylogeny, phylum, subgrouping*
CLANS, 304, 305, 308, 309, 313, 322, 324, 325
cluster, 12, 15–17, 29, 32, 36, 38–41, 46–51, 65, 66, 150, 154, 185, 240, 241, 243, 303–309, 312, 322–325, 349, 359–361, 409, 414, 417, 460, 464–466, 469, 471, 503
~ analysis, 12, 29, 32, 36, 38, 304, 360, 409, 414, 417
clustering, 12, 15, 46, 65, 154, 185, 240, 241, 303–305, 307–309, 322–325, 349, 361, 453, 460, 461, 464–466, 471, 503
see also *hierarchical clustering, k-means clustering*
~ algorithm, 15, 154, 303, 361, 464
~ coefficient, 453, 460, 461
~ method, 304
Cofan, 332, 343
cognate, 8, 12, 14, 16, 18, 38, 40–42, 141–143, 150–154, 157, 158, 175, 178–181, 201, 202, 204, 207, 231, 232, 235, 239–241, 249–251, 254, 255, 258, 259, 261–264, 273, 274,

Index 535

286, 306, 307, 310, 312, 313, 329, 375–378, 381, 382, 384, 391, 399, 404–406, 423, 425, 431, 439, 442, 486, 487, 507, 508, 510, 518, 528
collocation, 10, 387–389, 398, 399, 404–409, 411, 412, 416–420, 422–425, 476, 479, 480, 482, 483
comparative method, 6, 13, 20, 83, 92, 141, 143, 147, 151, 179, 200–202, 204, 207, 421, 423, 429, 447, 448, 450, 477, 486, 487, 501
complex predicate, 387
    see also *compound verb construction, CVC*
compound verb construction, 16, 387, 389, 425
    see also *complex predicate, CVC*
compression, 17, 18, 429, 430, 432–435, 437–439, 441, 442, 522–524, 526, 528
    see also *Lempel-Ziv algorithm, Normalized Compression Distance, zipping*
computational linguistics, 3, 9, 16, 19, 20, 293, 358, 384, 447, 448, 478, 485
    see also *language technology, natural language processing*
constructional distance, 387, 425
    see also *formal distance, grammatical distance, morphosyntactic distance, structural distance*
contact linguistics, 288
    see also *areal linguistics, diffusion, language contact, linguistic area, Sprachbund*
co-occurrence, 359, 360, 494, 495
core vocabulary, 33
    see also *ASJP list, basic meaning, basic vocabulary, Intercontinental Dictionary Series, Leipzig-Jakarta list, lexicostatistical list, Natural Semantic Metalanguage, Swadesh list, universal concept, word list*
corpus (linguistics), 6, 7, 10, 16, 18, 288, 313–316, 325, 326, 353–364, 366, 368, 370, 371, 375, 381, 383, 470, 476, 478, 493–497, 503
Creole languages, 486, 487, 492, 498
crowdsourcing, 293
cultural concept, 287
culture matrix (model), 31, 32
Cushitic, 252, 265, 314
CVC, 16, 17, 387–395, 398, 399, 401, 405, 409, 413, 417, 420, 421, 423, 425
    see also *complex predicate, compound verb construction*

Daly (River), 252, 265, 388, 389
database, 5, 10–13, 15–19, 36–38, 40, 45, 142–144, 147, 148, 150–158, 162, 164, 166–170, 181, 196, 200, 202, 205–210, 221, 231, 235, 236, 240, 241, 251, 261, 264, 285, 287, 289, 291–296, 304–307, 310, 313, 325, 329–331, 333–336, 338, 339, 342, 343, 345, 346, 360, 383, 458, 462, 464, 467, 507–511, 528, 529
data standardization, 295
dendrogram, 65, 240–243, 464, 466, 471
    see also *character-based method, cladistics, cladogram, distance-based method, genetic classification, genetic difference, genetic similarity, genus, language family, lineage, linguistic phylogeny, phylogenetic difference, phylogeny, phylum, subgrouping*
diachronic stability, 33, 44, 238, 239, 241
    see also *stability, stable feature, stable vocabulary*
dialect, 5–9, 11, 13, 32, 84, 98, 99, 107–133, 135, 147, 160, 166, 175, 179, 181, 184, 194, 231, 233, 240, 273, 295, 353, 354, 356, 360, 429, 432, 439, 444, 497
dialectometry, 5, 8, 13, 120, 175, 194, 231, 240, 354, 360, 429
Dice coefficient, 480, 481
dictionary, 7, 15–17, 142, 143, 145, 170, 285–287, 289, 290, 293, 295–297, 375–377, 379–381, 383, 384, 393,

447–452, 454–460, 462, 464, 467, 469–471, 478, 493, 494, 508–510
see also *bilingual dictionary*
diffusion, 47, 389, 391
see also *areal linguistics, contact linguistics, language contact, linguistic area, Sprachbund*
dissimilarity measure, 121, 122, 392, 399, 480, 501, 502
see also *distance measure, linguistic distance measure*
distance-based method, 142–144, 148, 201
see also *character-based method, cladistics, cladogram, dendrogram, genetic classification, genetic difference, genetic similarity, genus, language family, lineage, linguistic phylogeny, phylogenetic difference, phylogeny, phylum, subgrouping*
distance measure, 4–7, 9, 10, 12–14, 18–20, 157, 199–205, 207, 208, 212, 218, 219, 221, 222, 261, 303, 319, 324, 329, 337, 340, 341, 345, 349, 356, 357, 366, 368, 370, 391–393, 401, 420, 424, 462, 464, 477, 478, 483, 485, 487, 489, 491, 495, 497, 501, 528
see also *dissimilarity measure, linguistic distance measure*
DKB database, 304–307
Dravidian, 13, 141, 143–157, 164, 166, 169, 170, 252, 268, 292, 314, 322
Dutch (regional speech)
Belgian ~, 107, 112, 115, 117, 119, 128–131, 135
Netherlandic ~, 107, 112, 115, 119, 128, 357

Eastern Sudanic, 253, 270
edit distance, 9, 179, 202, 526, 527
see also *Levenshtein distance, LDND, Normalized Edit Distance*
effluvia, 14, 232–244
see also *BEET, body-part term, ephemera*

Eleman, 253, 272
ephemera, 8, 14, 114, 232–241, 244
see also *BEET, body-part term, effluvia*
Eskimo-Aleut, 486
Ethiosemitic, 253, 265
Ethnologue, 40, 147, 148, 170, 176, 193, 196, 251, 429, 433, 438, 447
evaluation, 6, 10, 17, 19, 20, 153, 156, 157, 202, 315, 320, 370, 384, 429, 439, 442, 448, 477, 493, 498, 507, 508, 522, 524, 528
see also *gold standard*

feature dependency, 335, 336, 340, 343, 346, 349
see also *functional dependency*
Finisterre, 253, 272
Finno-Ugric, 496, 511, 524, 528
formal
~ distance (measure), 4, 130
see also *constructional distance, grammatical distance, morphosyntactic distance, structural distance*
~ feature, 391–394
see also *grammatical feature, morphological feature, morphosyntactic feature, structural feature, syntactic feature, typological feature*
~ similarity (measure), 377, 381, 383, 393
see also *language similarity, lexical similarity, linguistic similarity, orthographic similarity, phonetic similarity, semantic similarity, similarity measure, string similarity, structural similarity, syntactic similarity, typological similarity, word similarity*
functional dependency, 329, 335, 345
see also *feature dependency*

Ge, 252, 269

genetic
~ classification, 5–7, 12–14, 17–20, 57, 61–65, 72, 90, 122, 151, 175, 178–180, 193, 196, 250, 285, 289, 291, 304, 309, 325, 330, 334, 336, 342, 343, 387, 421, 422, 425, 429, 430, 439, 442, 443, 447, 450, 477, 487, 490, 492, 496–498, 500–503
see also *character-based method, cladistics, cladogram, dendrogram, distance-based method, genetic difference, genetic similarity, genus, language family, lineage, linguistic phylogeny, phylogenetic difference, phylogeny, phylum, subgrouping*
~ difference, 142, 143, 204, 208, 387, 430, 439, 487, 501
see also *character-based method, cladistics, cladogram, dendrogram, distance-based method, genetic classification, genetic similarity, genus, language family, lineage, linguistic phylogeny, phylogenetic difference, phylogeny, phylum, subgrouping*
~ similarity, 46, 432
see also *character-based method, cladistics, cladogram, dendrogram, distance-based method, genetic classification, genetic difference, genus, language family, lineage, linguistic phylogeny, phylogenetic difference, phylogeny, phylum, subgrouping*
genus, 63, 72, 73, 209, 261, 447, 486, 487, 492, 496–500
see also *character-based method, cladistics, cladogram, dendrogram, distance-based method, genetic classification, genetic difference, genetic similarity, language family, lineage, linguistic phylogeny, phylogenetic*

difference, phylogeny, phylum, subgrouping
Geographical Information System (GIS), 12, 29, 36, 37, 41
Germanic, 57, 63, 64, 69, 72, 73, 84, 86, 87, 90, 91, 93, 98, 99, 180, 208, 221, 306, 322, 429, 465, 466, 486, 491, 492, 496, 497, 503
GIS, see *Geographical Information System*
glossing, 424, 478–480, 482–484
glottochronology, 5, 33, 141, 149, 150, 175, 180, 256, 262
gold standard, 19, 145, 179, 485, 522, 528
see also *evaluation*
Gower coefficient, 329, 337, 340–343, 345, 349
grammatical
~ distance, 477
see also *constructional distance, formal distance, morphosyntactic distance, structural distance*
~ feature, 7, 16, 51, 176, 335, 387, 398, 424
see also *formal feature, morphological feature, morphosyntactic feature, structural feature, syntactic feature, typological feature*
grammaticalization, 92, 262, 390, 391, 393, 421
Grand Valley Dani, 253, 272
Greater Madang, 253, 272, 273
Greek, 60, 62, 64, 66, 74, 75, 84–87, 92, 93, 98, 99, 224, 269, 306, 379, 458, 486, 487, 489, 490, 496, 499, 500, 503
Greek-Armenian, 98, 99
Guahibo, 433–436, 443
Gur, 252, 270

Hamming distance, 67, 142, 153, 155, 306, 329
hierarchical clustering, 65, 154, 464, 471
see also *clustering, k-means clustering*
Himalayan region, 14, 175–177, 292

Hmong-Mien, 252, 268
homonymy, 3, 378, 457, 479
Huon, 253, 260, 272

IDS, see *Intercontinental Dictionary Series*
imputation, 18, 20, 524, 526–530
Indo-Aryan, 92, 150–152, 292, 306
Indo-European, 8, 12, 13, 44, 58, 63, 64, 72–75, 83–86, 88–95, 97–99, 143, 151, 179, 199, 200, 202, 204–206, 208, 221, 222, 250, 252, 253, 268, 286, 304–306, 310, 312, 322, 381, 429, 430, 486, 487, 500
Indo-Hittite hypothesis, 95
Indo-Iranian, 85, 91, 92, 98, 99, 151, 306
innovation, 13, 83, 85, 86, 91, 95–99, 122, 141, 199, 202, 391, 420, 425
Intercontinental Dictionary Series (IDS), 15, 176, 285–297
   see also *ASJP list, basic meaning, basic vocabulary, core vocabulary, Leipzig-Jakarta list, lexicostatistical list, Natural Semantic Metalanguage, Swadesh list, universal concept, word list*
inter-language variation, 324
intra-language variation, 315, 324
Iranian, 77, 85, 91, 92, 98, 99, 151, 306
Italic, 84–86, 90, 91, 98, 185, 264, 489
Italo-Celtic, 91, 92, 98, 99
Iwaidjan, 252, 264, 265, 273

Japonic, 252, 254, 269
Jarrakan, 389, 409
Jicaquean, 332

Kadai, 253, 260, 271, 314
Kamasau, 253, 271, 273
Kamsa, 332, 433, 443
Kiwaian, 253, 272
k-means clustering, 503
   see also *clustering, hierarchical clustering*

Koiarian, 253, 272
koineization, 89, 110–113
Kolopom, 253, 272
Kwa, 113, 252, 270

L2 Dutch, 12, 199, 200, 204, 205, 221, 225
L2 English, 12, 217
L2 learning, 199, 200, 222, 288
   see also *language learning*
language
   ~ classification, 8, 10, 15, 19, 141, 143, 250, 273, 303, 305, 311, 313, 325, 430, 435
   ~ comparison, 6, 15, 20, 285, 431, 457, 501
   ~ contact, 6, 12, 29, 31–37, 41, 43–50, 89, 90, 97, 99, 112, 142, 151, 155, 262, 285, 286, 288, 292, 325, 334, 346, 395–397, 423, 449, 477, 487, 490, 496
      see also *areal linguistics, contact linguistics, diffusion, linguistic area, Sprachbund*
   ~ distance (measure), 6, 9, 14, 15, 17, 18, 143, 153–155, 202, 240, 241, 305, 468, 475–478, 484, 485, 487, 489, 491, 492, 497, 500–502, 522, 524, 528
      see also *linguistic distance*
   ~ family, 8, 13, 14, 18, 30, 37, 41, 44, 53, 62, 141, 143–145, 147, 151, 152, 155–157, 169, 175, 193, 200, 201, 205, 232, 241, 249, 251, 257, 258, 261, 264, 286, 291, 292, 307, 322, 382, 429, 433–436, 438, 442, 447, 448, 469, 470, 490, 501, 507, 510, 511, 517
      see also *character-based method, cladistics, cladogram, dendrogram, distance-based method, genetic classification, genetic difference, genetic similarity, genus, lineage, linguistic phy-*

logeny, phylogenetic difference, phylogeny, phylum, subgrouping
~ learning, 20, 57–59, 61–64, 66–68, 71–75, 199, 200, 202, 203, 205, 216, 222, 288
see also *L2 learning*
~ similarity (measure), 64, 199, 305, 500
see also *formal similarity, lexical similarity, linguistic similarity, orthographic similarity, phonetic similarity, semantic similarity, similarity measure, string similarity, structural similarity, syntactic similarity, typological similarity, word similarity*
~ technology, 286
see also *computational linguistics, natural language processing*
~ typology, 5, 8, 458
see also *lexical typology, morphological typology, semantic typology, typological linguistics*
LCSR (Longest Common Subsequence Ratio), 379–383, 430, 432
LDND (Levenshtein Distance Normalized Divided), 156, 249, 250
see also *edit distance, Levenshtein distance, Normalized Edit Distance*
Leipzig-Jakarta list, 290
see also *ASJP list, basic meaning, basic vocabulary, core vocabulary, Intercontinental Dictionary Series, lexicostatistical list, Natural Semantic Metalanguage, Swadesh list, universal concept, word list*
Lempel-Ziv algorithm, 430, 432
see also *compression, Normalized Compression Distance, zipping*
Lencan, 332, 333
Levenshtein distance, 9–14, 17, 116, 120–122, 124, 143, 154, 156, 170, 179, 202, 240, 249, 311, 319–321, 324, 429–432, 434, 435, 438–440, 442, 444, 526

see also *edit distance, LDND, Normalized Edit Distance*
lexical
~ borrowing, 99, 376
see also *borrowing, loan, loanword*
~ diffusion, 141, 150
~ distance (measure), 16, 46, 154, 201, 212, 353, 356, 357, 365–369, 477
~ feature, 7, 8, 13, 16, 40, 41, 43, 48, 50, 87, 88, 142, 143, 176, 285, 292, 304, 355, 398, 477
~ replacement, 9, 150, 157, 258, 263, 289
~ semantics, 292, 353, 354, 447–449, 454, 456–458, 462, 467–470
see also *word meaning, word semantics*
~ similarity (measure), 46, 47, 50, 258, 261
see also *formal similarity, language similarity, linguistic similarity, orthographic similarity, phonetic similarity, semantic similarity, similarity measure, string similarity, structural similarity, syntactic similarity, typological similarity, word similarity*
~ typology, 285, 288
see also *language typology, morphological typology, semantic typology, typological linguistics*
~ variation, 16, 353–363, 366, 368, 370
lexicostatistical list, 251
see also *ASJP list, basic meaning, basic vocabulary, core vocabulary, Intercontinental Dictionary Series, Leipzig-Jakarta list, Natural Semantic Metalanguage, Swadesh list, universal concept, word list*
lexicostatistics, 5–8, 12–14, 33, 141, 143, 149, 175, 178–180, 192, 194, 201, 250, 251, 264, 421, 422

lineage, 53, 200, 389, 393, 401, 404, 409, 423, 425, 447
    see also *character-based method, cladistics, cladogram, dendrogram, distance-based method, genetic classification, genetic difference, genetic similarity, genus, language family, linguistic phylogeny, phylogenetic difference, phylogeny, phylum, subgrouping*
linguistic
    ~ area, 73, 88, 142, 292, 500, 501
        see also *diffusion, areal linguistics, contact linguistics, language contact, Sprachbund*
    ~ distance (measure), 4, 5, 9, 12, 18, 19, 29, 32, 37, 38, 59, 107, 109, 120, 199–205, 207, 208, 212–216, 218, 219, 221, 222, 479
        see also *language distance*
    ~ phylogeny, 141–143, 153, 170, 447
        see also *ccharacter-based method, cladistics, cladogram, dendrogram, distance-based method, genetic classification, genetic difference, genetic similarity, genus, language family, lineage, phylogenetic difference, phylogeny, phylum, subgrouping*
    ~ similarity (measure), 33, 182, 202
        see also *formal similarity, language similarity, lexical similarity, orthographic similarity, phonetic similarity, semantic similarity, similarity measure, string similarity, structural similarity, syntactic similarity, typological similarity, word similarity*
    ~ variable, 130, 353, 354, 360
loan, 32–34, 41, 42, 45, 52, 88, 89
    see also *borrowing, lexical borrowing, loanword*

loanword, 16, 251, 287, 293, 375–381
    see also *borrowing, lexical borrowing, loan*
Loanword Typology Project, 287, 290, 293–297
Lolo-Burmese, 253, 271
LWT, see *Loanword Typology Project*

Macro-Ge, 252, 269
Macú-Puinave, 433, 443
Malagasy, 252, 266, 314, 318–320, 323
Malayo-Polynesian, 323
Mayan, 252, 260, 264, 269, 273, 332, 333, 486, 492
Mayi, 252, 265
MDL, see *Minimum Description Length*
MDS, see *multidimensional scaling*
Melanesian, 253, 266
Miao-Yao, 253, 268
Minimum Description Length (MDL), 18, 512
Misumalpan, 331, 333
Mixe-Zoque, 252, 253, 269, 274
Mon-Khmer, 253, 266
Morobe, 253, 266
morphological
    ~ feature, 235, 236, 448
        see also *formal feature, grammatical feature, morphosyntactic feature, structural feature, syntactic feature, typological feature*
    ~ typology, 482, 488, 489, 492
        see also *language typology, lexical typology, semantic typology, typological linguistics*
morphosemantic distance, 17, 18, 475, 478, 481, 482, 487, 489, 495, 497, 500–502
morphosyntactic
    ~ distance, 313
        see also *constructional distance, formal distance, grammatical distance, structural distance*

~ feature, 304, 307, 309, 324, 325, 335, 346
    see also *formal feature, grammatical feature, morphological feature, structural feature, syntactic feature, typological feature*
multidimensional scaling (MDS), 150, 364–367, 369, 492

Na-Dene, 252, 269
national variety, 356, 364
natural language processing, 19, 294, 315, 375
    see also *computational linguistics, language technology*
Natural Semantic Metalanguage (NSM), 290
    see also *ASJP list, basic meaning, basic vocabulary, core vocabulary, Intercontinental Dictionary Series, Leipzig-Jakarta list, lexicostatistical list, Swadesh list, universal concept, word list*
NCD, see *Normalized Compression Distance*
NED, see *Normalized Edit Distance*
Neighbor Joining (NJ), 142, 151, 154–157, 159–161, 163–171, 325, 343–345, 528
NeighborNet, 17, 32, 434–438, 491, 492, 495, 496
network analysis, 17, 447, 448, 451
New Hebrides, 253, 267
n-gram model, 429–431, 435, 442
    see also *bigram, unigram*
Niger-Congo, 90, 252, 269, 314, 486, 489
Nilo-Saharan, 253, 270
NJ, see *Neighbor Joining*
Normalized Compression Distance (NCD), 433, 524, 528
    see also *compression, Lempel-Ziv algorithm, zipping*

Normalized Edit Distance, 526–528
    see also *edit distance, LDND, Levenshtein distance*
North Halmahera, 253, 273
NSM, see *Natural Semantic Metalanguage*
Nyulnyulan, 389, 393, 395, 397–399, 401, 404–406, 408, 409, 416, 422, 423

Ok, 253, 272
Omotic, 252, 265
open content, 296
    see also *open source*
open source, 15, 296
    see also *open content*
orthographic similarity, 57, 72, 73, 375, 379
    see also *formal similarity, language similarity, lexical similarity, linguistic similarity, phonetic similarity, semantic similarity, similarity measure, string similarity, structural similarity, syntactic similarity, typological similarity, word similarity*
orthography, 9, 10, 58, 64–66, 243, 487, 488
    see also *script, writing system*
Oto-Manguean, 486, 490

Paez, 332, 334, 343
Paman, 252, 265
Pama-Nyungan, 389, 423
parallel corpus, 6, 16, 18, 313–315, 470, 476, 493
    see also *bitext, parallel corpus, translation corpus*
parallel text, 17, 305, 314, 315, 475, 476, 478, 492, 493, 497, 500, 501, 503
    see also *bitext, parallel corpus, parallel text, translation corpus*
Philippines languages, 223, 253, 267, 314
phonetic
    ~ difference, 182
        see also *pronunciation difference*

~ distance, 119–122, 126, 128, 131
~ feature, 6, 113, 514, 519, 528
~ similarity (measure), 10, 375, 378, 447
  see also *formal similarity, language similarity, lexical similarity, linguistic similarity, orthographic similarity, semantic similarity, similarity measure, string similarity, structural similarity, syntactic similarity, typological similarity, word similarity*
phonological change, 257, 258, 261
  see also *sound correspondence*
phylogenetic difference, 208
  see also *character-based method, cladistics, cladogram, dendrogram, distance-based method, genetic classification, genetic difference, genetic similarity, genus, language family, lineage, linguistic phylogeny, phylogeny, phylum, subgrouping*
phylogeny, 9, 13, 15, 18, 19, 141–144, 150–157, 170, 201, 202, 207, 208, 221, 241, 243, 250, 303, 304, 325, 408–410, 421, 430, 434, 439, 442, 447, 508, 524, 527, 528, 530
  see also *character-based method, cladistics, cladogram, dendrogram, distance-based method, genetic classification, genetic difference, genetic similarity, genus, language family, lineage, linguistic phylogeny, phylogenetic difference, phylum, subgrouping*
phylum, 44
  see also *character-based method, cladistics, cladogram, dendrogram, distance-based method, genetic classification, genetic difference, genetic similarity, genus, language family, lineage, linguistic phylogeny, phylogenetic difference, phylogeny, subgrouping*

polysemy, 3, 232, 356, 357, 457, 469
power law, 15, 453, 461, 462
  see also *Zipf's law*
pronunciation
~ difference, 13, 107, 115, 116, 121, 122, 124
  see also *phonetic difference*
~ distance, 120, 121, 130
Proto-Anatolian, 84, 85, 91, 96, 98
protolanguage, 44, 47, 92, 143, 178, 250, 309, 391, 404, 405, 420, 421

Quechuan, 253, 270, 331, 333, 433, 443

reconstruction, 18, 40–42, 52, 63, 83–86, 90–92, 96, 98, 153, 231, 243, 309, 405, 507, 510, 529
regional speech (regiolect), 13, 107–117, 120, 123–133
retention, 13, 32, 85, 91, 96, 141, 239, 391, 392, 420, 421
Romance, 93, 207, 306, 322, 429, 465, 469, 486, 492, 496, 497, 500, 503

Sáliba-Piaroa, 433, 443
Salishan, 253, 271, 274
script, 8–10, 18, 19, 36, 40, 57, 58, 64–66, 73–75, 78, 79, 84, 109, 112, 119, 120, 122, 145, 152, 179, 182, 183, 209, 225, 257, 263, 285, 287, 295, 306, 321, 337, 358, 375, 416, 424, 442, 502, 510, 512
  see also *orthography, writing system*
semantic
~ distance (measure), 18, 169, 398, 449, 464, 466, 475, 476, 478, 481, 482, 495, 501
~ feature, 16, 392, 393, 398
~ network, 456, 470, 471
~ similarity (measure), 313, 359, 376, 377, 395, 424, 448, 449, 451, 458, 459, 467, 477, 483, 488, 493, 500, 501
  see also *formal similarity, language similarity, lexical similar-*

ity, linguistic similarity, orthographic similarity, phonetic similarity, similarity measure, string similarity, structural similarity, syntactic similarity, typological similarity, word similarity
~ typology, 17, 447, 448, 450, 451, 468, 470
  see also *language typology, lexical typology, morphological typology, typological linguistics*
Semantic Vector Space model (SVS), 16, 357–361, 363, 364, 370
Semitic, 253, 265, 314, 322
sentence alignment, 375, 493
  see also *alignment, word alignment*
similarity measure, 9, 11, 16, 17, 67, 180, 202, 249, 255, 261, 303, 310–314, 317, 319–322, 339, 363, 377, 379, 384, 392, 399, 432, 493, 500
  see also *formal similarity, language similarity, lexical similarity, linguistic similarity, orthographic similarity, phonetic similarity, semantic similarity, string similarity, structural similarity, syntactic similarity, typological similarity, word similarity*
Sino-Tibetan, 151, 175, 253, 254, 271, 486
Slavic, 84–88, 98, 99, 207, 306, 323, 324, 429, 468, 486, 492, 493, 495–497, 500
small world property, 453
sound correspondence, 18, 122, 179, 250, 262, 378, 439, 442, 486, 487, 507, 511, 522
  see also *phonological change*
South American languages, 330–334, 338, 339, 342, 346, 430, 433, 442
South Asia, 144, 151, 287, 289, 291, 292
Sprachbund, 391, 500, 503
  see also *areal linguistics, contact linguistics, diffusion, language contact, linguistic area*
SSA database, 265, 270, 510, 522, 528

stability (in language), 8, 32–35, 41, 43–46, 48, 238–241, 261, 262
  see also *diachronic stability, stable feature, stable vocabulary*
stable
  ~ feature, 48
    see also *diachronic stability, stability, stable vocabulary*
  ~ vocabulary, 192
    see also *diachronic stability, stability, stable feature*
standard language, 13, 107, 108, 112, 113, 115, 117, 124, 127, 129–131, 199
StarLing database, 510, 522, 524, 528
string similarity (measure), 9, 379
  see also *formal similarity, language similarity, lexical similarity, linguistic similarity, orthographic similarity, phonetic similarity, semantic similarity, similarity measure, structural similarity, syntactic similarity, typological similarity, word similarity*
structural
  ~ distance, 200, 201, 219, 497–499
    see also *constructional distance, formal distance, grammatical distance, morphosyntactic distance*
  ~ feature, 7, 33, 36, 43, 51, 57, 61, 66, 67, 85, 145, 330, 387, 447, 450, 478, 481, 487, 488
    see also *formal feature, grammatical feature, morphological feature, morphosyntactic feature, syntactic feature, typological feature*
  ~ similarity, 66, 67, 476, 479
    see also *formal similarity, language similarity, lexical similarity, linguistic similarity, orthographic similarity, phonetic similarity, semantic similarity, similarity measure, string similarity, syntactic similarity, typological similarity, word similarity*

544 *Index*

subgrouping, 13, 32, 38, 83–86, 90, 98, 99, 141–145, 147, 148, 152–156, 157, 159–161, 164, 166, 168–170, 175, 193, 196, 217, 219, 306, 322, 391, 429, 439
  see also *character-based method, cladistics, cladogram, dendrogram, distance-based method, genetic classification, genetic difference, genetic similarity, genus, language family, lineage, linguistic phylogeny, phylogenetic difference, phylogeny, phylum*
SVS, see *Semantic Vector Space model*
Swadesh list, 7–15, 142, 143, 151–154, 156, 169, 176, 178, 180, 185, 192, 194, 201, 202, 207, 264, 288–290, 310, 447
  see also *ASJP list, basic meaning, basic vocabulary, core vocabulary, Intercontinental Dictionary Series, Leipzig-Jakarta list, lexicostatistical list, Natural Semantic Metalanguage, universal concept, word list*
synonymy, 16, 179, 251, 286, 290, 295, 360, 377, 378, 404, 411, 412, 448, 450
syntactic
  ~ feature, 94, 143, 153, 304, 307, 309, 315, 324, 325, 335, 346
    see also *formal feature, grammatical feature, morphological feature, morphosyntactic feature, structural feature, typological feature*
  ~ similarity, 313, 315
    see also *formal similarity, language similarity, lexical similarity, linguistic similarity, orthographic similarity, phonetic similarity, semantic similarity, similarity measure, string similarity, structural similarity, typological similarity, word similarity*

Tai-Kadai, 253, 271, 314
text semantics, 358, 359

Tibeto-Burman, 5, 13, 175, 193, 196, 292, 314
Tibeto-Kanauri, 13, 175, 176, 178, 179, 182, 184, 194, 196
Tocharian, 84–86, 91, 92, 97–99
Torricelli, 253, 271, 273
translation
  ~ corpus, 16, 313–316, 383, 495, 496
    see also *bitext, parallel corpus, parallel text*
  ~ equivalent, 6, 16, 17, 316, 375, 383, 411, 475
Trans-New Guinea, 253, 271, 273
Tucano, 44, 53, 431–443
Turama-Kikorian, 253, 272
Turkic, 252, 265, 486
typological
  ~ bias, 18, 501
  ~ classification, 17, 309, 343–346, 467, 471, 492, 496, 498, 500
  ~ database, 15, 143, 295
  ~ distance, 15, 202, 329, 485
  ~ feature, 12, 14, 15, 38, 40–45, 67, 74, 90, 143, 203, 295, 329, 330, 345, 346, 387, 423, 478, 488, 498, 500
    see also *formal feature, grammatical feature, morphological feature, morphosyntactic feature, structural feature, syntactic feature*
  ~ linguistics, 5, 6, 17, 18, 53, 92, 94, 98, 284, 295, 343, 345, 477, 478, 497, 501
    see also *language typology, lexical typology, morphological typology, semantic typology*
  ~ pressure, 32–34, 43–45, 52
  ~ sampling, 477, 497
  ~ similarity, 58, 72, 73, 86, 89, 387, 392
    see also *formal similarity, language similarity, lexical similarity, linguistic similarity, orthographic similarity, phonetic*

similarity, semantic similarity, similarity measure, string similarity, structural similarity, syntactic similarity, word similarity

unigram, 17, 430–442
  see also *bigram, n-gram model*
universal concept, 287
  see also *ASJP list, basic meaning, basic vocabulary, core vocabulary, Intercontinental Dictionary Series, Leipzig-Jakarta list, lexicostatistical list, Natural Semantic Metalanguage, Swadesh list, word list*
UPGMA, 142, 151, 154–157, 161, 163, 164, 166–170
Uralic, 18, 314, 486, 507, 510, 511, 522
Uto-Aztecan, 253, 254, 273, 486

WALS, see *World Atlas of Language Structures*
West Australian languages, 253, 265
West Barkly, 253, 266
West Papuan languages, 253, 273, 486
Wiktionary, 293–295, 297
Witoto, 433–435, 443
word
  ~ alignment, 316, 375, 381, 478, 483
    see also *alignment, sentence alignment*
  ~ list, 7–9, 15, 17, 18, 133, 149, 153, 156, 175, 176, 181, 182, 184, 191, 194, 207, 249–251, 257–260, 263, 264, 297, 310, 311, 447
    see also *ASJP list, basic meaning, basic vocabulary, core vocabulary, Intercontinental Dictionary Series, Leipzig-Jakarta list, lexicostatistical list, Natural Semantic Metalanguage, Swadesh list, universal concept*

~ meaning, 364
  see also *lexical semantics, word semantics*
~ order, 43–45, 49, 51, 53, 69, 70, 200, 206, 309, 313, 315, 423
~ semantics, 358, 359
  see also *lexical semantics, word meaning*
~ similarity (measure), 16, 310, 312, 360, 361, 375, 384, 432
  see also *formal similarity, language similarity, lexical similarity, linguistic similarity, orthographic similarity, phonetic similarity, semantic similarity, similarity measure, string similarity, structural similarity, syntactic similarity, typological similarity*
WordNet, 295, 448, 471
World Atlas of Language Structures (WALS), 7, 12, 36, 52, 53, 61, 67, 68, 73, 75, 77, 145–147, 289, 296, 304, 305, 307–310, 329, 447, 498
Worrorran, 252, 266, 389, 404, 405, 409, 422, 423
writing system, 12, 57, 58, 64, 65, 67, 72, 73, 225
  see also *orthography, script*

Xincan, 333

Yapen, 252, 268
Yawa, 253, 273

Zipf's law, 15, 158, 261, 290, 383, 401
  see also *power law*
zipping, 429, 430, 432–435, 437–439, 441, 442, 522
  see also *compression, Lempel-Ziv algorithm, Normalized Compression Distance*

www.ingramcontent.com/pod-product-compliance
Lightning Source LLC
Chambersburg PA
CBHW070746230426
43665CB00017B/2263